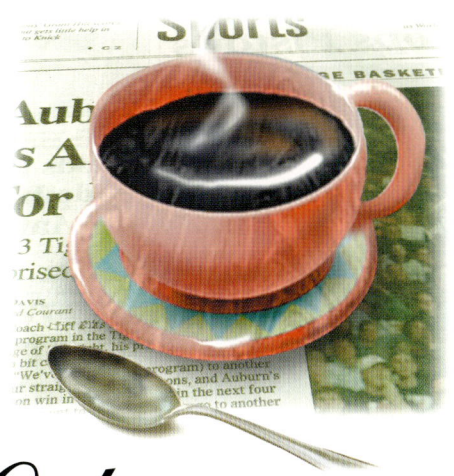

20th edition THE BEST OF NEWSPAPER DESIGN

BOOK CREDITS

Designer & Editor
C. Marshall Matlock
S.I. Newhouse School of
Public Communications
Syracuse University

Associate Designer
Shamus Walker
Syracuse, N.Y.

Copy Editor
Barbara Hines
Howard University
Washington, D.C.

Cover & Chapter Illustrations
Russ Ball
Albuquerque Journal
Albuquerque, N.M.

Cover & Chapter Design
Carolyn Flynn
Albuquerque Journal
Albuquerque, N.M.

Production Consultant
Dave Gray
Providence, R.I.

FOREWORD	3
INTRO	4
WORLD'S BEST-DESIGNED NEWSPAPERS	5
BEST OF SHOW, JUDGES' SPECIAL RECOGNITION	42
NEWS	53
FEATURES	89
MAGAZINE	143
SPECIAL SECTIONS	169
DESIGN PORTFOLIO	179
ILLUSTRATION	201
PHOTOJOURNALISM	223
INFOGRAPHICS	237
MISCELLANEOUS	257
JUDGES	265
INDEX	268

THE SOCIETY FOR NEWS DESIGN ■ 129 Dyer Street ■ Providence, RI 02903-3904

Judging takes place at The S.I. Newhouse School of Public Communications
Syracuse University, Syracuse, NY

FIRST PUBLISHED IN THE U.S.A. BY ROCKPORT PUBLISHERS, INC.
GLOUCESTER, MASS.

SPECIAL THANKS

S.I. Newhouse School of Public Communications
Syracuse University

Judging Assistants

John Allen, sports page designer, Atlanta Journal-Constitution, Atlanta, Ga.
G.W. Babb, design director, American-Statesman, Austin, Texas
Sara Bines, page designer, Tampa Tribune, Tampa, Fla.
Stephen Cavendish, ANE, The Washington Post, Washington, D.C.
Elizabeth Cromer, SND membership director, Providence R.I.
Steve Dorsey, design director, Detroit Free Press, Detroit, Mich.
Bill Dunn, visual content editor, Star Tribune, Minneapolis, Minn.
Carolyn Flynn, AME/photo & design, Albuquerque Journal, Albuquerque, N.M.
Kelly Frankeny, AME/design, San Francisco Examiner, San Francisco, Calif.
Dave Gray, SND executive director, Providence, R.I.
Scott Goldman, sports layout editor, The Washington Post, Washington, D.C.
Barbara Hines, Department of Journalism chair, Howard University, Washington, D.C.
Jim Jennings, VP & editorial director, Thomson Newspapers, Lexington, Ky.
Marshall Matlock, associate professor, School of Public Communications, Syracuse, N.Y.
Jim Michalowski, photo director, The Citizen, Auburn, N.Y.
Kenny Monteith, news designer, Savannah Morning News, Savannah, Ga.
Andrew Phillips, artist/designer, The Star-Ledger, Newark, N.J.
Debra Page-Trim, designer, The Boston Globe, Boston, Mass.
Jami Smith, copy editor/designer, Mercury News, San Jose, Calif.
Randy Stano, professor, University of Miami, Miami, Fla.
Shamus Walker, judging audit director, Syracuse University, Syracuse, N.Y.
Syracuse Students: Erin Banning, Penny Colston, Maile Chow-Hanson, Davis Janowski, Heather Johnson, Joanne Marciano, Erin Randolph, Jim Rodenbush, Jane Rushmore.
University of Miami Students: Nathan Estep, Damian Glover, Chris Melchiondo, Cheryl Milbrandt, Stephanie Reneau, April Robinson.

1999 SND OFFICERS

President
Ed Kohorst
Dallas Morning News

First Vice President
Jean Dodd
Kansas City Star

Second Vice President
Lucie Lacava
Montreal, Canada

Treasurer
Svenåke Boström
Sundsvalls Tidning

Secretary
Jay Small
Evantage Consulting LLC.

Past President
Lynn Staley
Newsweek

Executive Director
Dave Gray
The Society for News Design

Copyright © 1999 The Society for News Design

All rights reserved.
No part of this book may be reproduced in any form without written permission of the copyright owners. All images in this book have been reproduced with the knowledge and prior consent of the artists concerned and no responsibility is accepted by producer, publisher or printer for any infringement of copyright or otherwise, arising from the contents of this publication. Every effort has been made to ensure that credits accurately comply with information supplied.

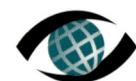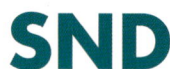

Society for News Design
129 Dyer Street
Providence, R.I. 02903-3904
Telephone: 401•276•2100
FAX: 401•276•2105
snd@snd.org
http://www.snd.org

Distributed to the book and art trade in the United States by:
North Light Books, an imprint of
F & W Publications
1507 Dana Avenue
Cincinnati, Ohio 45207
Telephone: 800•289•0963

Other distribution by:
Rockport Publishers, Inc.
Gloucester, Mass. 01930-5089

ISBN 1-56496-619-4
ISBN 1-878107-10-0 (Softcover edition)
ISSN: 1520-4251

THE SOCIETY FOR NEWS DESIGN
20 years of service to visual journalism

- For anyone with an interest in news and journalism design
- Founded in 1979
- More than 2,500 members in more than 50 countries
- Student and professional affiliates worldwide
- Quarterly DESIGN journal, frequent newsletters and other publications
- Workshops, Quick Courses and MacLabs in print, new media and information design
- Books, slides, tapes, videos, CDs and other teaching resources
- Annual Best of Newspaper Design, Malofiej information graphics and student design contests
- Scholarship and research awards and grants to students and faculty through the SND Foundation
- Online book browser, consultants directory, membership directory, workshop and seminar signup, job bank and media design connections via the web at http://www.snd.org

FOREWORD

This book represents the best work in the world in the field of newsprint journalism design for 1998. You will find the pages fascinating and inspiring.

You will find work that surprises you, creativity expressed in a way that hadn't occurred to you. You may find work that is flawless in its execution, the product of a news organization hitting on all cylinders. You will find work that advances the state of the art of visual storytelling, representing a quantum leap for us all.

Each year we receive thousands of entries — nearly 13,000 this year to break all records — from visual journalists who aspire to do work that is beyond mere competence. Indeed, this is work that makes a difference in how and why readers read. This year was the competition's biggest ever, with winners from 163 newspapers from 21 countries, totaling 1,055 awards.

The role of the competition, now in its 20th year, is to set a higher standard every year and inspire us to do the best we can. Each year as we work on this contest, whether we are among the hundreds who win or the thousands who hoped, we help establish a place for visual journalism in our newsrooms.

Putting this all together each year is a labor of love.

The judges who assembled at the S.I. Newhouse School of Public Communications at Syracuse University in February 1999 are multinational, multilingual and multitalented. They start the weekend strangers, some speaking languages the others don't understand. Though they are a diverse group, they share a passion for visual journalism. By the end of the weekend, they leave inspired.

So, too, for these folks, who deserve a special thanks:
- Marshall Matlock, who has run the competition out of Syracuse University for the past 11 years and has it running like a well-oiled machine; Shamus Walker, who takes care of all the little details at the judging site;
- Jim Jennings, for his help coordinating the World's Best-Designed Newspapers judging;
- the professional assistants who work 15-hour days at the judging site despite their aching feet and backs;
- the student assistants at Syracuse University and the invited guests from the University of Miami who helped us tremendously;
- David Gray and Elizabeth Cromer, from the SND office, who take care of everything from mailing the Call for Entries to data entry of winners to the letters that go out announcing the results; and
- the S.I. Newhouse School of Public Communications at Syracuse University and Dean David Rubin and his staff for continuing to support the competition as it expands and flourishes.

And now, turn the pages to see the work that made a difference in the world this year.

Carolyn Flynn
Carolyn Flynn, 20th edition coordinator

PREFACIO

Este libro representa la labor más destacada del mundo en el campo del diseño periodístico en 1998. Usted se sentirá fascinado e inspirado por sus páginas.

Encontrará obras que le sorprenderán, con una creatividad expresada en un modo que no se le había ocurrido a usted. Contemplará obras de ejecución impecable, el fruto de una organización de noticias que avanza a toda máquina, además de obras que adelantan el estado del arte fotográfico y representan un enorme paso de avance para todos nosotros.

Cada año recibimos miles de piezas — casi 13 000 este año, un número sin precedentes — de periodistas visuales cuya aspiración es crear obras que superen un trabajo meramente competente. Sin duda alguna, obras que marquen una diferencia en el modo de leer de los lectores y en los motivos que los llevan a leer. Este año fue el más exitoso del concurso, con ganadores de 163 periódicos procedentes de 21 países, para un total de 1055 premios.

El papel del concurso, ahora en su vigésima edición, es establecer mayores estándares cada año y servir de inspiración para dar nuestro máximo esfuerzo. Cada año que trabajamos para este concurso, ya estemos entre los cientos de ganadores o los miles de aspirantes, contribuimos a crear un lugar para el periodismo visual en nuestras salas de redacciones.

Lograr la realización del concurso cada año es una labor de amor.

Los miembros del jurado que se reunieron en S.I. Newhouse School of Public Communications, en Syracuse University en el mes de febrero de 1999 proceden de distintas naciones, son multilingües y tienen muchas dotes. Comienzan el fin de semana como extraños y algunos hablan idiomas que otros no entienden. Aunque son un grupo muy diverso, todos comparten su pasión por el periodismo visual. Cuando el fin de semana termina, parten llenos de inspiración.

Las personas mencionadas a continuación también merecen nuestro agradecimiento en particular:
- Marshall Matlock, quien ha dirigido el concurso desde Syracuse University durante los últimos 11 años y logrado que funcione de modo tan eficiente; Shamus Walker, quien se ocupa de los pequeños detalles en la sede del jurado.
- Jim Jennings, por ayudarnos a coordinar el criterio del jurado en la categoría "Periódicos con Mejor Diseño del Mundo."
- Los asistentes profesionales que trabajaron jornadas de 15 horas en la sede del jurado a pesar del cansancio.
- Los asistentes estudiantiles de Syracuse University y los invitados de University of Miami, quienes nos prestaron tanta ayuda.
- Davis Gray y Elizabeth Cromer, de la oficina de la SND, quienes se ocuparon de todo, desde enviar por correo la convocatoria a los concursantes e ingresar los datos de los ganadores hasta mandar las cartas que anunciaron los resultados.
- S.I. Newhouse School of Public Communications en Syracuse University y el Decano David Rubin y su personal, por continuar apoyando al concurso en tanto se amplía y prospera.

Acto seguido, hojee las páginas para ver la labor que marcó la diferencia en el mundo este año.

Carolyn Flynn
Carolyn Flynn, coordinador de la 10na edición

INTRODUCTION

We wish there was a magical way to explain what takes place each year at the competition. There isn't. Many hours are spent by editors, judges and assistants to make the process work. The judges have an awesome task: to determine which entries represent the best of the work being done in the world's newsrooms.

What judges look for in winners changes each year depending on the judges' personalities and the quality of the entries. That's what makes our industry exciting and challenging. Design is subjective; however, our definitions for the various awards remain the same.

Best of Show is the best of the Gold Medal winners. Any discussion for this award takes place at the conclusion of the judging. Judges have an opportunity to view all Silver and Gold winners at the same time. There is no limit as to the number of Best of Show awards that may be presented in one or more categories. This year only one was awarded.

A Gold Medal is granted for work that defines the state of the art. Such an entry stretches the limits of creativity. It should be impossible to find anything deficient in a gold-winning entry. It should be near perfect.

A Silver Medal is granted for work that goes beyond excellence. The technical proficiency of the Silver Medal should stretch the limits of the medium. These entries should shine.

An Award of Excellence is granted for work that is truly excellent. This award goes beyond mere technical or aesthetic competency. But to receive an Award of Excellence, these entries need not be "perfect." It is appropriate to honor entries for such things as being daring and innovative if the entry is outstanding, but less than 100 percent in other aspects.

The Judges' Special Recognition can be awarded by a team of judges or by all judges for work that is outstanding in a particular aspect, not necessarily singled out by the Award of Excellence, Silver or Gold award structure. This recognition has been granted for such things as use of photography, use of informational graphics and the use of typography throughout a body of work. This body of work may be a particular publication, section or sections by an individual or staff. The special recognition does not supplant any Award of Excellence, Silver or Gold and should be seen as an adjunct. This year nine A of E's were given.

In addition to the Award of Excellence and the two medals, two special honors are also possible: the Judges' Special Recognition and the Best of Show. These honors are given only when special circumstances warrant the awards.

Anyone who has attended the judging will agree the days are long and the work intensive. Some categories have too many entries to be displayed at the same time. When this is the case we do a "first cut" by having judges pick the pages they'd like to see again. It only takes one vote to make the cut. Depending on the number of entries in the category, this process may be repeated several times.

Once the first cut is completed and all entries in a category can be viewed at one time, the actual voting begins. Each judge has a single chip color to cast his or her vote. The judge must vote yes or no by placing a chip in one of the cups in front of each entry. Every judge must vote unless there is a conflict.

A conflict occurs when a judge comes across an entry from his or her publication, a publication he or she has done recent consulting work for (recent is defined as an 18-month period immediately prior to judging) or a publication with which he or she directly competes. In this case the judge places a yellow cup on the entry signifying to the team captain that a conflict exists. It is at this point the "floating" judge votes for or against the entry.

It takes three or more "yes" votes to get into the show.
- Entries receiving three votes receive an Award of Excellence.
- Entries receiving four or more votes in the first round go directly into the medal round.
- Any entry receiving four votes during the medal round is awarded a Silver Medal.
- Any entry receiving five votes (unanimous vote of the judging panel) is awarded a Gold Medal.
- At the end of the entire judging, judges re-examine all the Silver and Gold Medal winners. Medal winners can be renegotiated up or down the award scale at this time.

In the following pages, the medal won is indicated above the name of the publication. Publications without any references won an Award of Excellence.

Again, there is no magical way to explain what takes place during judging. Hopefully this information will put the winners that follow in perspective.

INTRODUCCIÓN

Ojalá que hubiese una manera mágica de explicar todo lo que ocurre cada año en el concurso, pero no la hay. Los editores, jueces y asistentes dedican muchas horas a lograr su éxito. Los miembros del jurado tienen una tarea imponente: determinar qué piezas representan lo mejor del trabajo que se realiza en las redacciones del mundo.

Las cualidades que los miembros del jurado buscan en los ganadores cambian cada año según la personalidad de los jueces y la calidad de las piezas concursantes. Es esto lo que hace que nuestra industria sea emocionante y desafiante. El diseño es subjetivo; sin embargo, nuestras definiciones de los diferentes premios siguen sin cambiar.

"Lo mejor del concurso" es lo mejor de los ganadores de la medalla de oro. Todo análisis de este premio tiene lugar después de la conclusión de la labor del jurado. Los miembros del jurado tienen la oportunidad de considerar todos los ganadores de las medallas de oro y plata a la vez. No hay ningún límite respecto al número de premios "Lo mejor del concurso" que se pueden presentar en una o más categorías. Este año, sólo se otorgó un premio de este tipo.

La medalla de oro se otorga a las obras que definen lo más novedoso del diseño. Estas obras amplían los límites de la creatividad. Debe ser imposible encontrar defectos en una obra galardonada con la medalla de oro; debe ser casi perfecta.

La medalla de plata se otorga a las obras que superan la excelencia. El nivel de competencia técnica exigido por la medalla de plata debe ampliar los límites del trabajo promedio. Estas obras deben sobresalir.

El "Premio a la excelencia" se otorga a las obras sin duda excelentes. Este premio supera las obras meramente competentes desde el punto de vista ético o técnico. Pero para recibir el "Premio a la Excelencia," no es necesario que estas obras sean "perfectas." Se acostumbra rendir honores a tales obras por cualidades como ser atrevidas e innovadoras si la obra sobresale, aunque no alcance el 100% de perfección en otros aspectos.

La "Mención especial de los jueces" puede otorgarse por un equipo de miembros o por todos los miembros del jurado a aquellas obras concursantes que sobresalgan en un aspecto en particular no enfatizado necesariamente por los criterios del "Premio a la excelencia," la medalla de oro, o la medalla de plata. Este reconocimiento se otorga por aspectos tales como el empleo de la fotografía, el uso de gráficos informativos y en uso de la tipografía en un conjunto de obras. Este conjunto de obras puede ser una publicación en particular o una sección o secciones realizadas por un individuo o por el plantel. Esta mención especial no sustituye ningún "Premio a la excelencia," ni a las medallas de oro y plata, sino que se debe considerar un complemento. se otorgaron nueve "JSRs

Además del "Premio a la excelencia" y las dos medallas, se contemplaron dos honores especiales: la Mención especial del jurado y "Lo mejor del concurso." Estos honores se conceden sólo cuando circunstancias especiales ameritan tales premios.

Todo el que haya presenciado la labor del jurado será del parecer que las jornadas son prolongadas y el trabajo intenso. Algunas categorías tienen demasiadas obras concursantes como para mostrarse a la misma vez. Cuando esto sucede, tenemos una ronda eliminatoria en la que hacemos que los miembros del jurado escojan las páginas que les gustaría ver de nuevo. Sólo hace falta una votación para clasificar. Según el número de piezas concursantes en cada categoría, se puede repetir este proceso varias veces.

Una vez que se realiza la primera ronda eliminatoria y se pueden ver todas las obras concursantes en una categoría a la vez, comienza la votación real. Cada miembro del jurado tiene un color de ficha para dar su voto. El miembro del jurado debe votar a favor o en contra colocando una ficha en una de las copas situadas al frente de cada obra. Todos los miembros del jurado deben votar a menos que exista un conflicto de intereses.

Un conflicto de intereses ocurre cuando un miembro del jurado se encuentra con una obra de su propia publicación, una publicación para la cual ha trabajado como consultor recientemente ("recientemente" se define como un período de 18 meses inmediatamente anterior al comienzo de la labor del jurado) o una publicación con la cual compite directamente. En este caso, el miembro del jurado coloca una copa amarilla sobre la obra concursante, lo que indica al capitán del equipo que existe un conflicto. En este punto interviene el juez "sustituto" para votar a favor o en contra de la obra.

Se necesitan tres o más votos a favor para entrar en el concurso.
- Las obras que obtengan tres votos reciben el "Premio a la excelencia."
- Las obras que obtengan cuatro o más votos en la primera ronda pasan directamente a la ronda de medallas.
- Toda obra que obtenga cuatro votos durante la ronda de medallas es galardonada con una medalla de plata.
- Toda obra que obtenga cinco votos (votación unánime del jurado) es galardonada con una medalla de oro.
- A la conclusión de la labor del jurado, sus miembros vuelven a examinar todos los ganadores de las medallas de oro y plata. Los ganadores de medallas pueden ascender o descender en la escala de premios en es momento si así lo estima el jurado.

En las páginas siguientes, se indica la medalla ganada encima del nombre de la publicación. Las publicaciones que no tengan referencia alguna ganaron un "Premio a la excelencia."

Como ya se dijo, no hay una manera mágica de explicar lo que ocurre durante la labor del jurado. Esperamos que esta información logre dar un panorama de las obras ganadoras a continuación.

WORLD'S BEST-DESIGNED NEWSPAPERS

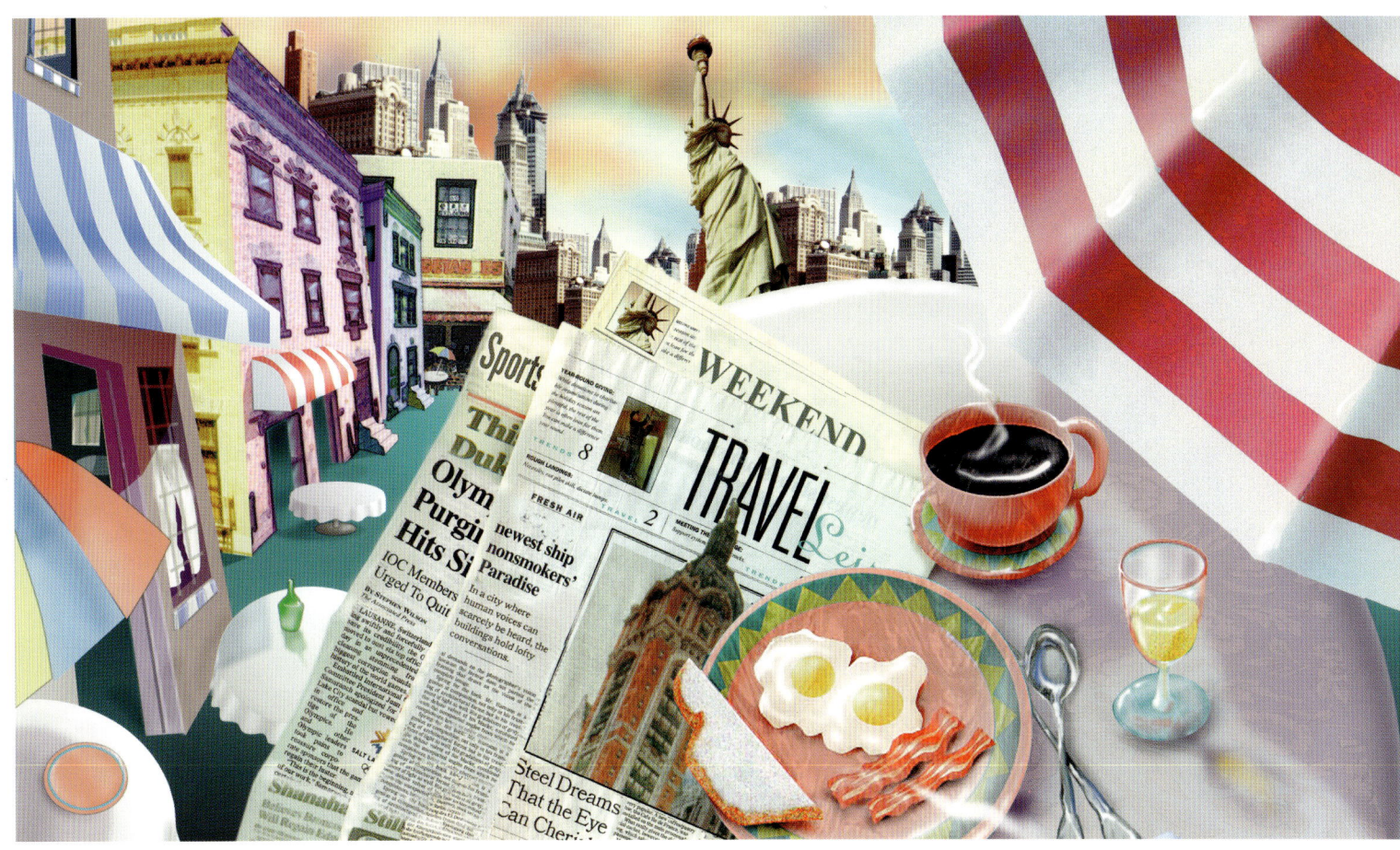

CHAPTER ONE

ALSO IN THIS CHAPTER:
BEST OF SHOW

As the name implies, this is the best of the Gold Medal winners. Any discussion for this award takes place at the conclusion of the judging. Judges have an opportunity to view all Silver and Gold winners at the same time. There is no limit as to the number of Best of Show awards that may be presented. For the 20th Edition judging, one Best of Show was given.

JUDGES' SPECIAL RECOGNITION

This honor can be awarded by a team of judges or by all judges for work that is outstanding in a particular respect. This recognition has been granted for such things as use of photography, use of informational graphics and the use of typography throughout a body of work. This body of work may be a particular publication, section or sections by an individual or staff.

WORLD'S BEST-DESIGNED NEWSPAPERS INTRODUCTION

The designation of a "World's Best-Designed Newspaper" are for those publications that excel in design and content. The judges look very carefully at the publication's content as well as the design. These newspapers must serve their readers.

Any list purporting to announce the "Best" of anything is subject to debate. People will naturally second-guess the judges' decision to include some, while excluding others. That is the nature of competition. A hand-scrawled note sitting on the fax machine brought this home ever so clearly.

There, across the top of a press release announcing the winners of SND's World's Best-Designed Newspapers was the following; "Is this a joke? How could (the name of a newspaper indicated by a bold circle on the release) make this list? I used to respect this organization!" These three short sentences from an otherwise astute senior newspaper executive summarized how far the society's competition had come in two decades, and how far it has yet to go.

The individual failed to understand that the fundamentals of design — use of the grid, typography, color, information graphics, photojournalism, etc. — were not the primary force behind the judges' decisions as they faced the 323 entries in this category. They were but a consideration among many including accessibility, content, discipline, presentation, restraint, risk-taking, story-telling, understanding of market, use of resources and design, with the emphasis on content.

The judges spent three days reading, discussing and debating the entries. In the end, 37 finalists sat on the table. The final discussion lasted just under four hours and centered as much on what was missing from the overall group of entries, as what was present in the finalists and ultimate winners.

"It is amazing how predictable everything began to look," one judge said. "I mean so many of the papers had a sameness about them. There was very little sense of community, having an audience, about them."

"You're right," another said. "it was hard to get an understanding of who they were trying to reach... of who their readers were."

"That's especially true with the North American papers," added a third. "There was little sense of place or culture. If you removed the nameplate they could be from anywhere."

The winning entries, the judges said, demonstrated a more rounded approach to the design process. "I voted for content. It was as simple as that," said one judge. "With this many entries you are looking for the surprises. The things that stand out from the mass and go beyond the obvious. Things that add value and relevance for the reader," added another. "I gave a lot of credit for the willingness to take risks... to try new things and dare to be different," said a third.

So, what lessons have we learned from the winners of the 20th edition's World's Best-Designed Newspapers category? Some of them repeat what we have heard in previous editions. Others are new.

1. Allow content to drive design: Remember that content is king. The judges had little time for heavily formatted design that restricted the ability to tell a story effectively. The winners avoided cookie-cutter solutions, choosing rather to use many elements in the design toolbox — typography, illustration, infographics, photography, etc. — to display the day's content in the most effective way possible.

2. Create a sense of place, community and culture: The judges were quick to note the sameness in many of the entries. The winning entries displayed a "clear understanding of not only their own identity, but that of their community," one judge noted. Another judge said, "Design should enhance content while reflecting the identity of the community. Design can take away from the sense of place, and it did a number of times. A lot of newspapers began to look exactly alike. Every design tool used on a page should have a reason for being."

3. Provide relevant content within an understandable context: Institutional coverage was viewed as an "easy out," often covering for a lack of planning. The winning papers provided relevant content in an understandable format. They told the readers not only what they needed to know, but also what they wanted to know as well.

4. Engage and interact with the reader: "The reader should not only be able to relate to the newspaper, but interact with it," explained one judge. The winning papers not only helped establish an agenda for their communities, but provided opportunities for the reader to participate in the process.

5. Experiment — seek new solutions to old problems: The judges applauded those papers willing to break out of the mold — taking risks and "pushing the envelope" in seeking well thought out design solutions to existing problems. The winning papers broke away from the predictability of the group, reflecting the "vitality of community life."

6. Give the same care and attention to the words as to the design: The judges considered headlines and captions in many of the entries "uninspired." This was viewed as a result of increased production demands on the copydesk. Headlines and captions should say something, and not be left to the end of the editing process.

7. Design the entire paper: The judges noted that the attention to detail in many of the entries stopped at section fronts, with inside pages presenting a sense of having been ignored. The winning papers demonstrated a sense of internal logic, movement and pacing offering the reader a consistent level of presentation throughout the edition.

8. Treat photography with respect: Pretty pictures without strong visual content were seen as a waste of space. The judges saw photojournalism as a fundamental story-telling tool that has diminished as visual content has been replaced with color, lighting, the use of photo manipulation and glitz for its own sake. The power of good black & white photography was noted, as was the power of a well-told picture story. Image manipulation was criticized as a gimmick or a "crutch" propping-up a lack of planning or creative thinking.

9. Practice restraint: The judges quickly tired of the overuse of technology and color. They suggested restraint when working with the various design tools, noting that the availability of a wide range of tools (color, graphics, photographs, typography, etc.) did not require the use of all of them at once.

10. Create a daily surprise for the reader: The judges believed that each day's paper should contain something special that stops the reader and makes them take notice. Something that goes beyond the norm. Something serendipitous that they will look forward to each day. What follows are the 17 winners. Those who have been here before, as well as true newcomers — including a newspaper that did not even exist four months before the judging — represent some of the standards of the industry.

James Jennings, category 1 team captain

INTRODUCCIÓN ■ BEST-DESIGNED NEWSPAPERS

LOS MEJORES DEL MUNDO INTRODUCCIÓN

La designación de "Periódico con el mejor diseño del mundo" es para aquellas publicaciones que se destacan en diseño y contenido. Los jueces consideran con gran detenimiento el contenido de la publicación así como el diseño. Estos periódicos deben estar al servicio de sus lectores.

Cualquier lista que pretenda anunciar "lo mejor" de algo es objeto de debate. La gente, naturalmente, criticará la decisión del jurado de incluir algunas obras y excluir a otras. Es la naturaleza de los concursos. Una nota escrita a mano enviada por fax mostró esto con claridad.

Allí, en la parte superior de un comunicado de prensa que anunciaba los ganadores del concurso "Los periódicos con mejor diseño del mundo" de la SND se encontraba lo siguiente: "¿Esto es una broma? ¿Cómo puede (nombre del periódico encerrado en un círculo en el comunicado) ser parte de esta lista? ¡Yo respetaba a esta organización!" Esta breve nota, proveniente de un alto ejecutivo por lo demás astuto de un diario, resumió los avances logrados por el concurso de la sociedad en dos décadas y el largo camino aún por recorrer.

Esta persona no entendió que los principios del diseño — uso de la cuadrícula, la tipografía, el color, los gráficos informativos, el periodismo gráfico, etc. — no fueron los criterios fundamentales que motivaron las decisiones del jurado al considerar las 323 obras concursantes en esta categoría. Estos fueron tan sólo algunos de los muchos actores usados, como también lo fueron la accesibilidad, el contenido, la disciplina, la presentación, la moderación, los riesgos corridos, el recuento fotográfico de las historias, la comprensión del mercado, el uso de recursos y el diseño, con énfasis en el contenido.

Los jueces dedicaron tres días a leer, analizar y debatir las obras concursantes. Al final, quedaron 37 finalistas. El debate final duró un poco menos de cuatro horas y se centró tanto en lo que faltaba en el grupo de obras en general como en lo que estaba presente en los finalistas y los ganadores definitivos.

"Es increíble el aspecto tan predecible que todo comenzó a tener'" afirmó un miembro del jurado. "Tantos periódicos tenían un aire tan similar. No se podía apreciar el sentido de comunidad, de su público en particular."

"Tienes razón," aseguró otro miembro. "Era difícil tener una idea de a quiénes estaban tratando de llegar... de quiénes eran sus lectores."

"Eso es particularmente cierto con los periódicos de Norteamérica," señaló un tercero. "Tenían muy poco sentido de lugar o cultura. Si se les quita el nombre, podrían ser de cualquier parte."

Las obras ganadoras, según el jurado, demostraron un enfoque más integral del proceso de diseño. "Yo voté por el contenido. Fue así de fácil," declaró un miembro del jurado. "Con tantas obras concursantes, uno busca las sorpresas. Lo que sobresale y va más allá de lo obvio. Cualidades que añadan valor y significación para el lector," agregó otro. Un tercero comentó: "Consideré que el mérito radicaba en estar dispuesto a correr riesgos, a probar lo novedoso y a tratar de ser diferente.

Entonces, ¿qué lecciones hemos aprendido de los ganadores de la vigésima edición del concurso "Los periódicos con mejor diseño del mundo"? Algunas de ellas son lo que habíamos escuchado en ediciones previas. Otras son nuevas.

1. Deje que el contenido impulse el diseño: recuerde que el contenido es lo principal. Los miembros del jurado no dedicaron su tiempo a considerar diseños con demasiado formato que restringían la capacidad de narrar una historia con eficacia. Los ganadores evitaron soluciones perfectas y decidieron utilizar los elementos en el cuadro de herramientas de diseño —tipografía, ilustración, infografía, fotografía, etc. — para mostrar el contenido del día del modo más eficaz posible.

2. Cree una sensación de lugar, comunidad y cultura. Los jueces señalaron inmediatamente la similitud entre muchas de las obras concursantes. Las obras ganadoras mostraron "una clara idea no sólo de su propia identidad, sino también la de su comunidad," declaró un miembro del jurado. Otro afirmó: "el diseño debe mejorar el contenido a la vez que refleja la identidad de la comunidad. El diseño puede disminuir la sensación de lugar, como sucedió varias veces. Muchos periódicos comenzaron a parecer idénticos. Cada herramienta de diseño utilizada en una página debe tener una razón."

3. Ofrezca contenido pertinente dentro de un contexto que se pueda entender: la cobertura de instituciones se consideró como una salida fácil y a menudo compensó la falta de planificación. Los periódicos ganadores ofrecieron contenido pertinente en un formato que se podía entender. Informaban a los lectores no sólo lo que éstos necesitaban saber sino también lo que querían saber.

4. Se identifique con el lector e interactúe con él: "el lector no sólo debe identificarse con el periódico, sino también interactuar con él," explicó un miembro del jurado. Los diarios ganadores no sólo ayudaron a plantear un programa para sus comunidades sino que también ofrecieron la oportunidad a los lectores de participar en el proceso.

5. Experimente, busque nuevas soluciones para resolver viejos problemas: el jurado alabó aquellos periódicos dispuestos a ser creativos, correr riesgos e idear soluciones de diseño novedosas para viejos problemas. Los diarios ganadores, a diferencia del resto, no eran predecibles y reflejaron la "vitalidad de la vida de la comunidad."

6. Preste la misma atención y cuidado a las palabras que al diseño: el jurado consideró que muchos titulares y leyendas de obras concursantes "carecían de inspiración." Esto se atribuyó a la mayor exigencia de producción en las redacciones. Los titulares y las leyendas deben tener un sentido, y no dejarse para el final del proceso de edición.

7. Diseñe todo el periódico: el jurado señaló que la atención prestada a los detalles en muchas de las obras concursantes sólo llegaba hasta el frente de las secciones, y que las páginas interiores parecían desatendidas. Los periódicos ganadores demostraron un sentido de lógica, movimiento y ritmo internos que ofrecía al lector un nivel de presentación coherente en toda la edición.

8. Respete la fotografía: las fotos bonitas sin contenido visual impactante se consideraron como un derroche de espacio. El jurado vio al periodismo gráfico como una herramienta fundamental para narrar la historia que ha sido desplazada a medida que el contenido visual ha sido reemplazado por el color, la iluminación, el empleo de manipulación de imágenes y lo glamoroso sin razón alguna. El jurado observó el poder de la buena fotografía en blanco y negro, así como el poder de una historia fotográfica bien narrada. Se criticó la manipulación de imágenes y se le desechó como un truco o "recurso efectista," cuyo objetivo es "apuntalar" la falta de planificación o de talento creativo.

9. Practique la moderación: el jurado se cansó rápidamente del uso excesivo de la tecnología y el color. Recomendaron la moderación al trabajar con las distintas herramientas de diseño, y observaron que la disponibilidad de una amplia gama de herramientas (color, gráficos, fotografías, tipografía, etc.) no implicaba el uso de todas estas herramientas a la vez.

10. Cree una sorpresa diaria para el lector: el jurado consideró que los diarios debían tener algo especial todos los días, que atrajera la atención del lector y lo forzara a detenerse. Algo que sobrepase la norma y que el lector busque sin proponérselo y que lo haga esperar la llegada de cada día. A continuación se exponen los 17 ganadores. Esos que ya han participado, así como otros que asisten por primera vez —como por ejemplo, un periódico que ni siquiera existía cuatro meses antes de que comenzara el concurso— representan algunos de los modelos de diseño en la industria de noticias.

James Jennings, Jefe de equipo de la categoría 1

BEST-DESIGNED NEWSPAPERS ■ a.m. De León

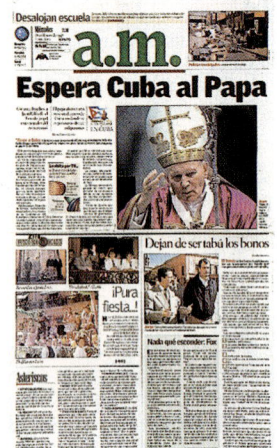
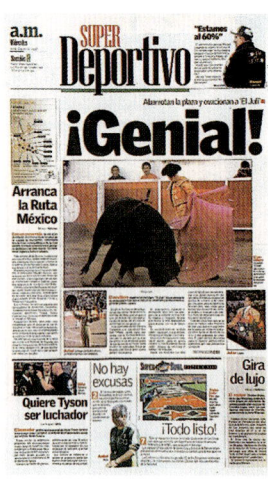
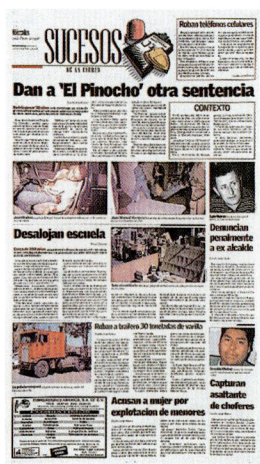
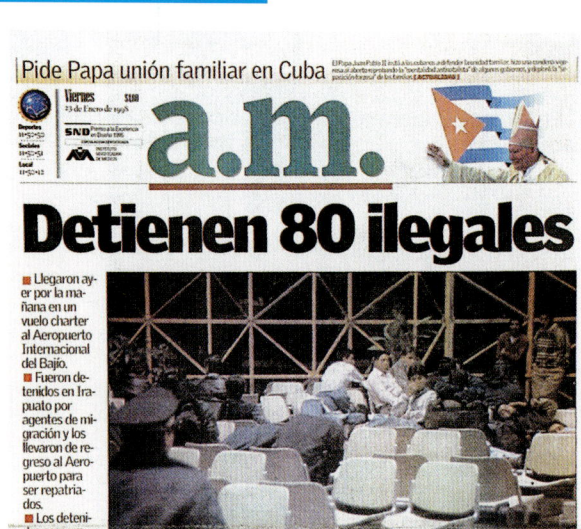

a.m. De León
León, México

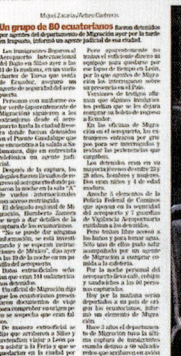
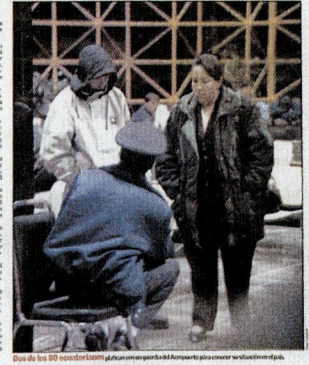

The a.m. is the liveliest newspaper in the group of winners. There is a wonderful sense of energy and vitality at work here. It has a "creative intelligence" about its presentation. There are two — or possibly three — designs working at once to meet the needs of the diversity of the readership. The content is well-crafted. The color palette is incredibly bright, yet controlled. This is a nice publication.

The a.m. es el periódico más animado de entre el grupo de los ganadores. Tiene un maravilloso sentido de la energía y la vitalidad y su presentación se realiza con "inteligencia creativa." Consta de dos o quizás de hasta tres diseños que funcionan a la vez para satisfacer las necesidades de los diversos lectores. El contenido está bien hilvanado y los colores empleados son increíblemente brillantes aunque controlados. Es una publicación muy agradable.

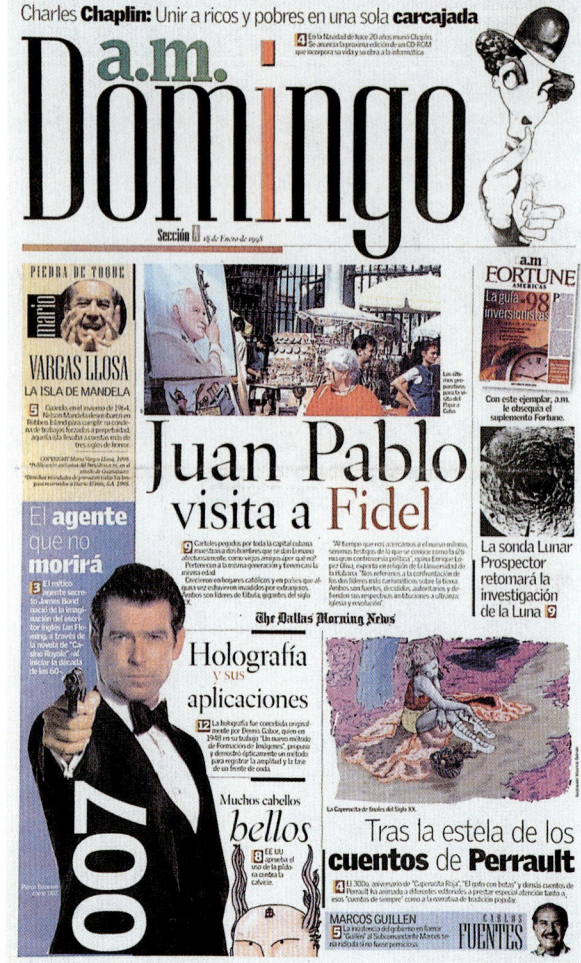

8 ■ THE BEST OF NEWSPAPER DESIGN

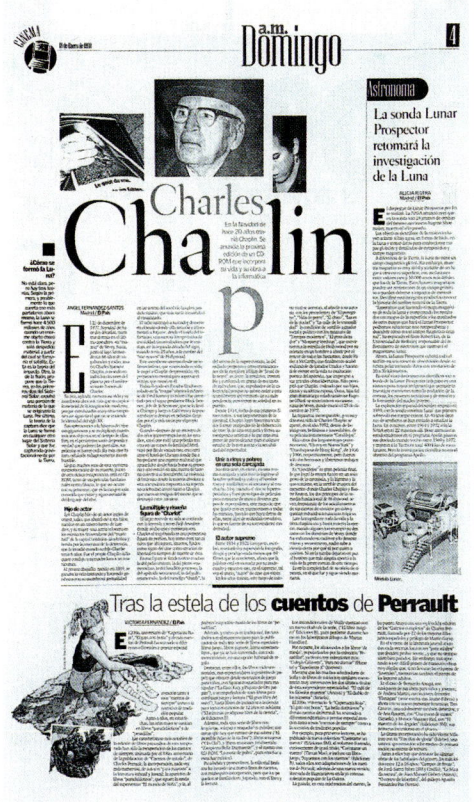
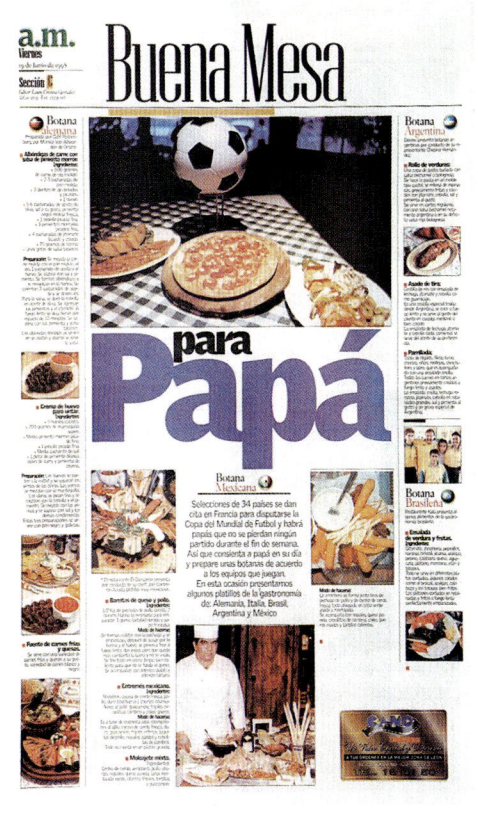
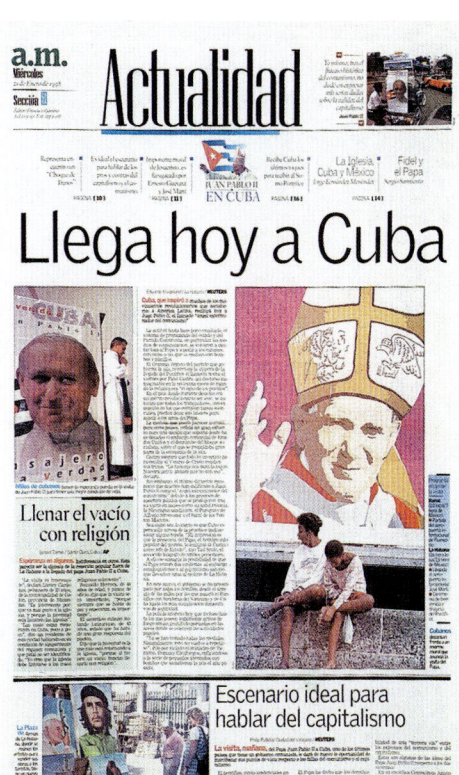
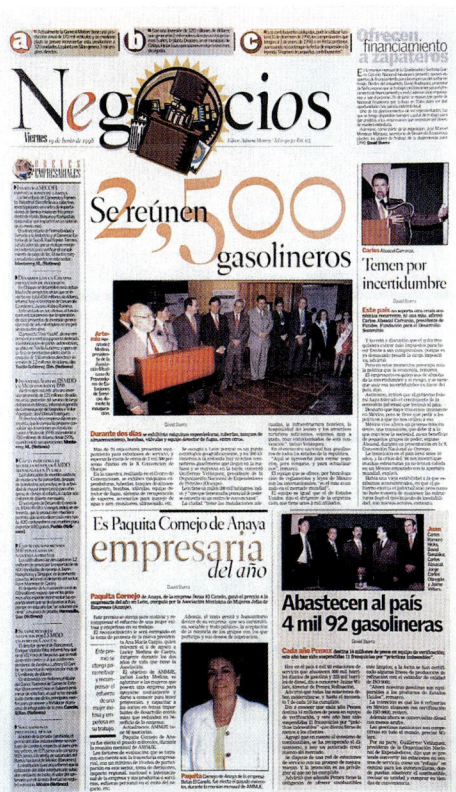
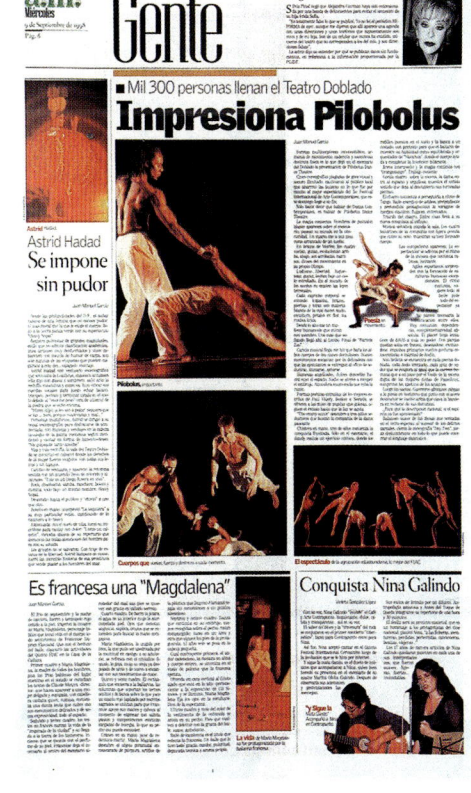
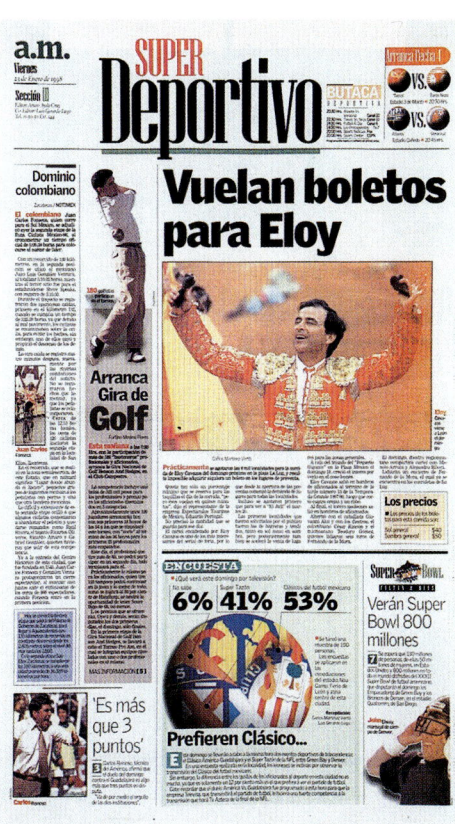

BEST-DESIGNED NEWSPAPERS ■ Centre Daily Times

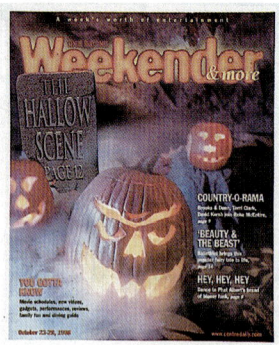 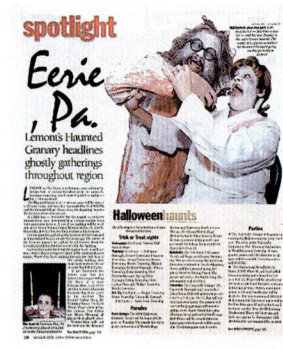 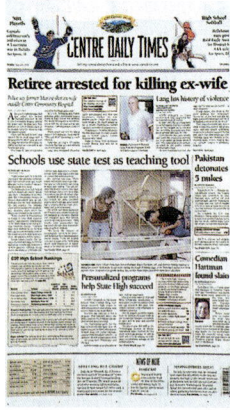 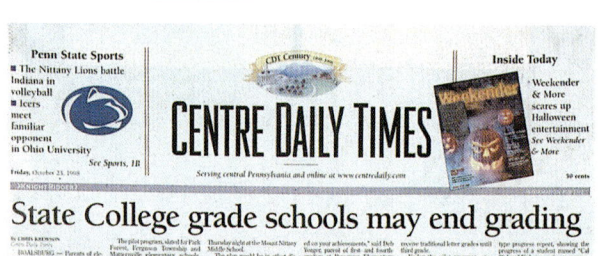

Centre Daily Times
State College, PA

The Centre Daily Times is a solid newspaper that speaks to its readers and is not afraid to take risks. There is a lot of good thinking about what makes a good local paper going on here. It is very local in story selection and play and uses all of its resources effectively to tell stories. The packaging is well-organized and its typography is handled well. The paper has great local photography and isn't afraid to use it for good effect. The inside pages also show an understanding of the community and the paper's audience.

The Centre Daily Times es un diario muy sólido que se dirige a sus lectores y no teme correr riesgos. Demuestra que tiene ideas muy buenas acerca de lo que hace falta para ser un buen periódico local. La selección de historias hace mucho hincapié en lo local y se emplean todos los recursos con eficacia para contar las historias de sus artículos. La presentación está muy bien organizada y la tipografía se maneja muy bien. El diario tiene una fotografía local estupenda y no teme utilizarla para lograr un efecto determinado. Las páginas interiores demuestran que se comprende a la comunidad y a los lectores del diario.

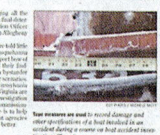 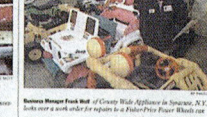 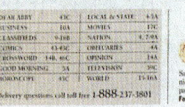 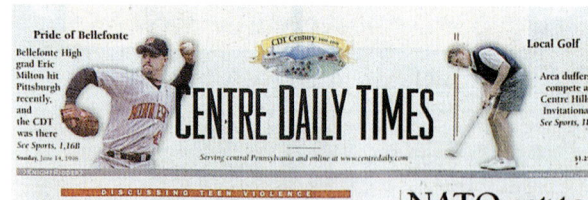 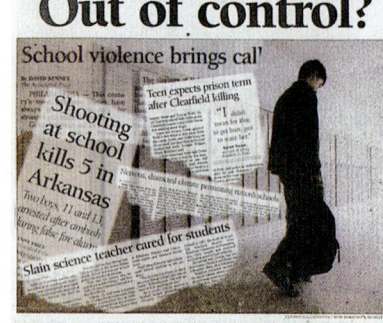

10 ■ THE BEST OF NEWSPAPER DESIGN

CIRCULATION 26,000 ■ BEST-DESIGNED NEWSPAPERS

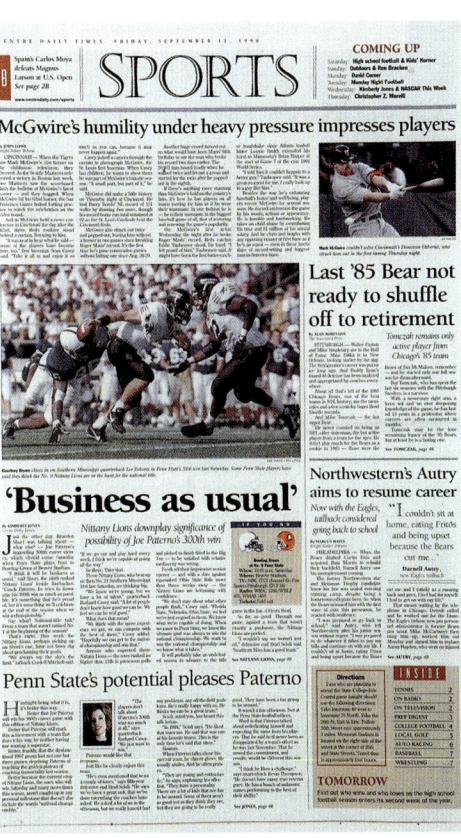
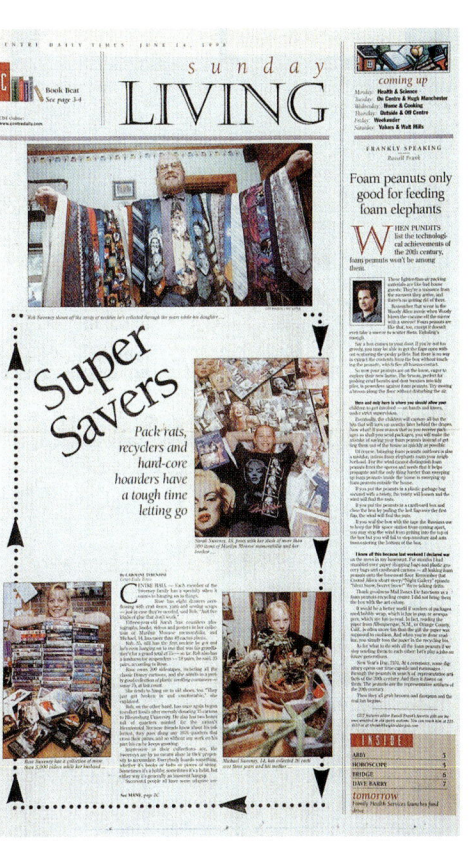
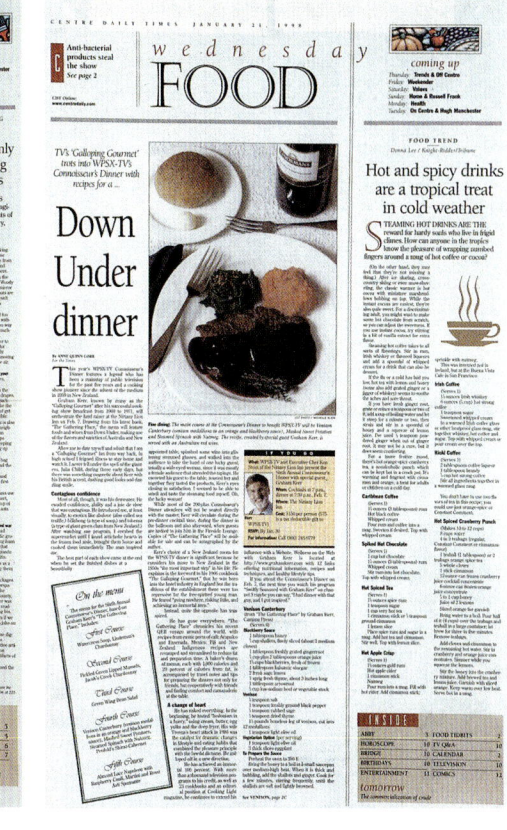
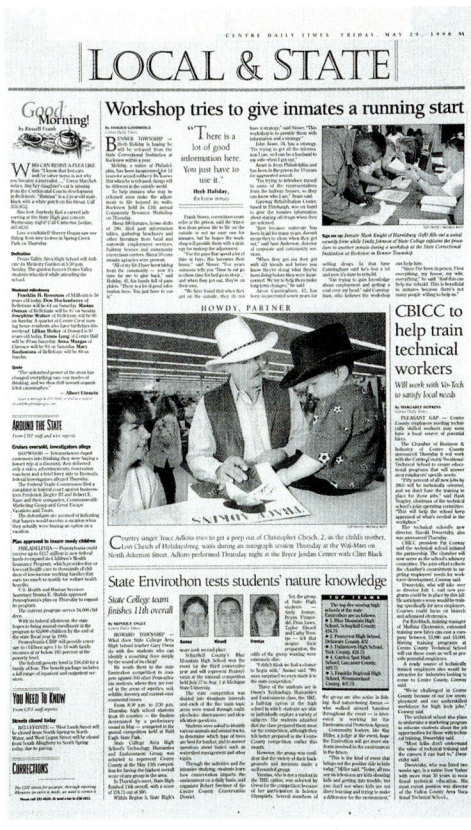
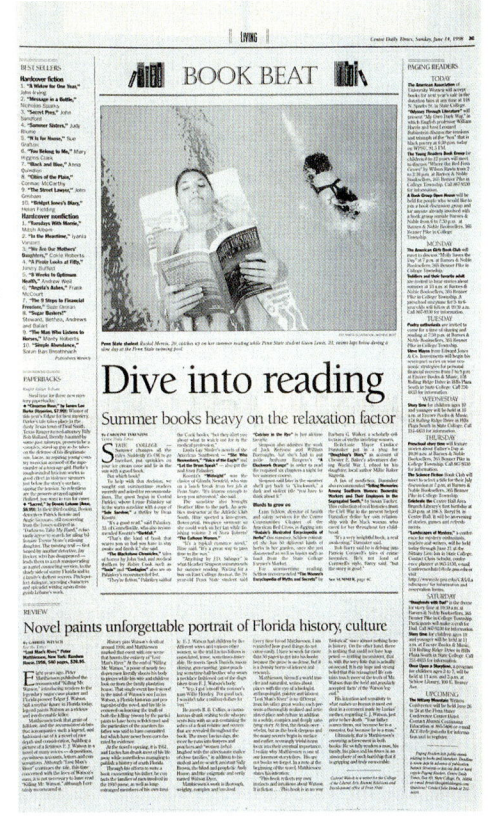
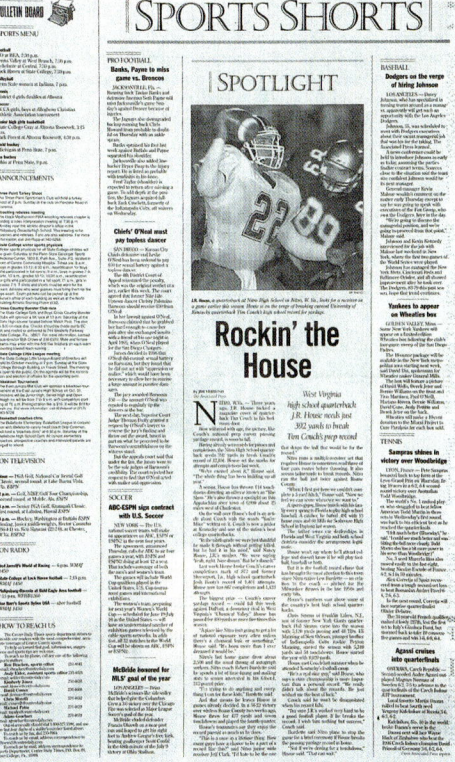

TWENTIETH EDITION ■ 11

BEST-DESIGNED NEWSPAPERS ■ Diario de Noticias

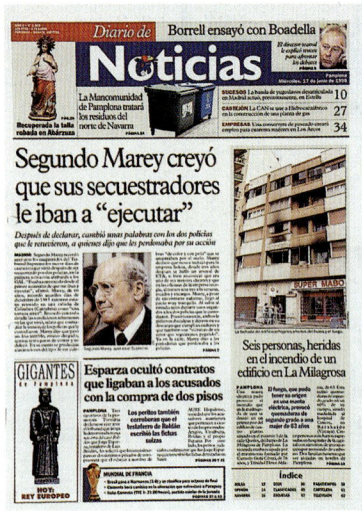
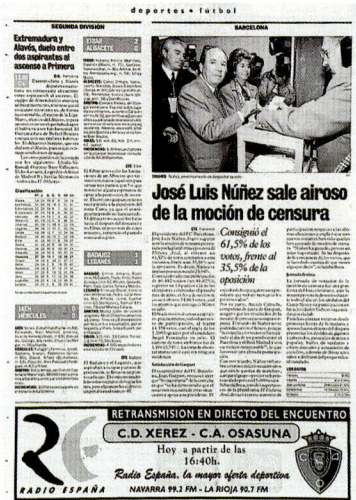
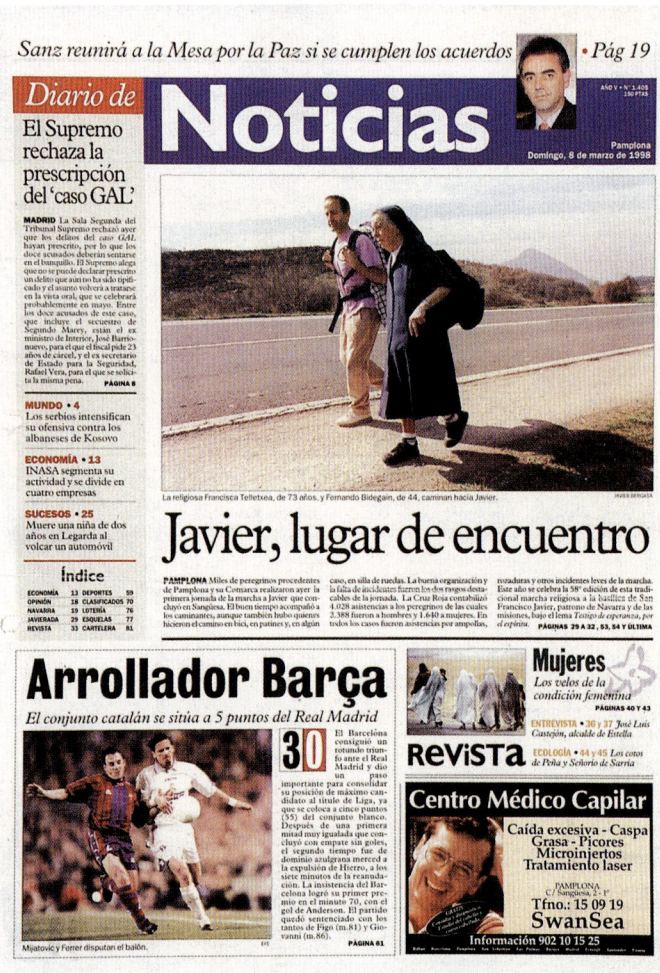

Diario de Noticias
Pamplona, Spain

Diario de Noticias is a very organized paper. It knows its audience and writes to it. Its design is consistent from front-to-back, without looking formatted. There is a lot of movement on every page, especially the inside pages which were the strongest part of the entry. There is a texture about this design that sets it apart from many of the others in the competition. The publication makes excellent use of its photography and illustrations. It uses technology to advance the content without allowing it to take control of the overall package.

Diario de Noticias es un periódico muy bien organizado, que conoce a su público y escribe para él. Su diseño posee coherencia desde las primeras hasta las últimas páginas, sin que parezca que ha sido formateado. Cada página tiene mucho movimiento, particularmente las páginas interiores, su punto más fuerte. Su diseño posee una textura que lo distingue de muchos de los demás concursantes. Esta publicación hace un uso excelente de la fotografía y las ilustraciones. Utiliza la tecnología para promover el contenido, pero sin dejar que ella asuma el control de toda la presentación

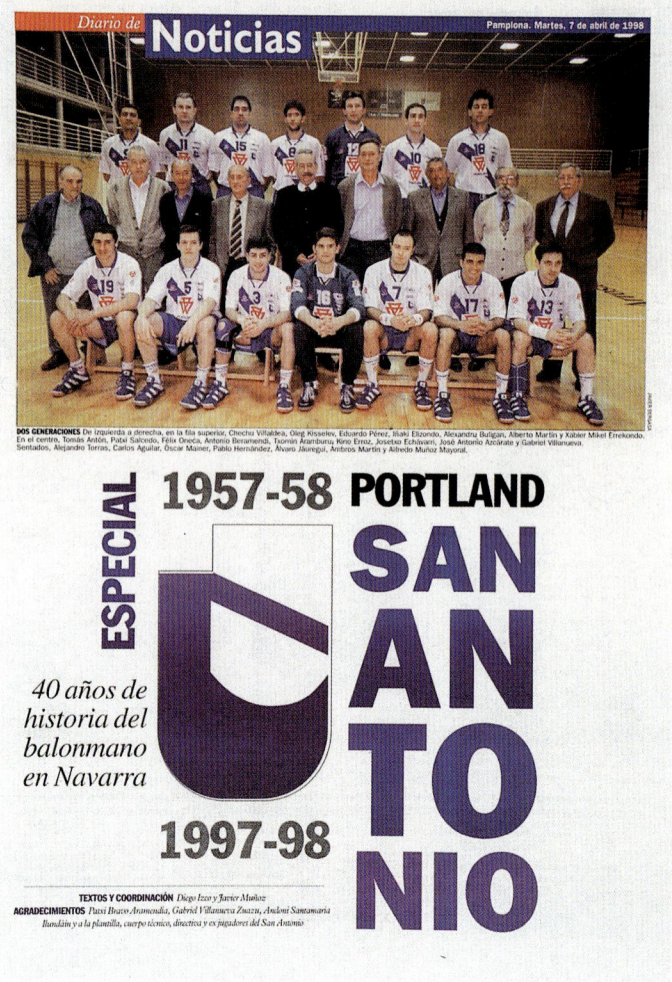

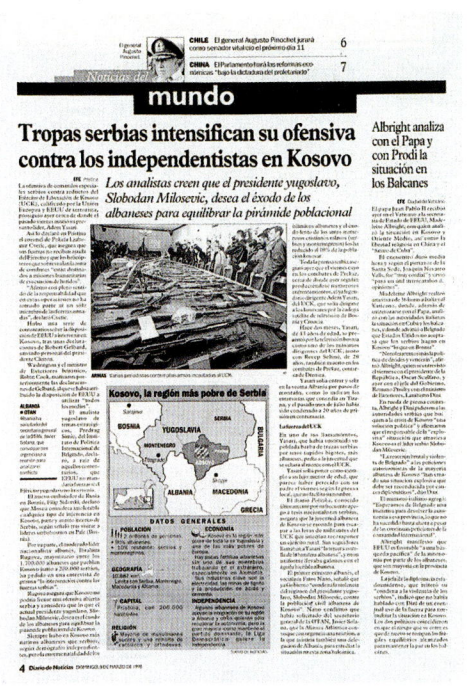
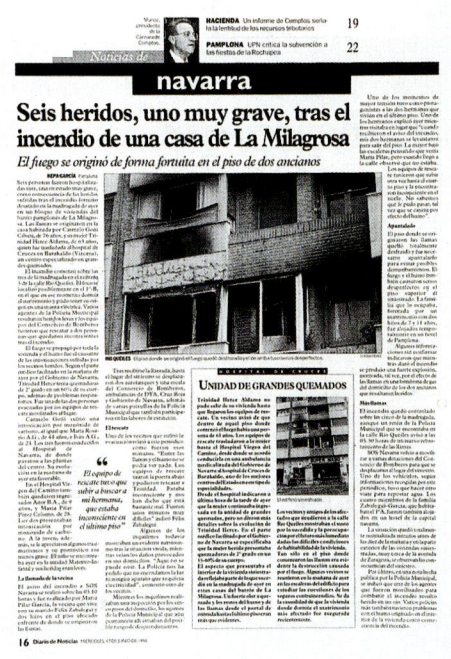
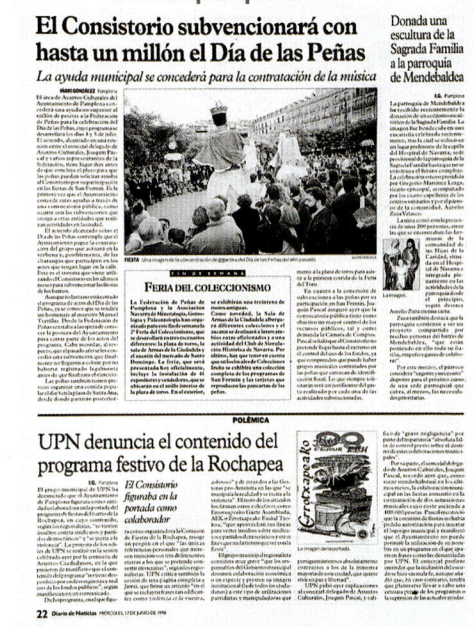
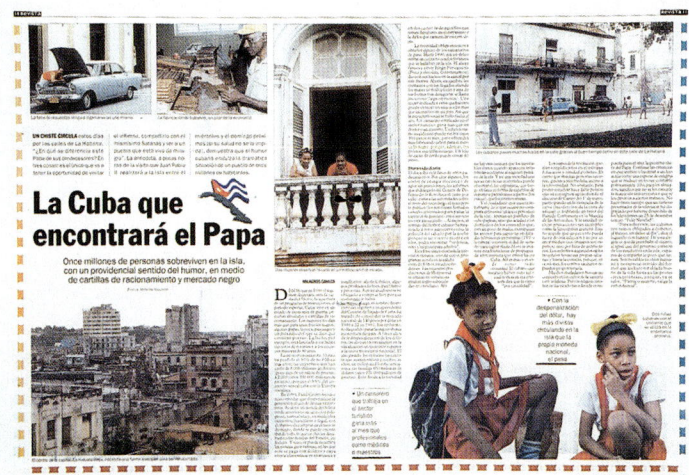
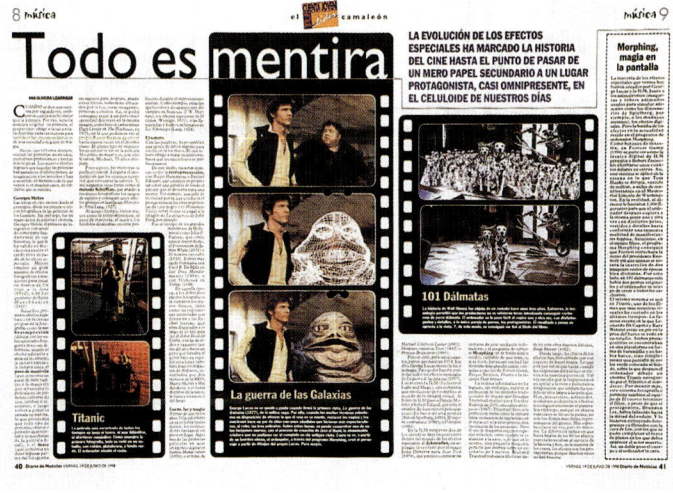
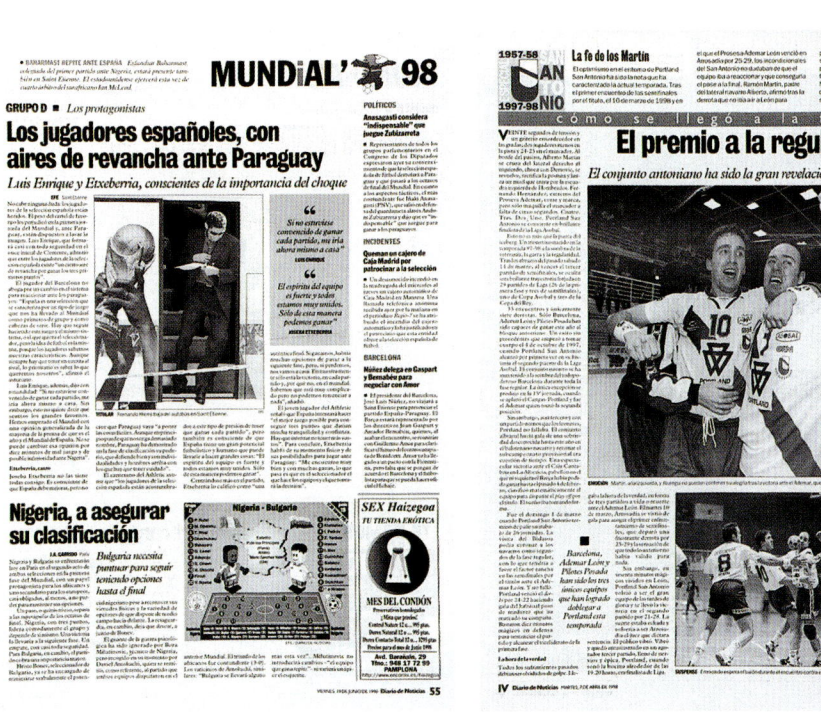
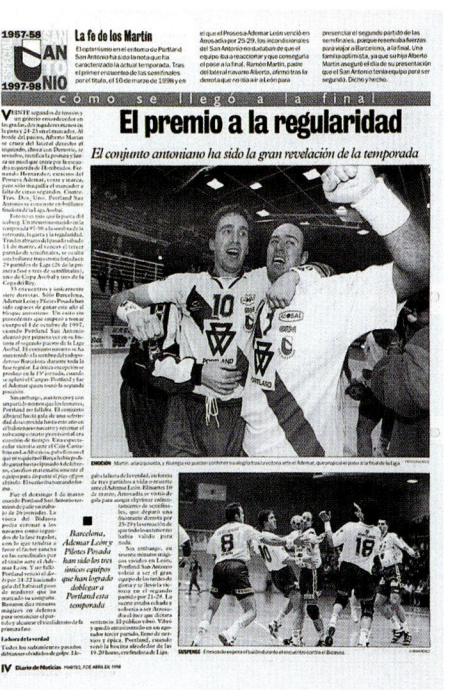
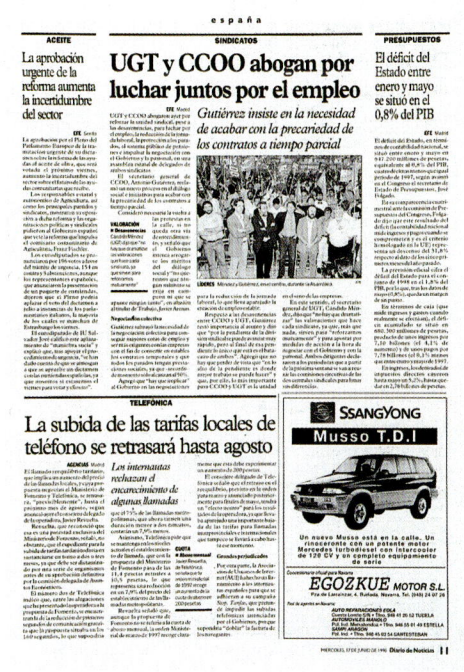

BEST-DESIGNED NEWSPAPERS ■ Correio Braziliense

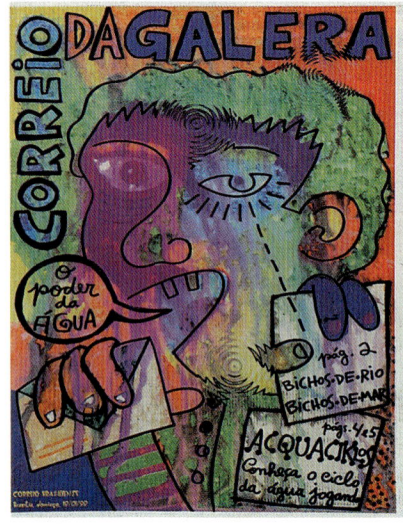
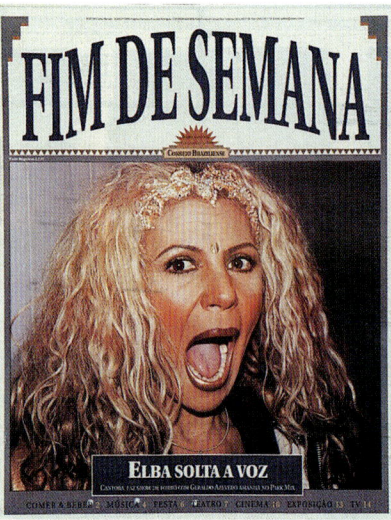
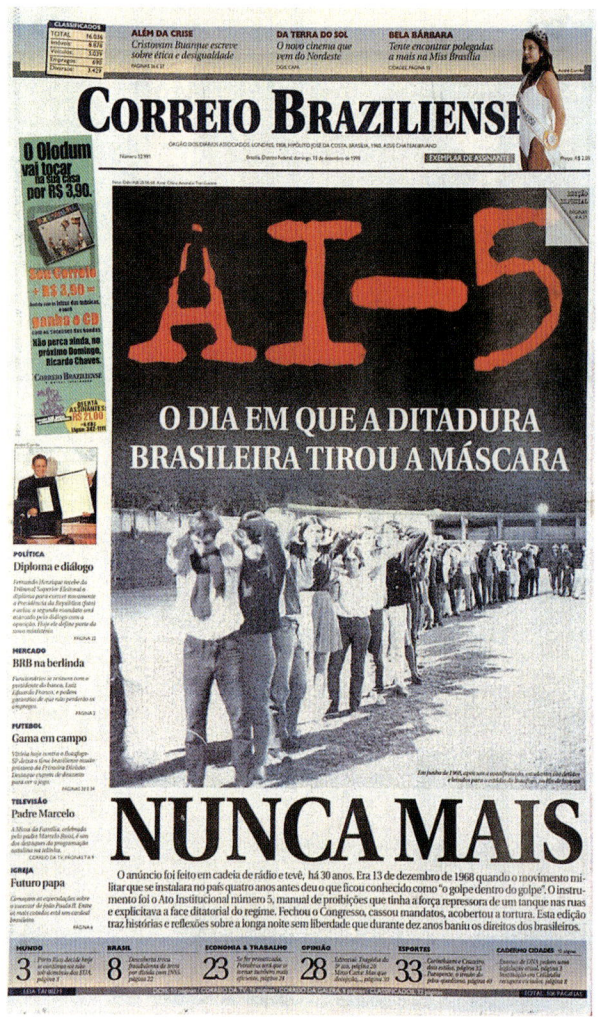

Correio Braziliense
Brasília, Brasil

Correio Braziliense is the market leader for a reason. It has a young, well-educated readership and knows how to meet its needs. Its content is also interesting. The strength of the paper's design is in its attention to detail. It's extremely refined and its inside pages are wonderfully consistent. The newspaper takes care to provide the reader with multiple points of entry to almost every piece. There are lots of layering devices used, all of which are well done.

Correio Braziliense es el líder del mercado por una razón: sus lectores son jóvenes y están bien informados, y conoce cómo satisfacer sus necesidades. Su contenido también es de gran interés. El punto fuerte del diseño de este diario radica en la atención que le presta a los detalles. Es refinado en extremo y sus páginas interiores mantienen la coherencia y el atractivo. El periódico se esfuerza por brindarle al lector varios puntos de entrada para cada artículo. Se emplean numerosos recursos de sombreado, realizados con eficacia

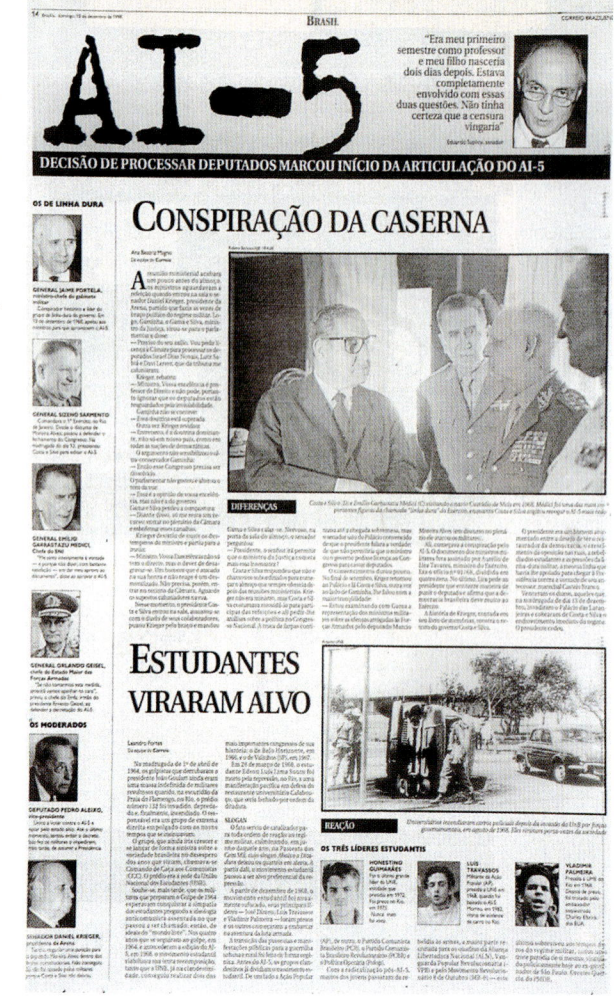

14 ■ THE BEST OF NEWSPAPER DESIGN

CIRCULATION 80,000 ■ BEST-DESIGNED NEWSPAPERS

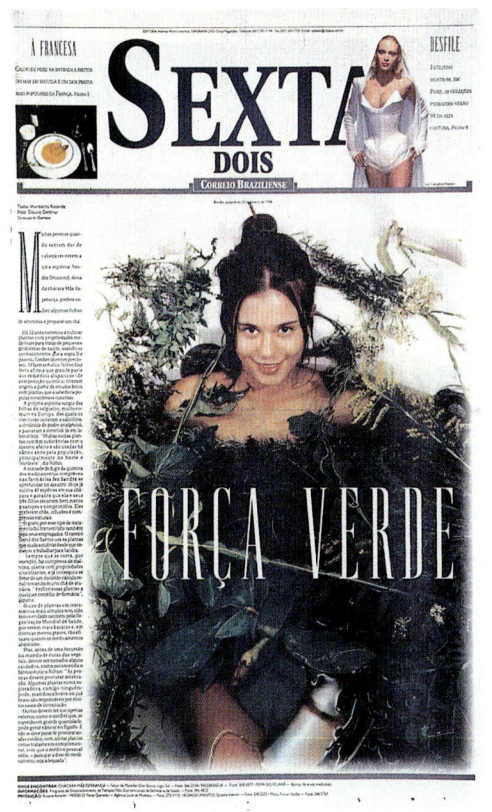
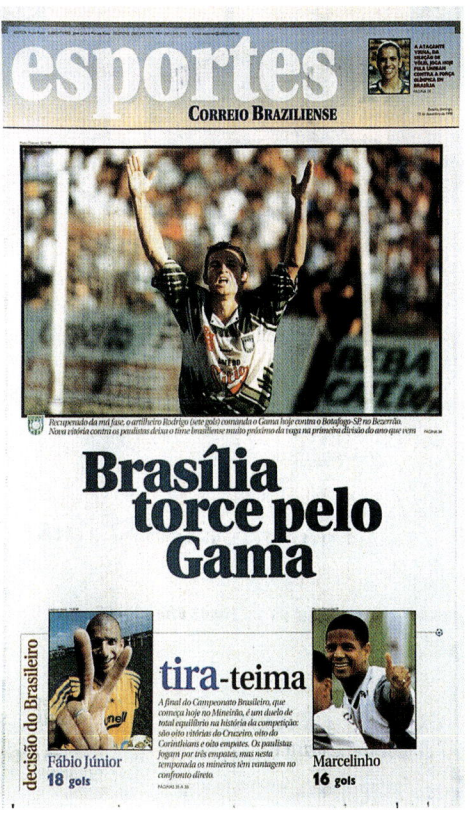
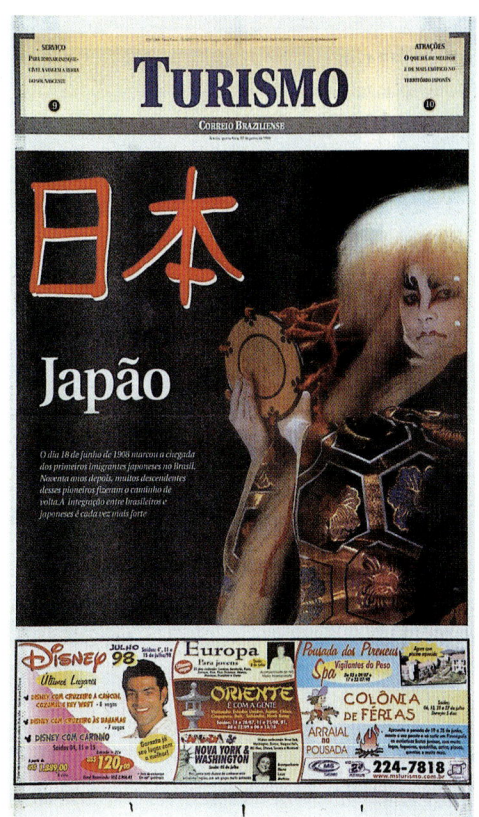
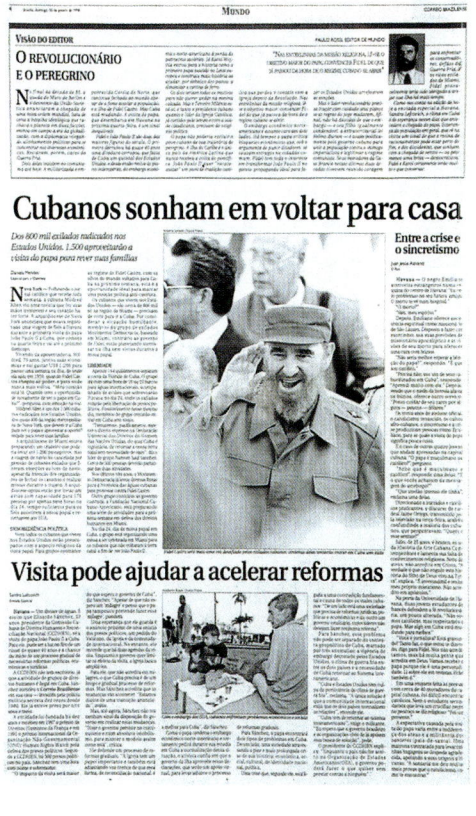
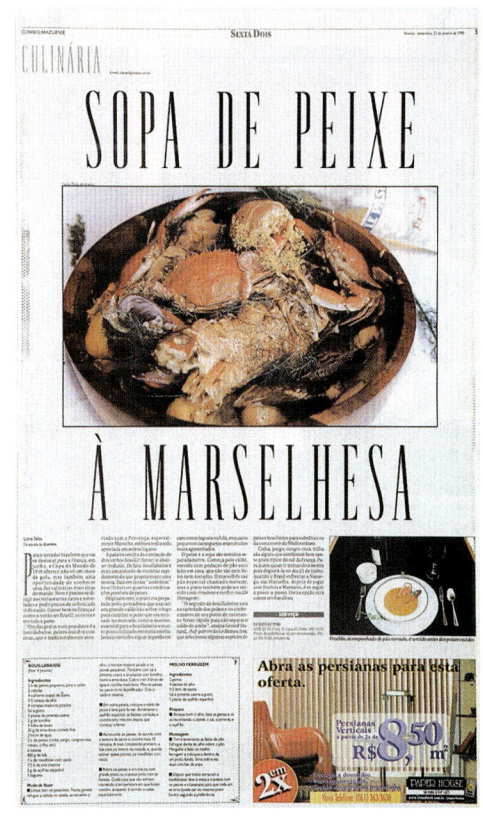
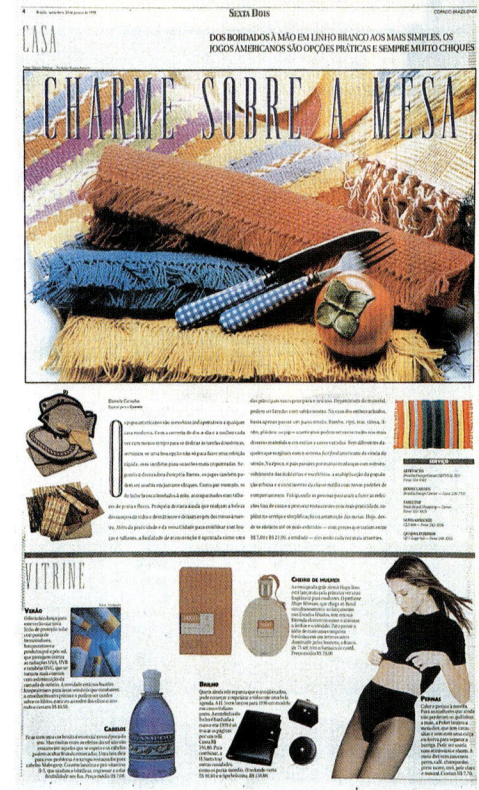

TWENTIETH EDITION ■ 15

BEST-DESIGNED NEWSPAPERS ■ El Correo

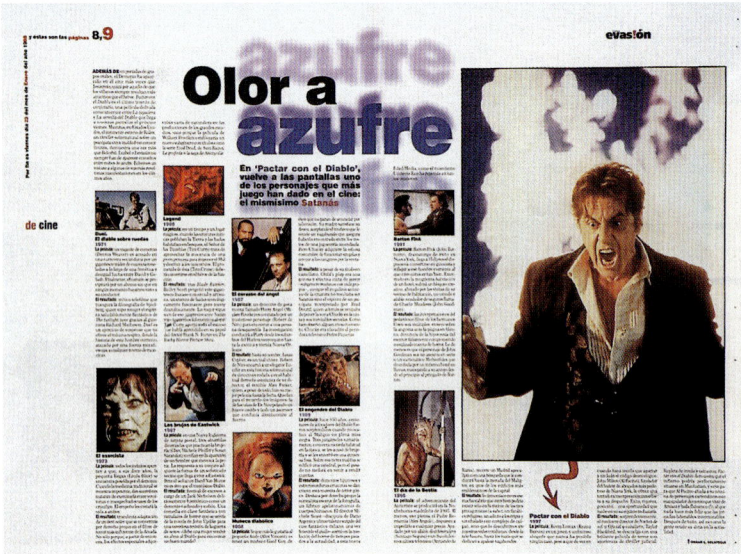

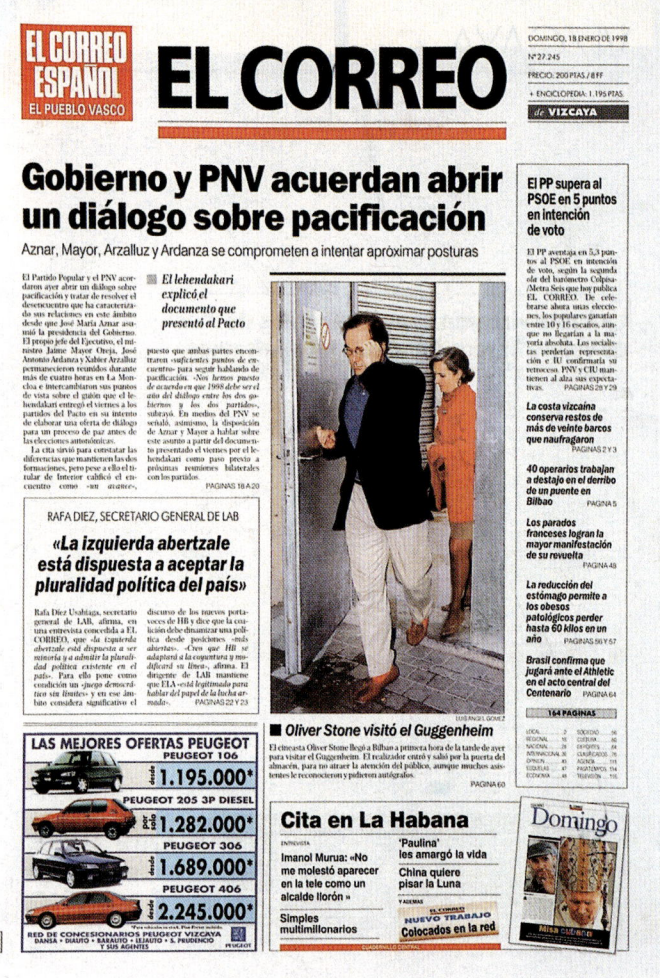

El Correo
Bilbao, Spain

El Correo is clearly text-driven, targeting a conservative readership. It is serious and filled with great writing. The publication presents its readers with a passionate voice and presentation. It is nicely done with a quiet, crisp, scripted — almost understated — sense of design. There is an understanding of scale and balance in everything it does. It lets the content carry its message. The photography and graphics are handled well.

El Correro hace un claro énfasis en el texto, y se dirige a lectores muy conservadores. Es un diario muy serio y sus artículos están muy bien redactados. Esta publicación le ofrece a sus lectores una voz y una presentación apasionadas. Tiene una realización muy buena y un sentido del diseño muy sutil, conciso y preparado, casi discreto. Tiene una idea muy clara de la escala y el equilibrio en todo lo que hace, y deja que el contenido se encargue de trasmitir su mensaje. La fotografía y los gráficos se manejan con gran eficacia.

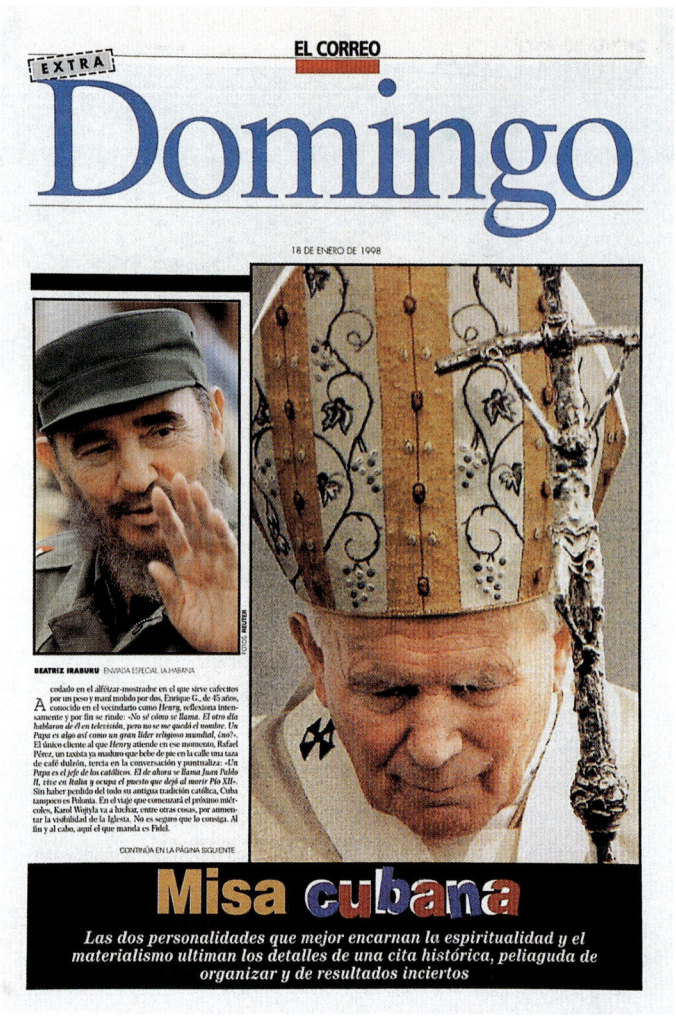

CIRCULATION 130,000 ■ BEST-DESIGNED NEWSPAPERS

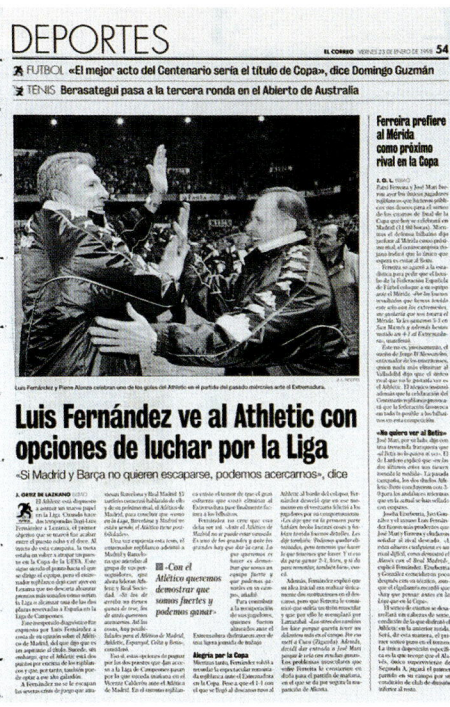
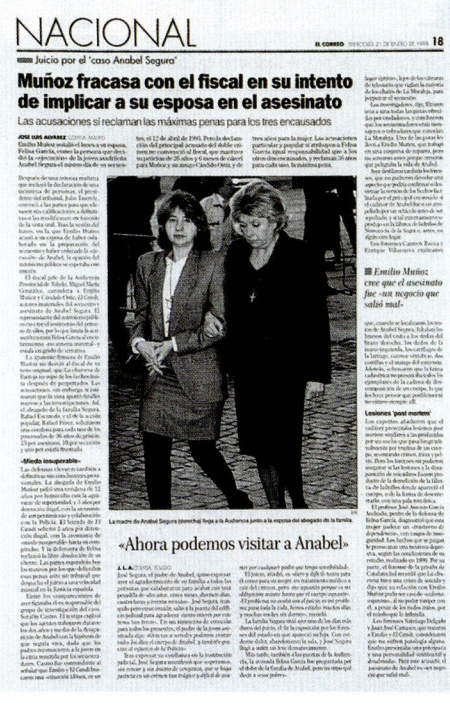
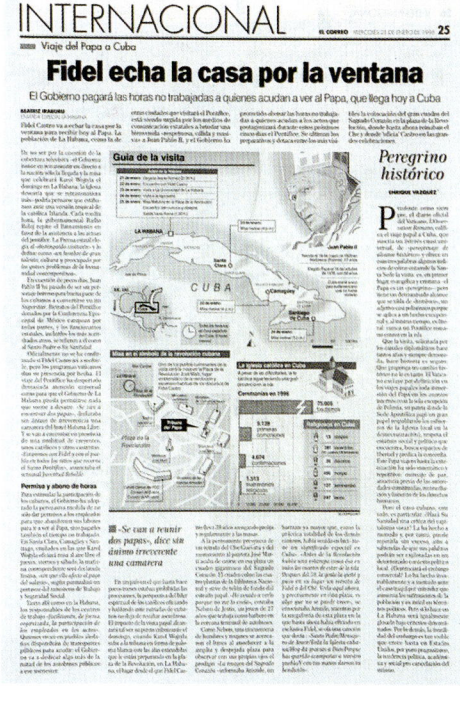
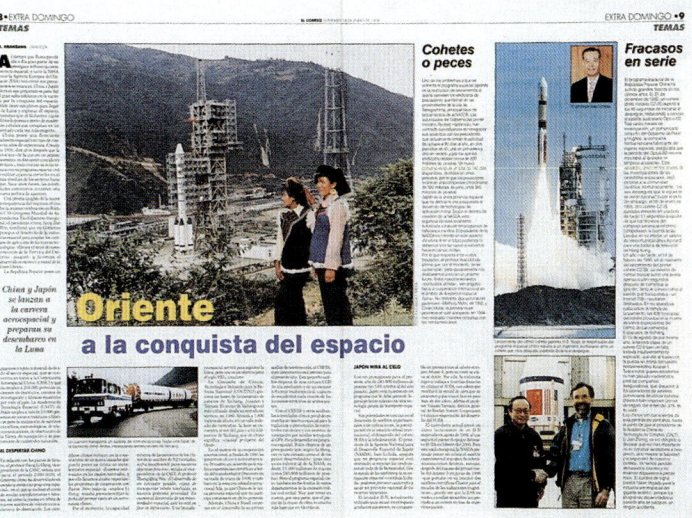
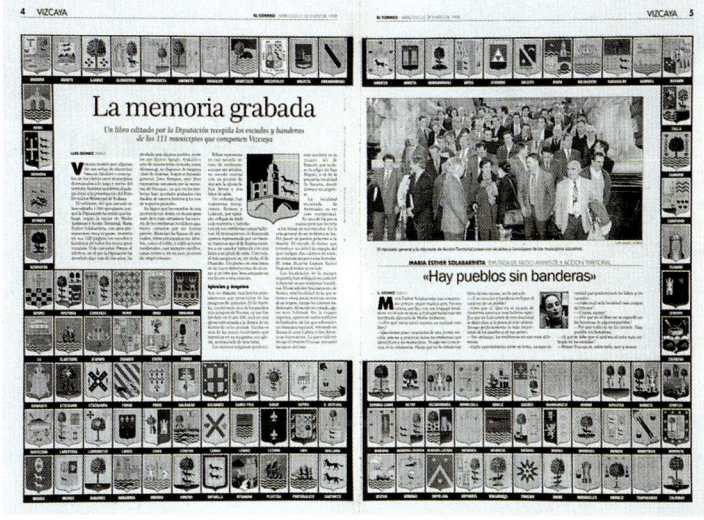
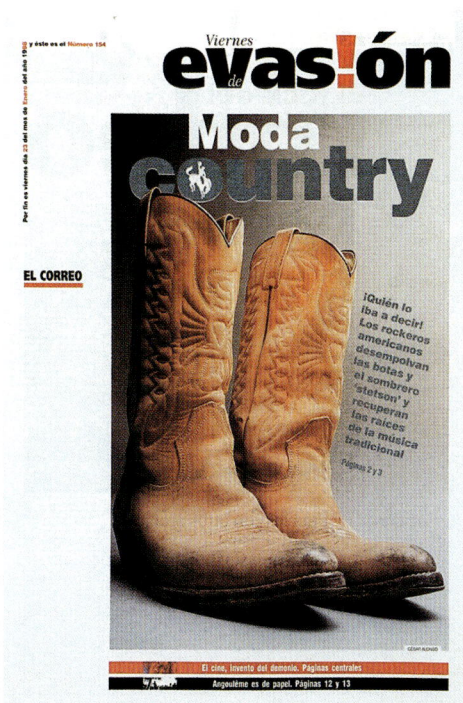
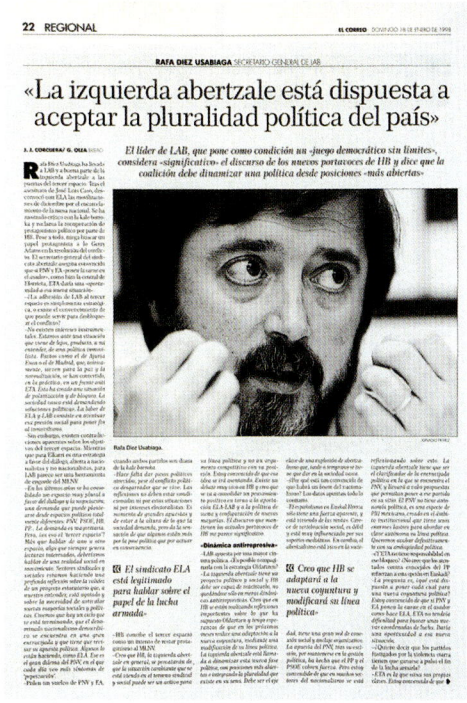
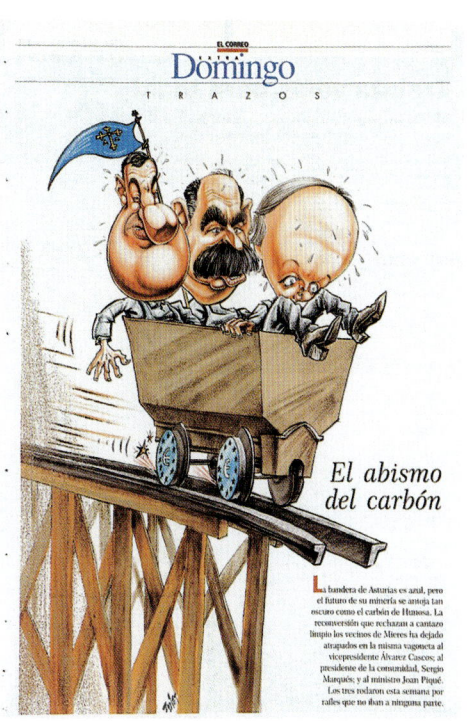

TWENTIETH EDITION ■ 17

BEST-DESIGNED NEWSPAPERS • The Gainesville Sun

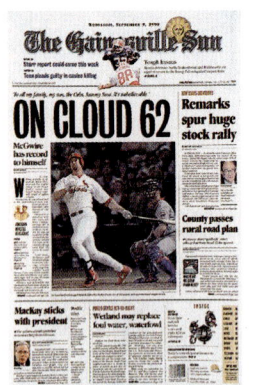
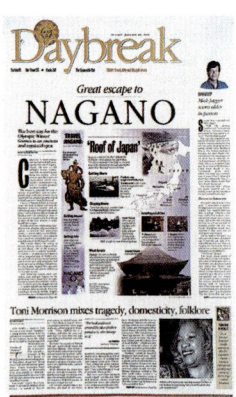
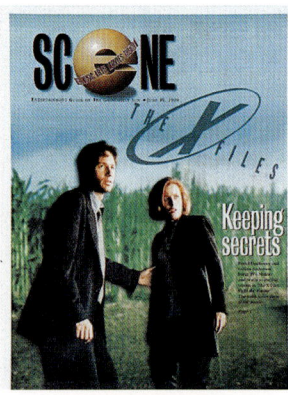
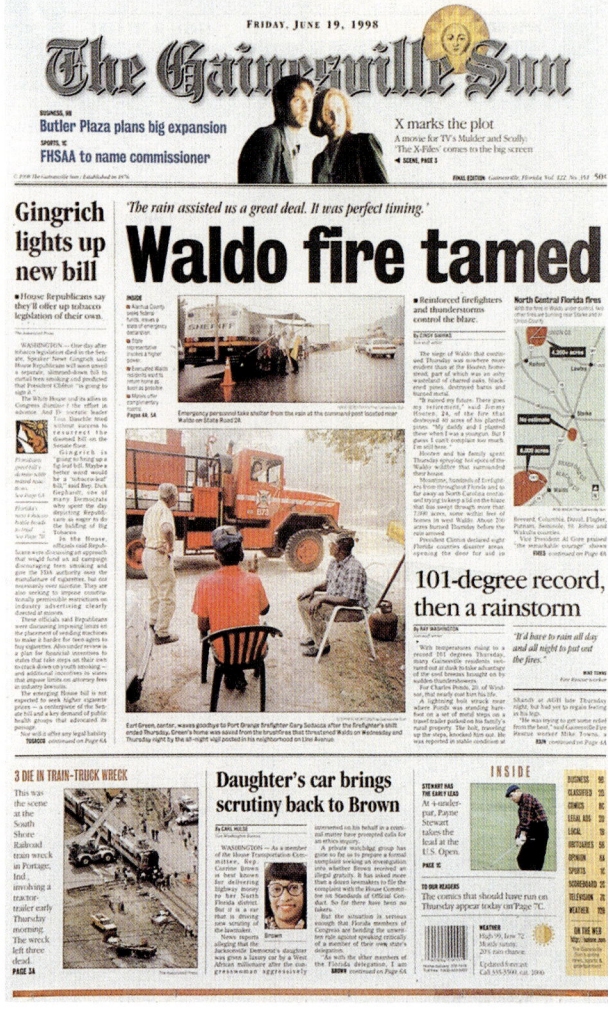

The Gainesville Sun
Gainesville, FL

The Gainesville Sun is a well-organized package with a strong sense of place about it. Its design uses all of its resources to help the reader to navigate its pages. There is a sense of energy at work on these pages. The packaging is obviously planned, even in breaking news stories. The internal design structure carries the entire package. This paper is well done.

The Gainesville Sun tiene una presentación muy bien organizada que enfatiza el color local. Su diseño utiliza todos los recursos para ayudar al lector a navegar por sus páginas, las mismas que denotan energía. Es obvio que la presentación ha sido planificada, incluso cuando se da una noticia de último minuto. La estructura de diseño interna sostiene todo el periódico. Es un periódico muy bien realizado.

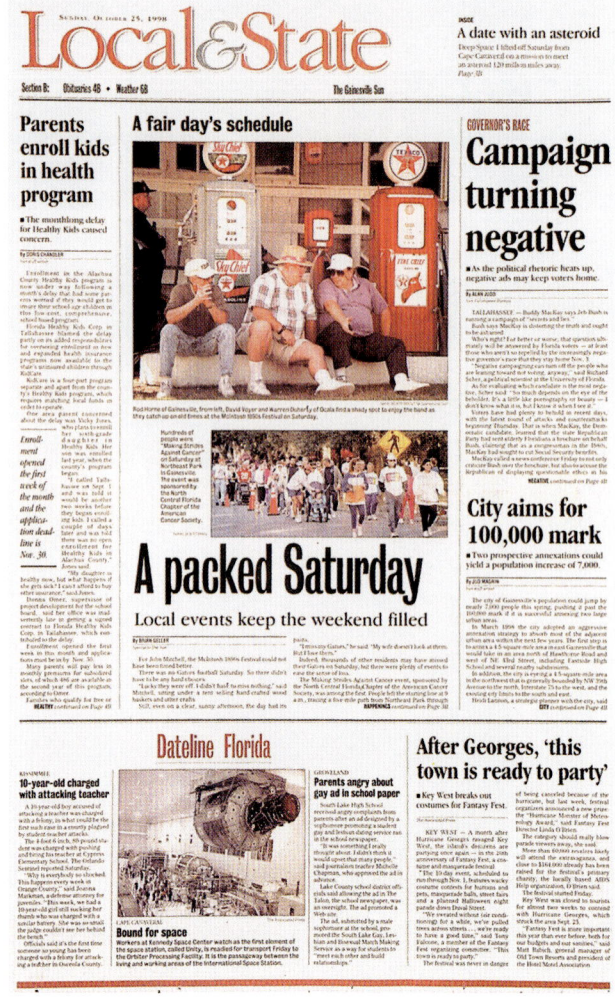

18 ■ THE BEST OF NEWSPAPER DESIGN

CIRCULATION 54,000 ■ BEST-DESIGNED NEWSPAPERS

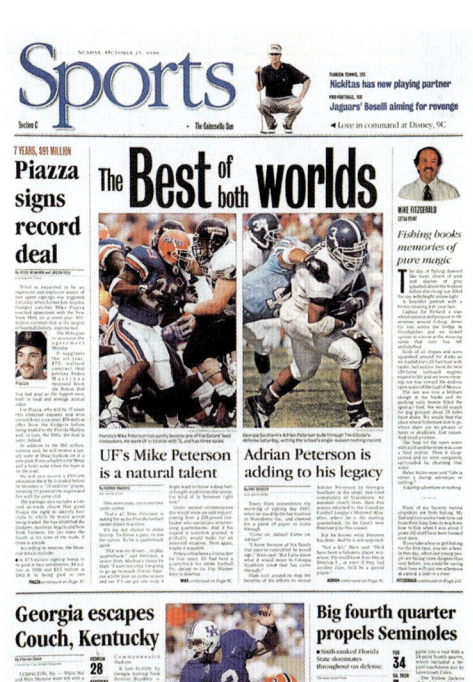
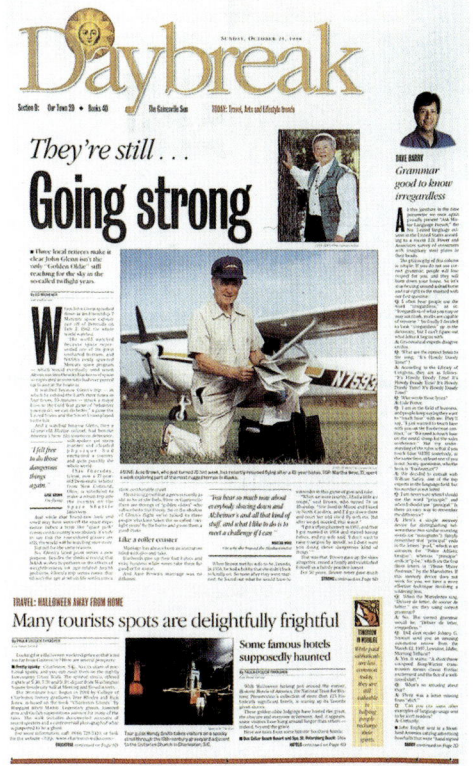
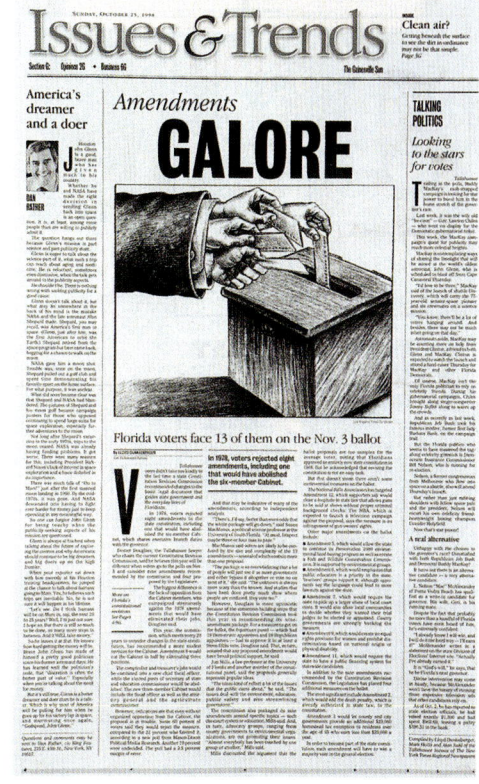
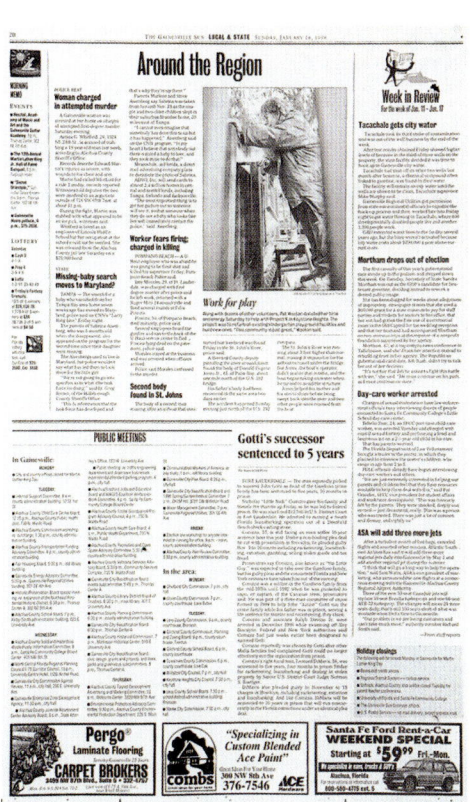
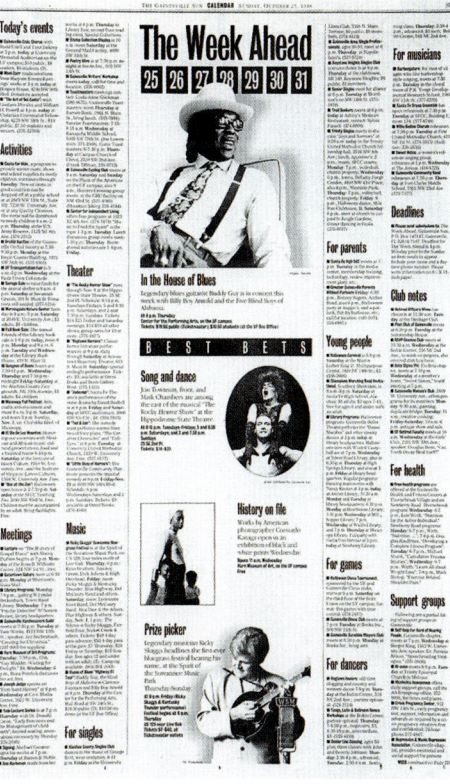
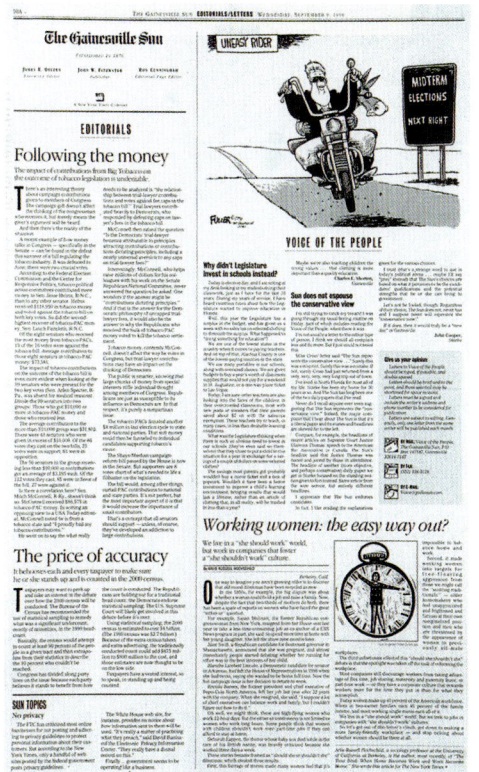

TWENTIETH EDITION ■ 19

BEST-DESIGNED NEWSPAPERS ■ Lexington Herald-Leader

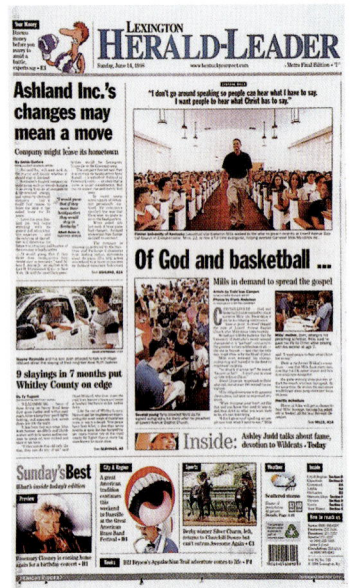
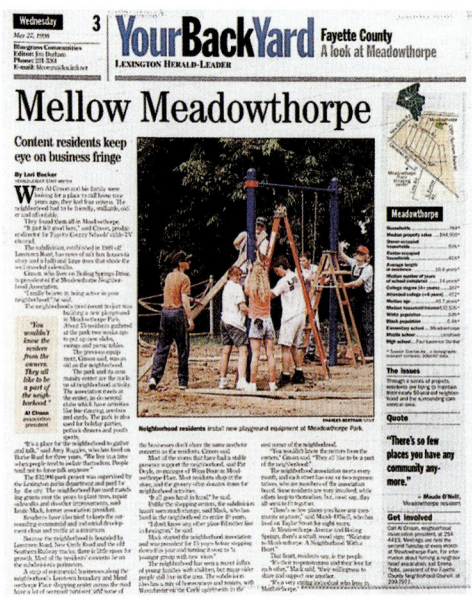
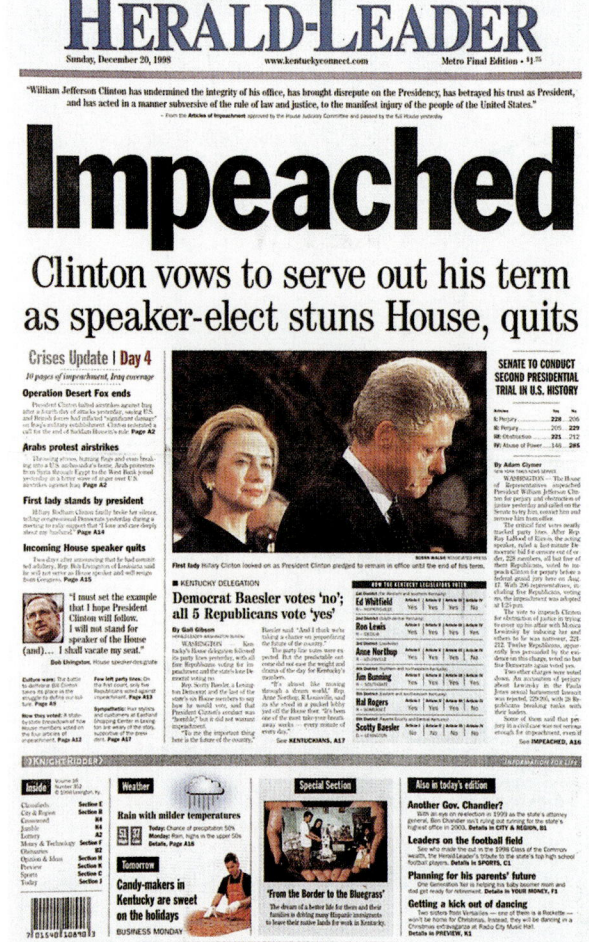

Lexington Herald-Leader
Lexington, KY

Everything the Lexington Herald-Leader does is clearly labeled and accessible. The design flows easily to the inside pages with lots of content throughout in the paper. The special sections were some of the best we saw in any of the entries. It handles its photography and typography well.

The Lexington Herald-Leader es un periódico muy bien organizado. Todo lo que hace tiene la referencia adecuada y es accesible. El diseño fluye con facilidad hacia las páginas interiores y el contenido es abundante. Las secciones especiales fueron de lo mejor que vimos entre los concursantes, y maneja la fotografía y la tipografía con eficacia.

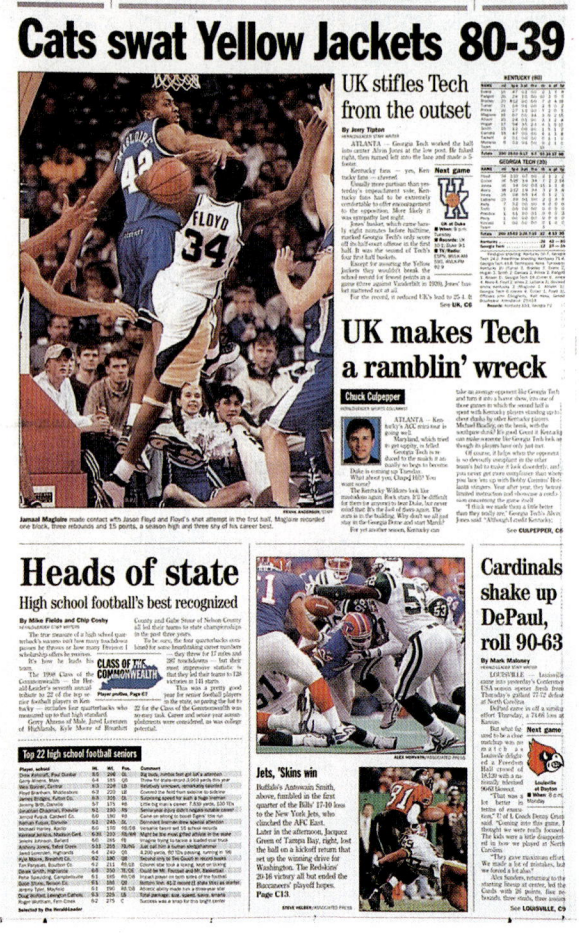

20 ■ THE BEST OF NEWSPAPER DESIGN

CIRCULATION 160,000 ■ BEST-DESIGNED NEWSPAPERS

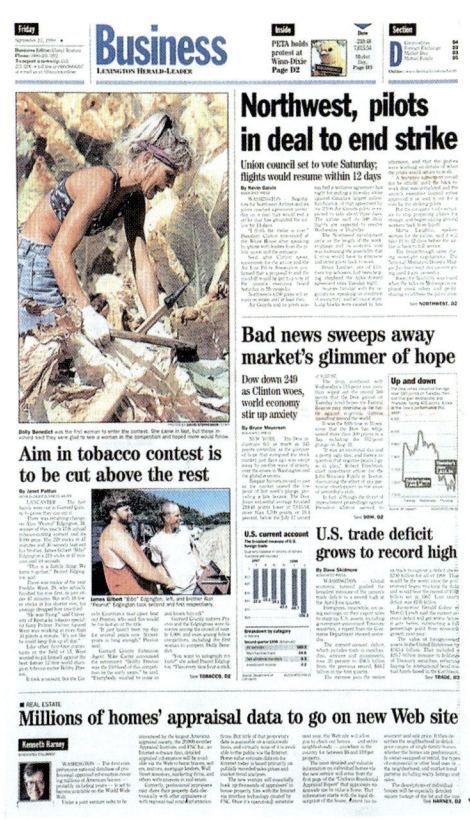
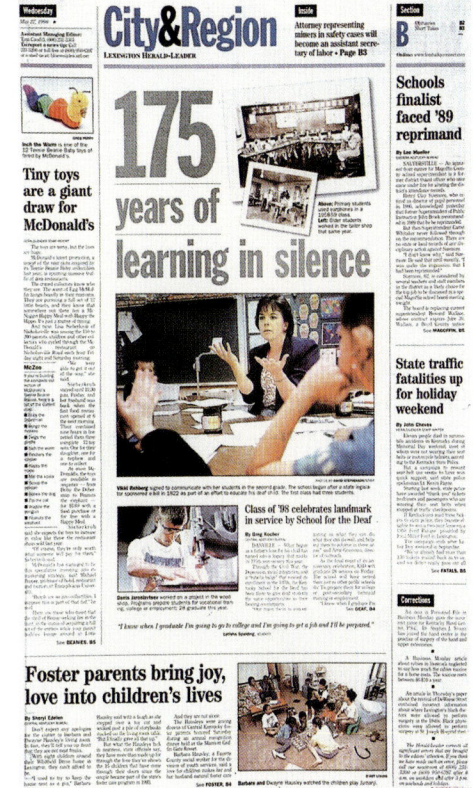
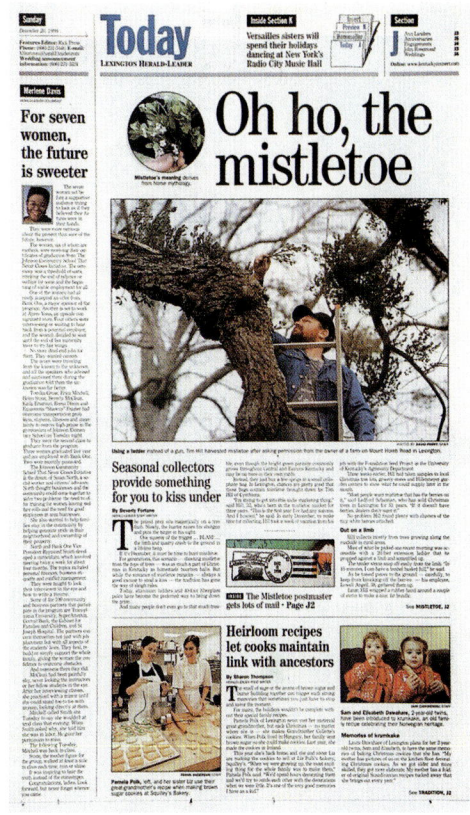
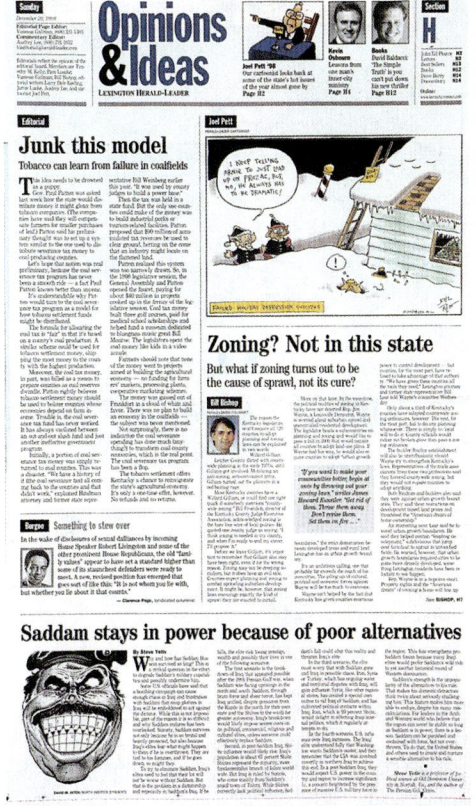
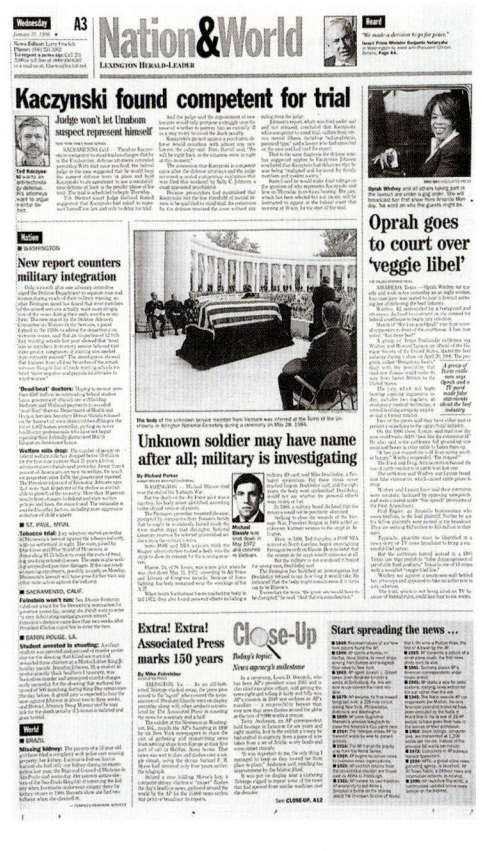
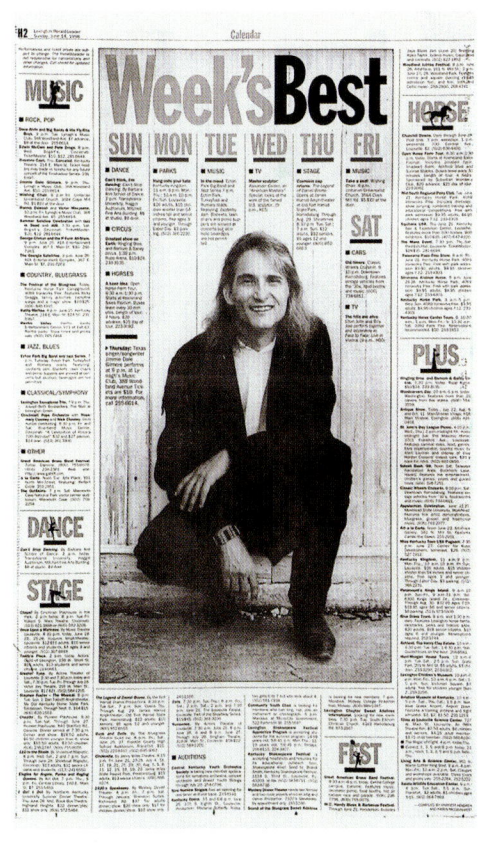

TWENTIETH EDITION ■ 21

BEST-DESIGNED NEWSPAPERS ■ The News & Observer

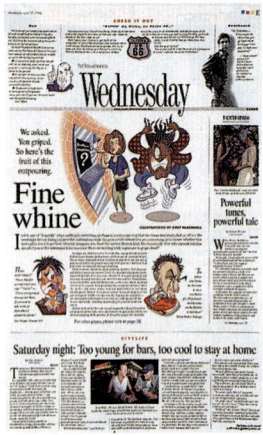
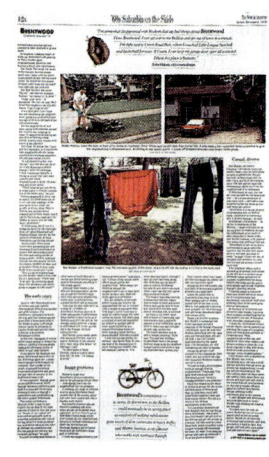
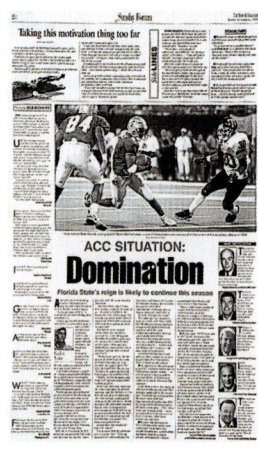
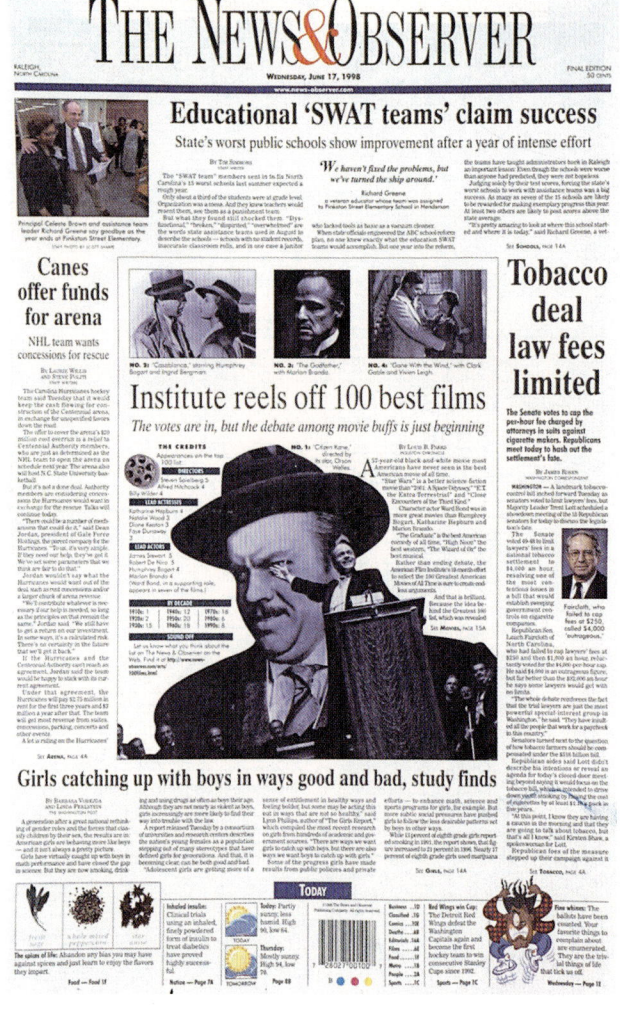

The News & Observer
Raleigh, NC

The News & Observer is an eloquently packaged local paper. It understands the interests of its readers and appears to address them daily. The paper is full of surprises. The design conforms to the day's news. There is nothing formula about this package. Each day presents a creative solution to the challenge of packaging the news. The constant changing of rhythm throughout the entry indicates it is definitely not afraid to experiment. It has wonderful typography and makes good use of its photography and illustration.

The News & Observer es un diario local con una elocuente presentación. Está al tanto de los intereses de sus lectores y parece dirigirse a ellos a diario. Es un diario lleno de sorpresas y el diseño se ajusta a las noticias del día. No hay nada que no denote creatividad. Cada día se ofrecen nuevas soluciones para enfrentar el reto de presentar las noticias. El constante cambio de ritmo indica que, sin dudas, no temen experimentar. Su tipografía es magnífica y se hace un uso excelente de la fotografía y las ilustraciones.

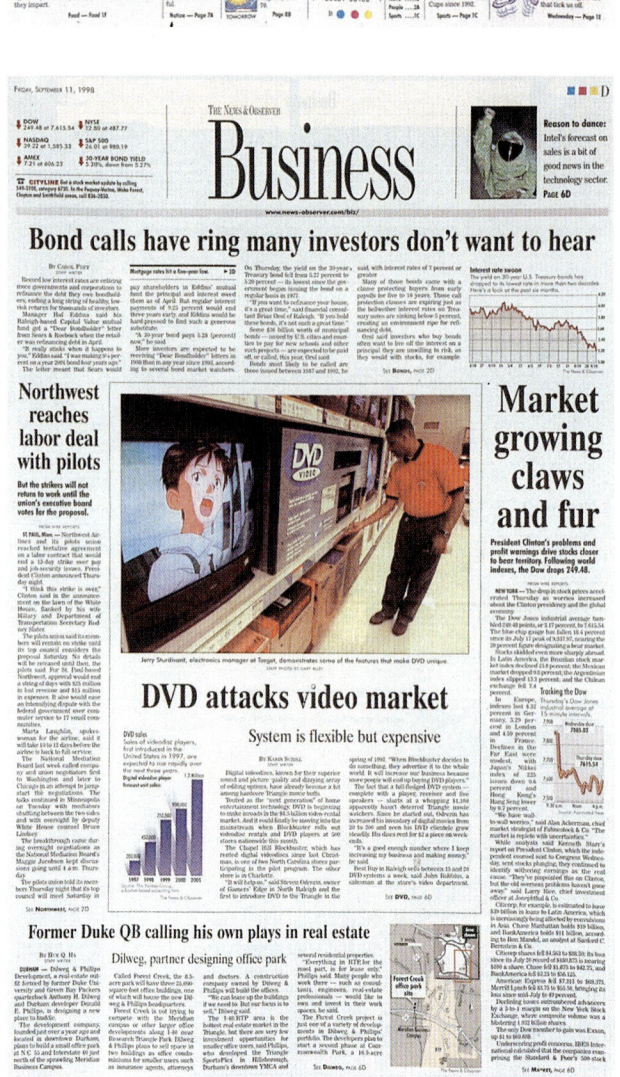

22 ■ THE BEST OF NEWSPAPER DESIGN

CIRCULATION 160,000 ■ BEST-DESIGNED NEWSPAPERS

• Award of Excellence for Special News Topics

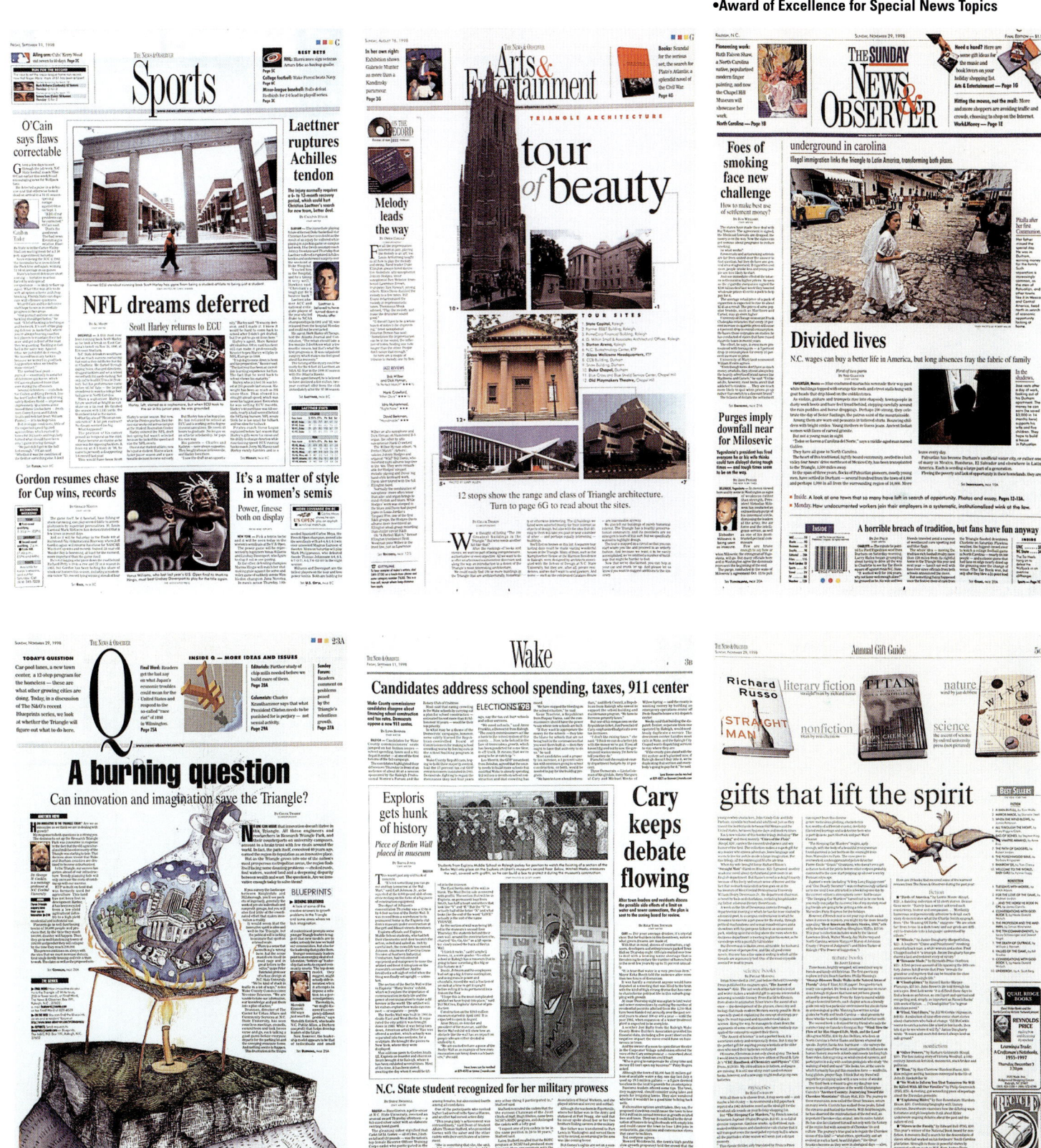

TWENTIETH EDITION ■ 23

BEST-DESIGNED NEWSPAPERS ■ Le Soleil

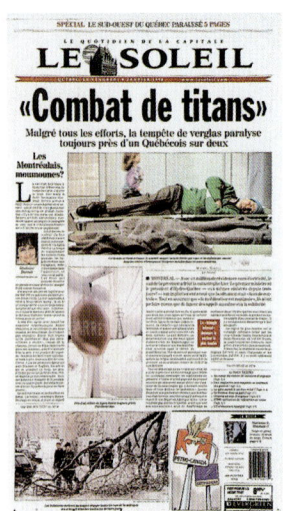
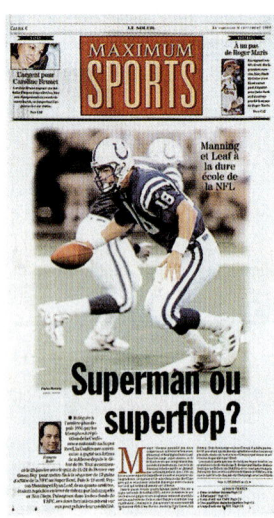
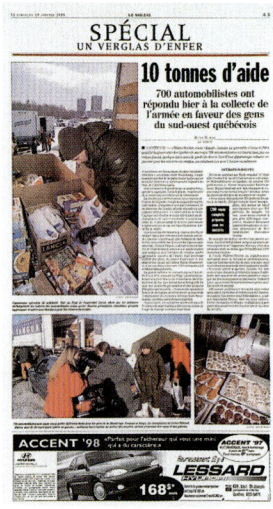
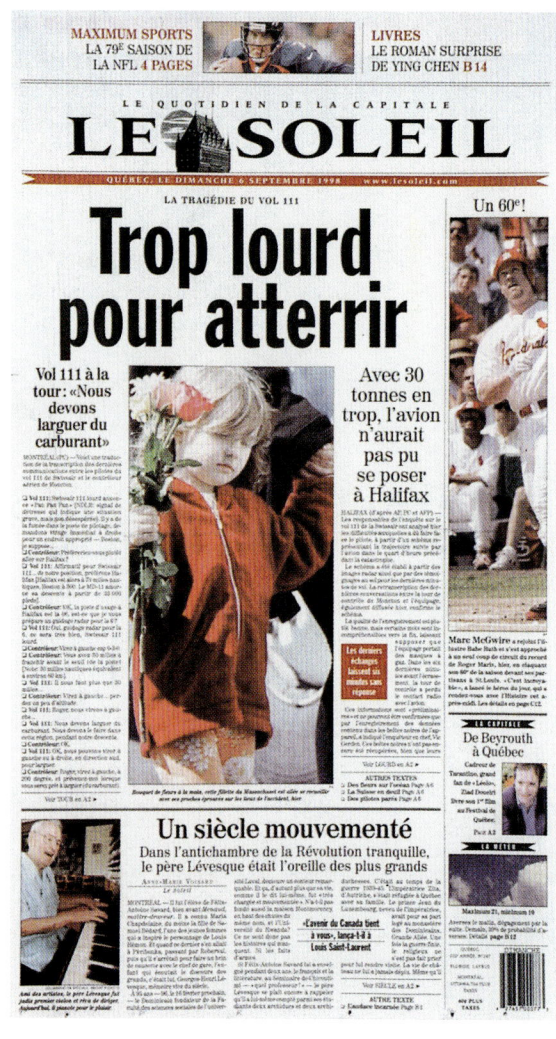

Le Soleil
Québec, Canada

Le Soleil is not a formula newspaper. It seems to reinvent itself daily. There are lots of surprises. The design is handled well with a balance between the words and the visuals. Care and attention to detail are given to each inside page. It is well packaged. The architecture of its pages and the use of color, typography and photography is sophisticated. It reflects its community and the culture of its readers. It is really beautiful.

Le Soleil no es un periódico fácil de encasillar. Parece volver a inventarse a diario y abundan las sorpresas. El diseño se maneja con mucha eficacia y se alcanza un equilibrio entre las palabras y las imágenes visuales. Se presta gran atención y cuidado a cada página interior, y su presentación está muy bien lograda. La arquitectura de sus páginas y el empleo del color, la tipografía y la fotografía son muy sofisticados. Refleja a su comunidad de lectores y su cultura. Es muy atractivo.

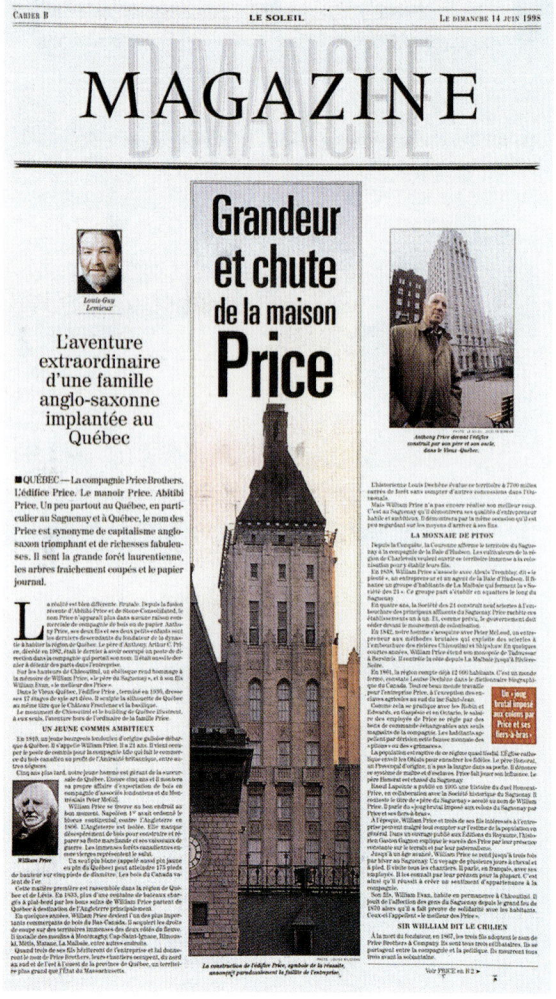

24 ■ THE BEST OF NEWSPAPER DESIGN

CIRCULATION 95,000 ■ BEST-DESIGNED NEWSPAPERS

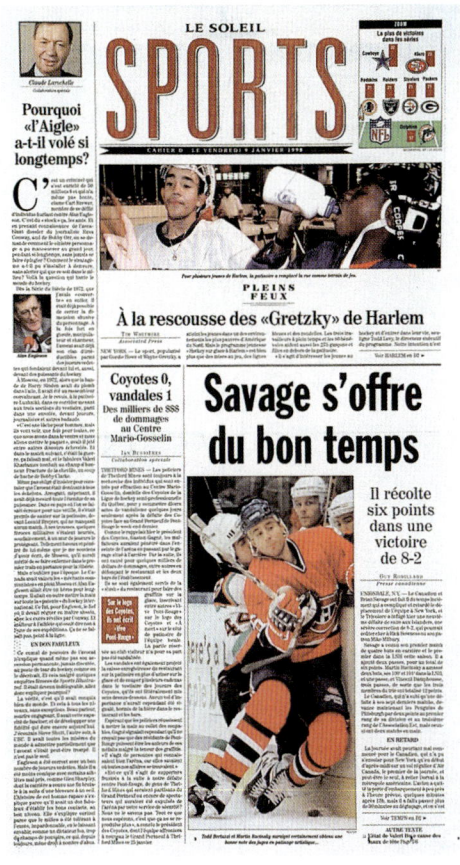
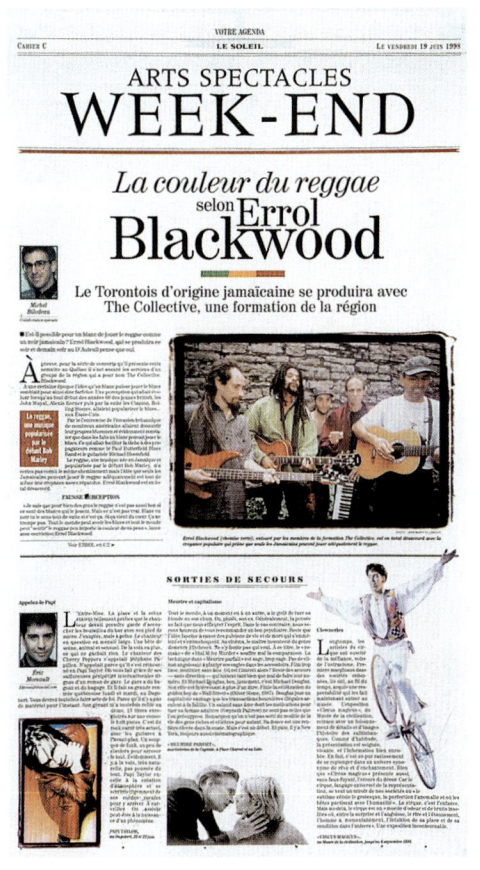
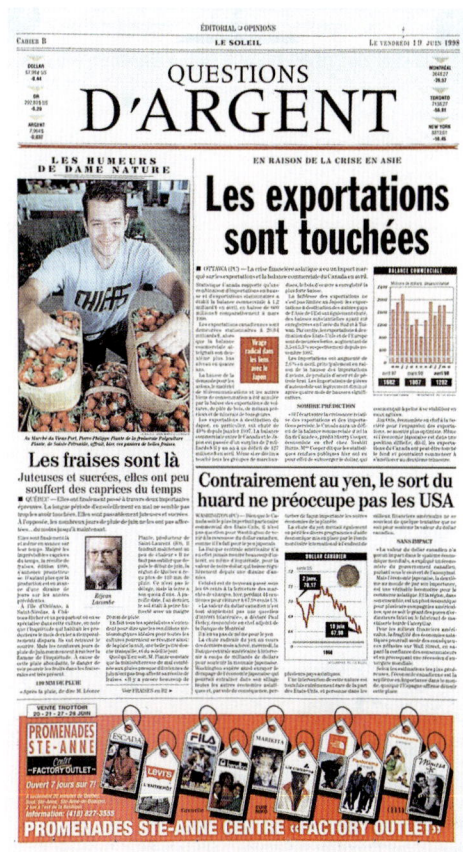
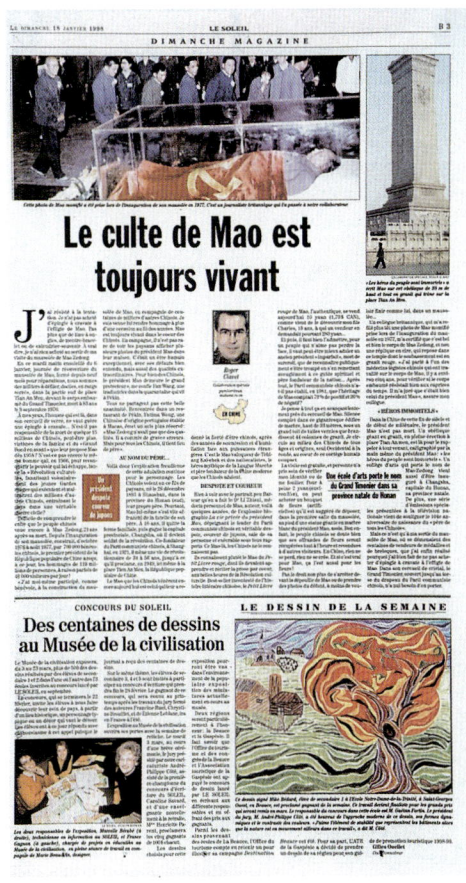
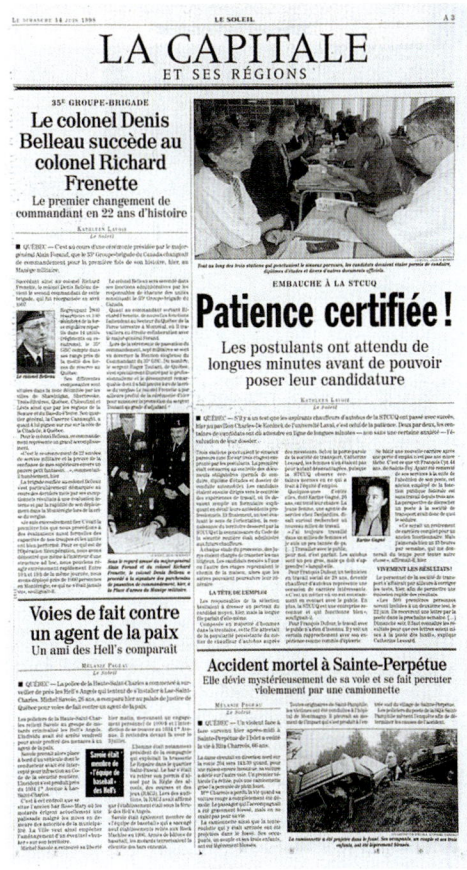
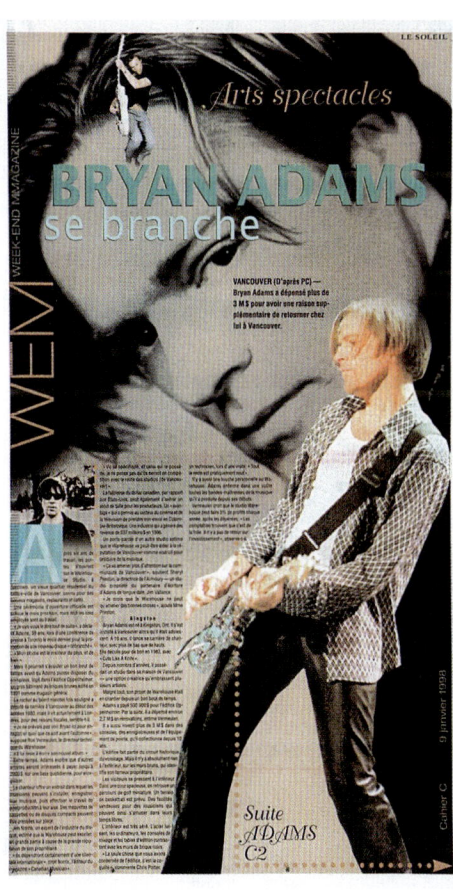

TWENTIETH EDITION ■ 25

BEST-DESIGNED NEWSPAPERS ■ The Spokesman-Review

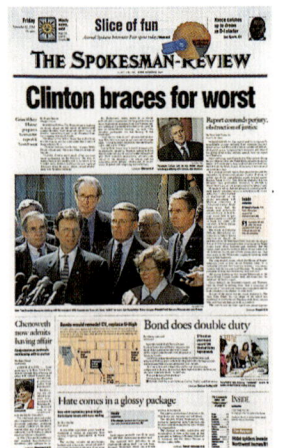
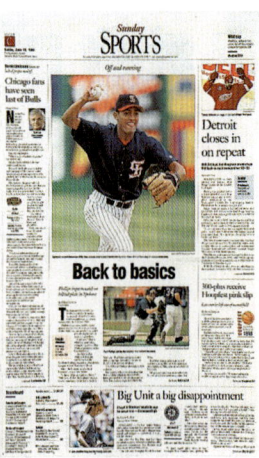
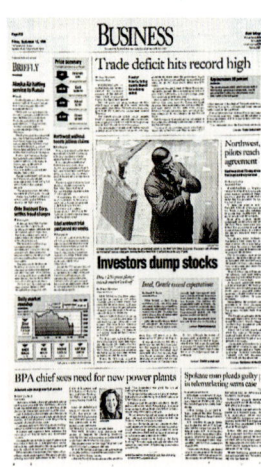
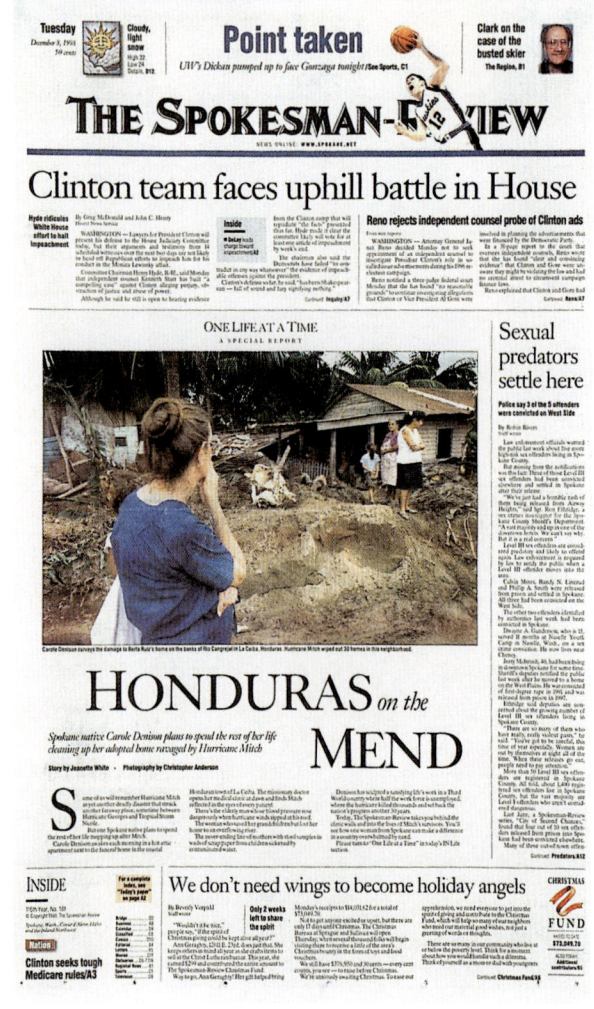
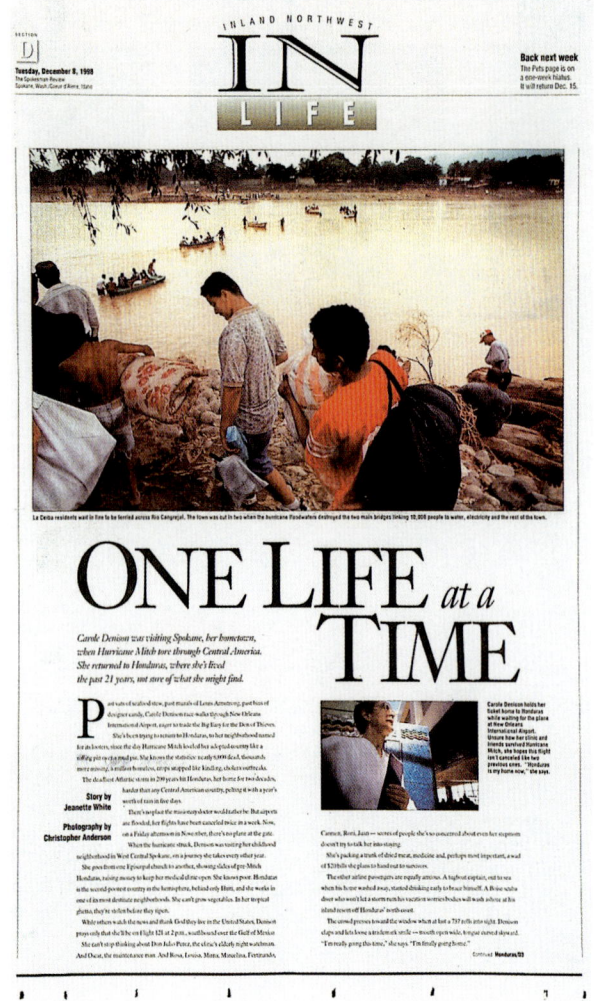

The Spokesman-Review
Spokane, WA

The Spokesman-Review knows its readers and its community. It seems to be having a lot of fun in what it does. The design is consistent throughout the paper with a lot of attention to detail that was missing in many of the entries. The feature sections are filled with surprises and contain a lot of texture in the presentation. The paper keeps everything simple by using photography well; maintaining a sense of clean, elegant typography; incorporating white space into the core of the design; and packaging everything, including the inside pages.

The Spokesman-Review conoce a sus lectores y su comunidad, y parece disfrutar lo que hace. El diseño tiene coherencia en todo el periódico y, a diferencia de otros muchos concursantes, se presta gran atención a los detalles. Las secciones regulares están llenas de sorpresas y contienen una gran textura en la presentación. Este diario mantiene la sencillez mediante el uso eficaz de la fotografía, la tipografía limpia y elegante, la incorporación de espacio blanco en el núcleo del diseño y una presentación integral que abarca las páginas interiores.

CIRCULATION 114,000 ■ BEST-DESIGNED NEWSPAPERS

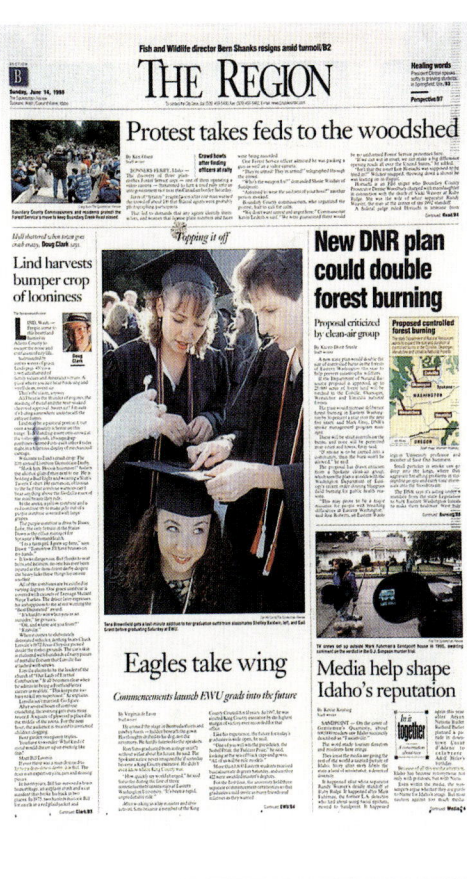
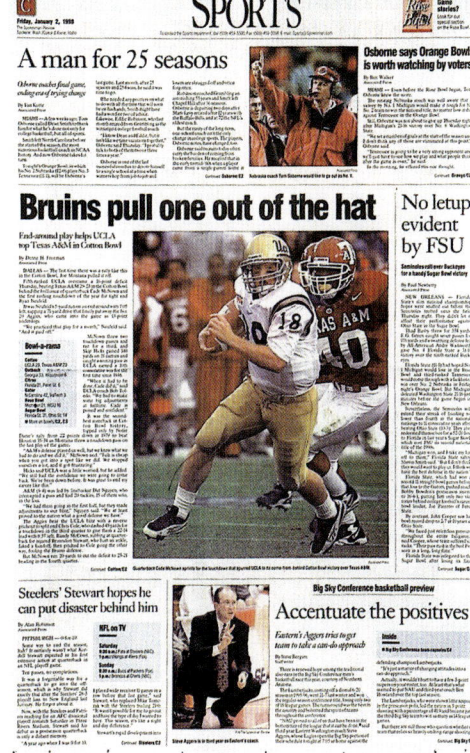
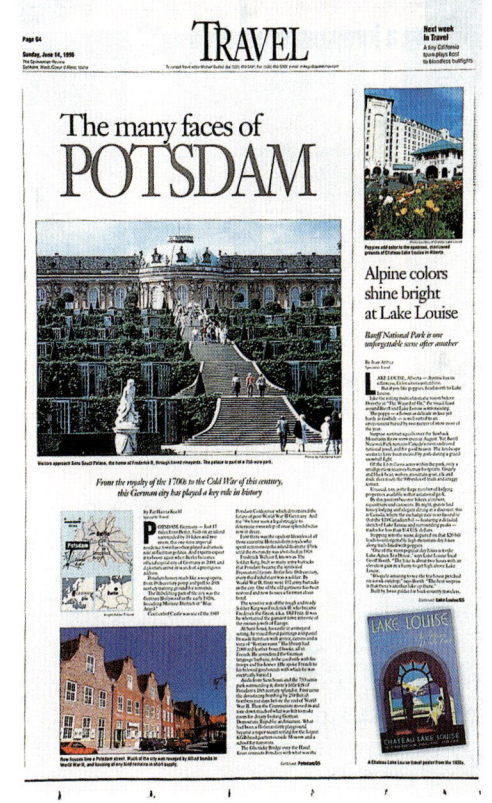
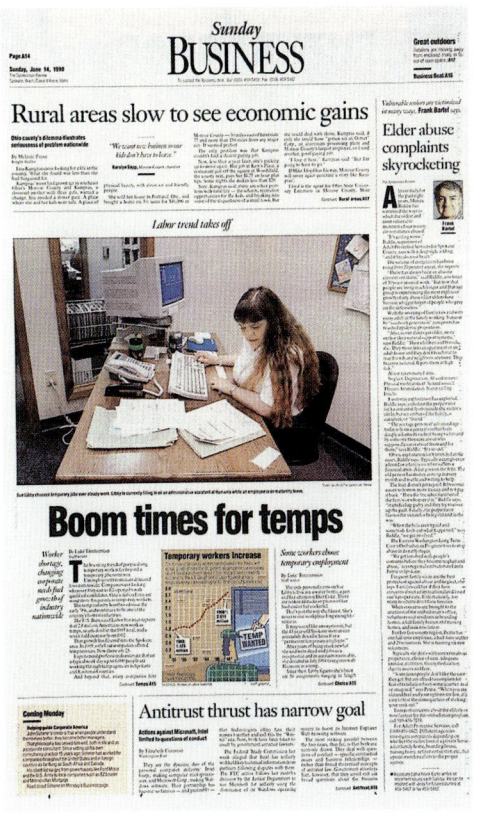
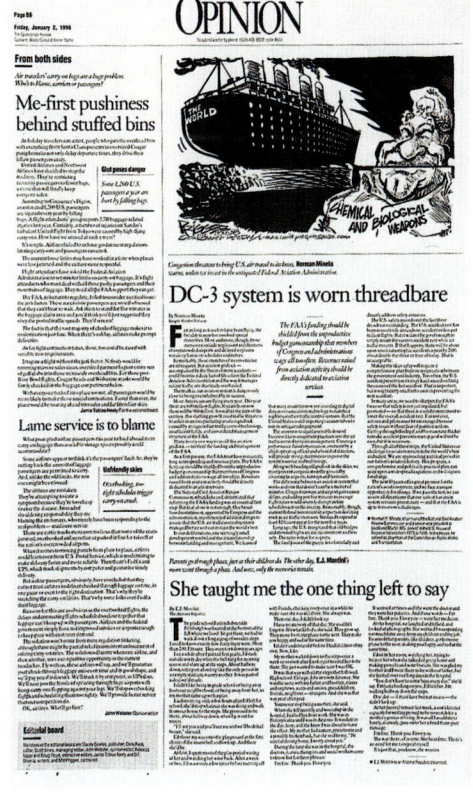
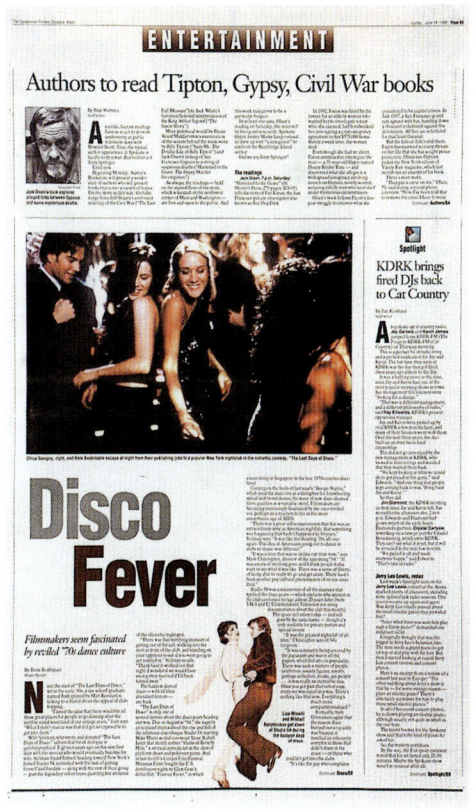

TWENTIETH EDITION ■ 27

BEST-DESIGNED NEWSPAPERS ■ Tomskaya Nedelya

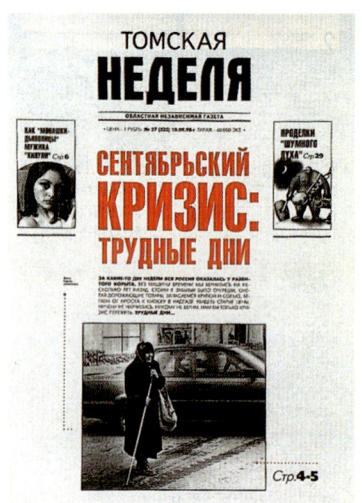
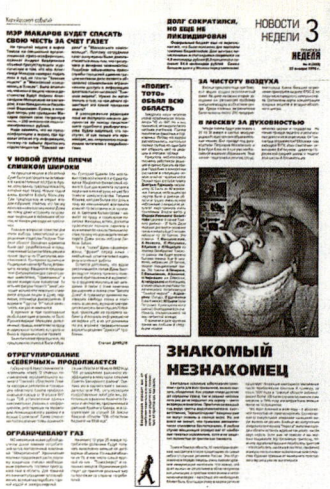
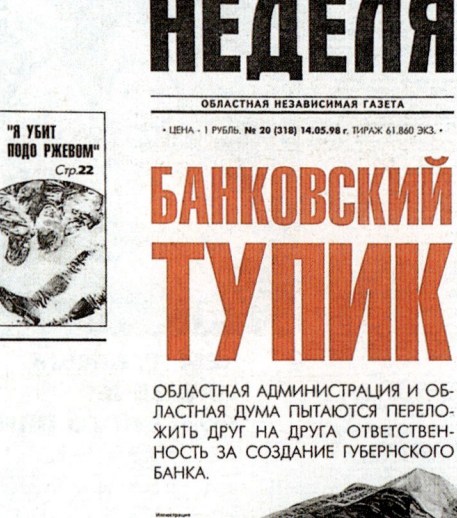
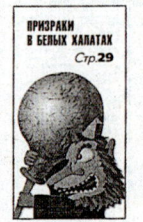
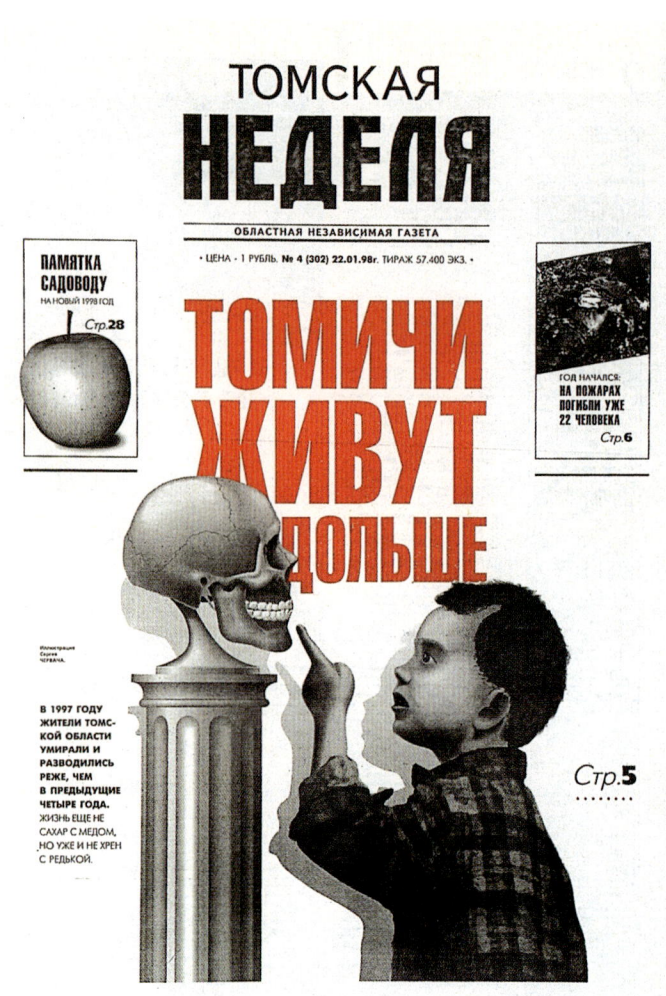

Tomskaya Nedelya
Tomsk, Russia

Tomskaya Nedelya breaks with Russia's past in dramatic form. The paper gives the reader a sense of place and community, not party. The design has a nice typographical sense that is contemporary and fresh, yet with a historical perspective about it. There is an innocence about this design. The photography is well handled. The inside pages are well packaged, with lots of attention to detail. Its minimal use of color (red and black) is superb.

Tomskaya Nedelya rompe con el pasado de Rusia de un modo dramático. Este diario les brinda a sus lectores una sensación de color local y comunidad, y no de partido alguno. El diseño tiene un agradable sentido tipográfico tanto contemporáneo como fresco que, sin embargo, mantiene la perspectiva histórica. Este diseño refleja cierta inocencia. La fotografía está muy bien lograda. Las páginas interiores tienen una presentación impecable que presta gran atención a los detalles. El poco uso del color (rojo y negro) es excelente.

CIRCULATION 61,000 — BEST-DESIGNED NEWSPAPERS

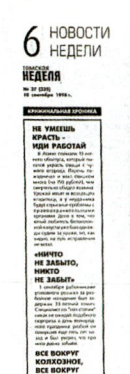
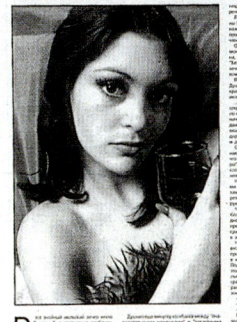
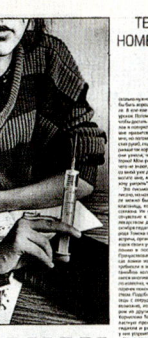
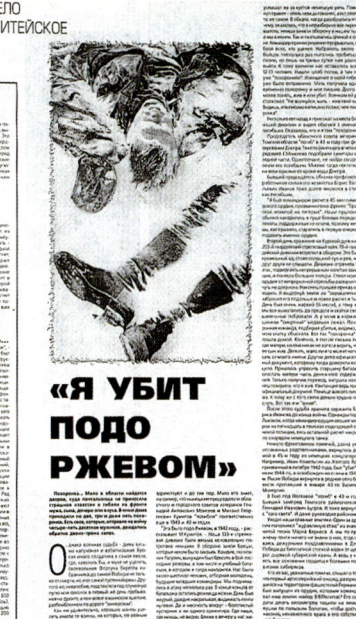
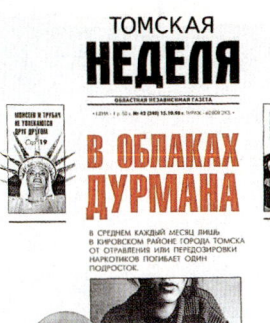
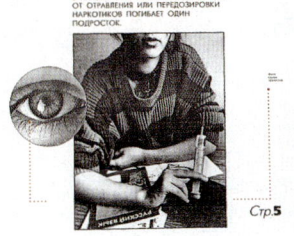
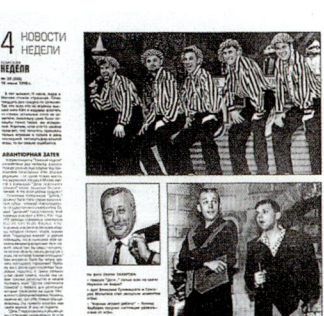
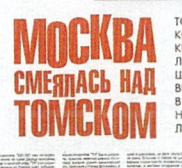
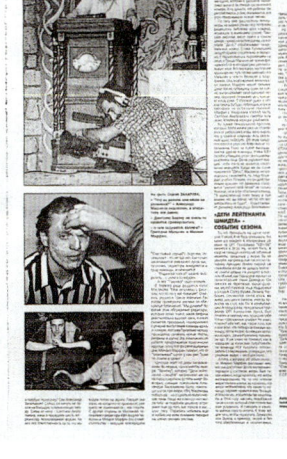
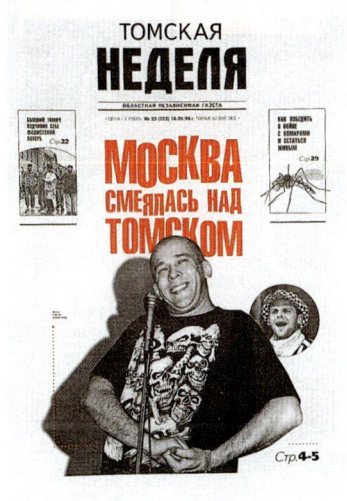
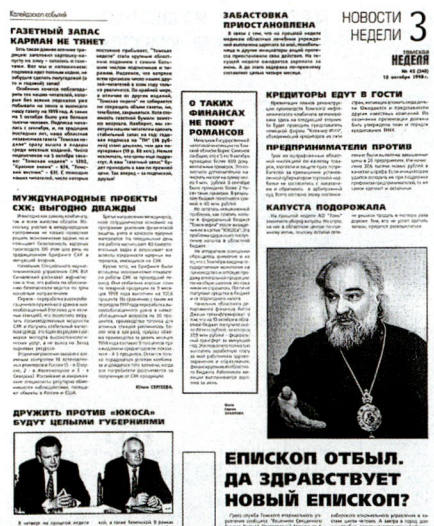
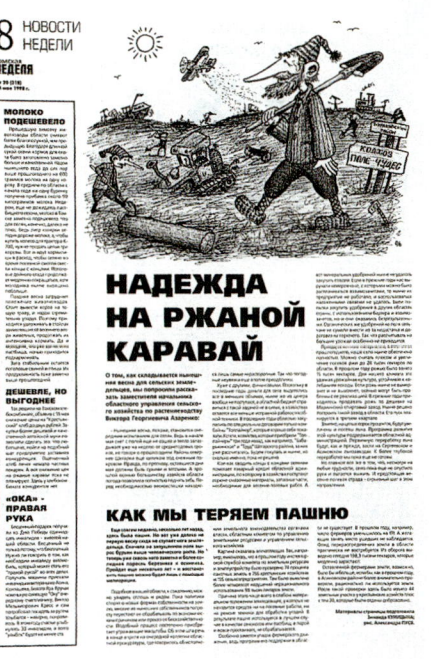
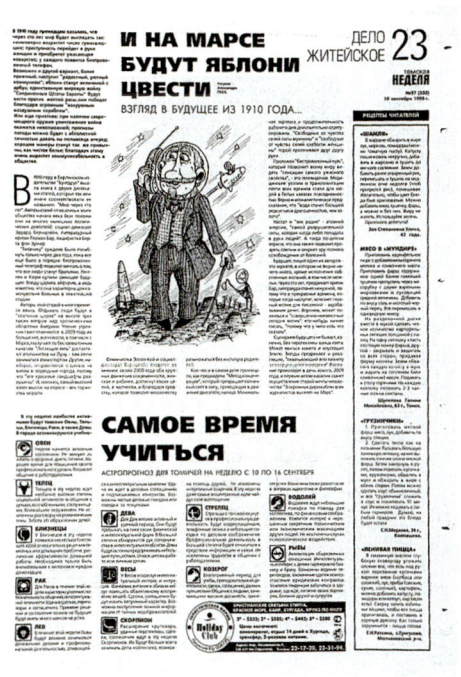

BEST-DESIGNED NEWSPAPERS ■ Die Woche

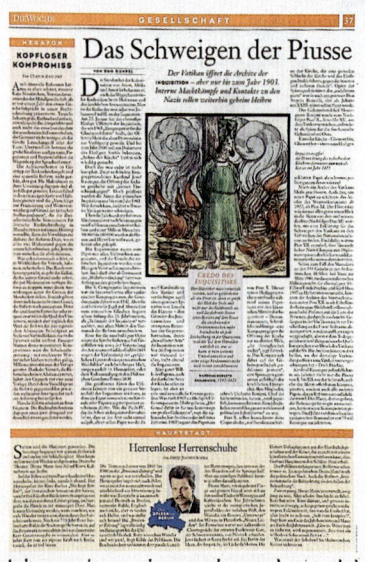
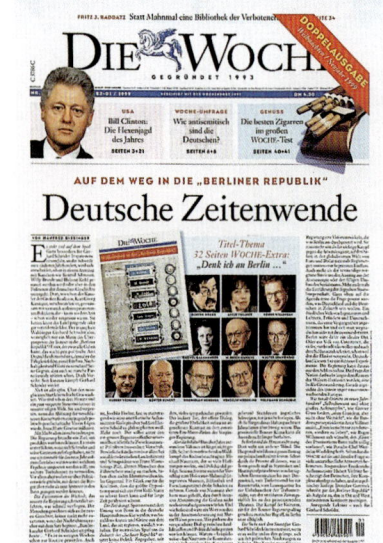
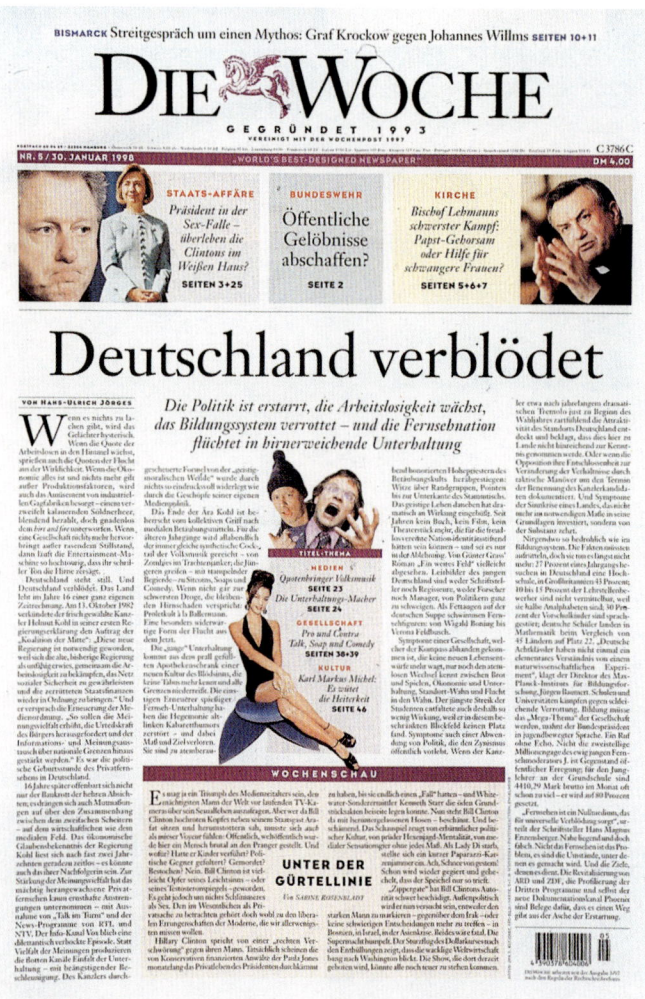

Die Woche
Hamburg, Germany

Die Woche is a sophisticated paper with a lot of energy on its pages. The packaging is aimed at making things accessible for the reader. The design is well-structured without getting in the way of the content. The paper is an elegant, handsome, piece of work. Every aspect of the design — color choice, photography, typography — is refined and treated with respect. All of this is in support of great writing, superb editing and wonderful headlines. This is a truly beautiful newspaper.

Die Woche es un periódico muy sofisticado que desprende gran energía en sus páginas. La presentación tiene el objetivo de poner todo al alcance del lector. El diseño está bien estructurado y no interfiere con el contenido. Es un diario elegante y atractivo. Cada aspecto de su diseño —selección de colores, fotografía, tipografía— es refinado y tratado con respeto. Todo lo anterior apoya la excelente redacción, la inmejorable edición y los estupendos titulares. Sin duda alguna, es un diario hermoso.

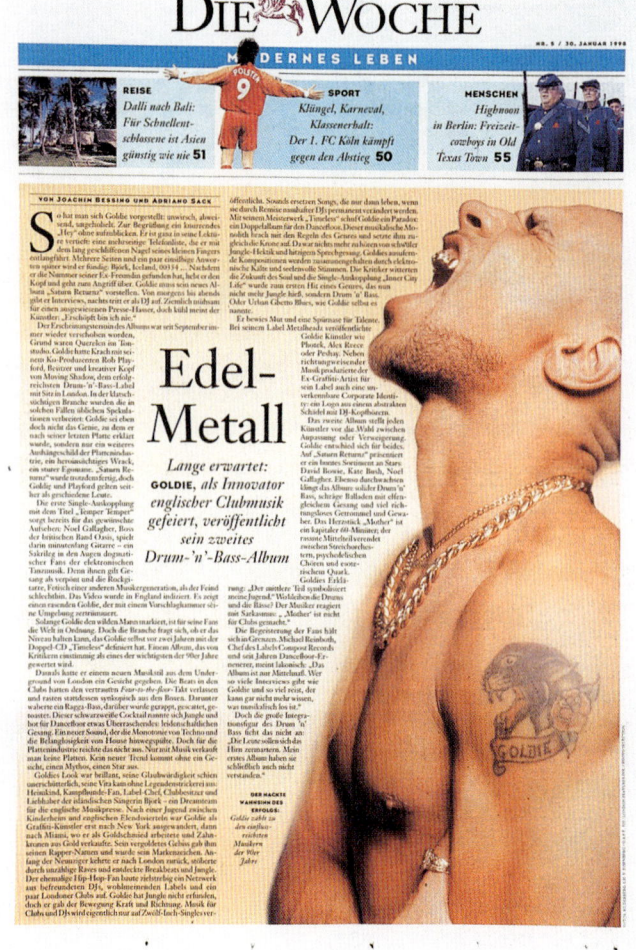

30 ■ THE BEST OF NEWSPAPER DESIGN

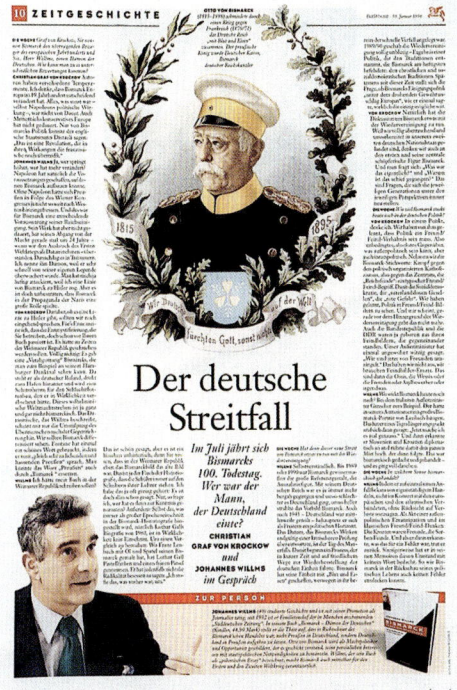
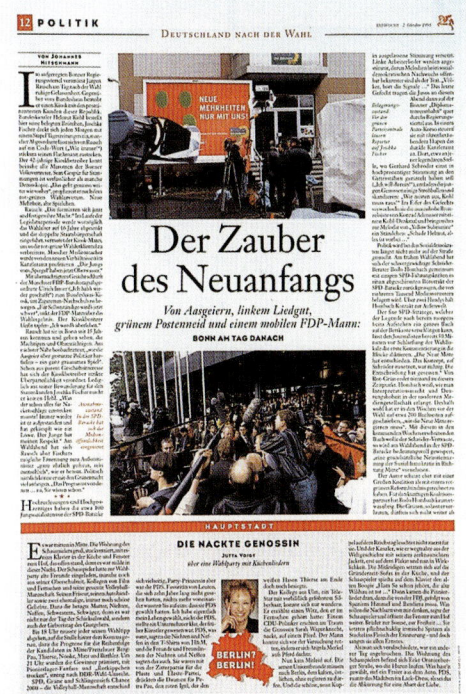
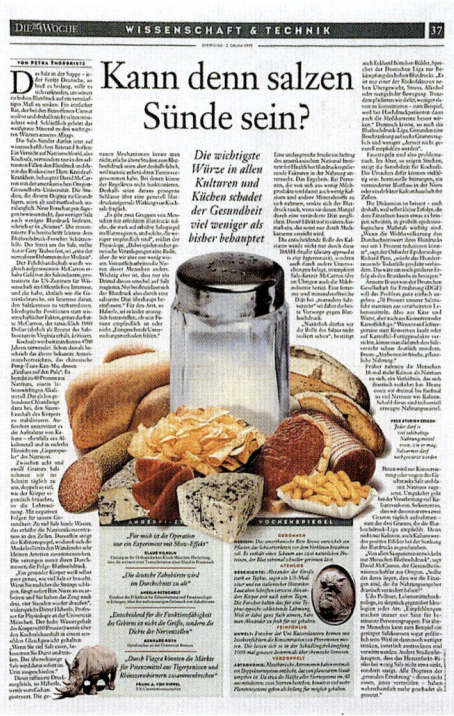
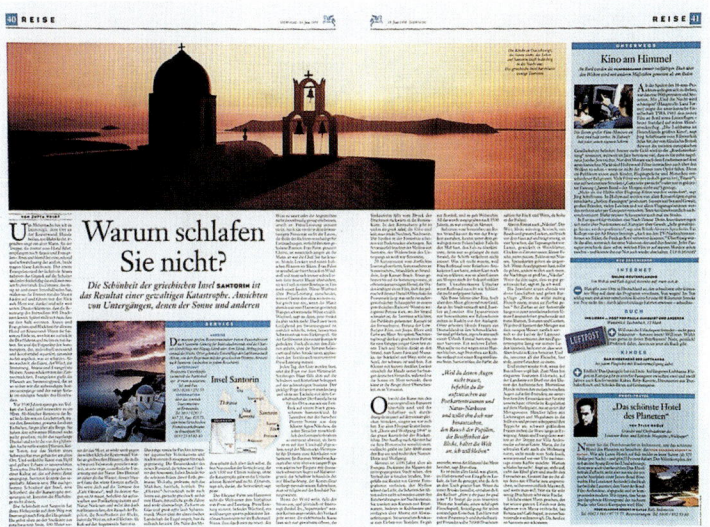
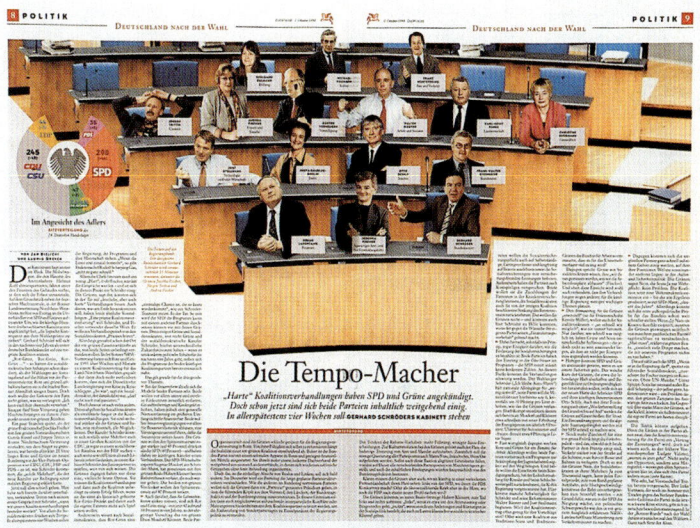
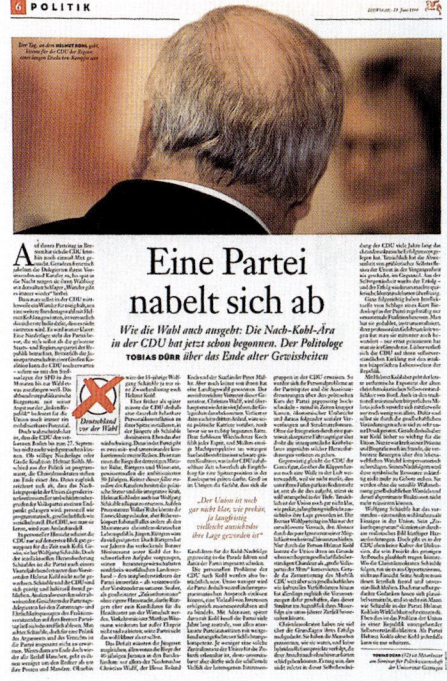
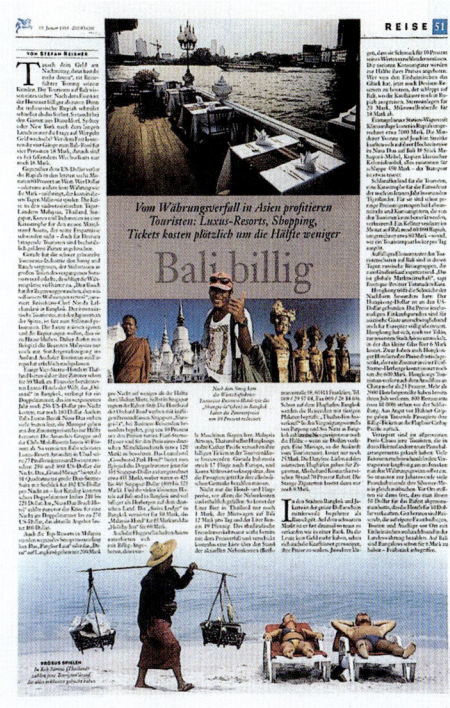
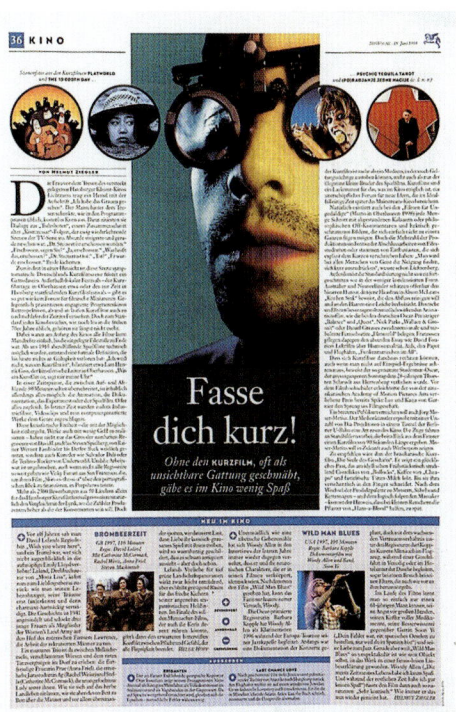

BEST-DESIGNED NEWSPAPERS ■ The Sun

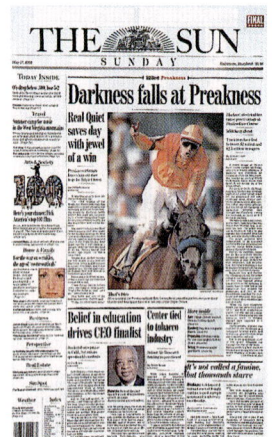
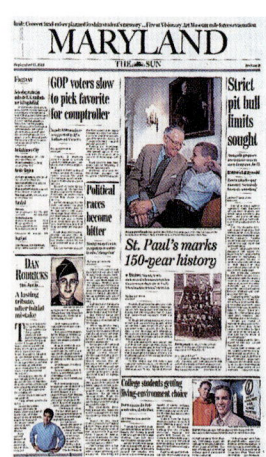
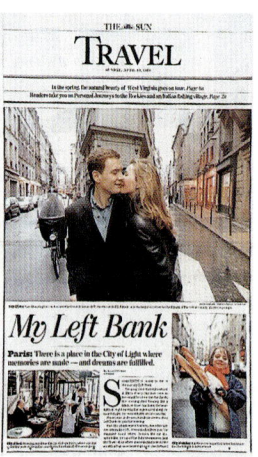
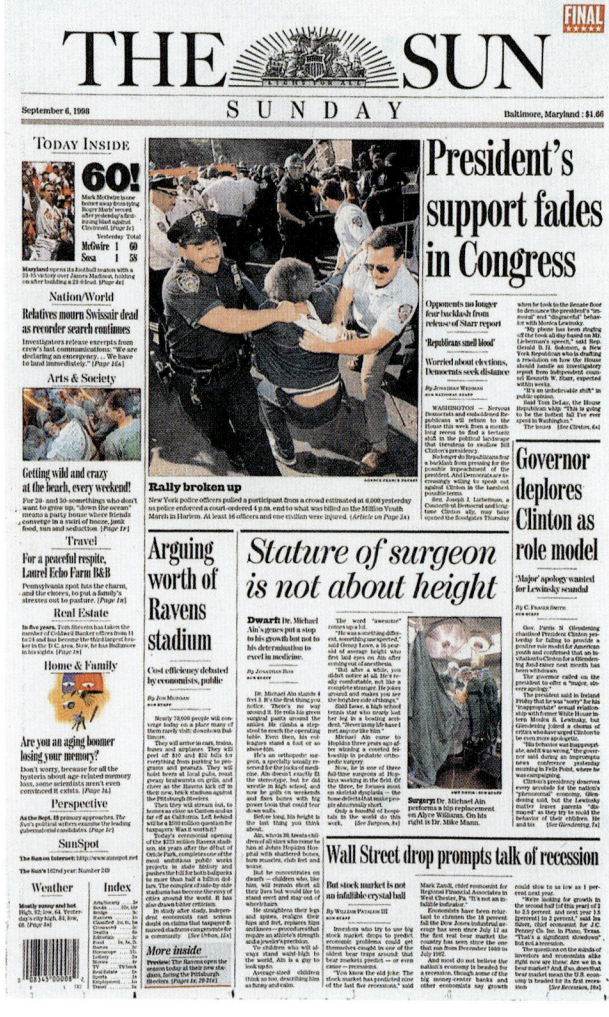

The Sun
Baltimore, MD

The (Baltimore) Sun is really top quality journalism. It is a text-driven paper with a classic and elegant design. The publication is unique and innovative. It doesn't look like the rest of the American papers in the group. The typography sends a reader-friendly message to its audience. The story selection is the personification of local content. The paper makes excellent use of photography, with each picture edited for maximum impact. It is one of the best papers we've seen, and it seems to have a lot of fun with its design.

The (Baltimore) Sun es un claro ejemplo de periodismo de la mejor calidad. Es un diario que enfatiza los textos y posee un diseño clásico y elegante. Es una publicación singular e innovadora. No se asemeja al resto de los diarios estadounidenses de su tipo. La tipografía envía a los lectores un mensaje que les resulta fácil de entender. La selección de artículos es la personificación del énfasis en las noticias locales. Se hace un uso excelente de la fotografía y cada foto se edita para lograr el mayor efecto en el lector. Es uno de los mejores diarios que hemos visto y parece que se siente muy a gusto con su diseño.

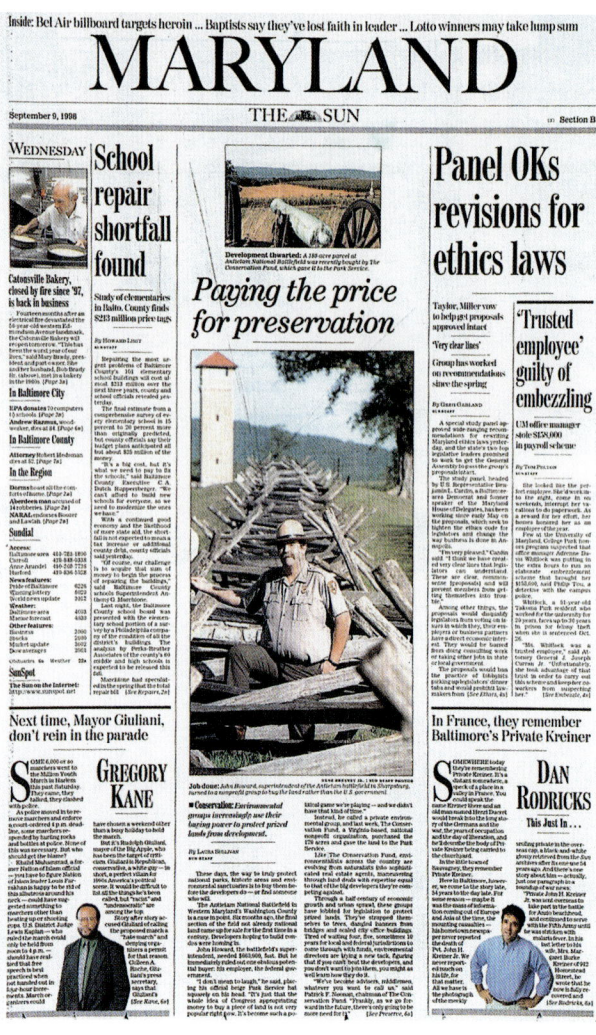

CIRCULATION 315,000 ■ BEST-DESIGNED NEWSPAPERS

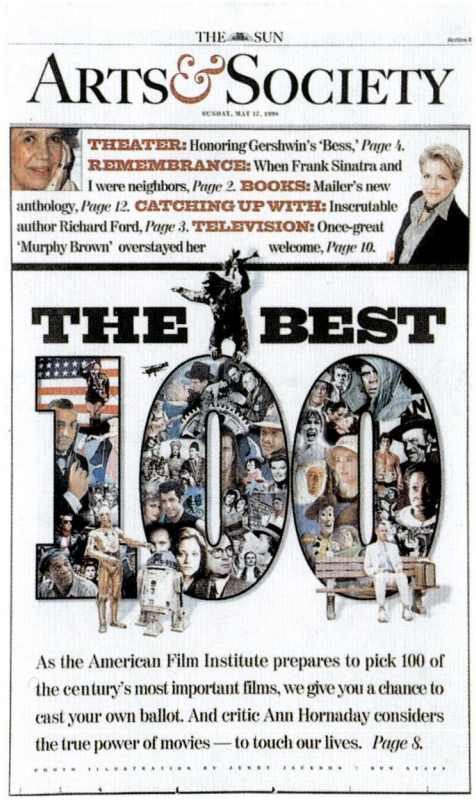
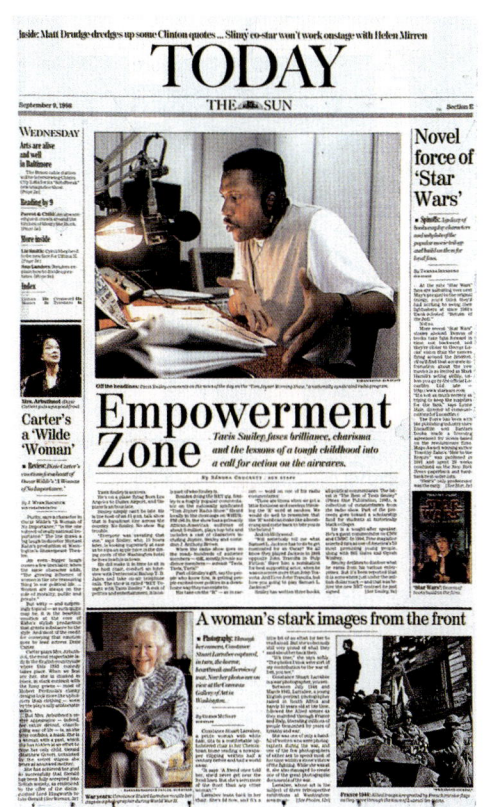
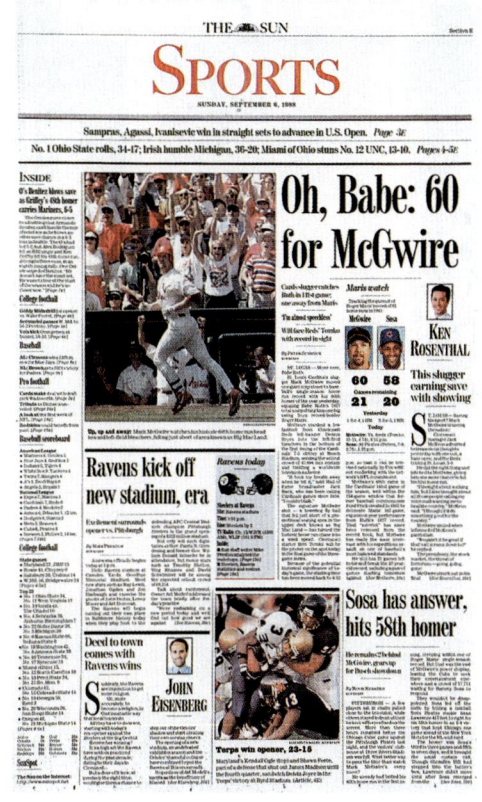
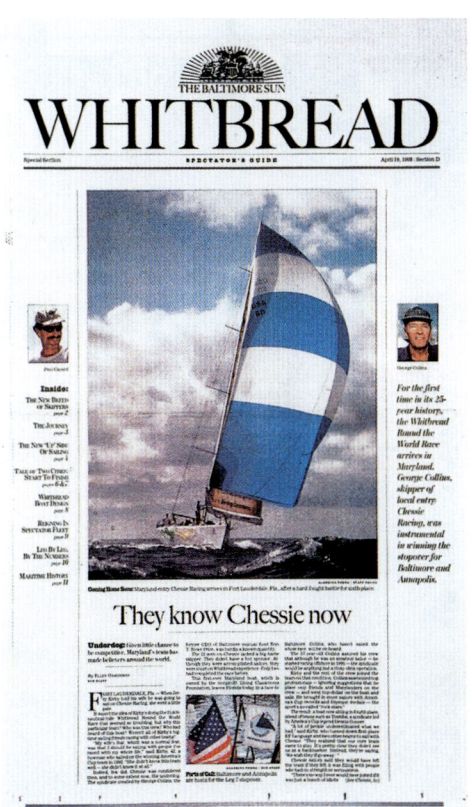
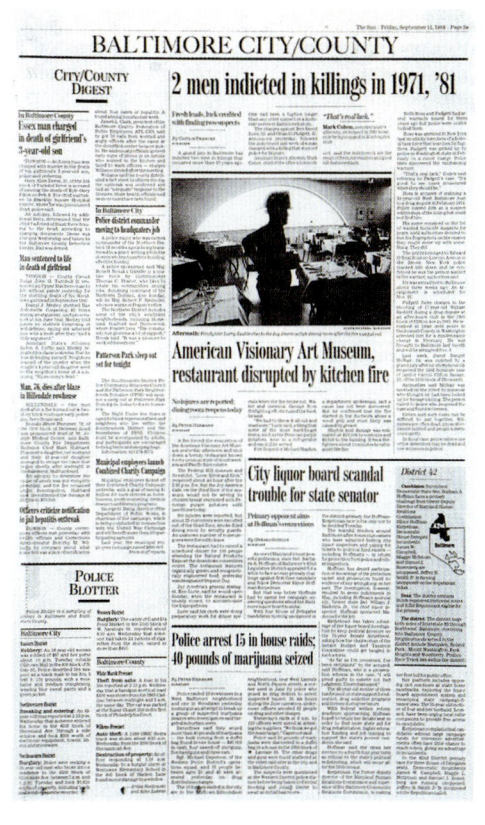
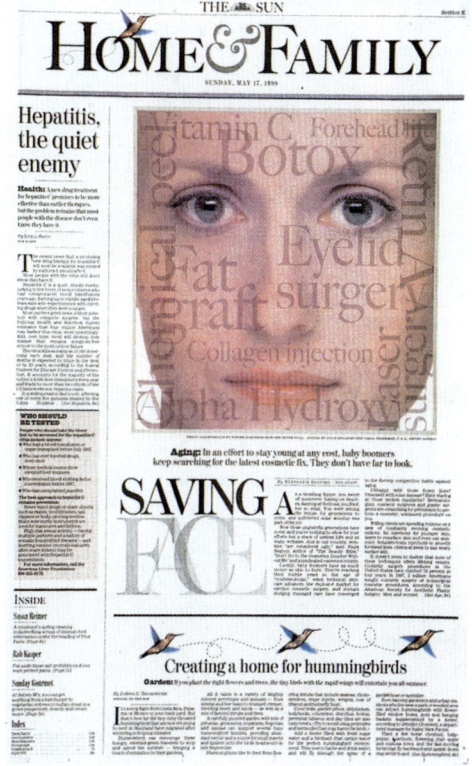

TWENTIETH EDITION ■ 33

BEST-DESIGNED NEWSPAPERS — The Globe and Mail

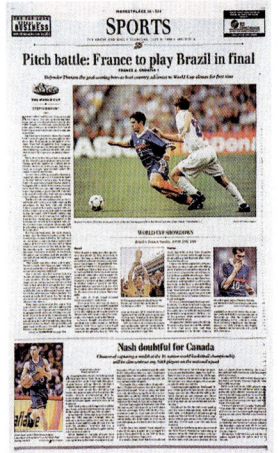
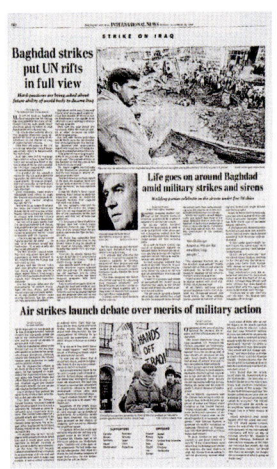
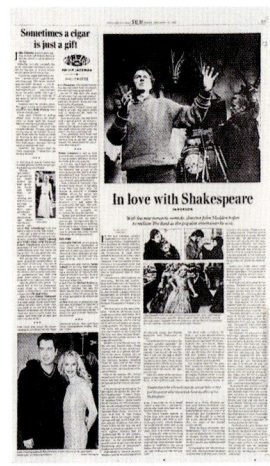
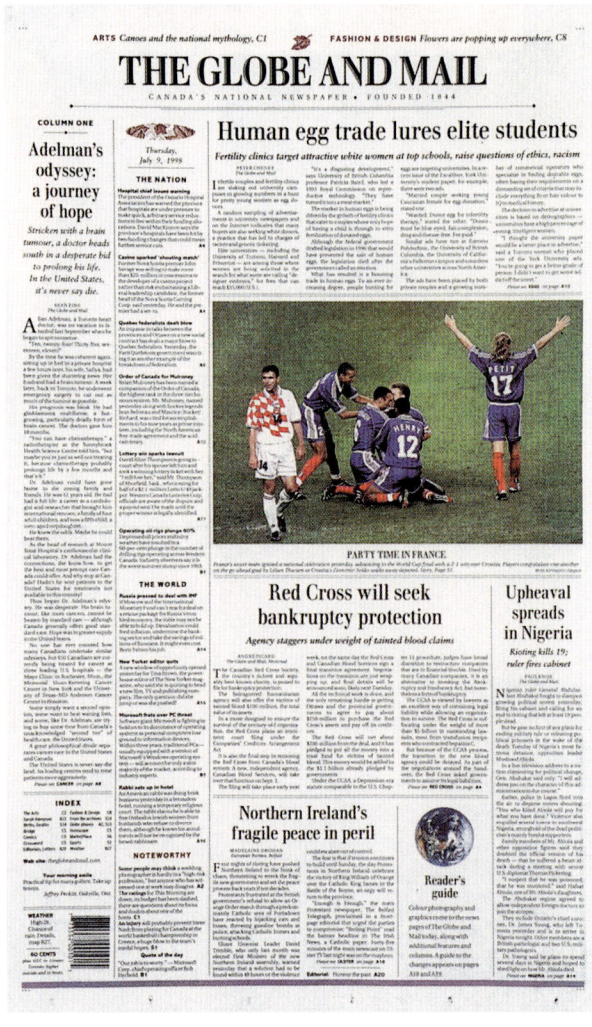

The Globe and Mail
Toronto, Canada

The Globe and Mail shows what you can do with just a little bit of color. The publication uses color very subtly. The staff did an excellent job transforming a good paper and modernizing it. The design has a sense of planning — a framework about it. There is a sense of consistency in the design from front to back, with lots of nice touches sprinkled throughout. This is a paper for people who like to read. It has wonderful inside spreads.

The Globe and Mail demuestra lo que se puede lograr con sólo un poco de color. Esta publicación emplea el color de un modo muy sutil. El plantel logró transformar y modernizar con eficacia un excelente periódico. El diseño da la impresión de que fue planificado, como en torno a una estructura. El lector siente que hay coherencia en el diseño desde las primeras páginas hasta las últimas, con muchos detalles agradables en toda la publicación. Es un diario para personas que les gusta leer y tiene magníficas imágenes a doble plana en su interior.

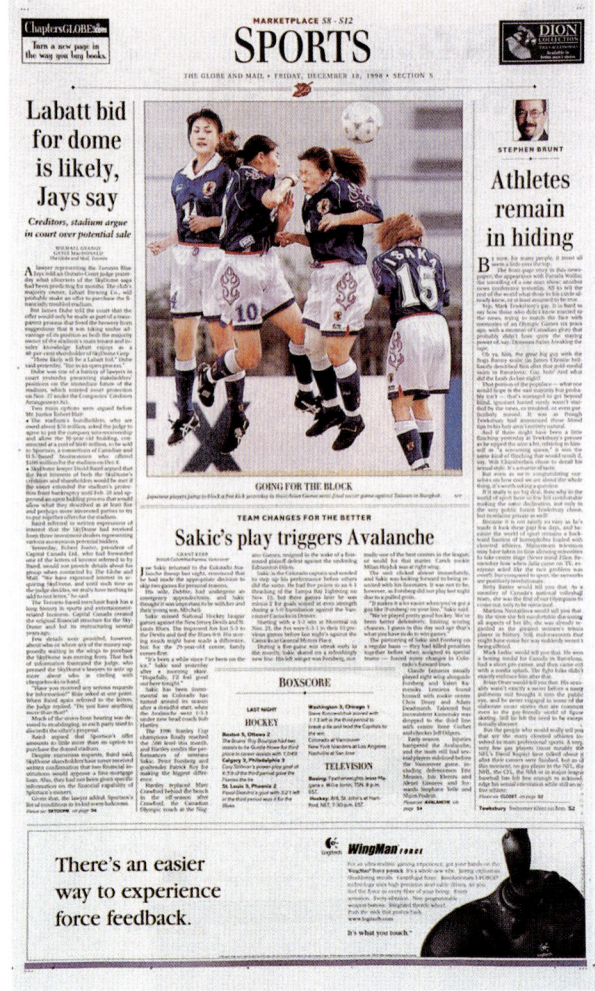

34 ■ THE BEST OF NEWSPAPER DESIGN

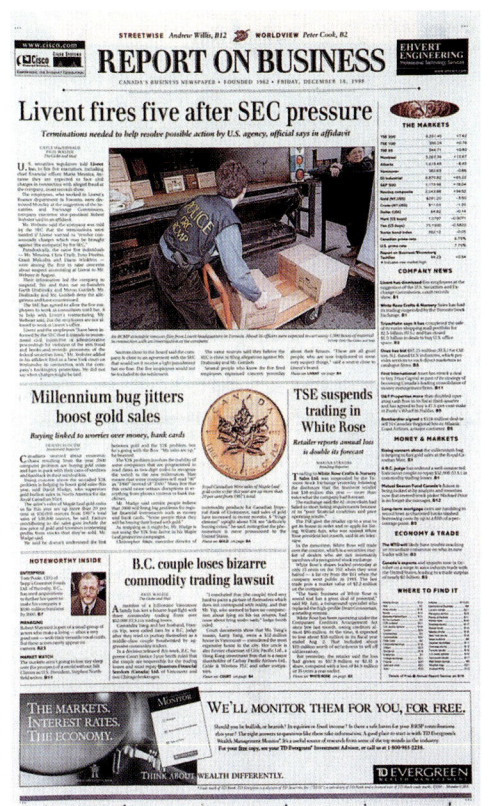
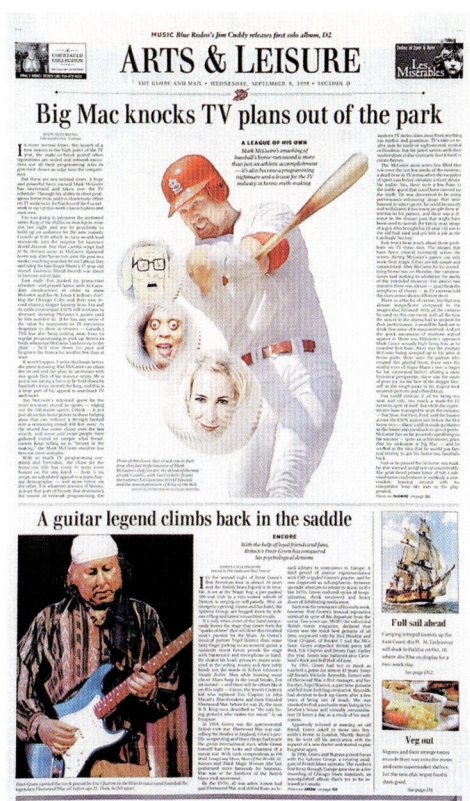
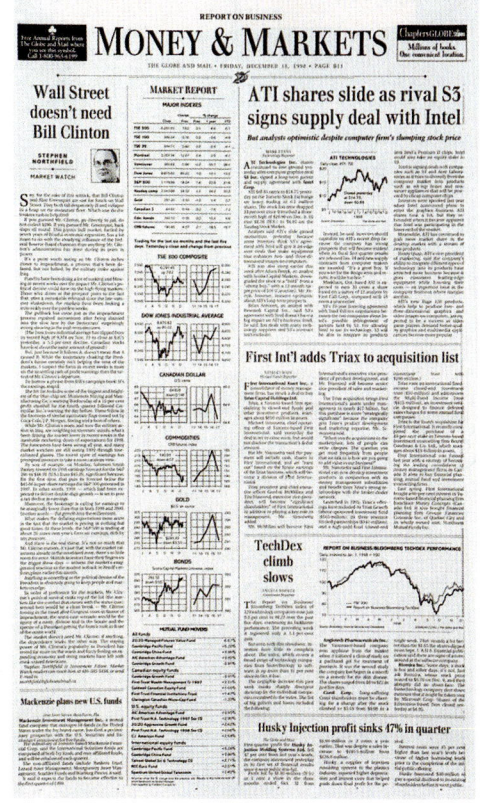
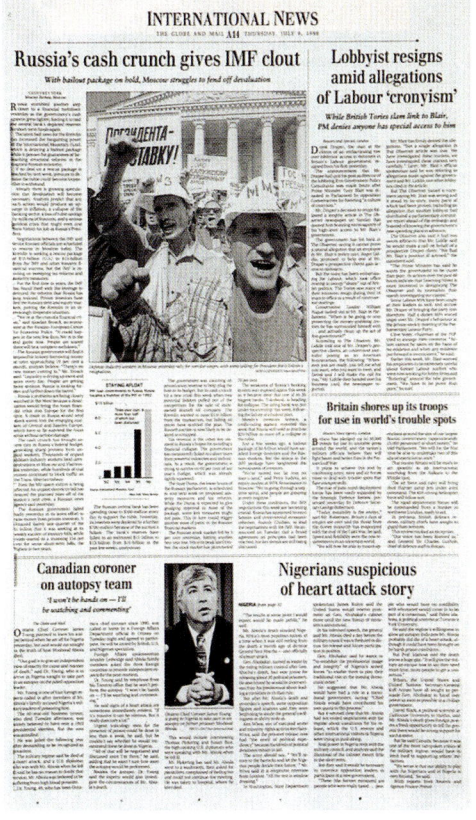
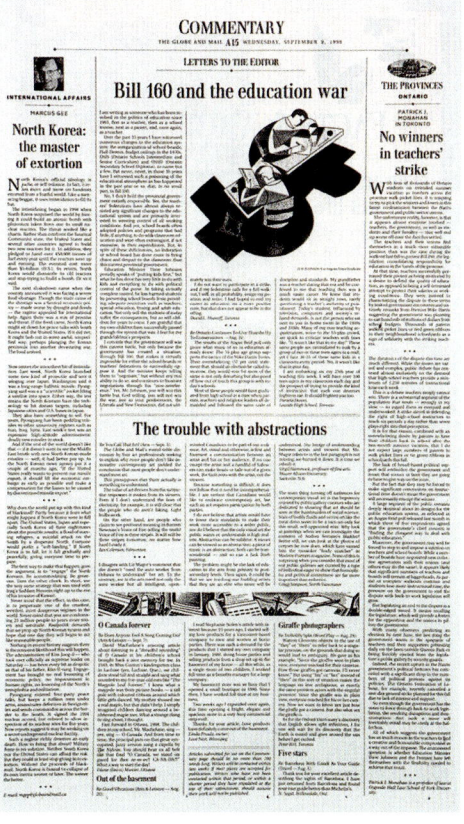
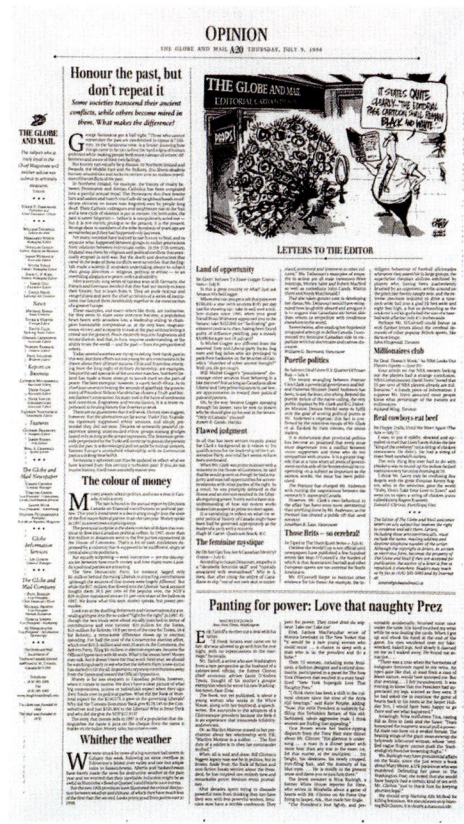

BEST-DESIGNED NEWSPAPERS ■ The National Post

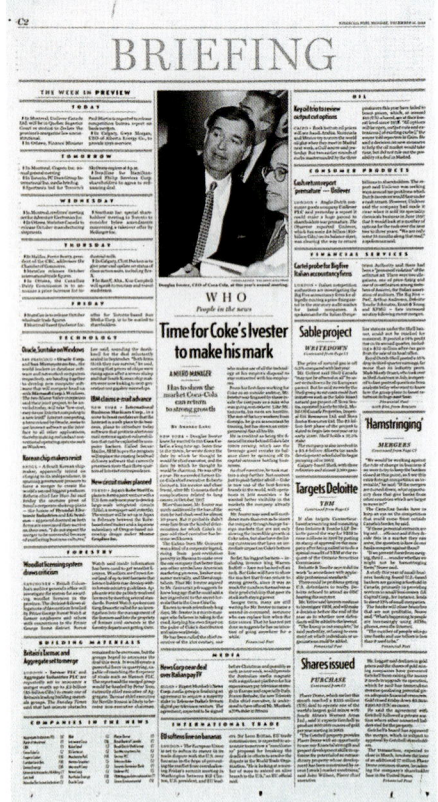
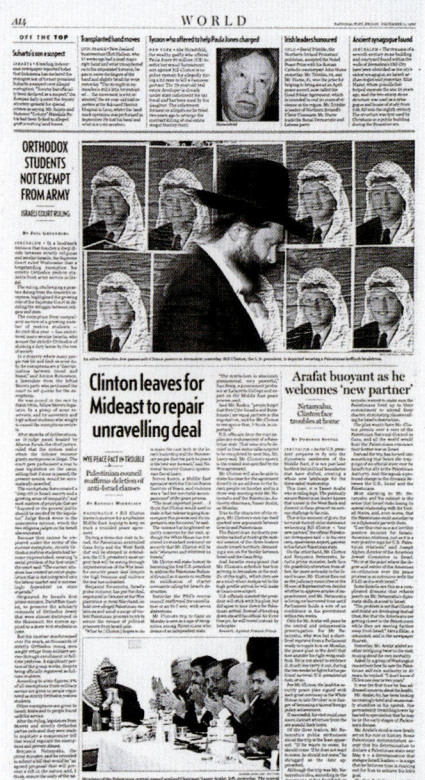
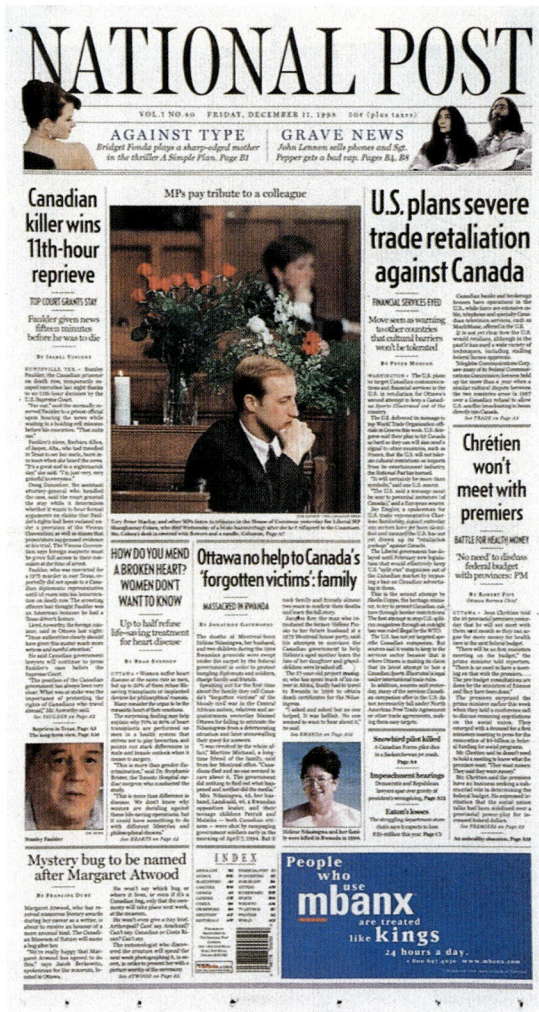

The National Post
Don Mills, Canada

The National Post is beautifully executed and masterfully done, especially considering it began from scratch just a few months ago. Its retro-design almost looks modern with appealing packaging. It invites the reader to sit back and read each page. The use of the top of the page for "finger reading" is well done. The attention to detail in this paper is phenomenal.

The National Post, por su parte, cuenta con una bella ejecución y se realiza con gran maestría, particularmente si tomamos en cuenta que comenzó de cero hace unos pocos meses. Su diseño retro casi parece moderno y la presentación es muy atractiva. Invita al lector a relajarse y leer cada página. El uso de la parte superior de la página para "leer con el dedo" está muy bien logrado. La atención prestada a los detalles es fenomenal.

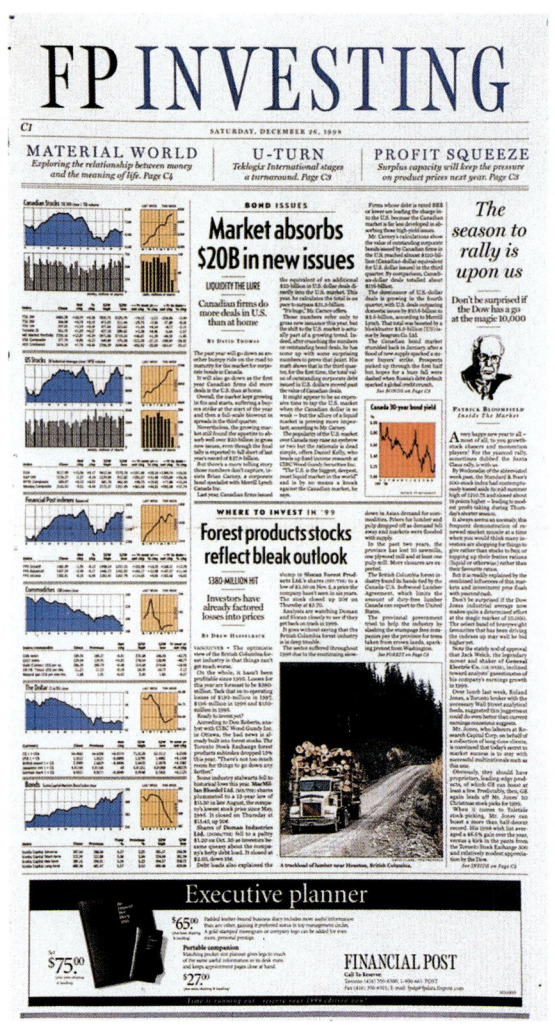

CIRCULATION 266,000 ■ BEST-DESIGNED NEWSPAPERS

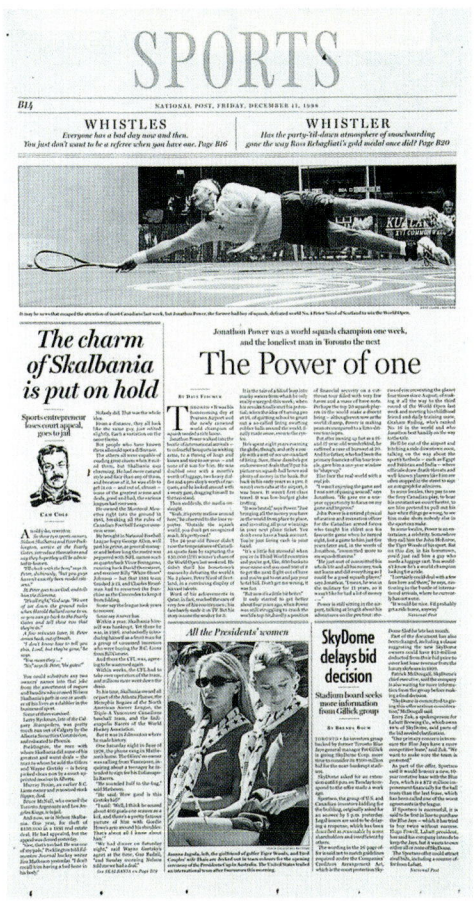
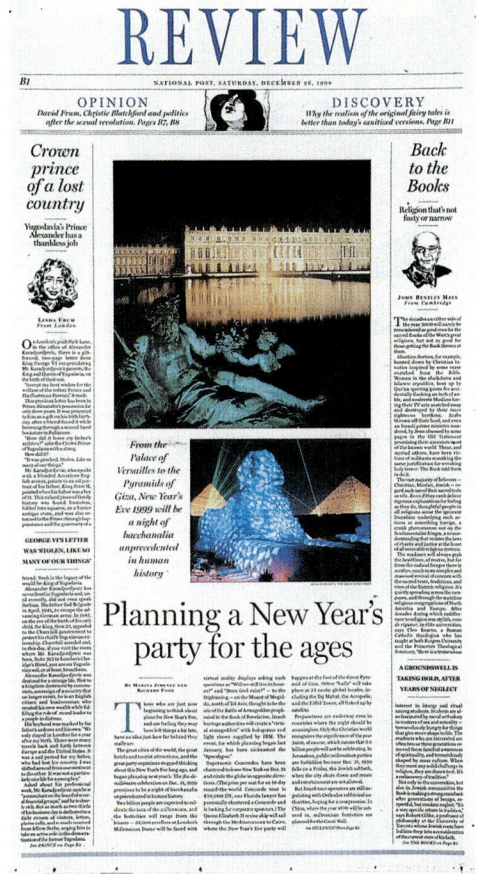
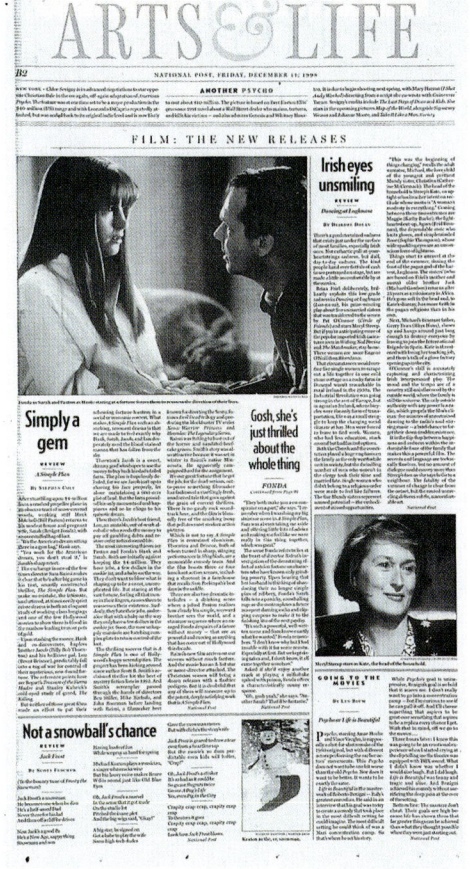
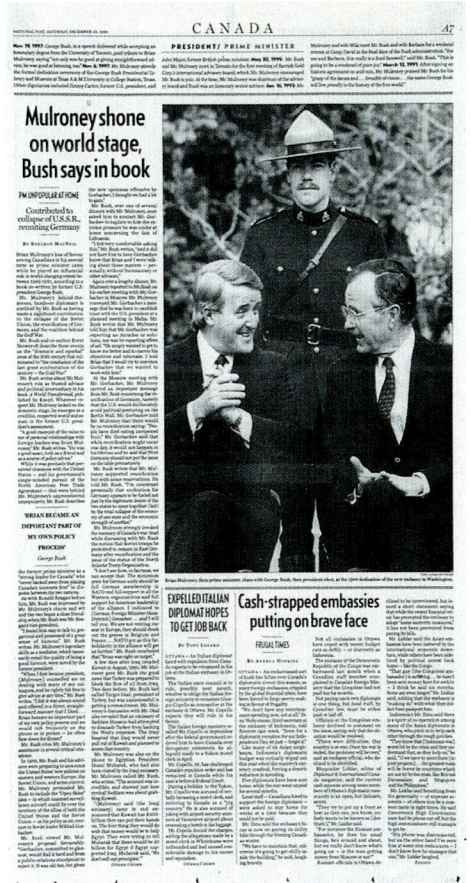
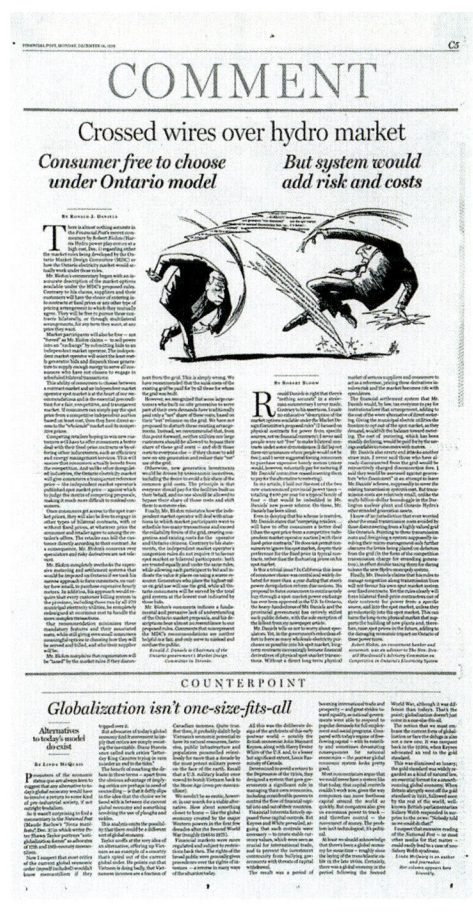
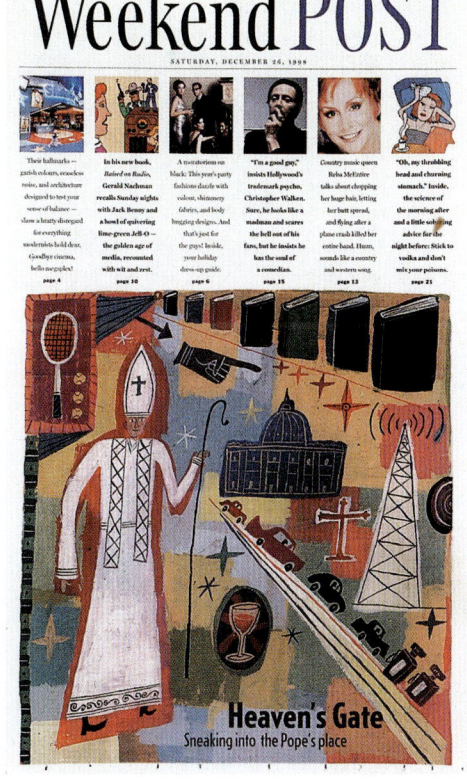

TWENTIETH EDITION ■ 37

BEST-DESIGNED NEWSPAPERS ■ The New York Times

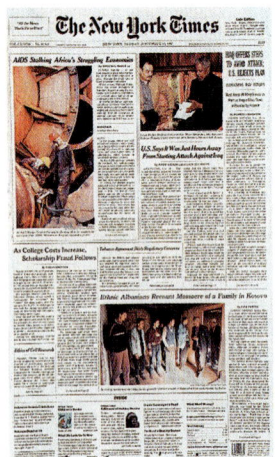
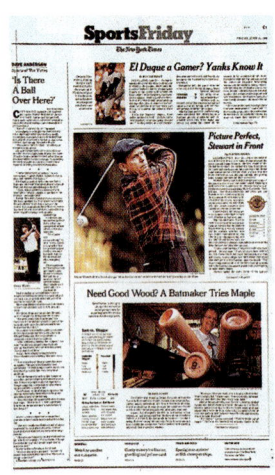
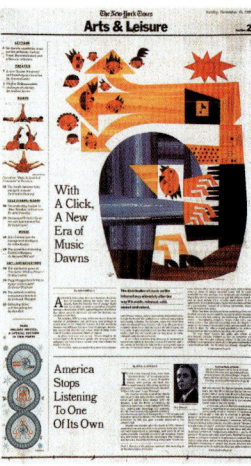
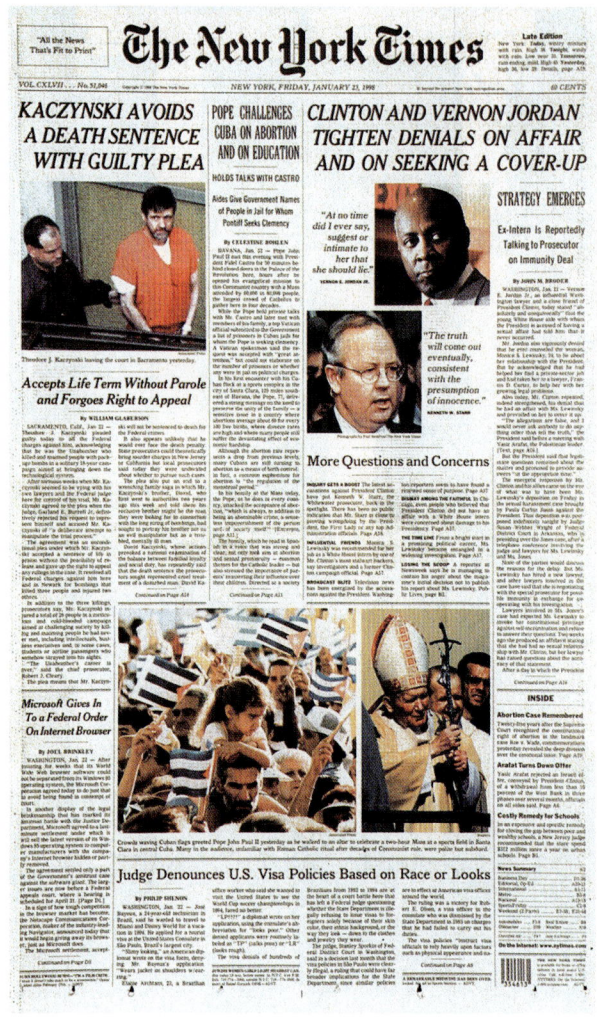

The New York Times
New York, NY

The New York Times is an impressive publication. It makes everything it does look almost effortless. Its content is a joy to read and is the ultimate example of WED (Writing/Editing/Design). It has a sense of credibility about everything it does. There is a distinct sense of attention to detail throughout the publication. It's consistent from section to section. The packaging makes it easy to maneuver with a lot of changes of pace throughout the paper. It knows its readership and presents its material accordingly.

The New York Times es una publicación impresionante. Todo lo que hace parece realizado casi sin esfuerzo alguno. Su contenido atrapa el interés de sus lectores y es el máximo ejemplo de redacción, revisión y diseño. Aporta a todo lo que hace un sentido de credibilidad, y se presta una atención increíble a los detalles en toda la publicación. Es coherente de una sección a otra. Su presentación permite hojearlo con muchos cambios de ritmo en todo el periódico. Es un diario que conoce a sus lectores y presenta sus materiales en concordancia con ello.

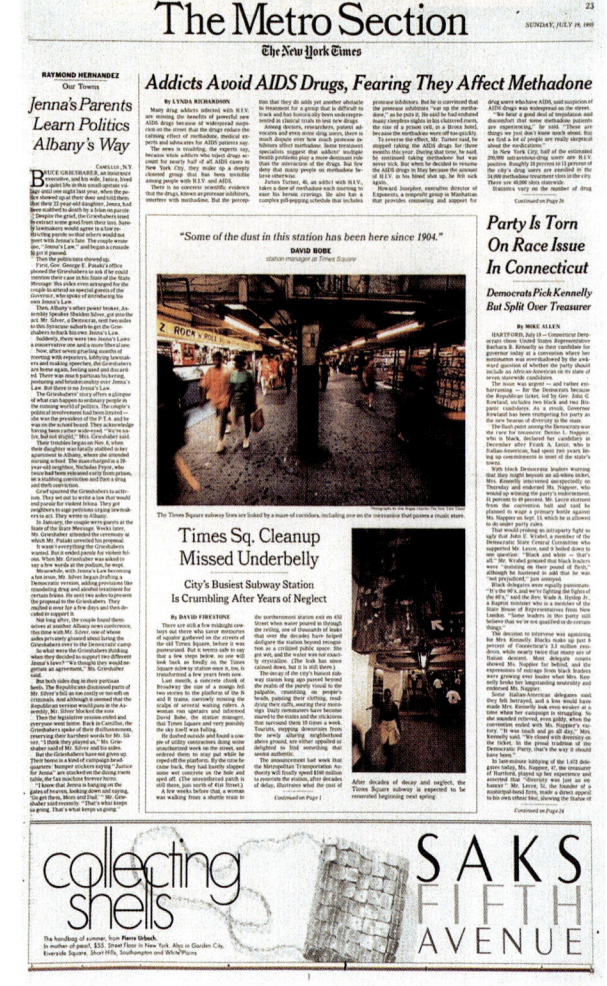

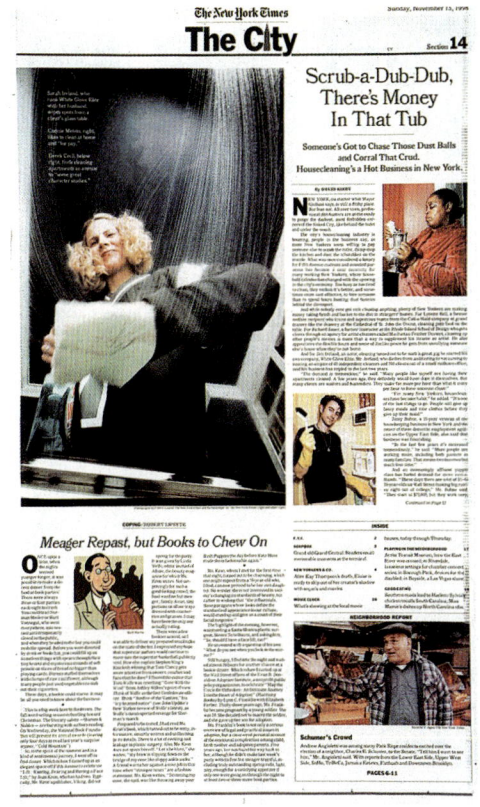
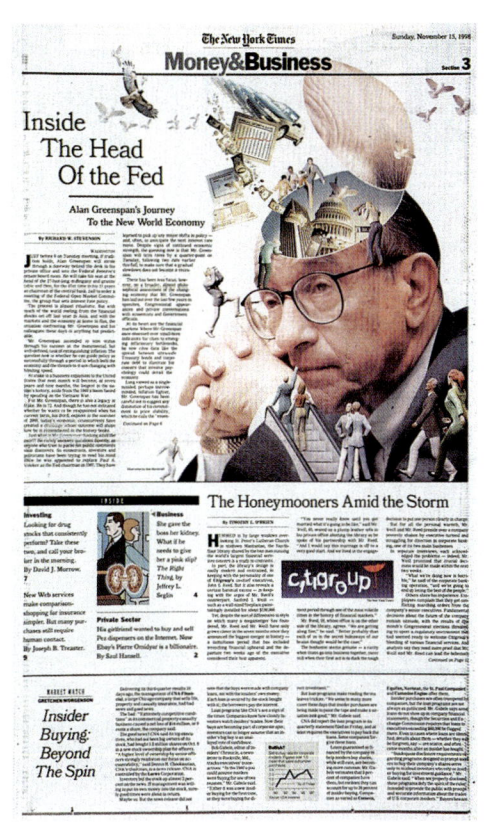
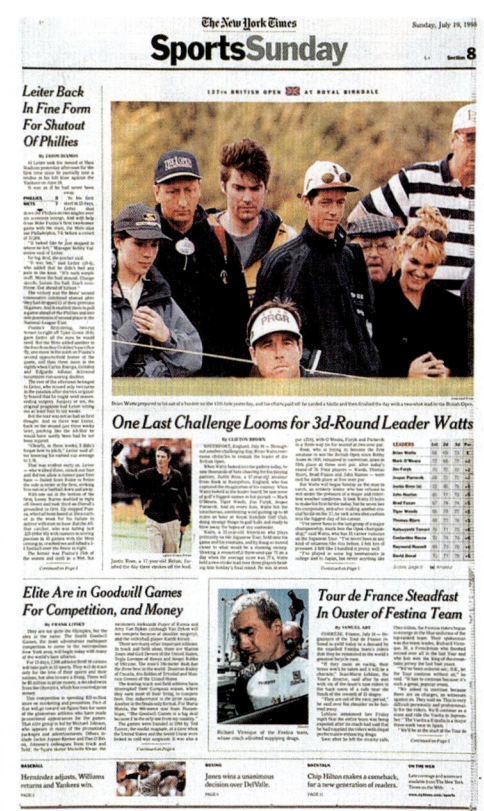
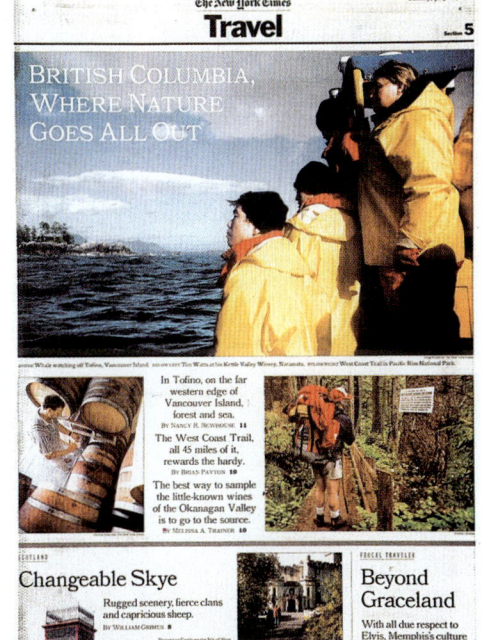
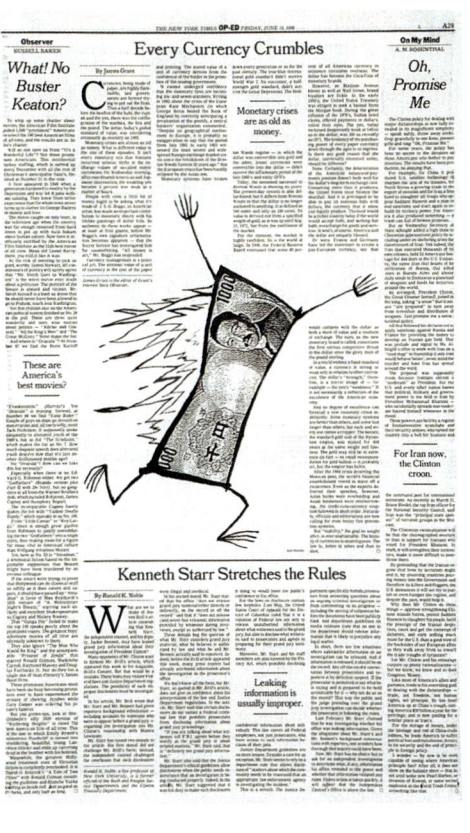
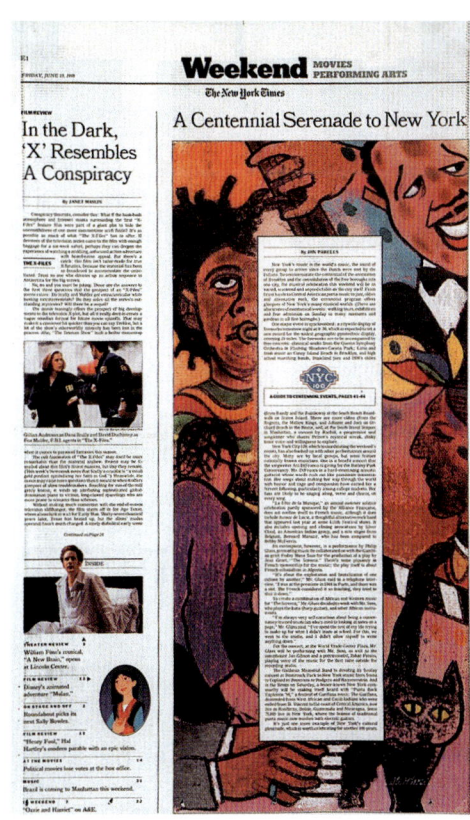

BEST-DESIGNED NEWSPAPERS ■ Die Zeit

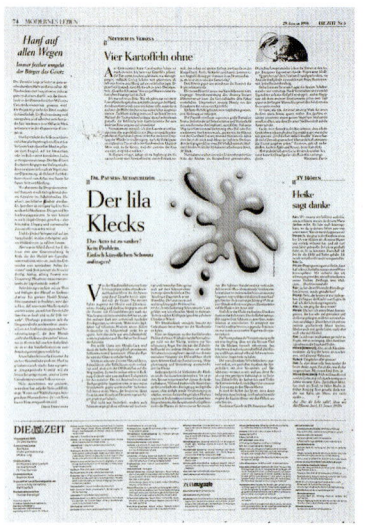
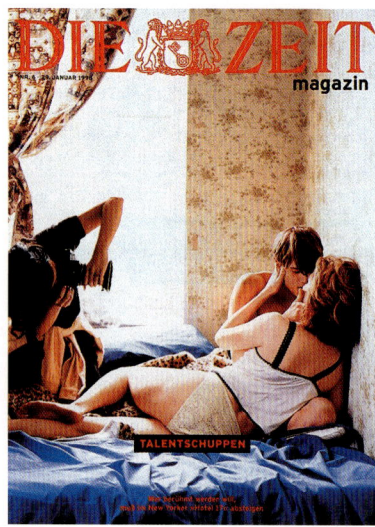
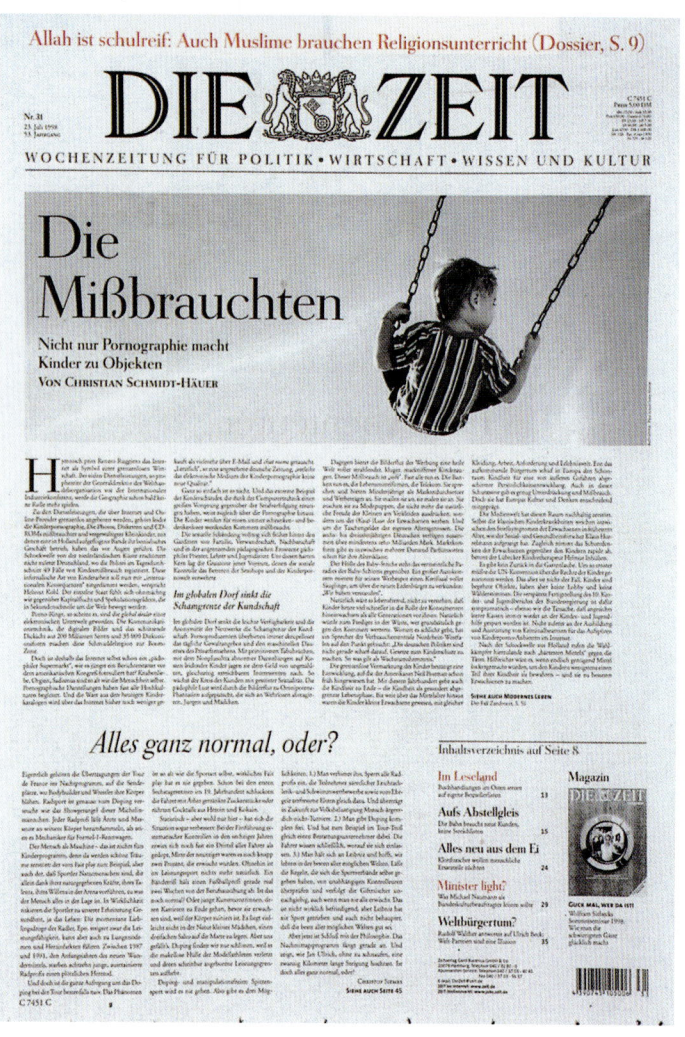

Die Zeit
Hamburg, Germany

Die Zeit was easily the best newspaper in the entire competition. It is a serious paper that really knows its readers. It is inviting with solid content that is superbly presented. This is a stunning example of the power of black and white, combined with subtle use of color. There is a creative sense of continuity throughout the paper that ties everything together.

Die Zeit fue sin duda alguna el mejor periódico del concurso. Se trata de un periódico muy serio que conoce muy bien a sus lectores. Atrapa el interés con un contenido bien argumentado y presentado de modo inmejorable. Es un ejemplo increíble del poder de la impresión en blanco y negro, combinado con el empleo sutil del color. Hay un sentido creativo de la continuidad en todo el periódico que aglutina a todas sus secciones.

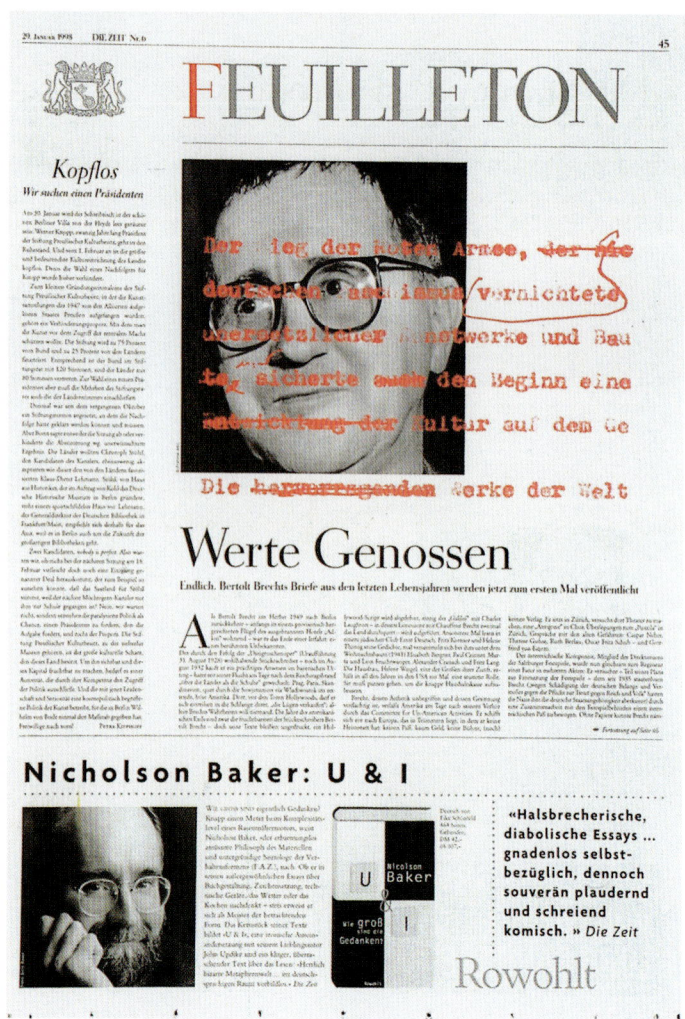

40 ■ THE BEST OF NEWSPAPER DESIGN

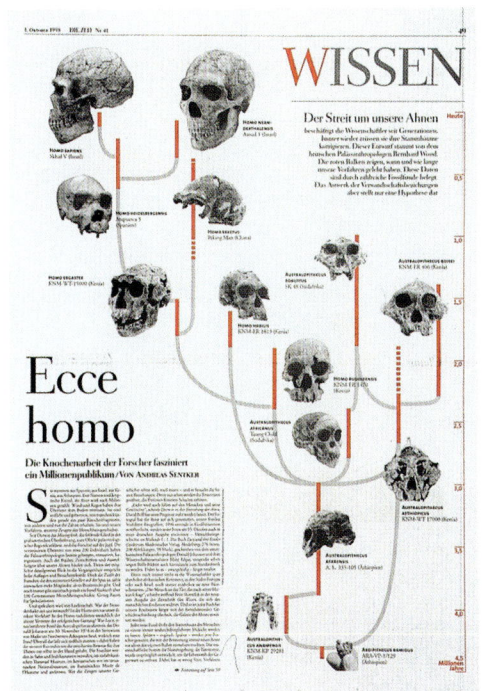
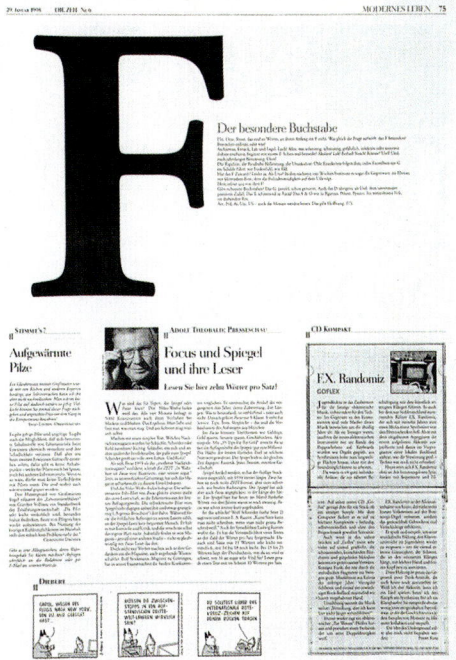
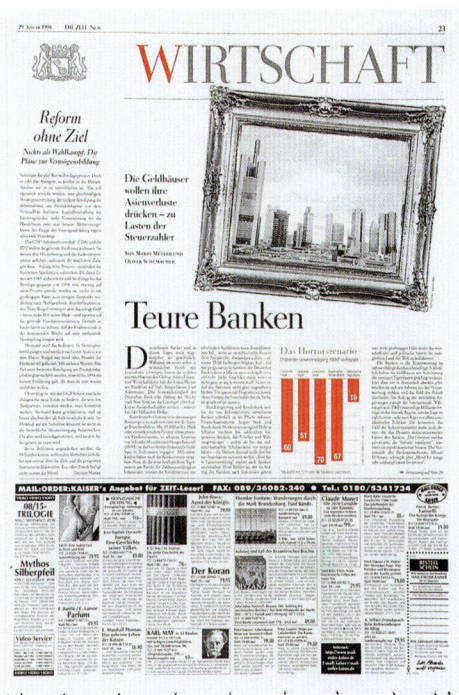
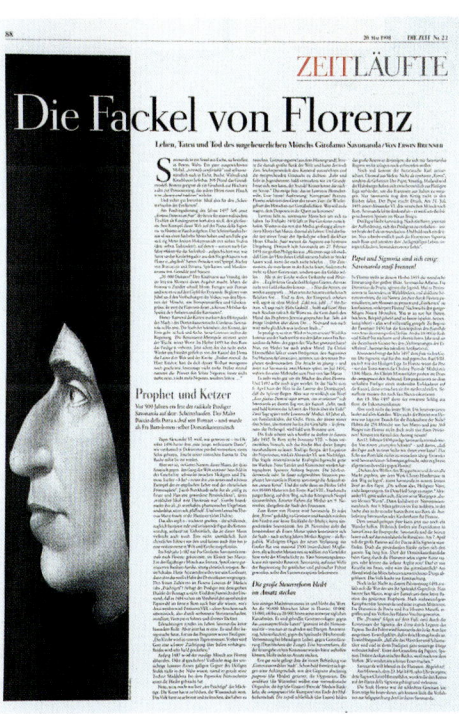
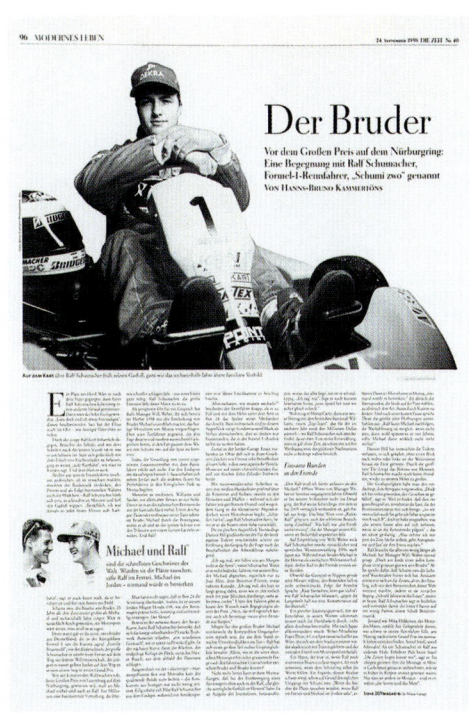
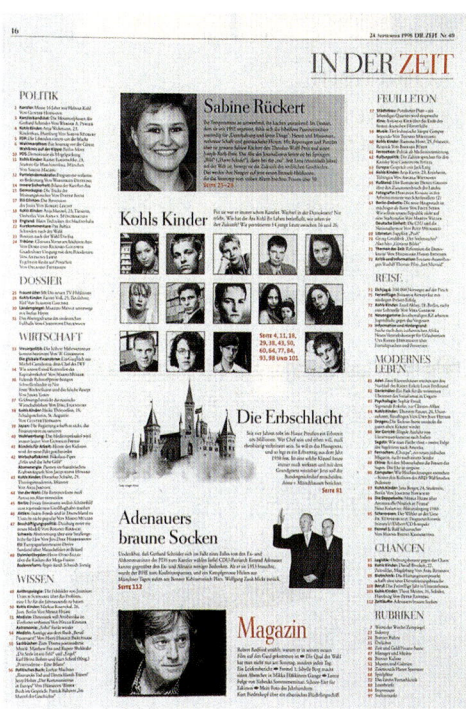

BEST OF SHOW ■ El Mundo Supplements

The judges awarded the supplements of El Mundo for overall visual presentation. What stood out about these sections was creativity, a constant level of originality, consistency and execution.
La Luna reflects a consistency that is flawless from cover to cover and features innovative typography that remains respectful to photography. The strong portraiture is treated lavishly and respectfully.
Metropoli, a weekly entertainment guide, features innovative conceptual covers so strong they often don't depend on headlines.
Tendencias, the trend and fashion magazine, is a combination of bold photography and perfectly blended typography.
Ricardo Martinez excels on the **opinion pages**. This masterful hand-drawn art, in rich detail, was lauded as a return to high craftsmanship, flying in the face of a disturbing trend for the prevalence of computer imagery.

La Luna
Madrid, Spain
Rodrigo Sánchez, Art Director; **Francisco Dorado**, Designer; **Chano del Río**, Designer; **Carmelo Caderot**, Design Director; **Mark Seliger**, Photographer

El jurado otorgó este premio a los suplementos de El Mundo, por su presentación visual en general, su creatividad, su constante nivel de originalidad, coherencia y ejecución.
La Luna refleja una coherencia que fue impecable de portada a portada y presentó una innovadora tipografía que demostraba su respeto por la fotografía. El firme empleo de los retratos se trata con esplendidez y respeto.
Metrópoli, una guía semanal de entretenimiento, presentó portadas con conceptos innovadores tan impactantes que a menudo no dependen de los titulares.
Tendencias, la revista que sigue el mundo de la moda y lo que está de moda, es una combinación de atrevida fotografía y una tipografía mezclada a la perfección. Ricardo Martínez tiene una labor muy destacada en las **páginas de opiniones**. Estas geniales imágenes dibujadas a mano, con abundancia de detalles, fueron alabadas como una vuelta al trabajo artístico de alta calidad, en oposición a una preocupante tendencia hacia el dominio de las imágenes diseñadas por computadora.

• Award of Excellence for Entertainment Page

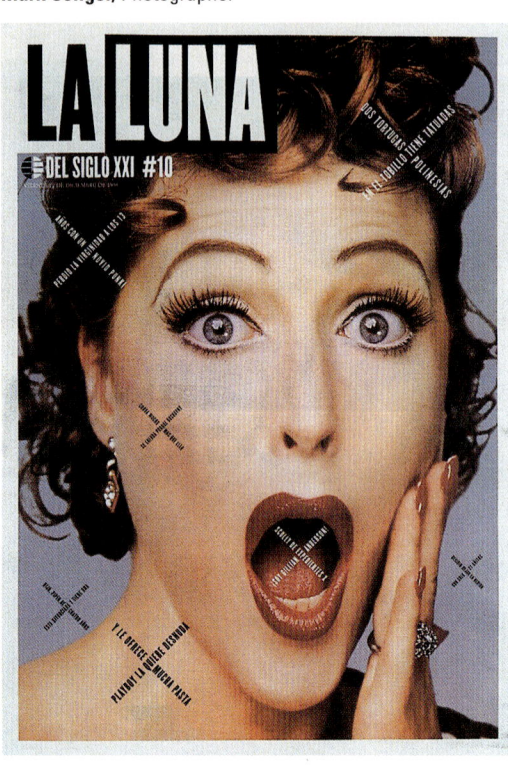

• Silver for Entertainment Page

Gold • for Entertainment Section
The quality of this entry never dies. It's consistently outstanding throughout the magazine. There is energy on every page, including the index pages.

La calidad de este concursante siempre está presente. Se destaca con coherencia en toda la revista. En cada página abunda la energía, incluso en el índice.

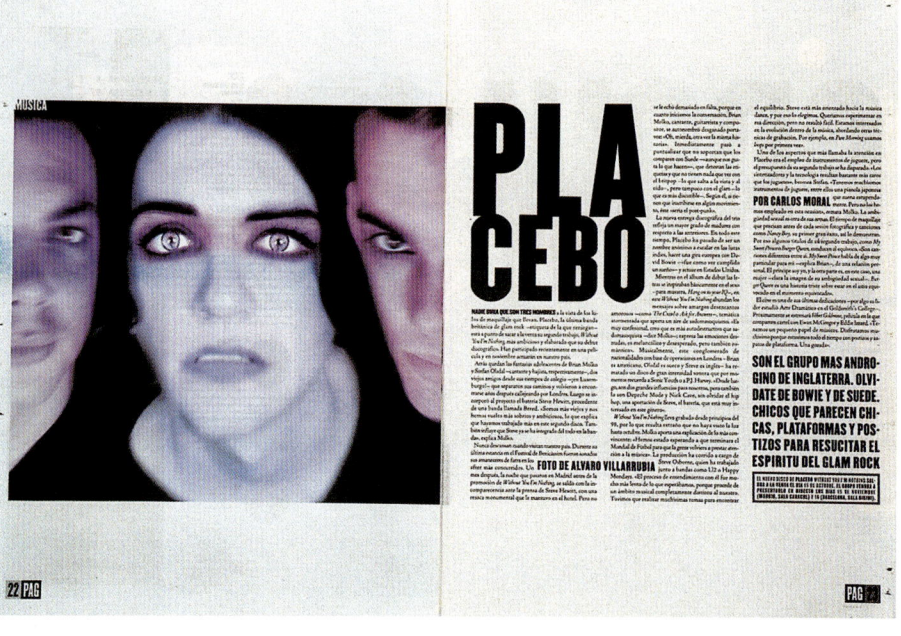

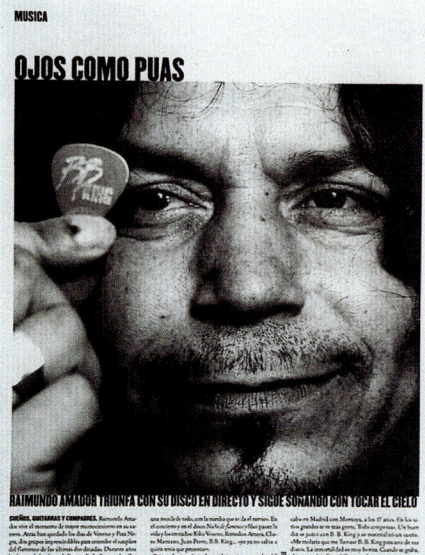
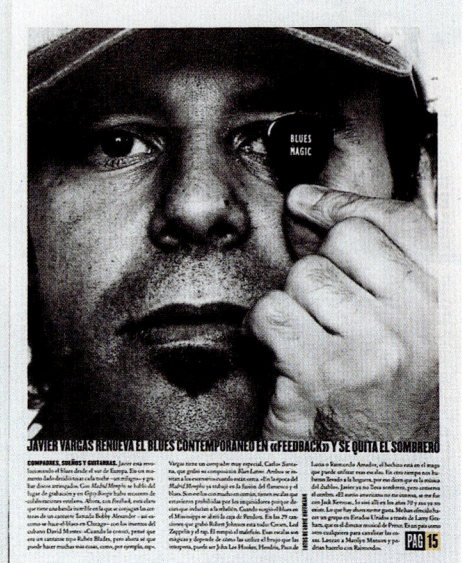

El Mundo Supplements — BEST OF SHOW

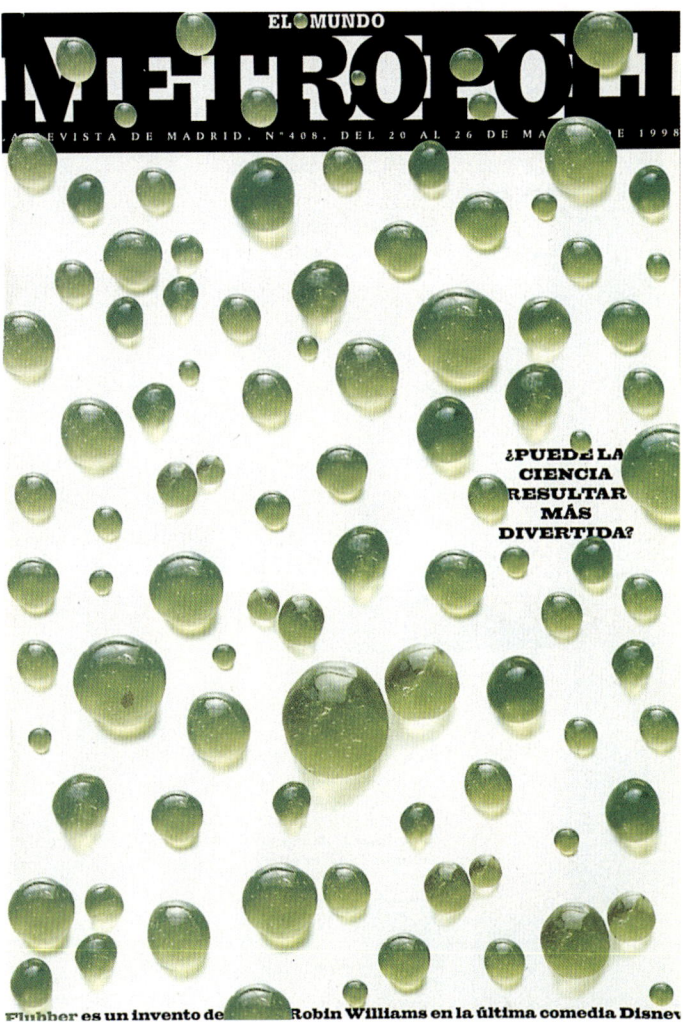

El Mundo Metropoli
Madrid, Spain
Rodrigo Sánchez, Art Director; **Maria Gonzalez**, Designer; **Carmelo Caderot**, Design Director

Gold • for Magazine Cover Black or Black and One Color
Can science be more fun? It has such dimension to it. You want to put your hand in front of it. Innovative.

¿La ciencia puede ser más entretenida? Sí se le puede encontrar ese ángulo. Uno siente ganas de tocarlo con las manos. Innovador.

Gold • for Magazine Cover Black or Black and One Color
This goes far beyond the obvious about "Saving Private Ryan:" it's about saving all the soldiers. It's used like a language with no words — real information in its most sophisticated and alarming form. The eye goes right to Ryan.

Va mucho más allá de lo obvio acerca de la película "Saving Private Ryan": se trata de salvar a todos los soldados. Se utiliza como un lenguaje sin palabras — la información real se presenta en su forma más sofisticada y alarmante. El ojo va directamente a Ryan.

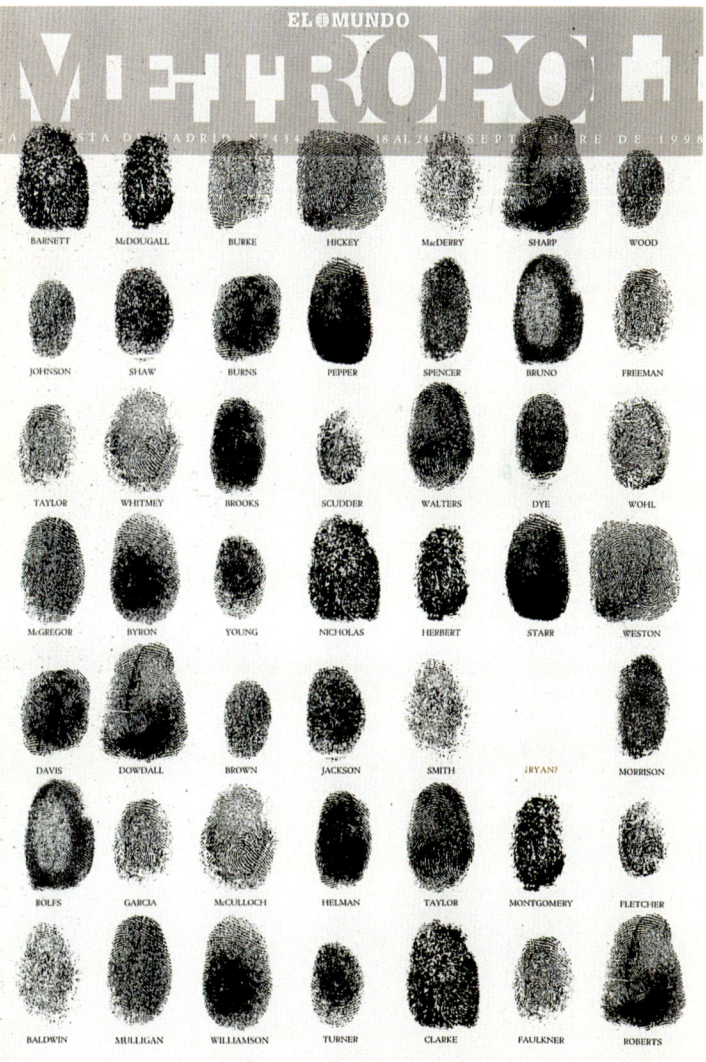

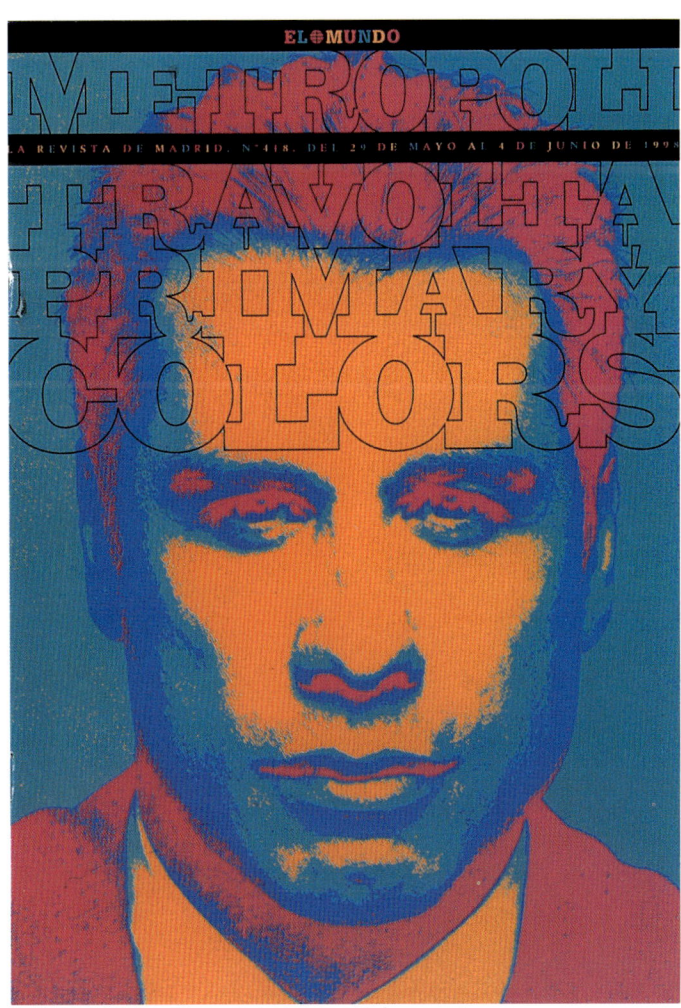

Gold • for Magazine Cover Three or More Colors
We like the play off of the colors, which are incredible. The nameplate grows out of the content.

Nos gusta el juego con los colores, que son increíbles. La placa de nombre crece y se sale del contenido.

BEST OF SHOW ■ El Mundo Supplements

• Award of Excellence for Magazine Page Design

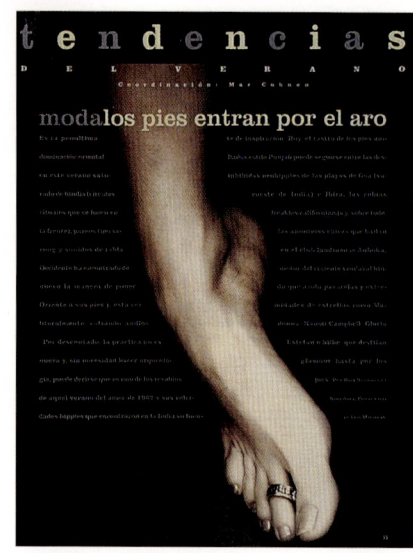

La Revista de El Mundo
Madrid, Spain
Rodrigo Sánchez, Art Director; **Maria Gonzalez,** Designer; **Carmelo Caderot,** Design Director; **Amparo Redondo,** Designer; **Alain Duplantier,** Photographer

• Silver for Magazine Page Design

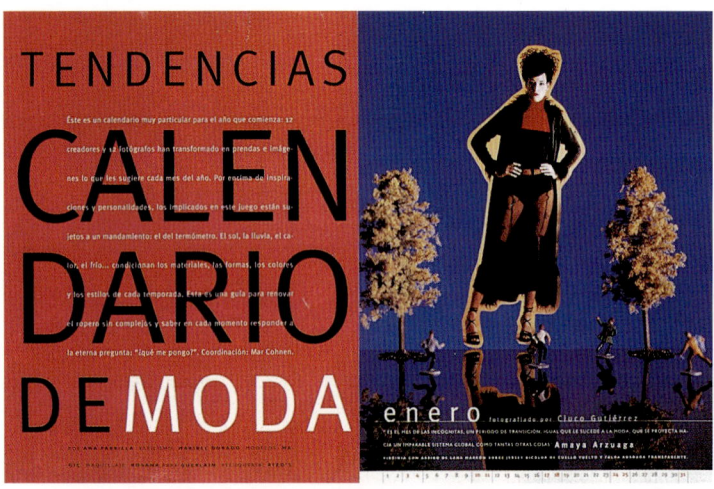
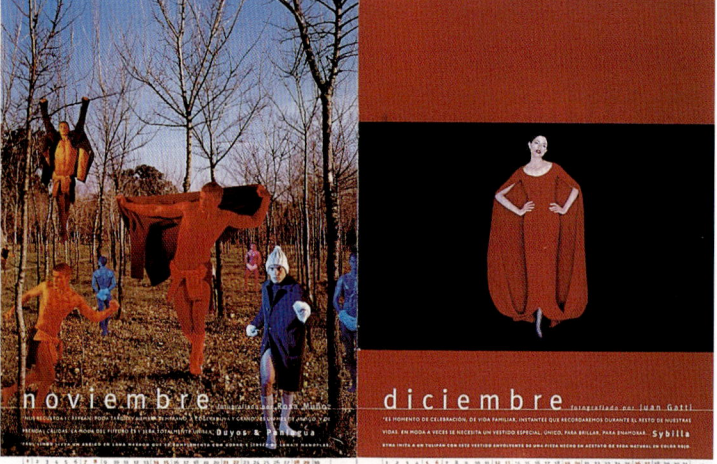

• Silver for Magazine Page Design

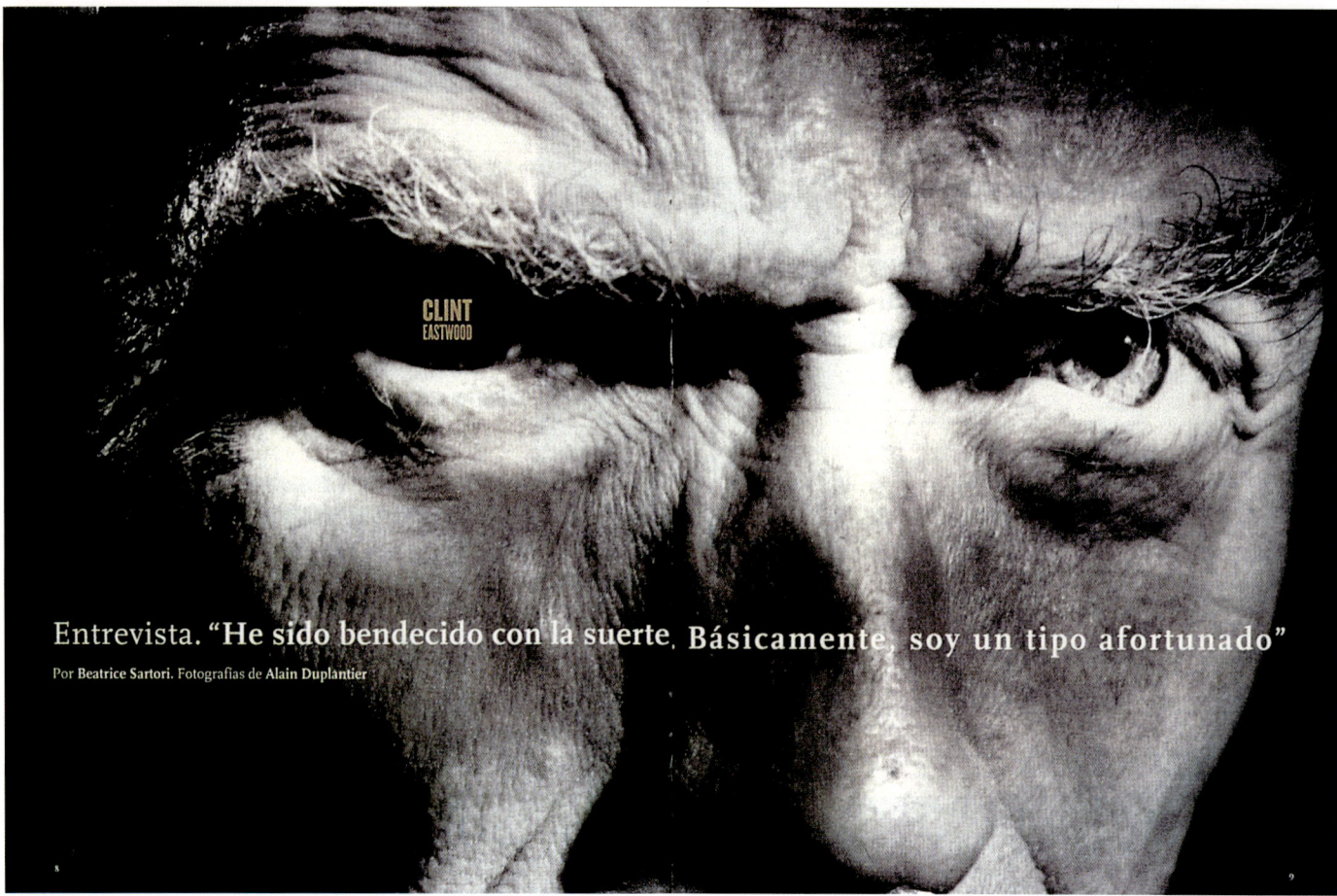

El Mundo Del Siglo XXI
Madrid, Spain
Ricardo Martinez, Illustrator

Gold • for Illustration Black, or Black and One Color

The artist has a special way of illustrating ideas. This sends a message that the American way of illustrating — where everything is on the page — isn't always successful. Here, a partial image adds to the strength of the message. There is a sense of emotion — all done by hand. The illustration works well with the overall design. The presentation is strong and clever.

El artista ilustra las ideas de modo especial. Esto trasmite el mensaje de que la manera estadounidense de ilustrar —en la que todo está en la página— no siempre tiene éxito. En este caso, una imagen parcial subraya la fuerza del mensaje. Hay una sensación de emoción, todo ello hecho a mano. La ilustración armoniza con el diseño en general. La presentación es potente e inteligente.

Gold & JSR • for Illustration Black, or Black and One Color

This hand-drawn art makes a statement that computer art is often over used. This piece speaks in a loud voice: read me, touch me, see me.

Esta imagen dibujada a mano subraya que las imágenes diseñadas por computadora a menudo se utilizan demasiado. Esta pieza nos habla en voz alta: léeme, tócame, mírame.

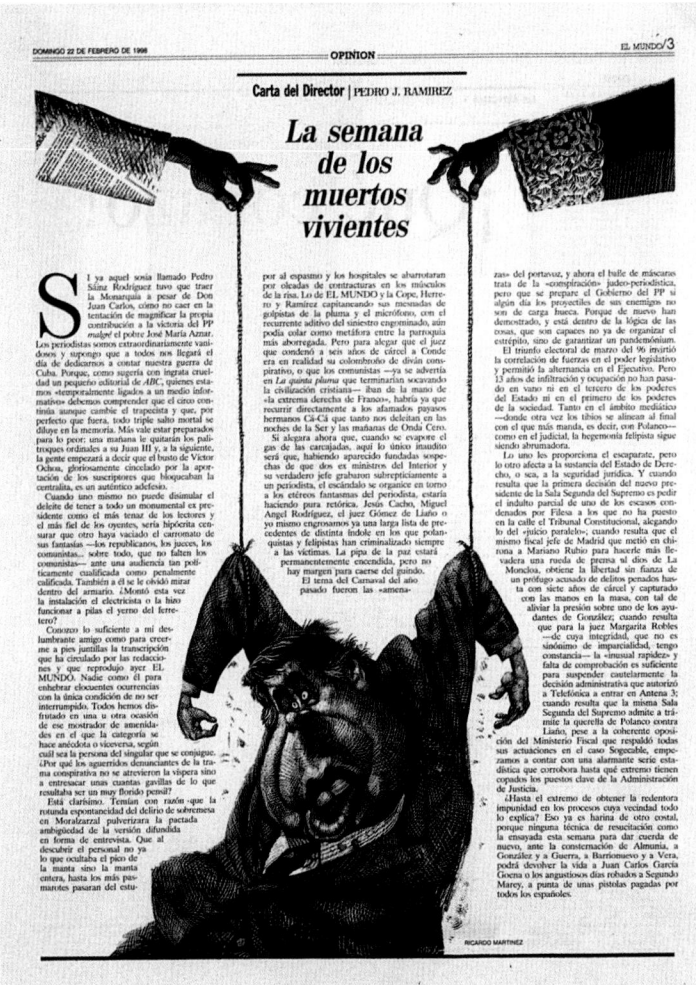

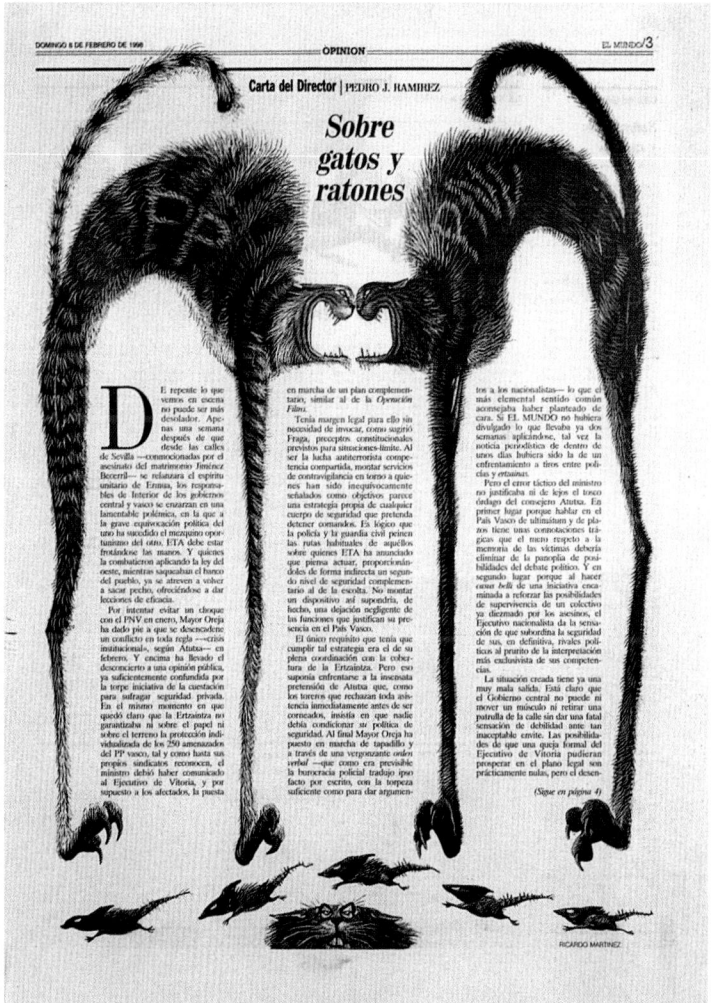

JUDGES' SPECIAL RECOGNITION ■ The Spokesman-Review

Gold & JSR • for Single-Subject Series

The storytelling photographs in the series, "City of Second Chances," propelled the entry to Gold recognition. The photographer's spontaneous and sensitive images took the readers behind the scenes of complicated and difficult-to-access human dreams, and epitomized the highest standards of documentary photojournalism.

Also, a JSR was awarded for the extraordinary commitment to covering a community issue. It is difficult to get photos like this without a sustained investment in gaining the trust of the subjects. "I have not seen anything like this in all my years of being a newspaper photographer," said one judge. The photography achieves a a flawless intimacy with the subjects, time and time again. This is simply presented and tightly edited.

The Spokesman-Review
Spokane, WA
John Nelson, Design Editor; **John Sale,** Photo Editor; **Colin Mulvany,** Photographer; **Vince Grippi,** Graphics

Las elocuentes fotografías de la serie "City of Second Chances" fueron el factor que catapultó a este concursante a la medalla de oro. Las sensibles y espontáneas imágenes del fotógrafo transportaron a los lectores al mundo de los sueños humanos complicados e inaccesibles, y representaron el más alto nivel del periodismo fotográfico documental.

Además, se le otorgó una mención especial del jurado por la extraordinaria dedicación a cubrir un problema de la comunidad. Es difícil conseguir fotos como éstas ganándose la confianza de los sujetos. "No he visto nada semejante en todos los años que llevo de fotógrafo para diarios," aseguró un miembro del jurado. La fotografía logra una impecable intimidad con los sujetos, una y otra vez. La presentación es sencilla y la edición es sobria.

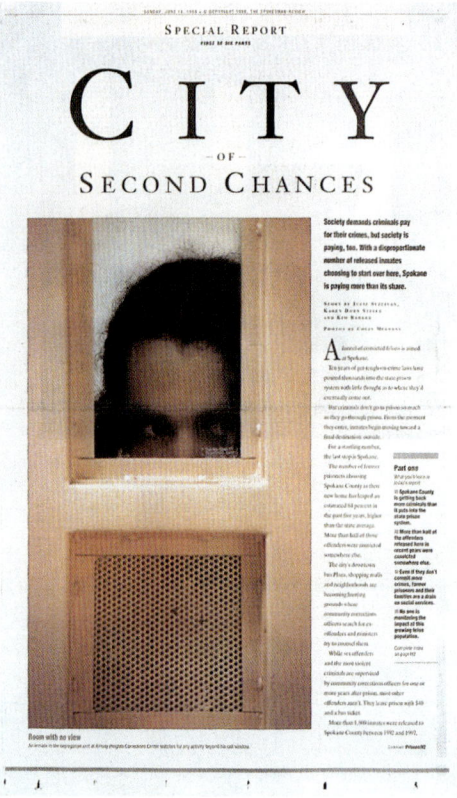
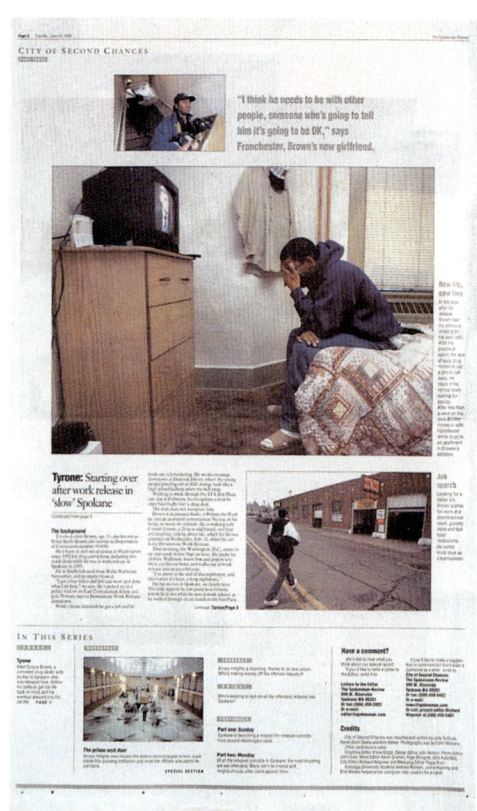

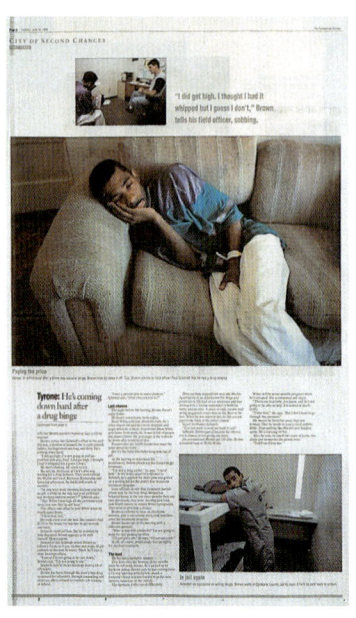
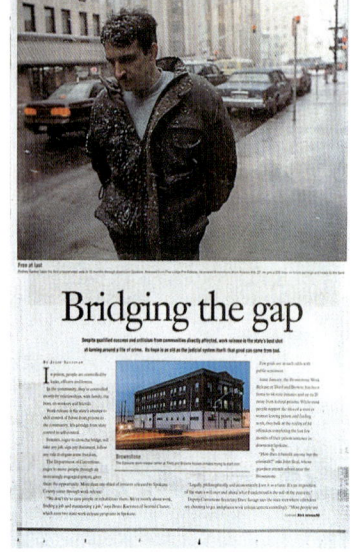
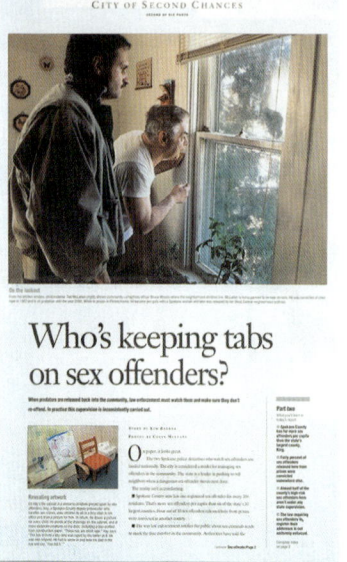
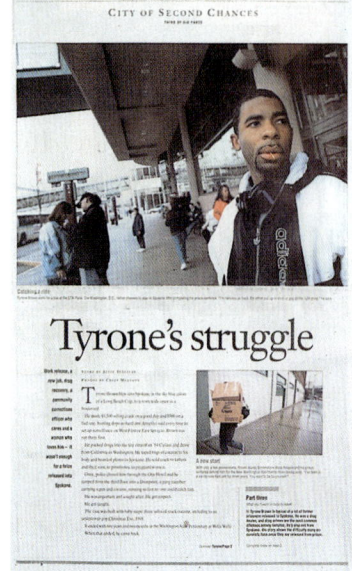

The Scotsman ■ JUDGES' SPECIAL RECOGNITION

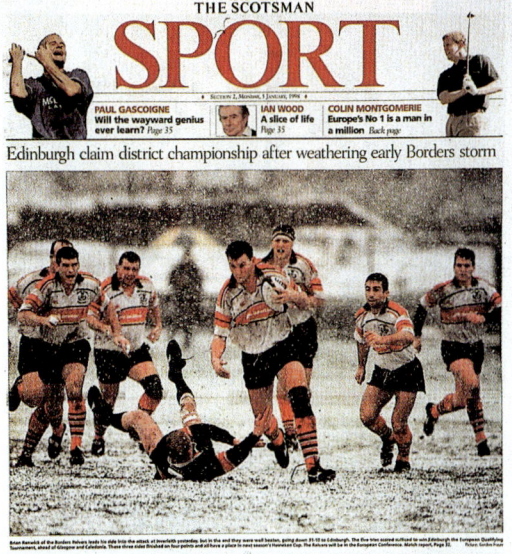

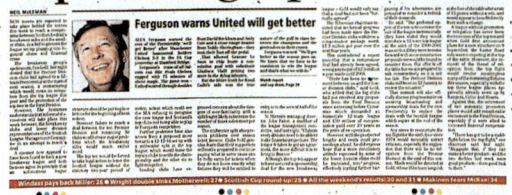

The Scotsman
Edinburgh, Scotland
Staff

Silver & JSR • for Sports Section

This paper has made a commitment to reporting sports photographically, more than any other news section we saw. The Scotsman delivers photography that has impact, content, color and space. Readers must love seeing this publication's sports coverage.

Este diario se ha comprometido a realizar el reportaje deportivo mediante fotografías, más que las demás secciones de noticias que vimos. The Scotsman presenta una fotografía que tiene impacto, contenido, color y espacio. Con seguridad los lectores disfrutan la cobertura deportiva que ofrece esta publicación.

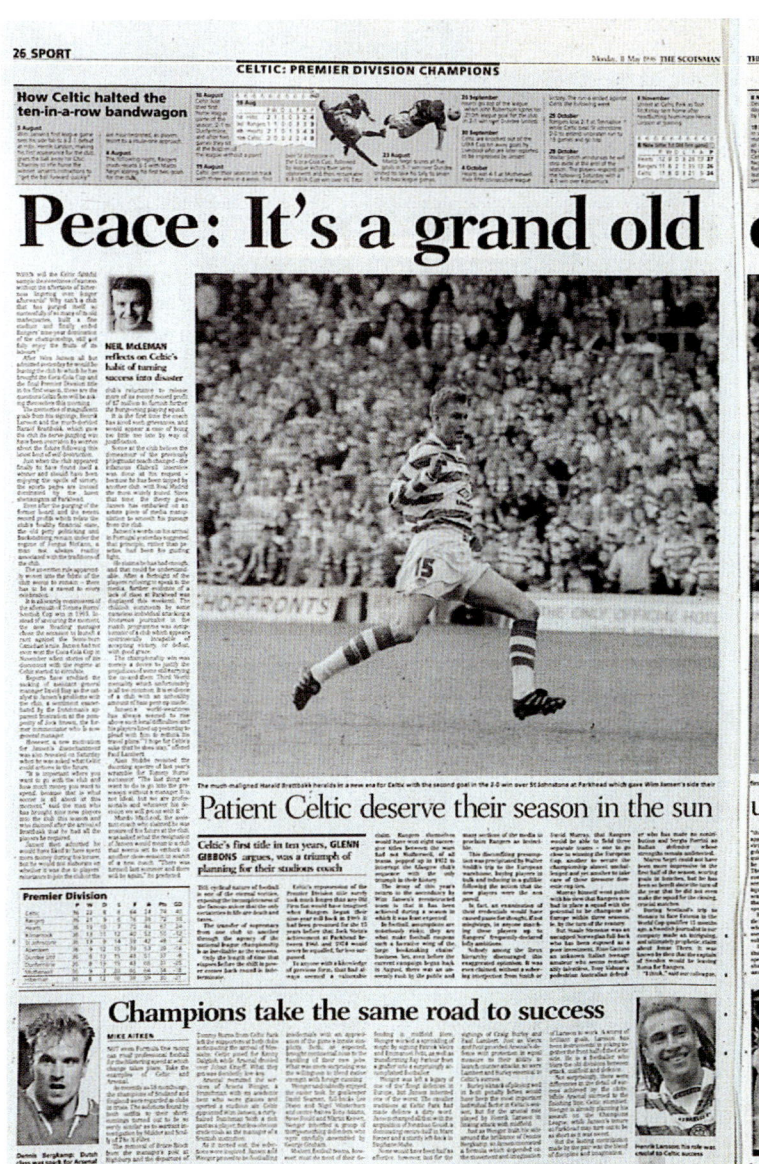

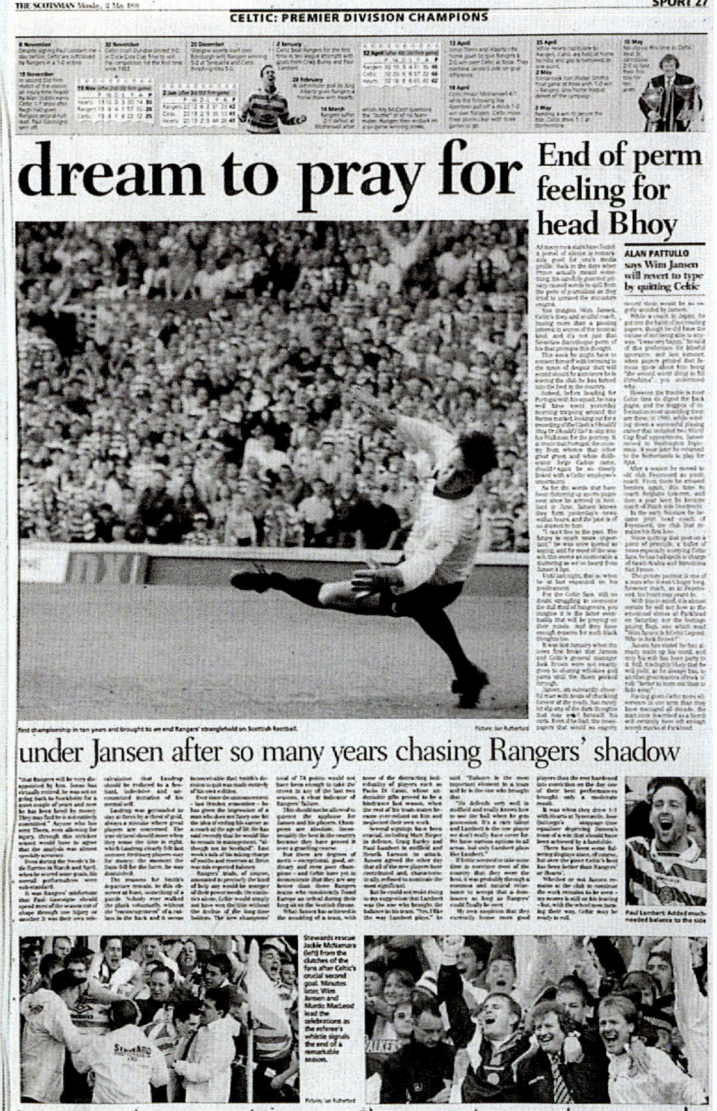

JUDGES' SPECIAL RECOGNITION ■ The Chicago Tribune

The Chicago Tribune
Chicago, IL

Joan Cairney, Art Director; **David Cowles,** Illustrator; **Mark Anderson,** Illustrator; **Andrew Skwish,** Illustrator; **Tom Bachtell,** Illustrator; **Stephen Kroninger,** Illustrator; **Rakefet Keenan,** Illustrator; **Devin Rose,** Editor

Gold • for Illustration
Gold • for Illustration Portfolio Staff

This was solid Gold: a crowd-stopper. It gets readers involved day to day, building the illustration on a kid's wall in Chicago — what a wonderful thing for kids and art. The concept is unique among today's publications in an age when it seems as though everyone is copying everyone else. It's refreshing when different artists come together to make something special.

This was the finest example of creativity the judges have seen in many, many years. It is exciting and daring. This newspaper made a commitment to honor the city's favorite son and has done so in a way that transcends any other recognition it could have given him.

Una medalla de oro bien merecida: atrajo la atención de todos. Logra captar a los lectores a diario y la ilustración se construyó en torno a la pared de un niño de Chicago, ¡qué bueno para los niños y el arte! El concepto es único en su tipo y se distingue entre todas las publicaciones actuales, que parecen que se copian unas a otras. Es reconfortante que diferentes artistas se reúnan para lograr algo especial.

Este fue el mejor ejemplo de creatividad que el jurado haya visto en muchísimos años. Es emocionante y atrevido. Este diario se comprometió a honrar al hijo favorito de la ciudad y lo ha hecho de un modo que trasciende cualquier otro reconocimiento que le pudieran haber dado.

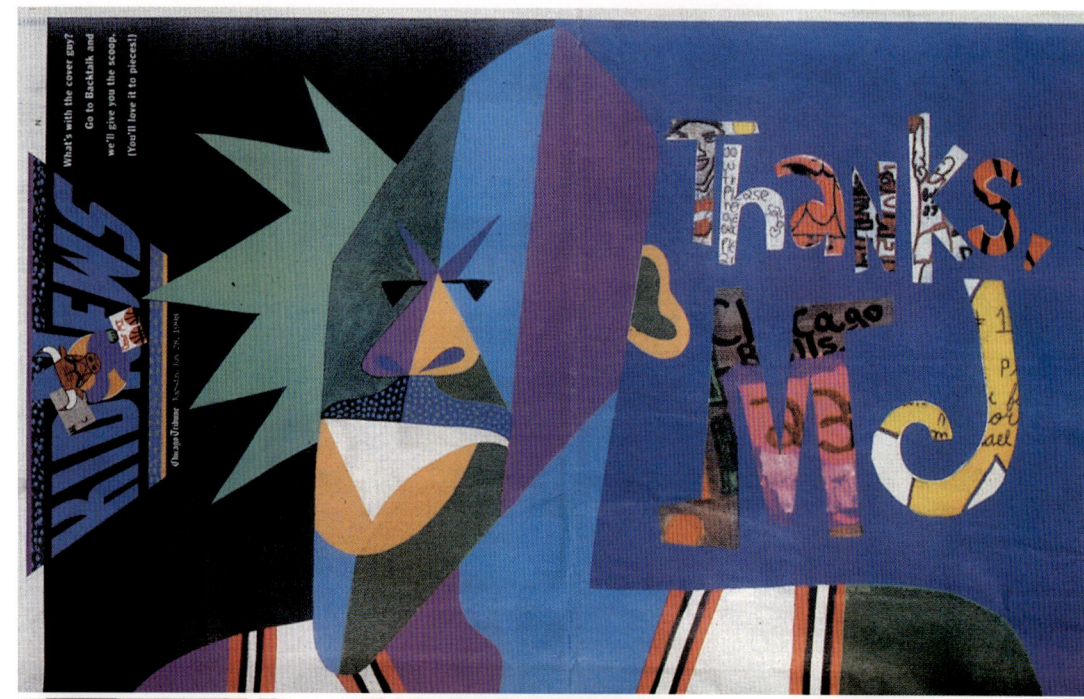

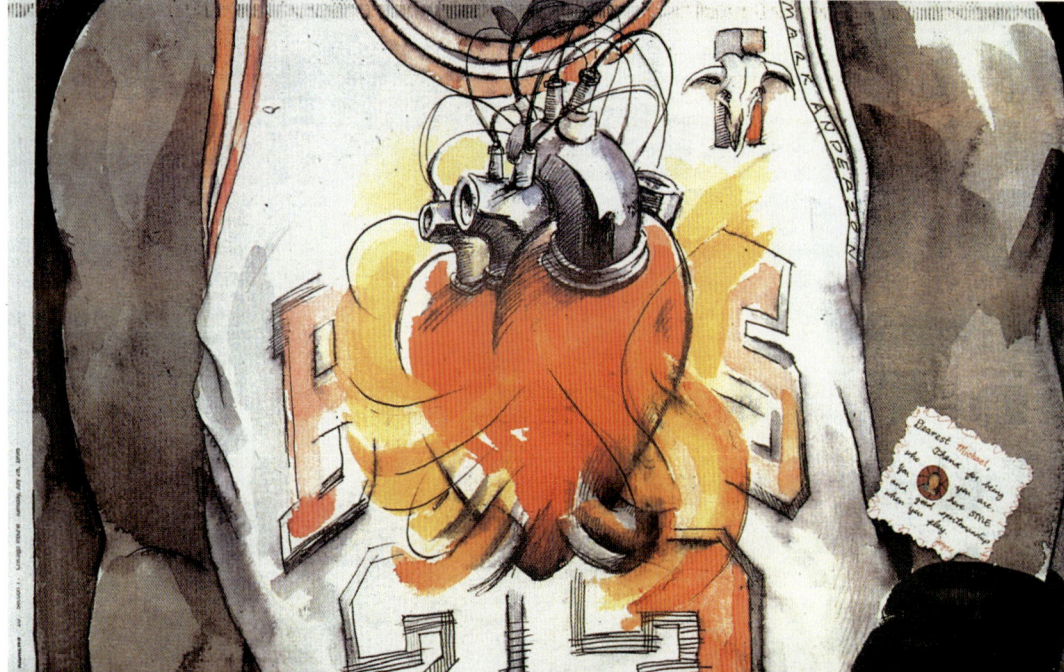

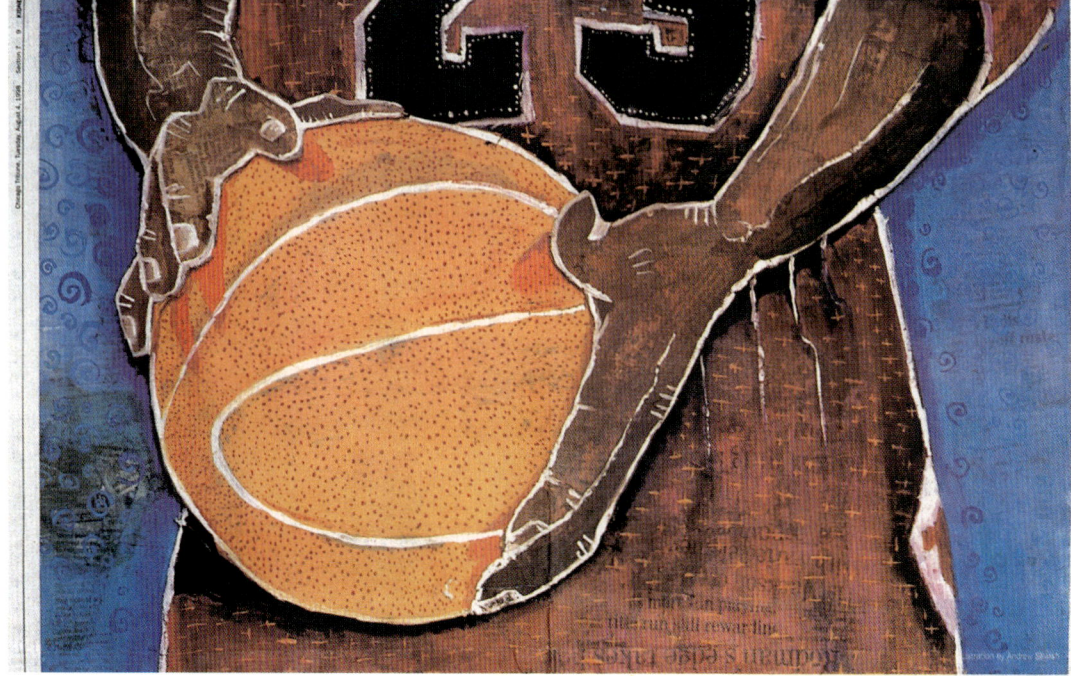

48 ■ THE BEST OF NEWSPAPER DESIGN

The Chicago Tribune ■ JUDGES' SPECIAL RECOGNITION

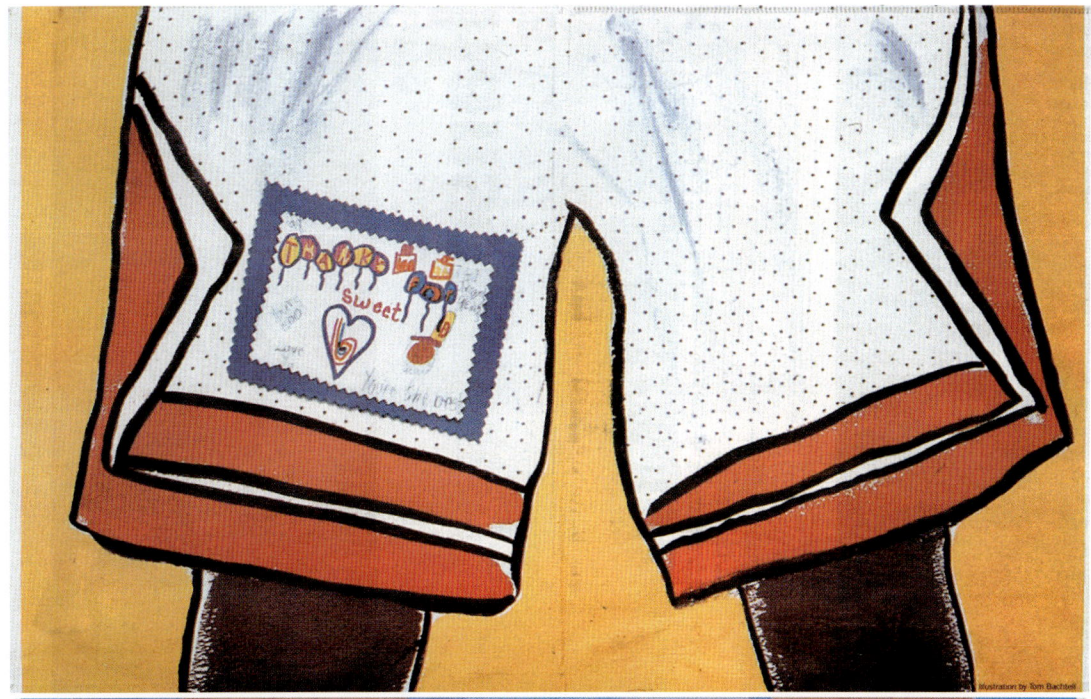

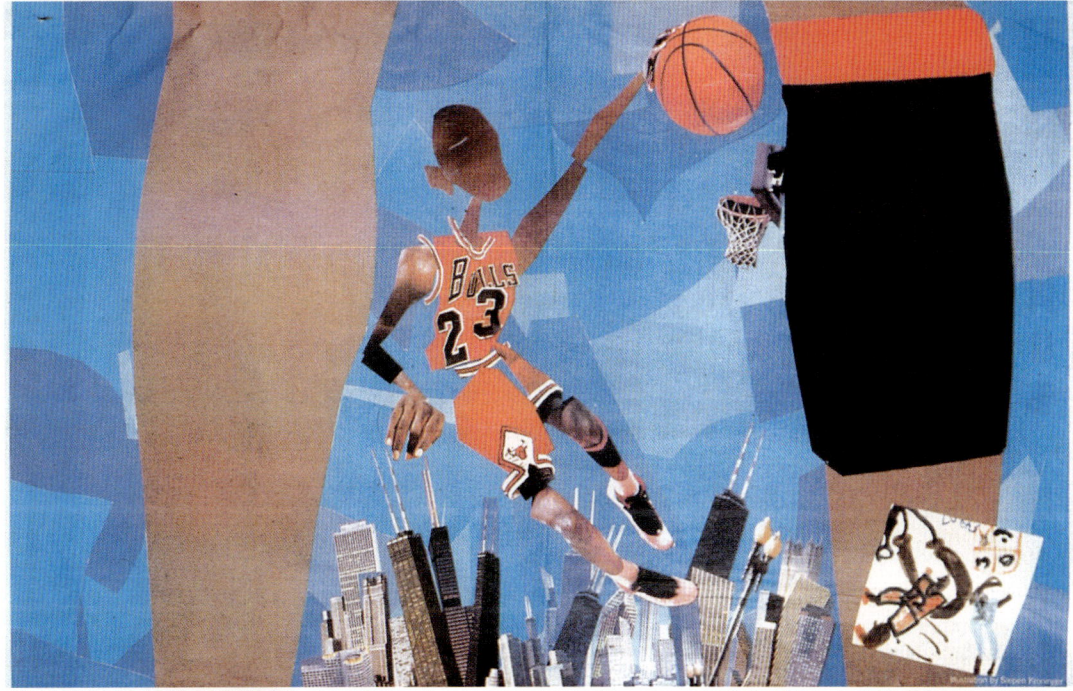

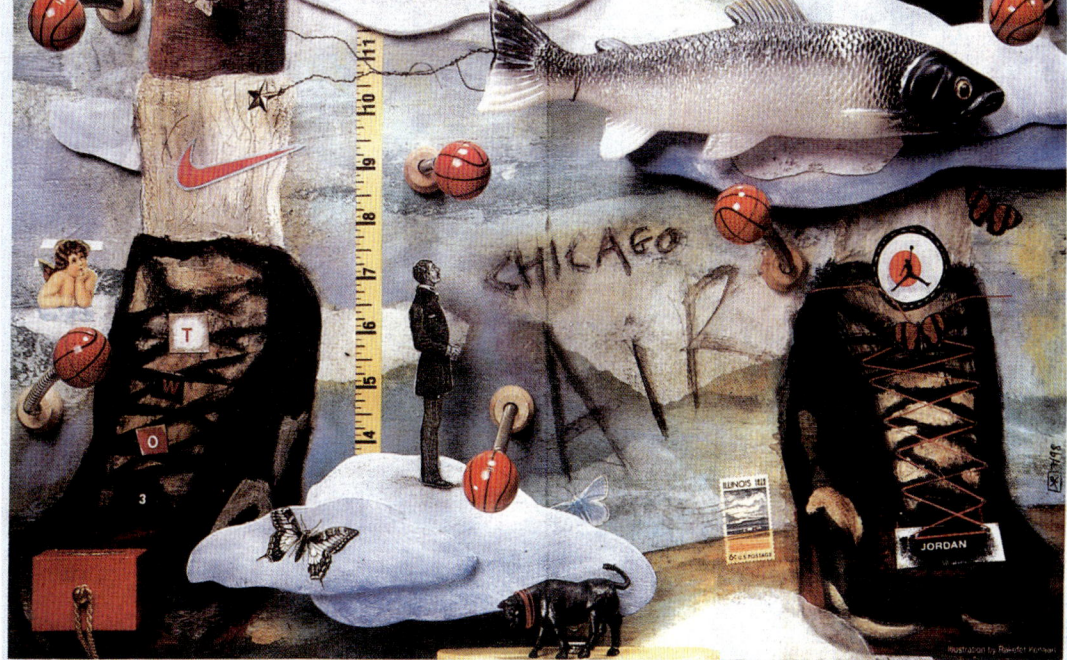

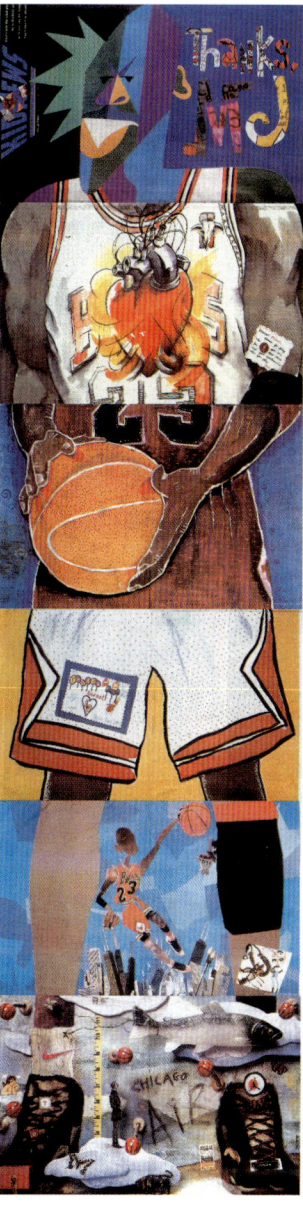

When assembled, the six pages formed a life-sized poster of Michael Jordan.

JUDGES' SPECIAL RECOGNITION ■ Göteborgs-Posten

Göteborgs-Posten
Göteborg, Sweden
Staff

Gold • for Special News Topics Editor's Choice, Local/Regional

The photos are very good, played at the right size, and provide great information. There is a strong visual impact on every page. This is a classic example of how to do breaking news right. The judges found the effort used in this breaking news story "amazing." This is the best of what can be done on deadline.

Las fotos son muy buenas, tienen el tamaño adecuado y ofrecen mucha información. Cada página trasmite un gran efecto visual. Este es un ejemplo clásico de cómo anunciar una noticia de último minuto con eficacia. El jurado estimó que el esfuerzo empleado para anunciar esta noticia de última minuto fue "increíble." Es una muestra de lo mejor que puede hacerse dentro del plazo dado.

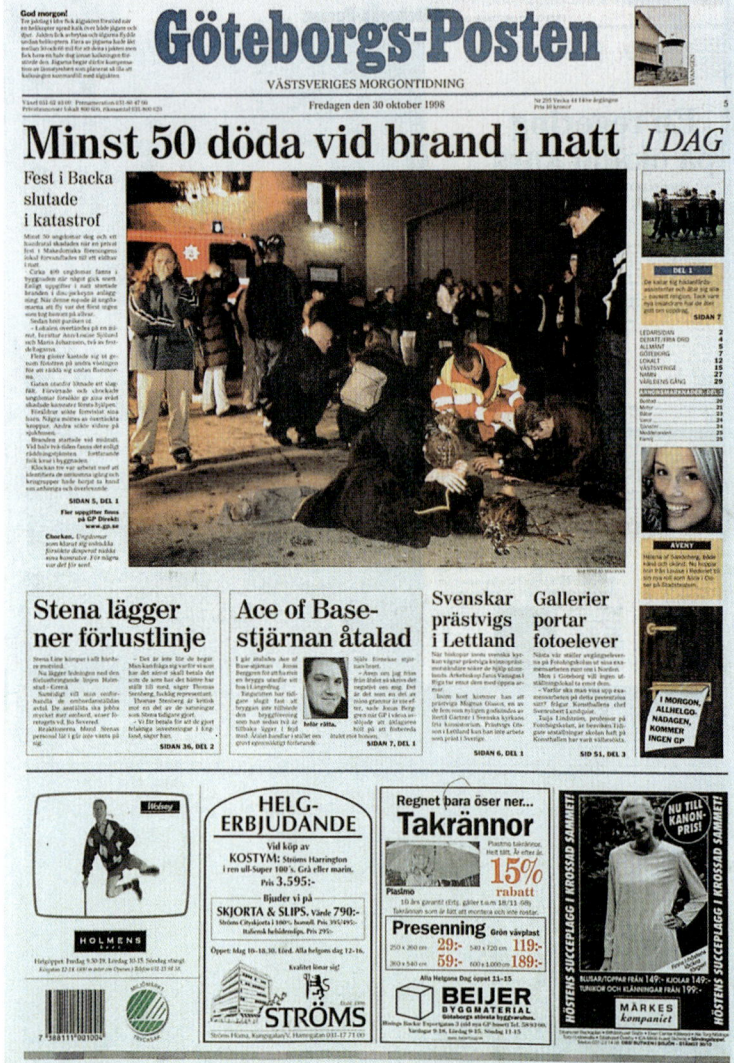
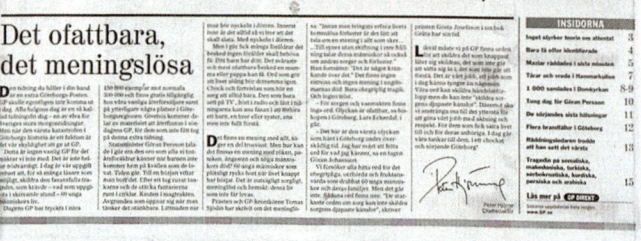
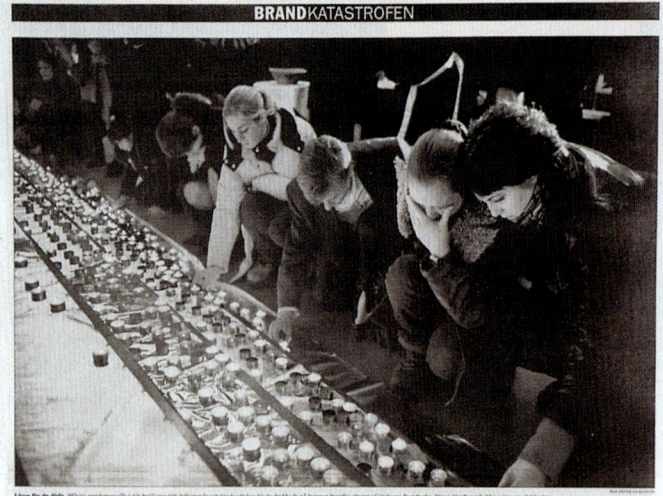
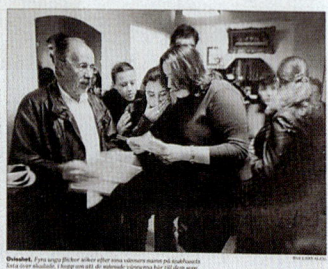

50 ■ THE BEST OF NEWSPAPER DESIGN

Diario de Noticias / DNA ■ JUDGES' SPECIAL RECOGNITION

Diario de Noticias / DNA
Lisbon, Portugal
Mário B. Resendes, Editor-in-Chief; **José Maria Ribeirinho**, Art Director; **Pedro Rolo Duarte**, Editor; **Luís Silva Dias**, Design Editor; **Miguel Pedroso**, Designer

Gold • for Magazine Page Design
Gold • for Magazine Cover Black or Black and One Color
Silver • for Photo Series

This was poetry. The idea was far better and more powerful than a portrait of the poet on the cover. It's nice they kept the flag muted.

Esto fue poesía. La idea fue mucho mejor y más impactante que un retrato del poeta en la portada. La cabecera apagada es un detalle muy atractivo.

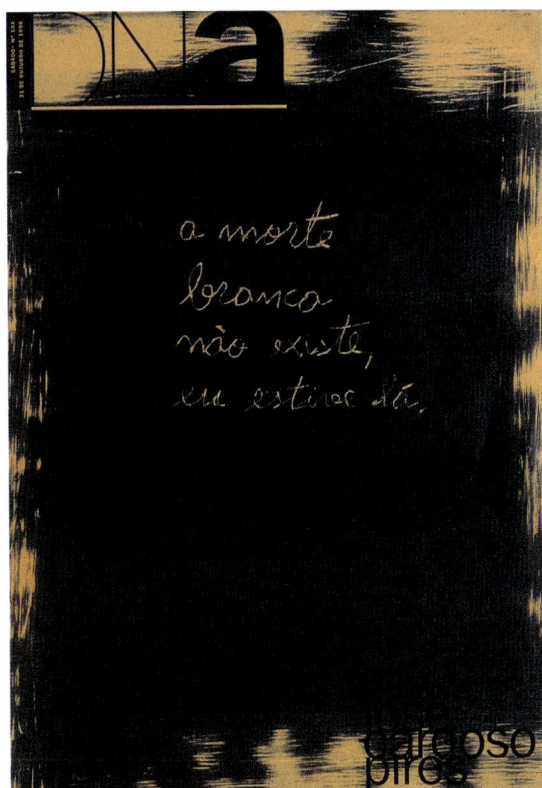

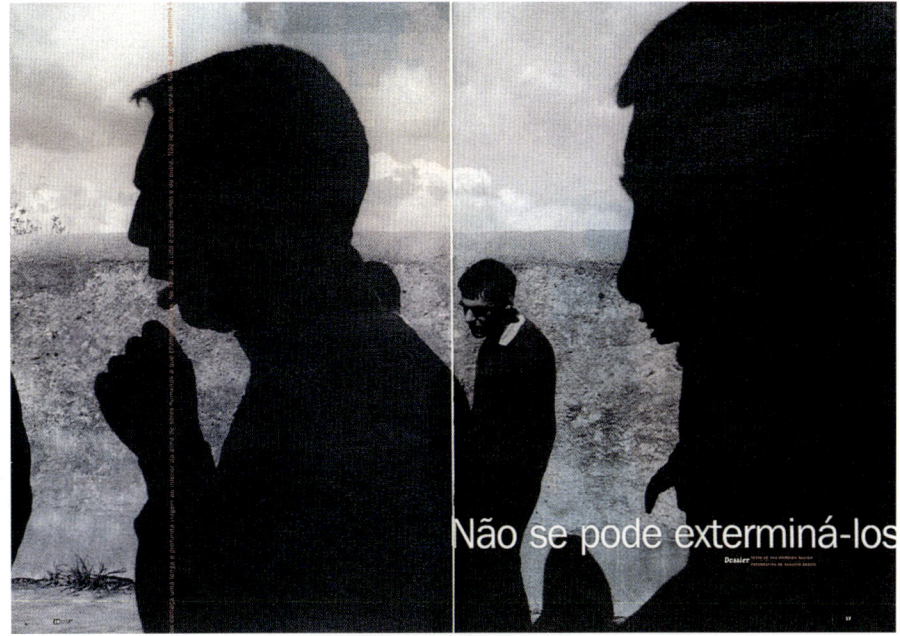

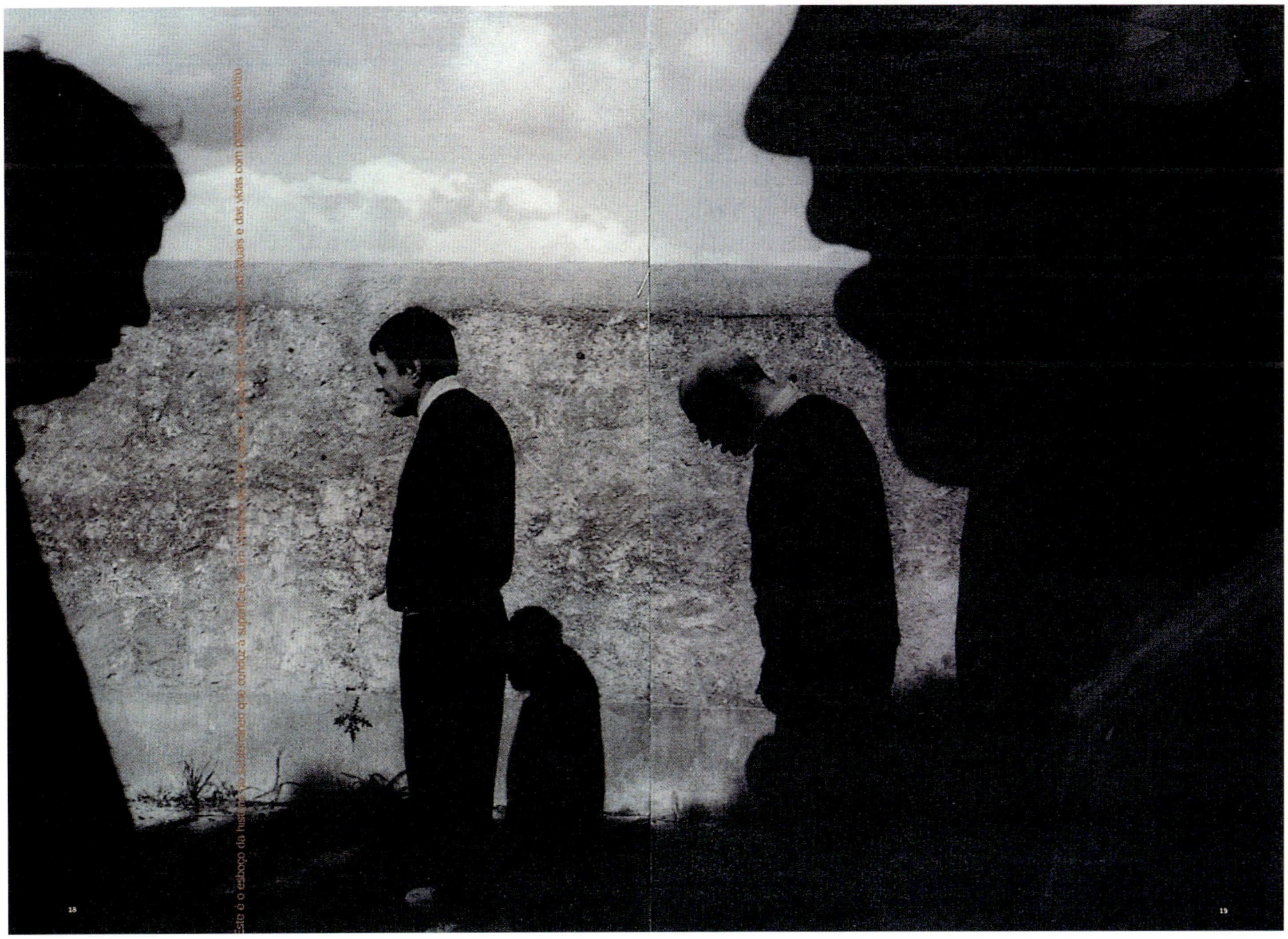

TWENTIETH EDITION ■ 51

JUDGES' SPECIAL RECOGNITION ■ The National Post

The National Post
Don Mills, Canada

Gayle Grin, Design Editor; **Kenneth Whyte,** Editor in Chief; **Martin Newland,** Deputy Editor; **Kirk Lapointe,** Executive Editor; **Marvin Zivitz,** Deputy M.E.; **Lucie Lacava,** Design Consultant; **Roland-Yves Carignan,** Design Editor; **Alison Uncles,** National Editor; **John Racovali,** Foreign Editor; **Denis Paquin,** Photo Editor

Gold • Section A

Everything from the photo display to the attention to detail is excellent. Little things make it a Gold winner. What stands out about this paper is that, from top to bottom, the architecture is top of the line. They have taken what The New York Times does to a higher level. They have used the 50-inch web to enhance the design. The color palette is rich and original.

Todo, desde el despliegue de fotos hasta la atención prestada a los detalles, es excelente. Los pequeños detalles hacen que sea merecedor de la medalla de oro. Lo que sobresale de este periódico es que, desde la primera hasta la última página, la arquitectura es de primera. Lo que The New York Times hace, ellos lo han llevado a nuevas alturas. Han empleado la red de 50 pulgadas para realzar el diseño. La gama de colores es rica y original.

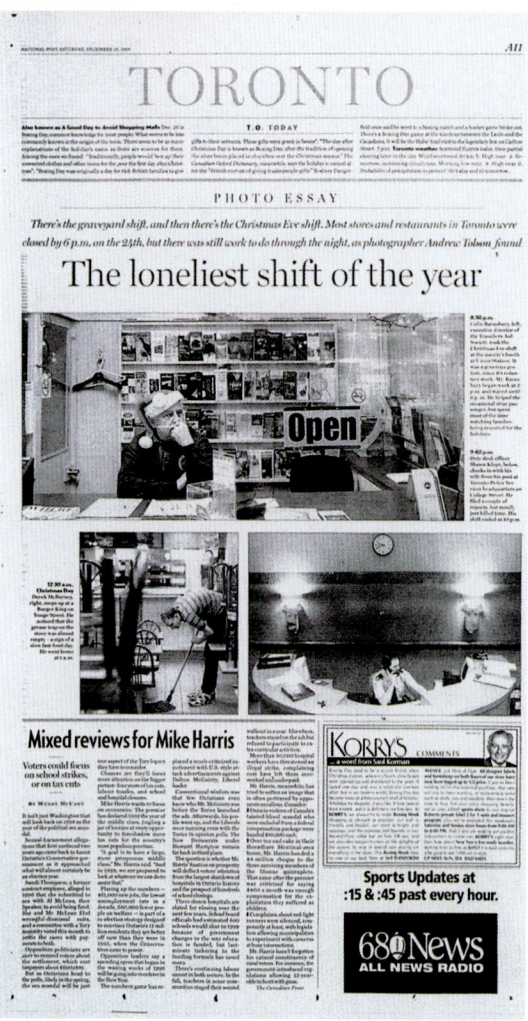

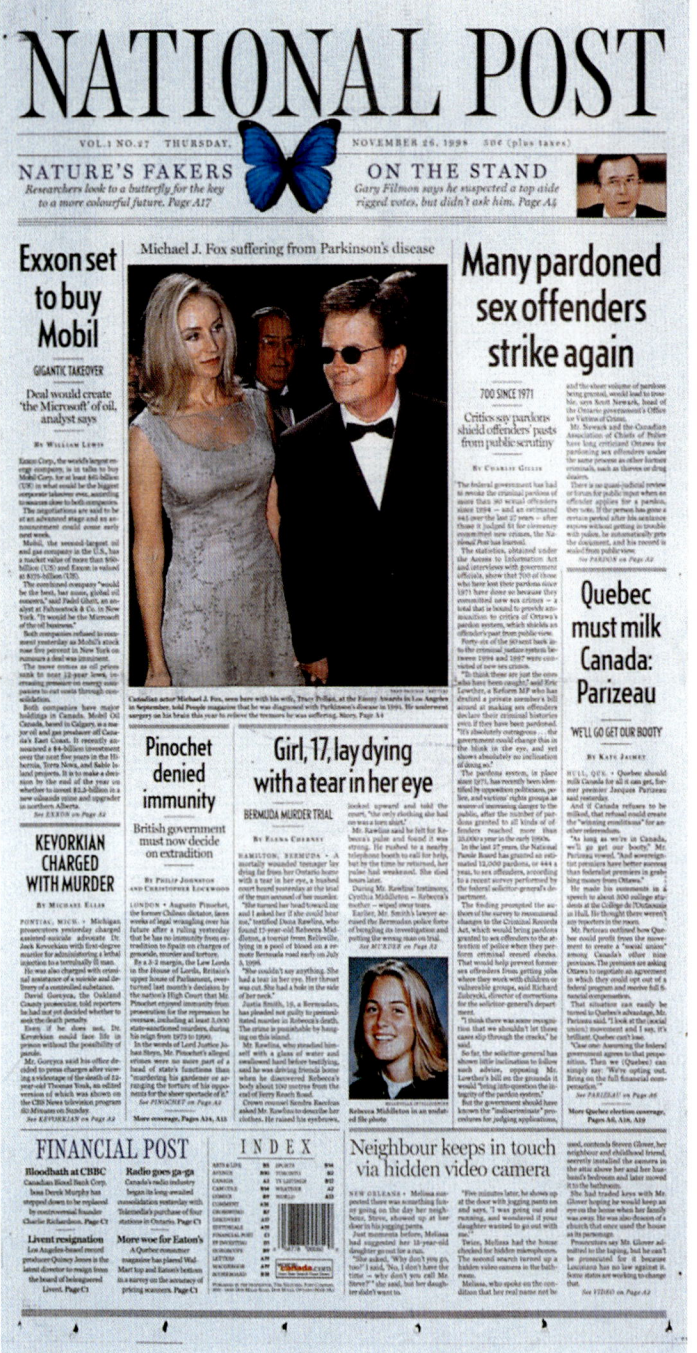

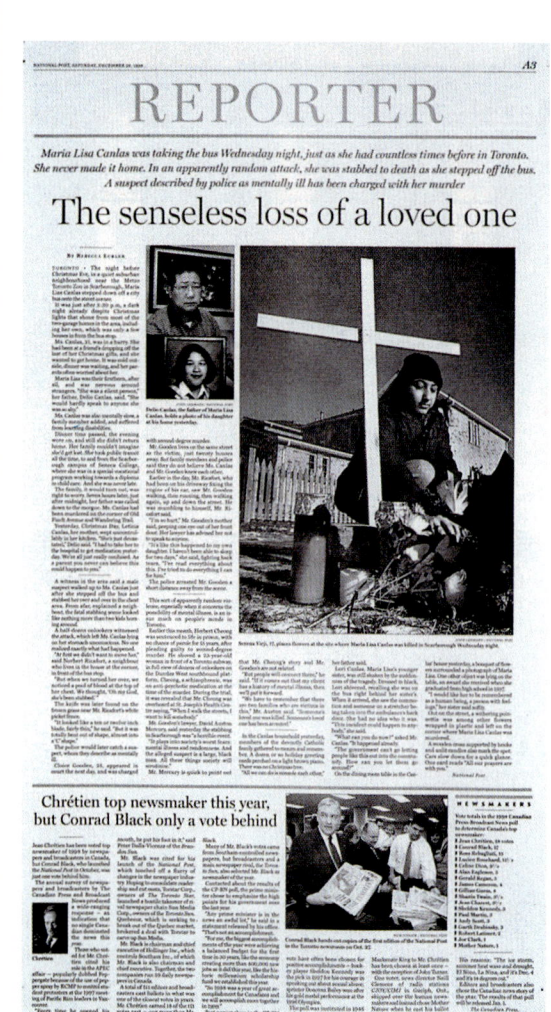

52 ■ THE BEST OF NEWSPAPER DESIGN

NEWS

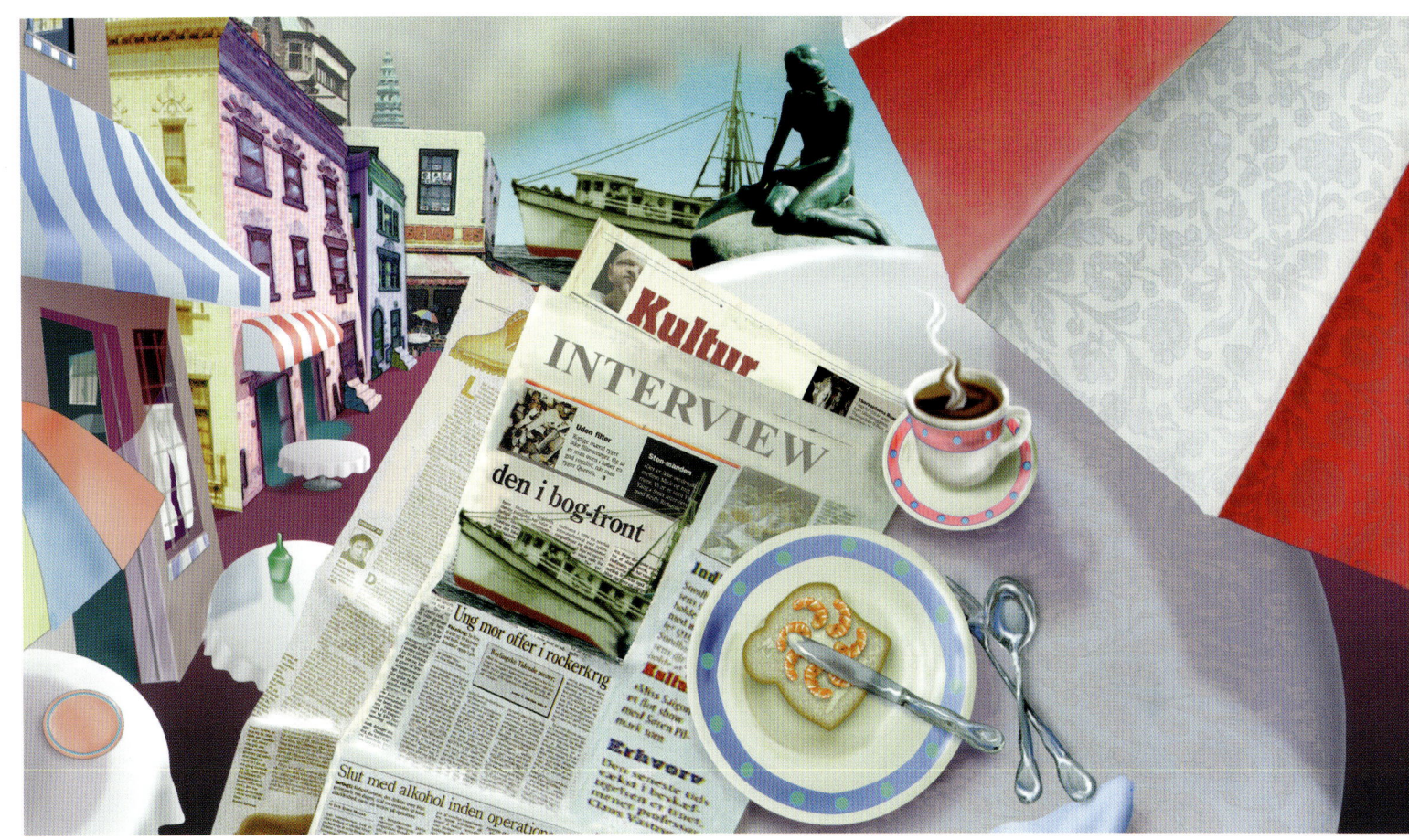

CHAPTER TWO

NEWS SECTIONS

NEWS PAGES

BREAKING NEWS PAGES

SPECIAL NEWS TOPICS

NEWS ■ Section A, Sports Section

Berlingske Tidende
Copenhagen, Denmark
Staff; **Niels Hjerrild**, Photo Editor; **Carsten Gregersen**, Design Editor

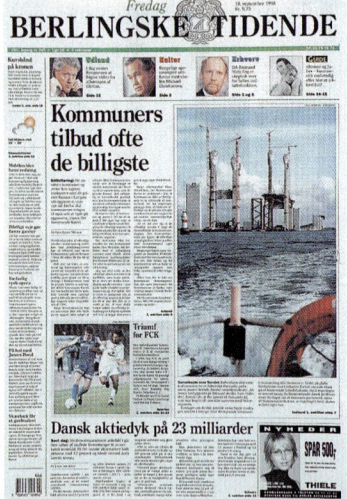

Politiken
Copenhagen, Denmark
Staff

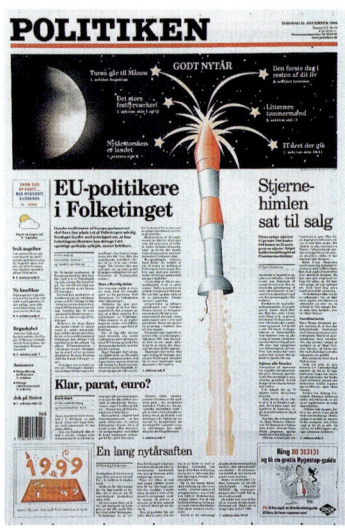

The Globe and Mail
Toronto, Canada
Staff

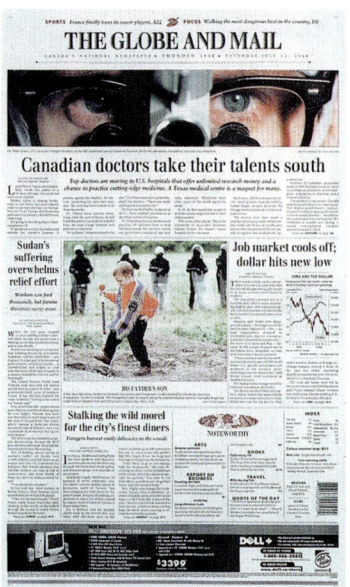

The Times
Munster, IN
Kevin Poortinga, Design Director; **Craig Newman**, Design Team Leader; **Epha Good**, Design Team Leader; **Matt Mansfield**, Deputy Managing Editor; **Paul Mullaney**, Deputy Managing Editor/Nights; **Marilyn Kucer**, Night Editor; Staff

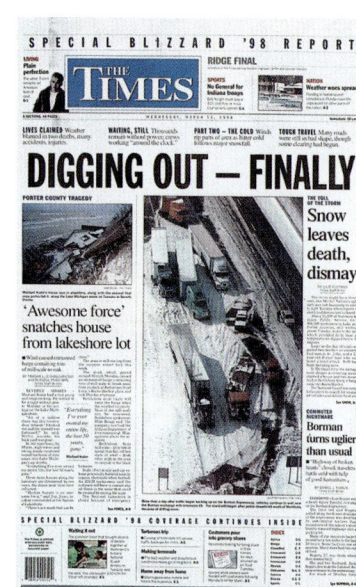

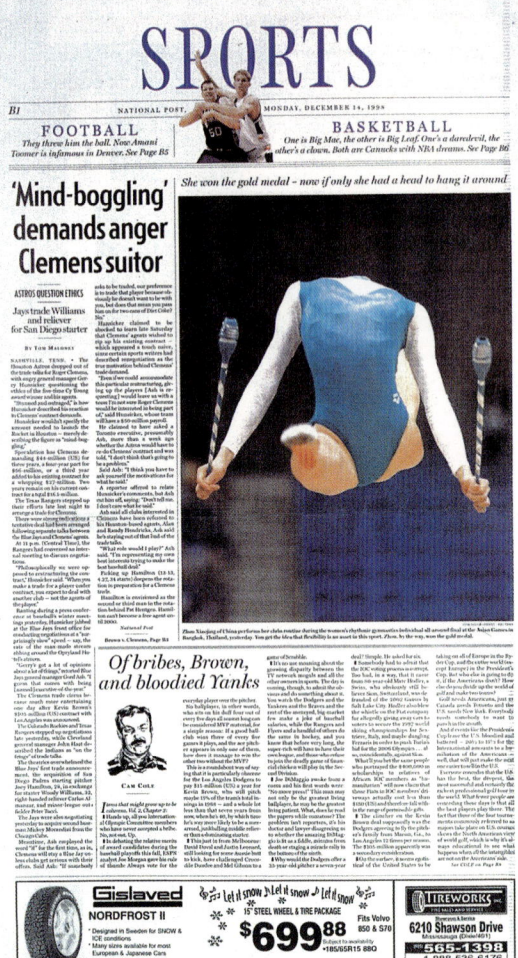

Silver
The National Post
Don Mills, Canada
Kenneth Whyte, Editor-in-Chief; **Lucie Lacava**, Design Consultant; **Gayle Grin**, Design Editor; **Graham Parley**, Sports Editor; **Ron Wadden**, Design Sports Editor & Designer

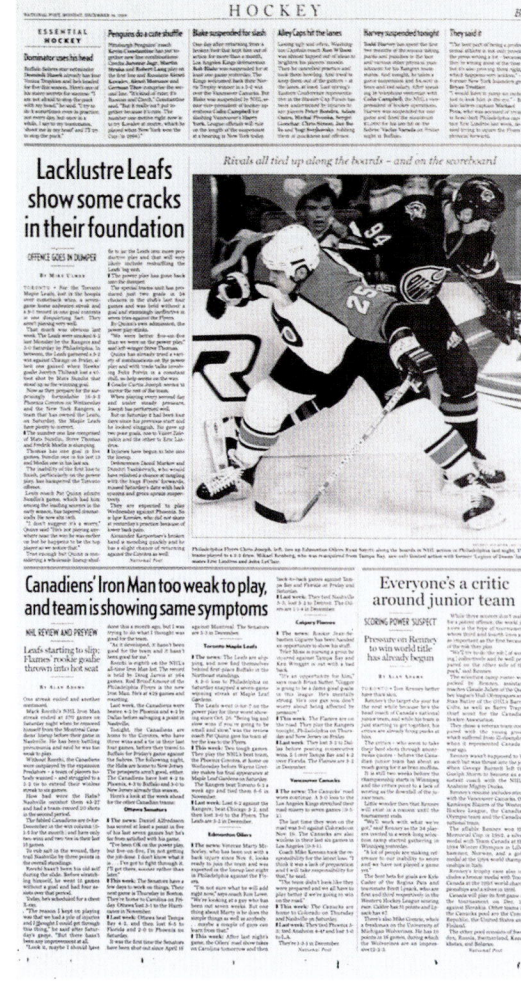

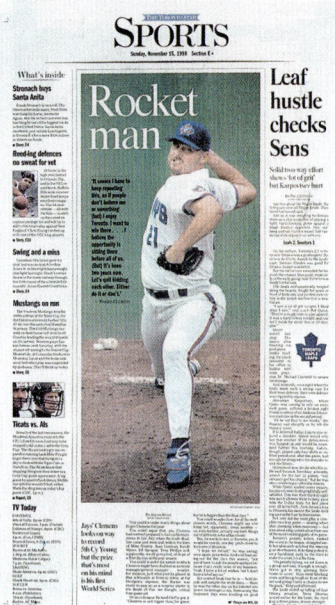

The Toronto Star
Toronto, Canada
Staff

54 ■ THE BEST OF NEWSPAPER DESIGN

Sports Section, Business Section, Other Section ■ NEWS

The News & Observer
Raleigh, NC
Teresa Kriegsman, Assistant Director/News Design; **Jessaca Senechal**, Designer; **Justin Scheef**, Designer

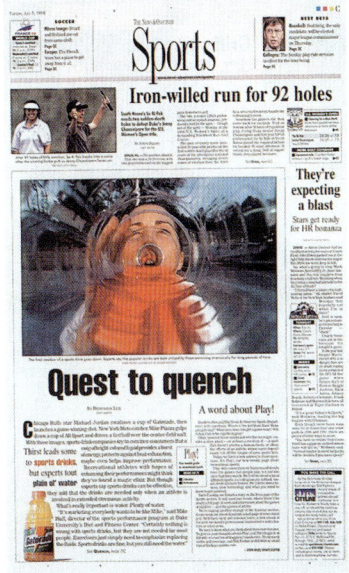

The Beacon-News
Aurora, IL
Michael W. Whitley, Sports Design Editor; **James Denk**, Director/Design & Graphics; **Staff**

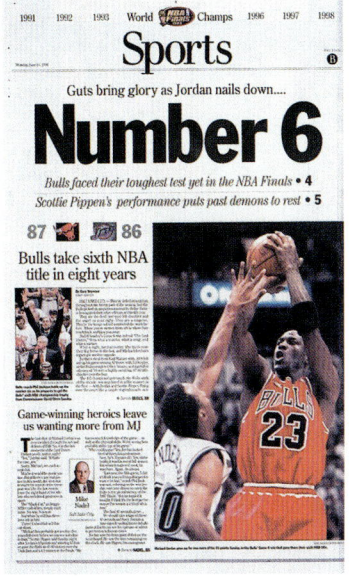

Le Soleil
Québec, Canada
Marcel Colbert, Front Page Designer & Editor; **Staff**

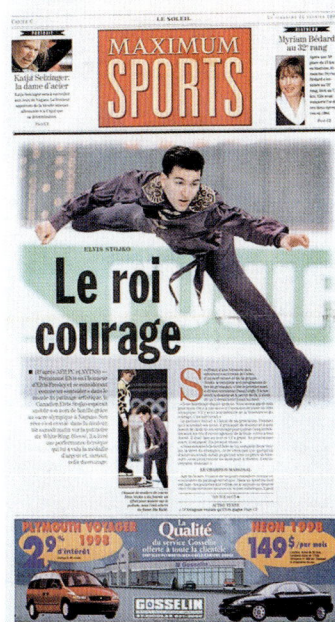

The Beacon-News
Aurora, IL
Michael W. Whitley, Sports Design Editor; **James Denk**, Director/Design & Graphics; **Staff**

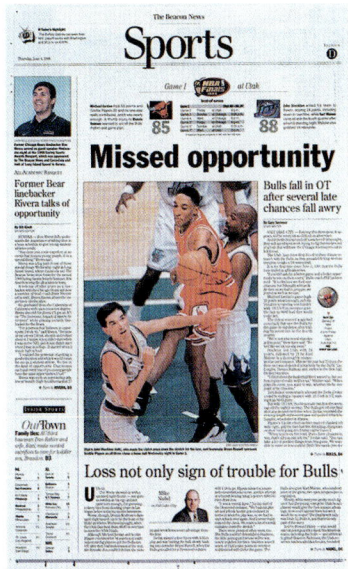

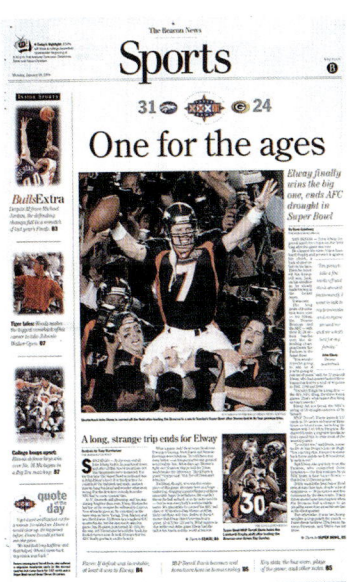

The Beacon-News
Aurora, IL
Michael W. Whitley, Sports Design Editor; **James Denk**, Director/Design & Graphics; **Staff**

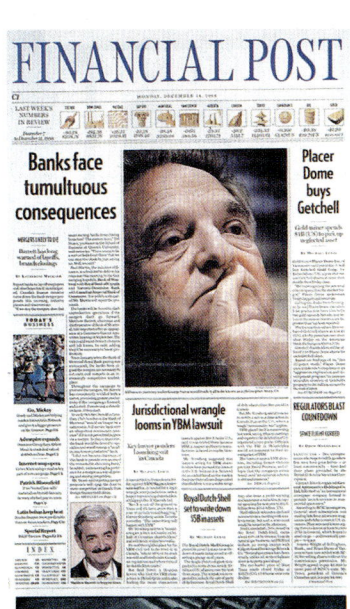

The National Post
Don Mills, Canada
Kenneth Whyte, Editor-in-Chief; **Chris Watson**, Deputy Managing Editor; **Kirk Lapointe**, Executive Editor; **Lucie Lacava**, Design Consultant; **Gayle Grin**, Design Editor; **Roland-Yves Carignan**, Design Editor; **Howard Intrator**, Business News Editor

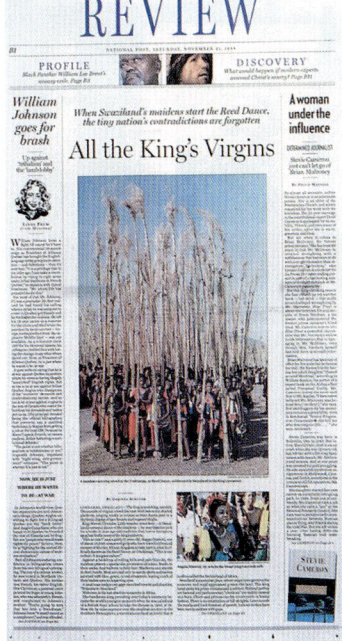

The National Post
Don Mills, Canada
Martin Newland, Editor-in-Chief; **Kirk Lapointe**, Executive Editor; **Mark Stevenson**, Section Editor; **Kenneth Whyte**, Editor-in-Chief; **Chuck Davies**, Section Editor; **Gerald Owen**, Copy Editor; **Lucie Lacava**, Design Consultant; **Roland-Yves Carignan**, Design Editor

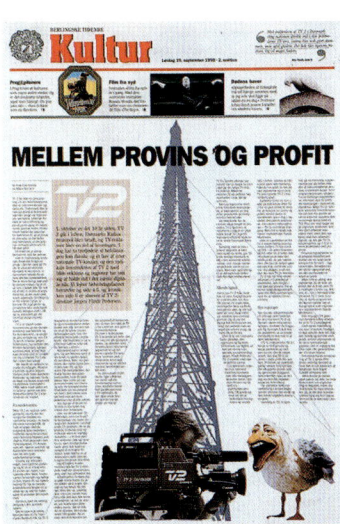

Berlingske Tidende
Copenhagen, Denmark
Gregers Jensen, Page Designer; **Kirsten Lauritzen**, Page Designer; **Dorthe Ravn**, Page Designer; **Jørgen Falck**, Page Designer; **Lars Henrik Aagaard**, Culture Editor; **Carsten Gregersen**, Design Editor

TWENTIETH EDITION ■ 55

NEWS — Front Page

The Charlotte Observer
Charlotte, NC
Monica Moses, Design Director; **Craig Paddock,** Designer; **Stephanie Grace Lim,** Photographer; **Brian Melton,** Senior Editor; **Tom Murray,** Photo Editor; **John Vaughn,** Writer

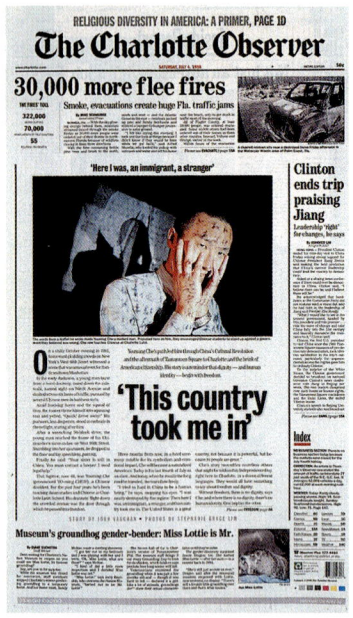

Dagens Nyheter
Stockholm, Sweden
Mia Holmgren, Front Page Editor; **Linda Wikström,** Photographer; **Sören Johansson,** Photo Editor

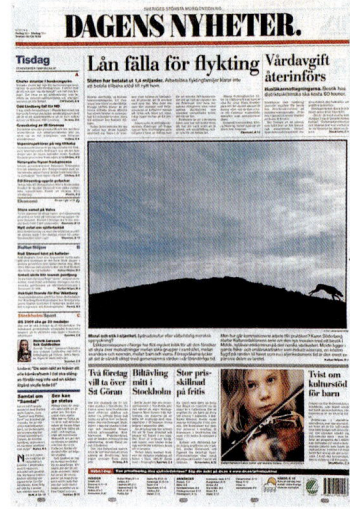

Detroit Free Press
Detroit, MI
Steve Anderson, Designer; **Rick Nease,** Graphics Editor; **Thom Fladung,** News Editor; **Todd Winge,** Picture Editor

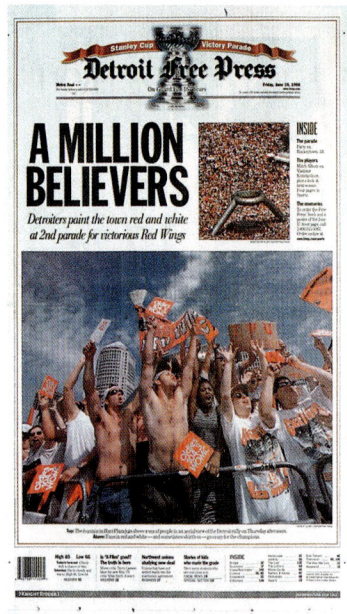

The Detroit News
Detroit, MI
David Kordalski, A.M.E./Presentation; **Joe Greco,** Designer; **Steve Haines,** Photo Editor; **Bill McMillan,** News Editor; **Charles V. Tines,** Photographer

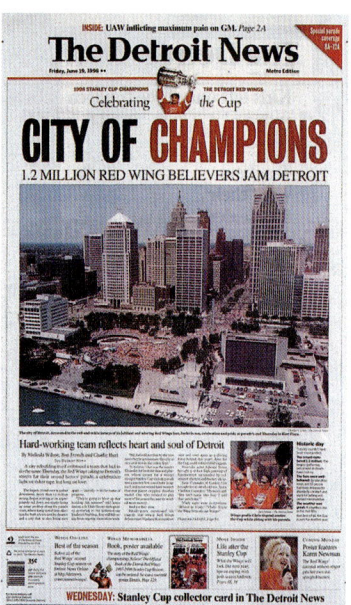

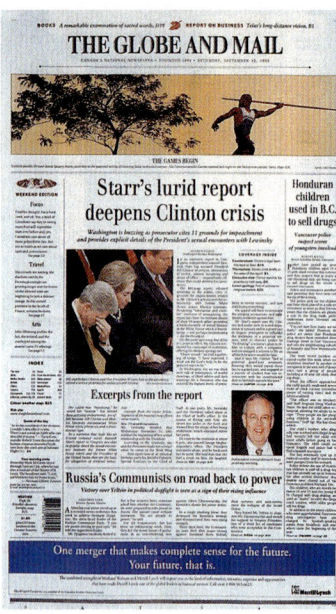

The Globe and Mail
Toronto, Canada
Staff

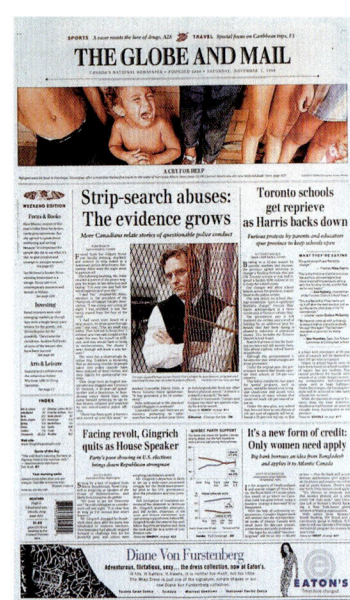

The Globe and Mail
Toronto, Canada
Staff

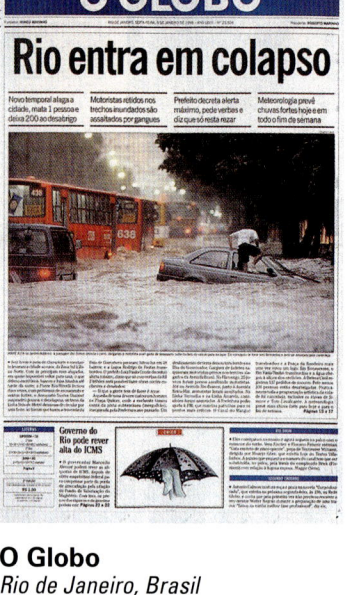

O Globo
Rio de Janeiro, Brasil
Claudio Prudente, Designer; **Rodolfo Fernandes,** Editor; **Ricardo Leoni,** Photographer

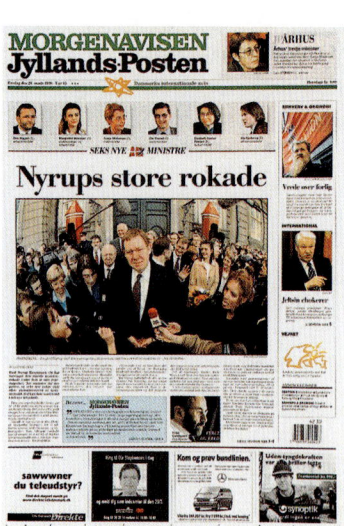

Morgenavisen Jyllands-Posten
Viby J., Denmark
Torben Møldrup, Editor; **Steen Hansen,** News Editor; **Lars Krabbe,** Photographer

Front Page ■ NEWS

The National Post
Don Mills, Canada
Kenneth Whyte, Editor-in-Chief; **Martin Newland,** Deputy Editor; **Kirk Lapointe,** Executive Editor; **Marvin Zivitz,** Deputy M.E.; **Lucie Lacava,** Design Consultant; **Gayle Grin,** Design Editor; **Stephen Meurice,** Copy Editor/Design; **Rob Roberts,** Copy Editor/Design

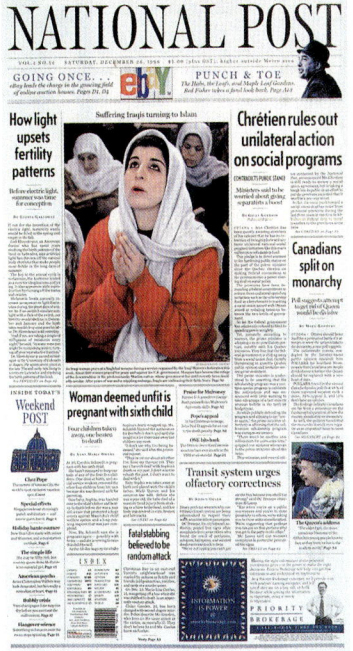

The Star-Ledger
Newark, NJ
George Frederick, Deputy Design Director; **Chris Collins,** Photo Editor; **Charles Cooper,** M.E./Production; **Andrew Phillips,** Graphic Artist

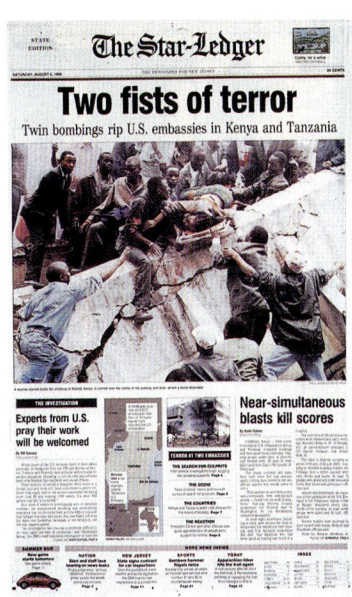

The San Diego Union-Tribune
San Diego, CA
Michael Whitley, Designer

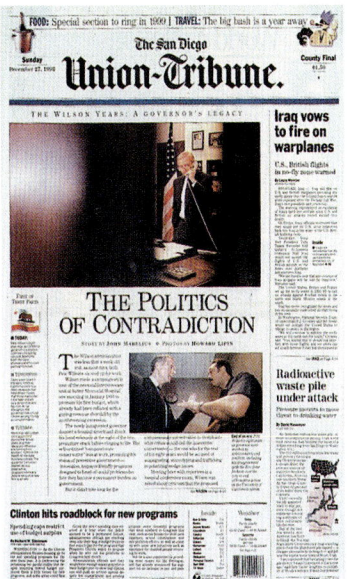

La Vanguardia
Barcelona, Spain
Staff

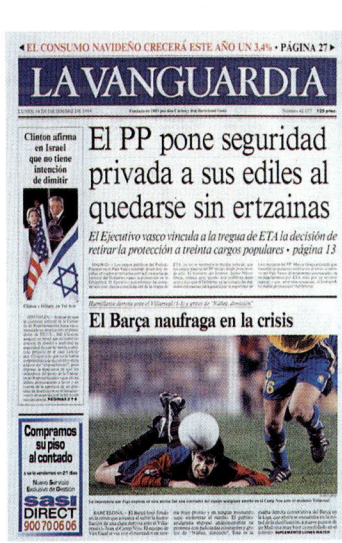

San Jose Mercury News
San Jose, CA
Steve Cavendish, Design Director/News; **Annette J. Vazquez,** News Designer; **Mark Damon,** Photo Editor; **Bryan Monroe,** A.M.E./News, Visuals & Technology; **Ann Hurst,** Deputy M.E./Projects Editor; **Luci S. Houston,** Photographer

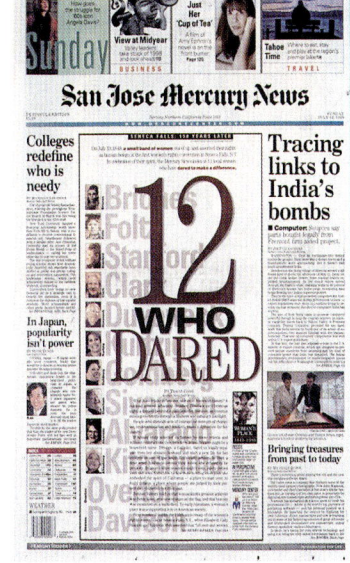

The Virginian-Pilot
Norfolk, VA
Paul Nelson, Designer; **Denis Finley,** News Editor; **Eric Seidman,** Art Director; **Jim Collins,** Photo Editor; **Courtney Murphy,** Projects Designer; **Lisa Cowan,** Designer
• also for Breaking News

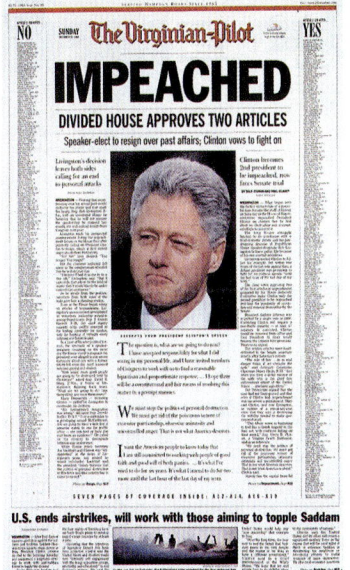

Star Tribune
Minneapolis, MN
Greg Branson, Assistant Graphics Director; **Judy Romanowich-Smith,** A1 Night Coordinator; **Terry Sauer,** A1 Coordinator; **Dave Denney,** Photo Director; **Ray Grumney,** Graphics Director; **Anders Ramberg,** Design Director; **Bill Dunn,** Visual Content Editor; **Pam Fine,** M.E.; **Glen Stubbe,** Photo Editor; **Staff**

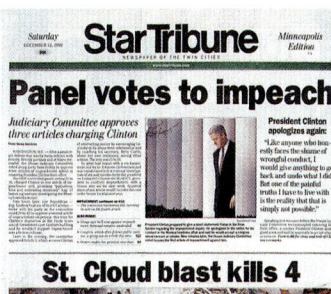
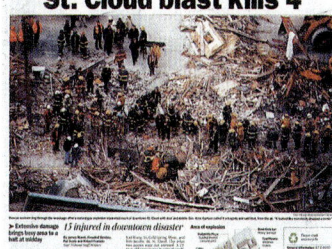

Berlingske Tidende
Copenhagen, Denmark
Bo Tornvig, Photographer; **Staff**

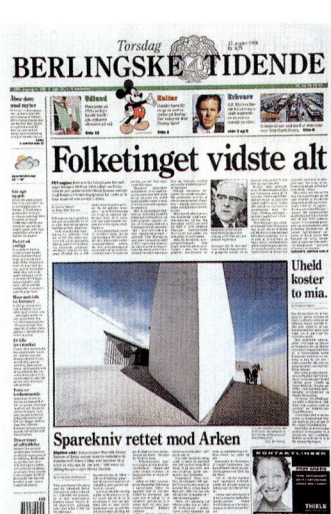

NEWS — Front Page

Silver
Politiken
Copenhagen, Denmark
Søren Nyeland, Design Editor; **Søren-Mikael Hansen,** News Editor; **Kristoffer Løve Østerbye,** Designer; **Ole Kjærhus,** Copy Editor

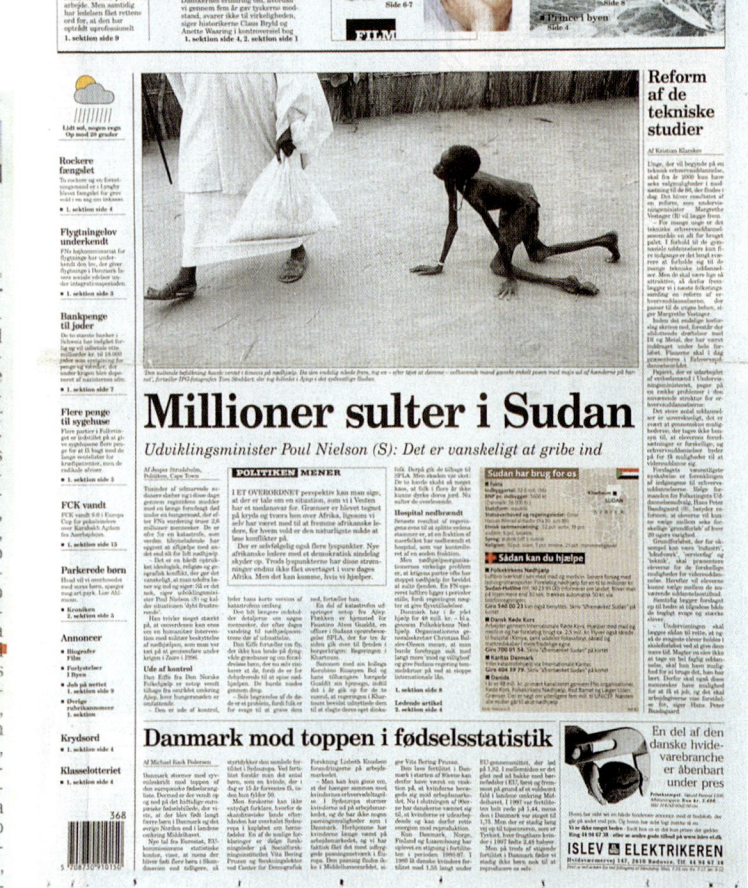

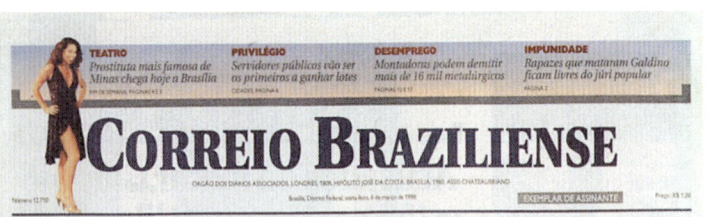

Silver
Correio Braziliense
Brasília, Brasil
Ricardo Noblat, Executive Editor; **Francisco Amaral,** Art Director; **Cláudio Versiani,** Photo Editor

Front Page ■ NEWS

The Providence Journal
Providence, RI

Cecilia Prestamo, Picture Editor/Designer; **Connie Grosch**, Photographer; **Mary Beth Meehan**, Photographer

The Register-Guard
Eugene, OR

Carl Davaz, A.M.E./Graphics & Technology; **George Millener**, Director/Graphics; **Rob Romig**, News Page Designer; **Paul Carter**, Photographer; **Tom Penix**, News Artist; **Chris Frisella**, News Editor; **Chris Pietsch**, Photographer; **Wayne Eastburn**, Photographer; **Thomas Boyd**, Photographer; **Nicole DeVito**, Photographer
• also for Special News Topics

Savannah Morning News
Savannah, GA

Kenny Monteith, News Planner/Designer

The Irish News
Belfast, Northern Ireland

Staff

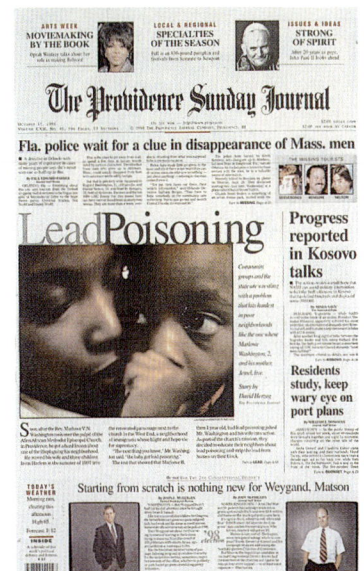
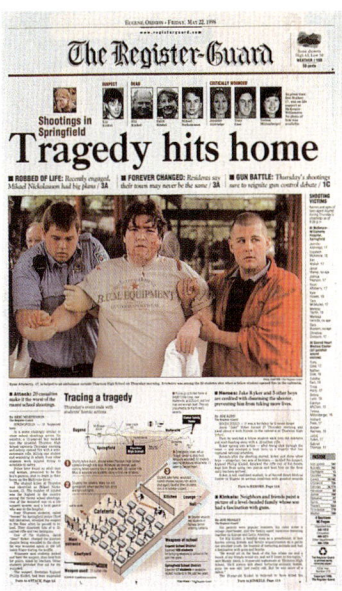
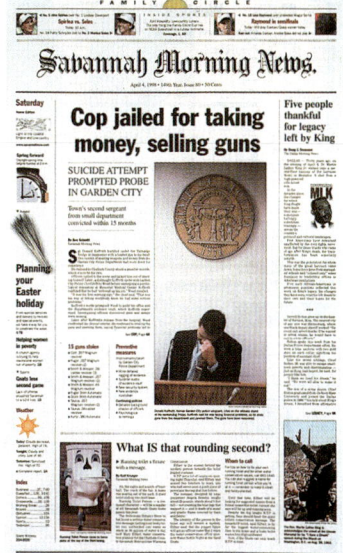

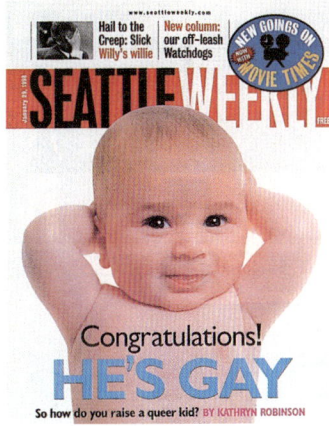

Savannah Morning News
Savannah, GA

Robbie McBride, Sports Planner/Designer; **Kenny Monteith**, News Planner/Designer; **Stephen D. Komives**, Sports/Features Planning Editor

Seattle Weekly
Seattle, WA

Barbara Dow, Art Director & Designer; **Penny Gentieu**, Photographer; **Tony Stone**, Photographer

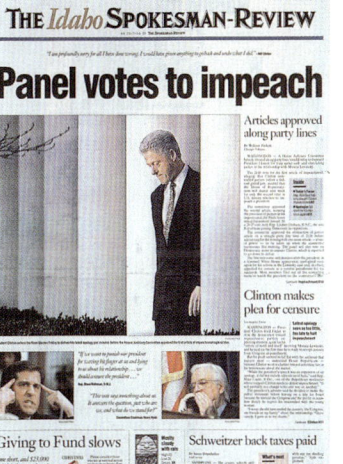

The Spokesman-Review
Spokane, WA

John Kafentzis, Designer

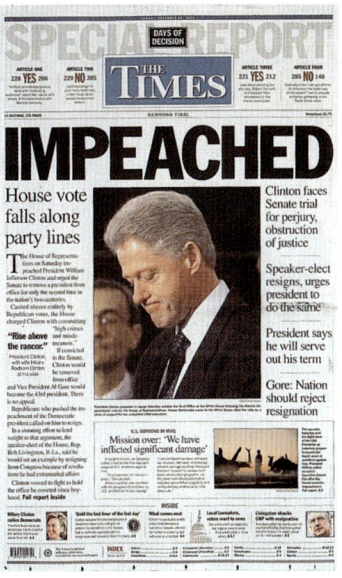

The Times
Munster, IN

Matt Mansfield, Deputy M.E.; **Epha Good**, Design Team Leader; **Craig Newman**, Design Team Leader

TWENTIETH EDITION ■ 59

NEWS ▪ Front Page, Local News Page

The Albuquerque Tribune
Albuquerque, NM
Leanne Potts, Designer

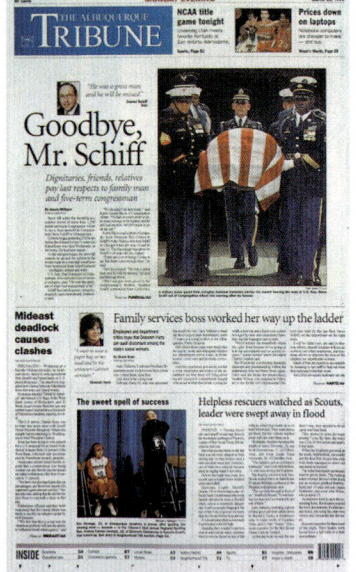

The Albuquerque Tribune
Albuquerque, NM
David Carrillo, News Editor

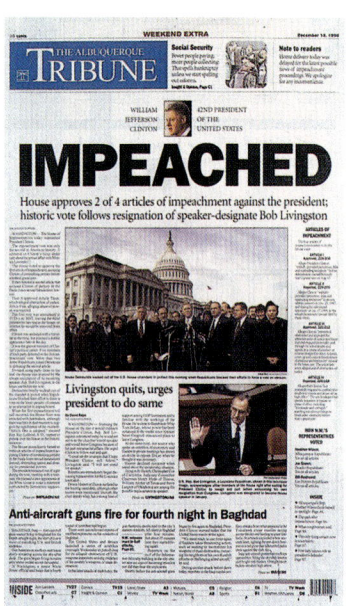

The Beacon-News
Aurora, IL
Karen Wolden, Designer; **James Denk,** Director/Design & Graphics

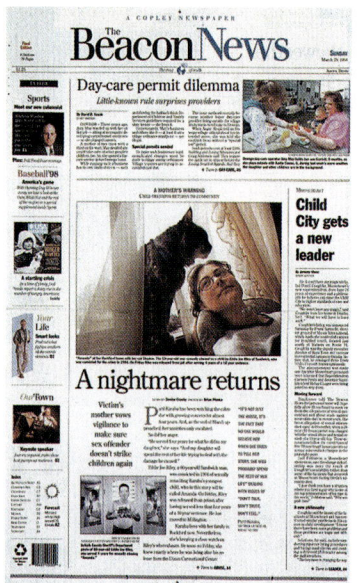

The Beacon-News
Aurora, IL
Karen Wolden, Designer; **James Denk,** Director/Design & Graphics

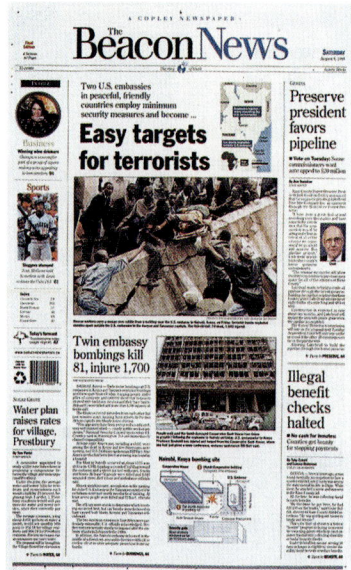

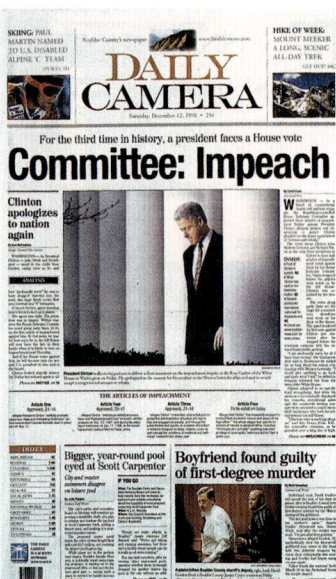

Boulder Daily Camera
Boulder, CO
Brian MacQueen, Designer

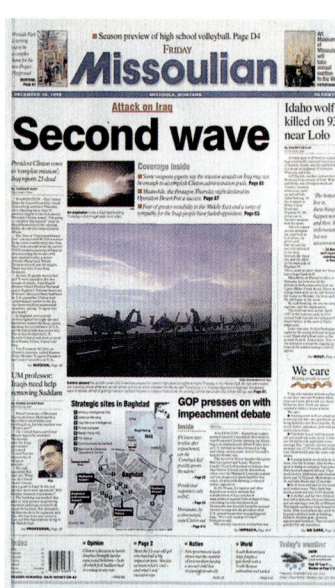

Missoulian
Missoula, MT
Jake Ellison, Assistant News Editor

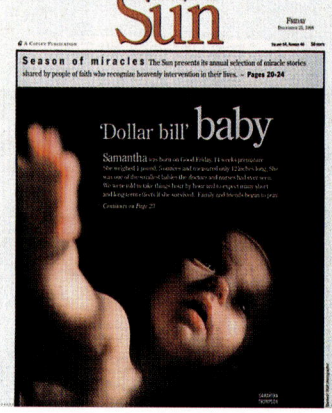

The Naperville Sun
Naperville, IL
Robb Montgomery, Design Editor; **Chris Stanford,** Photographer

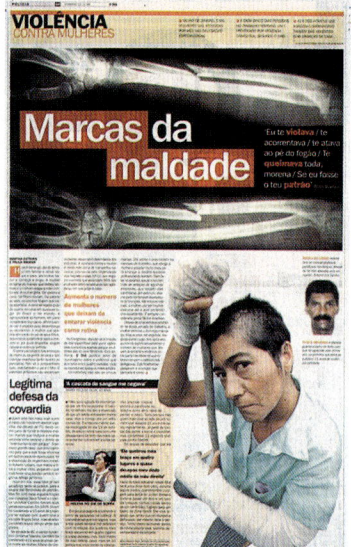

O Dia
Rio de Janeiro, Brasil
André Renato Malvar, Designer; **André Hippertt,** Art Director

Local News Page ■ NEWS

The Hartford Courant
Hartford, CT

Toni Finch-Kellar, Designer/Photo Editor; **Christian P. Drury,** Art Director; **Patrick Raycraft,** Photographer

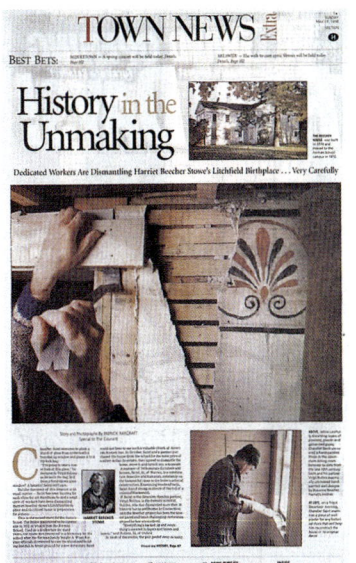

The Hartford Courant
Hartford, CT

Bruce Moyer, Designer/Photo Editor; **Christian P. Drury,** Art Director; **David Roberts,** Photographer

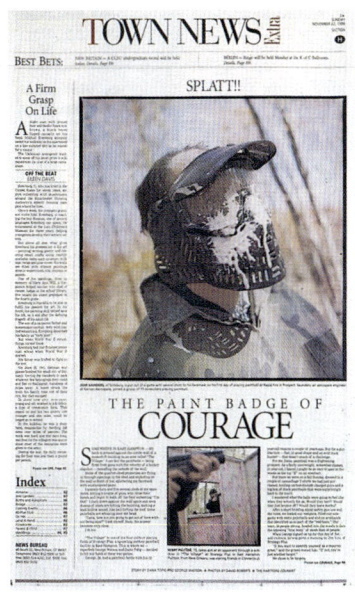

The St. Petersburg Times
St. Petersburg, FL

Dave Murray, Copy Editor; **Tracey Logsdon,** Copy Editor; **Stan Alost,** Dep. Director/Photography; **Don Morris,** Art Director

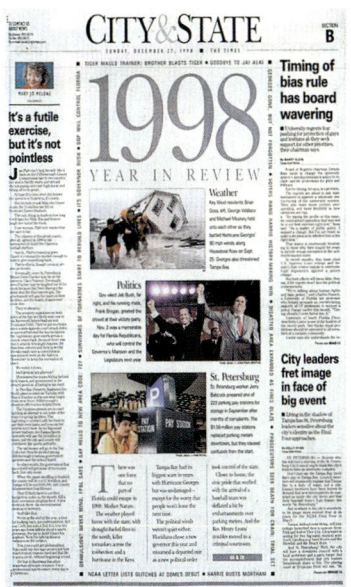

Estado de Minas
Belo Horizonte, Brasil

Álvaro Duarte, Art Director; **Rogério Carnevali,** Design Editor; **Julio Moreira,** Designer; **Cesar Motta,** Graphic Artist; **Wagner Seixas,** News Editor

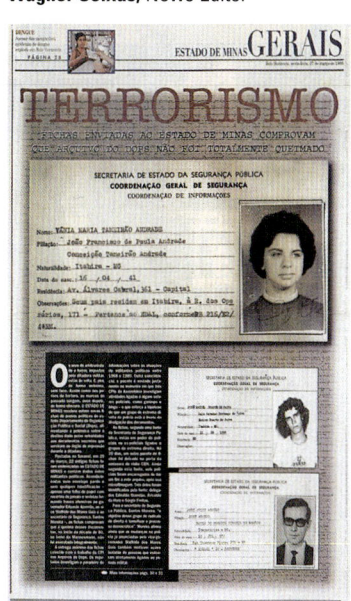

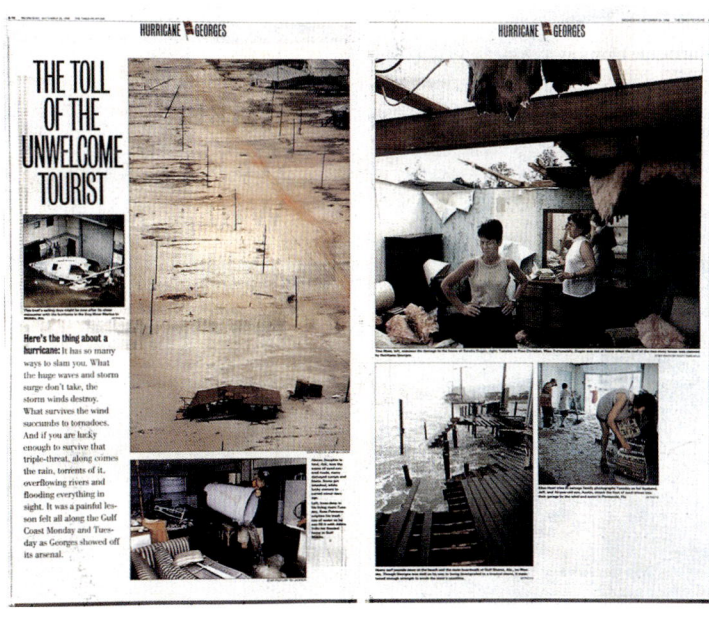

The Times-Picayune
New Orleans, LA

George Berke, Design Director; **Ted Jackson,** Photographer; **John McCusker,** Photographer; **Scott Threlkeld,** Photographer; **Doug Parker,** Photo Editor

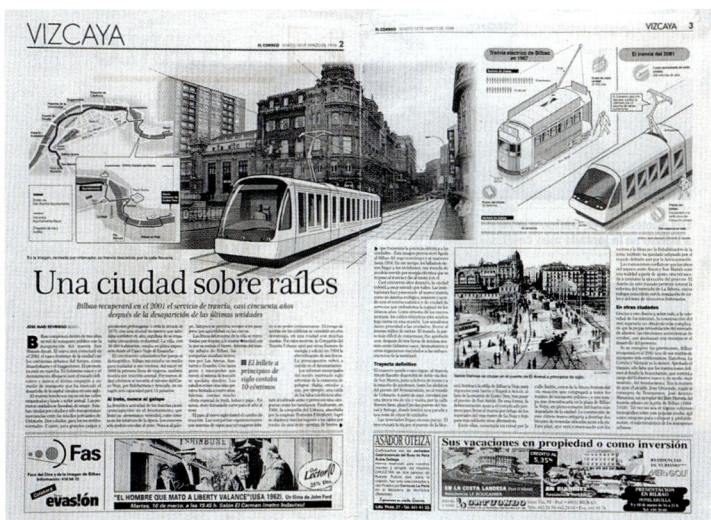

El Correo
Bilbao, Spain

Javier Zarracina, Graphic Artist; **Fernando G. Baptista,** Graphic Artist; **Jesús Ayart,** Art Director & Designer; **Alberto Torregros,** Editorial Art & Design Consultant

NEWS — Local News Page

El Norte
Monterrey, México
Carlos Arce, Designer & Design Editor; **Eddie Macías**, Illustrator; **José Antonio Chávez**, Photographer; **Humberto Castro**, Section Editor; **Raúl Braulio Martinez**, Art Director; **Alexandro Medrano**, Design M.E.; **Ramón Alberto Garza**, General Editor Director; **Martín Pérez Cerda**, Editor Director

El Norte
Monterrey, México
José Ramirez, Photographer; **Eric Gallegos**, Designer; **Carlos Arce**, Designer & Design Editor; **Alexandro Medrano**, Design Manager Editor; **Raúl Braulio Martinez**, Art Director; **Martin Pérez Cerda**, Editor/Director; **Ramón Alberto Garza**, General Editor Director; **Norma Rodriguez**, Section Editor

Reforma
México City, México
Daniel Esqueda, Designer; **Alberto Fabela**, Designer; **Oscar Yañez**, Section Designer; **Héctor Zamarrón**, Editor; **Gustavo Adolfo Hernández**, Editor; **Rubelio Fernández**, Photographer; **Ricardo del Castillo**, Graphics Coordinator; **Emilio Deheza**, Art Director; **Eduardo Danilo**, Design Consultant

Reforma
México City, México
Oscar Yáñez, Section Designer; **Héctor Zamarrón**, Editor; **Alejandro Ramos**, Editor; **Agustín Márquez**, Photographer; **José Luis Guzmán**, Photographer; **Ricardo del Castillo**, Graphics Coordinator; **Emilio Deheza**, Art Director; **Eduardo Danilo**, Design Consultant

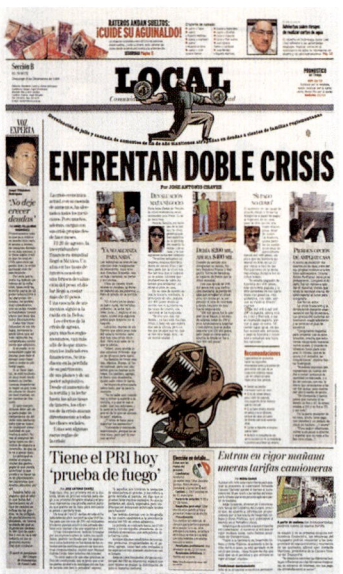 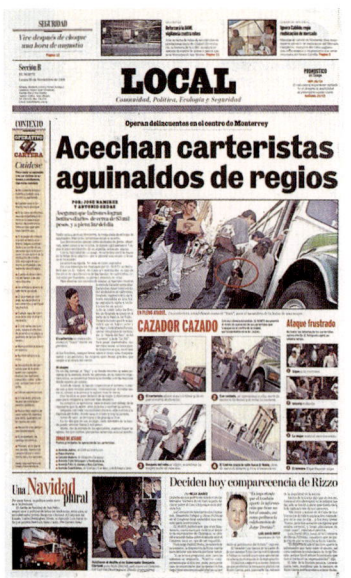 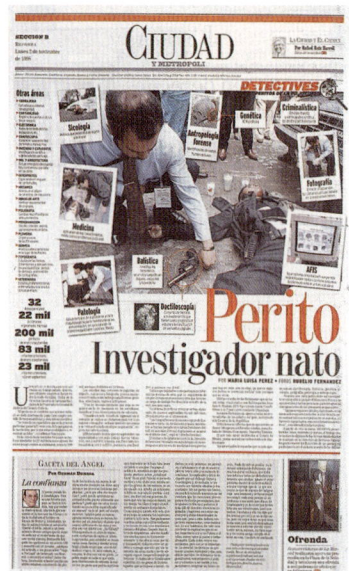 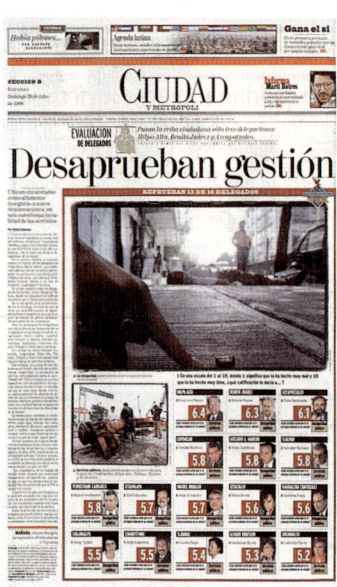

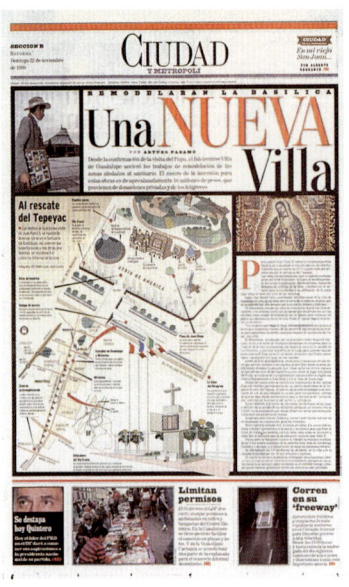 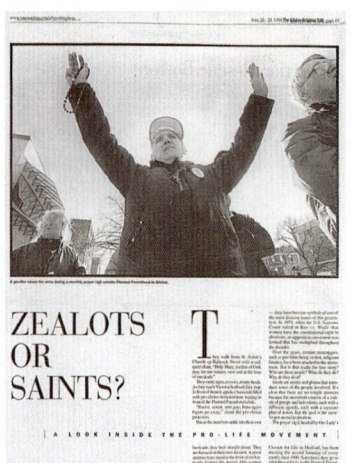 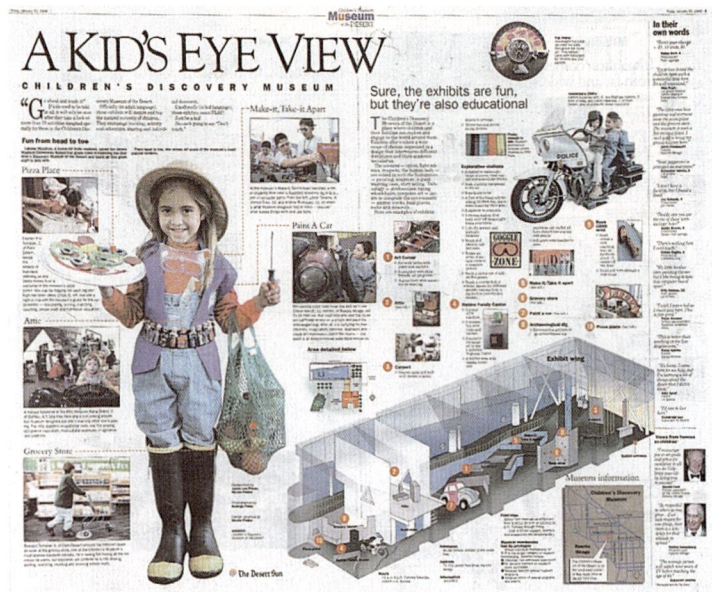

Reforma
México City, México
Eduardo Danilo, Design Consultant; **Emilio Deheza**, Art Director; **Alejandro Ramos**, Editor; **Ricardo Vargas**, Photographer; **Juan Jesús Cortes**, Illustrator; **Oscar Santiago Méndez**, Designer; **Oscar Yáñez**, Section Designer

Allston/Brighton Tab
Needham, MA
Mark Gabrenya, Design Director; **David Del Poio**, Photo Editor; **Darren McCollester**, Photographer; **Melissa Soloman**, Editor

The Desert Sun
Palm Springs, CA
Nicole Peake, Artist; **James Abundis**, Graphics Editor; **Jamie Lee Pricer**, Features Writer; **Fielding Buck**, Features Editor; **Rodrigo Peña**, Photographer; **Vikki Porter**, Executive Editor

The Desert Sun
Palm Springs, CA

Brian Cragin, Assistant Graphics Director; **Gabriel Campanario,** Graphics Editor; **Nicole Peake,** Artist; **Tracy Green,** Artist; **Leita Cowart,** Photographer; **Matt Fitzsimons,** Reporter

Silver
Marca
Madrid, Spain

José Juan Gámez, Graphics Editor; **Antonio Martín Hervás,** Graphic Designer; **César Galera,** Graphic Designer; **Pablo Mª Ramírez,** Graphic Designer; **Manuel Romero,** Graphic Designer; **Ramón Franco,** Graphic Designer

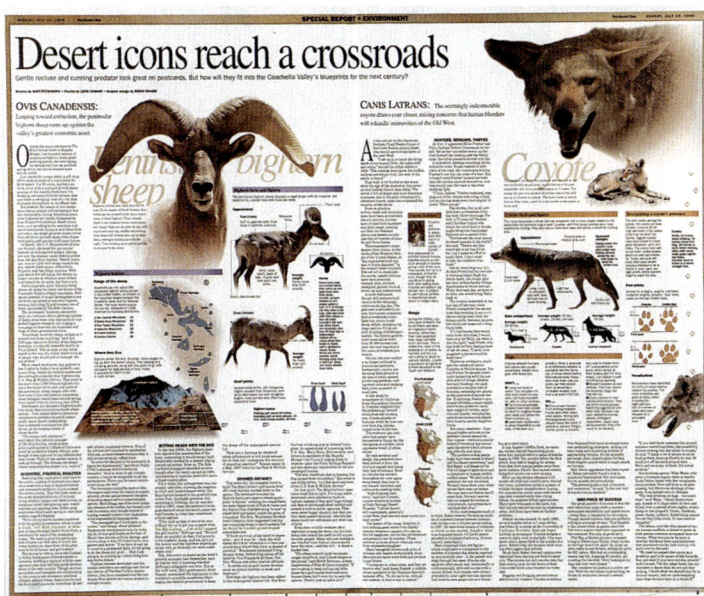

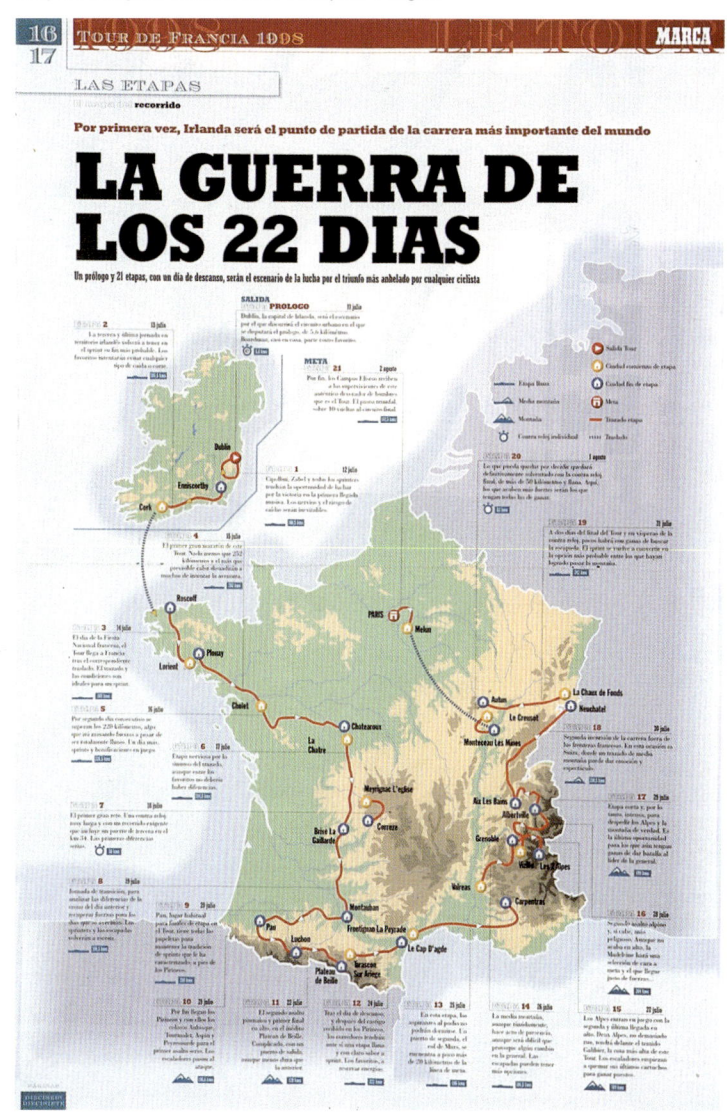

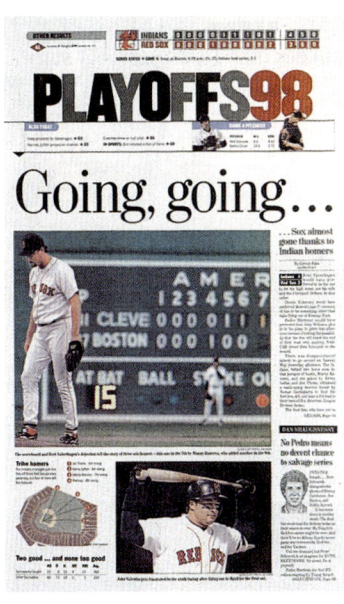

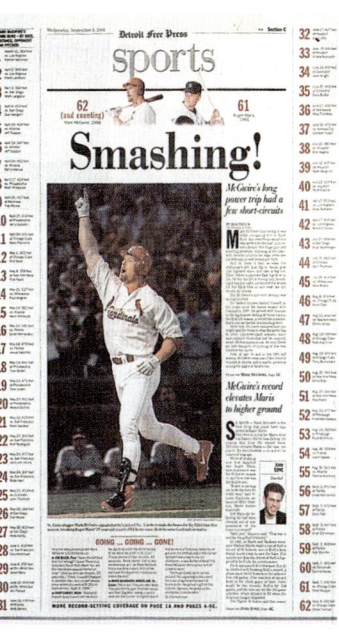

The Boston Globe
Boston, MA

Janet L. Michaud, Art Director & Designer; **Richard Sanchez,** Graphic Artist; **Ken Fratus,** Editor; **Jim Davis,** Photographer

Detroit Free Press
Detroit, MI

Brian James, Designer; **Gene Myers,** Sports Editor

NEWS Sports Page

Marca
Madrid, Spain
José Juan Gámez, Graphics Editor/Designer; **Manuel Romero,** Graphic Designer; **César Galera,** Graphic Designer; **Alfredo Prados,** Graphic Designer

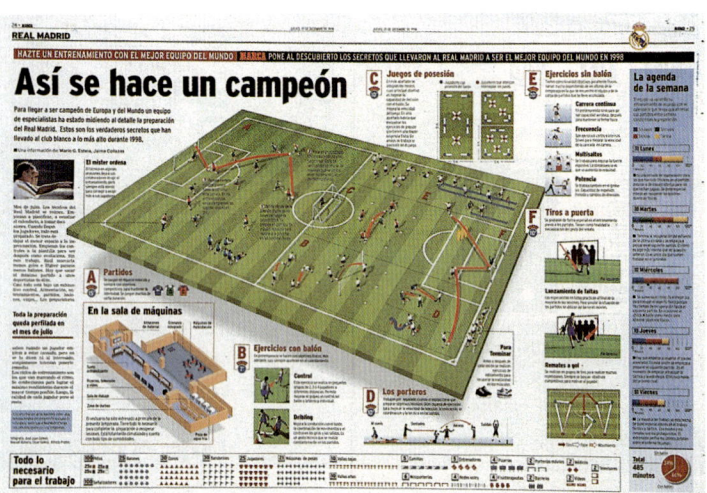

Marca
Madrid, Spain
José Juan Gámez, Graphics Editor; **Antonio Martín Hervás,** Graphic Designer

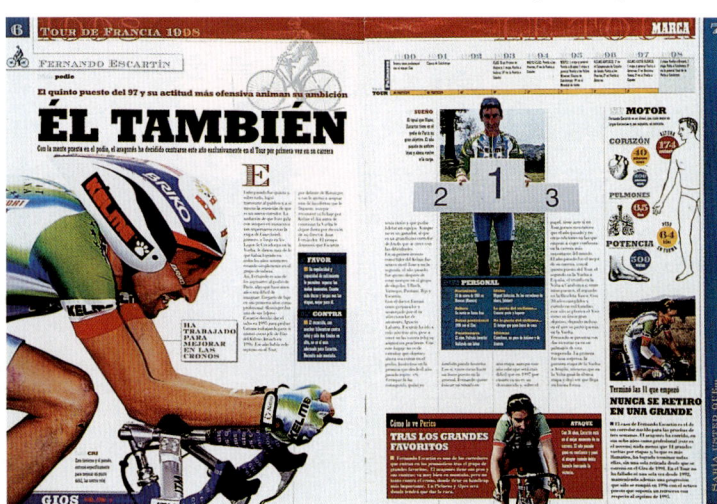

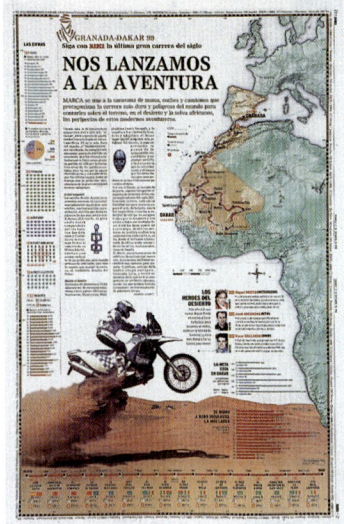

Marca
Madrid, Spain
José Juan Gámez, Graphics Editor/Designer

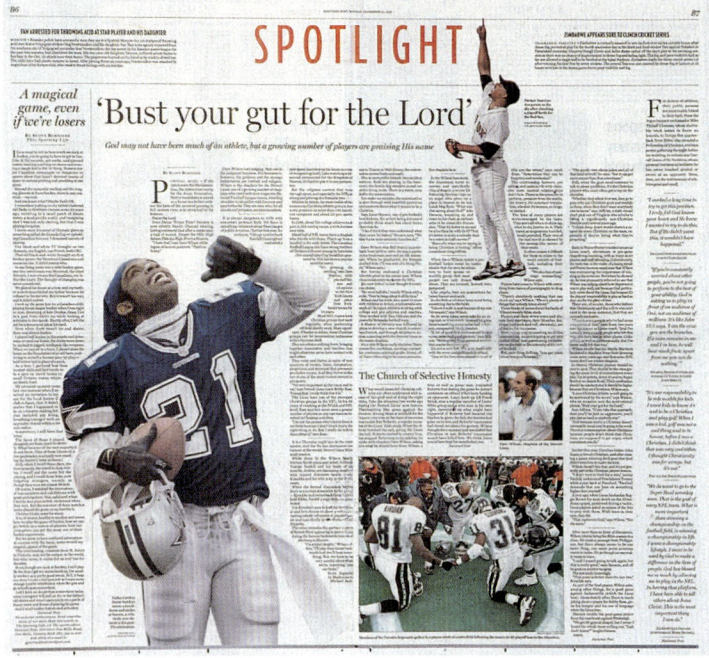

The National Post
Don Mills, Canada
Gayle Grin, Designer/Design Editor; **Graham Parley,** Sports Editor; **Ron Wadden,** Deputy Sports Editor/Designer; **Scott Burnside,** Writer; **Kenneth Whyte,** Editor-in-Chief; **Lucie Lacava,** Design Consultant

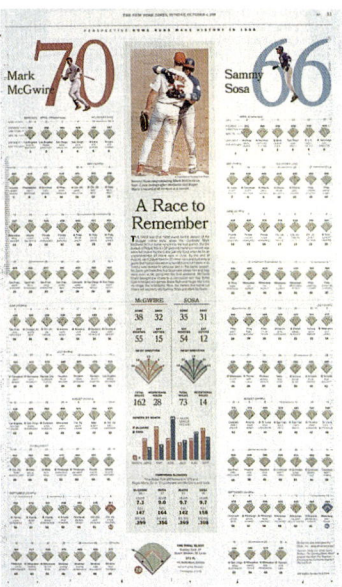

The New York Times
New York, NY
Joe Ward, Graphics Editor/Designer

Sports Page ■ NEWS

The Seattle Times
Seattle, WA
Michael Kellams, Designer/Graphics; **Ken Oelerich,** Graphic Artist; **James McFarlane,** Graphic Artist; **David Miller,** Art Director

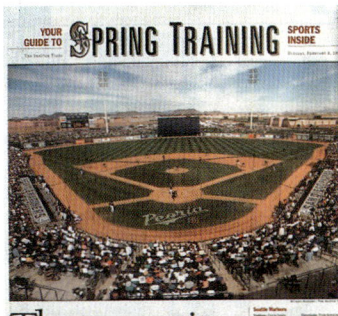

El Tiempo
Santa Fe de Bogota, Colombia
Beiman Pinilla, Graphics Editor; **Yesid Vargas,** Designer

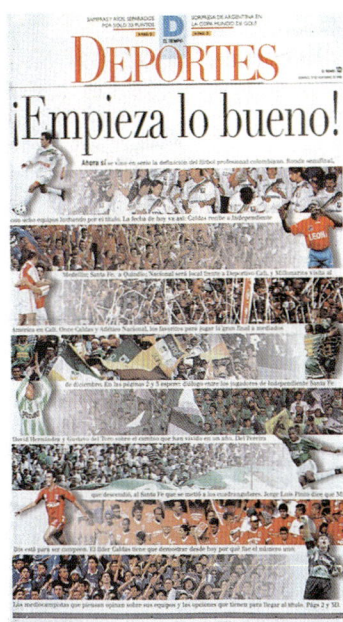

El Tiempo
Santa Fe de Bogota, Colombia
Beiman Pinilla, Graphics Editor; **Yesid Vargas,** Designer; **Hugo Torres,** Illustrator

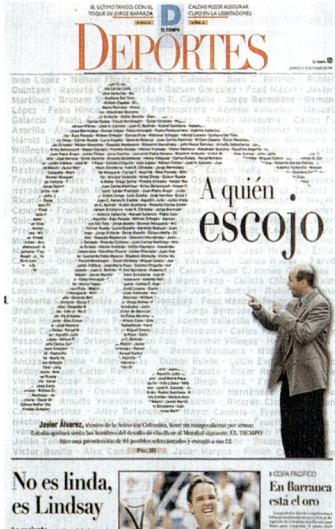

Albuquerque Journal
Albuquerque, NM
Wendy Cromwell, Assistant Design Director/Designer; **Joe Kirby,** Design Director; **Julie Aicher,** Sports Editor; **Karen Moses,** A.M.E./News & Sports; **Carolyn Flynn,** A.M.E. Photo/Design

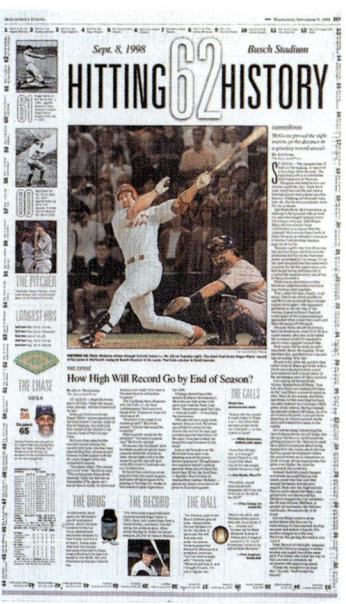

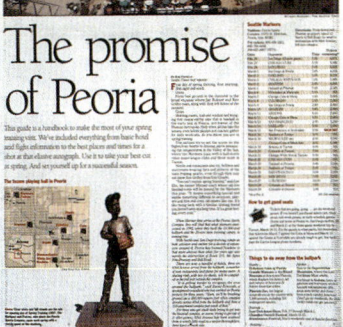

Anchorage Daily News
Anchorage, AK
Craig Lancaster, Designer; **Richard Murphy,** Photo Editor

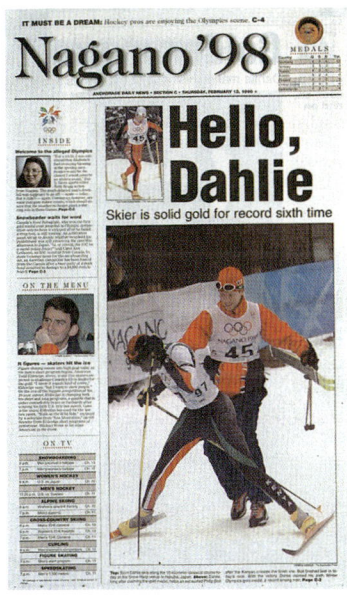

The Asbury Park Press
Neptune, NJ
Christine A. Birch, News & Sports Designer; **Jeff Paslay,** Sports & News Designer; **Gary Potosky,** Assistant Sports Editor; **Celeste LaBrosse,** Night Photo Editor; **Andrew Prendimano,** Art & Photo Director; **Harris G. Siegel,** M.E./Design & Photography

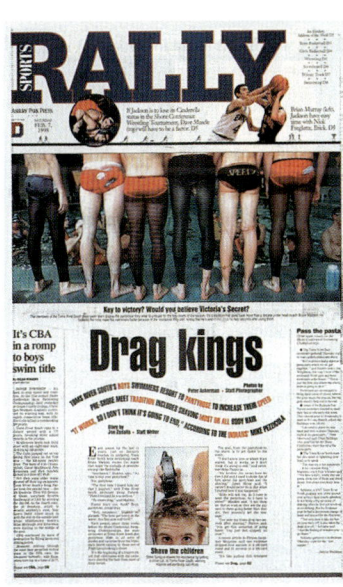

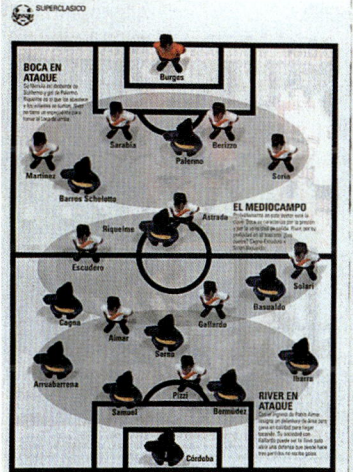

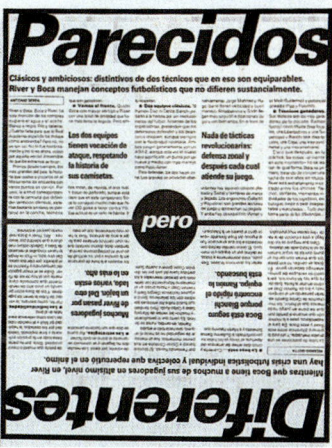

Olé
Buenos Aires, Argentina
Martín Marotta, Art Editor; **Jorge Doneiger,** Art Editor; **Diego Bianchi,** Designer; **Matías Kirschenbaum,** Designer; **Sergio Maraggi,** Designer; **Mariano Nuñez,** Designer; **Gastón Pérsico,** Designer; **Ana Saidon,** Designer; **Cecilia Szalkowicz,** Designer

TWENTIETH EDITION ■ 65

NEWS — Sports Page

Olé
Buenos Aires, Argentina
Martín Marotta, Art Editor; **Jorge Doneiger**, Art Editor; **Diego Bianchi**, Designer; **Juan Martín Cucurulo**, Designer; **Sergio Maraggi**, Designer; **Mariano Nuñez**, Designer; **Gastón Pérsico**, Designer; **Ana Saidon**, Designer; **Cecilia Szalkowicz**, Designer; **Matías Kirschenbaum**, Designer

Olé
Buenos Aires, Argentina
Martín Marotta, Art Editor; **Jorge Doneiger**, Art Editor; **Diego Bianchi**, Designer; **Juan Martín Cucurulo**, Designer; **Sergio Maraggi**, Designer; **Mariano Nuñez**, Designer; **Gastón Pérsico**, Designer; **Ana Saidon**, Designer; **Cecilia Szalkowicz**, Designer; **Matías Kirschenbaum**, Designer

The Register-Guard
Eugene, OR
Carl Davaz, A.M.E. Graphics & Tech./Designer; **Tom Penix**, News Artist/Designer

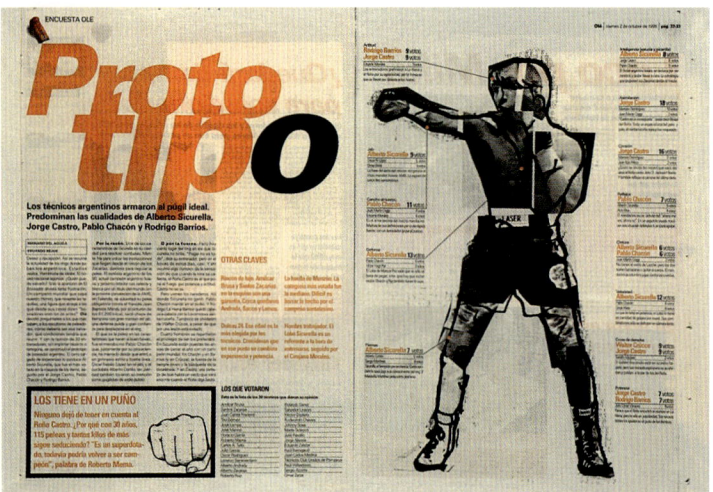
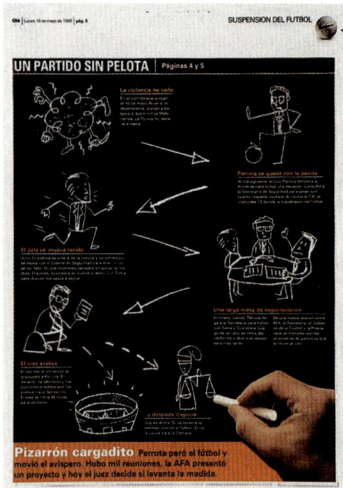
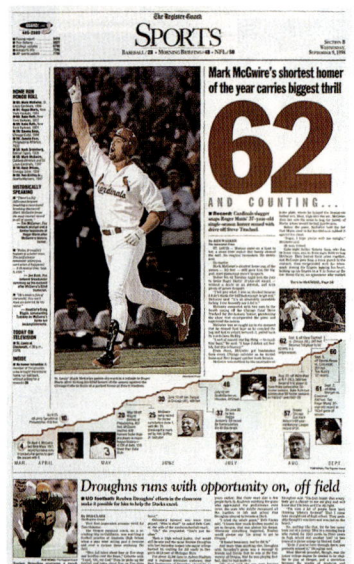

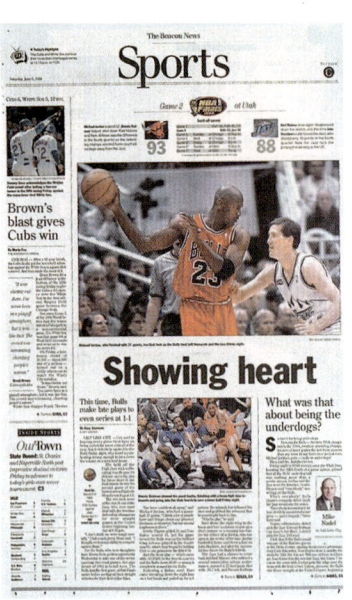
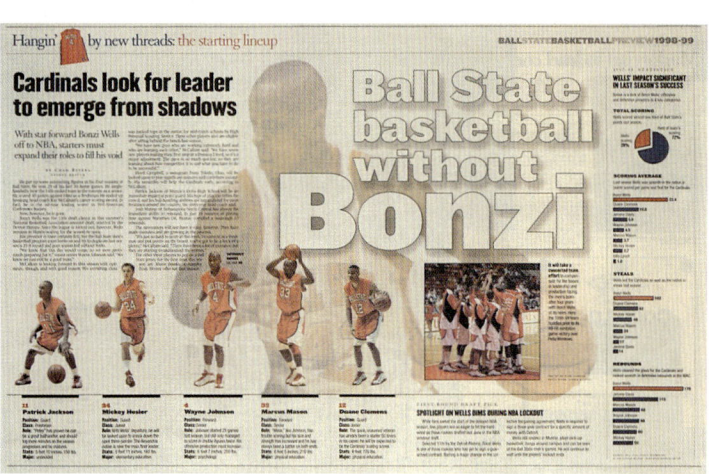
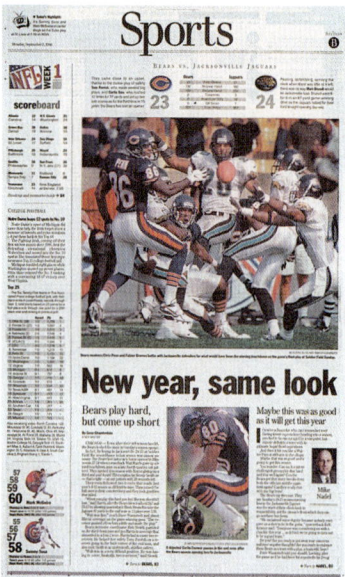

The Ball State Daily News
Muncie, IN
Chris Barber, Design Editor; **Chris Meighan**, Design Editor

The Beacon-News
Aurora, IL
Michael Whitley, Design Editor; **James Denk**, Director/Design & Graphics

The Beacon-News
Aurora, IL
Michael Whitley, Design Editor; **James Denk**, Director/Design & Graphics; **Rob Finch**, Photographer; **Tim Reck**, Designer

Sports Page, Business Page ■ NEWS

The Beacon-News
Aurora, IL
Tim Reck, Designer; **James Denk,** Director/Design & Graphics

The Beacon-News
Aurora, IL
Tim Reck, Designer; **James Denk,** Director/Design & Graphics; **Michael Whitley,** Director/Design & Graphics; **Martin Stockwell,** Designer

The Desert Sun
Palm Springs, CA
Brian Cragin, Assistant Graphics Editor; **Gabriel Campanario,** Graphics Editor; **Vikki Porter,** Executive Editor

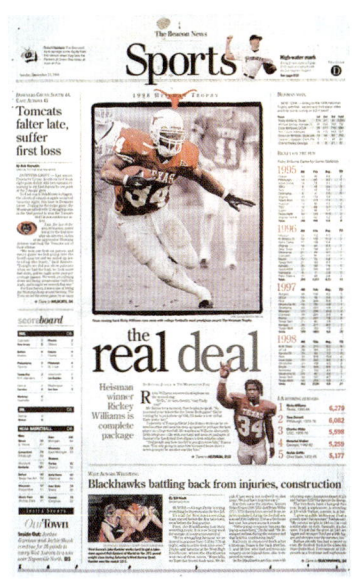
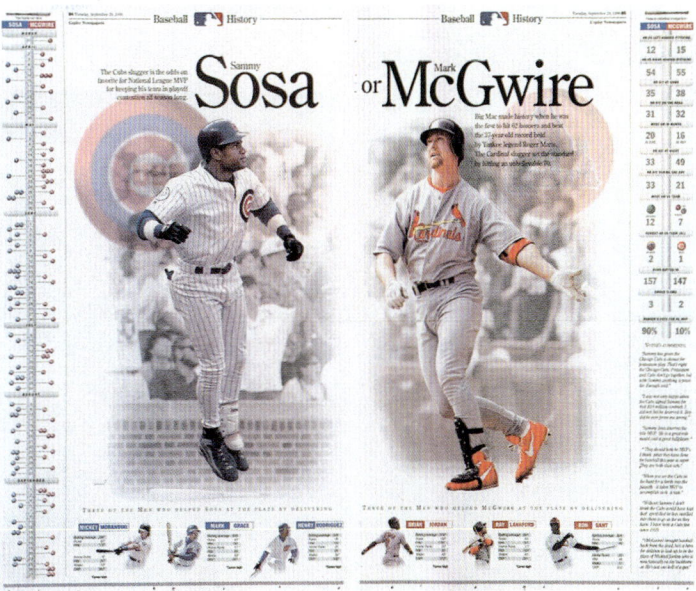
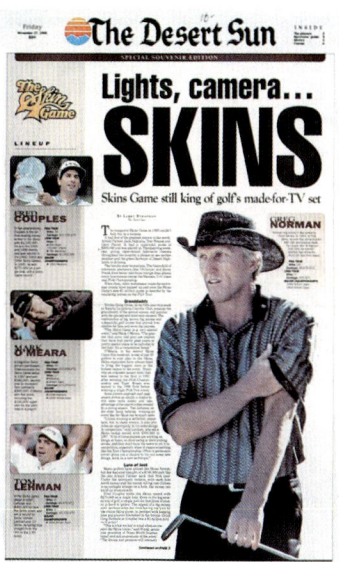

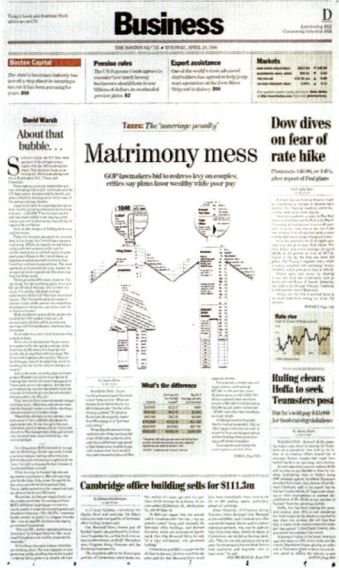
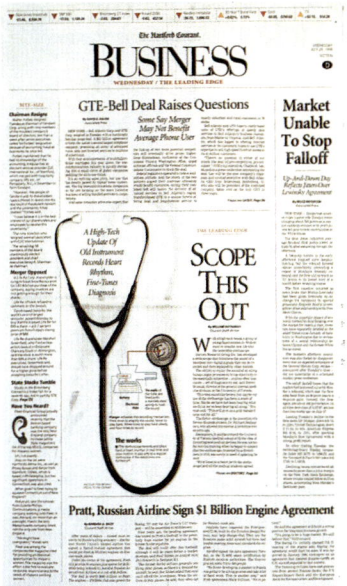
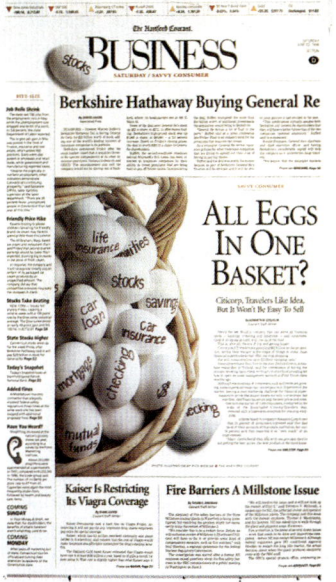
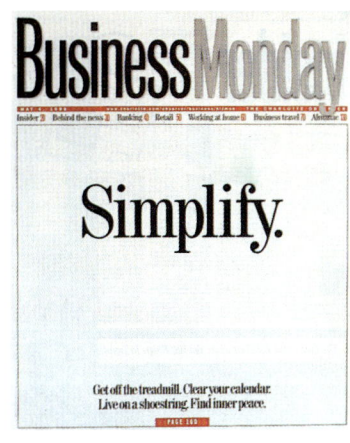

The Boston Globe
Boston, MA
Sue Dawson, Art Director & Designer

The Hartford Courant
Hartford, CT
Scott Johnson, Assistant Art Director; **Joan McLaughlin,** Designer

The Hartford Courant
Hartford, CT
Scott Johnson, Assistant Art Director; **Joan McLaughlin,** Designer

The Charlotte Observer
Charlotte, NC
Monica Moses, Design Director; **Barry Kolar,** Page Designer; **Chin Wang,** Page Designer; **Elizabeth Gelgud,** Copy Editor; **Jon Talton,** Business Editor

NEWS ■ Business Page

The Virginian-Pilot
Norfolk, VA

Terry Chapman, Designer; **Carl Fincke,** Editor; **John Corbitt,** Illustrator

The Honolulu Advertiser
Honolulu, HI

David F. Montesino, A.M.E. Design; **Stephen Downes,** Art Director; **Michael Bergen,** Illustrator

La Gaceta
San Miguel de Tucuman, Argentina

Daniel Fontanarrosa, Photo Illustrator; **Sergio Fernandez,** Art Director & Designer; **Mario García,** Design Consultant

Pittsburgh Post-Gazette
Pittsburgh, PA

Kim Germosek, Deputy Graphics Editor & Designer

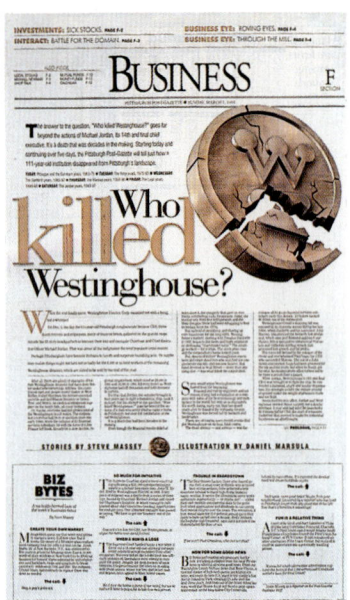

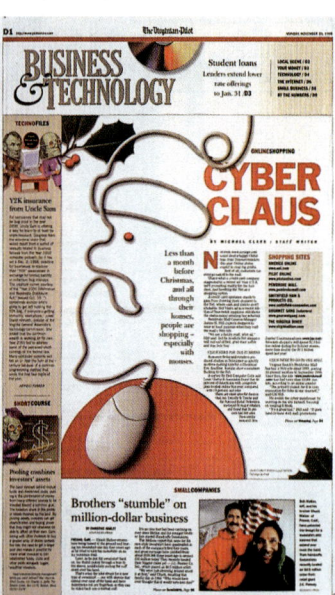

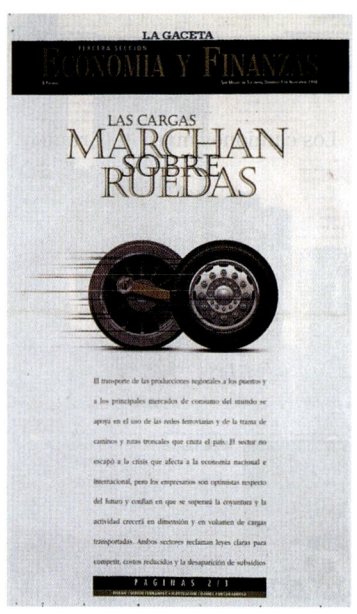

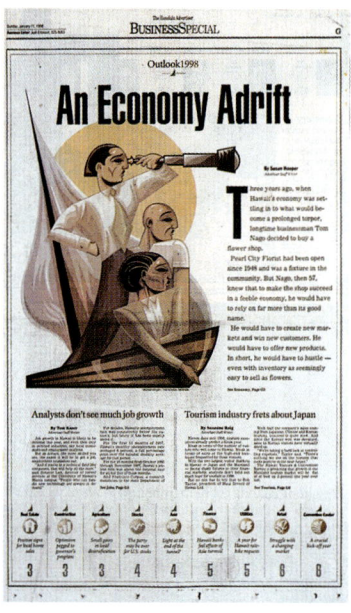

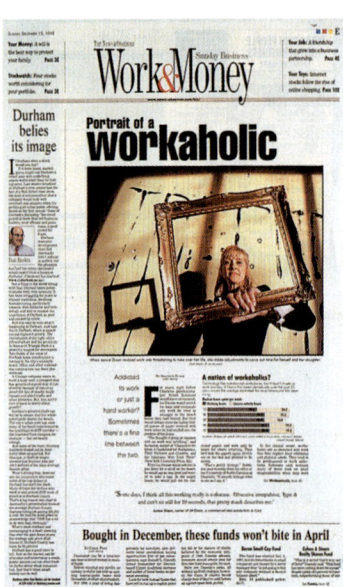

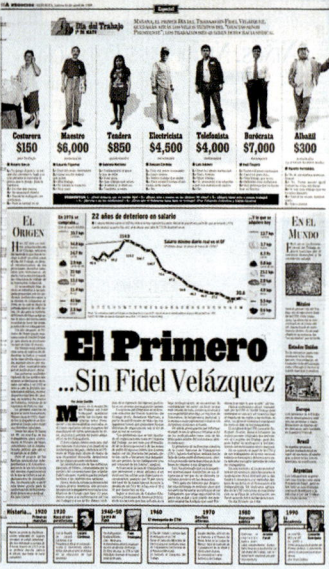

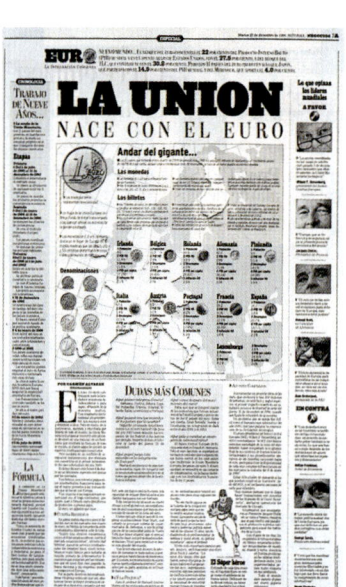

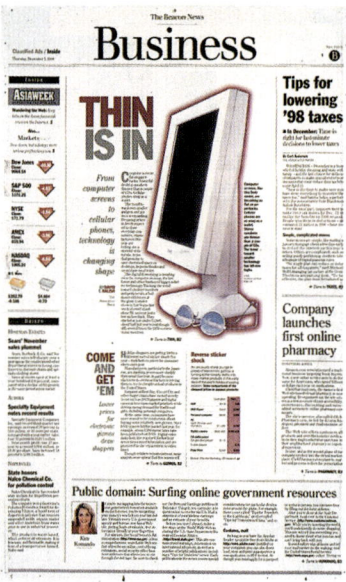

Reforma
México City, México

Eduardo Danilo, Design Consultant; **Emilio Deheza,** Art Director; **Alejandro Páez,** Editor; **Ernesto Carrillo,** Graphic Editor; **Ricardo Péna,** Section Designer; **Enrique Santiago,** Designer

The Beacon-News
Aurora, IL

Dan Ray, Designer; **James Denk,** Director/Design & Graphics

The News & Observer
Raleigh, NC

Adelaide Nash, Designer; **Mary Cornatzer,** Section Editor

Reforma
México City, México

Eduardo Danilo, Design Consultant; **Emilio Deheza,** Art Director; **Alejandro Páez,** Editor; **Ricardo Pena,** Section Designer; **Gustavo Cabrera,** Illustrator; **Ernesto Carrillo,** Graphics Editor; **Gabriel Ortiz,** Designer

68 ■ THE BEST OF NEWSPAPER DESIGN

Silver
Expansión
Madrid, Spain
Pablo Mª Ramírez, Designer; **Jose Juan Gámez**, Art Director; **Ignacio de Haro**, Graphic Artist

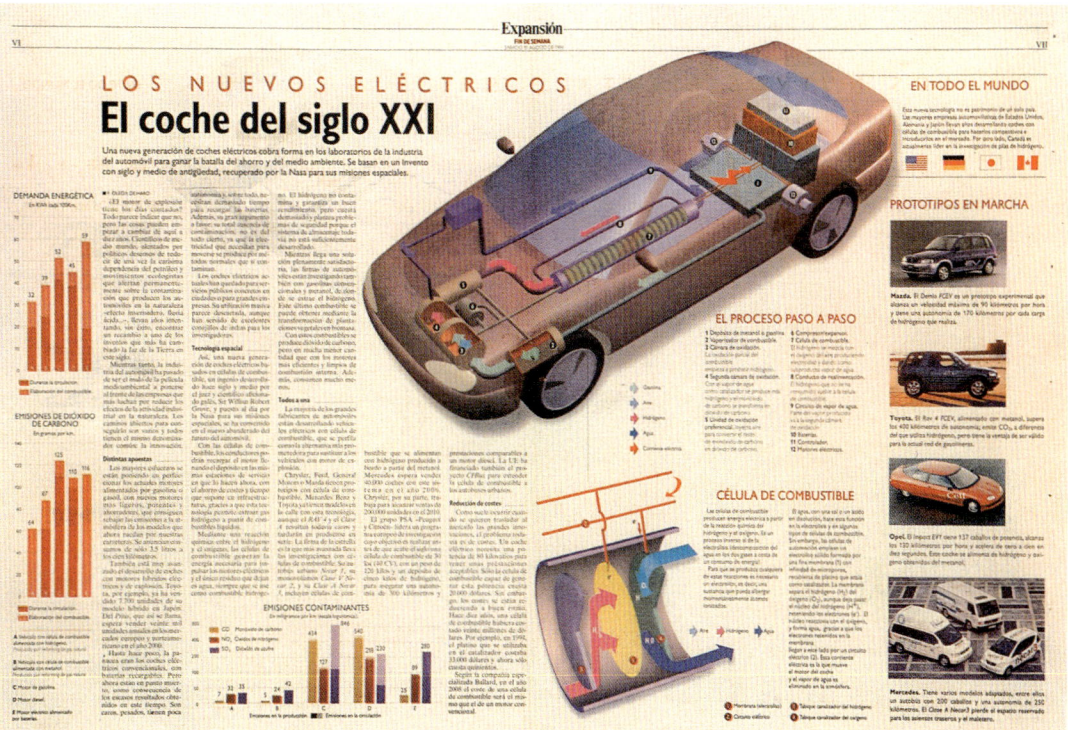

Expansión
Madrid, Spain
Pablo Mª Ramírez, Graphic Artist; **Jose Juan Gámez**, Art Director

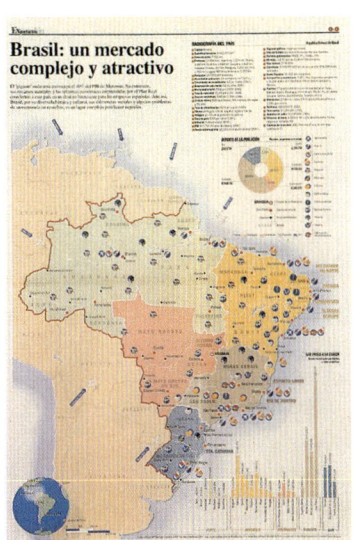

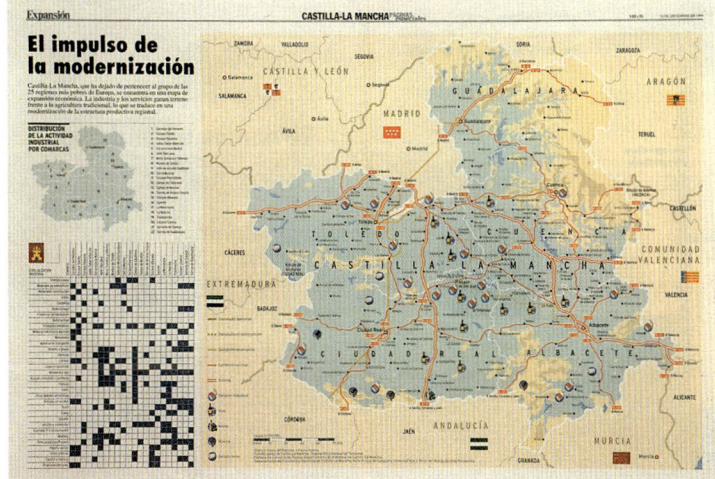

Expansión
Madrid, Spain
Pablo Mª Ramírez, Designer & Graphic Artist; **Jose Juan Gámez**, Art Director; **Pedro Pablos**, Graphic Artist

Expansión
Madrid, Spain
Antonio Martín Hervás, Designer; **Jose Juan Gámez**, Art Director

NEWS Business Page, Other News Page

Expansión
Madrid, Spain
Pablo Mª Ramírez, Designer; **Jose Juan Gámez,** Art Director; **Beatriz Santacruz,** Graphic Artist; **Diego Arambillet,** Designer

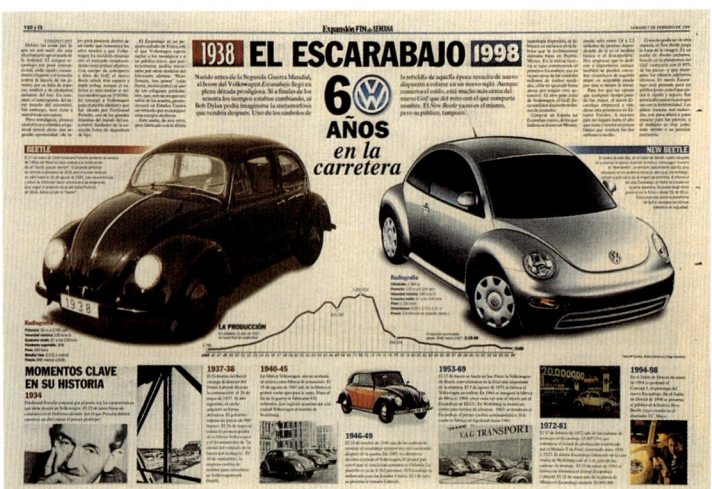

Clarín
Buenos Aires, Argentina
Iñaki Palacios, Art Director; **Paula Mizraji,** Design Editor; **Corina Mascotti,** Graphic Designer

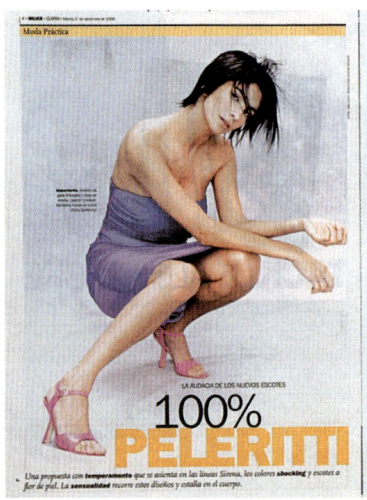
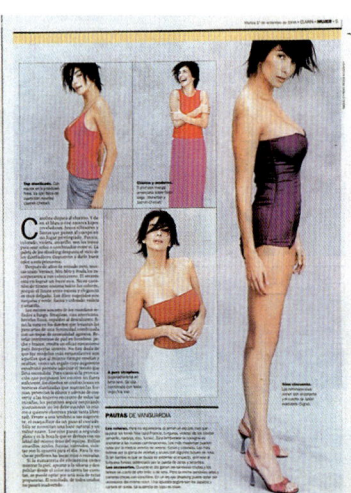

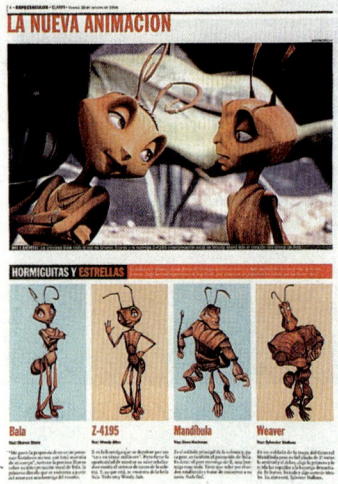
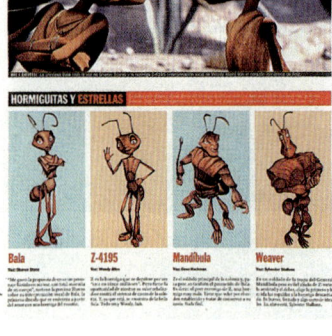
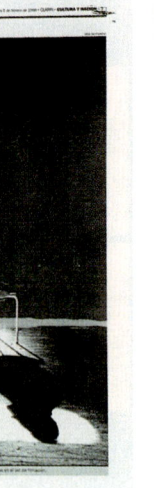

Clarín
Buenos Aires, Argentina
Iñaki Palacios, Art Director; **Tea Alberti,** Design Editor; **Oscar Bejarano,** Graphic Designer; **Valeria Castresana,** Graphic Designer; **Omar Olivella,** Graphic Designer; **Matilde Oliveros,** Graphic Designer; **Pablo Ruiz,** Graphic Designer; **Carolina Wainsztok,** Graphic Designer; **Silvina Fuda,** Graphic Designer

Clarín
Buenos Aires, Argentina
Iñaki Palacios, Art Director; **Tea Alberti,** Design Editor; **Oscar Bejarano,** Graphic Designer; **Valeria Castresana,** Graphic Designer; **Omar Olivella,** Graphic Designer; **Maltilde Oliveros,** Graphic Designer; **Pablo Ruiz,** Graphic Designer; **Carolina Wainsztok,** Graphic Designer; **Silvina Fuda,** Graphic Designer

El País
Madrid, Spain
Jesus Martines, Designer; **Luis Galán,** Designer

Other News Page ■ NEWS

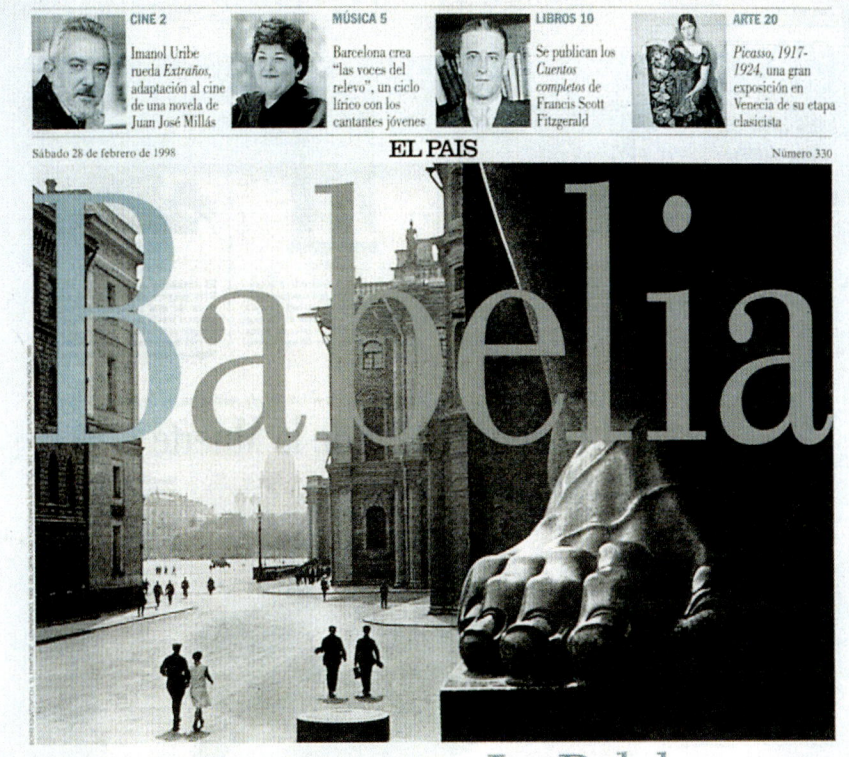

Silver
El País
Madrid, Spain
Luis Galán, Designer; **Jesus Martinez,** Designer

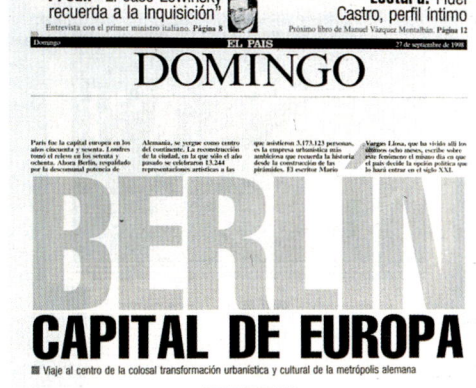

El País
Madrid, Spain
Manuel M. Fuentes, Designer; **Marta Calzada,** Designer

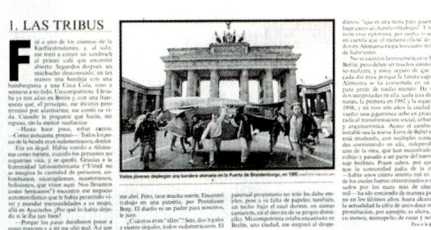

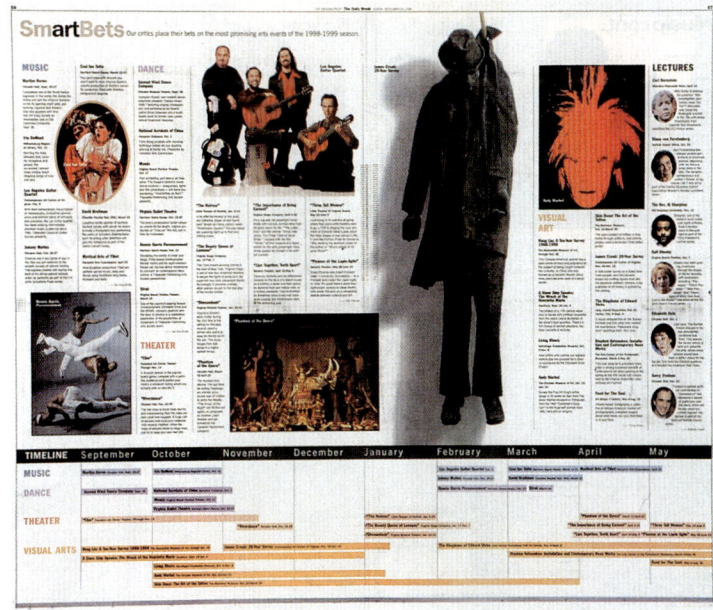

The Virginian-Pilot
Norfolk, VA
Sam Hundley, Illustrator & Designer; **Bob Fleming,** Editor; **Maria Carrillo,** Editor

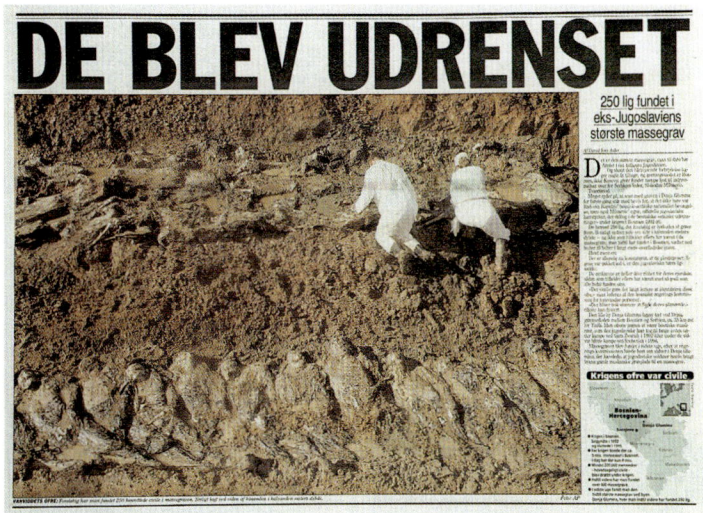

B.T.
Copenhagen, Denmark
Kim Henningsen, Sub-Editor

TWENTIETH EDITION ■ 71

NEWS — Other News Page, Inside News Page

El Norte
Monterrey, México
Jorge Obregón, Designer; **Pedro Ocañas,** Section Editor; **Carlos Arce,** Designer & Design Editor; **Alexandro Medrano,** Design Manager Editor; **Raúl Braulio Martinez,** Art Director; **Martin Pérez Cerda,** Editor/Director; **Ramón Alberto Garza,** General Editor Director

El Norte
Monterrey, México
Victor Cabiedes, Designer; **Irineo Morales,** Editor; **Carlos Arce,** Design Editor; **Alexandro Medrano,** Design Manager Editor; **Raúl Braulio Martinez,** Art Director; **Martin Pérez Cerda,** Editor/Director; **Ramón Alberto Garza,** General Editor Director

B.T.
Copenhagen, Denmark
Helle Skoett, Sub-Editor

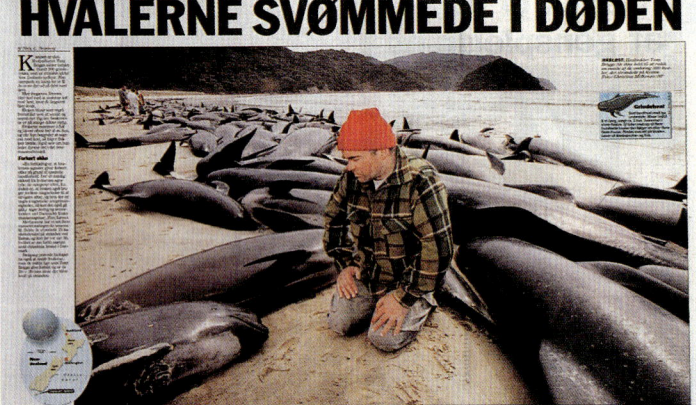

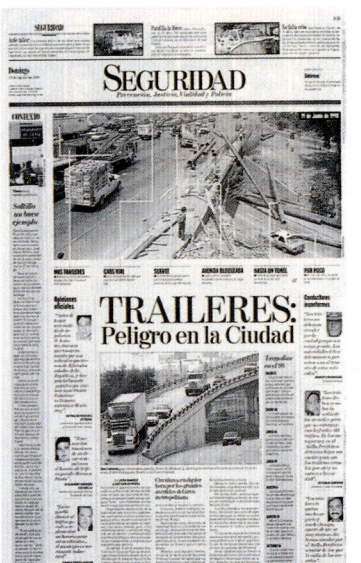

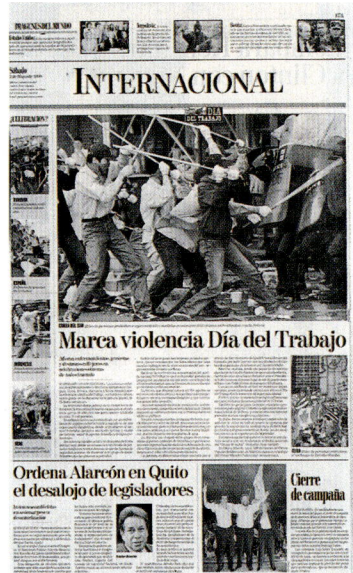

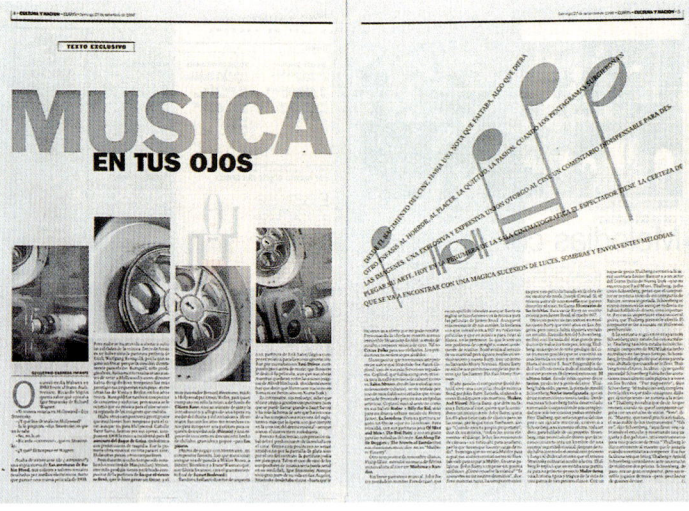

Clarín
Buenos Aires, Argentina
Iñaki Palacios, Art Director; **Tea Alberti,** Design Editor; **Oscar Bejarano,** Graphic Designer; **Valeria Castresana,** Graphic Designer; **Omar Olivella,** Graphic Designer; **Matilde Oliveros,** Graphic Designer; **Pablo Ruiz,** Graphic Designer; **Carolina Wainsztok,** Graphic Designer; **Silvina Fuda,** Graphic Designer

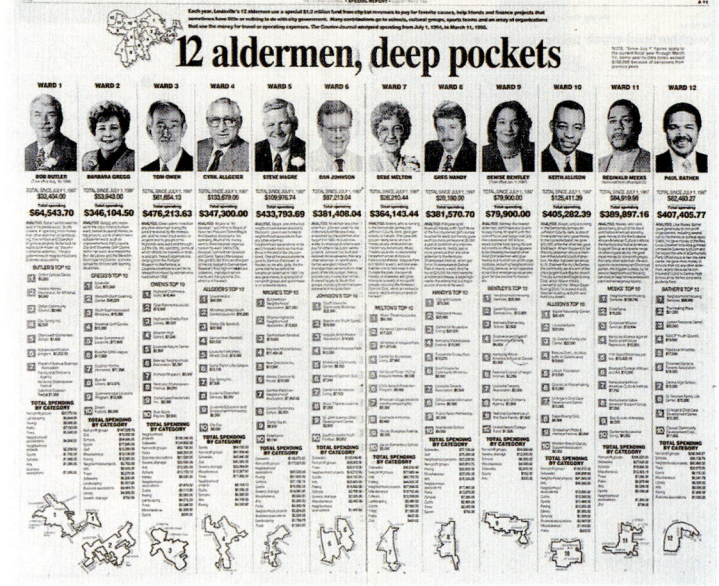

The Courier-Journal
Louisville, KY
Kim Kolarik, News Designer

Inside News Page, Breaking News ■ NEWS

The Hartford Courant
Hartford, CT

Cloe Poisson, Photographer; **Cecilia Prestamo**, Photo Editor/Designer

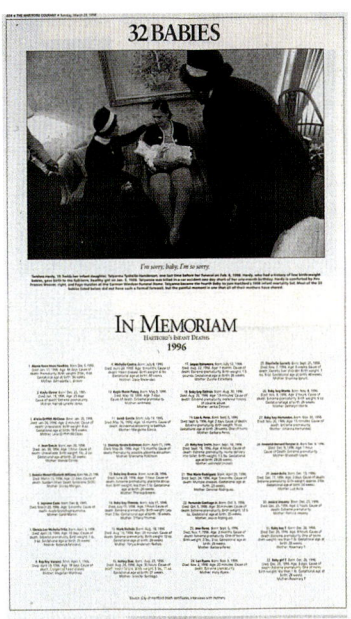

The Virginian-Pilot
Norfolk, VA

Courtney Murphy, Designer; **Ian Martin**, Photographer; **Mike Mather**, Reporter

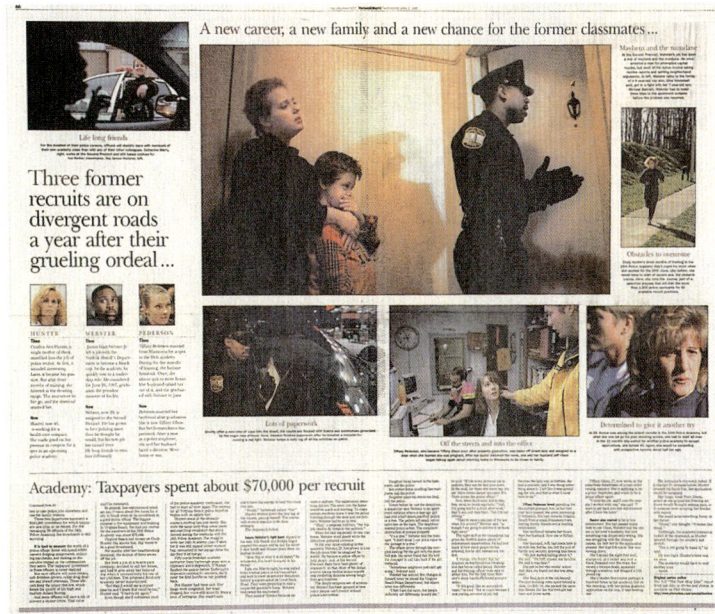

The Idaho Statesman
Boise, ID

Randy Wright, Presentation Editor; **Mark Bullard**, Designer; **Bill Roberts**, Reporter

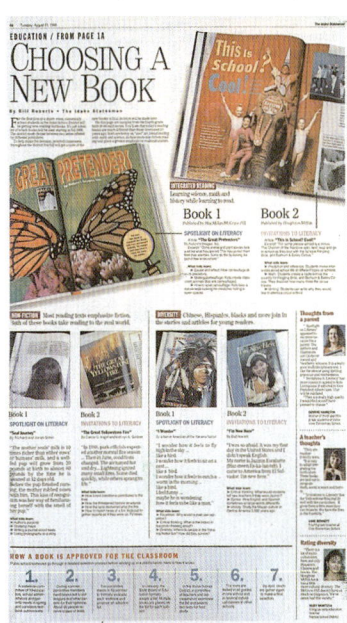

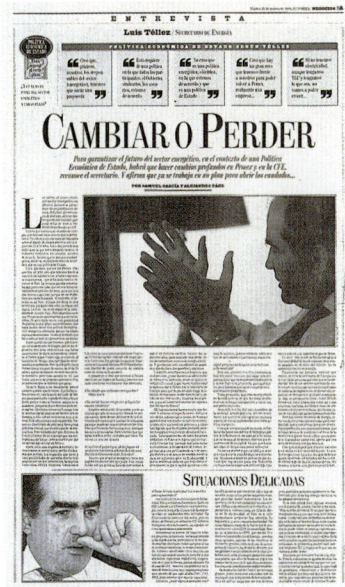

Reforma
México City, México

Eduardo Danilo, Design Consultant; **Emilio Deheza**, Art Director; **Alejandro Páez**, Editor; **Ricardo Pena**, Section Designer; **Gustavo Cabrera**, Illustrator; **Enrique Santiago**, Designer; **Diego Treviño**, Photographer; **Jaime Boites**, Photographer; **Ernesto Carrillo**, Graphics Editor

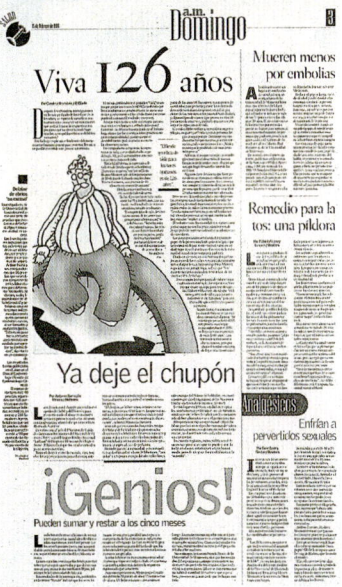

a.m. De León
León, México

Gustavo Belman, Designer; **Beatriz Zambrano**, Art Director

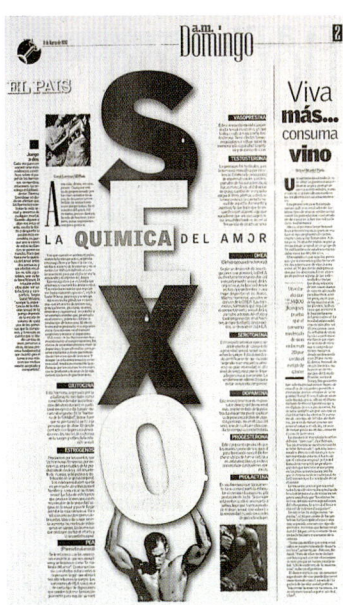

a.m. De León
León, México

Gustavo Belman, Designer; **Beatriz Zambrano**, Art Director; **Roberto Castañeda**, Editor

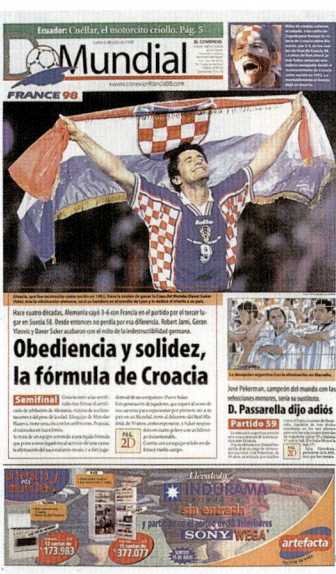

El Comercio
Quito, Ecuador

Ponto Moreno, Graphics Director; **Jorge Mantilla**, Graphics Editor; **Pancho Cajas**, Infographic Editor; **Guillermo Corral**, Photo Editor

TWENTIETH EDITION ■ 73

NEWS — Breaking News

Folha de São Paulo
São Paulo, Brasil

Marcos Augusto Gonçalves, Sunday Editor; **Melchiades Filho,** Sport Editor; **Vincenzo Scarpellini,** Art Director; **Fernanda Cirenza,** Art Editor; **Thales de Menezes,** Assistant Editor; **Toni Pires,** Image Editor; **Adilson Secco,** Infographic Designer; **Mario Kanno,** Infographic Designer; **Jair de Oliveira,** Page Designer; **Adailton Pereira Gontijo,** Page Designer

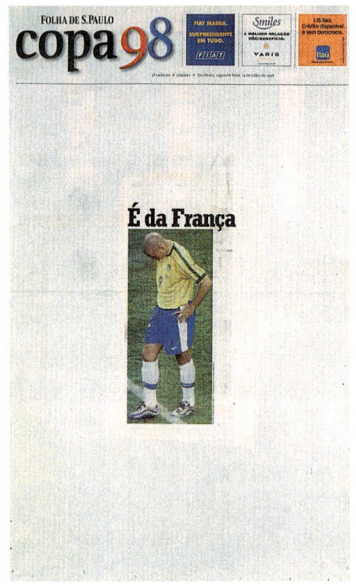

Correio Braziliense
Brasília, Brasil

Ricardo Noblat, Executive Editor; **Francisco Amaral,** Art Director; **Paulo Pestana,** Assistant Editor; **Carlos Marcelo,** Editor; **Conceição Freitas,** Editor; **Fredson Charlson,** Editor; **João Bosco Adelino,** Page Designer

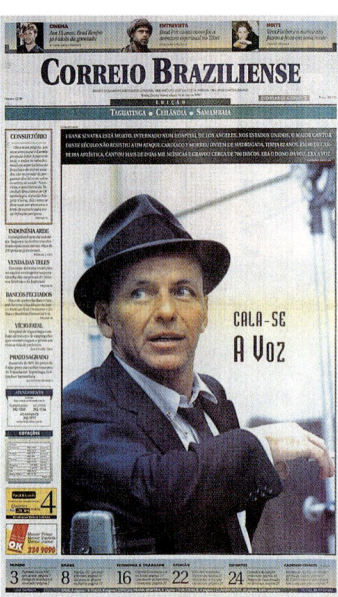

The Desert Sun
Palm Springs, CA

Brian Cragin, Assistant Graphics Editor; **James Abundis,** Graphics Editor; **Vikki Porter,** Executive Editor; **Nicole Peake,** Artist; **Tracey Green,** Artist; **Bruce Fessier,** Features Writer

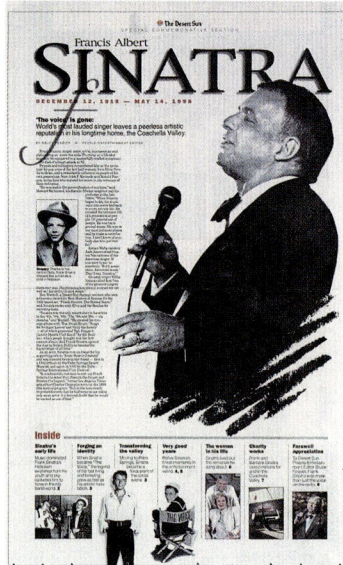

San Jose Mercury News
San Jose, CA

Steve Cavendish, Design Director; **Scott Demusey,** Photo Editor; **Mark Damon,** Photo Editor; **Susan Steade,** Designer; **Bryan Monroe,** A.M.E./News, Visuals & Technology

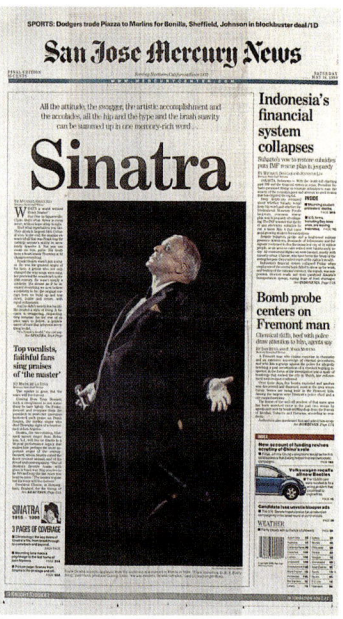

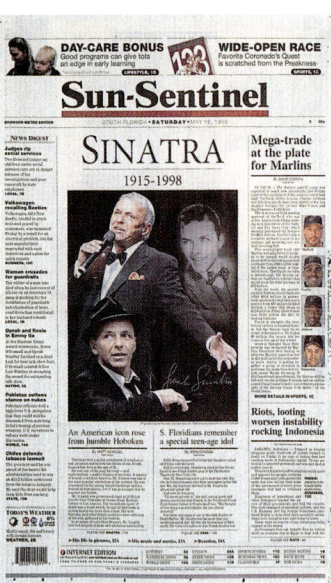

Sun-Sentinel
Ft. Lauderdale, FL

Jeanne Jordan, News Editor; **Bill Mcdonald,** Assistant News Editor; **Tan Ly,** Designer; **R. Scott Horner,** Graphics Reporter; **George Wilson,** Photo Editor; **Chris Kirkman,** Graphics Reporter

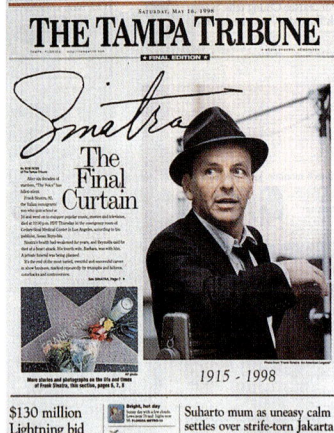

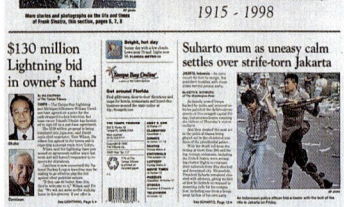

The Tampa Tribune
Tampa, FL

Len Howell, Designer; **Greg Williams,** Art Director; **Pat Mitchell,** Senior Editor/Graphics

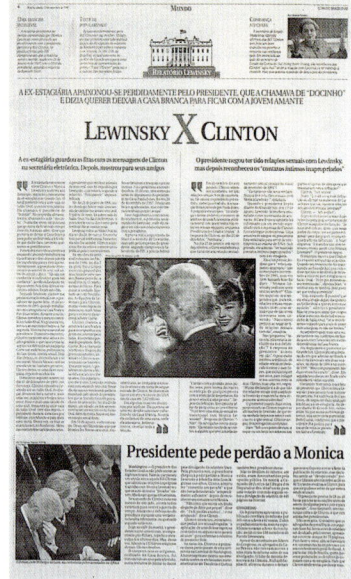

Correio Braziliense
Brasília, Brasil

Hélio Doyle, Editor; **Francisco Amaral,** Art Director; **Cláudio Versiani,** Photo Editor; **Amaro Júnior,** Illustrator; **André Rodriques,** Illustrator; **Ángela Valdilena,** Page Designer

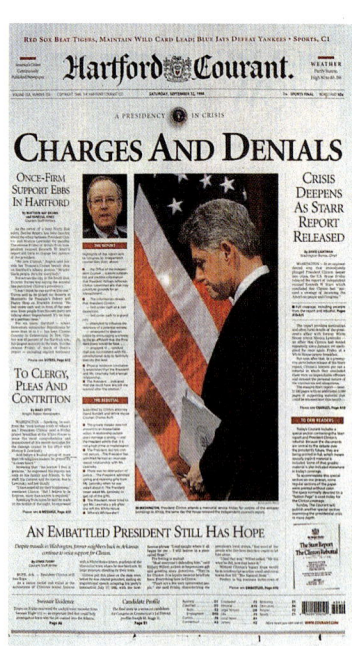

The Hartford Courant
Hartford, CT

Ingrid Muller, Page Designer; **Stephanie Heisler,** Photo Editor; **Christian P. Drury,** Art Director

Breaking News ■ NEWS

The Miami Herald
Miami, FL

Kris Strawser, News Design Editor

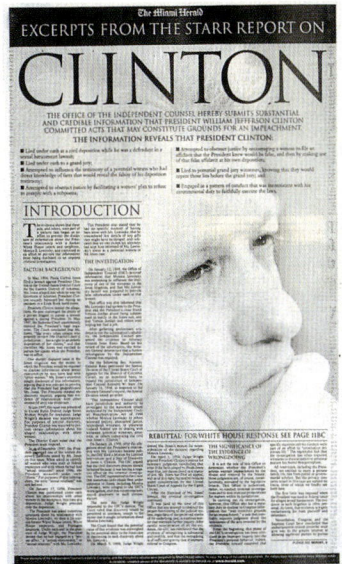

The Orange County Register
Santa Ana, CA

Karen Kelso, Presentation Editor & Art Director; **Patty Pitts,** Designer; **Joelle Beckett,** Designer; **Ken Niedziela,** Designer; **Marcia Prouse,** Photo Editor; **Bill Cunningham,** Designer

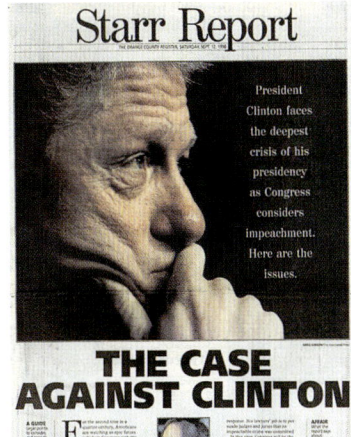

The Providence Journal
Providence, RI

Cecilia Prestamo, Picture Editor; **George Sylvia,** Artist

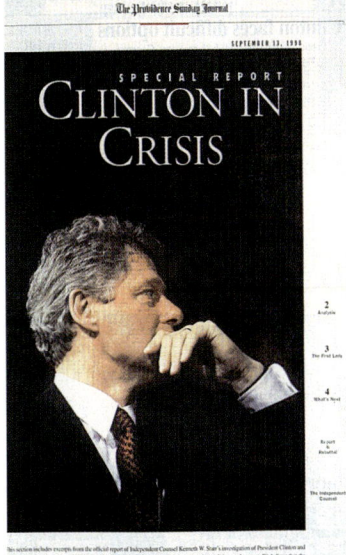

Star Tribune
Minneapolis, MN

Greg Branson, Assistant Graphics Director; **Judy Romanowich-Smith,** A1 Night Coordinator; **Terry Sauer,** A1 Coordinator; **Steve Rice,** Photo Director; **Ray Grumney,** Graphics Director; **Anders Ramberg,** Design Director; **Bill Dunn,** Visual Content Editor; **Pam Fine,** M.E.; Staff

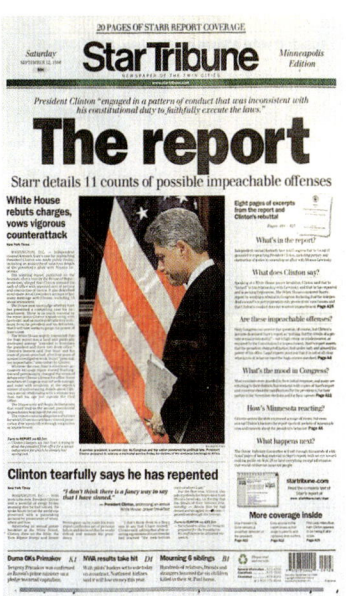

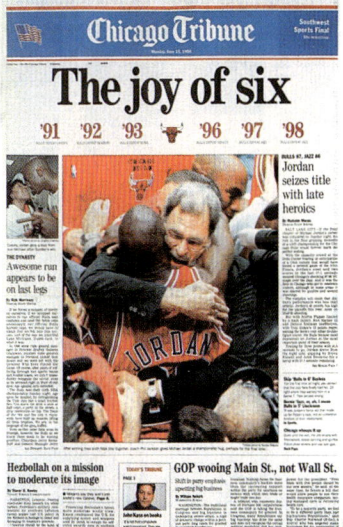

The Chicago Tribune
Chicago, IL

Stacy Sweat, Designer; **Bill Parker,** News Editor; **Torry Bruno,** Photo Editor; **Nuccio DiNuzzo,** Photographer

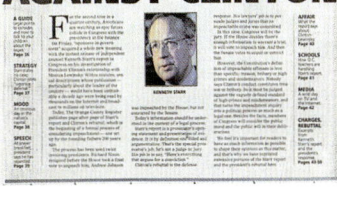

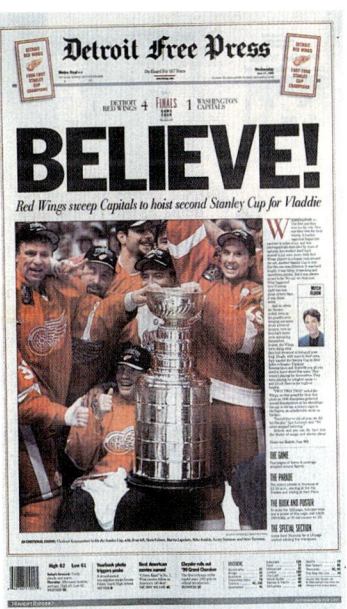

Detroit Free Press
Detroit, MI

Scott Albert, Designer; **Julian H. Gonzalez,** Photographer; **Rob St. John,** Picture Editor; **Caroline E. Couig,** Picture Editor

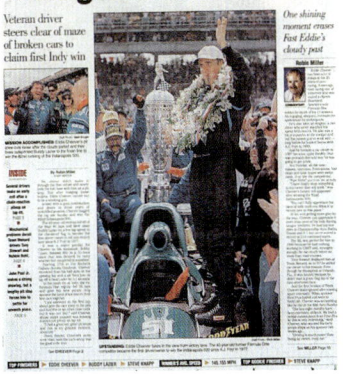

The Indianapolis Star
Indianapolis, IN

Channon Seifert, Art Director & Designer; **Mark Emmert,** Sports Operations Editor; **John Scott,** Graphics Team Leader; **Rich Miller,** Photographer; **Matt Kryger,** Photographer; **Greg Fisher,** Picture Editor; **Greg Nichols,** Graphic Artist

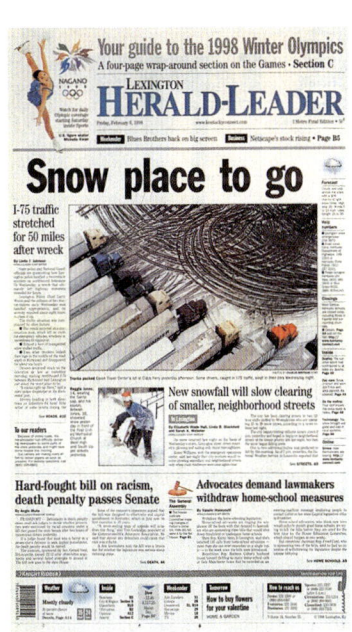

Lexington Herald-Leader
Lexington, KY

Harlen Makemson, Designer; **Dean Holt,** Designer; **Steve Dorsey,** Presentation Director & Designer; **Charles Bertram,** Photographer

NEWS ■ Breaking News

San Jose Mercury News
San Jose, CA
Steve Cavendish, Design Director/News; **Anna Buchmann,** Metro News Editor; **Herschel Kenner,** A.M.E./News; **Bryan Monroe,** A.M.E./News, Visuals & Technology; **David Yarnold,** M.E.

The Times
Munster, IN
Matt Mansfield, Deputy M.E.; **Epha Good,** Design Team Leader; **Tom Davies,** Copy Editor; **Dan Lee,** Designer; **David Lindquist,** Features Editor; **Geoff Black,** Director/Photography; **Staff**
• also for Front Page

The News Tribune
Tacoma, WA
Carmen Dybdahl, Designer; **Peter Haley,** Photographer; **Lee Waigand,** Presentation Editor; **Roy Gallop,** Graphic Artist

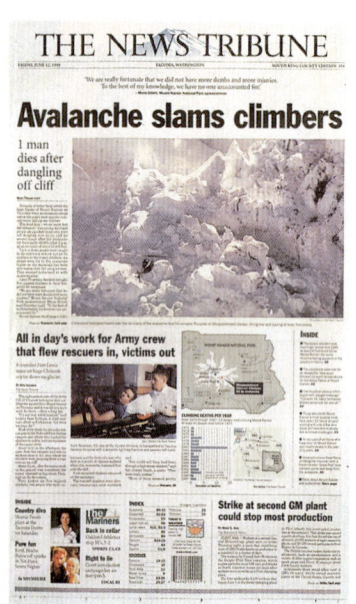

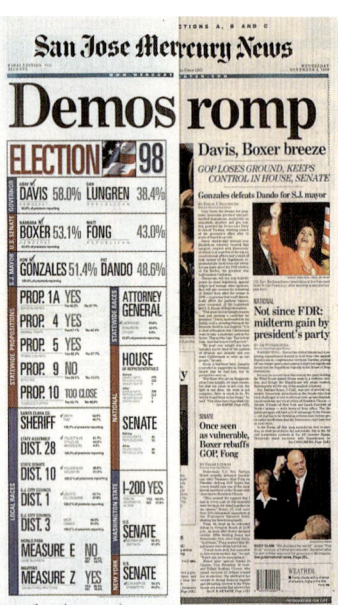

The Times
Munster, IN
Kevin Poortinga, Design Director; **Epha Good,** Design Team Leader; **Matt Mansfield,** Deputy M.E.; **Marilyn Kucer,** Night Editor; **Geoff Black,** Photo Director; **Staff**

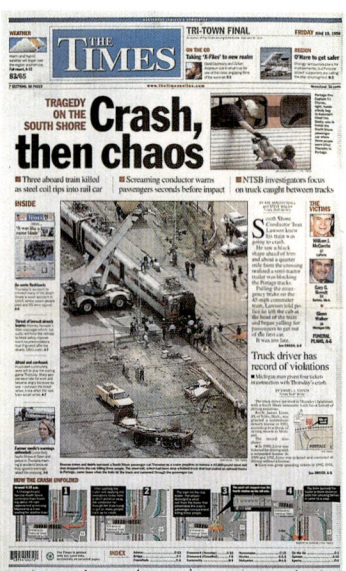

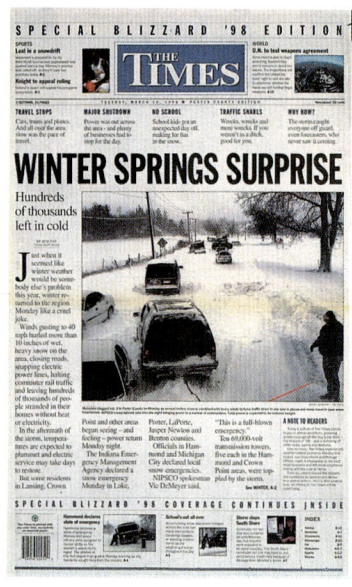

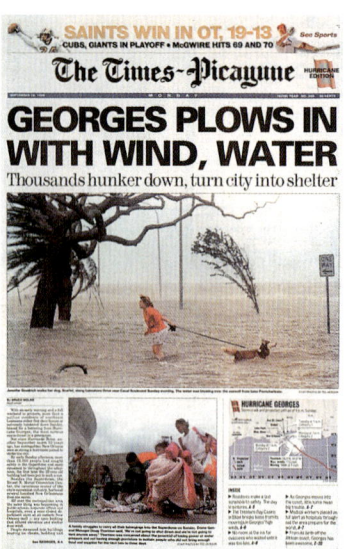

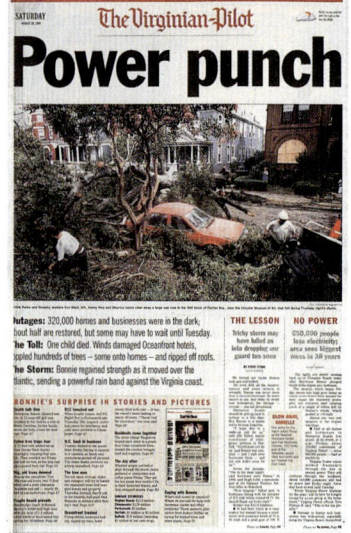

The Virginian-Pilot
Norfolk, VA
Buddy Moore, Designer; **Courtney Murphy,** Projects Designer; **Lisa Cowan,** Designer; **Denis Finley,** News Editor; **Janet Shaunessy,** Designer

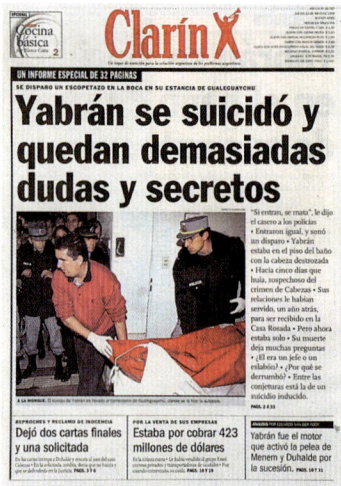

Clarín
Buenos Aires, Argentina
Iñaki Palacios, Art Director; **Juan Elissetche,** Design Editor; **Vicente Dagnino,** Design Editor; **Federico Sosa,** Design Editor; **Carlos Vazquez,** Graphic Designer; **Maureen Holboll,** Graphic Designer; **Osvaldo Estevao,** Graphic Designer; **Victoria Quintiero,** Graphic Designer
• also Special News Topics

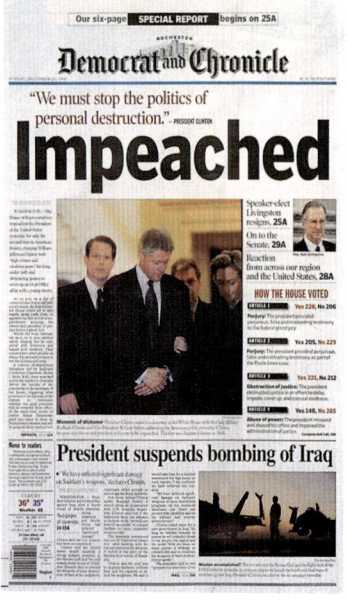

The Times-Picayune
New Orleans, LA
George Berke, Design Director; **Ted Jackson,** Photographer; **James O'Byrne,** Sunday Editor; **Laura Jayne,** News Editor; **Doug Parker,** Photo/Graphics Editor; **Dinah Rodgers,** Assistant Photo Editor

Democrat and Chronicle
Rochester, NY
Dennis R. Floss, A.M.E./Presentation/Graphics; **Stan Wischnowski,** A.M.E./News; **Paulina Reid,** Graphics Editor; **Henry Howard,** Assistant News Editor; **John Johnson,** Assistant News Editor; **Annette Meade,** Assistant Graphics Editor; **Yvonne Lin,** Artist; **Joanne Andrews,** Artist

Pittsburgh Post-Gazette
Pittsburgh, PA

Kim Germosek, Deputy Graphics Editor/Designer; **Chrisopher Pett-Ridge,** A.M.E. Graphics; **Tim Martin,** News Editor; **Dan Majors,** News Page Designer; **Catherine Tigano,** Graphic Artist
• also Special News Topics

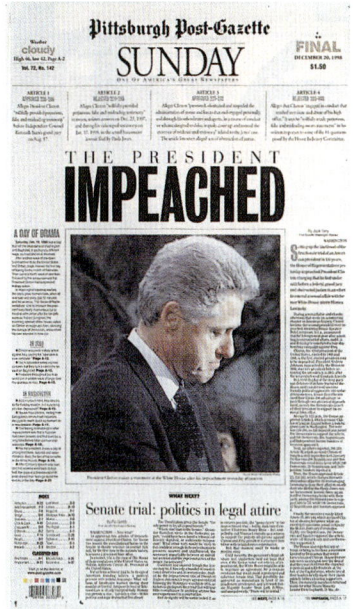

Silver
Berlingske Tidende
Copenhagen, Denmark

Gregers Jensen, Page Designer; **Rie Jerichow,** Graphic Designer; **Morten Juhl,** Photographer

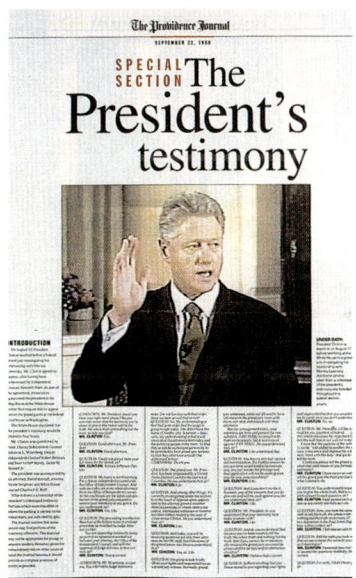

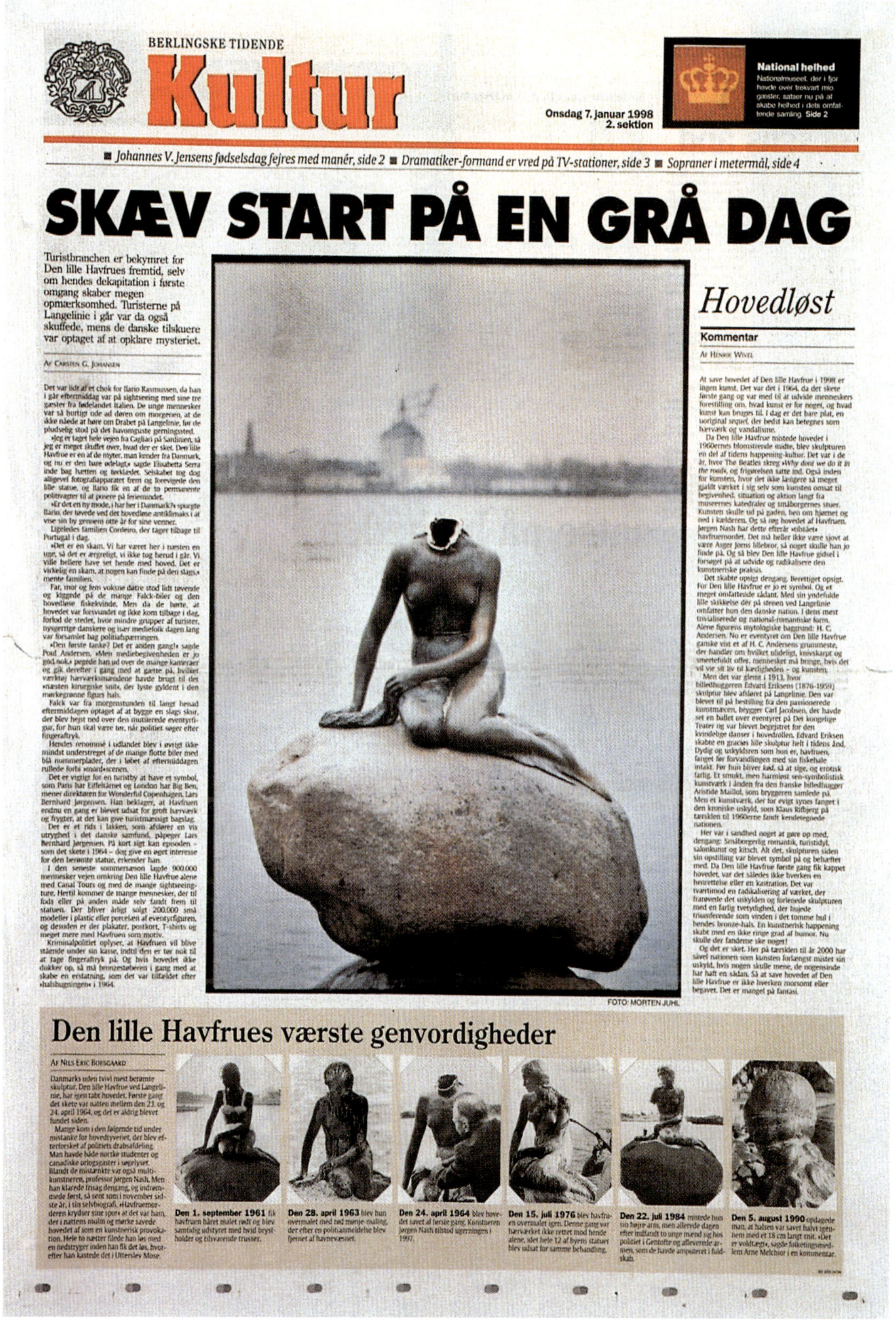

The Providence Journal
Providence, RI

Lynn Rognsvoog, Picture Editor/Designer; **Bill Ostendorf,** M.E./Visuals; **Molly McAllister,** Picture Editor/Designer

NEWS — Breaking News

Silver
Clarín
Buenos Aires, Argentina

Iñaki Palacios, Art Director; **Juan Elissetche**, Design Editor; **Vicente Dagnino**, Design Editor; **Federico Sosa**, Design Editor; **Carlos Vazquez**, Graphic Designer; **Maureen Holboll**, Graphic Designer; **Osvaldo Estevao**, Graphic Designer; **Victoria Quintiero**, Graphic Designer
• also an Award of Excellence for Front Page

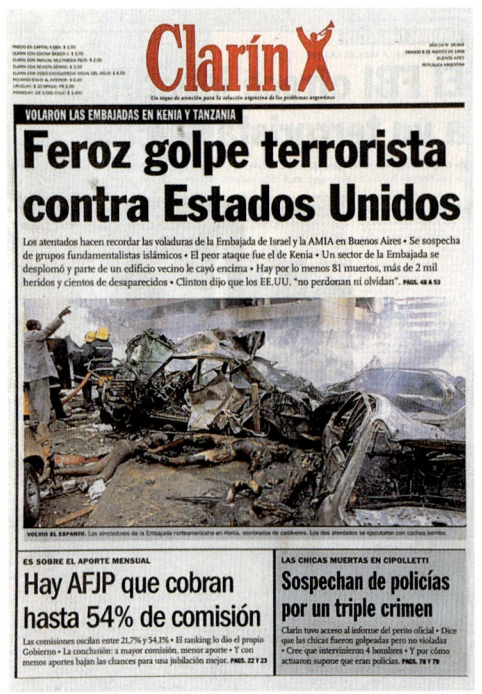
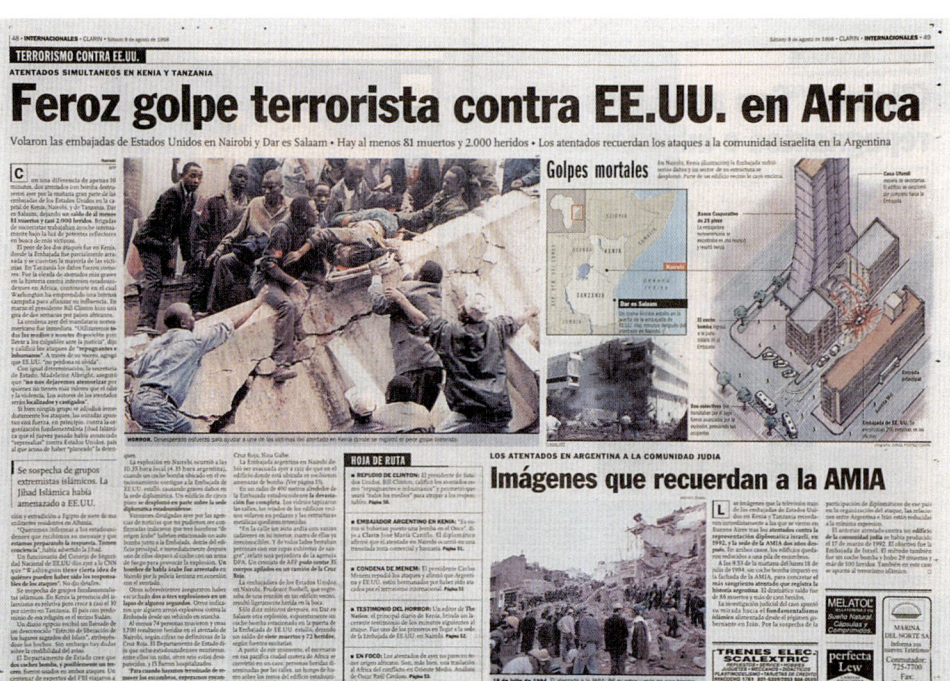

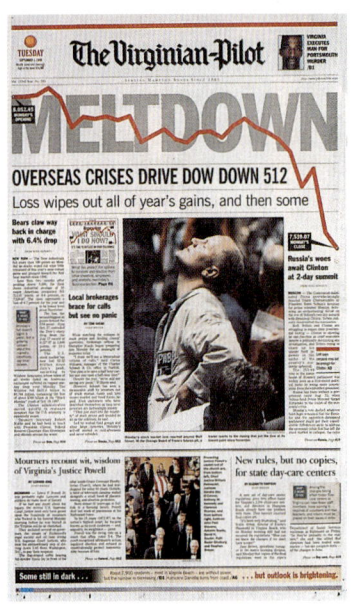
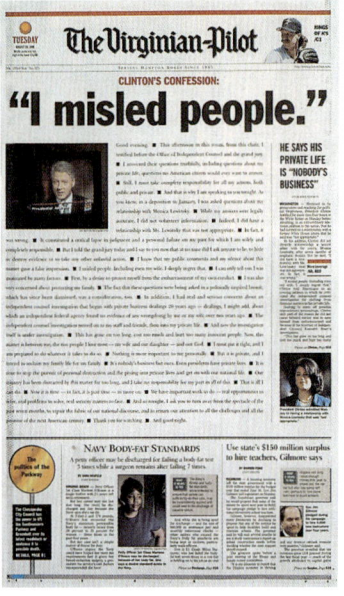
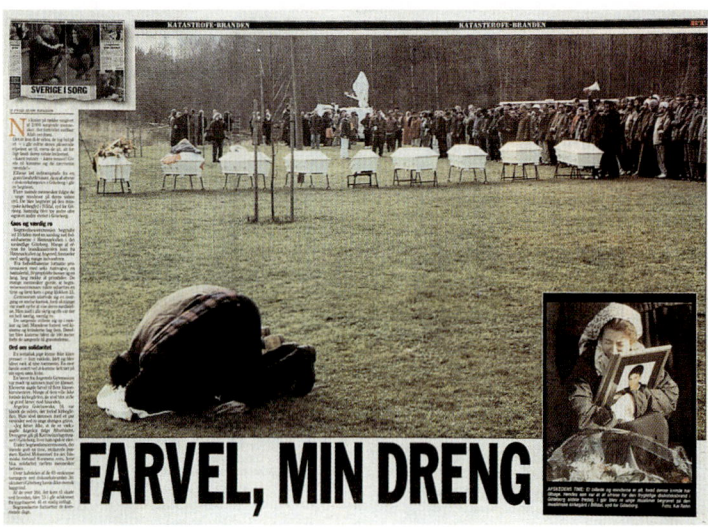

The Virginian-Pilot
Norfolk, VA
Buddy Moore, Designer; **Julie Elman**, Designer; **Norm Shafer**, Photo Editor; **Bob Voros**, Artist; **Eric Seidman**, Creative Director

The Virginian-Pilot
Norfolk, VA
Buddy Moore, Designer; **Dennis Hartig**, M.E.
• also for Front Page

B.T.
Copenhagen, Denmark
Helle-Lise Ritzau, Sub-Editor

Breaking News ■ NEWS

Clarín
Buenos Aires, Argentina

Iñaki Palacios, Art Director; **Juan Elissetche**, Design Editor; **Vicente Dagnino**, Design Editor; **Federico Sosa**, Design Editor; **Carlos Vazquez**, Graphic Designer; **Maureen Holboll**, Graphic Designer; **Osvaldo Estevao**, Graphic Designer; **Victoria Quintiero**, Graphic Designer

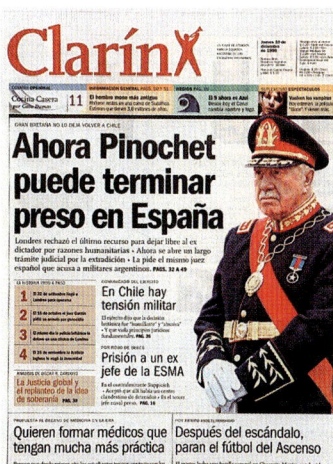

Correio Brasiliense
Brasília, Brasil

Ricardo Noblat, Executive Editor; **Francisco Amaral**, Art Director; **Cláudio Versiani**, Photo Editor; **Hélio Doyle**, Editor; **T. T. Catalão**, Editor; **Cynthia Garda**, Editor; **Toni Lucena**, Photo Illustrator; **Ângela Valdilena**, Page Designer

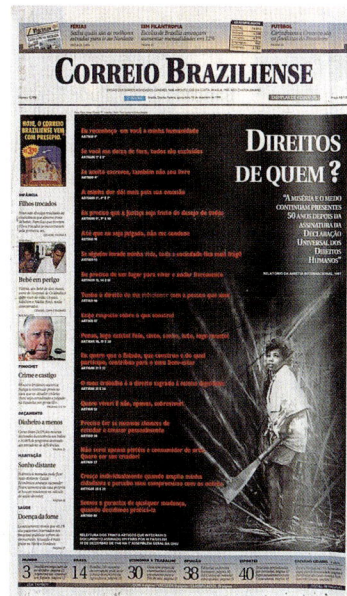

Dagens Nyheter
Stockholm, Sweden

Mars Odéen, Assistant Director; **Johan Jarnestad**, Graphic Artist; **Thomas Molén**, Graphic Artist; **Anders Nordlund**, Designer; **Erik Bergin**, Designer; **Mats Sjöberg**, Designer; **Lena Hansson**, Designer

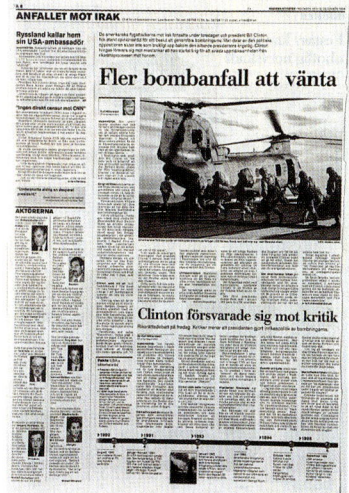

Morgenavisen Jyllands-Posten
Viby J., Denmark

Jane Nielsen, Page Designer/News Graphic Artist; **Lotte Overgaard**, News Graphic Artist; **Winnie Øvad**, News Graphic Artist; **Kent Olsen**, Reporter; **Hans Larsen**, Editor

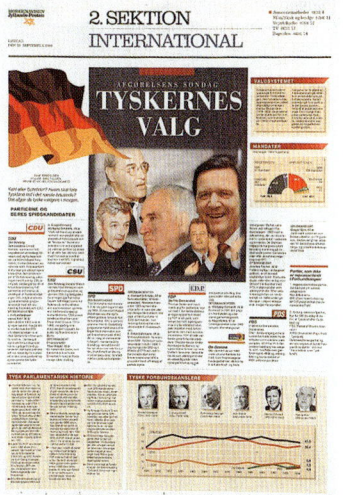

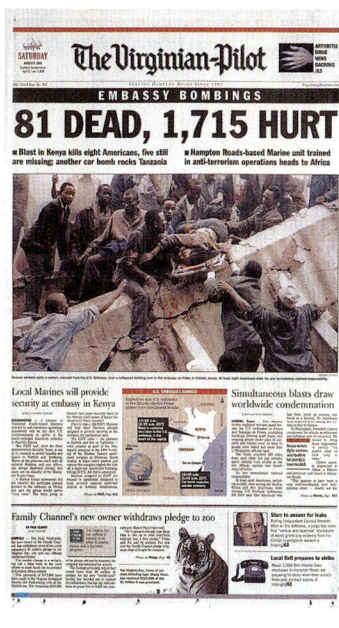

The Virginian-Pilot
Norfolk, VA

Harry Brandt, Designer; **Paul Nelson**, News Editor; **Jim Collins**, Photo Editor; **Denis Finley**, Design Team Leader; **Eric Seidman**, Creative director; **John Earle**, Artist

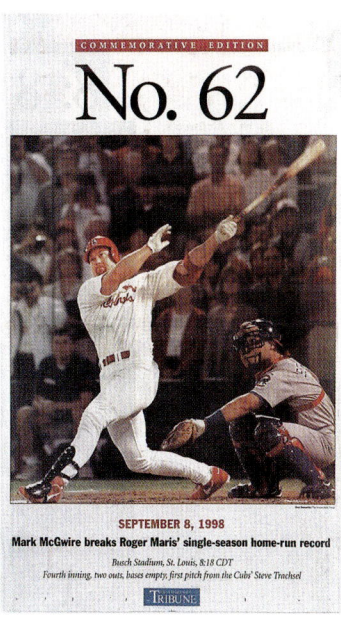

The Albuquerque Tribune
Albuquerque, NM

David Carrillo, News Editor; **Kevin Hellyer**, A.M.E.

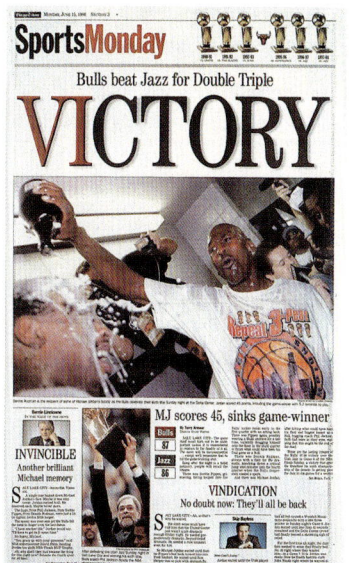

The Chicago Tribune
Chicago, IL

Therese Shechter, Designer; **Joe Knowles**, News Editor; **Terri Boyd**, Picture Editor; **Francisco Bernasconi**, Picture Editor; **Steve Layton**, Graphics Editor
• also for Special News Topics

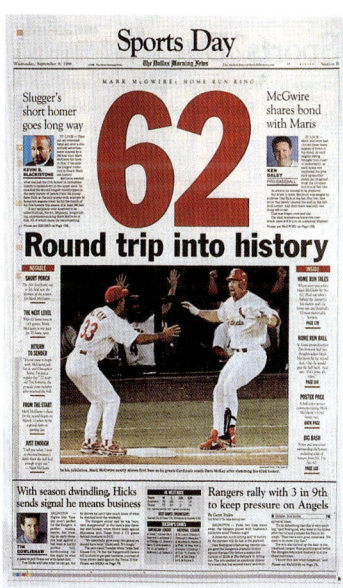

The Dallas Morning News
Dallas, TX

Dave Wilson, Designer; **John Banks**, Assistant Sports Editor

NEWS ■ Breaking News, Special News Topics

The New York Times
New York, NY
Joe Ward, Graphics Editor; **Wayne Kamidoi**, Designer

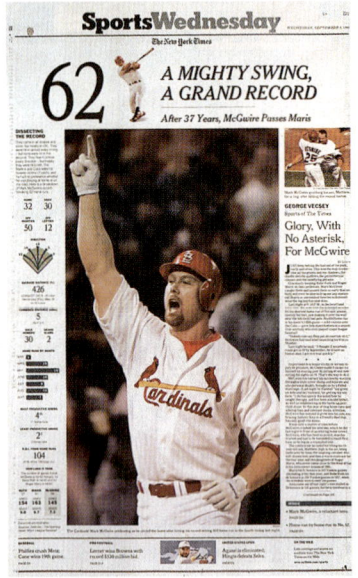

The Boston Globe
Boston, MA
Dan Zedek, Design Director; **Janet Michaud**, Designer; **Rena Sokolow**, Designer; **Jim Karaian**, Graphics Director; **David Schutz**, Graphic Artist; **Ed Wiederer**, Graphic Artist

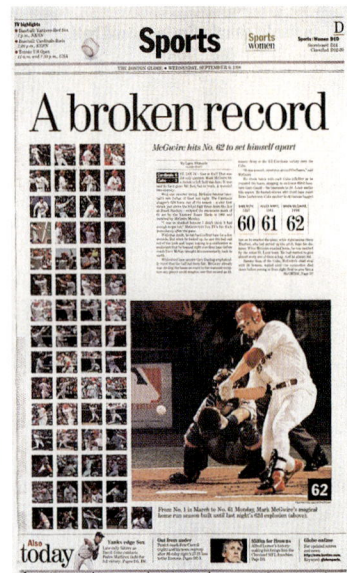

The Hartford Courant
Hartford, CT
Scott Johnson, Art Director & Designer; **Bruce Moyer**, Photo Editor

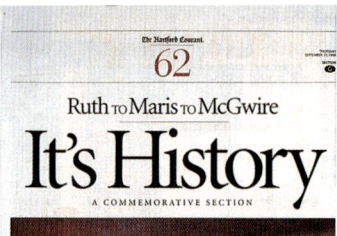

The New York Times
New York, NY
Joe Ward, Graphics Editor; **Wayne Kamidoi**, Designer; **Lee Yarosh**, Designer; **Sports Staff**

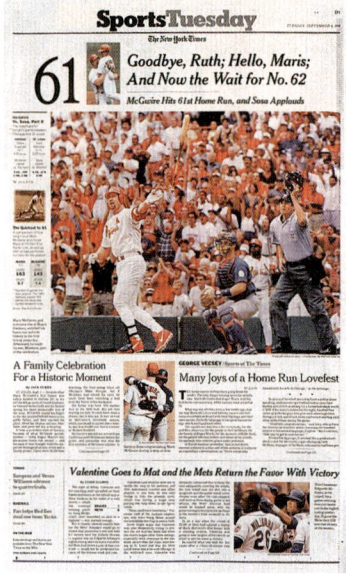

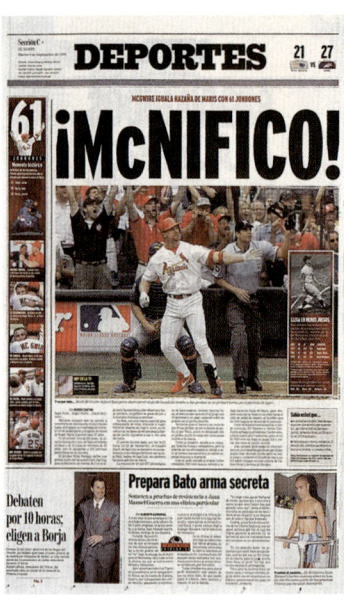

El Norte
Monterrey, México
Arturo Ortega, Section Editor; **Martin Pérez Cerda**, Editor Director; **Alexandro Medrano**, M.E./Design; **Ramón Alberto Garza**, General Editor Director; **Raúl Braulio Martinez**, Art Director; **Sandra de León**, Designer; **José Grajeda**, Graphic Coordinator

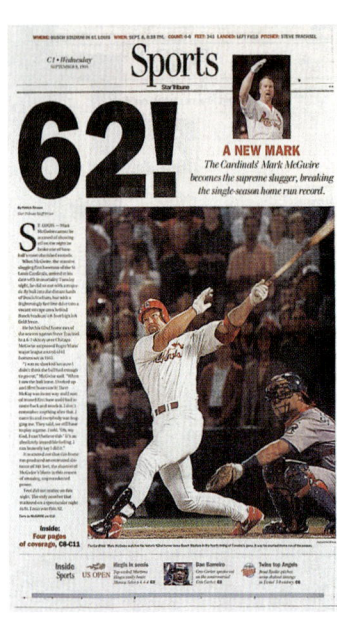

Star Tribune
Minneapolis, MN
Derek Simmons, Designer; **Mark Wolleman**, Night Sports Section Coordinator; **Glen Crevler**, Sports Editor; **Tim Wheatley**, Sports Section Coordinator; **Anders Ramberg**, Design Director; **Bill Dunn**, Visual Content Editor

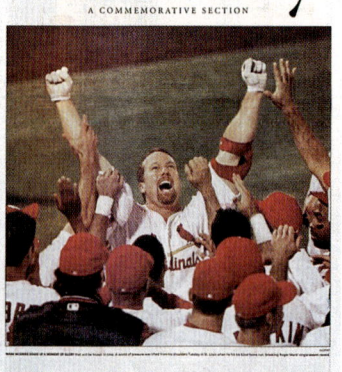

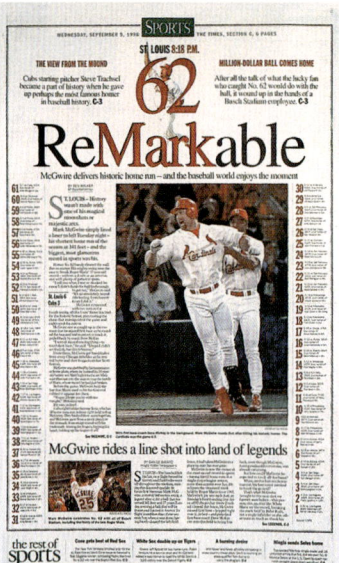

The Times
Munster, IN
Staff

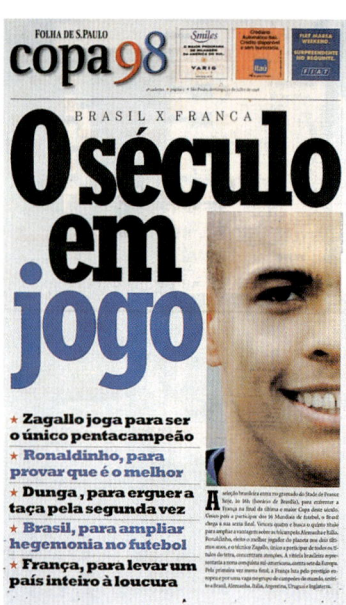

Folha de São Paulo
São Paulo, Brasil
Marcos Augusto Gonçalves, Sunday Editor; **Melchiades Filho**, Sport Editor; **Vincenzo Scarpellini**, Art Director; **Fernanda Cirenza**, Art Editor; **Thales de Menezes**, Assistant Editor; **Toni Pires**, Image Editor; **Adilson Secco**, Infographic Designer; **Mario Kanno**, Infographic Designer; **Jair de Oliveira**, Page Designer; **Adailton Pereira Gontijo**, Page Designer

Special News Topics ■ NEWS

Folha de São Paulo
São Paulo, Brasil

Marcos Augusto Gonçalves, Sunday Editor; **Melchiades Filho,** Sport Editor; **Vincenzo Scarpellini,** Art Director; **Fernanda Cirenza,** Art Editor; **Thales de Menezes,** Assistant Editor; **Toni Pires,** Image Editor; **Adilson Secco,** Infographic Designer; **Mario Kanno,** Infographic Designer; **Jair de Oliveira,** Page Designer; **Adailton Pereira Gontijo,** Page Designer

Zero Hora
Porto Alegre, Brasil

Marcelo Rech, Director; **Luiz Adolfo,** Art Director; **David Coimbra,** Sports Editor

The New York Daily News
New York, NY

Thomas Ruis, Design Director; **William St. Angelo,** Design Director/News

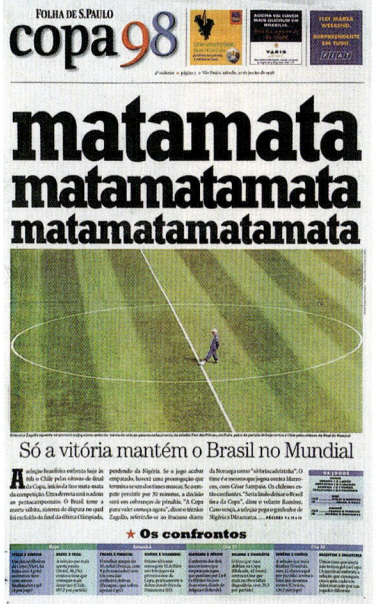
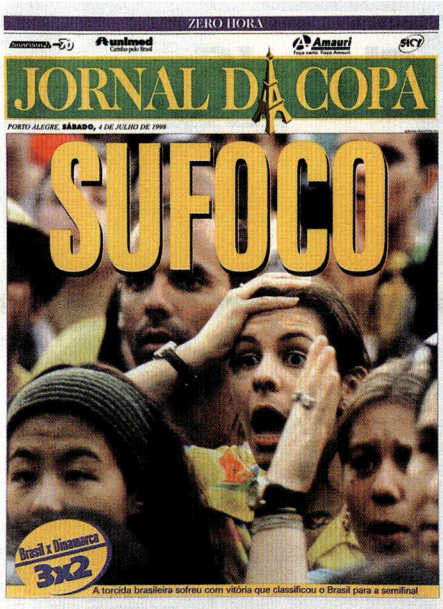
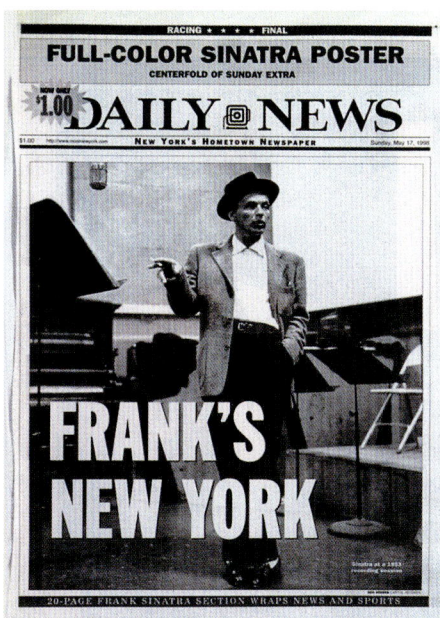

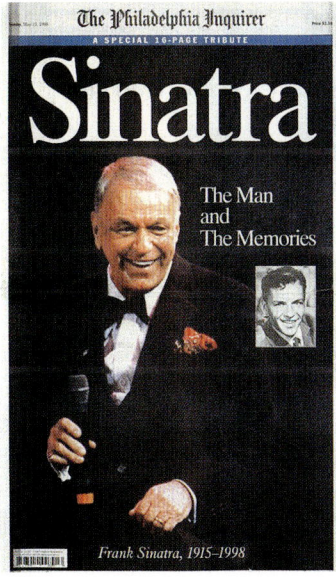
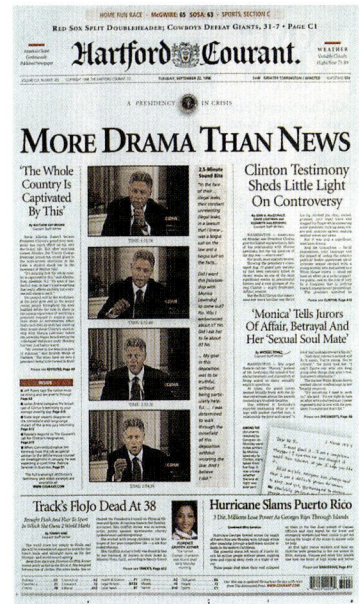
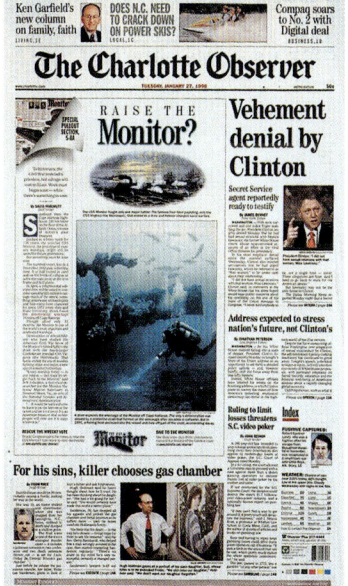
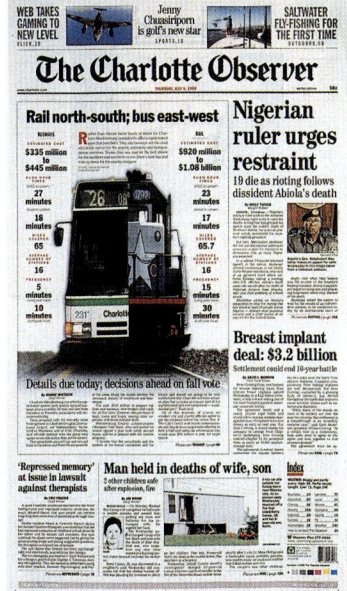

The Philadelphia Inquirer
Philadelphia, PA

Lisa A. Zollinger, Page Designer; **David Milne,** A.M.E. Design; **Matthew Ericson,** Graphic Artist/Page Designer; **Bill Marsh,** Art Director; **Clem Murray,** Director/Photography; **Charles Knittle,** Special Sections Editor

The Hartford Courant
Hartford, CT

Ingrid Muller, Designer; **Bill Sikes,** Photo Editor; **Christian P. Drury,** Art Director

The Charlotte Observer
Charlotte, NC

Monica Moses, Design Director; **Cory Powell,** Designer; **William Pitzer,** News Graphic Editor; **Tom Tozer,** Project Editor

The Charlotte Observer
Charlotte, NC

Monica Moses, Design Director; **Steve Johnston,** Copy Editor; **Danielle Parks,** Designer; **Brenda Pinnell,** Artist; **Joanne Miller,** Art Director; **George Breisacher,** Artist; **Mike Gordon,** Project Editor; **Dianne Whitacre,** Staff Writer; **L. Mueller,** Photographer

NEWS ■ Special News Topics

Silver
The Seattle Times
Seattle, WA
Deb Dahrling, Designer; **Rick Lund,** Designer; **Mike Kellams,** Designer; **David Miller,** Art Director & Designer; **Jeff King,** Designer; **Rod Mar,** Photographer; **Mark Harrison,** Photographer; **Dean Rutz,** Photographer; **Steve Ringman,** Photographer

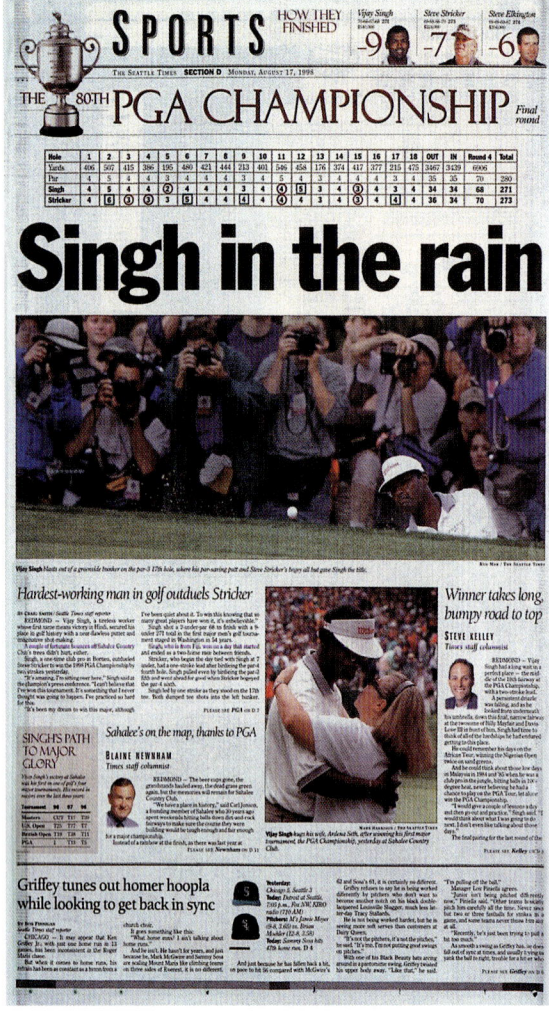
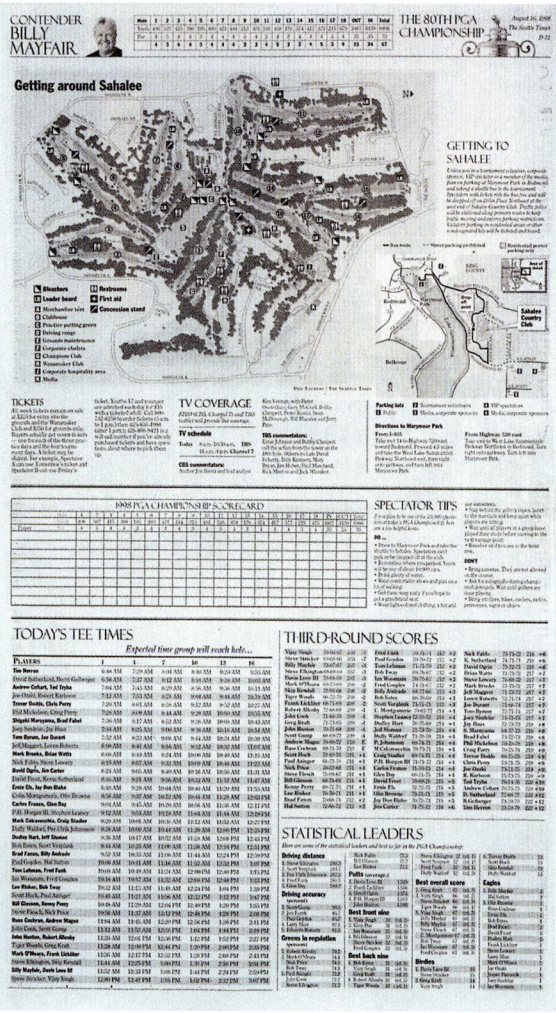

Silver
The Seattle Times
Seattle, WA
Tracy Porter, Designer; **Karen Klinkenberg,** Designer; **Michelle Kumata,** Infographic Artist; **James McFarlane,** Infographic Artist; **Karen Kerchelich,** Infographic Artist; **David Miller,** Art Director

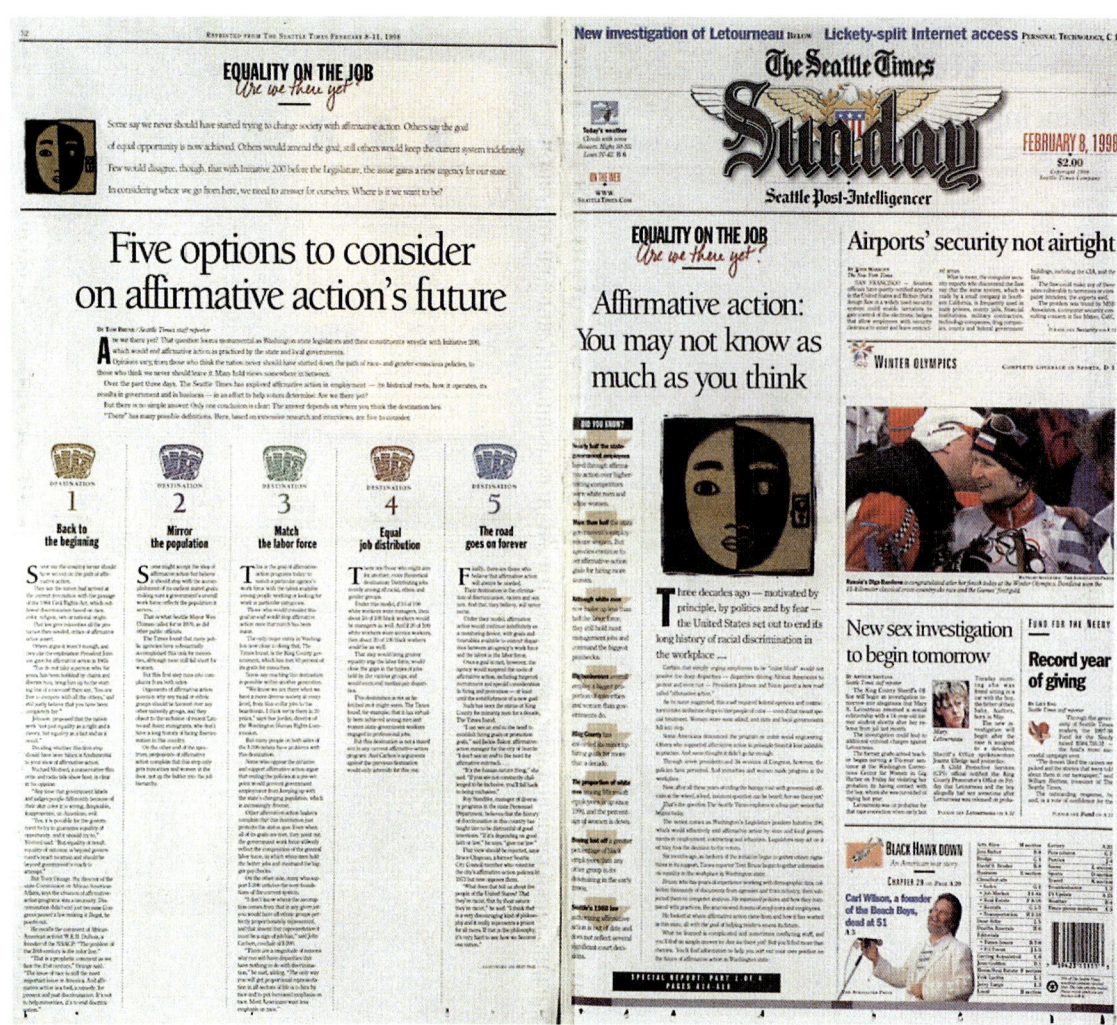

82 ■ THE BEST OF NEWSPAPER DESIGN

Special News Topics ■ NEWS

Silver
The Spokesman-Review
Spokane, WA
Scott Stoddard, Designer; **Torsten Kjellstrand**, Photographer

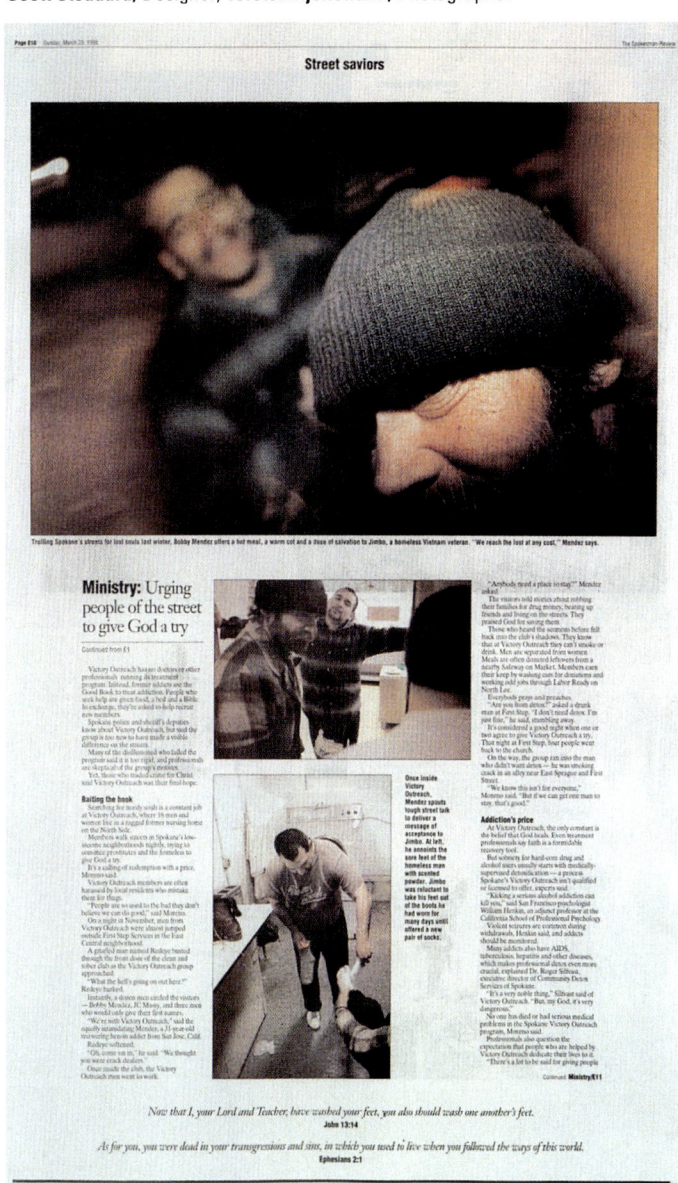

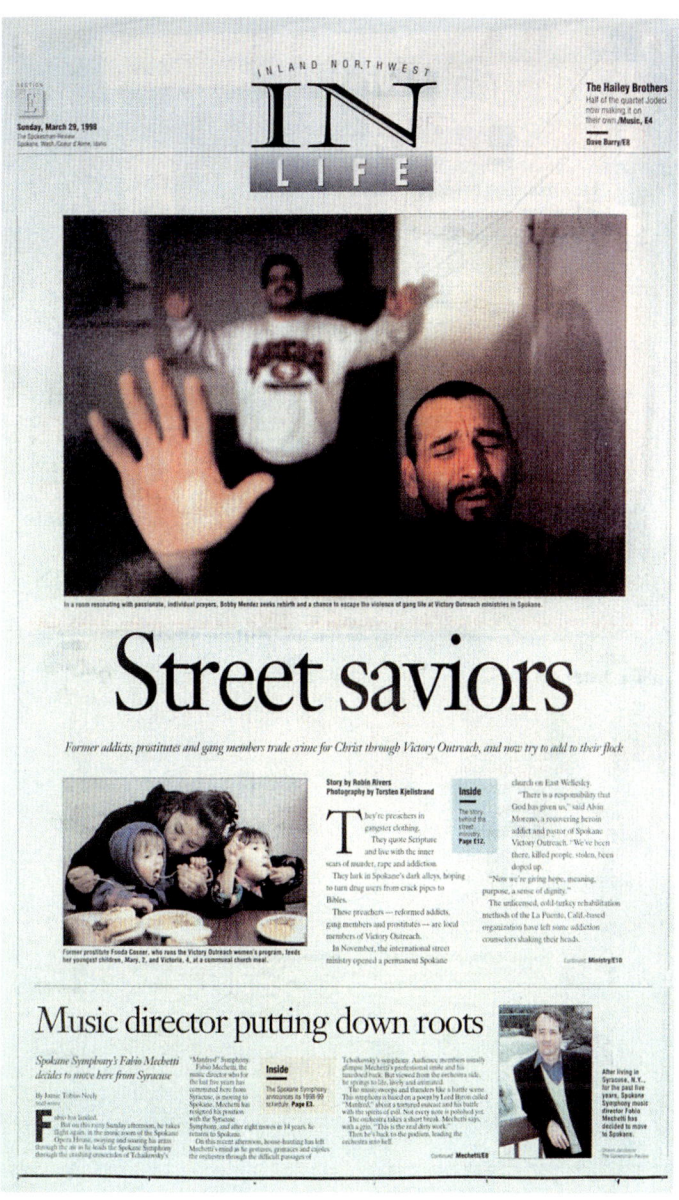

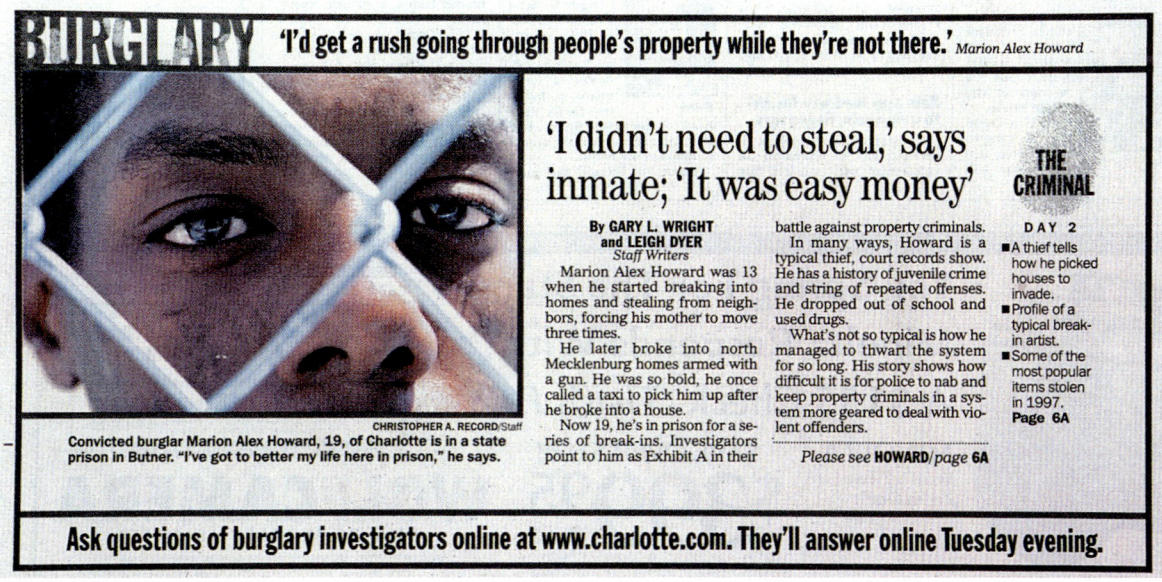

The Charlotte Observer
Charlotte, NC
Monica Moses, Design Director; **Christopher A. Record**, Photographer; **Susan Gilbert**, Director/Photography

TWENTIETH EDITION ■ 83

NEWS ▪ Special News Topics

The Charlotte Observer
Charlotte, NC

Monica Moses, Design Director/Designer; **Steve Gunn,** Projects Editor; **Patrick Schneider,** Photographer; **Anna Griffin,** Staff Writer; **Joanne Miller,** Art Director

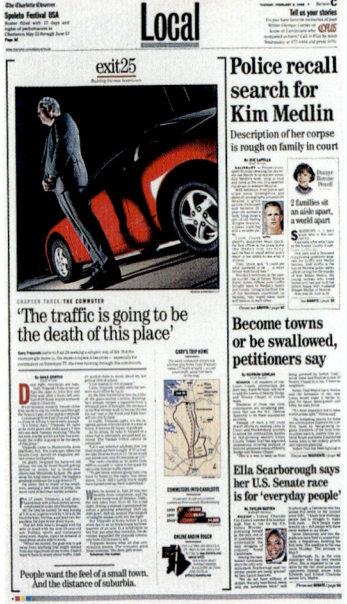

The Courier-Journal
Louisville, KY

Kim Kolarik, News Designer; **Joanne Meshew,** Graphic Artist

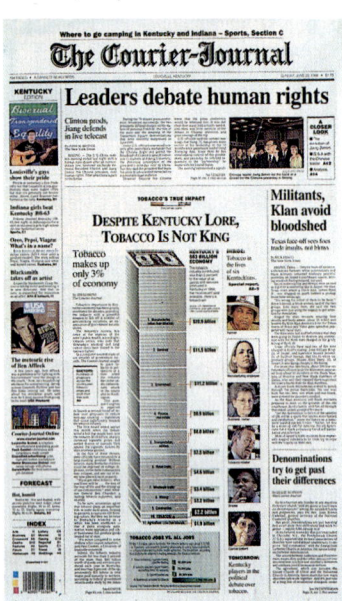

The Florida Times-Union
Jacksonville, FL

Dave Horn, News Designer; **Carole Fader,** A1 Editor

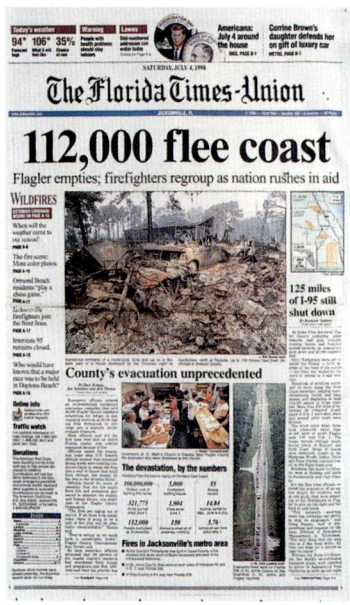

The Hartford Courant
Hartford, CT

Staff

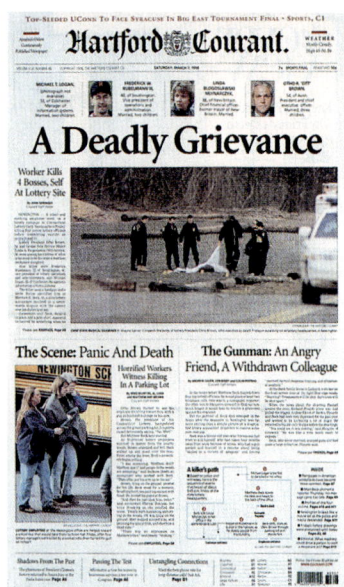

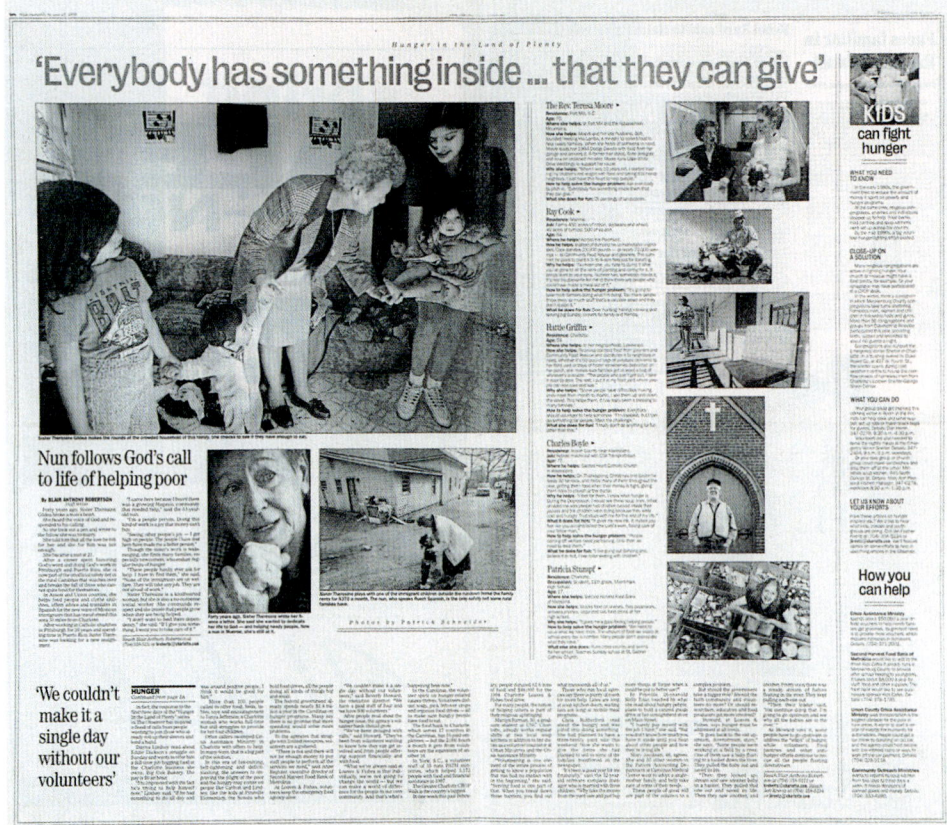

The Charlotte Observer
Charlotte, NC

Monica Moses, Design Director/Designer; **Danielle Parks,** Designer; **Susan Gilbert,** Director/Photography; **Steve Gunn,** Project Editor; **Blair Anthony Robertson,** Staff Writer; **Jeri Fischer Krentz,** Staff Writer; **Patrick Schneider,** Photographer

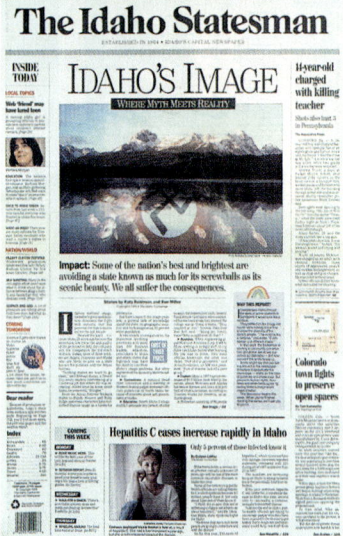

The Idaho Statesman
Boise, ID

Randy Wright, Designer; **Dennis Joyce,** Editor; **Patrick Davis,** Graphic Artist; **Brad Talbutt,** Photographer; **Katherine Jones,** Photographer; **Ken Miller,** Staff Writer; **Katy Robinson,** Staff Writer

84 ▪ THE BEST OF NEWSPAPER DESIGN

Special News Topics ■ NEWS

The Irish News
Belfast, Northern Ireland
Staff
• also for Front Page

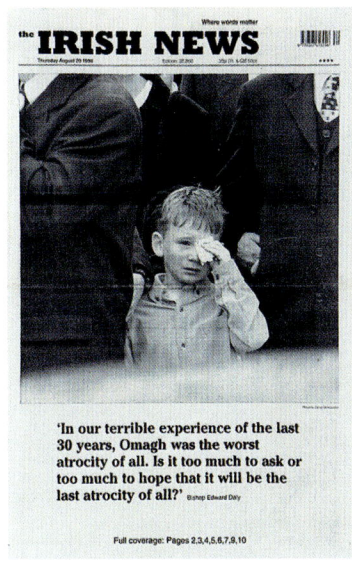

The Orange County Register
Santa Ana, CA
Molly Zisk, Artist; **Helayne Perry,** Designer; **Kris Viesselman Onuigbo,** Art Director; **Ygnacio Nanetti,** Photographer; **Michele Cardon,** Photo Editor; **April Jackson,** Graphics Reporter

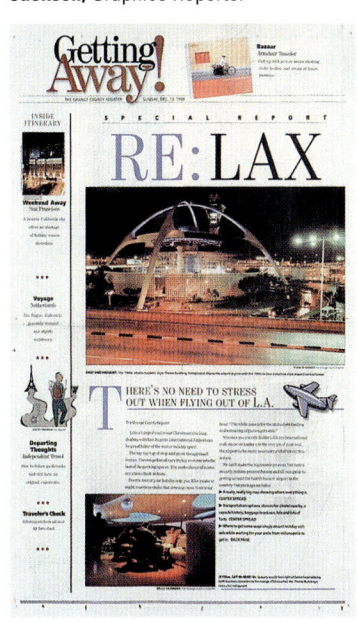

The Spokesman-Review
Spokane, WA
Scott Stoddard, Designer; **Christopher Anderson,** Photographer

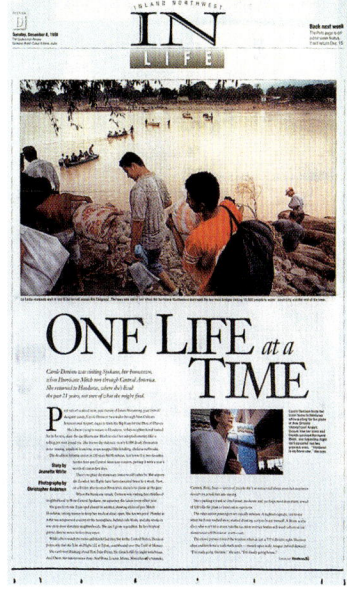

St. Louis Post-Dispatch
St. Louis, MO
Geof Dubson, Designer; **Tom Borgman,** Designer; **Scott Dine,** Photographer; **Bob Duffy,** Reporter; **Philip Kennicott,** Reporter

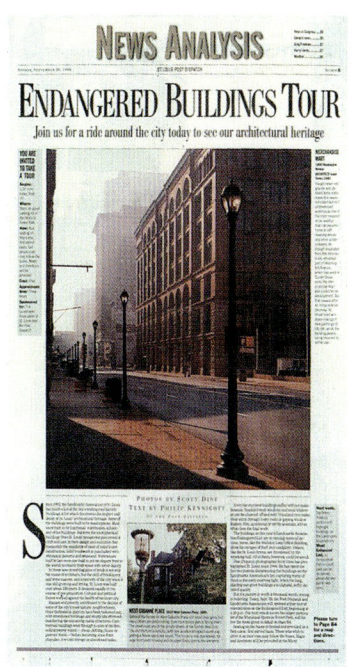

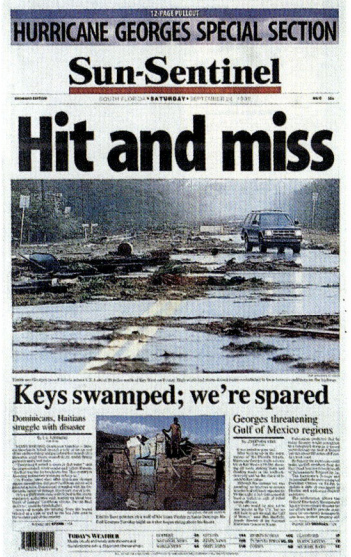

Sun-Sentinel
Ft. Lauderdale, FL
Staff

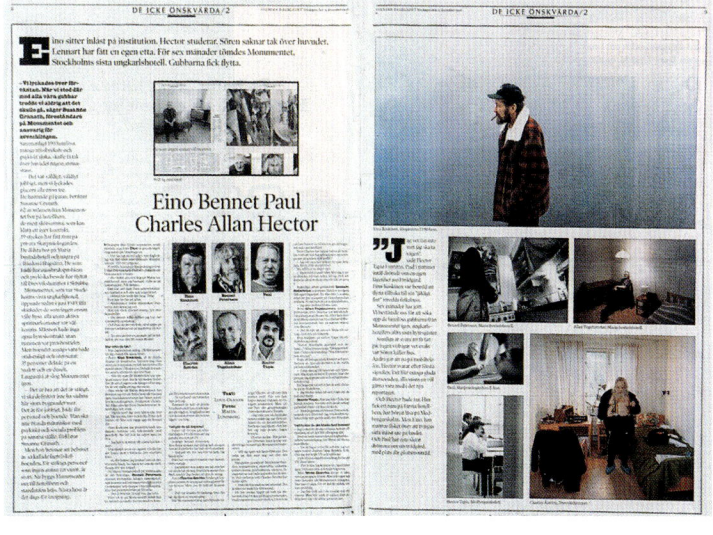

Svenska Dagbladet
Stockholm, Sweden
Lars Andersson, Design Editor

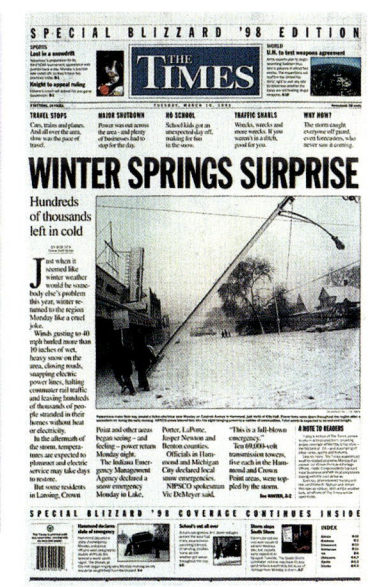

The Times
Munster, IN
Staff

NEWS ■ Special News Topics

The Times-Picayune
New Orleans, LA
Staff

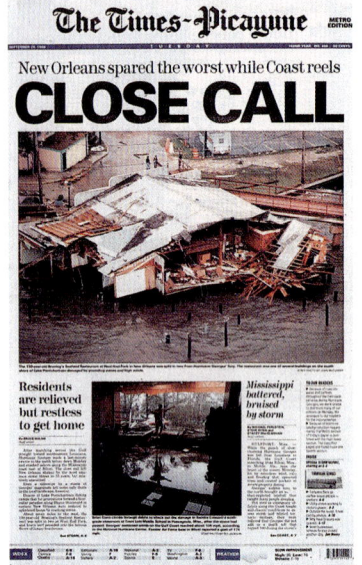

Svenska Dagbladet
Stockholm, Sweden
Lars Andersson, Design Editor

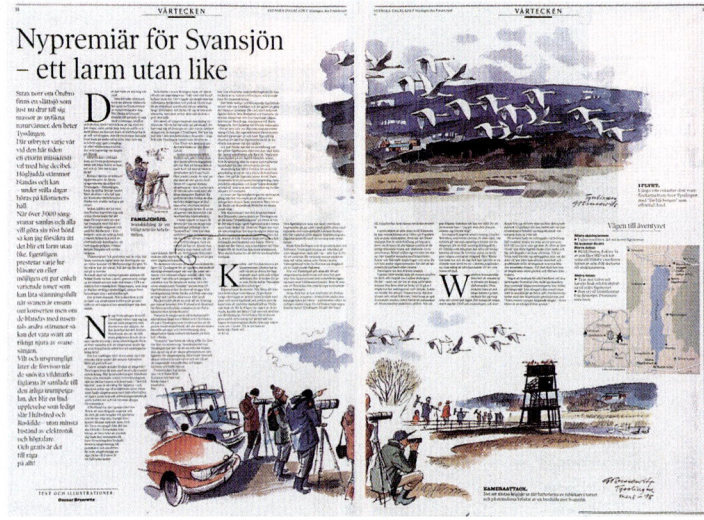

The Sun
Baltimore, MD

Jay Judge, News Page Designer; **Joseph Hutchinson,** A.M.E. Graphics/Design; **Andre F. Chung,** Photographer; **Jim Preston,** A.M.E. Photography; **Amy Deputy,** Picture Editor

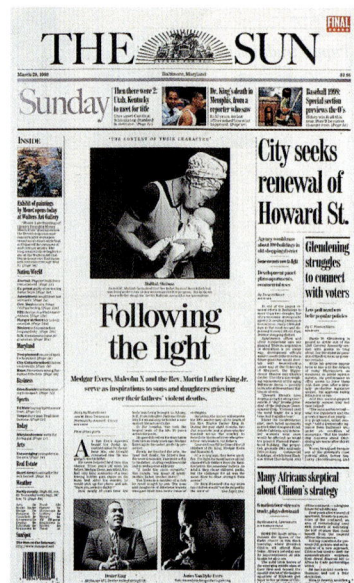

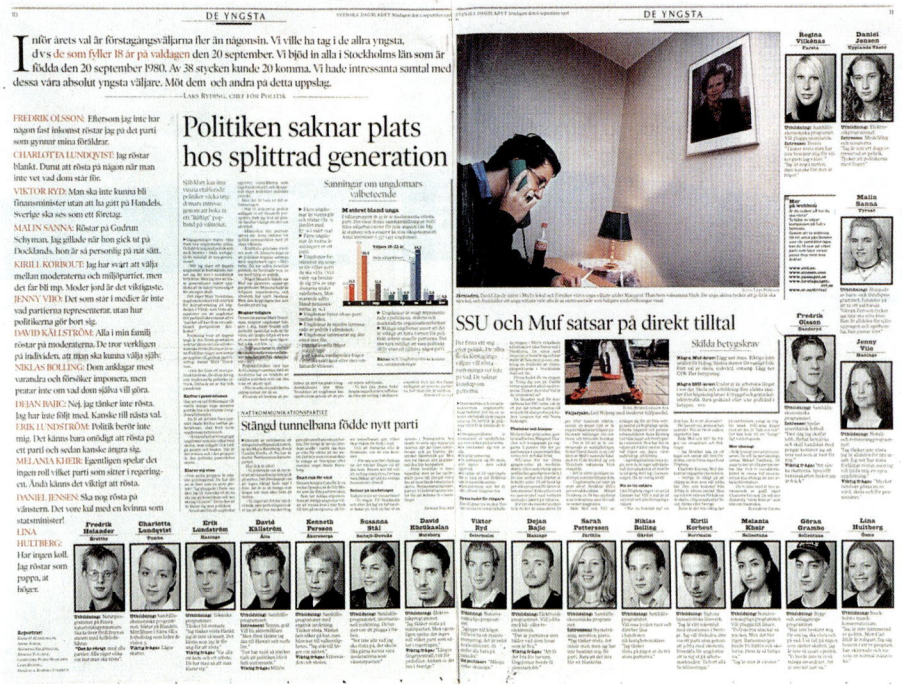

Svenska Dagbladet
Stockholm, Sweden
Lars Andersson, Design Editor

St. Louis Post-Dispatch
St. Louis, MO

Wade Wilson, News Editor; **Tom Borgman,** Design Director; **Steve Parker,** Sunday Editor

86 ■ THE BEST OF NEWSPAPER DESIGN

Special News Topics ■ NEWS

Gold
Svenska Dagbladet
Stockholm, Sweden

Lars Andersson, Design Editor; **Dan Hansson**, Photographer

The use of the signature, instead of the usual headline, and the layout as a whole are excellent concepts. The designer has a unique split between the introduction, story and picture over separate pages. The photo, different than the usual big shot of a face, is a great idea. A work of art.

El uso de la firma, en lugar del titular normal, y la composición en general son excelentes conceptos. El diseñador logra una pausa singular entre la introducción, la historia y la imagen en páginas separadas. La foto, diferente a la común imagen de grandes dimensiones de un rostro, es una magnífica idea. Una obra de arte.

NEWS ■ Special News Topics

The Chicago Tribune
Chicago, IL

Stacy Sweat, Graphics & Design Editor; **Therese Shechter,** Designer; **Jeanie Adams Smith,** Picture Editor; **José Moré,** Photographer; **Mark Hinojosa,** Photo Editor; **Bill Parker,** News Editor

The Commercial Appeal
Memphis, TN

Richard Robbins, Designer; **Lance Murphey,** Photographer; **Bartholomew Sullivan,** Reporter

Folha de São Paulo
São Paulo, Brasil

Paula Cesarino Costa, Special Features Editor; **Vincenzo Scarpellini,** Art Director; **Jair de Oliveira,** Page Designer; **Joana Brasileiro,** Page Designer; **Adi Leite,** Image Editor; **Eudardo Asta,** Infographic Designer

The New York Times
New York, NY

Tom Bodkin, Associate M.E./Design Director; **Linda Brewer,** Deputy Design Director; **Anne Leigh,** Art Director; **Marilyn Shapiro,** News Design Editor; **Daphne Angles,** Picture Editor; **Philip Gefter,** Picture Editor; **Jim Perry,** Graphics Editor

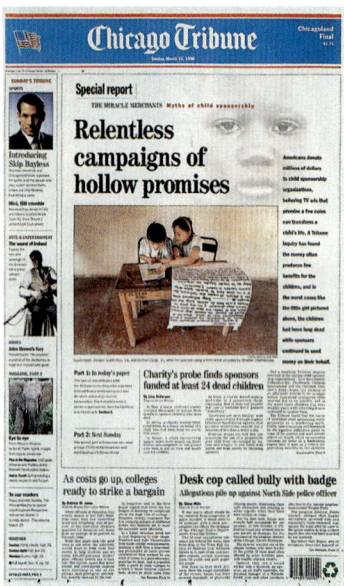
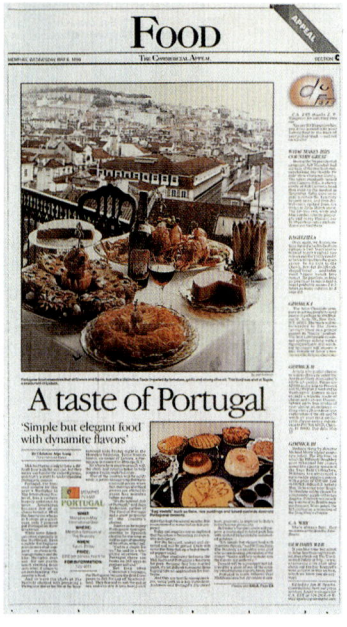
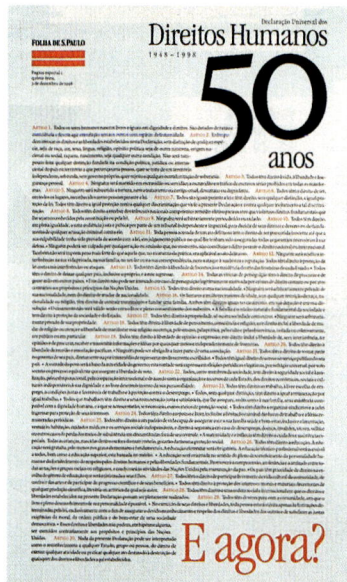
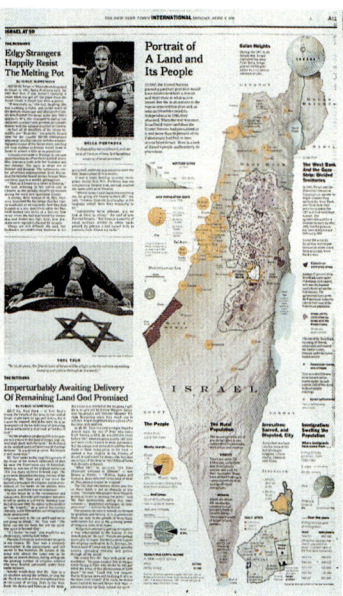

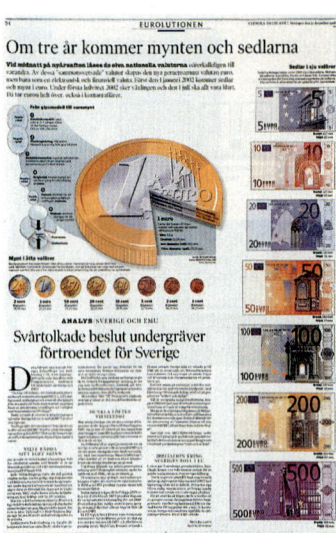

Svenska Dagbladet
Stockholm, Sweden

Lars Andersson, Design Editor; **Rickard Frank,** Graphic Artist

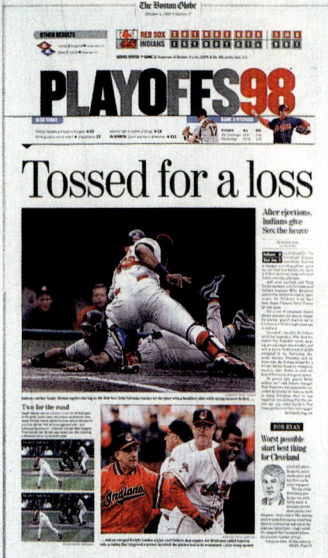

The Boston Globe
Boston, MA

Janet Michaud, Art Director & Designer; **Ken Fratus,** Editor/Designer; **Richard Sanchez,** Graphic Artist; **Ed Weiderer,** Graphic Artist; **Jim Karaian,** Graphics Editor; **Jim Davis,** Photographer; **Barry Chin,** Photographer; **John Tlumacki,** Photographer; **Don Skwar,** Sports Editor

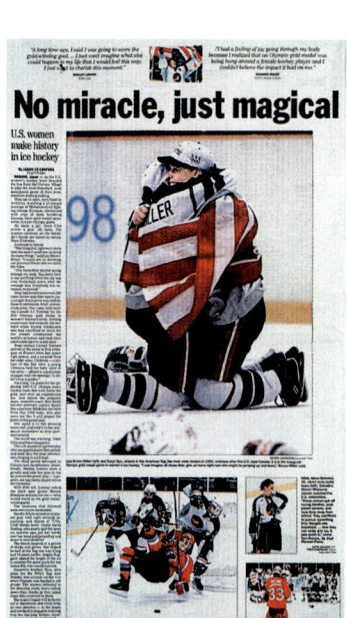

The Charlotte Observer
Charlotte, NC

Monica Moses, Design Director; **Scott Goldman,** Assistant Sports Editor; **Larry Davidson,** Designer; **Mike Bambach,** Designer; **Gina Davidson,** Designer; **Gary Schwab,** Sports Editor; **Joanne Miller,** Art Director; **Susan Gilbert,** Director/Photography

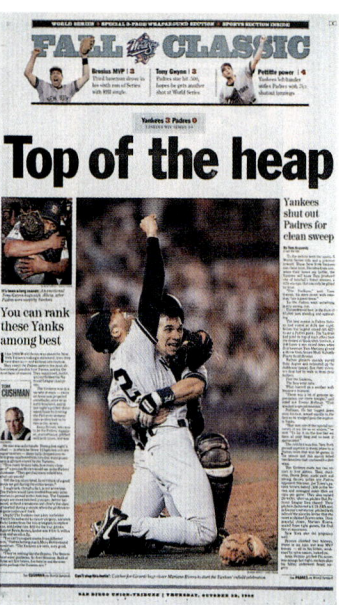

The San Diego Union-Tribune
San Diego, CA

Bill Dawson, Designer; **Bill Gaspard,** Designer; **Sean M. Haffey,** Photographer; **Jim Baird,** Photographer; **Peggy Peattie,** Photographer; **John Gastaldo,** Photographer; **Robert York,** Photo Editor; **Michael Franklin,** Photo Editor

FEATURES

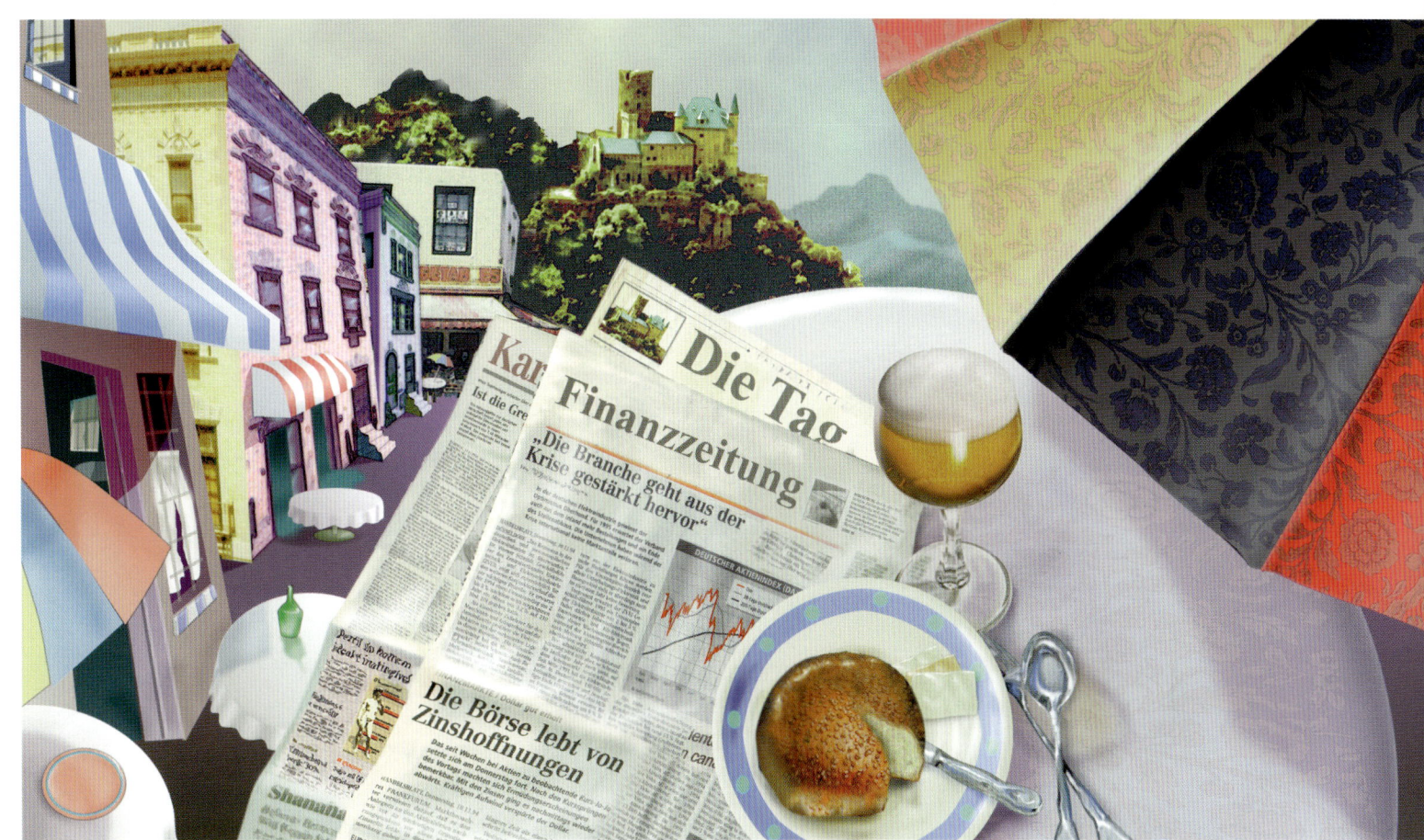

CHAPTER THREE

**REGULARLY
APPEARING
SECTIONS**

PAGE DESIGN

FEATURES ■ Sections: Opinion, Entertainment, Home/Real Estate

Silver
Estado de Minas
Belo Horizonte, Brasil

Álvaro Duarte, Art Director; **Rogério Carnevali,** Design Director; **Heliane Souza,** Designer; **Alexandre Coelho,** Illustrator; **Angelo Oswaldo,** News Editor; **Carlos Perez Diaz,** Design Consultant
• also an Award of Excellence for Opinion Page

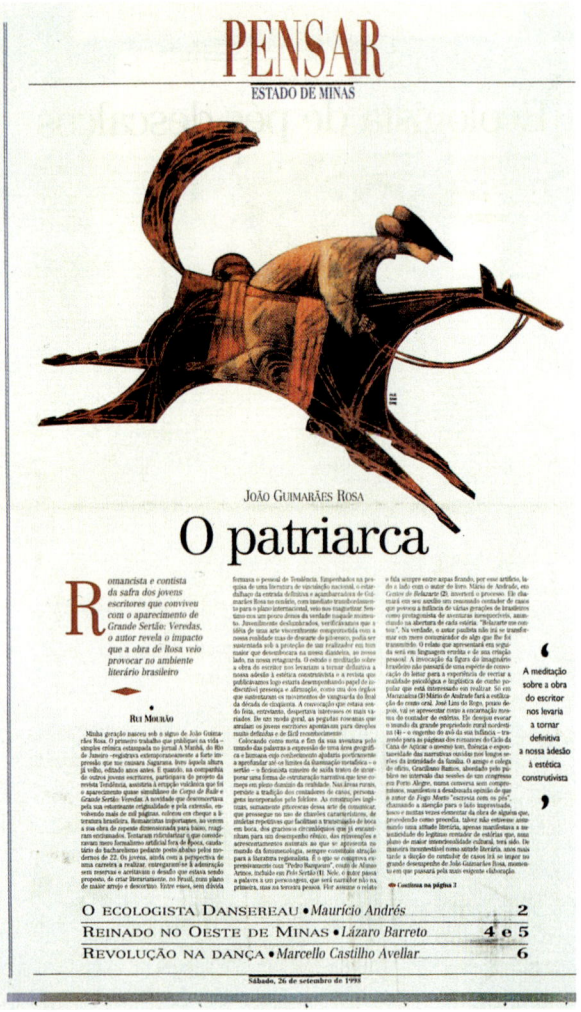
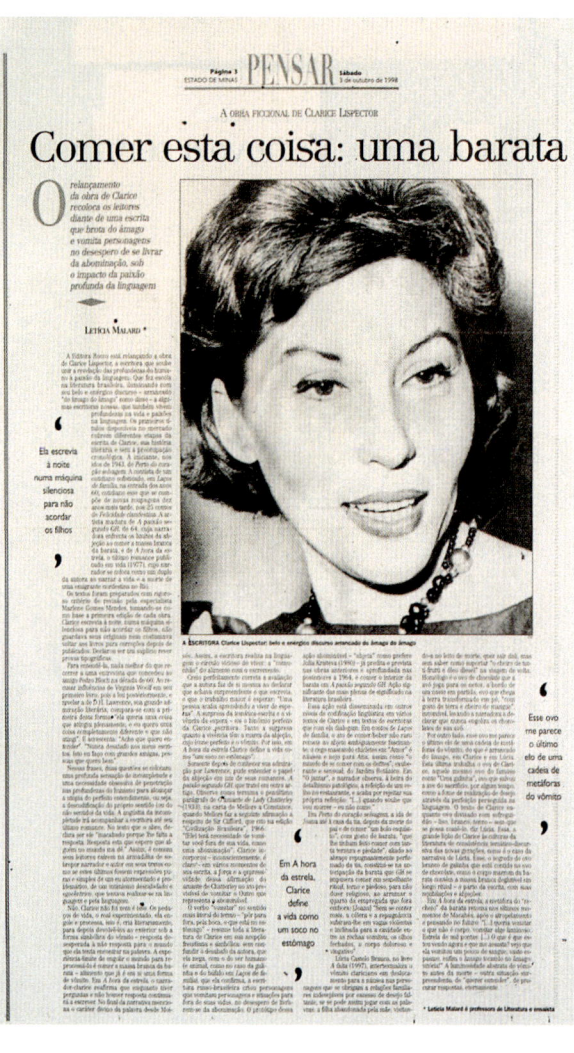

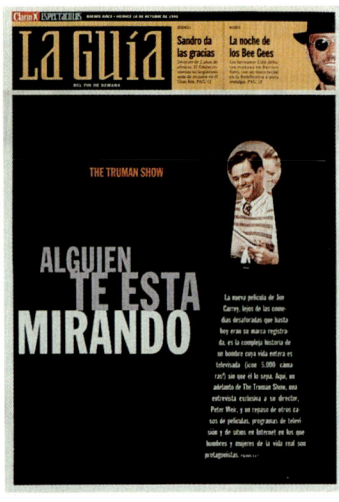

Clarín
Buenos Aires, Argentina

Iñaki Palacios, Art Director; **Tea Alberti,** Design Editor; **Oscar Bejarano,** Graphic Designer; **Valeria Castresana,** Graphic Designer; **Omar Olivella,** Graphic Designer; **Matilde Oliveros,** Graphic Designer; **Pablo Ruiz,** Graphic Designer; **Carolina Wainsztok,** Graphic Designer; **Silvina Fuda,** Graphic Designer

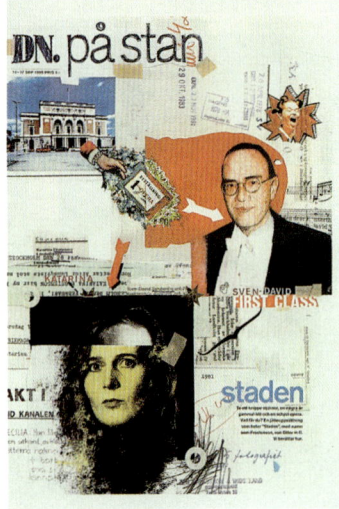

Dagens Nyheter
Stockholm, Sweden

Peter Alenäs, Art Director; **Pompe Hedengren,** Art Director; **Magnus Naddermier,** Art Director; **Nina Jakobson,** Layout

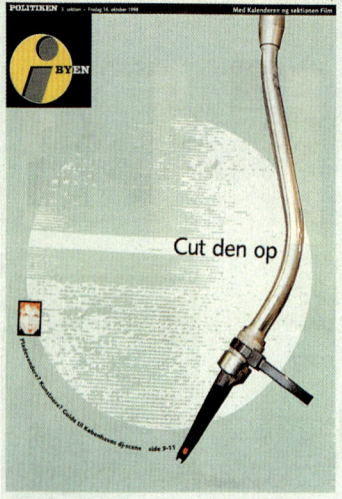

Politiken
Copenhagen, Denmark

Søren Nyeland, Design Editor; **Katinka Bukh,** Designer; **Per Bergsbo,** Designer; **Kristoffer Løve Østerbye,** Designer; **Jeanne Olsen,** Designer; **Mikkel Henssel,** Designer; **Karina Kofoed,** Junior Designer; **Stig Dyre,** Editor; **Charlotte Sejer,** Editor; **Else Bjørn,** Copy Editor

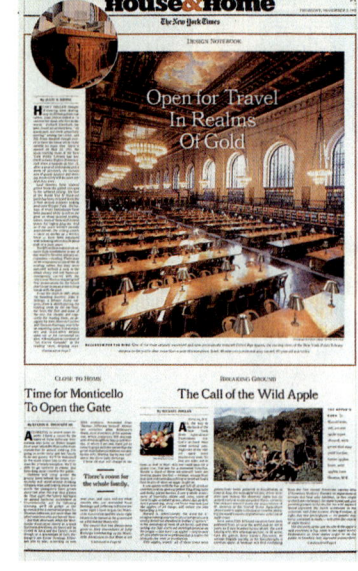

The New York Times
New York, NY

Nancy Kent, Art Director; **Barbara Graustark,** Editor; **Jeffrey Scales,** Photo Editor

Sections: Lifestyle, Other ■ FEATURES

Silver
Politiken
Copenhagen, Denmark
Søren Nyeland, Design Editor; **Jes Stein Pedersen,** Editor; **Søren Vinterberg,** Editor; **Katinka Bukh,** Designer; **Mads Holm Lauridsen,** Designer; **Jeanne Olsen,** Designer; **Anette Vestergaard,** Copy Editor; **Michael Quist Møller,** Copy Editor

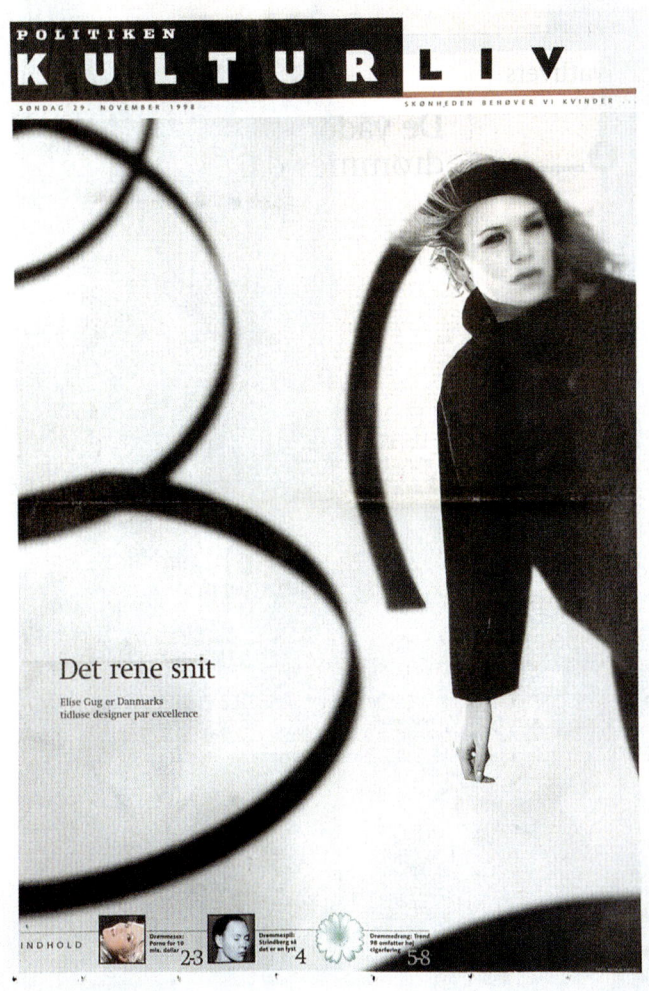
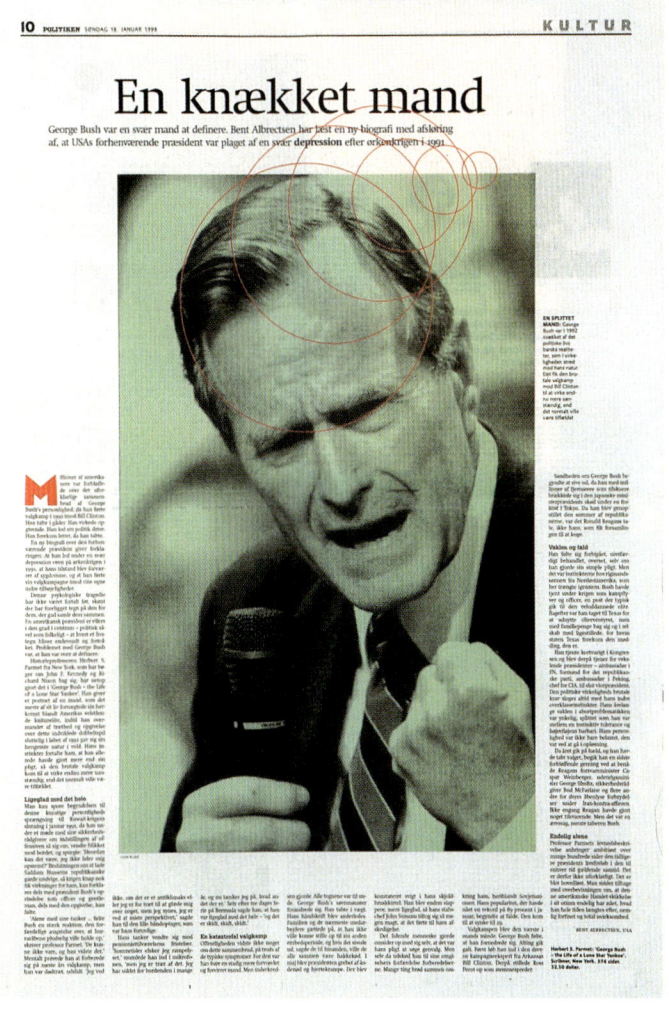

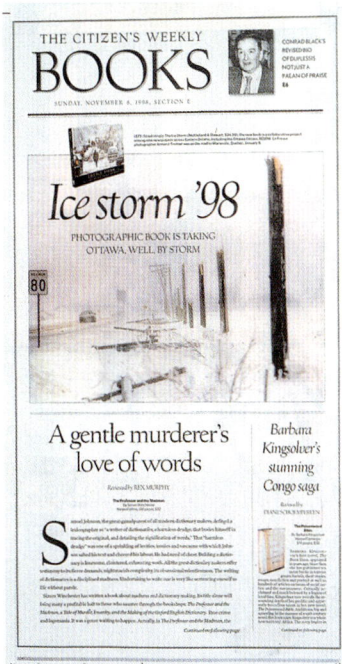

The Ottawa Citizen
Ottawa, Canada
Russell Mills, Publisher; **Neil Reynolds,** Editor; **Lynn McAuley,** Section Editor; **Kit Collins,** Designer; **Jordan Juby,** Designer; **Robert Cross,** Artist

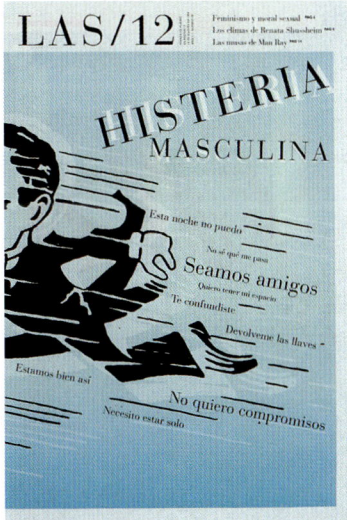

Página/12
Buenos Aires, Argentina
Alejandro Ros, Art Director; **Florencia Helguera,** Graphic Designer

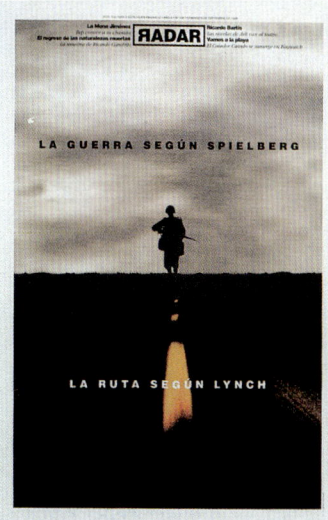

Página/12
Buenos Aires, Argentina
Alejandro Ros, Art Director; **Florencia Helguera,** Graphic Designer

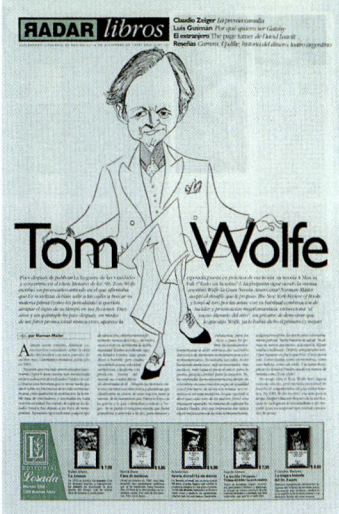

Página/12
Buenos Aires, Argentina
Alejandro Ros, Art Director; **Florencia Helguera,** Graphic Designer

FEATURES ■ Opinion Page

The Boston Globe
Boston, MA

Jane Martin, Art Director & Designer; **Chris Chinlund,** Editor; **Julie Dalton,** Copy Editor; **Daniel B. Kopans,** Staff Writer

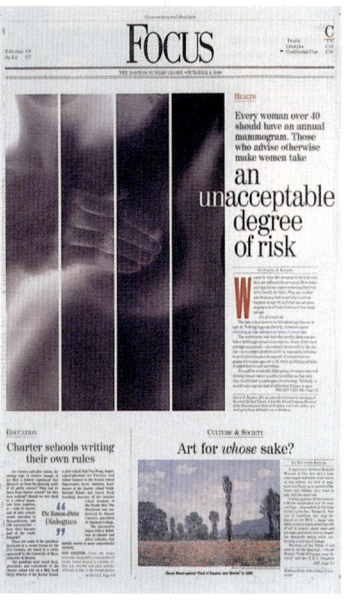

The Boston Globe
Boston, MA

Rena Anderson Sokolow, Art Director & Designer; **Jim Concannon,** Editor; **Mary Leonard,** Staff Writer; **Julie Dalton,** Copy Editor

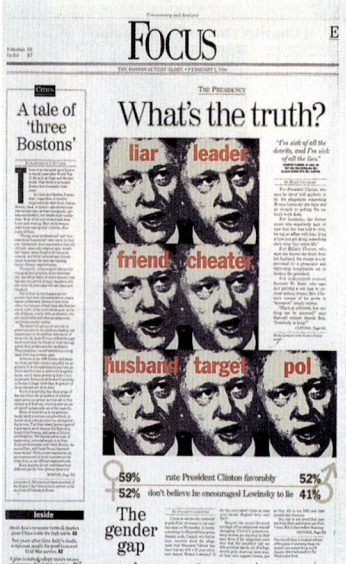

Politiken
Copenhagen, Denmark

Søren Nyeland, Design Editor; **Per M. E. Christiansen,** Editor; **John Bach,** Designer

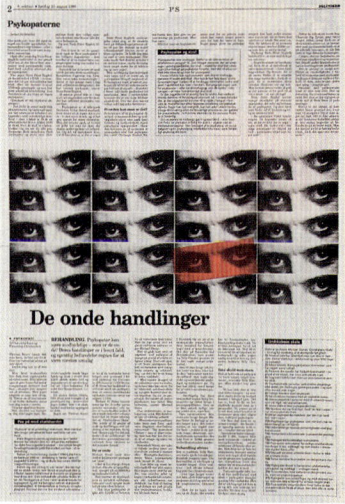

The Boston Globe
Boston, MA

Jane Martin, Art Director & Designer; **Chris Chinlund,** Editor; **Julie Dalton,** Copy Editor; **Matthew Brelis,** Staff Writer

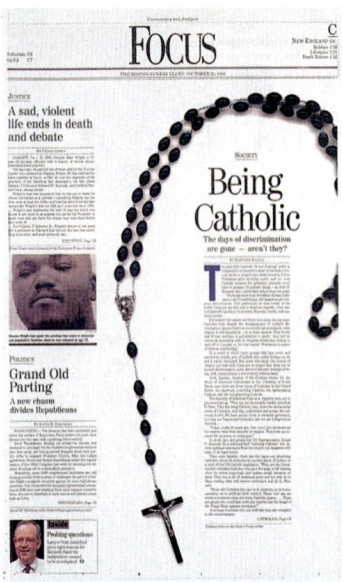

The Seattle Times
Seattle, WA

Betty Anderson, Designer; **Deb Dahrling,** Infographics Artist; **David Miller,** Art Director; **Paul Schmid,** Illustrator

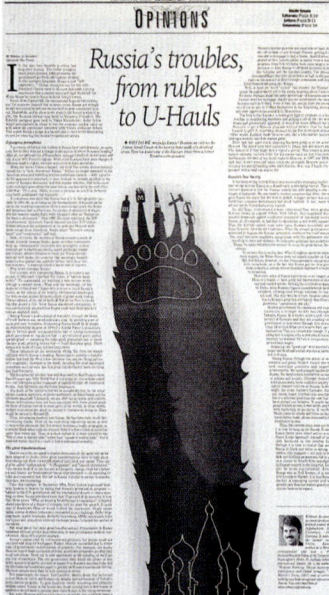

Star Tribune
Minneapolis, MN

Eddie Thomas, Page Designer

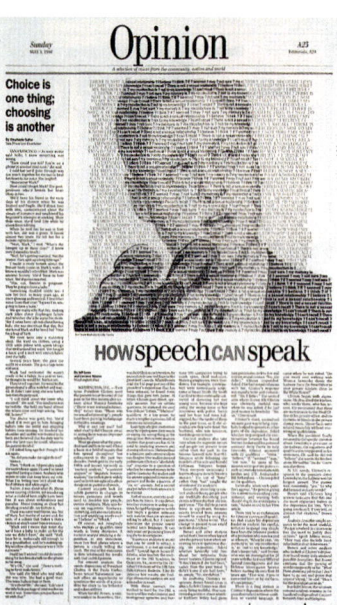

Estado de Minas
Belo Horizonte, Brasil

Álvaro Duarte, Art Director; **Rogério Carnevali,** Design Editor; **Heliane Souza,** Designer; **Alexandre Coelho,** Illustrator; **Angelo Oswaldo,** News Editor; **Carlos Perez Diaz,** Design Consultant

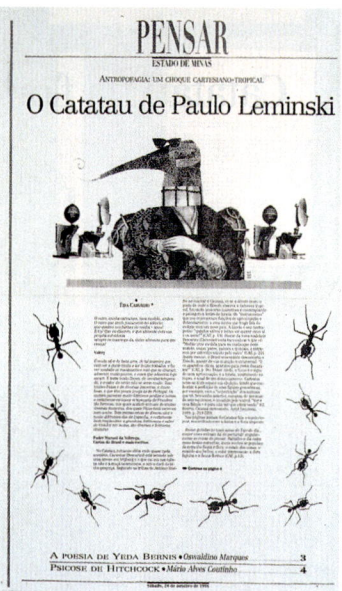

Politiken
Copenhagen, Denmark

Søren Nyeland, Design Editor; **Per M. E. Christiansen,** Editor; **Jeanne Olsen,** Designer

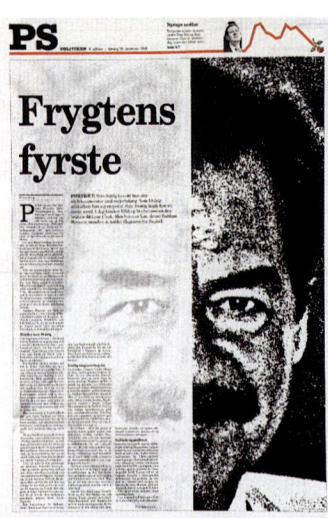

Opinion Page ■ FEATURES

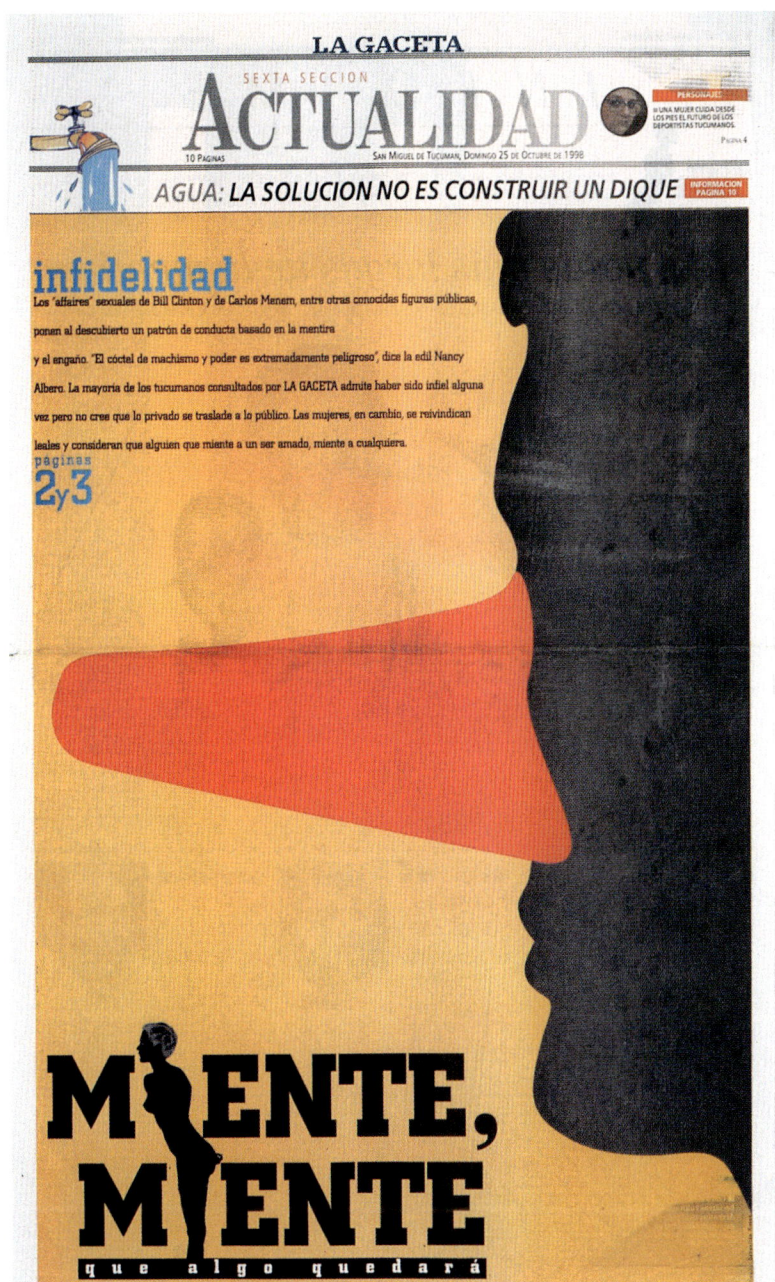

Silver
La Gaceta
San Miguel de Tucuman, Argentina
Sebastian Rosso, Designer; **Sergio Fernandez**, Art Director; **Mario García**, Design Consultant; **Federico Türpe**, Editor

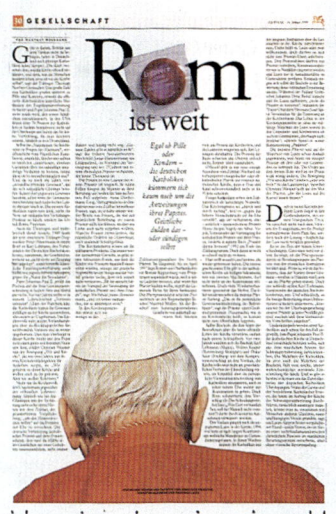

Die Woche
Hamburg, Germany
Manfred Bissinger, Editor-in-Chief; **Kurt Breme**, Executive Editor; **Hans-Ulrich Joerges**, Executive Editor; **Dirk Linke**, Art Director; **Andreas Schomberg**, Associate Art Director; **Armin Ogris**, Designer; **Stefan Semrau**, Designer; **Jessica Winter**, Designer; **Reinhard Schulz-Schaeffer**, Designer/Info Graphics; **Florian Poehl**, Designer/Info Graphics

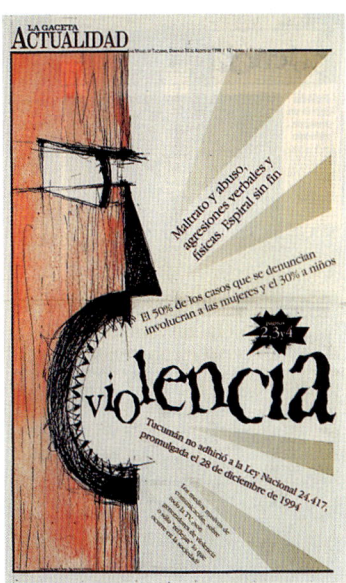

La Gaceta
San Miguel de Tucuman, Argentina
Sebastian Rosso, Illustrator & Designer; **Sergio Fernandez**, Art Director; **Mario García**, Design Consultant

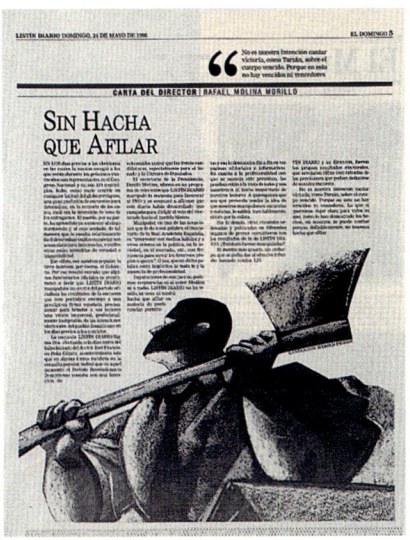

Listin Diario
Arazuri, Spain
Bega Communicacíon, Consultants; **Iban Campo**, Editor; **Julián Cobos**, Art Director; **Germán Larrañaga**, Assistant Art Director; **Harold Priego**, Illustrator

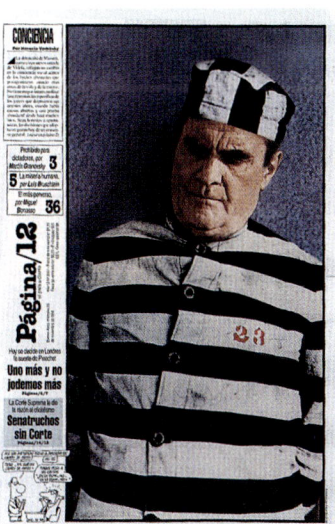

Página/12
Buenos Aires, Argentina
Eduardo Iglesias Brickles, Art Director; **Carlos Zicarelli**, Graphic Designer; **Claudio Andreotti**, Graphic Designer; **Alberto Otamendi**, Graphic Designer; **Juliana Rossato**, Graphic Designer; **Marcelo Cofan**, Graphic Designer; **Walter Molina**, Graphic Designer; **Andrea Max**, Graphic Designer

FEATURES ■ Opinion Page, Lifestyle Page

Silver
The Boston Globe
Boston, MA
Keith A. Webb, Art Director & Designer

Boulder Daily Camera
Boulder, CO
Steve Miller, Design Leader; **Scott Luxor**, Deputy M.E./Presentation

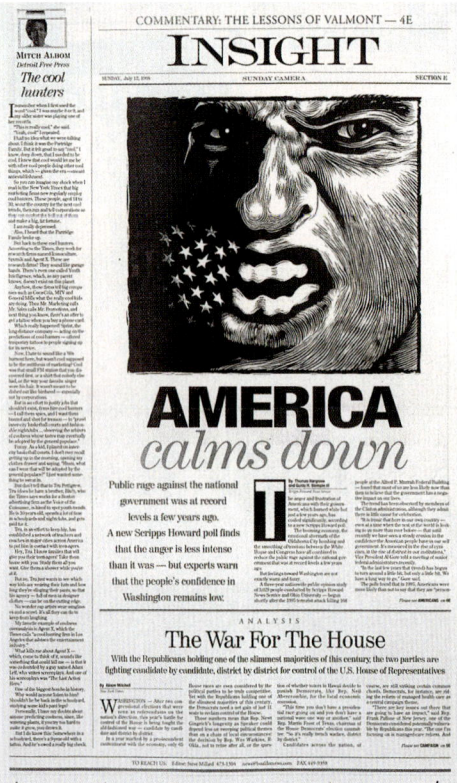

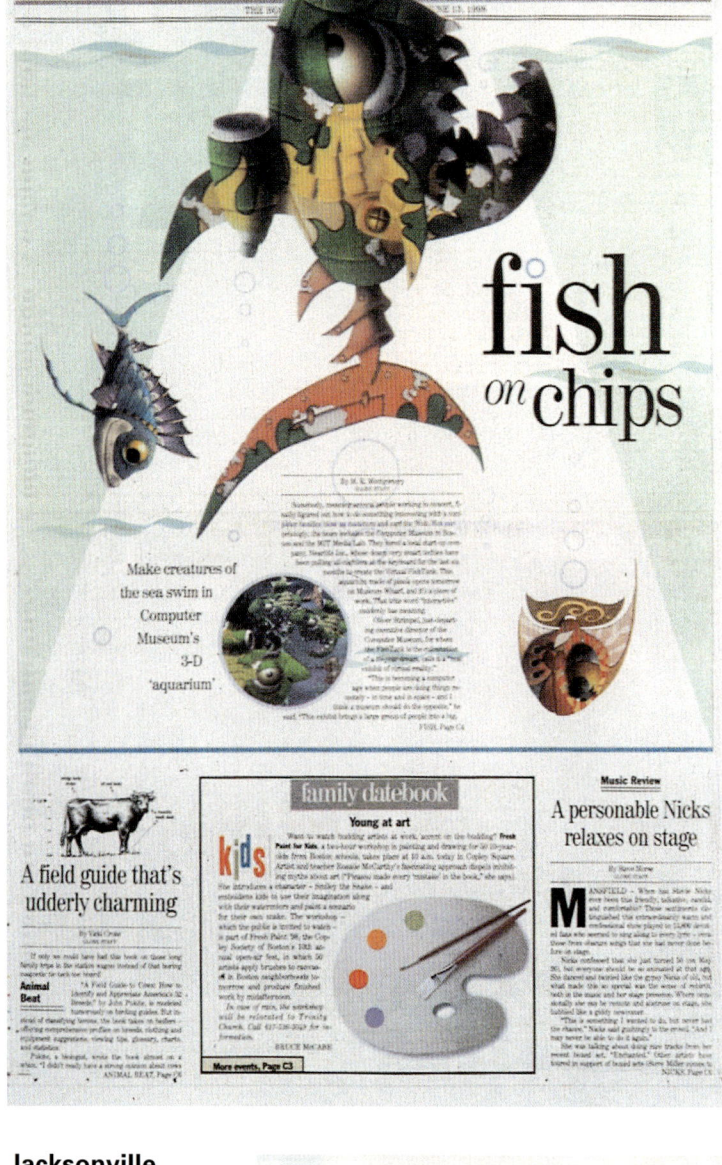

Palabra
Monterrey, México
Delgar Antonio García Quintero, Designer; **Carlos Mendoza**, Illustrator; **Sergio Lucio**, Section Editor; **Lucía Rodríguez**, Design Managing Editor; **Raúl Braulio Martínez**, Art Director

Jacksonville Journal-Courier
Jacksonville, IL
Mike Miner, Editor/Designer

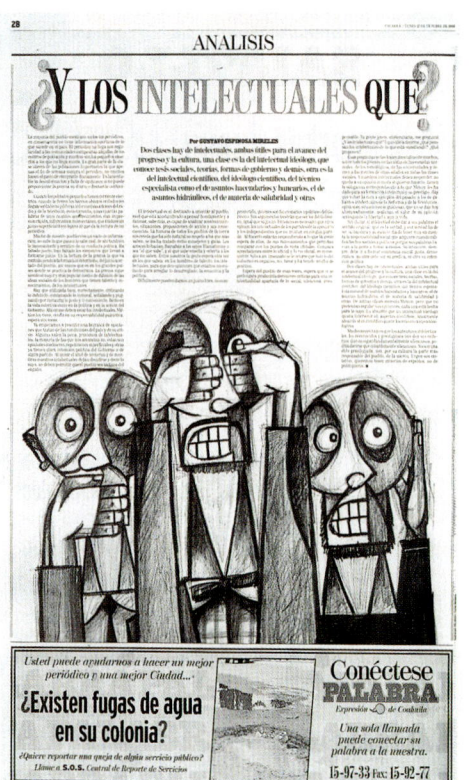

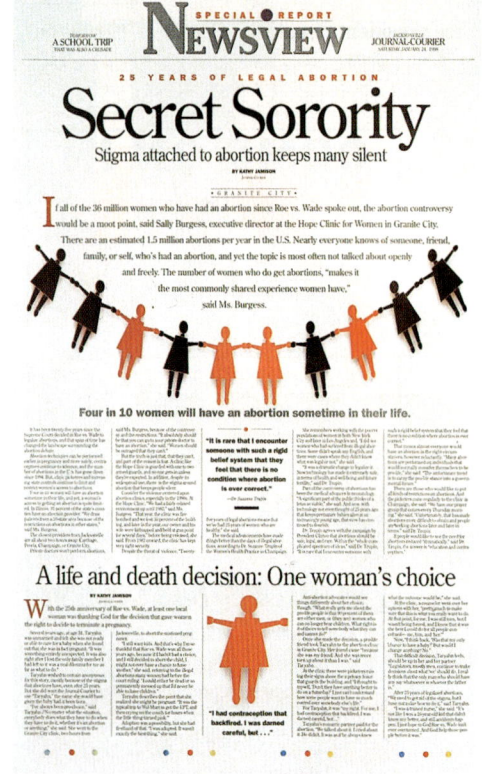

Gold
Morgenavisen Jyllands-Posten
Viby J., Denmark
Bodil Krogh, Editor/Page Designer/Illustrator; **Stig Olesen**, Reporter

The simple drawing adds to this well-designed page. What better way to illustrate the topic? Simplicity worked for the designer.

El sencillo dibujo contribuye a esta página bien diseñada. ¿Qué mejor manera de ilustrar el tema? La simplicidad trabajó a favor del diseñador.

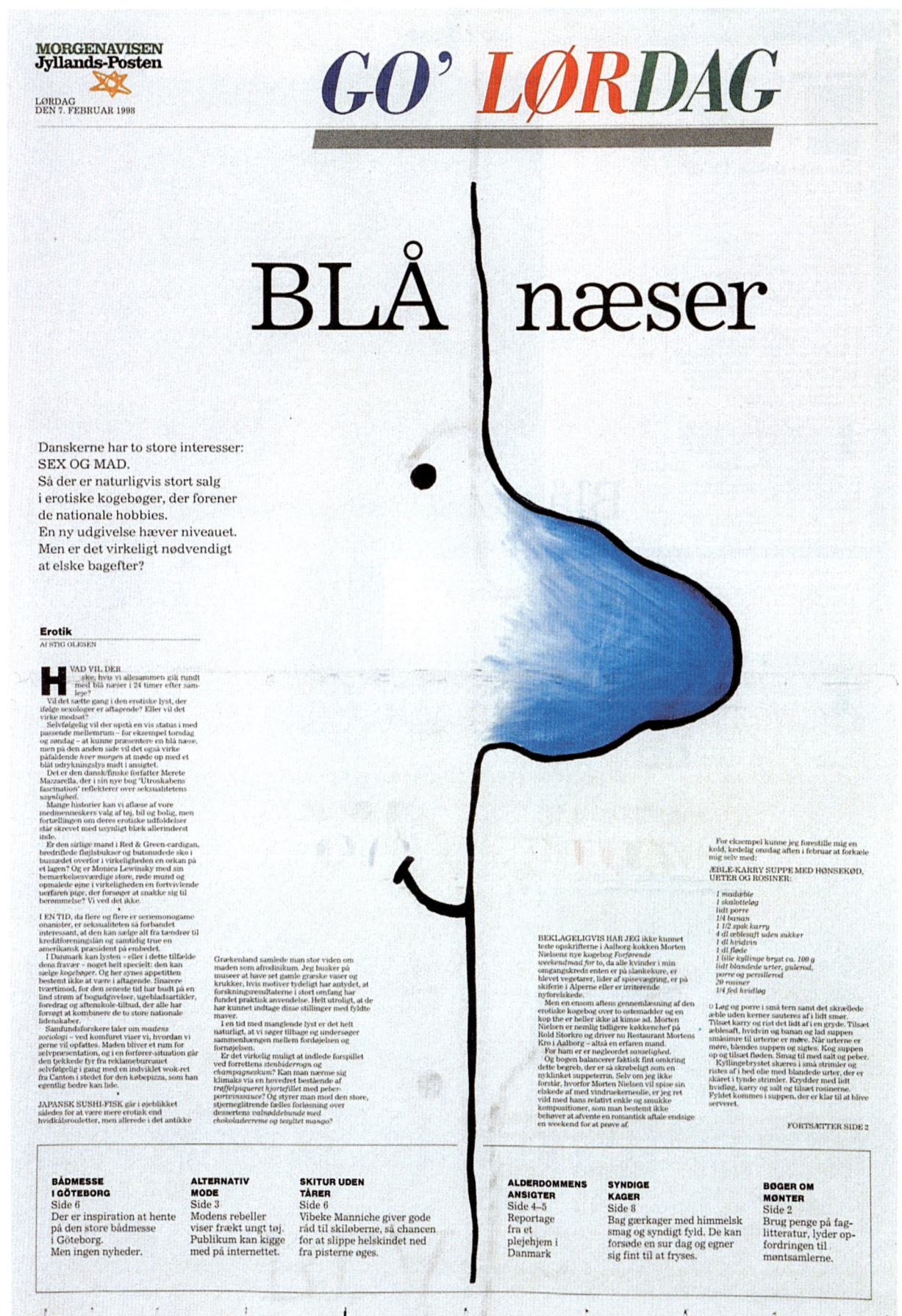

FEATURES — Lifestyle Page

Silver
The National Post
Don Mills, Canada

Gayle Grin, Designer/Design Editor; **Rene Zamie,** Illustrator; **Peter Scowen,** Toronto Editor; **Kenneth Whyte,** Editor-in-Chief

Silver
The Charlotte Observer
Charlotte, NC

Monica Moses, Design Director; **Ted Yee,** Designer; **Gina Nania,** Copy Editor; **Anna Griffin,** Staff Writer; **The' Pham,** Photo Editor; **Mike Weinstein,** Section Editor; **Laura Mueller,** Photographer

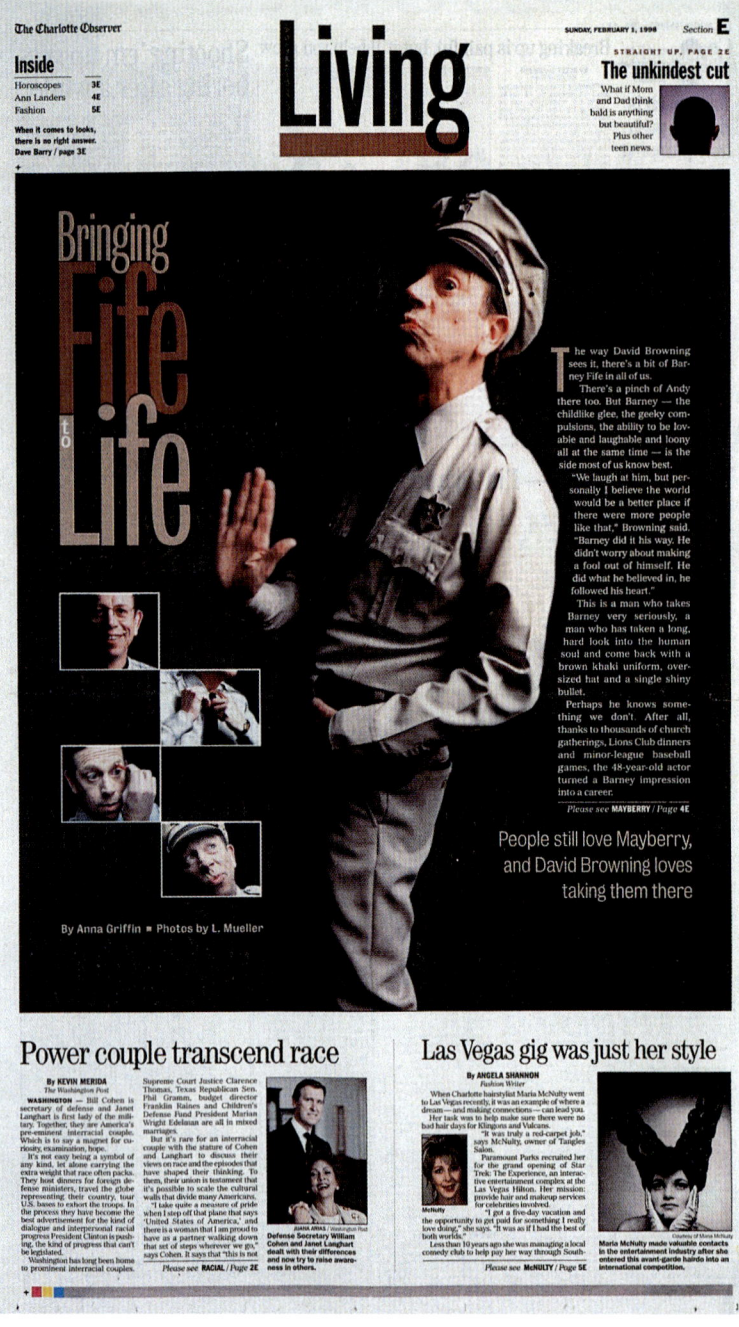

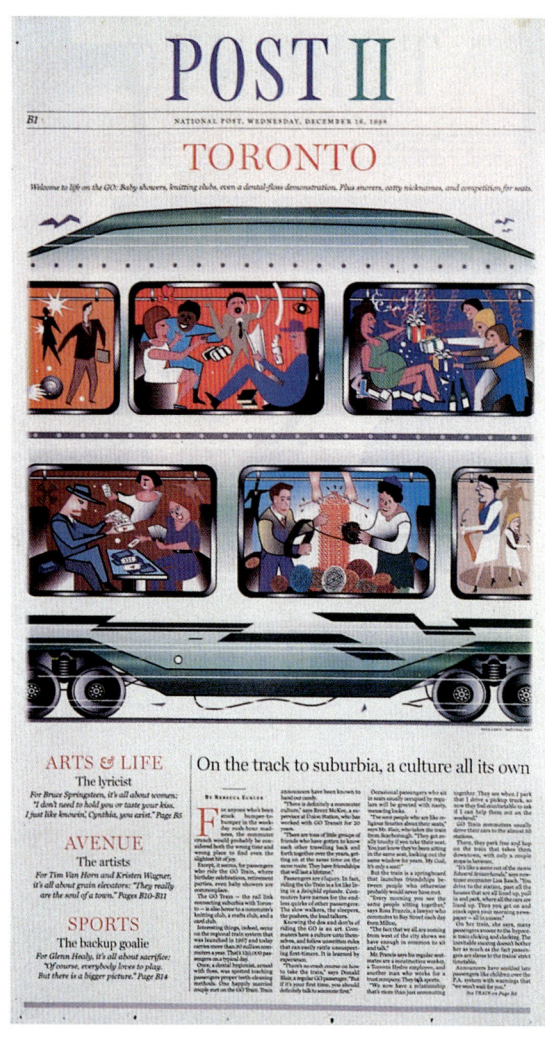

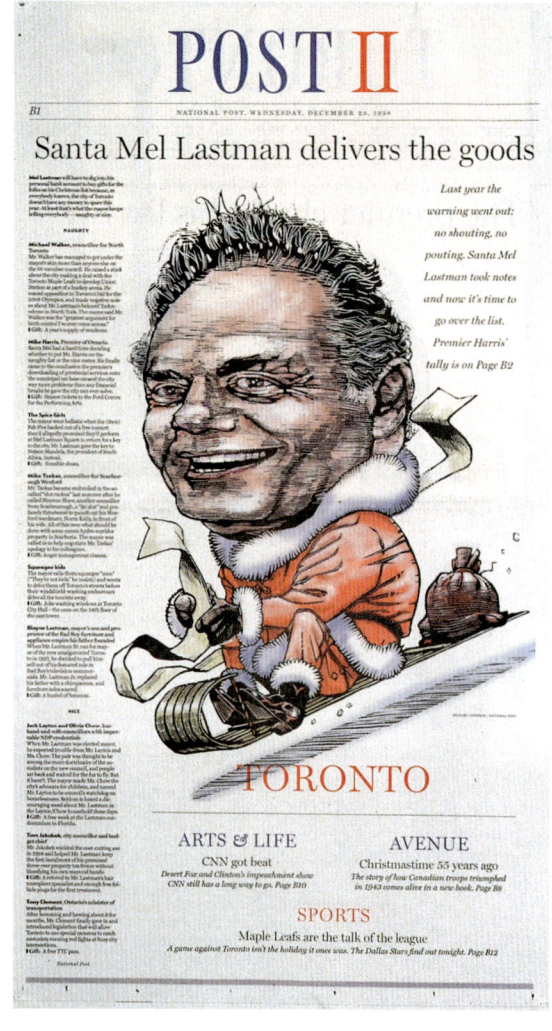

Silver
The National Post
Don Mills, Canada

Gayle Grin, Designer/Design Editor; **Richard Johnson,** Illustrator; **Peter Scowen,** Toronto Editor; **Tim Rostrum,** Arts Editor; **Diane de Fenoyl,** Living Editor; **Kenneth Whyte,** Editor-in-Chief; **Lucie Lacava,** Design Consultant
• also an Award of Excellence for Lifesyle Section

Lifestyle Page ■ FEATURES

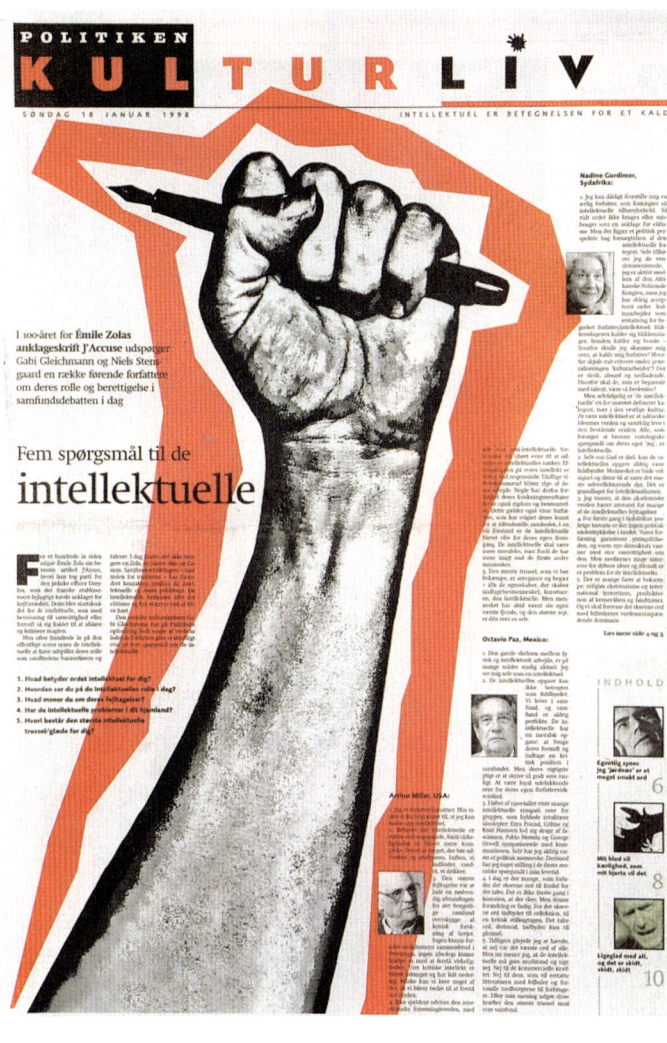

Silver
Politiken
Copenhagen, Denmark
Søren Nyeland, Design Editor; **Søren Vinterberg,** Editor; **Katinka Bukh,** Designer

Silver
Morgenavisen Jyllands-Posten
Viby J., Denmark
Bodil Krogh, Editor/Page Designer; **Lars Pryds,** Illustrator

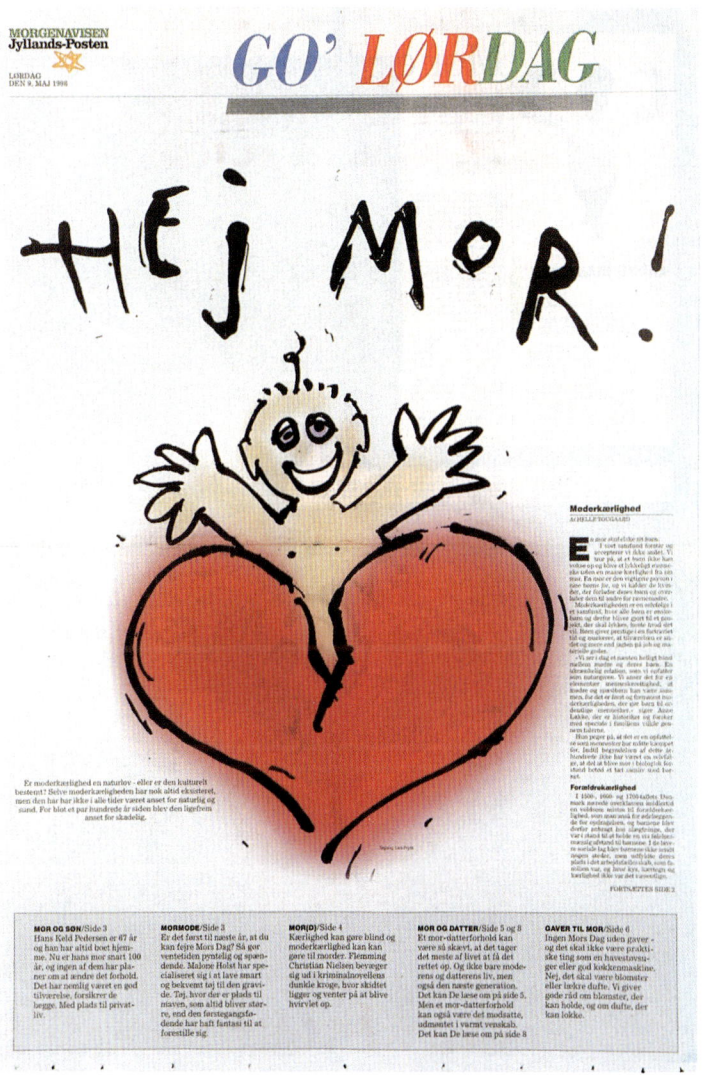

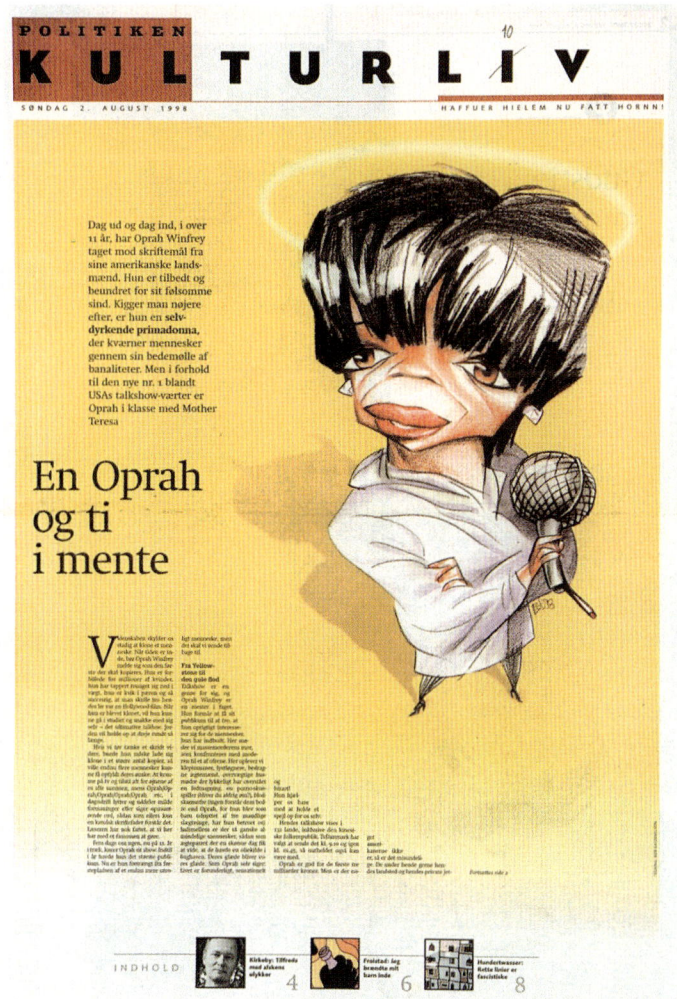

Silver
Politiken
Copenhagen, Denmark
Søren Nyeland, Design Editor; **Søren Vinterberg,** Editor; **Peter Sætternissen,** Designer; **Bob Katzenelson,** Artist

TWENTIETH EDITION ■ 97

FEATURES — Lifestyle Page

Silver
Pittsburgh Post-Gazette
Pittsburgh, PA
K.C. Conner, Artist

Silver
San Jose Mercury News
San Jose, CA
David Frazier, Page Designer
• also an Award of Excellence for Features Portfolio

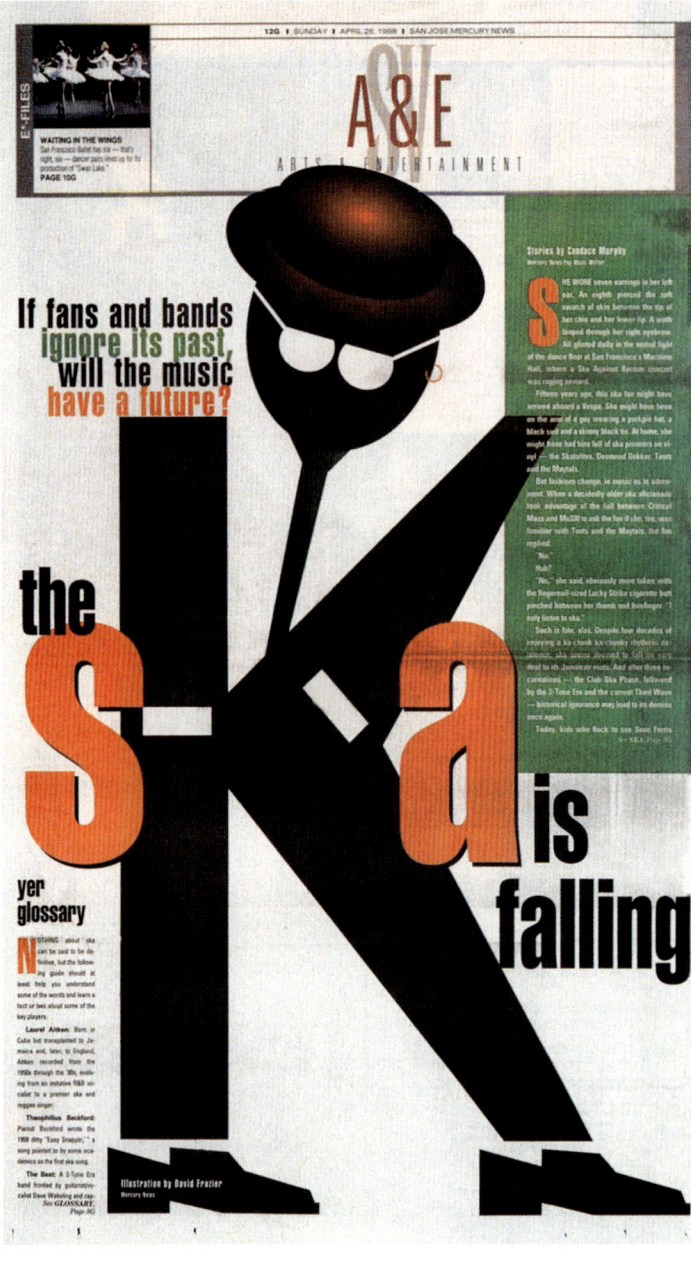

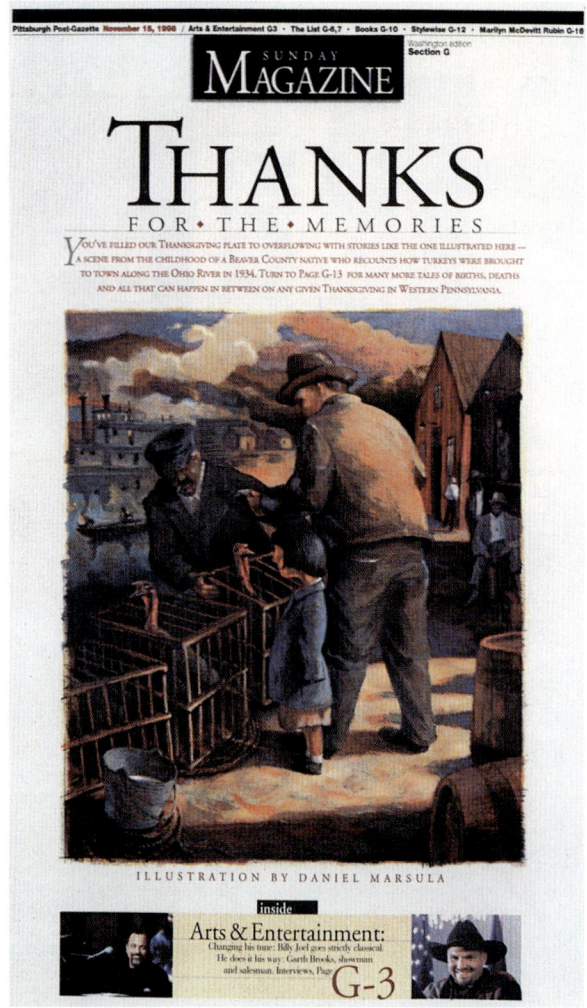

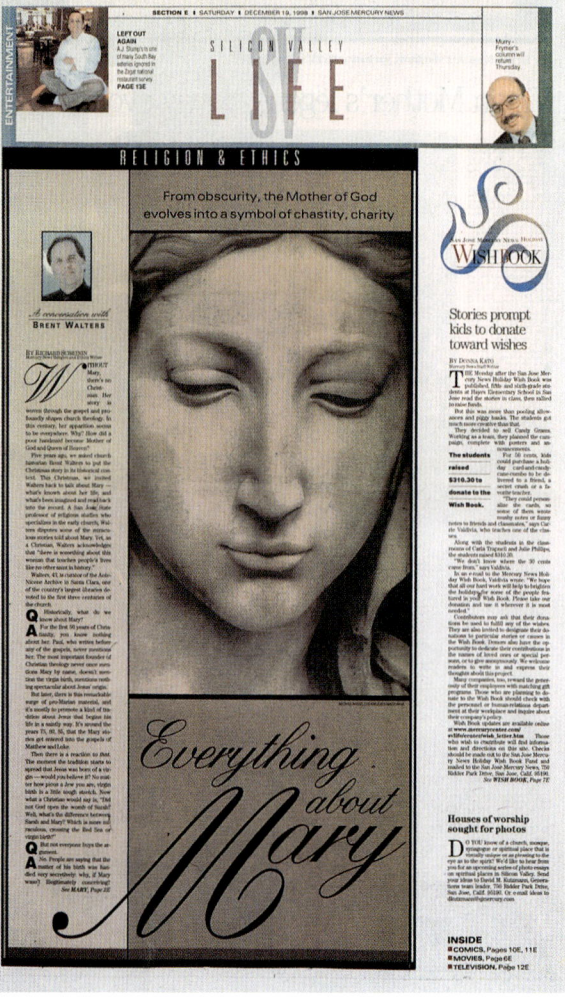

Silver
San Jose Mercury News
San Jose, CA
Jenny Anderson, Features Designer; **Sue Morrow**, Features Design Director

Lifestyle Page ■ FEATURES

The Charlotte Observer
Charlotte, NC
Monica Moses, Design Director; **Ted Yee,** Designer; **Gayle Shomer,** Photographer; **Susan Gilbert,** Director/Photography; **The' Pham,** Photo Editor; **Leigh Dyer,** Staff Writer; **Caroline Beyrau,** Editor; **Alix Felsing,** Copy Editor; **David Vest,** Copy Editor

The Charlotte Observer
Charlotte, NC
Monica Moses, Design Director; **Ted Yee,** Designer; **Gayle Shomer,** Photographer; **Susan Gilbert,** Director/Photography; **The' Pham,** Photo Editor; **Leigh Dyer,** Staff Writer; **Caroline Beyrau,** Editor; **Alix Felsing,** Copy Editor; **David Vest,** Copy Editor

Detroit Free Press
Detroit, MI
Jamila Robinson, Designer; **Susan Tusa,** Photographer; **Andrew Johnston,** Photo Editor

Dagens Nyheter
Stockholm, Sweden
Nina Andén, Designer

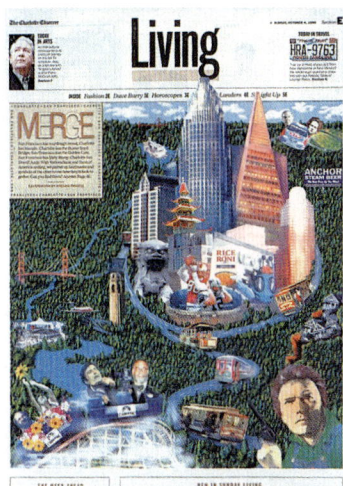
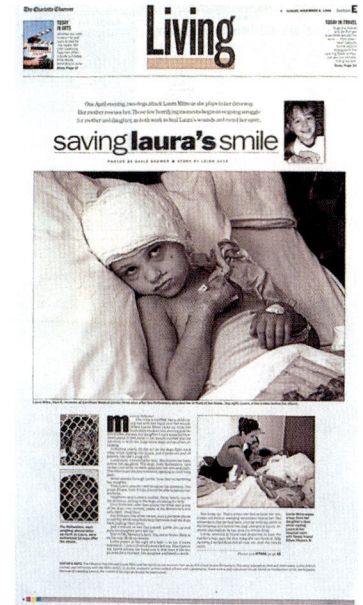
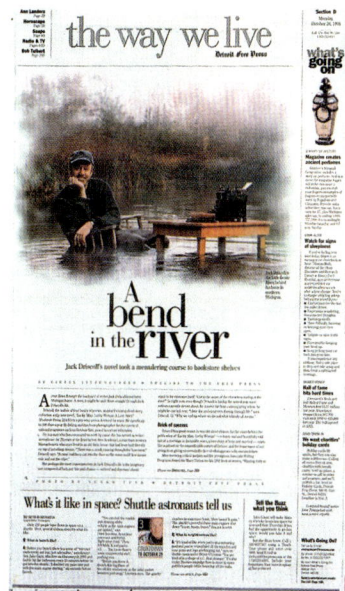
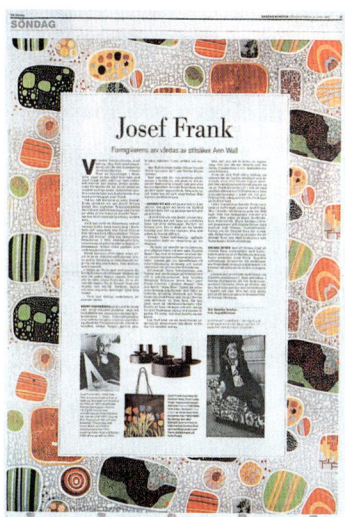

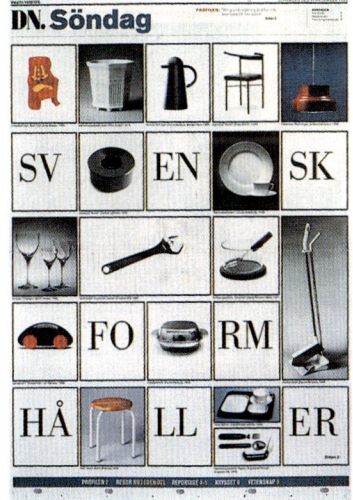
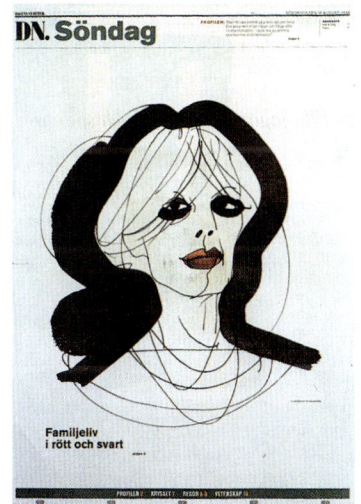
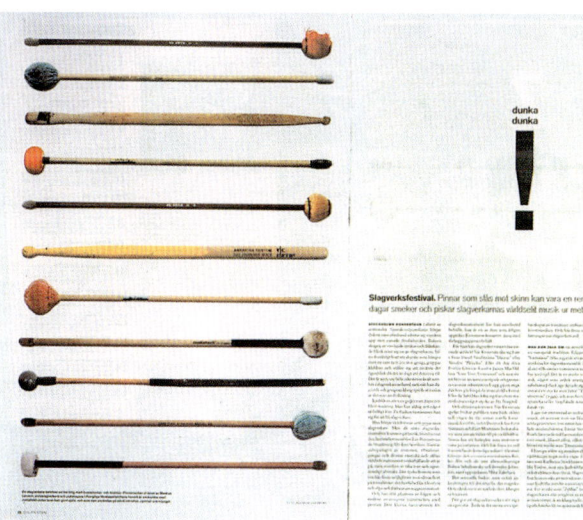

Dagens Nyheter
Stockholm, Sweden
Hakan Burell, Designer

Dagens Nyheter
Stockholm, Sweden
Maria Huldt, Designer; **Stina Wirsén,** Artist

Dagens Nyheter
Stockholm, Sweden
Magnus Naddermier, Art Director; **Beatrice Lundborg,** Photographer

FEATURES — Lifestyle Page

Dagens Nyheter
Stockholm, Sweden
Håkan Burell, Designer; **Jens Assur,** Photographer

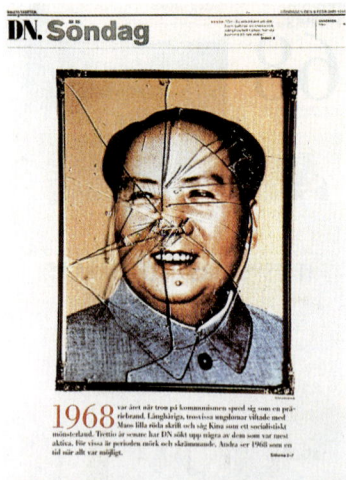

O Globo
Rio de Janeiro, Brasil
Leonardo Drummond, Designer; **Marilia Martins,** Editor

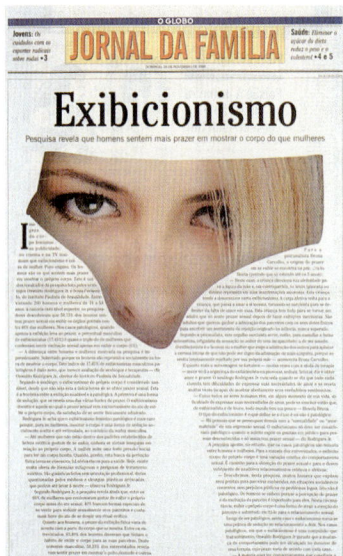

Göteborgs-Posten
Göteborg, Sweden
Thomas Andersson, Designer; **Brad White,** Photographer

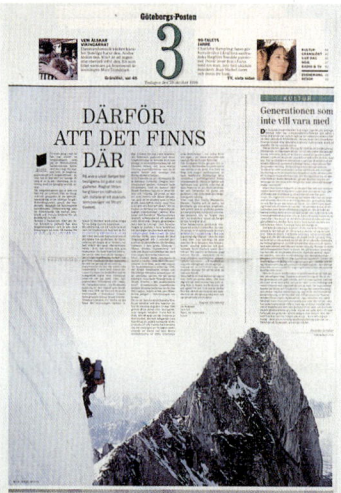

The Hartford Courant
Hartford, CT
Melanie Shaffer, Designer; **Scott Johnson,** Assistant Art Director

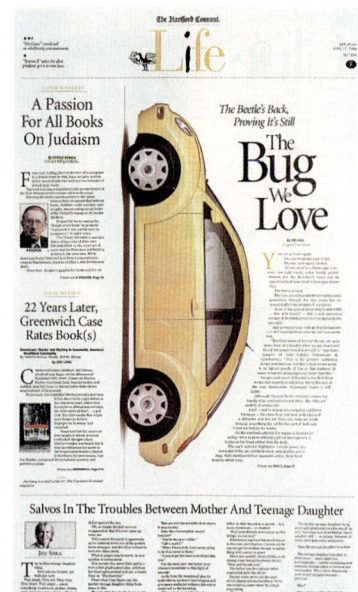

The Hartford Courant
Hartford, CT
Melanie Shaffer, Designer; **Christian P. Drury,** Art Director; **Scott Johnson,** Assistant Art Director

Morgenavisen Jyllands-Posten
Viby J., Denmark
Lars Pryds, Page Designer; **Finn Koch,** Editor; **Søren Lorenzen,** Photographer

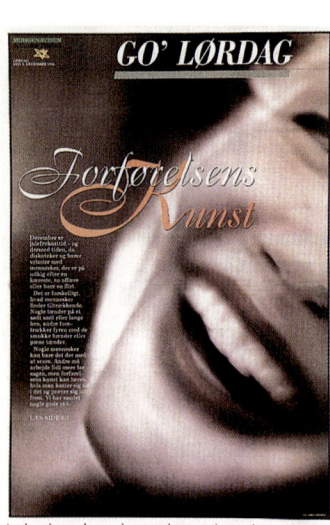

The National Post
Don Mills, Canada
Gayle Grin, Designer/Design Editor; **Jamie Bennett,** Illustrator; **Peter Scowen,** Toronto Editor; **Kenneth Whyte,** Editor-in-Chief; **Tim Rostrum,** Arts Editor; **Rebecca Eckler,** Writer
• also for Illustration Three or More Colors

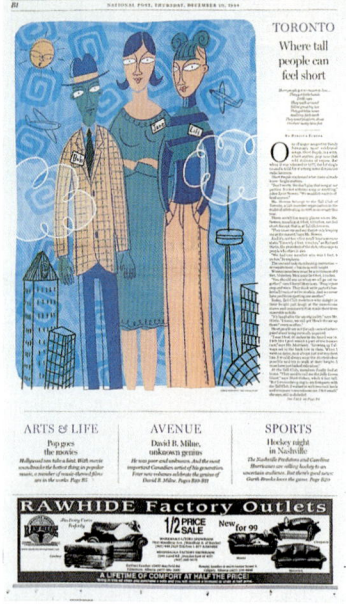

The National Post
Don Mills, Canada
Gayle Grin, Designer/Design Editor; **Tim Rostrum,** Arts Editor; **Peter Scowen,** Toronto Editor; **Kenneth Whyte,** Editor-in-Chief; **Diane de Fenoyl,** Living Editor

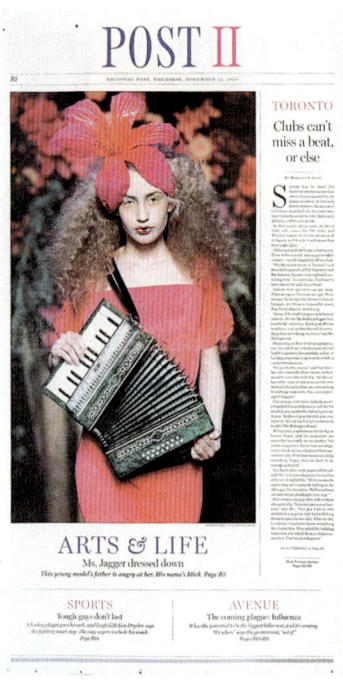

Lifestyle Page ■ FEATURES

The Orange County Register
Santa Ana, CA
Lewis Leung, Designer; **Kris Viesselman Onuigbo,** Art Director; **Dee Doyles,** Art Director

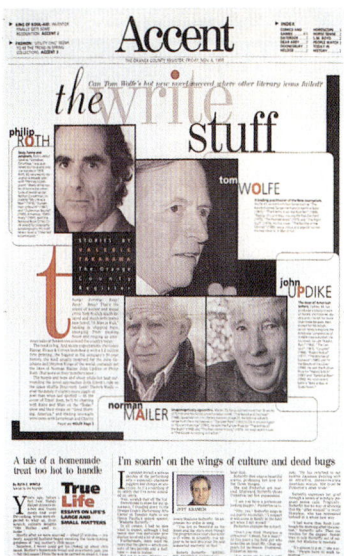

The Orange County Register
Santa Ana, CA
Dee Boyles, Illustrator & Designer

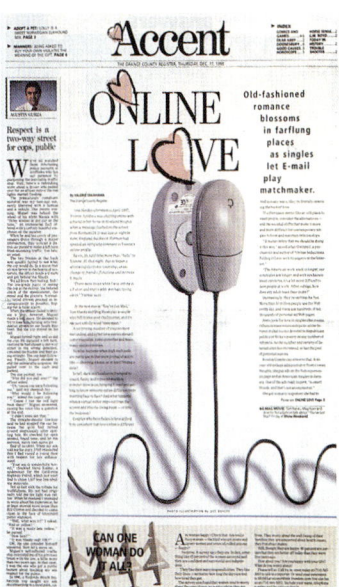

The Orange County Register
Santa Ana, CA
Dee Boyles, Art Director; **Martin Gee,** Designer; **Kris Viesselman Onuigbo,** Art Director

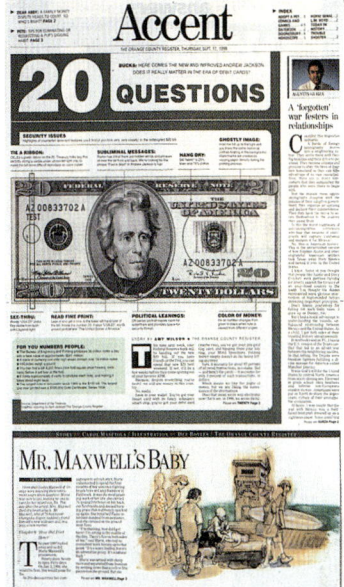

The Oregonian
Portland, OR
Patrick McLelland, Graphic Artist; **Lisa Russo,** Graphics Researcher; **Beth Weissman,** Page Designer; **Steve McKinstry,** Art Director

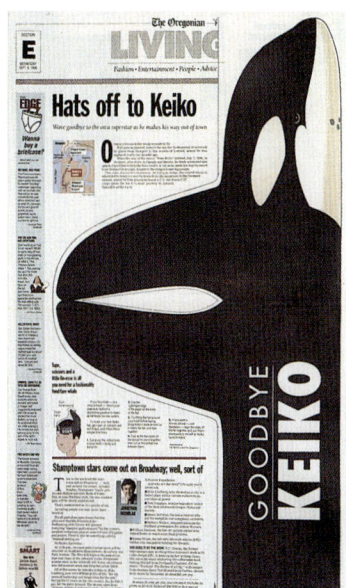

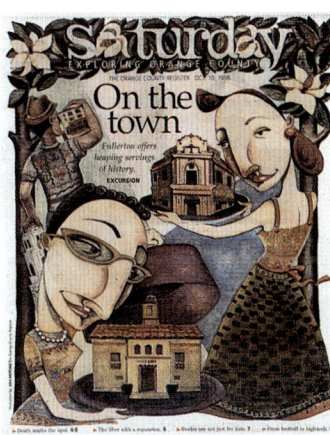

The Orange County Register
Santa Ana, CA
Patty Pitts, Designer; **Lisa Mertins,** Artist; **Kris Viesselman Onuigbo,** Art Director; **Dee Boyles,** Art Director

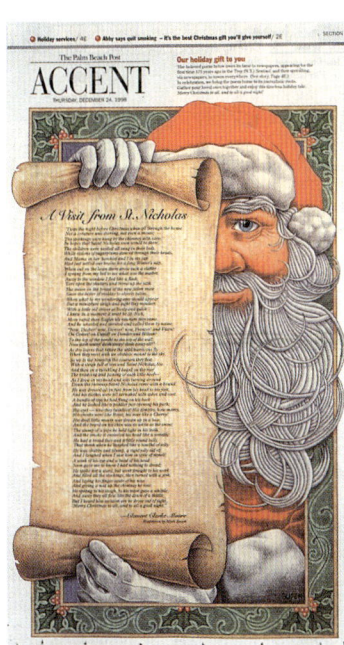

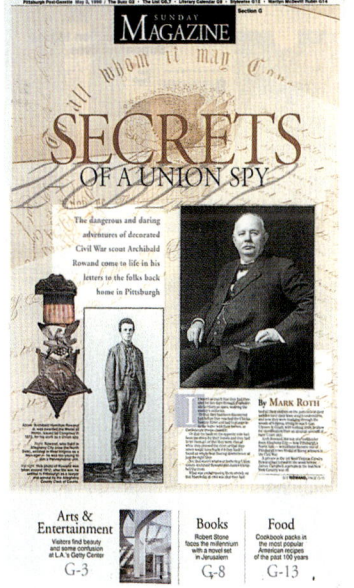

Pittsburgh Post-Gazette
Pittsburgh, PA
K.C. Conner, Artist

The Palm Beach Post
W. Palm Beach, FL
Mark Buzek, Artist/Designer

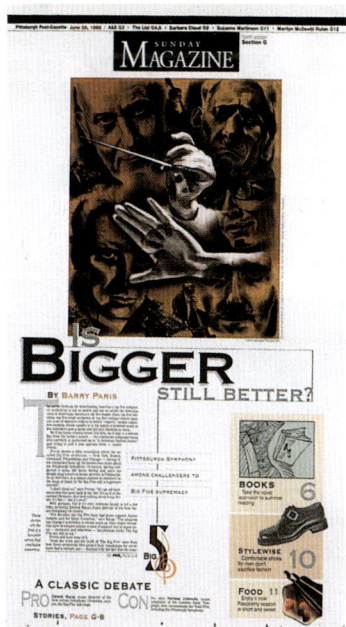

Pittsburgh Post-Gazette
Pittsburgh, PA
K.C. Conner, Staff Artist

TWENTIETH EDITION ■ 101

FEATURES — Lifestyle Page

San Jose Mercury News
San Jose, CA
Jenny Anderson, Features Designer/Illustrator; **Sue Morrow,** Features Design Director
• also for Illustration Three or More Colors

San Jose Mercury News
San Jose, CA
Rebecca Hall, Features Designer; **Sue Morrow,** Features Design Director; **Eugene Louie,** Photographer

The San Diego Union-Tribune
San Diego, CA
Martina Schimitschek, Designer

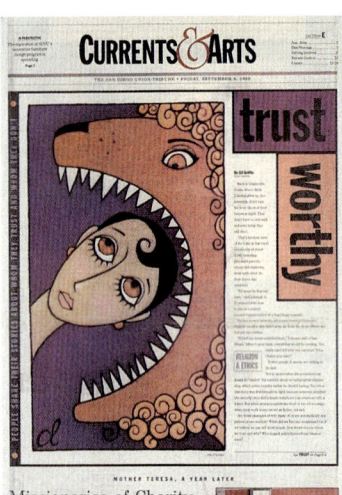

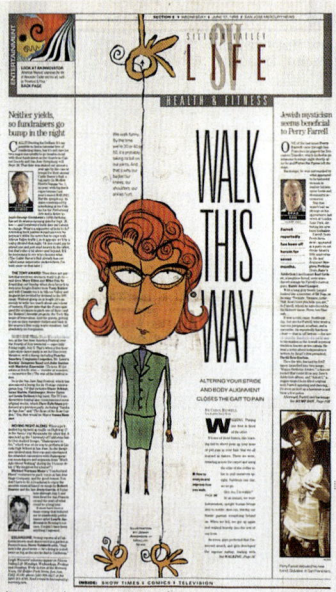

San Jose Mercury News
San Jose, CA
Rebecca Hall, Features Designer; **Sue Morrow,** Features Design Director; **Eugene Louie,** Photographer

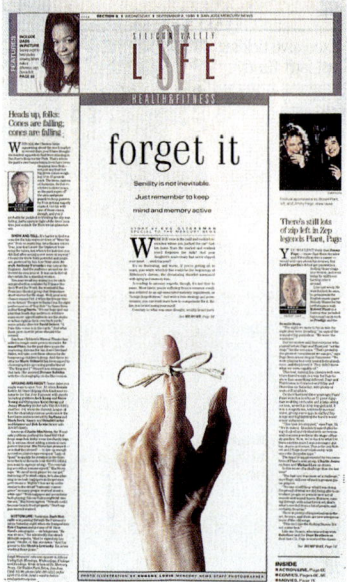

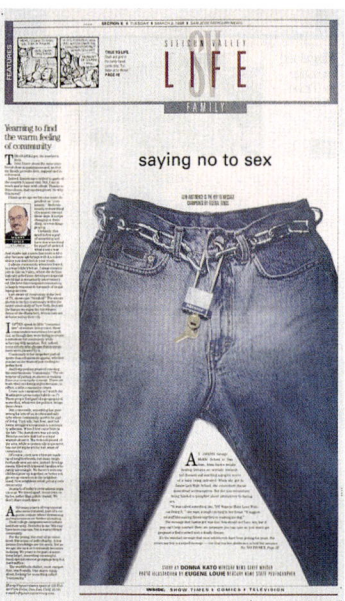

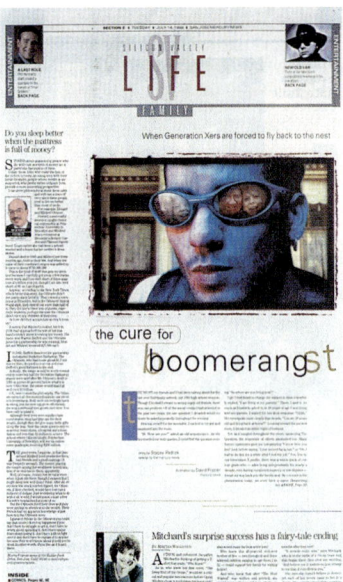

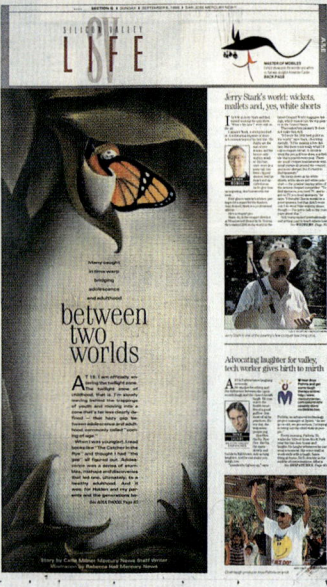

San Jose Mercury News
San Jose, CA
Rebecca Hall, Features Designer; **Sue Morrow,** Features Design Director

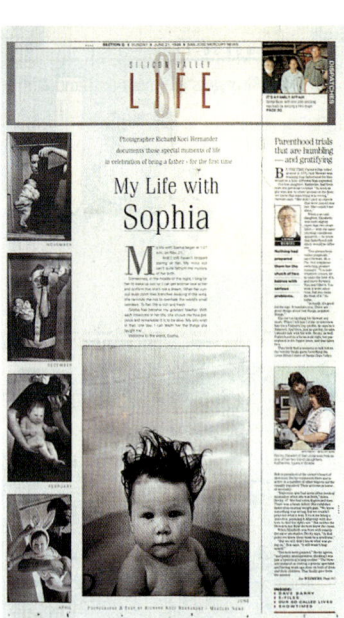

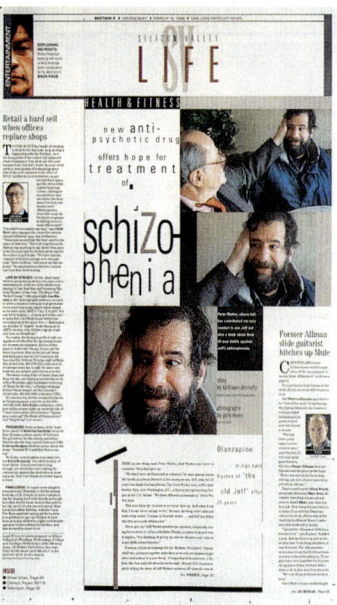

San Jose Mercury News
San Jose, CA
David Frazier, Page Designer

San Jose Mercury News
San Jose, CA
David Frazier, Page Designer

San Jose Mercury News
San Jose, CA
Sue Morrow, Features Design Director

Lifestyle Page ■ FEATURES

The Seattle Times
Seattle, WA
Tracy Porter, Designer; **David Miller**, Art Director

Star Tribune
Minneapolis, MN
Denise M. Reagan, Designer/Art Director

Seattle Post-Intelligencer
Seattle, WA
Duane Hoffmann, Designer

The St. Petersburg Times
St. Petersburg, FL
Gregory Perez, Designer; **Steve Persall**, Reporter

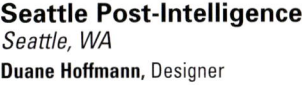
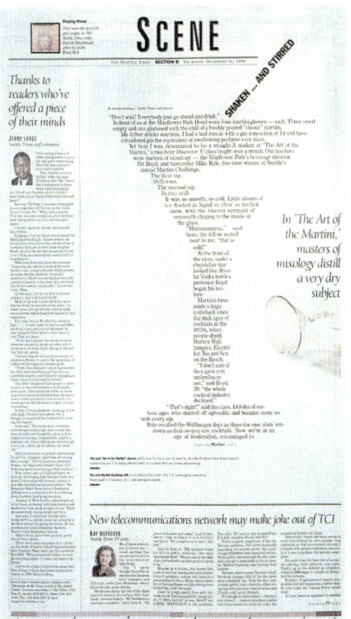
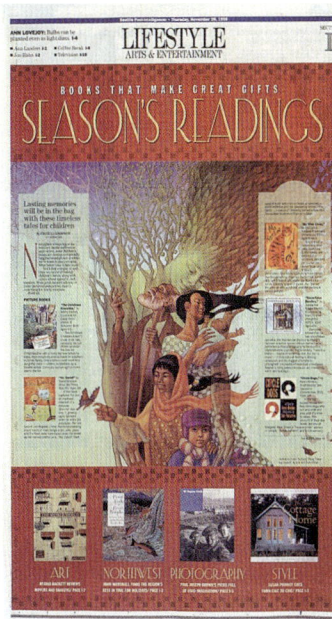
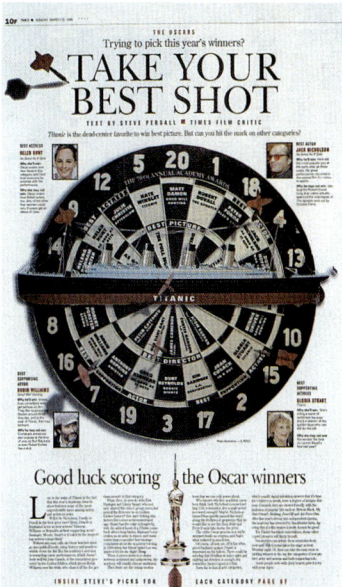
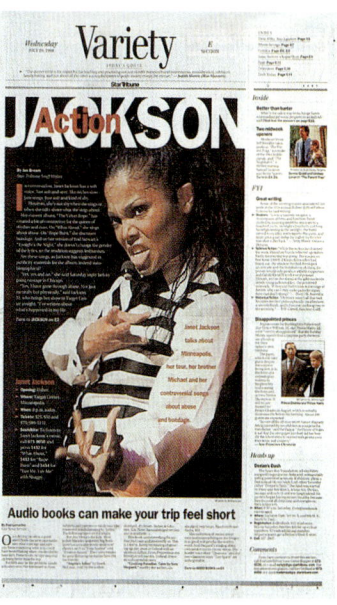

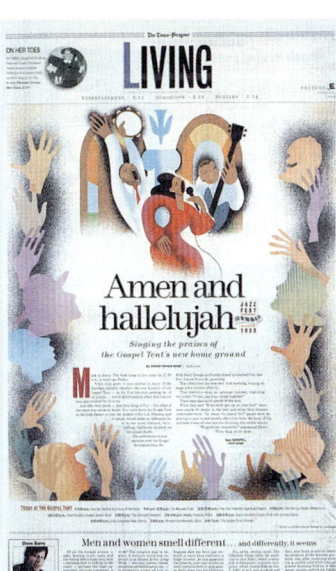
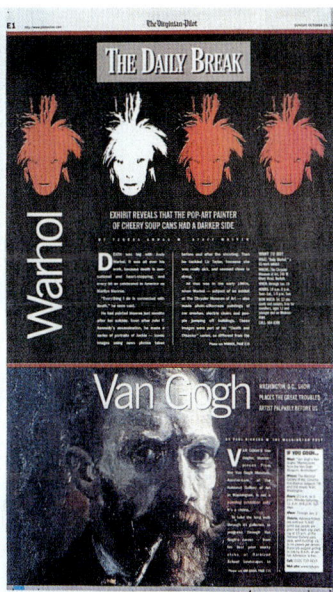
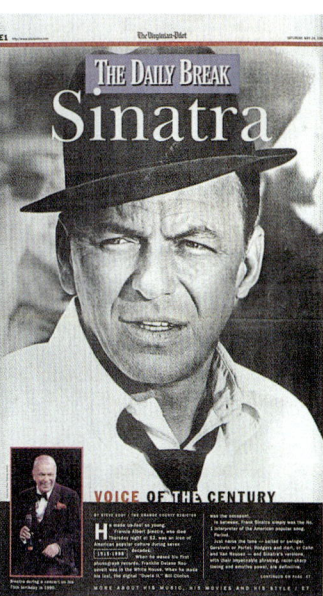
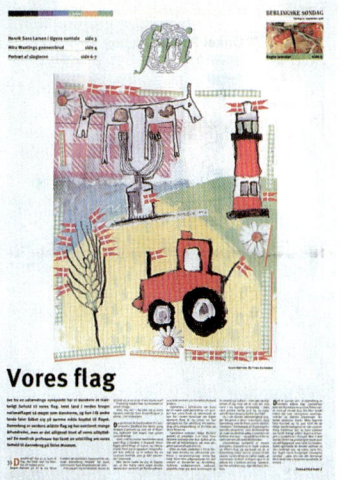

The Virginian-Pilot
Norfolk, VA
Latané Jones, Designer; **Bob Fleming**, Editor

Berlingske Tidende
Copenhagen, Denmark
Bettina Kofmann, Page Designer

The Times-Picayune
New Orleans, LA
Julia Nead, Designer; **Jean McIntosh**, Art Director; **Kenneth Harrison**, Illustrator; **Bettye Anding**, Editor

The Virginian-Pilot
Norfolk, VA
Sam Hundley, Designer; **Bob Fleming**, Editor

FEATURES ■ Lifestyle Page

Gold
Politiken
Copenhagen, Denmark
Søren Nyeland, Design Editor; **Katinka Bukh**, Designer

This page is music and has a lot of rhythm. Each individual photo has passion and energy. The way photos are stacked and designed gives the page the same energy.

Esta página es música y tiene mucho ritmo. Cada foto individual desprende pasión y energía. El modo en que las fotos están dispuestas y diseñadas le confiere a la página la misma energía.

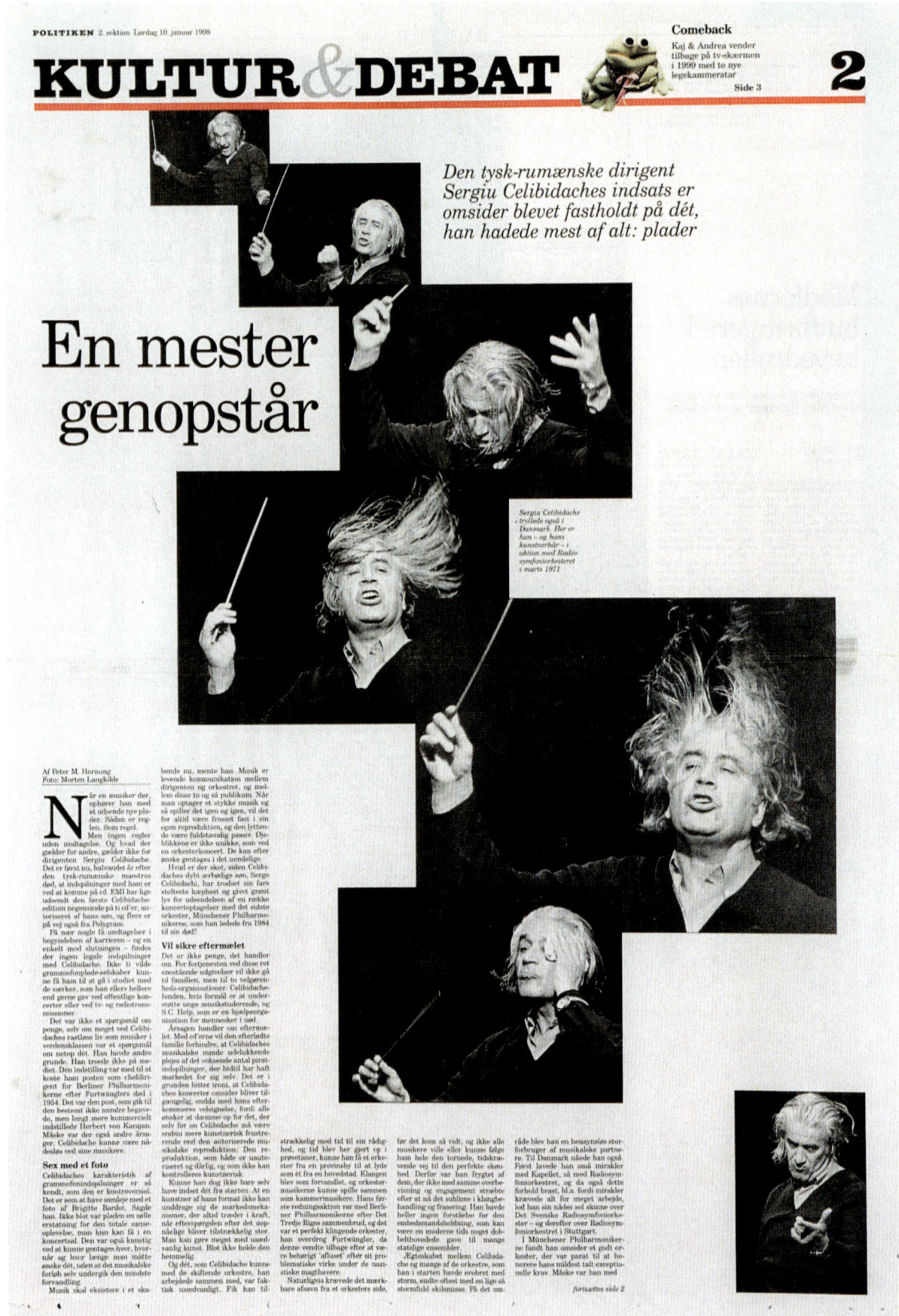

Lifestyle Page ■ FEATURES

Gold
Politiken
Copenhagen, Denmark
Søren Nyeland, Design Editor; **Per Bergsbo**, Designer

This is one of the pages you wish you had done. The page makes you smile. We love the humor in it. Every detail on the page has been taken care of. Many elements used, yet so simple.

Esta es una de las páginas que uno desearía haber realizado. La página nos hace sonreír y nos encanta el humor que tiene. Se ha prestado atención a cada uno de los detalles de la página. Se han utilizado numerosos elementos y, no obstante, es tan sencilla.

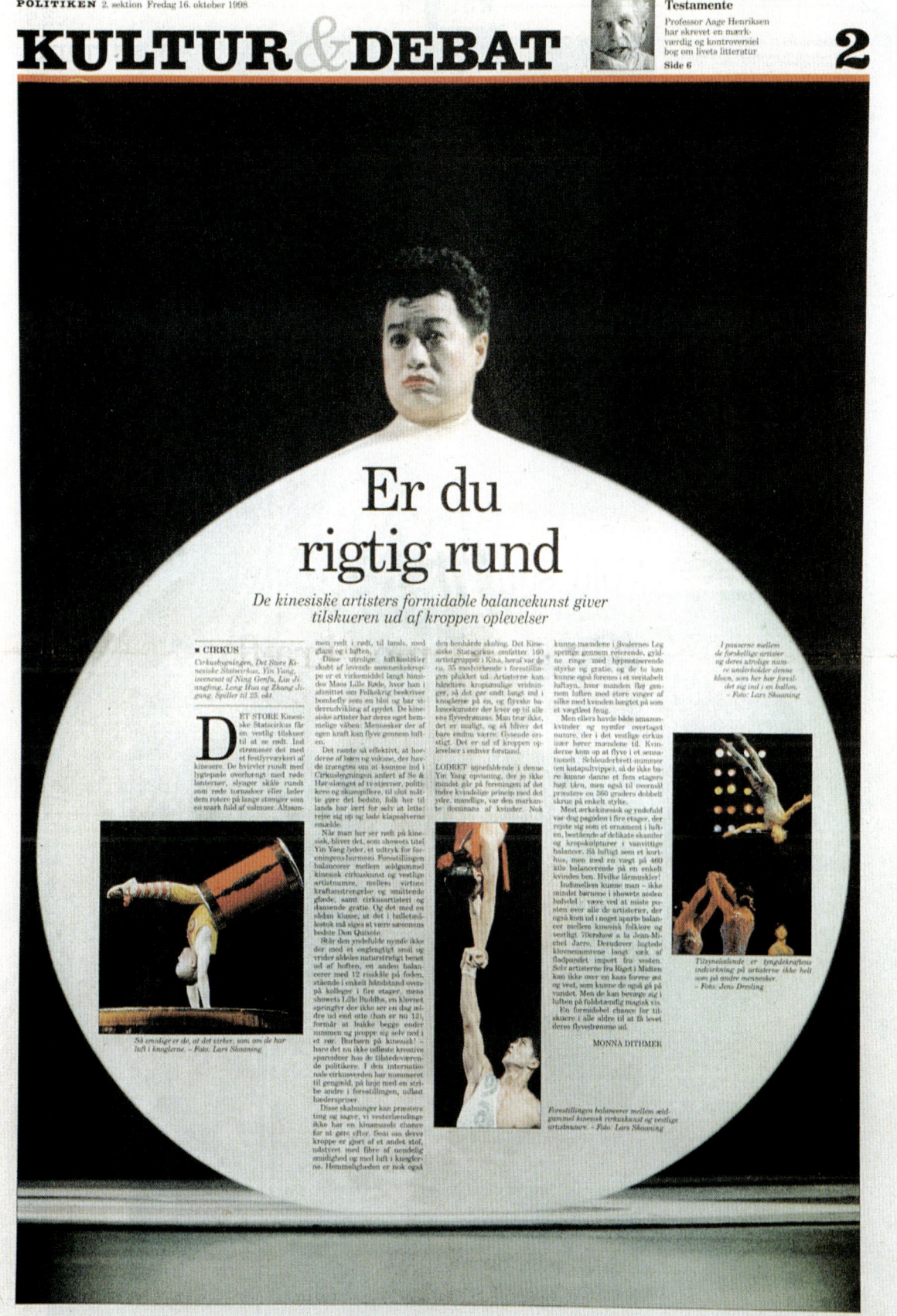

FEATURES — Lifestyle Page

Silver
La Gaceta
San Miguel de Tucuman, Argentina
Sebastian Rosso, Designer; **Sergio Fernandez,** Art Director; **Mario García,** Design Consultant; **Gustavo Rodriguez,** Editor

Silver
La Gaceta
San Miguel de Tucuman, Argentina
Sebastian Rosso, Designer; **Sergio Fernandez,** Art Director; **Mario García,** Design Consultant

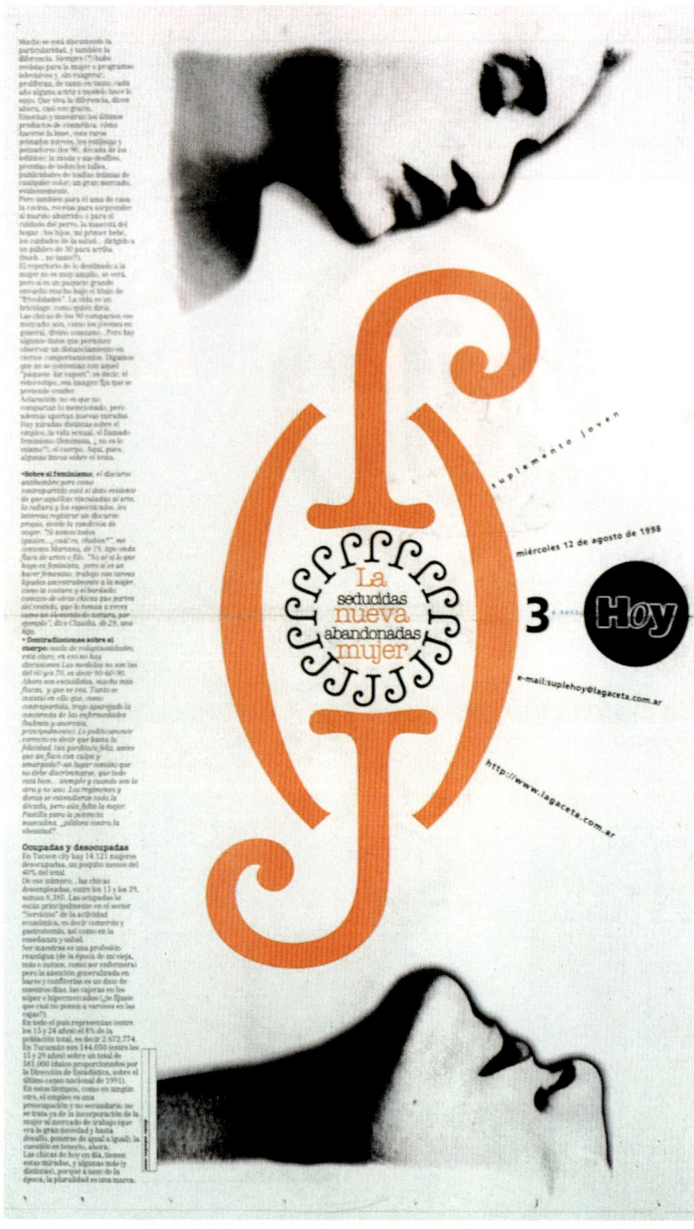

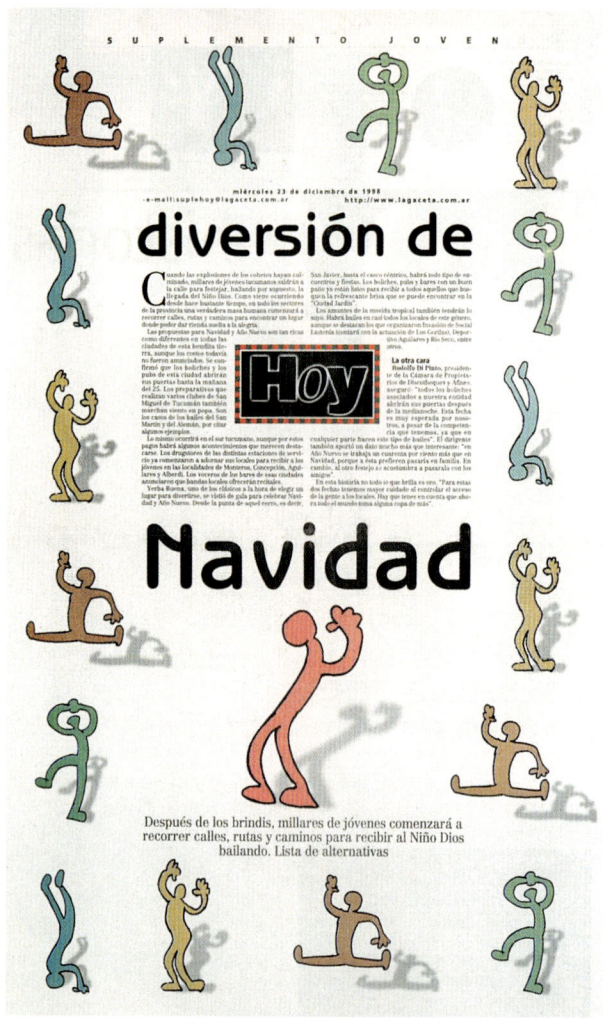

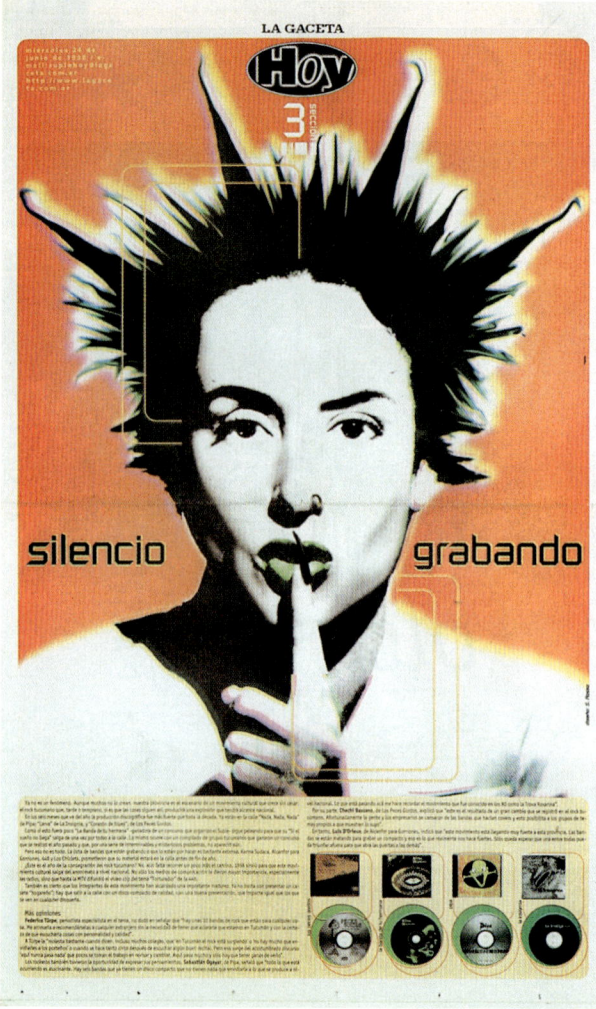

Silver
La Gaceta
San Miguel de Tucuman, Argentina
Sebastian Rosso, Designer; **Sergio Fernandez,** Art Director; **Mario García,** Design Consultant; **Gustavo Rodriguez,** Editor

Silver
La Voz del Interior
Córdoba, Argentina
Miguel De Lorenzi, Art Director; **Oscar Beguán,** Photo Editor; **Juan Carlos González,** Editor; **Carlos Jornet,** Publisher; **Mario García,** Design Consultant; **Javier Candellero,** Designer/Illustrator

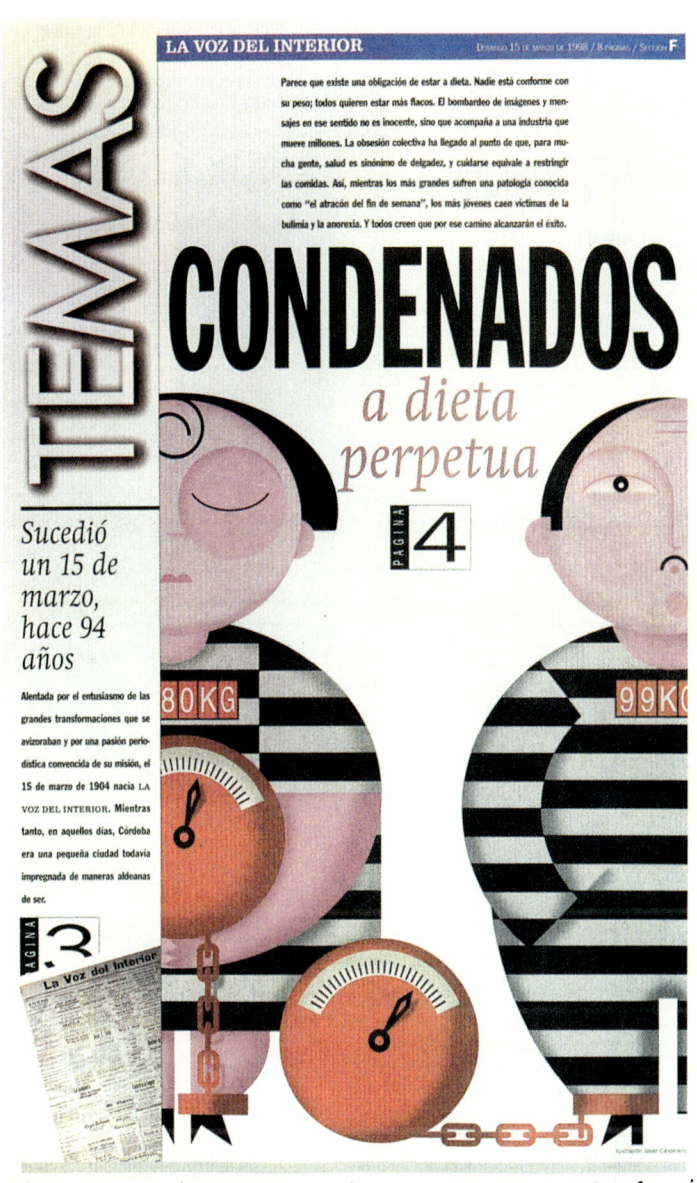

Silver
La Voz del Interior
Córdoba, Argentina
Miguel De Lorenzi, Art Director; **Oscar Beguán,** Photo Editor; **Juan Carlos González,** Editor; **Carlos Jornet,** Publisher; **Mario García,** Design Consultant; **Javier Candellero,** Designer/Illustrator

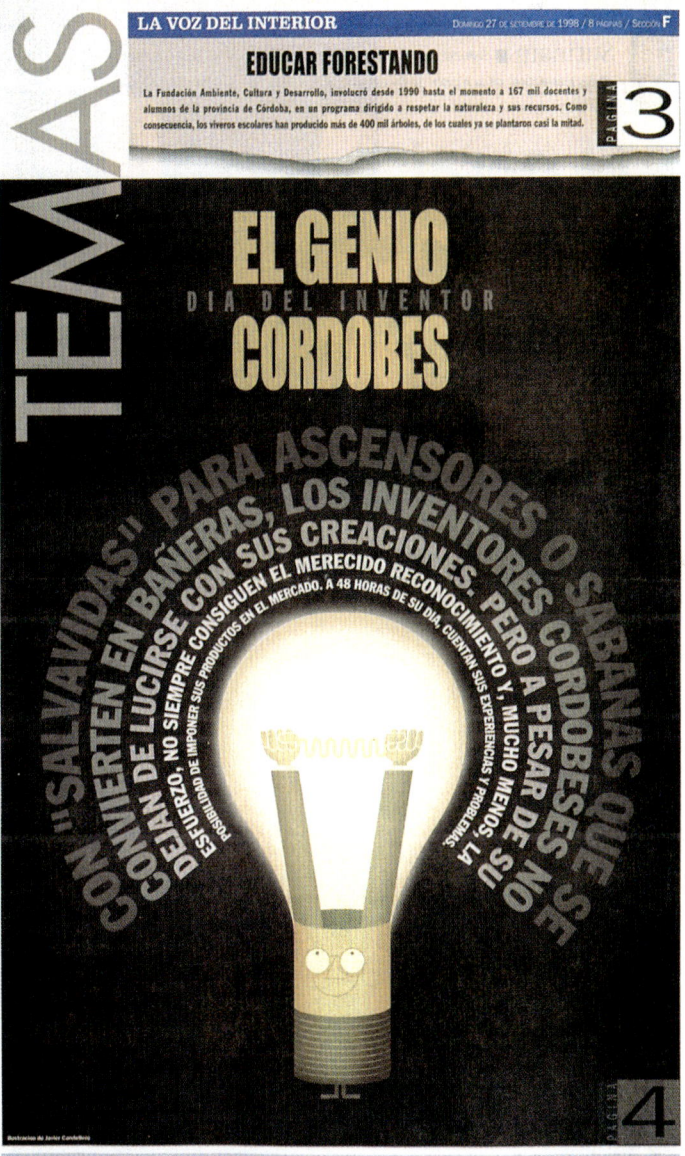

FEATURES ■ Lifestyle Page

Berlingske Tidende
Copenhagen, Denmark
Gregers Jensen, Page Designer

La Gaceta
San Miguel de Tucuman, Argentina
Sebastian Rosso, Designer; **Sergio Fernandez,** Art Director; **Mario García,** Design Consultant; **Maria Ester Veliz,** Editor

La Gaceta
San Miguel de Tucuman, Argentina
Héctor Reinoso Gallo, Designer; **Raúl Valverdi,** Art Director; **Sergio Fernandez,** Art Director; **Mario García,** Design Consultant

La Gaceta
San Miguel de Tucuman, Argentina
Sebastian Rosso, Designer; **Sergio Fernandez,** Art Director; **Mario García,** Design Consultant

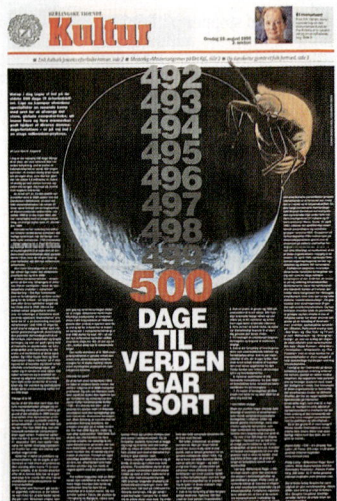
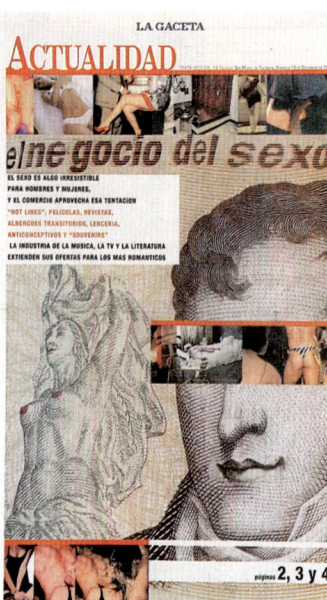
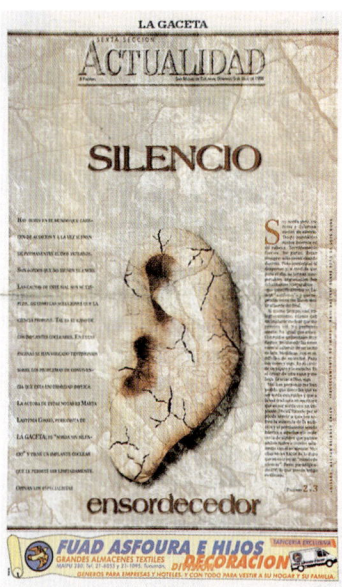
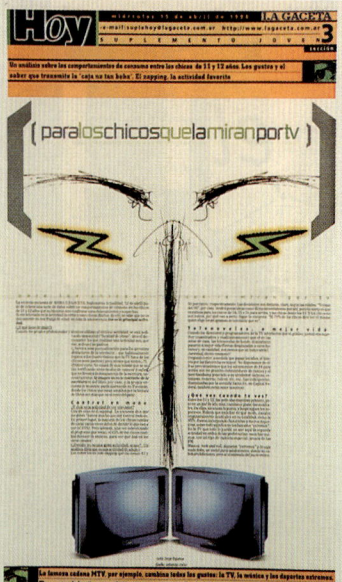

La Gaceta
San Miguel de Tucuman, Argentina
Sebastian Rosso, Designer; **Sergio Fernandez,** Art Director; **Mario García,** Design Consultant

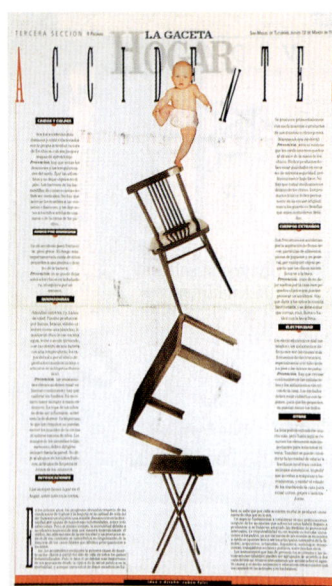
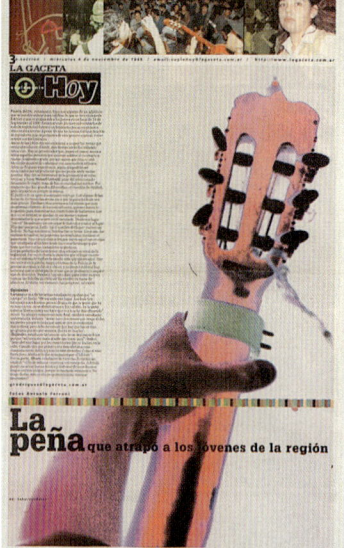
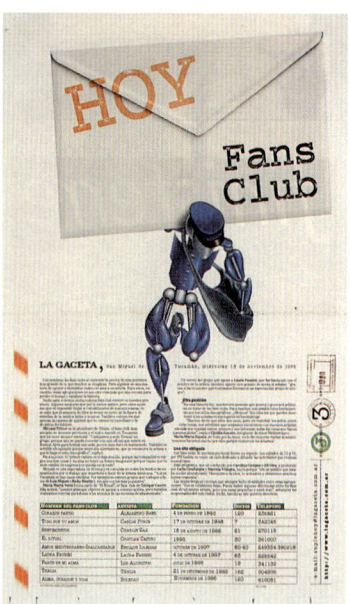

La Gaceta
San Miguel de Tucuman, Argentina
Falci Ruben, Designer; **Sergio Fernandez,** Art Director; **Mario García,** Design Consultant

La Gaceta
San Miguel de Tucuman, Argentina
Sebastian Rosso, Designer; **Sergio Fernandez,** Art Director; **Mario García,** Design Consultant; **Antonio Ferroni,** Photographer; **Gustavo Rodriguez,** Editor

La Gaceta
San Miguel de Tucuman, Argentina
Sebastian Rosso, Designer; **Sergio Fernandez,** Art Director; **Mario García,** Design Consultant; **Gustavo Rodriguez,** Editor; **Daniel Fontanarrosa,** Illustrator

Lifestyle Page ■ FEATURES

San Francisco Examiner
San Francisco, CA

Kelly Frankeny, A.M.E. Design; **Don McCartney**, Design Director; **Heidi Benson**, Style Editor; **Bill Prochnow**, Designer

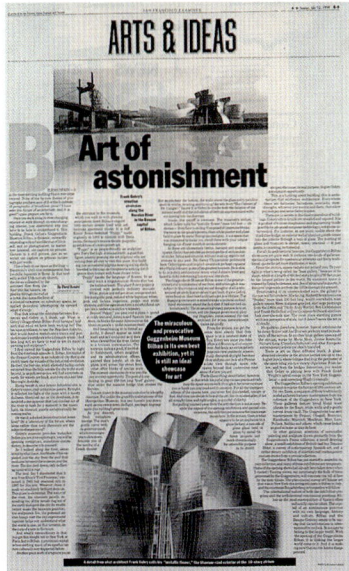

San Francisco Examiner
San Francisco, CA

Kelly Frankeny, A.M.E. Design; **Don McCartney**, Design Director; **Liz Mangelsdorf**, Photo Editor; **Richard Poali**, Director/Photography; **Heidi Benson**, Style Editor; **Pat Sedlar**, Designer

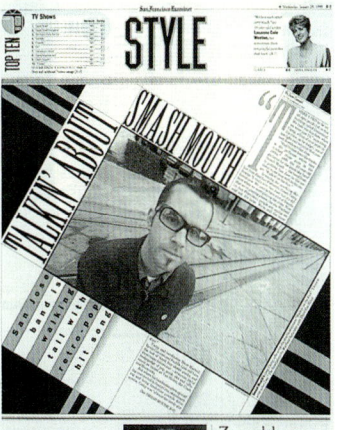

San Francisco Examiner
San Francisco, CA

Kelly Frankeny, A.M.E. Design; **Don McCartney**, Design Director; **Heidi Benson**, Style Editor; **Richard Paoli**, Director/Photography; **Kurt Rogers**, Photographer; **Andrew Skwish**, Designer

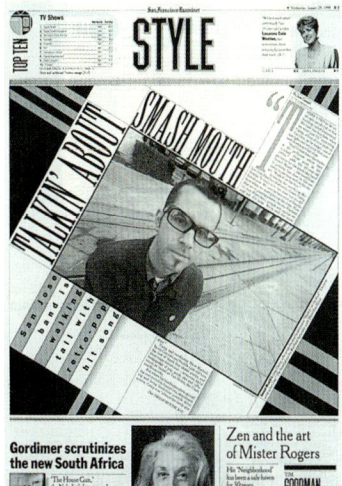

Savannah Morning News
Savannah, GA

Jill Jauch, Features Designer; **Gail Krueger**, Environmental Reporter; **Stephen D. Komives**, Sports/Features Planning Editor

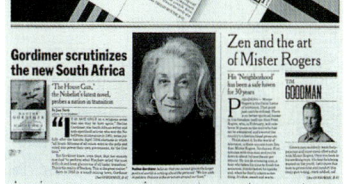

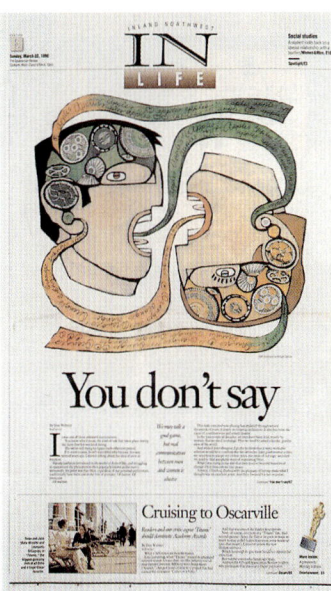

The Spokesman-Review
Spokane, WA

John Nelson, Design Editor; **Bridget Sawicki**, Illustrator
• also for Illustration Three or More Colors

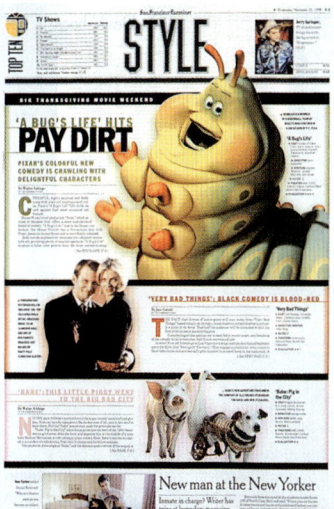

La Voz del Interior
Córdoba, Argentina

Miguel De Lorenzi, Art Director/Illustrator & Designer; **Oscar Beguán**, Photo Editor; **Juan Carlos González**, Editor; **Carlos Jornet**, Publisher; **Mario García**, Design Consultant

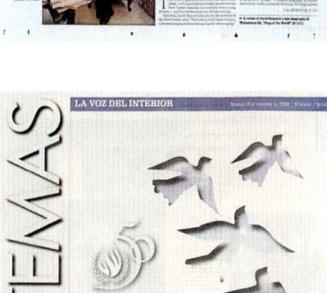

La Voz del Interior
Córdoba, Argentina

Miguel De Lorenzi, Art Director; **Oscar Beguán**, Photo Editor; **Juan Carlos González**, Editor; **Carlos Jornet**, Publisher; **Mario García**, Design Consultant; **Javier Candellero**, Illustrator & Designer

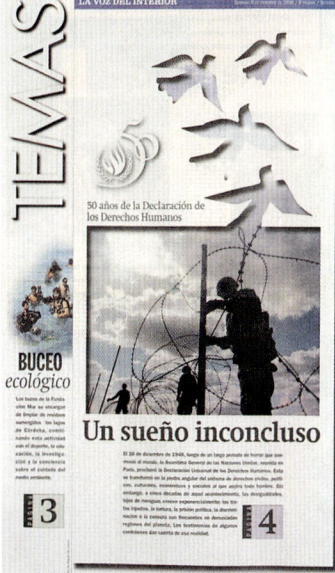

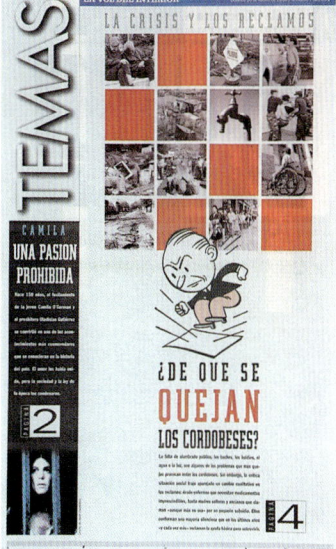

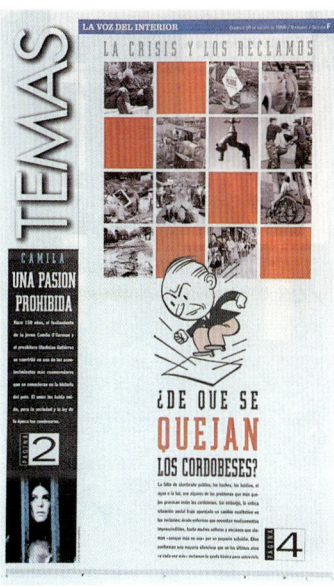

La Voz del Interior
Córdoba, Argentina

Miguel De Lorenzi, Art Director; **Oscar Beguán**, Photo Editor; **Juan Carlos González**, Editor; **Carlos Jornet**, Publisher; **Mario García**, Design Consultant; **Javier Candellero**, Illustrator & Designer

FEATURES ■ Lifestyle Page

La Voz del Interior
Córdoba, Argentina
Miguel De Lorenzi, Art Director & Designer; **Oscar Beguán,** Photo Editor; **Juan Carlos González,** Editor; **Carlos Jornet,** Publisher; **Mario García,** Design Consultant; **Javier Candellero,** Illustrator & Designer

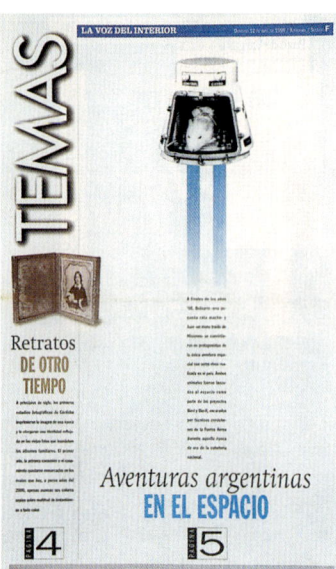

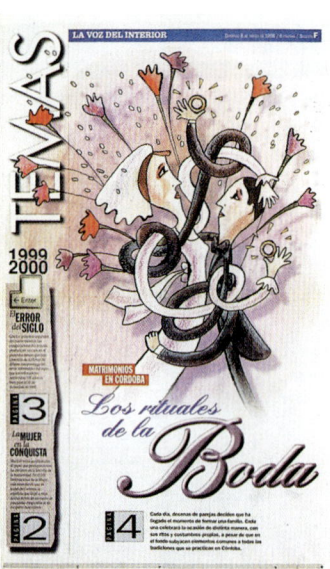

La Voz del Interior
Córdoba, Argentina
Miguel De Lorenzi, Designer/Illustrator/Art Director; **Oscar Beguán,** Art Director; **Juan Carlos González,** Editor; **Carlos Jornet,** Publisher; **Mario García,** Design Consultant

La Voz del Interior
Córdoba, Argentina
Miguel De Lorenzi, Art Director; **Oscar Beguán,** Photo Editor; **Juan Carlos González,** Editor; **Carlos Jornet,** Publisher; **Mario García,** Design Consultant; **Javier Candellero,** Illustrator & Designer

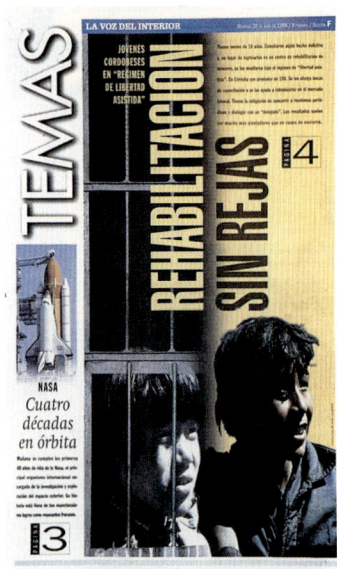

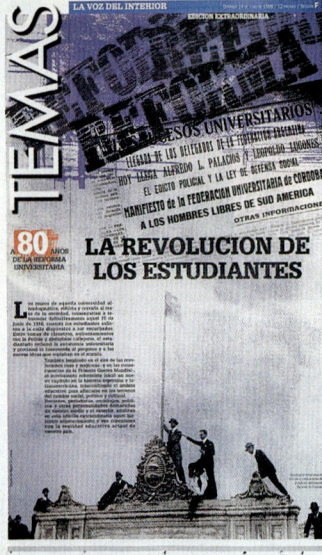

La Voz del Interior
Córdoba, Argentina
Miguel De Lorenzi, Designer/Illustrator/Art Director; **Oscar Beguán,** Photo Editor; **Juan Carlos González,** Editor; **Carlos Jornet,** Publisher; **Mario García,** Design Consultant

La Voz del Interior
Córdoba, Argentina
Miguel De Lorenzi, Art Director; **Oscar Beguán,** Photo Editor; **Juan Carlos González,** Editor; **Carlos Jornet,** Publisher; **Mario García,** Design Consultant; **Javier Candellero,** Illustrator & Designer

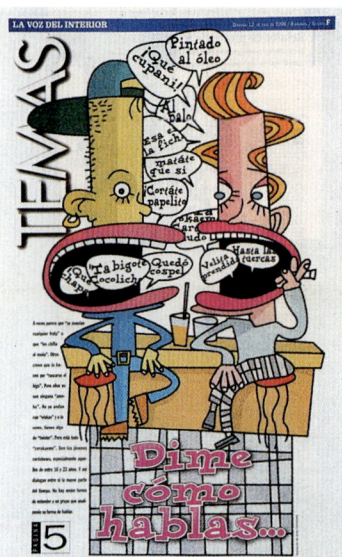

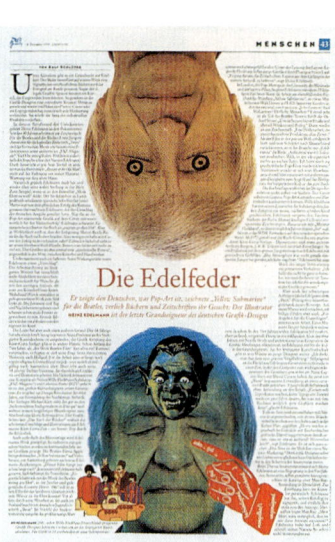

Die Woche
Hamburg, Germany
Manfred Bissinger, Editor in Chief; **Kurt Breme,** Executive Editor; **Hans-Ulrich Joerges,** Executive Editor; **Dirk Linke,** Art Director; **Andreas Schomberg,** Associate Art Director; **Armin Ogris,** Designer; **Stefan Semrau,** Designer; **Jessica Winter,** Designer; **Reinhard Schulz-Schaeffer,** Designer/Info Graphics; **Florian Poehl,** Designer/Info Graphics

La Voz del Interior
Córdoba, Argentina
Miguel De Lorenzi, Art Director; **Oscar Beguán,** Photo Editor; **Juan Carlos González,** Editor; **Carlos Jornet,** Publisher; **Mario García,** Design Consultant; **Javier Candellero,** Illustrator & Designer

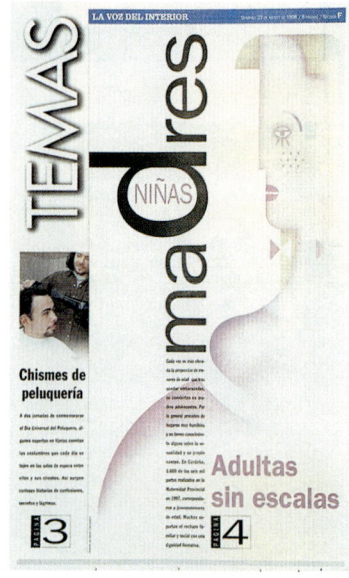

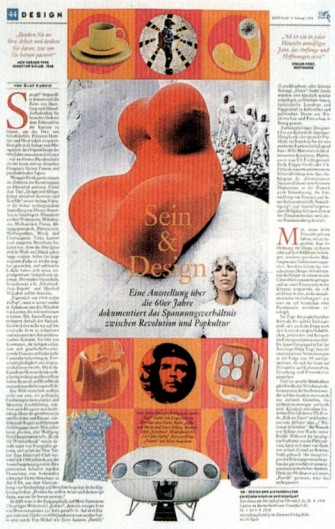

Die Woche
Hamburg, Germany
Manfred Bissinger, Editor in Chief; **Kurt Breme,** Executive Editor; **Hans-Ulrich Joerges,** Executive Editor; **Dirk Linke,** Art Director; **Andreas Schomberg,** Associate Art Director; **Armin Ogris,** Designer; **Stefan Semrau,** Designer; **Jessica Winter,** Designer; **Reinhard Schulz-Schaeffer,** Designer/Info Graphics; **Florian Poehl,** Designer/Info Graphics

Lifestyle Page, Entertainment Page ■ FEATURES

The Beacon-News
Aurora, IL
James Smith, Designer; **James Denk,** Director/Design & Graphics; **Brian Plonka,** Photographer

Le Devoir
Montréal, Canada
Christian Tiffet, Art Director

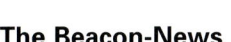

The Beacon-News
Aurora, IL
Dale Roe, Design Editor; **James Denk,** Director/Design & Graphics; **Brian Plonka,** Photographer

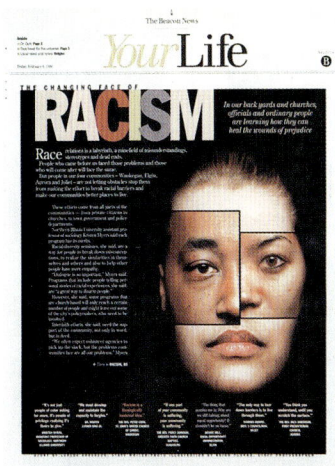

Le Devoir
Montréal, Canada
Christian Tiffet, Art Director

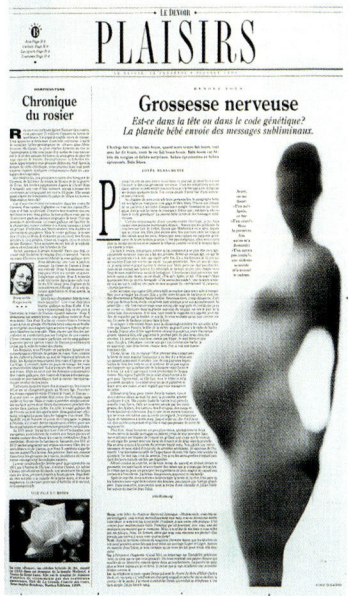

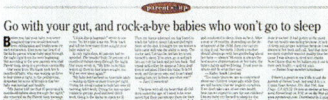

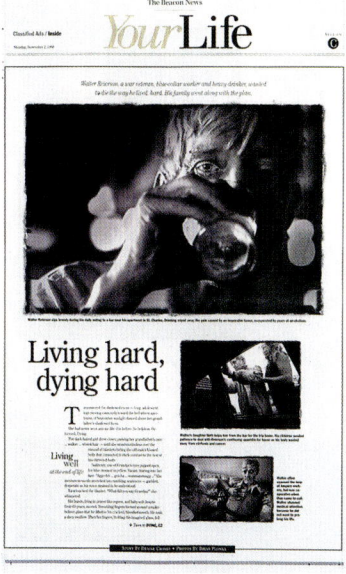

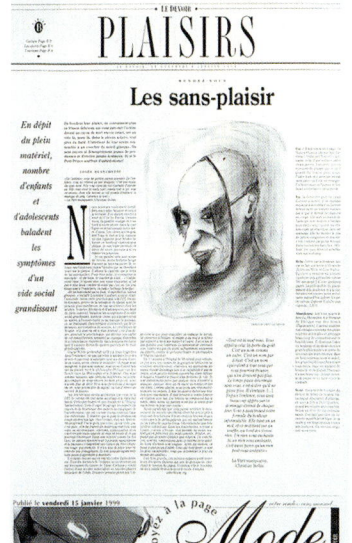

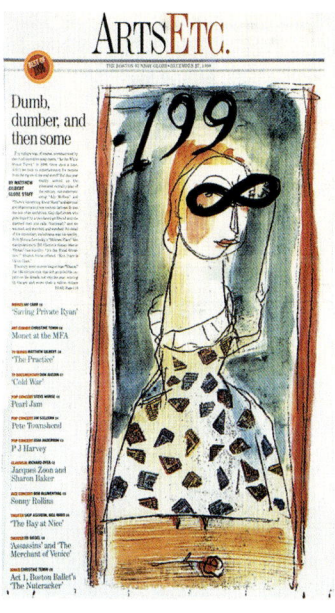

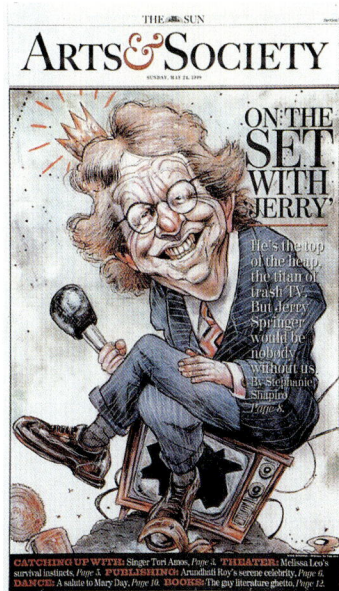

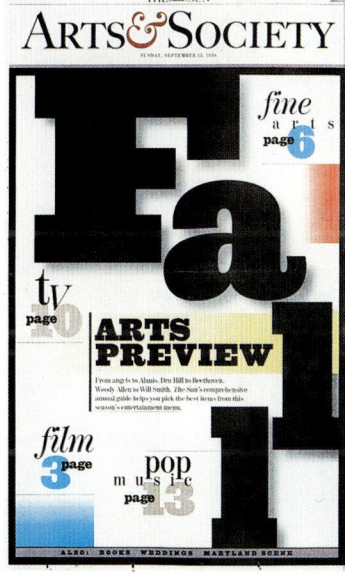

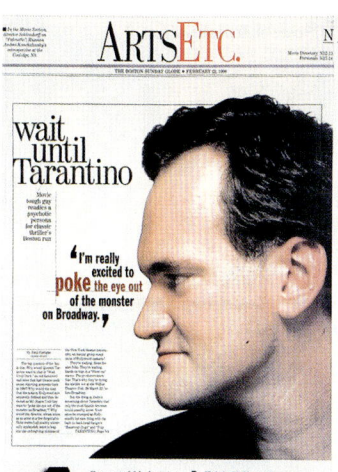

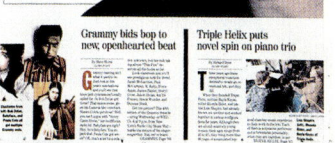

The Sun
Baltimore, MD
Joseph Hutchinson, A.M.E. Graphics/Design; **Victor Panichkul,** Features Design Director; **Peter Yuill,** Design Editor

The Boston Globe
Boston, MA
Sue Dawson, Art Director & Designer

The Boston Globe
Boston, MA
Rena Anderson Sokolow, Art Director & Designer; **Geneviève Côté,** Illustrator; **Scott Powers,** Editor; **John Ferguson,** Copy Editor

The Sun
Baltimore, MD
Joseph Hutchinson, A.M.E. Graphics/Design; **Victor Panichkul,** Features Design Director

TWENTIETH EDITION ■ 111

FEATURES ■ Entertainment Page

Gold
O Globo
Rio de Janeiro, Brasil
Claudio Duarte, Illustrator; **Telio Navega**, Designer

This is an overpowering illustration that gives the page energy. The circle of movement draws you into the story. The elegance on the page is perfect. It's appropriate that everything on the page becomes related. Excellent color treatment.

Es una ilustración impactante que confiere energía a la página y el círculo de movimiento te sumerge en la historia. La elegancia de la página es perfecta y se ha logrado que todo en la página se relacione. Excelente tratamiento del color.

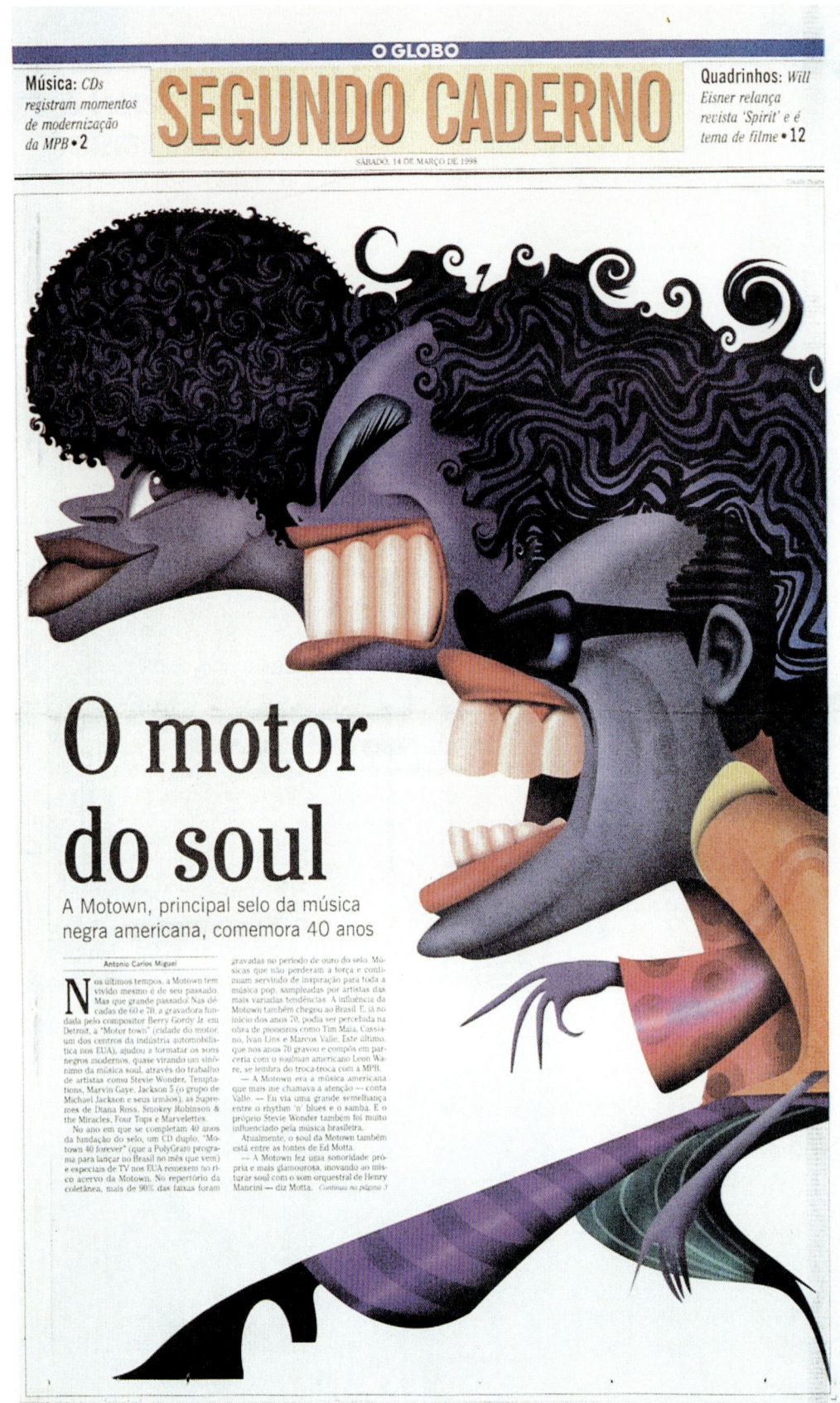

Gold
La Luna
Madrid, Spain
Rodrigo Sánchez, Art Director; **Francisco Dorado,** Designer; **Chano del Río,** Designer; **Carmelo Caderot,** Design Director; **James White,** Photographer

This page is simple, stylish, straightforward and elegant. It's cool. It's a show stopper.

Esta página es sencilla, atractiva, directa y elegante. Tiene un aire muy moderno y logra atrapar la atención de todos.

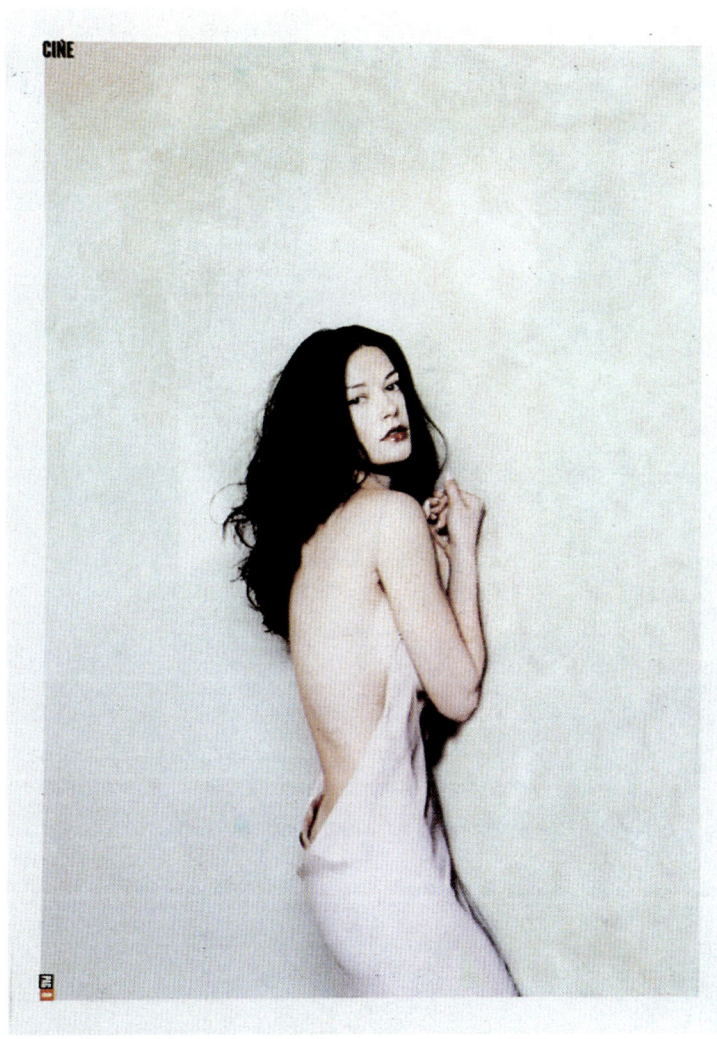
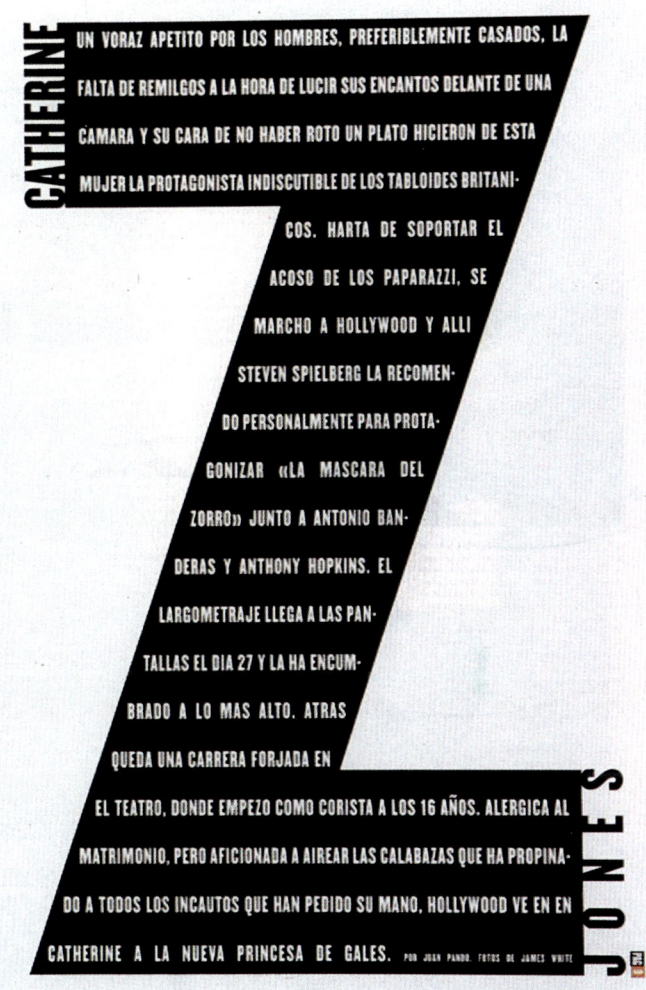

Silver
La Luna
Madrid, Spain
Rodrigo Sánchez, Art Director; **Francisco Dorado,** Designer; **Chano del Río,** Designer; **Carmelo Caderot,** Design Director; **The Douglas Bros,** Photographer

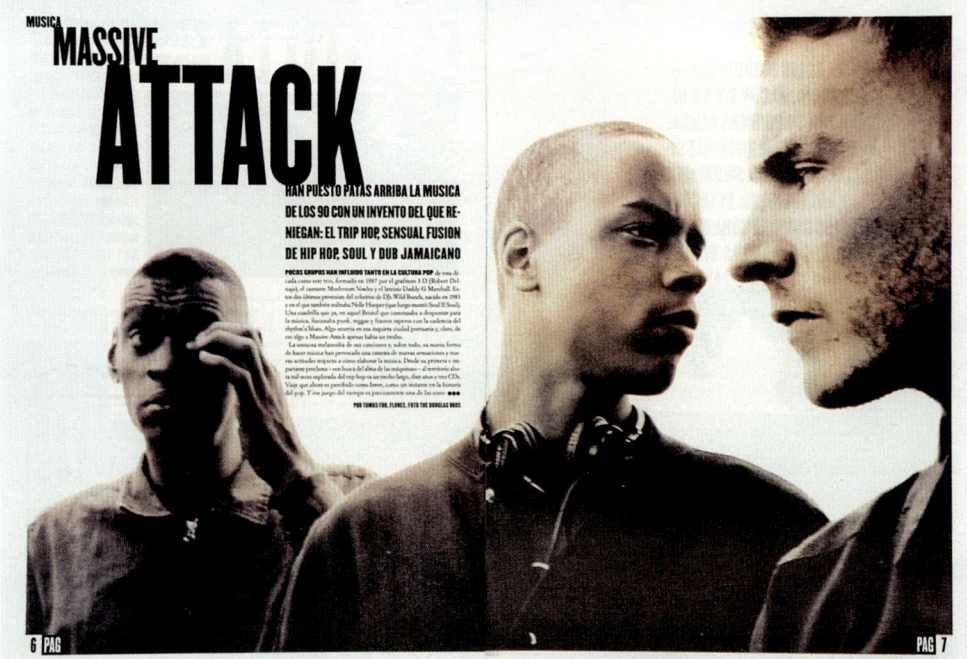

Silver
La Luna
Madrid, Spain
Rodrigo Sánchez, Art Director; **Francisco Dorado,** Designer; **Chano del Río,** Designer; **Carmelo Caderot,** Design Director; **Urraco,** Photographer

 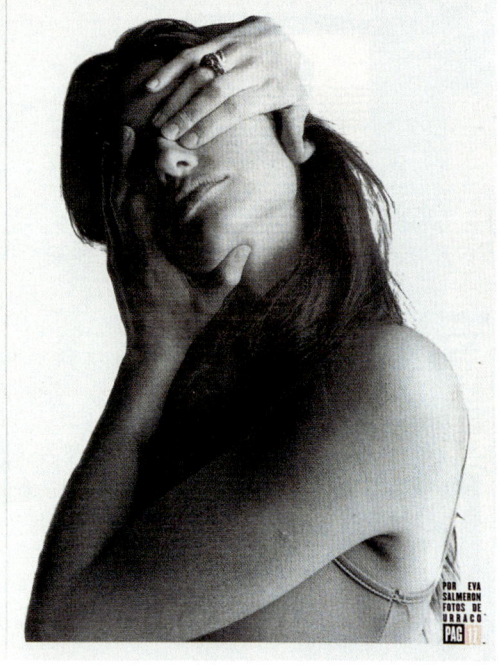

Silver
La Luna
Madrid, Spain
Rodrigo Sánchez, Art Director; **Francisco Dorado,** Designer; **Chano del Río,** Designer; **Carmelo Caderot,** Design Director; **Cristina Esperanza,** Photographer

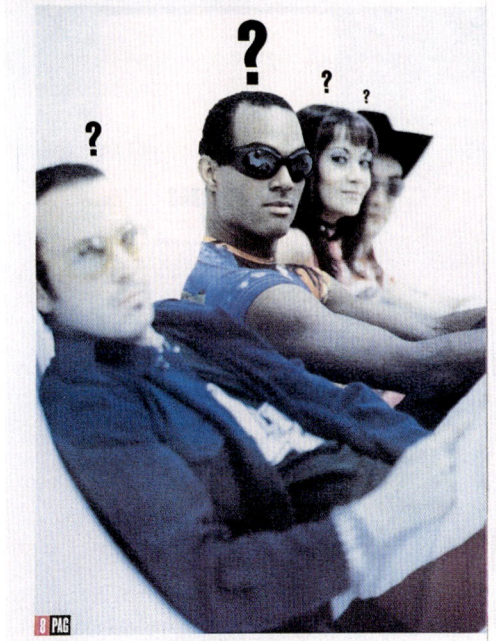 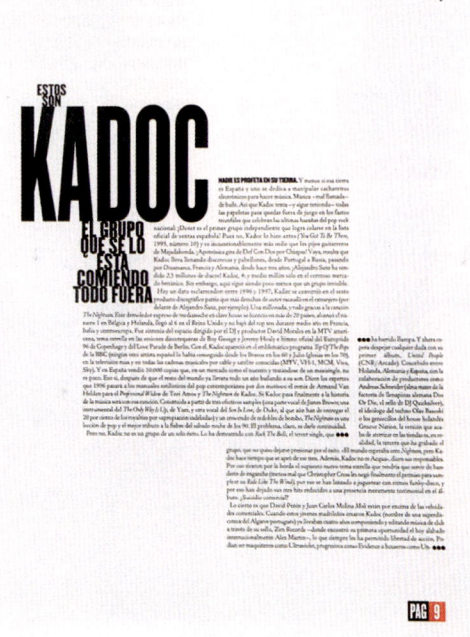

Entertainment Page ■ FEATURES

The Boston Globe
Boston, MA
Rena Anderson Sokolow, Art Director & Designer; **John Ferguson,** Copy Editor; **Scott Powers,** Editor

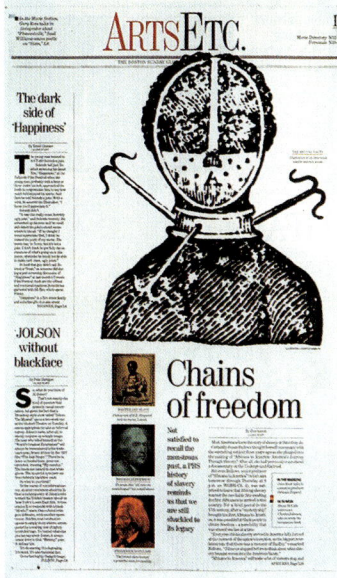

The Charlotte Observer
Charlotte, NC
Monica Moses, Design Director; **Kristen Powell,** Designer

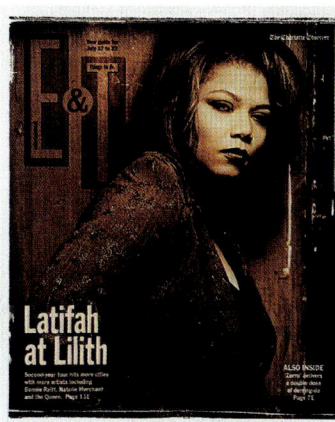

The Chicago Tribune
Chicago, IL
Stephen Ravenscraft, Designer; **Tim Bannon,** Editor; **Rancisco Caceres,** Illustrator

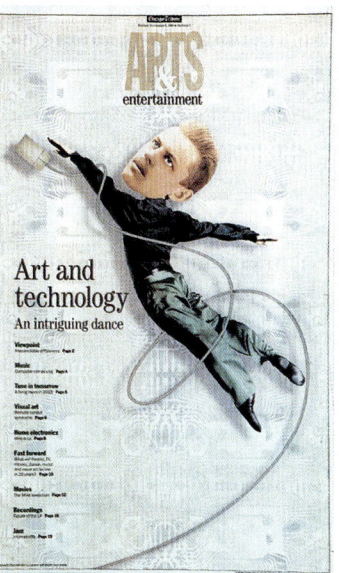

O Dia
Rio de Janeiro, Brasil
Renata Maneschy, Designer

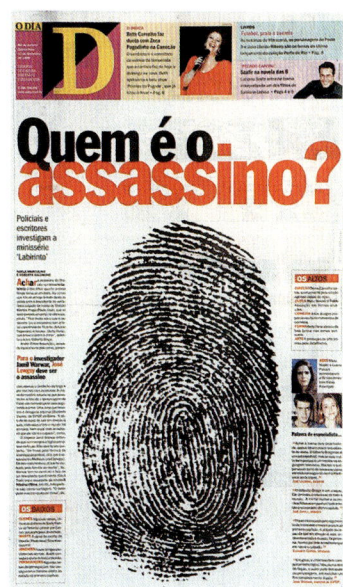

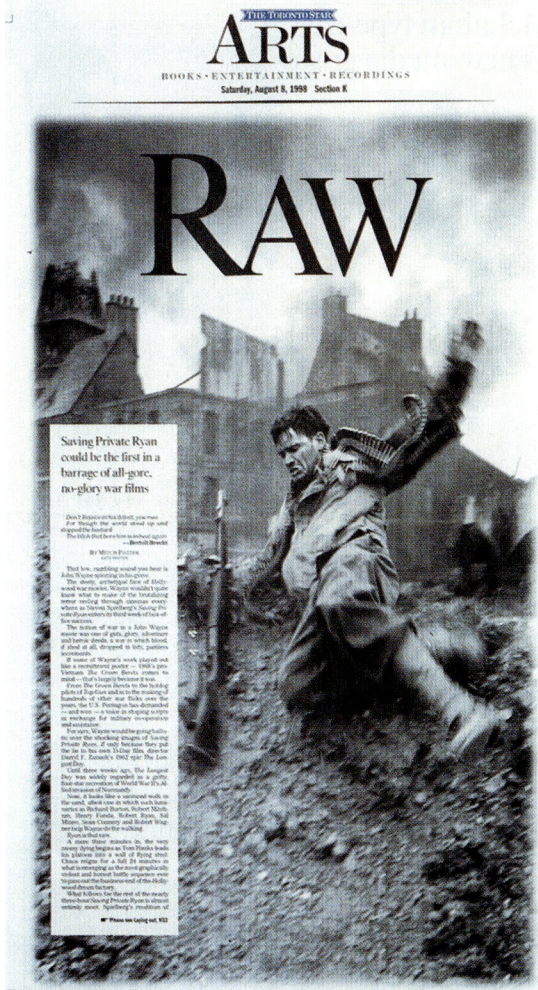

Silver
The Toronto Star
Toronto, Canada
Ian Somerville, Art Director; **Evelyn Stoynoff,** Designer; **Patrick McCormick,** Editor; **Mitch Potter,** Staff Writer

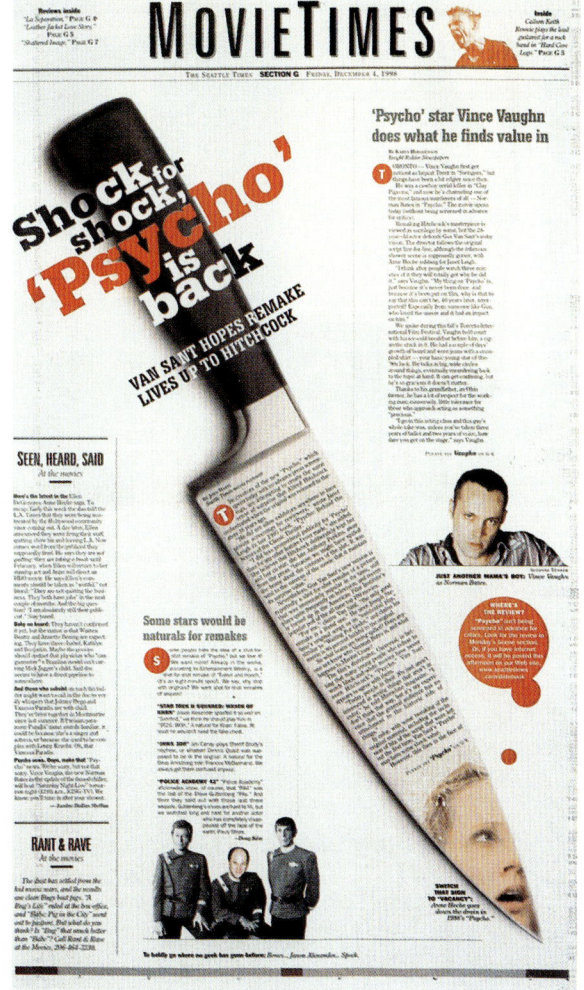

Silver
The Seattle Times
Seattle, WA
Jeff Neumann, Designer/Illustrator; **David Miller,** Art Director

TWENTIETH EDITION ■ 115

FEATURES — Entertainment Page

Dagbladet
Oslo, Norway
André Martinsen, Designer

Dagbladet
Oslo, Norway
Torfinn Solbrekke, Art Director & Designer

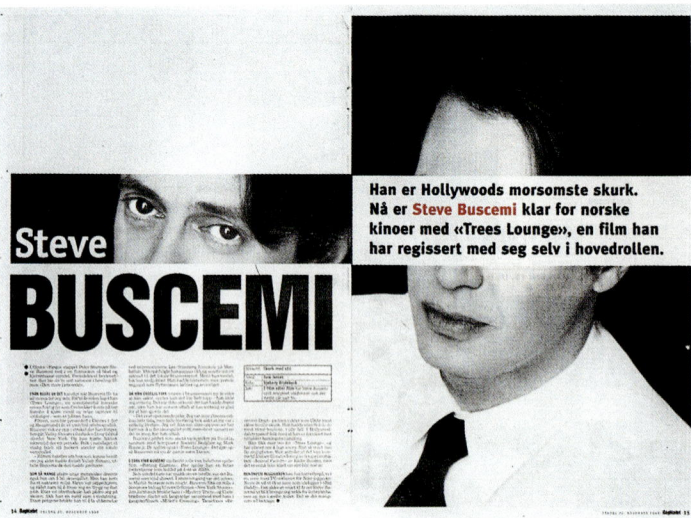

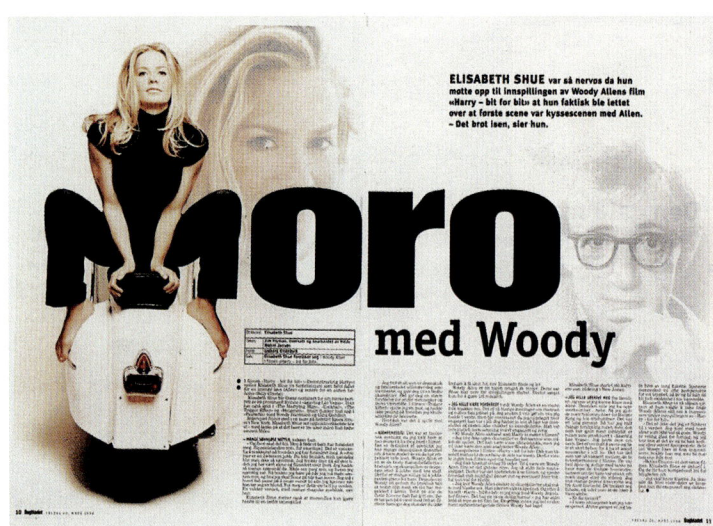

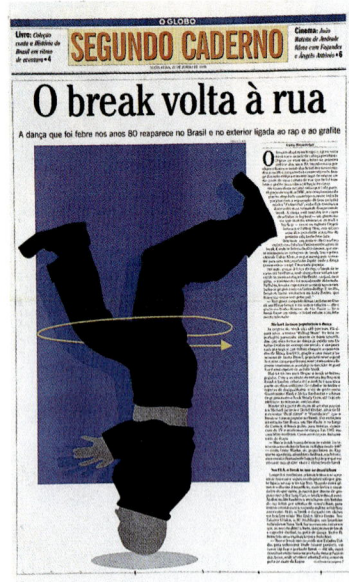

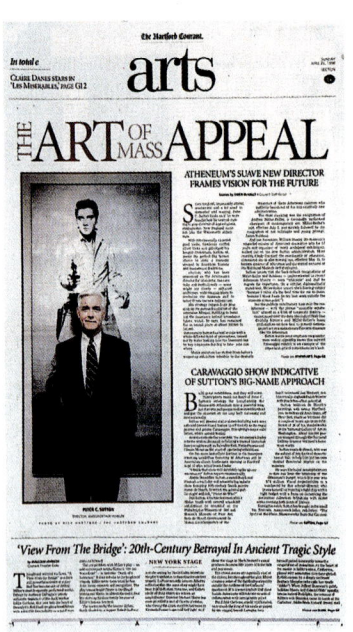

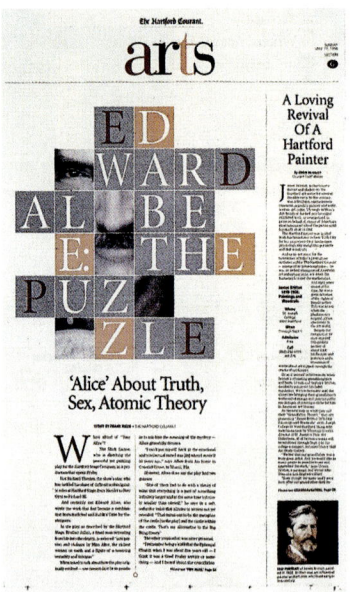

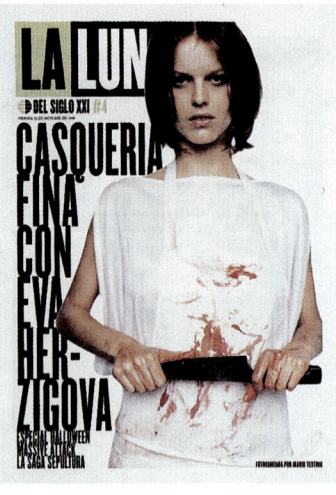

O Globo
Rio de Janeiro, Brasil
Claudio Duarte, Illustrator

The Hartford Courant
Hartford, CT
Melanie Shaffer, Designer; **Christian P. Drury,** Art Director; **Sherry Peters,** Photo/Graphics Editor; **Rick Hartford,** Photographer

The Hartford Courant
Hartford, CT
Melanie Shaffer, Designer; **Christian P. Drury,** Art Director

La Luna
Madrid, Spain
Rodrigo Sánchez, Art Director; **Francisco Dorado,** Designer; **Chano del Río,** Designer; **Carmelo Caderot,** Design Director; **Mario Testino,** Photographer

La Luna
Madrid, Spain

Rodrigo Sánchez, Art Director; **Francisco Dorado,** Designer; **Chano del Río,** Designer; **Carmelo Caderot,** Design Director

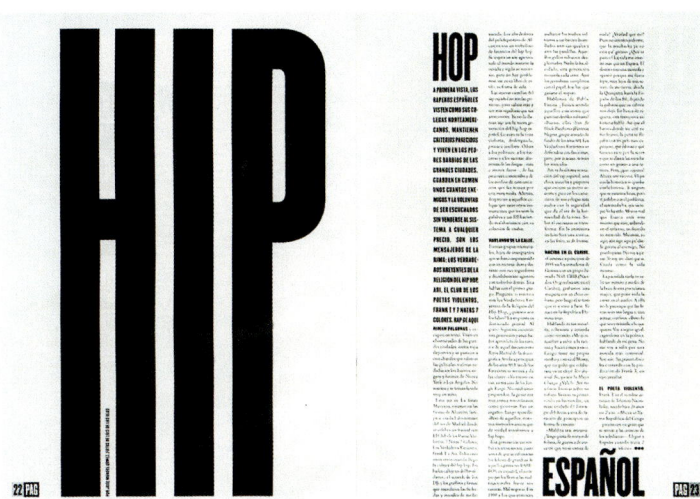

La Luna
Madrid, Spain

Rodrigo Sánchez, Art Director; **Francisco Dorado,** Designer; **Chano del Río,** Designer; **Carmelo Caderot,** Design Director; **Danny Clinch,** Photographer

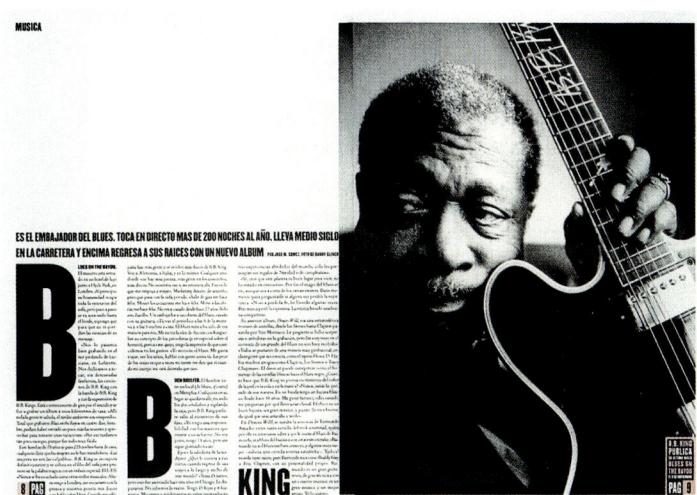

La Luna
Madrid, Spain

Rodrigo Sánchez, Art Director; **Francisco Dorado,** Designer; **Chano del Río,** Designer; **Carmelo Caderot,** Design Director; **Raul Arias,** Illustrator

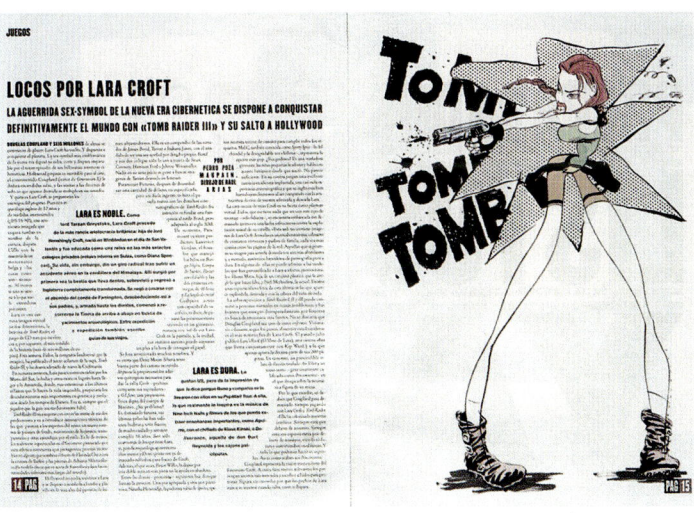

La Luna
Madrid, Spain

Rodrigo Sánchez, Art Director; **Francisco Dorado,** Designer; **Chano del Río,** Designer; **Carmelo Caderot,** Design Director; **Luis de las Alas,** Photographer

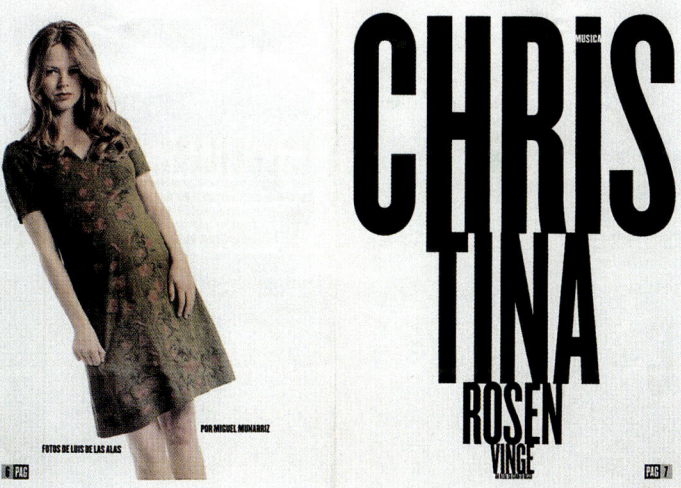

FEATURES ■ Entertainment Page

The Orange County Register
Santa Ana, CA
Dee Boyles, Artist/Designer

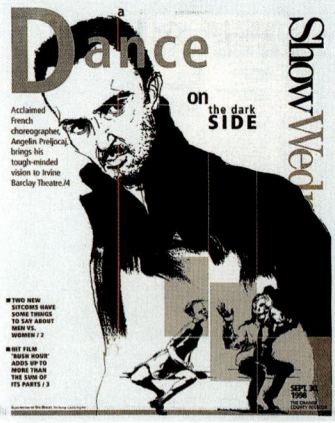

The Orange County Register
Santa Ana, CA
Martin Gee, Designer; **Kris Viesselman Onuigbo,** Art Director; **Dee Boyles,** Art Director

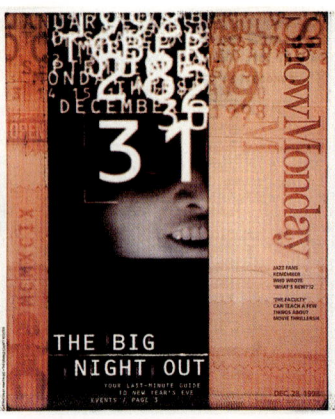

The Orange County Register
Santa Ana, CA
Peter Nguyen, Designer; **Kris Viesselman Onuigbo,** Art Director; **Dee Boyles,** Art Director

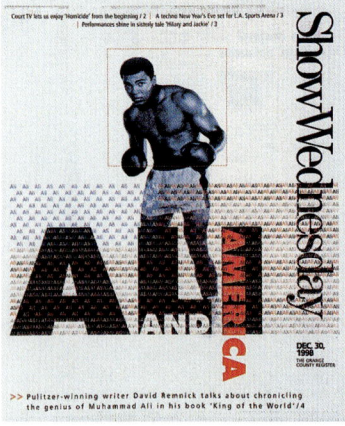

The Oregonian
Portland, OR
Reed Darmon, Designer; **Jonathan Barkat,** Illustrator; **Shawn Vitt,** Art Director; **Nancy Casey,** Art Director

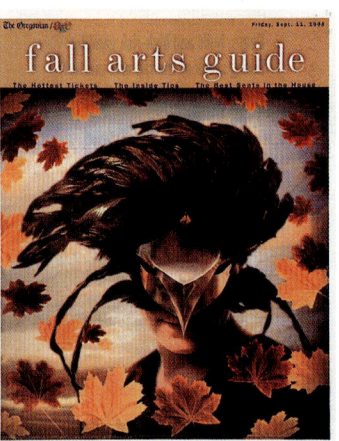

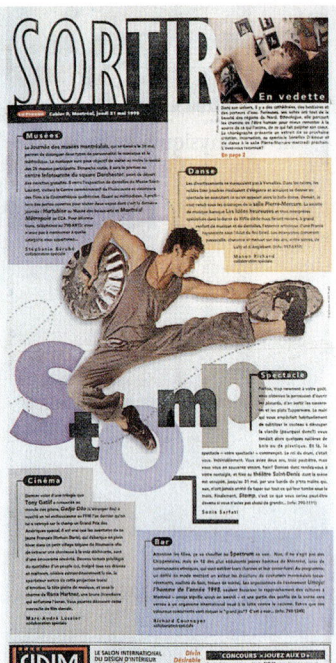

La Presse
Montréal, Canada
André Rivest, Graphic Designer; **Yves De Repentigny,** Section Editor

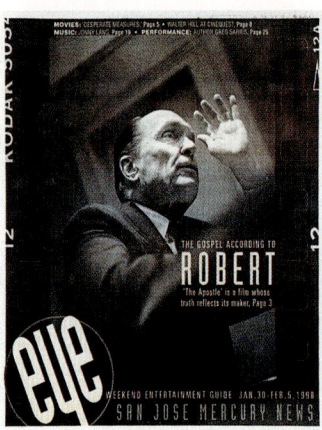

San Jose Mercury News
San Jose, CA
Sue Morrow, Features Design Editor; **Brian A. Griffin,** Designer; **Richard Koci Hernandez,** Photographer

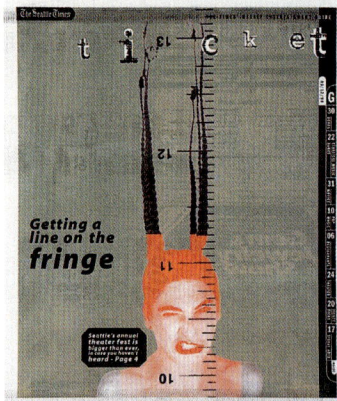

The Seattle Times
Seattle, WA
Jeff Neumann, Designer; **David Miller,** Art Director

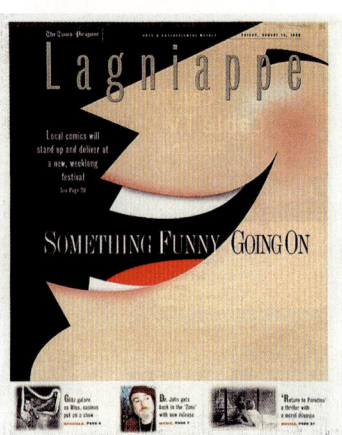

The Times-Picayune
New Orleans, LA
Julia Nead, Designer; **Jean McIntosh,** Art Director; **Karen Taylor-Gist,** Editor; **Tony O. Champagne,** Illustrator

Entertainment Page ■ FEATURES

Anchorage Daily News
Anchorage, AK
Greg Epkes, Designer; **Ruthie Stein,** Photographer

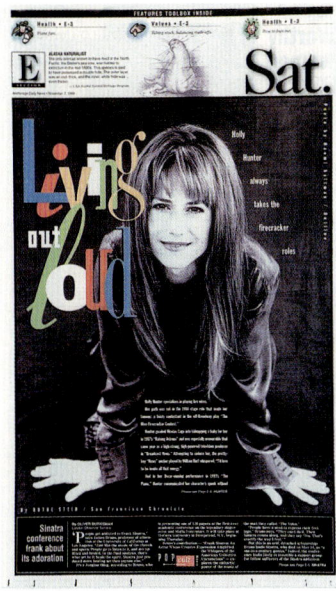

The Toronto Star
Toronto, Canada
Jo-Ann Dodds, Designer; **Ian Somerville,** Art Director; **Doug Cudmore,** Editor; **John Ferri,** Entertainment Editor

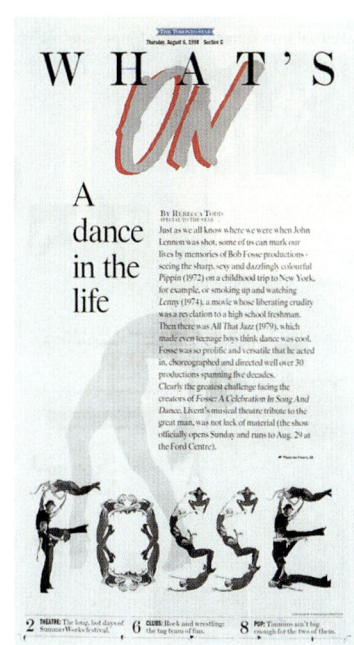

Silver
Anchorage Daily News
Anchorage, AK
Greg Epkes, Designer

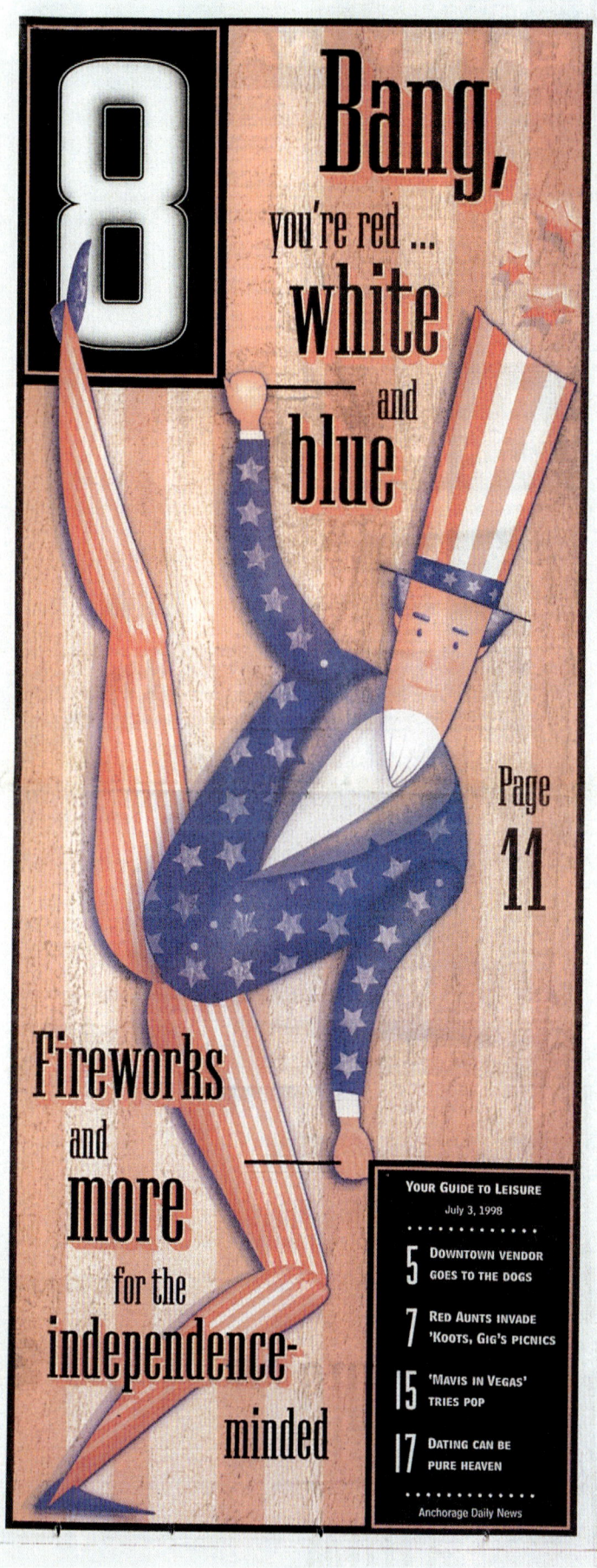

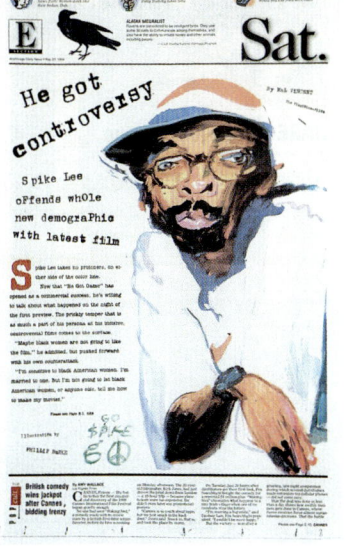

Anchorage Daily News
Anchorage, AK
Lance Lekander, Designer; **Phillip Burke,** Illustrator
• also for Illustration Three or More Colors

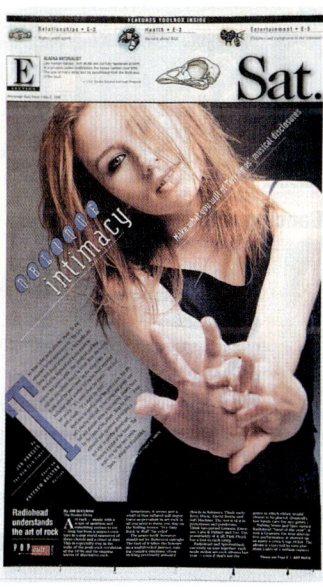

Anchorage Daily News
Anchorage, AK
Lance Lekander, Designer; **Matthew Rolston,** Photographer

TWENTIETH EDITION ■ 119

FEATURES — Entertaiment Page

Gold
La Gaceta
San Miguel de Tucuman, Argentina
Sebastian Rosso, Designer; **Sergio Fernandez**, Art Director; **Mario García**, Design Consultant

This has an intelligent use of illustration and photography that work well together. It stood out from all the other pages. They made a superb page out of a mediocre photo and showed how you can treat a press release intelligently. The page shows the character he plays in the movie and does it well.

Hace un uso inteligente de la ilustración y la fotografía, y la combinación de éstas surte un gran efecto. Sobresalió de entre todas las demás páginas. De una foto mediocre, lograron crear una página magnífica y probaron cómo se puede tratar un comunicado de prensa con inteligencia. La página muestra al personaje que él tiene en la película y lo hace con eficacia.

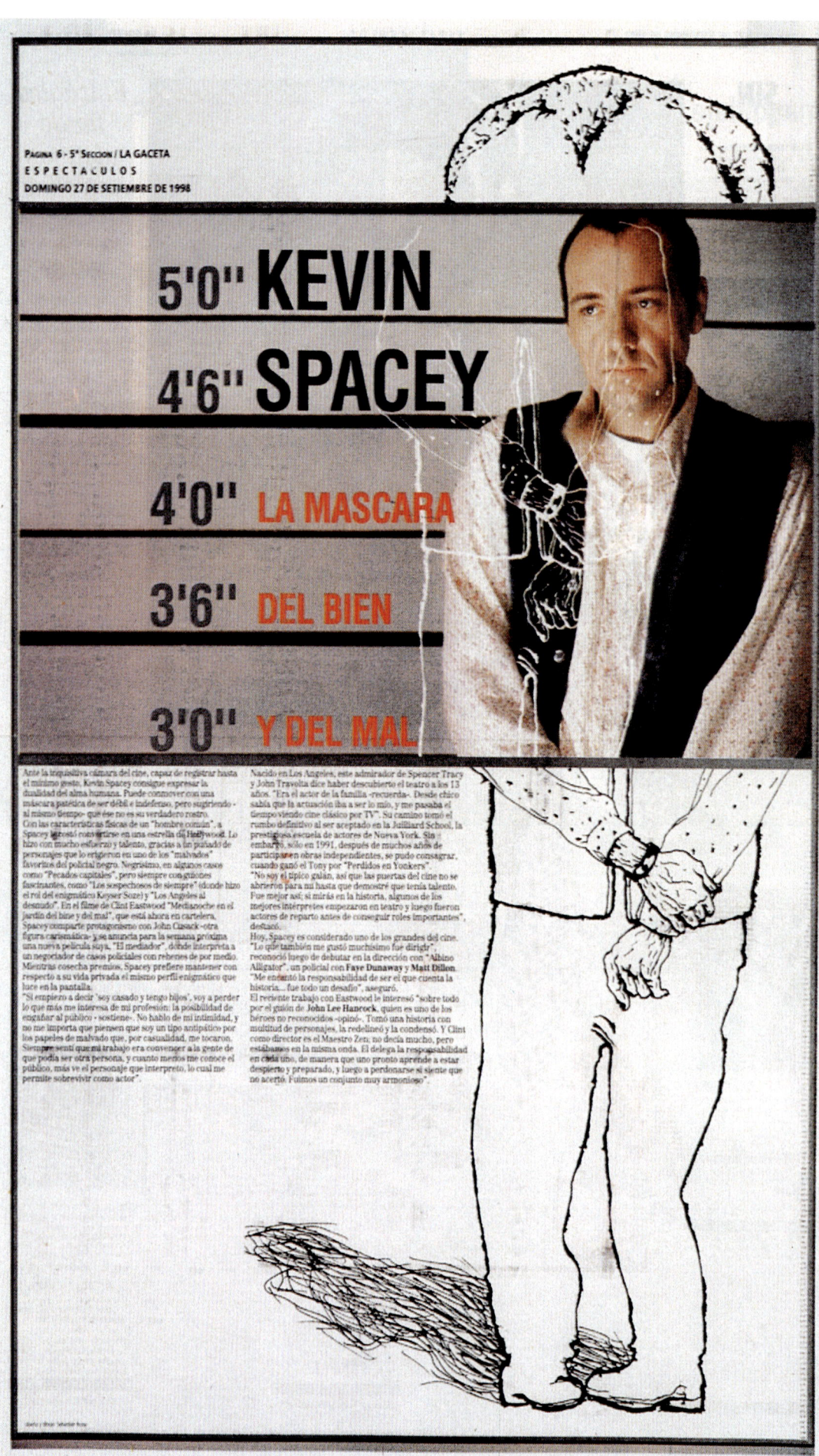

Entertainment Page ■ FEATURES

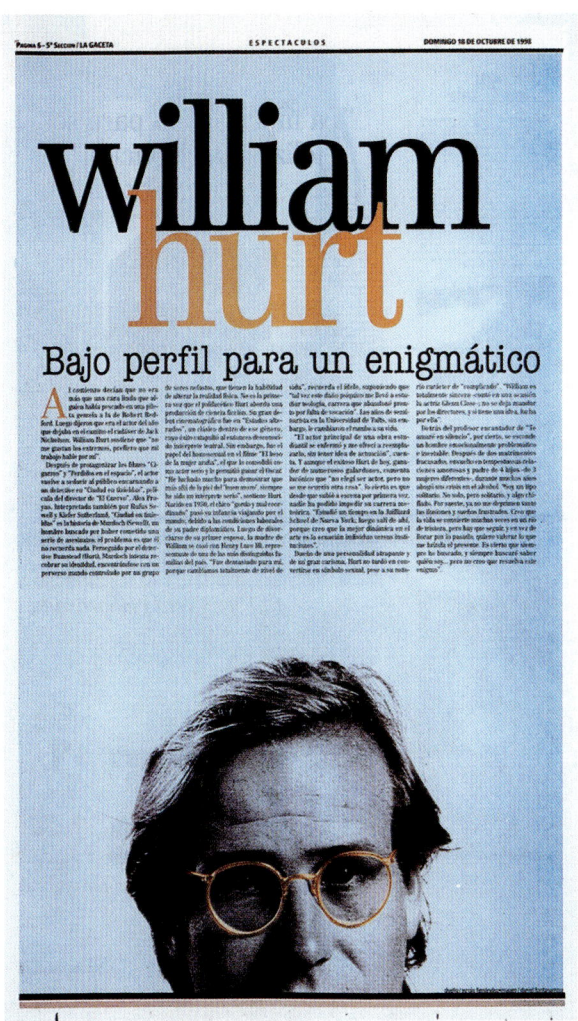

Silver
La Gaceta
San Miguel de Tucuman, Argentina
Sergio Fernandez, Art Director & Designer; **Daniel Fontanarrosa,** Photo Illustrator; **Mario García,** Design Consultant

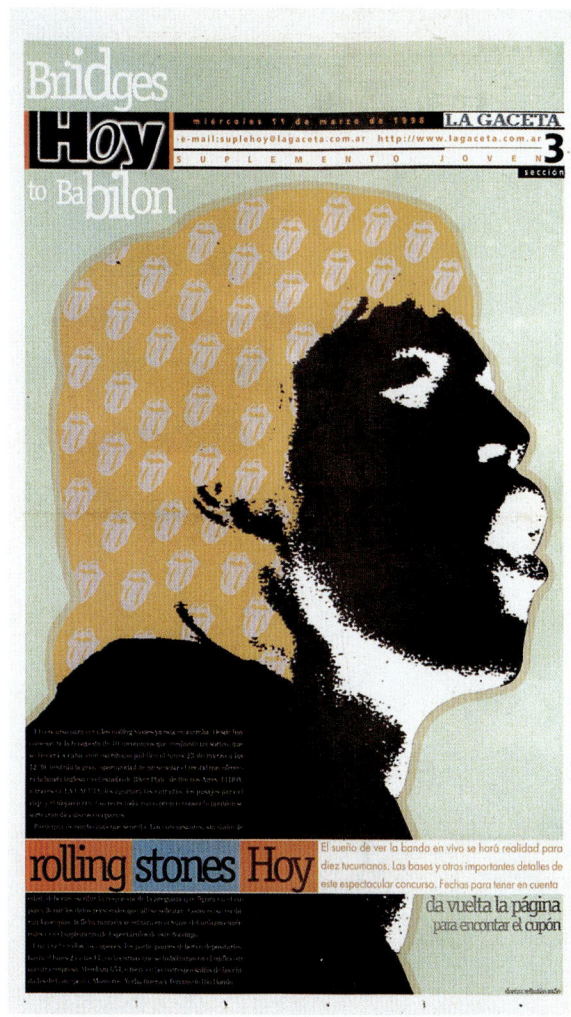

Silver
La Gaceta
San Miguel de Tucuman, Argentina
Sergio Fernandez, Art Director; **Sebastian Rosso,** Designer; **Mario García,** Design Consultant

Silver
La Gaceta
San Miguel de Tucuman, Argentina
Sergio Fernandez, Art Director; **Oscar Ferronato,** Designer; **Mario García,** Design Consultant; **Daniel Fontanarrosa,** Photo Illustrator

Silver
La Gaceta
San Miguel de Tucuman, Argentina
Sergio Fernandez, Art Director; **Sebastian Rosso,** Designer; **Mario García,** Design Consultant

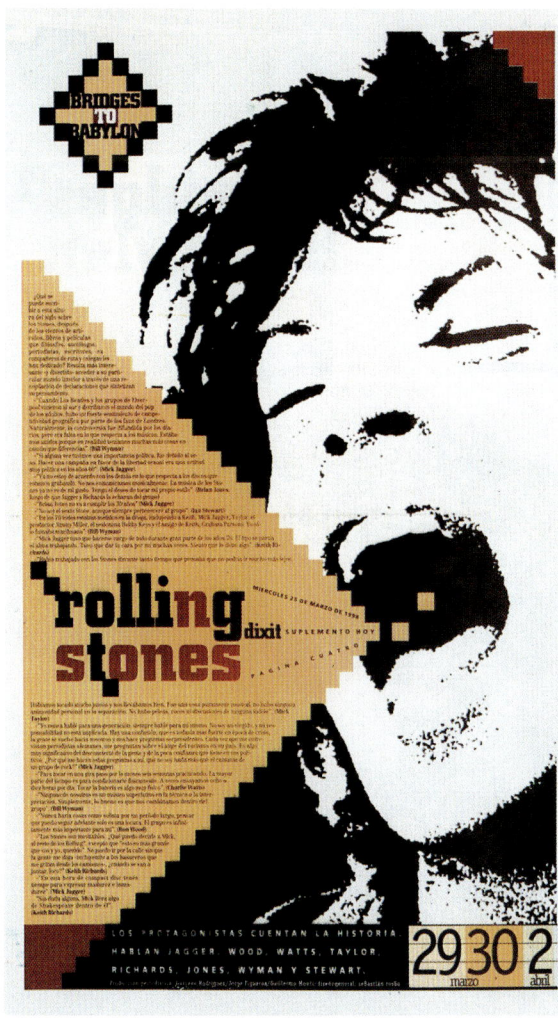

FEATURES ■ Entertainment Page

Anchorage Daily News
Anchorage, AK
Greg Epkes, Designer; **Sam Jones,** Photographer

La Gaceta
San Miguel de Tucuman, Argentina
Sebastian Rosso, Designer; **Sergio Fernandez,** Art Director; **Mario García,** Design Consultant; **Guillermo Monti,** Editor

La Gaceta
San Miguel de Tucuman, Argentina
Sebastian Rosso, Designer; **Sergio Fernandez,** Art Director; **Mario García,** Design Consultant

¡Exito! Newspaper
Chicago, IL
Victor Sánchez, Designer; **Antonio Pérez,** Photographer; **Alejandro Riera,** Reporter; **Alejandro Escalona,** Editor; **Arturo Jiménez,** Art & Production Director; **Anthony Majeri,** Senior Design Editor; **Francisco Caceres,** Illustrator

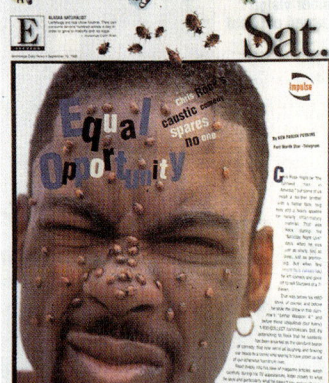

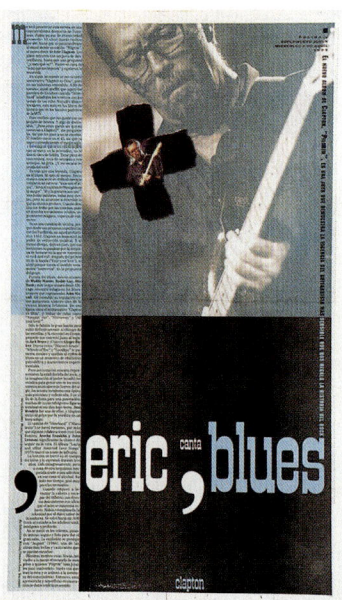

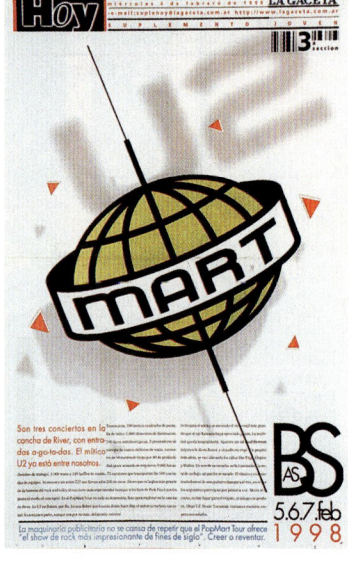

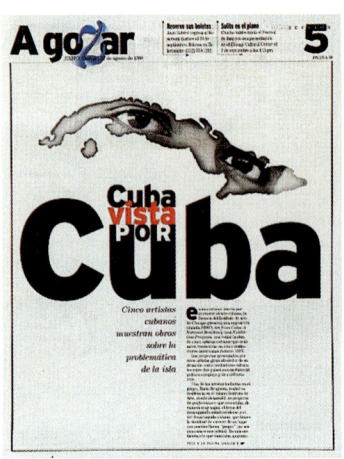

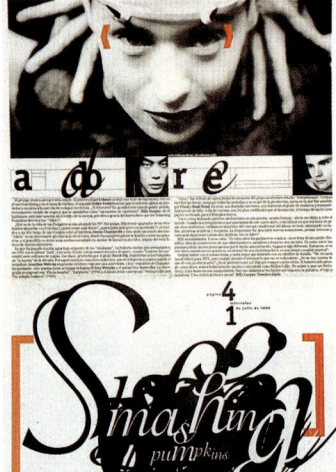

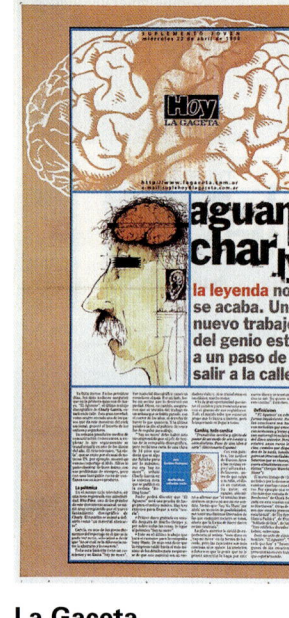

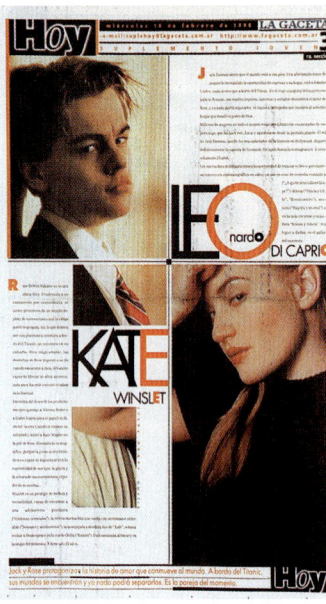

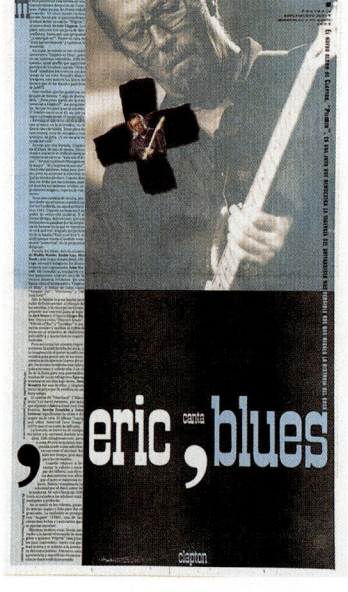

La Gaceta
San Miguel de Tucuman, Argentina
Falci Ruben, Designer; **Sergio Fernandez,** Art Director; **Mario García,** Design Consultant

La Gaceta
San Miguel de Tucuman, Argentina
Sebastian Rosso, Designer; **Sergio Fernandez,** Art Director; **Mario García,** Design Consultant; **Guillermo Monti,** Editor

La Gaceta
San Miguel de Tucuman, Argentina
Sebastian Rosso, Designer; **Sergio Fernandez,** Art Director; **Mario García,** Design Consultant; **A. Hugo Solarz,** Editor

La Gaceta
San Miguel de Tucuman, Argentina
Sebastian Rosso, Designer; **Sergio Fernandez,** Art Director; **Mario García,** Design Consultant; **Gustavo Rodriguez,** Editor

Entertainment Page ■ FEATURES

La Gaceta
San Miguel de Tucuman, Argentina
Sebastian Rosso, Illustrator & Designer; **Sergio Fernandez**, Art Director; **Mario García**, Design Consultant; **Gustavo Rodriguez**, Editor

La Gaceta
San Miguel de Tucuman, Argentina
Sebastian Rosso, Designer; **Sergio Fernandez**, Art Director; **Mario García**, Design Consultant; **Federico Türpe**, Editor

La Gaceta
San Miguel de Tucuman, Argentina
Sebastián Rosso, Designer; **Sergio Fernandez**, Art Director; **Mario García**, Design Consultant

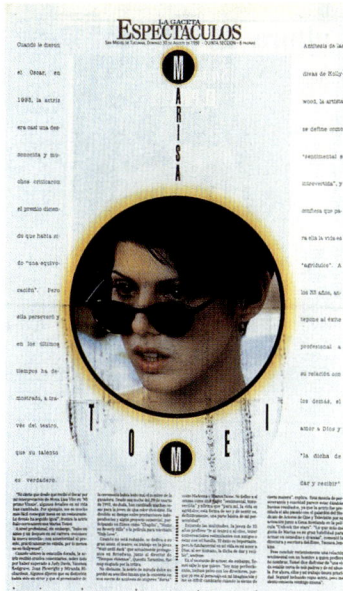

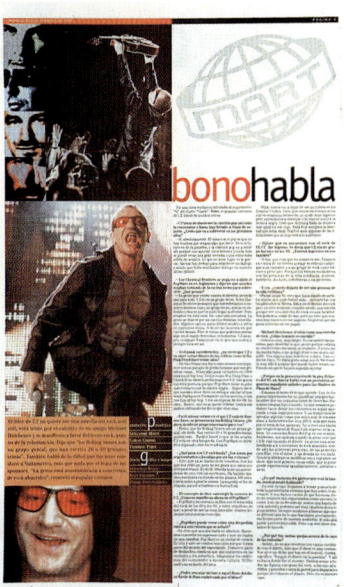

La Gaceta
San Miguel de Tucuman, Argentina
Oscar Ferronato, Designer; **Sergio Fernandez**, Art Director; **Mario García**, Design Consultant

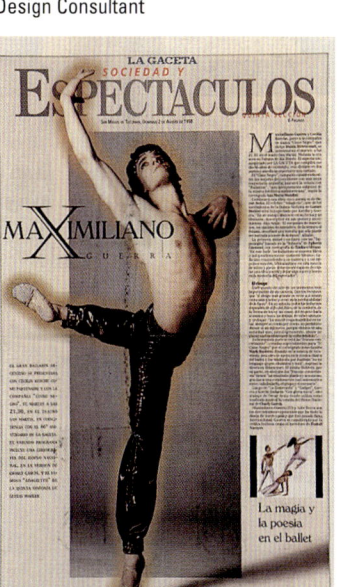

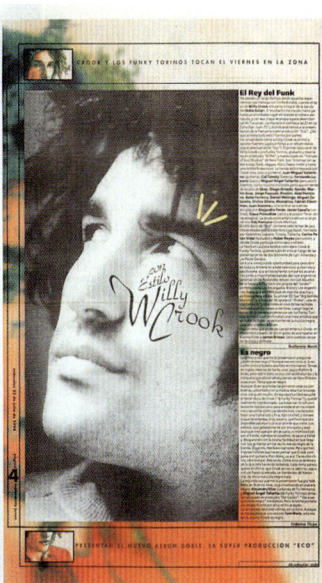

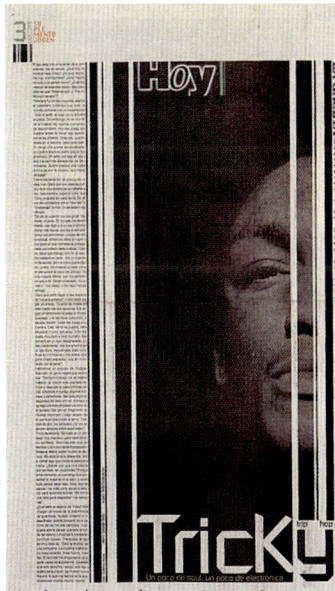

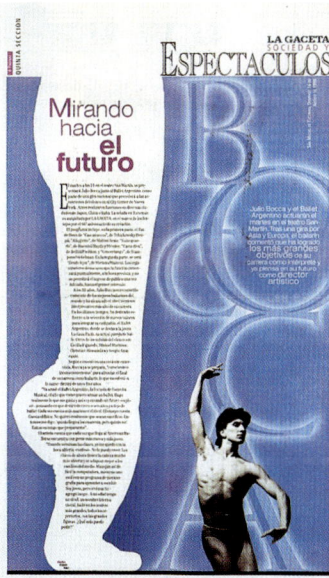

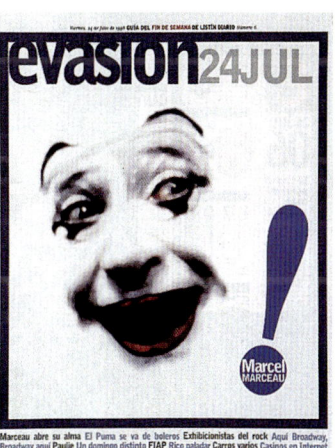

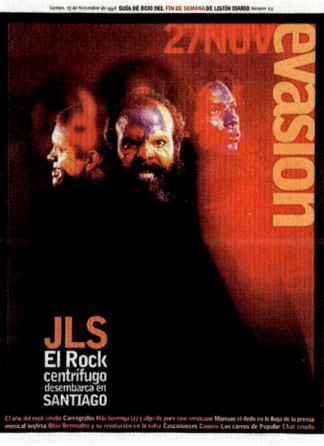

La Gaceta
San Miguel de Tucuman, Argentina
Sergio Fernandez, Art Director; **Falci Ruben**, Designer; **Mario García**, Design Consultant; **Raul Valverdi**, Photo Illustrator

Listin Diario
Arazuri, Spain
Pablo Ferrer, Editor; **Yoni Cruz**, Design Editor; **Bega Comunicación**, Design Consultant

Listin Diario
Arazuri, Spain
Pablo Ferrer, Editor; **Yoni Cruz**, Design Editor; **Bega Comunicación**, Design Consultant

La Gaceta
San Miguel de Tucuman, Argentina
Sebastian Rosso, Designer; **Sergio Fernandez**, Art Director; **Mario García**, Design Consultant; **Guillermo Monti**, Editor

FEATURES ■ Entertainment Page

Politiken
Copenhagen, Denmark
Søren Nyeland, Design Editor; **Katinka Bukh,** Designer; **Charlotte Sejer Pedersen,** Editor; **Else Bjørn,** Copy Editor

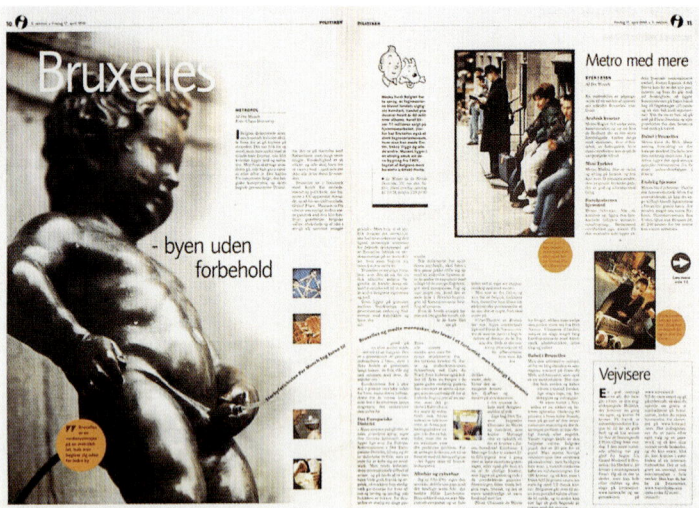

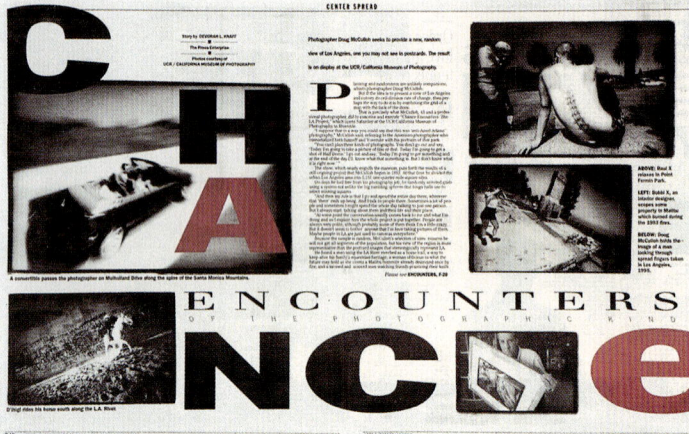

The Press-Enterprise
Riverside, CA
Veronica Hill, Designer/Asst. Entertainment Editor

Politiken
Copenhagen, Denmark
Søren Nyeland, Design Editor; **Stig Dyre,** Editor; **Katinka Bukh,** Designer

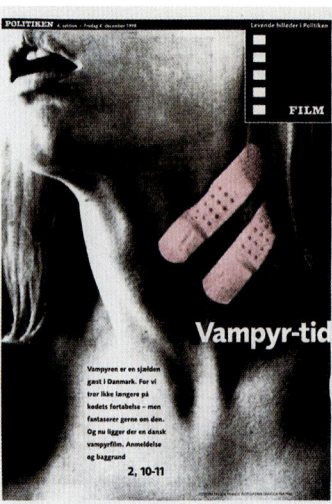

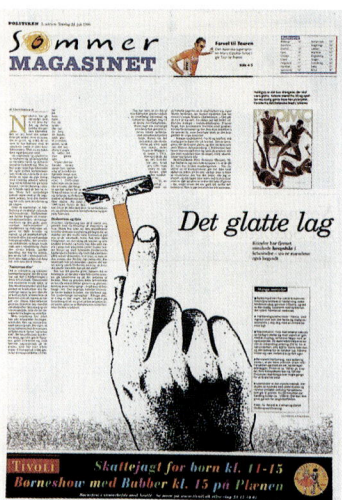

Politiken
Copenhagen, Denmark
Søren Nyeland, Design Editor; **Katinka Bukh,** Designer

Politiken
Copenhagen, Denmark
Søren Nyeland, Design Editor; **Katinka Bukh,** Designer

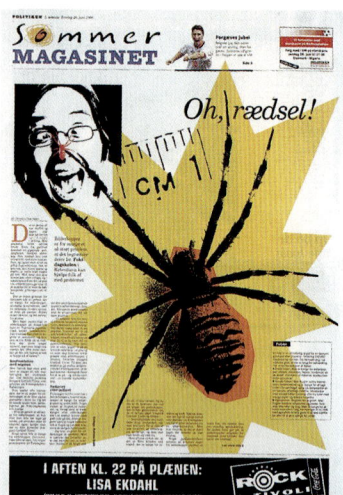

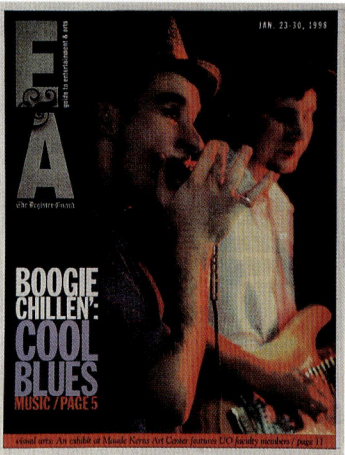

The Register-Guard
Eugene, OR
Tom Penix, Designer; **Thomas Boyd,** Photographer

Entertainment Page, Food Page ■ FEATURES

Tulsa World
Tulsa, OK
Mark Brown, Designer; **Cathy Logan,** Editor; **Kelly Kerr,** Photographer

Le Devoir
Montréal, Canada
Christian Tiffet, Art Director

Le Soleil
Quebec, Canada
Marie Delagrave, Designer

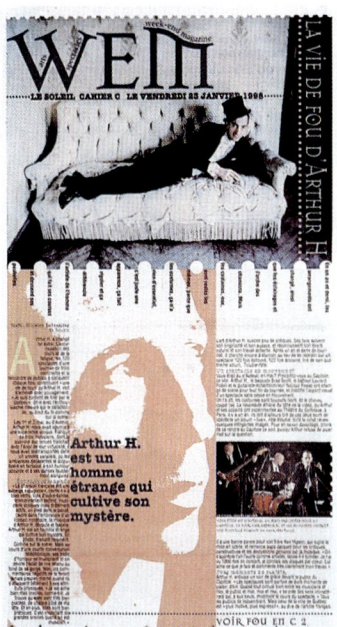

Le Devoir
Montréal, Canada
Christian Tiffet, Art Director

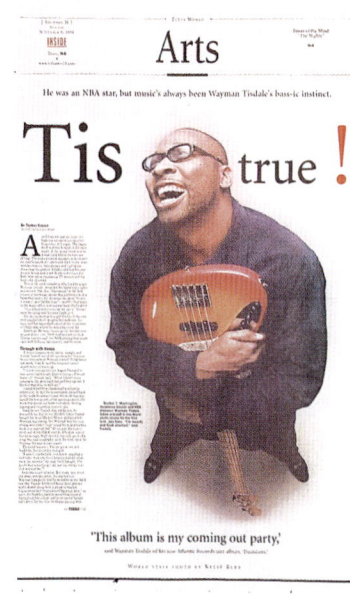

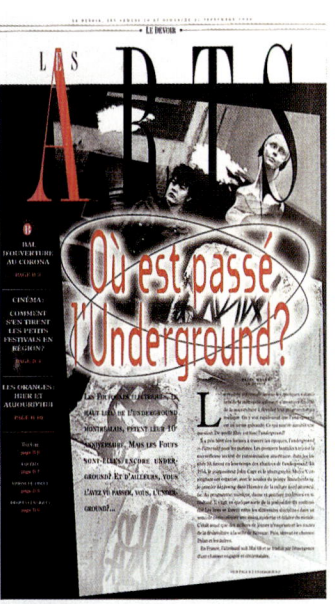

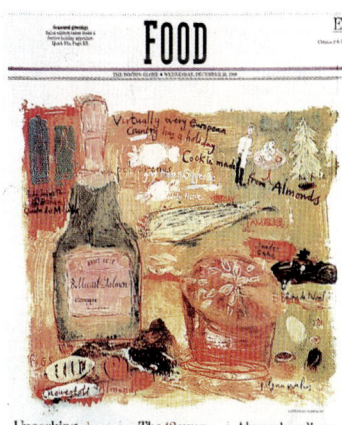

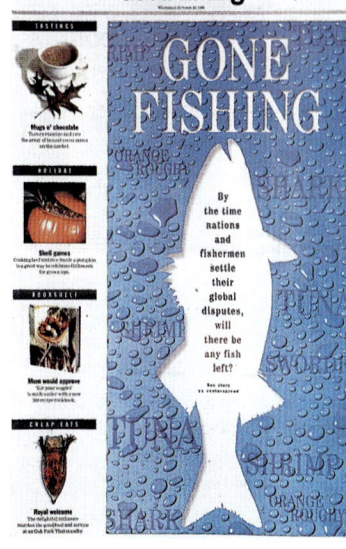

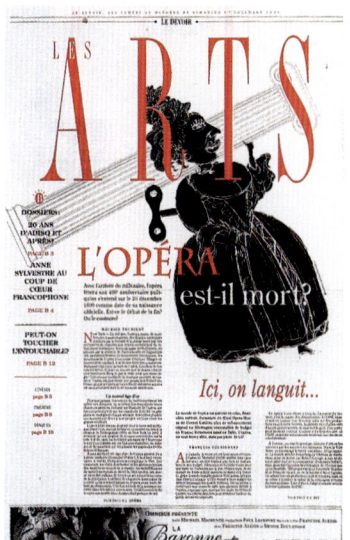

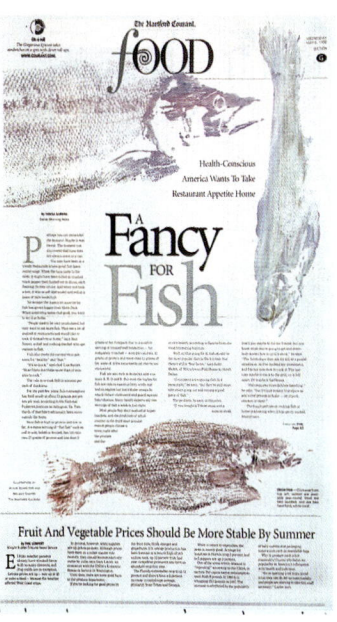

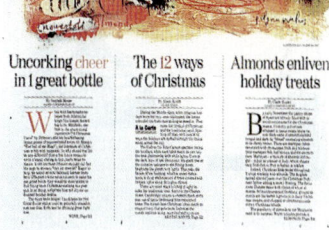

The Chicago Tribune
Chicago, IL
David Syrek, Designer

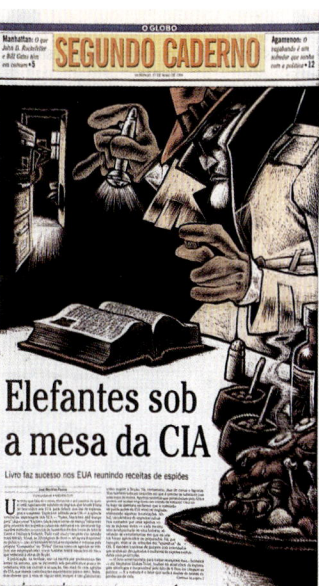

The Hartford Courant
Hartford, CT
Alison Schweitzer, Designer; **Christian P. Drury,** Art Director; **Melanie Shaffer,** Designer

The Boston Globe
Boston, MA
Jacqueline Berthet, Art Director & Designer; **Stephen Meuse,** Freelance Writer; **Suzy Pilgrim-Waters,** Illustrator; **Fiona Luis,** Editor; **Susan Epstein,** Copy Editor; **Alison Arnett,** Reporter; **Claire Hopley,** Free-lance Writer

O Globo
Rio de Janeiro, Brasil
Cruz, Illustrator; **Helio Hara,** Editor

TWENTIETH EDITION ■ 125

FEATURES ■ Food Page

The San Diego Union-Tribune
San Diego, CA
Laurie Harker, Designer/Art Director; **Anita L. Arambula**, Photographer

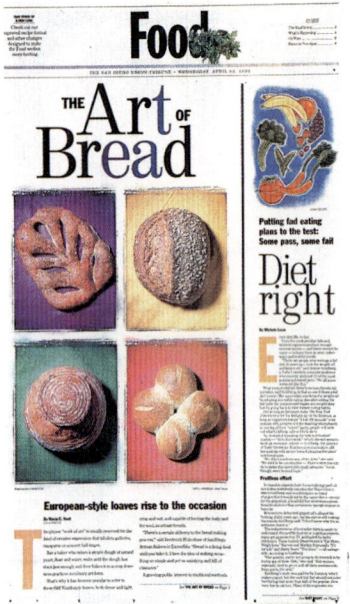

Anchorage Daily News
Anchorage, AK
Pamela Dunlap-Shohl, Designer; **Lin Mitchell**, Photographer

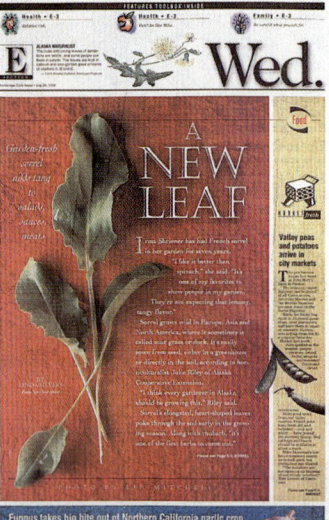

La Gaceta
San Miguel de Tucuman, Argentina
Sebastian Rosso, Designer; **Sergio Fernandez**, Art Director; **Mario García**, Design Consultant; **Daniel Fontanarrosa**, Illustrator; **Dante Erbetta**, Editor

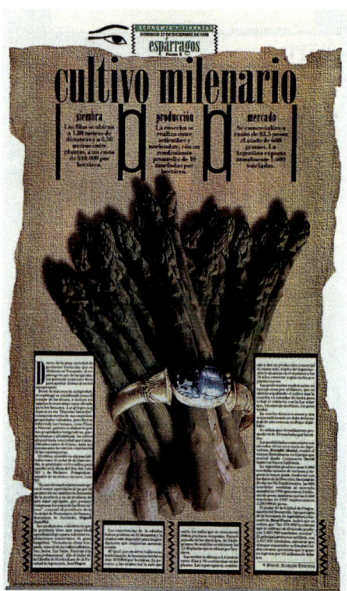

La Gaceta
San Miguel de Tucuman, Argentina
Sebastian Rosso, Designer; **Sergio Fernandez**, Art Director; **Mario García**, Design Consultant; **Ricardo Heredia**, Illustrator; **Dante Erbetta**, Editor

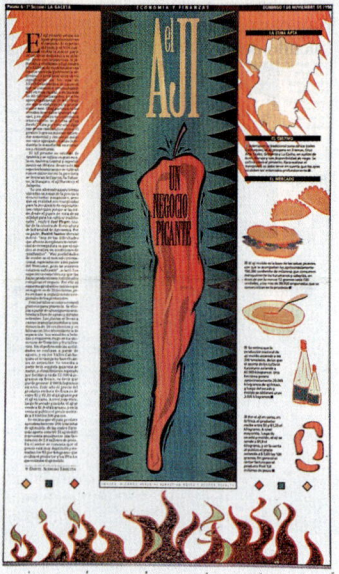

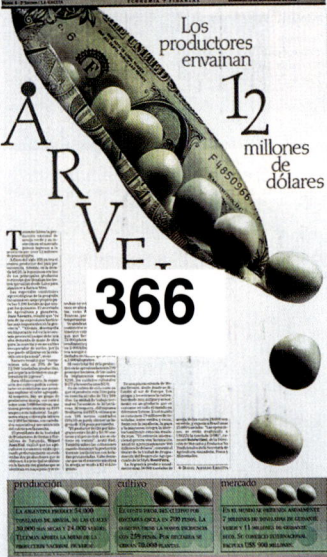

La Gaceta
San Miguel de Tucuman, Argentina
Sebastian Rosso, Designer; **Sergio Fernandez**, Art Director; **Mario García**, Design Consultant; **Dante Erbetta**, Editor

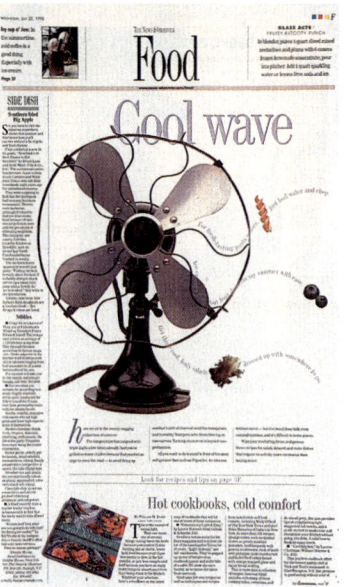

The News & Observer
Raleigh, NC
Robin Johnston, Features Design Director; **Debbie Moose**, Food Editor

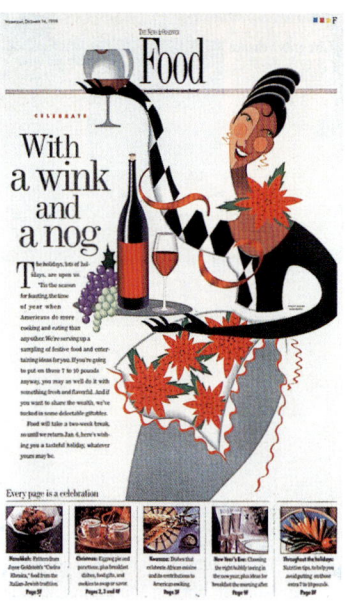

The News & Observer
Raleigh, NC
Robin Johnston, Features Design Director; **Susan Houston**, Food Editor

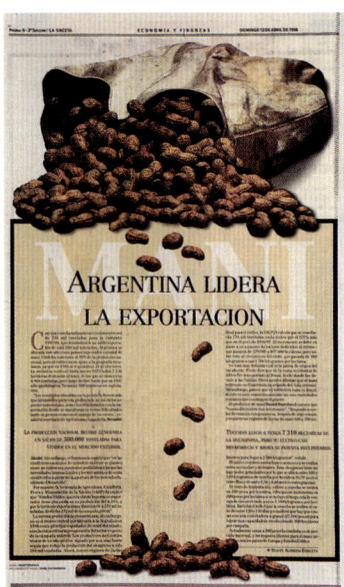

La Gaceta
San Miguel de Tucuman, Argentina
Oscar Ferronato, Designer; **Sergio Fernandez**, Art Director; **Mario García**, Design Consultant; **Daniel Fontanarrosa**, Photo Illustrator

Food Page, Fashion Page ■ FEATURES

Dagens Nyheter
Stockholm, Sweden
Peter Alenäs, Art Director & Designer; **Pompe Hedengren,** Art Director; **Karolina Henke,** Photographer; **Maria Schelin,** Stylist

Diario de Noticias
Pamplona, Spain
Silvia de Luis, Designer

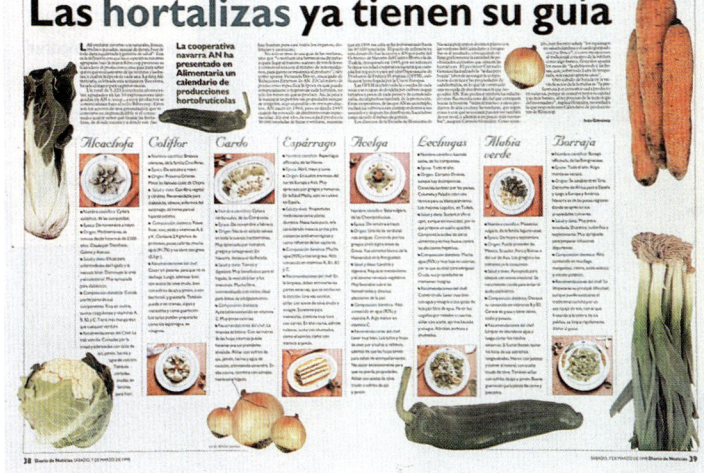

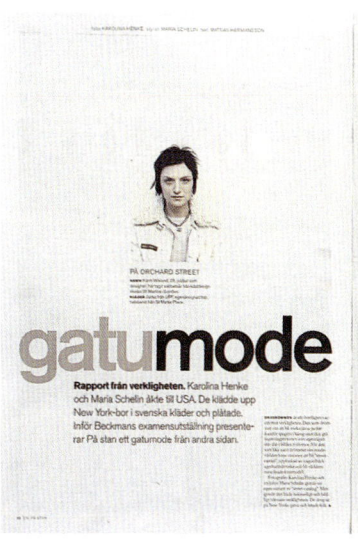
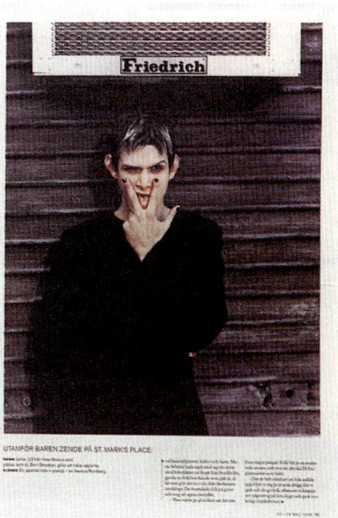

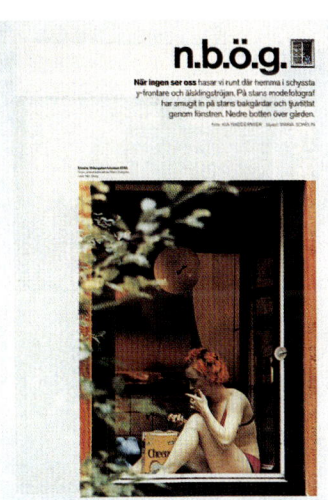
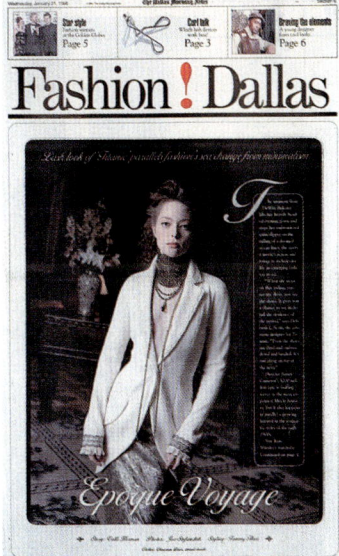
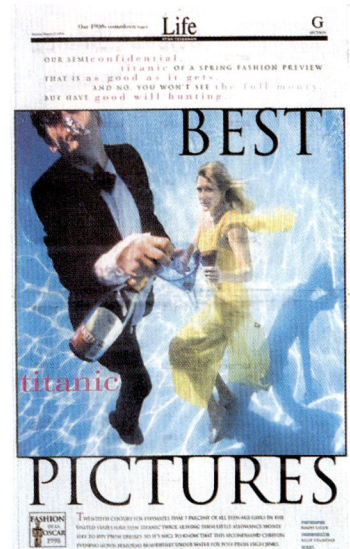
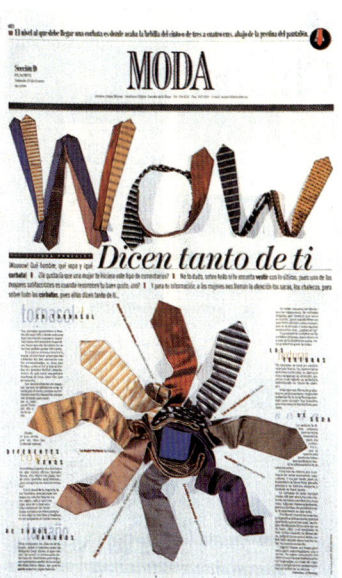

Dagens Nyheter
Stockholm, Sweden
Magnus Naddermier, Art Director; **Kia Naddermier,** Photographer; **Maria Schelin,** Stylist

The Dallas Morning News
Dallas, TX
Laura Betts Ford, Designer

Fort Worth Star-Telegram
Fort Worth, TX
Cynthia Wahl, Art Director & Designer; **Ralph Lauer,** Photographer; **Gaile Robinson,** Fashion Editor; **Kelly DeGarmo,** Staff Writer
• also for Photo Illustration

El Norte
Monterrey, México
Lourdes de la Rosa, Designer; **Miguel Angel Chavéz,** Photographer; **Diana Marcos,** Section Editor; **Carmen Escobedo,** Design Manager Editor; **Raúl Braulio Martinez,** Art Director; **Martha Treviño,** Editor/Director; **Ramón Alberto Garza,** General Editor Director

FEATURES ■ Fashion Page, Home/Real Estate

Göteborgs-Posten
Göteborg, Sweden
Gunilla Wernhamn, Designer; **Marcel Pabst,** Photographer

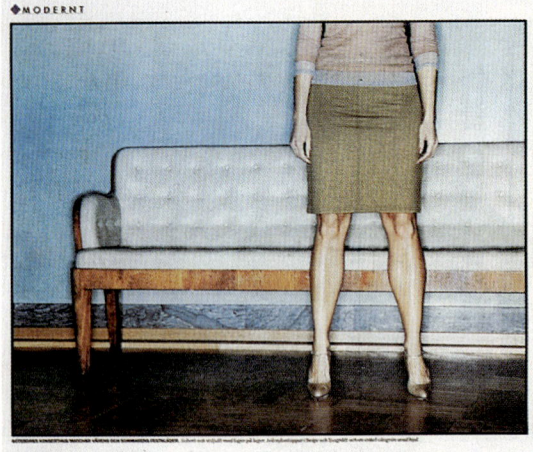

Politiken
Copenhagen, Denmark
Søren Nyeland, Design Editor; **Annete Vestergaard,** Editor; **Mikkel Hensel,** Designer

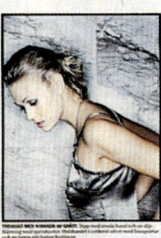

The Washington Times
Washington, DC
Joseph W. Scopin, A.M.E. Graphics; **Jennifer Pritchard,** Art Editor; **Daniel Rosenbaum,** Photographer

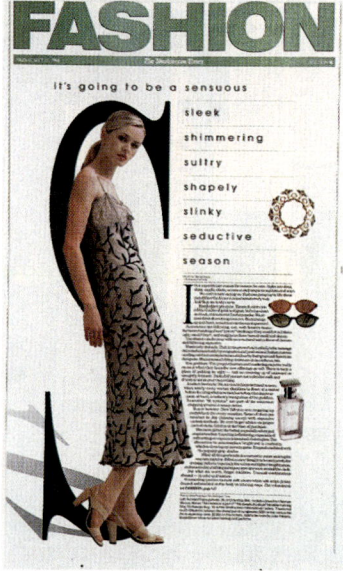

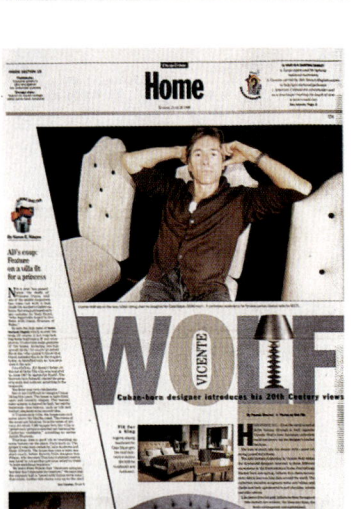

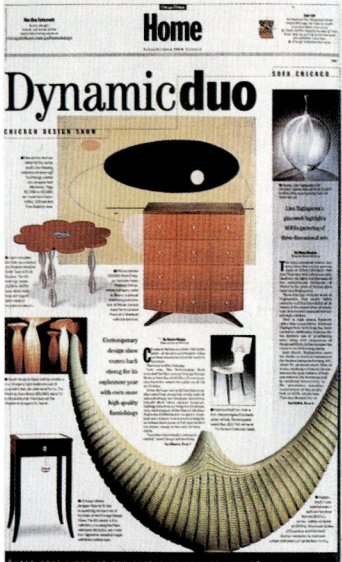

The Chicago Tribune
Chicago, IL
Herman Vega, Designer; **Bob Fila,** Photographer; **Elaine Matsushita,** Editor

The Chicago Tribune
Chicago, IL
Herman Vega, Designer; **Elaine Matsushita,** Editor

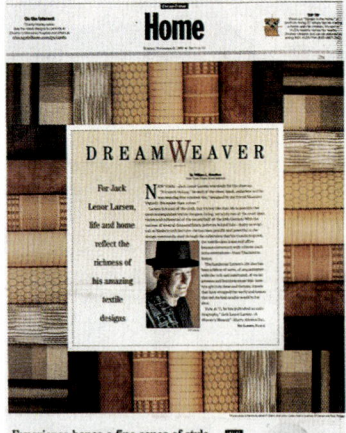
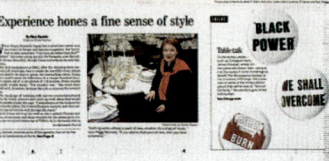

The Chicago Tribune
Chicago, IL
Herman Vega, Designer; **James F. Quinn,** Photographer; **Charles Osgood,** Photographer; **Elaine Matsushita,** Editor

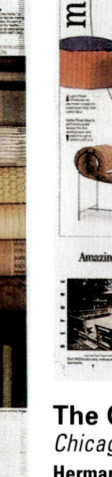
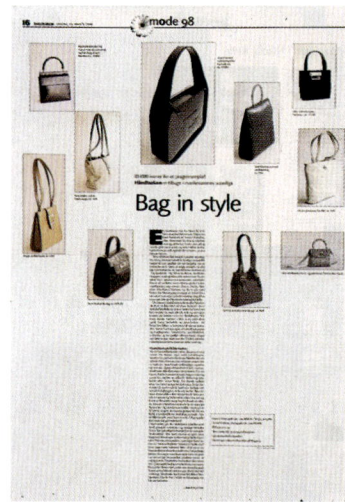

The Chicago Tribune
Chicago, IL
Herman Vega, Designer; **Scott Cavanah,** Photographer; **Pete Krumhardt,** Photographer; **Elaine Matsushita,** Editor

Home/Real Estate Page, Travel Page ■ FEATURES

O Globo
Rio de Janeiro, Brasil
Cruz, Illustrator; **Lea Cristina Gomes,** Editor

The Star-Ledger
Newark, NJ
Bob Bogert, Designer; **Deborah Jerome-Cohen,** Editor/Home & Garden

The Chicago Tribune
Chicago, IL
Herman Vega, Designer; **Pete Souza,** Photographer; **James E. Quinn,** Photographer; **Elaine Matsushita,** Editor

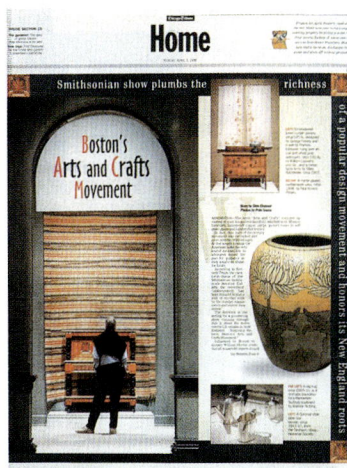

San Jose Mercury News
San Jose, CA
David Frazier, Page Designer

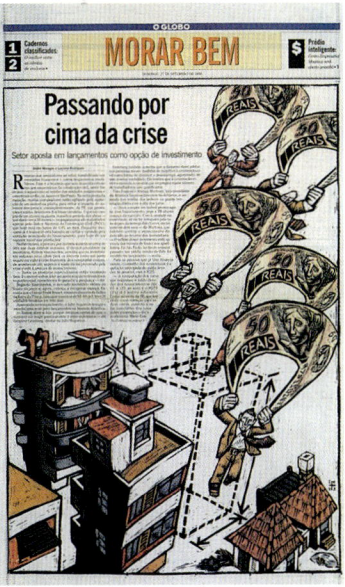

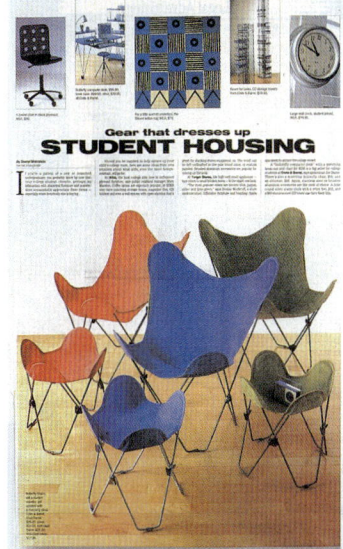

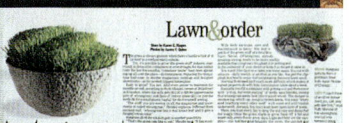

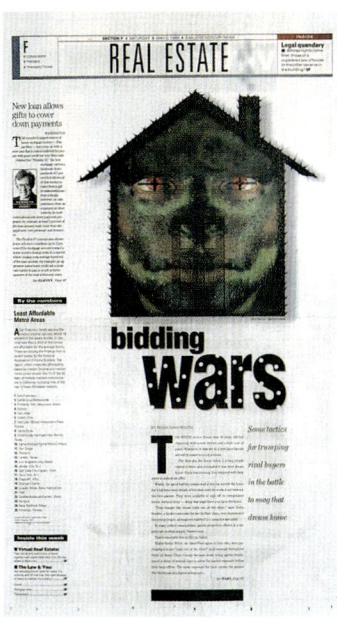

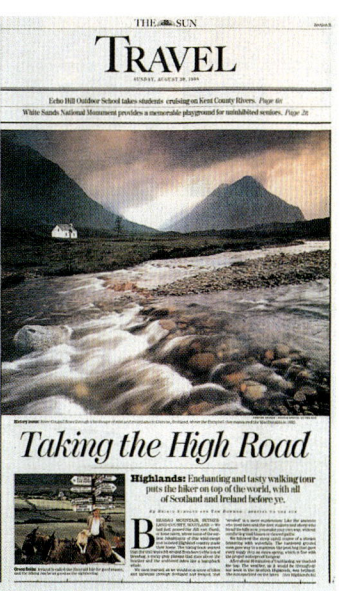

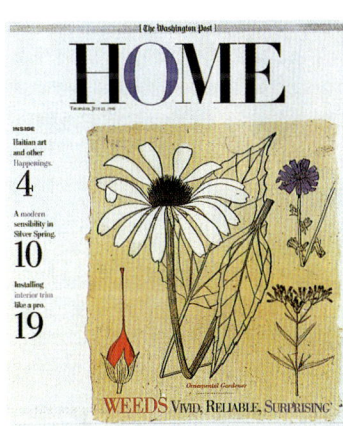

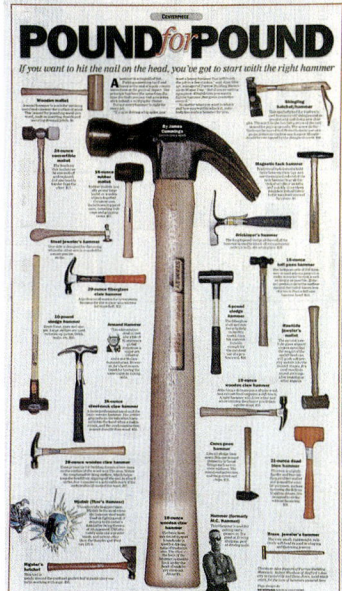

The Washington Post
Washington, DC
Alice Kress, Art Director/Illustrator

Dayton Daily News
Dayton, OH
M.B. Hopkins, Designer; **Jim Witmer,** Photographer; **Ted Pitts,** Art Director

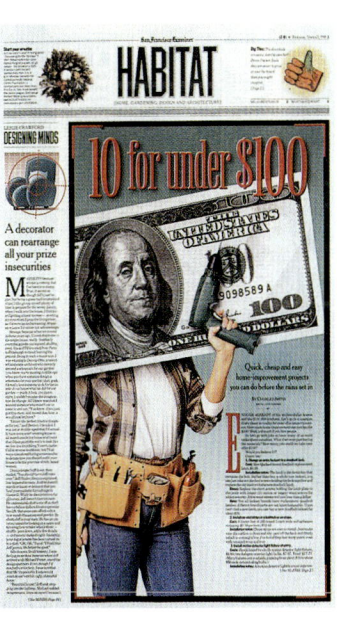

The Sun
Baltimore, MD
Peter Dishal, Designer; **Victor Panichkul,** Features Design Director; **Joseph Hutchinson,** A.M.E. Graphics/Design

San Francisco Examiner
San Francisco, CA
Kelly Frankeny, A.M.E. Design; **Don McCartney,** Design Director; **Jo Mancuso,** Habitat Editor; **Pat Sedlar,** Designer/Illustrator

TWENTIETH EDITION ■ 129

FEATURES ■ Travel Page

Silver
The Sun
Baltimore, MD

Peter Dishal, Designer; **Victor Panichkul,** Features Design Director; **Joseph Hutchinson,** A.M.E. Graphics/Design

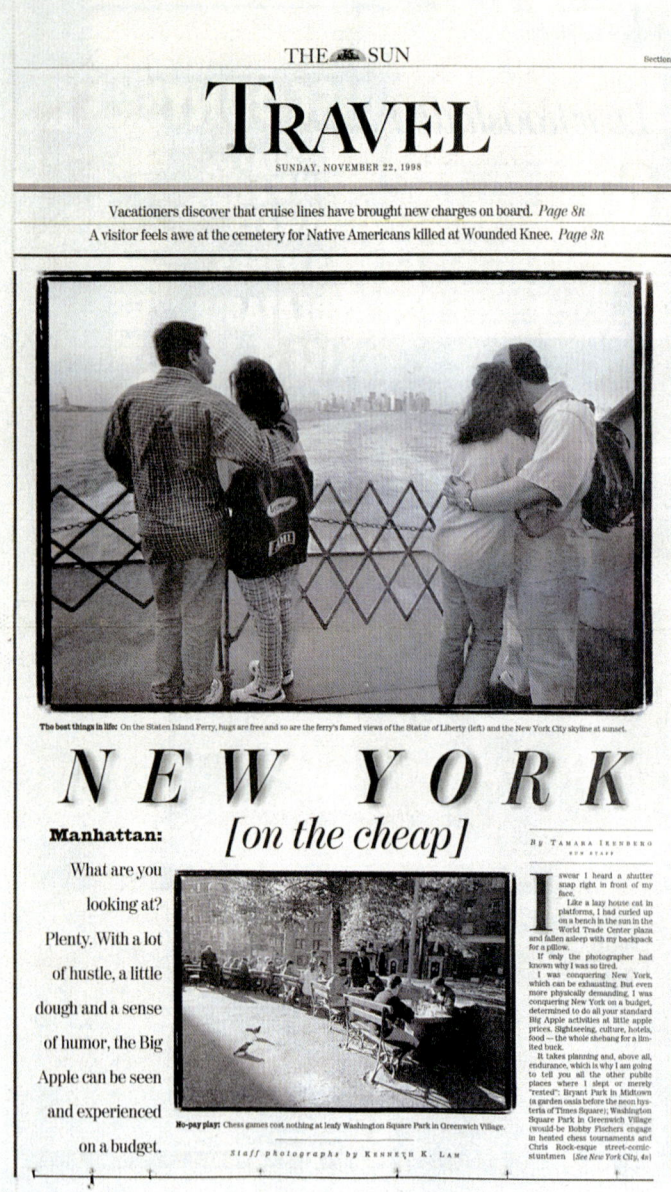

The Boston Globe
Boston, MA

Keith A. Webb, Art Director & Designer;
Dan Leeth, Photographer; **Eric Berger,** Photographer

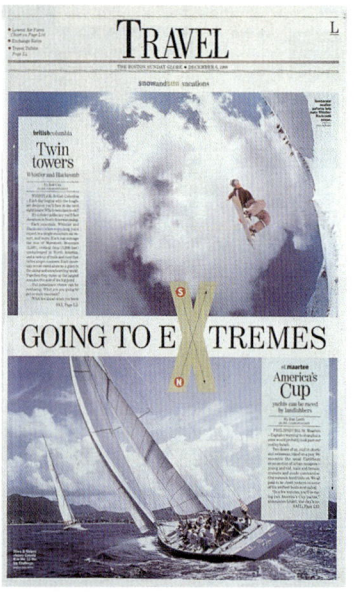

The Boston Globe
Boston, MA

Keith A. Webb, Art Director & Designer

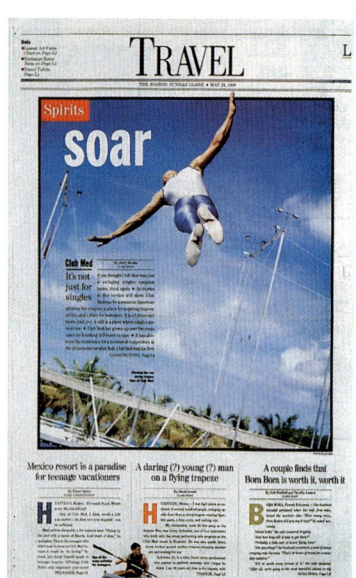

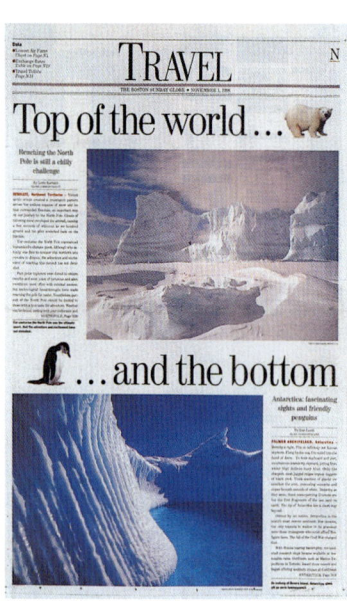

The Boston Globe
Boston, MA

Patty Alvarez, Art Director & Designer;
Neo Vision Photonica, Photographer;
Kevin Schafer, Photographer

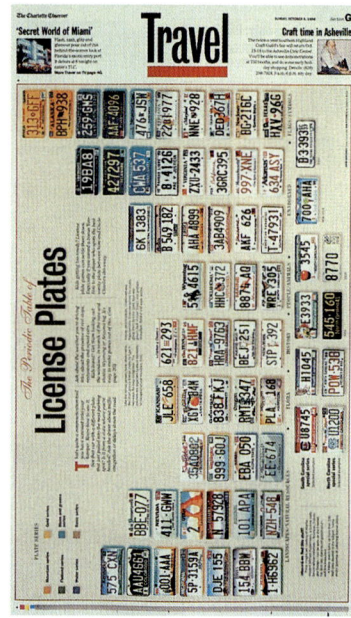

The Charlotte Observer
Charlotte, NC

William Pitzer, News Graphic Editor;
Joanne Miller, Art Director; **Jack Russell,** Designer; **John Bordsen,** Travel Editor; **Gina Nania,** Copy Editor

Travel Page ■ FEATURES

Fort Worth Star-Telegram
Fort Worth, TX
Clif Bosler, Designer

The Orange County Register
Santa Ana, CA
Helayne Perry, Designer; **Kris Viesselman Onuigbo,** Art Director; **Amy Ning,** Artist; **Dee Boyles,** Art Director

The Oregonian
Portland, OR
Nancy Casey, Page Designer

The Chicago Tribune
Chicago, IL
Kate Elazegui, Designer; **Randy Curwen,** Editor; **John Sayles,** Illustrator

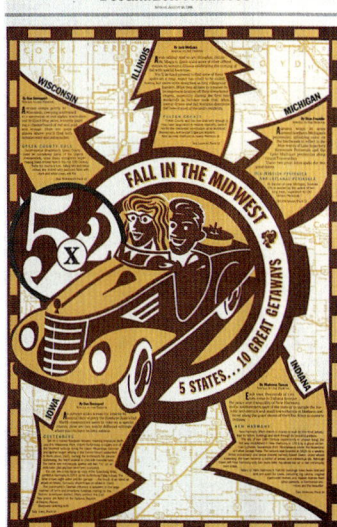

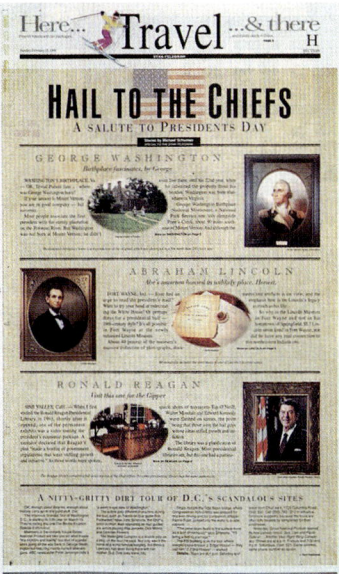

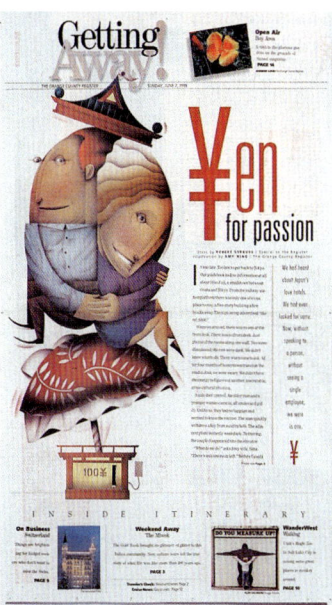

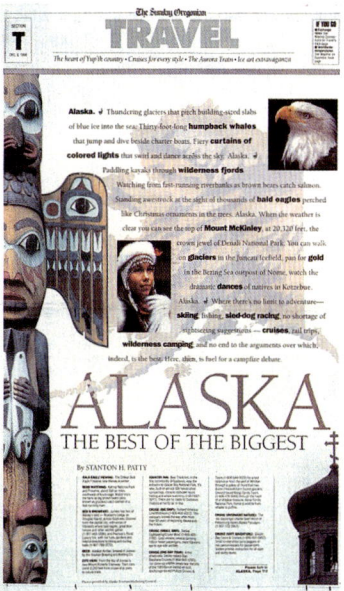

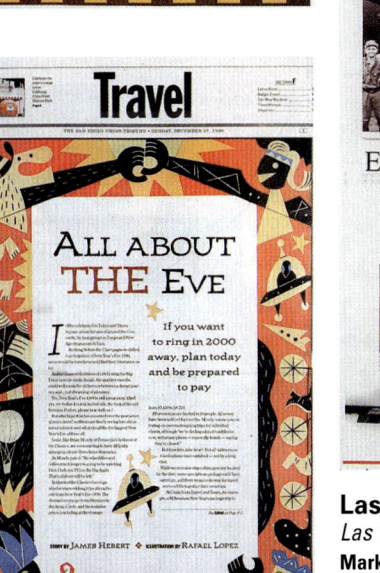

Las Vegas Review-Journal
Las Vegas, NV
Mark Antonuccio, Page Designer

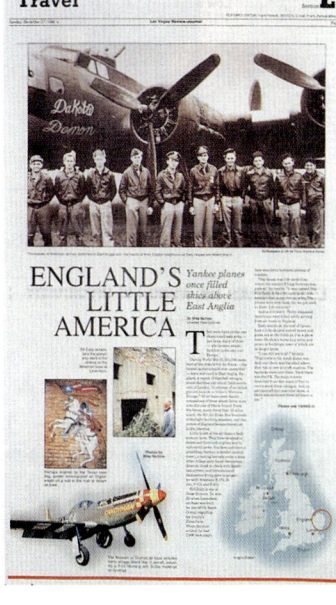

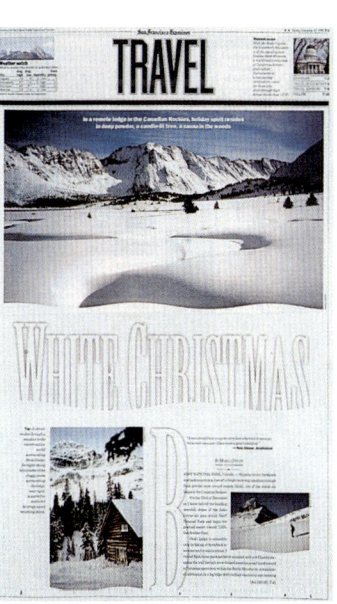

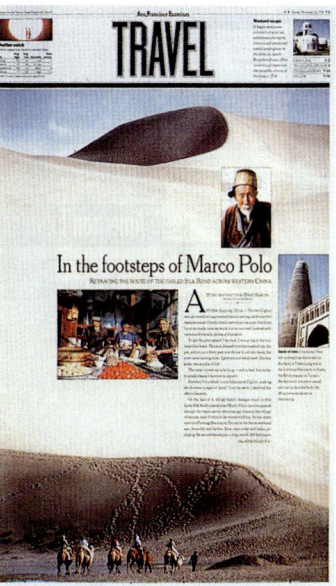

San Francisco Examiner
San Francisco, CA
Kelly Frankeny, A.M.E. Design; **Don McCartney,** Design Director; **John Flinn,** Travel Editor; **Andrew Skwish,** Designer

The San Diego Union-Tribune
San Diego, CA
Jean Fraser, Designer; **Raphael Lopez,** Illustrator

San Francisco Examiner
San Francisco, CA
Kelly Frankeny, A.M.E. Design; **Don McCartney,** Design Director; **John Flinn,** Travel Editor; **Andrew Skwish,** Designer

FEATURES ■ Science/Technology Page

Silver
The San Diego Union-Tribune
San Diego, CA
Laurie Harker, Designer/Art Director; **David Mollering,** Illustrator

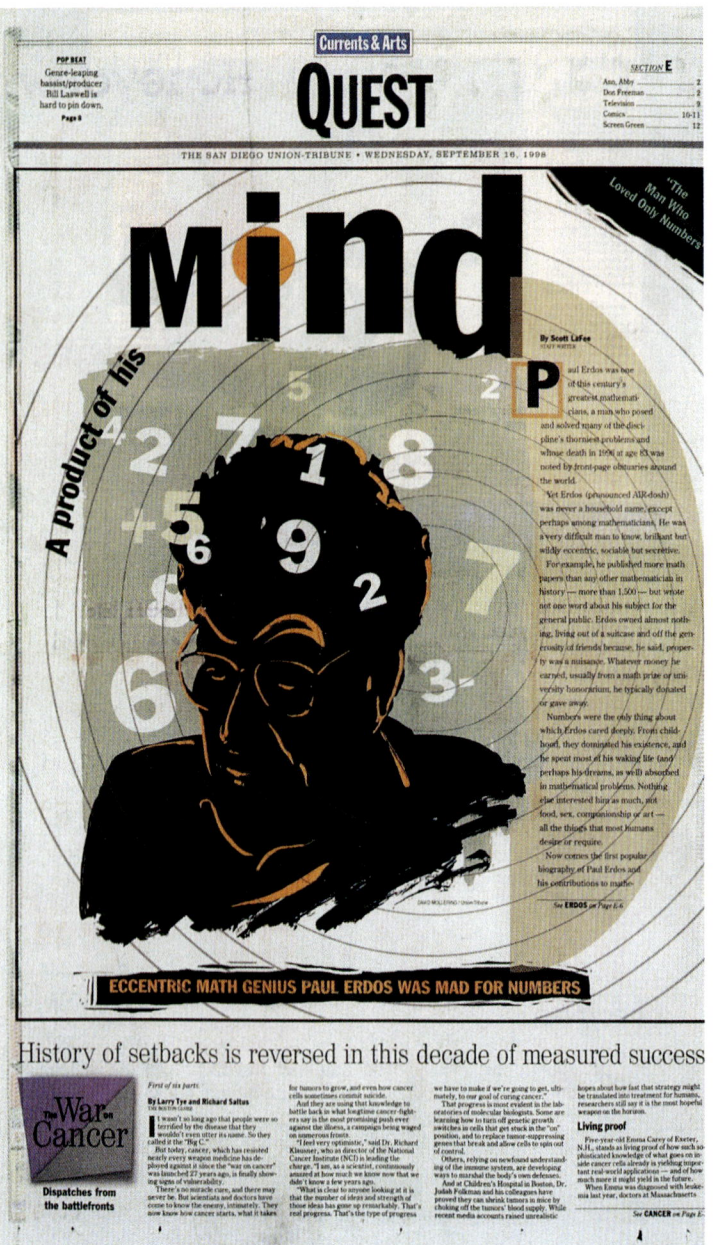

The Boston Globe
Boston, MA
Cindy Daniels, Art Director & Designer; **Nils Bruzelius,** Editor; **Katherine Everly,** Editor; **David Chandler,** Writer

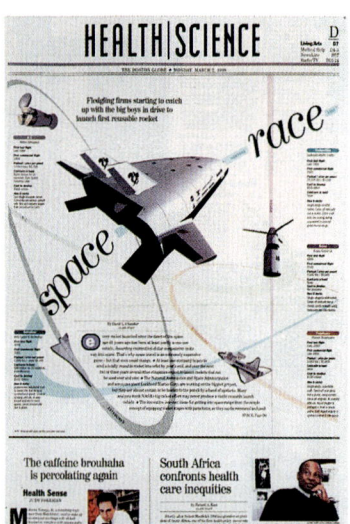

O Globo
Rio de Janeiro, Brasil
Leonardo Drummond, Designer; **Marilia Martins,** Editor; **Cláudio Duarte,** Illustrator

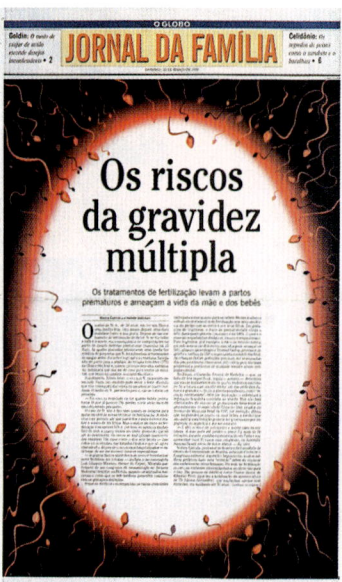

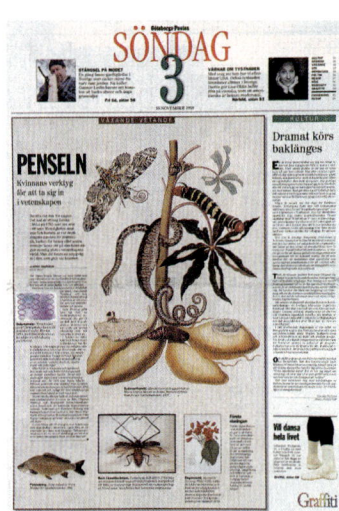

Göteborgs-Posten
Göteborg, Sweden
Barbro Dahrén, Editorial Designer

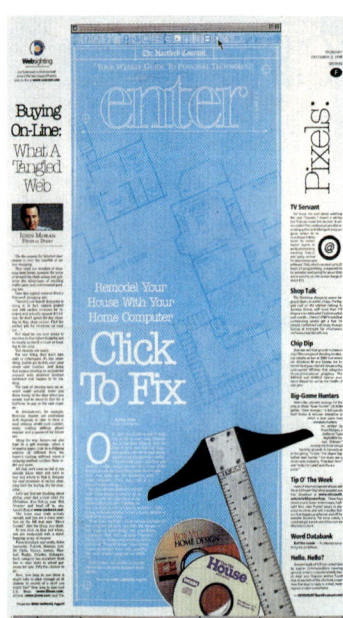

The Hartford Courant
Hartford, CT
Chris Moore, Designer; **Scott Johnson,** Assistant Art Director; **Christian P. Drury,** Art Director; **Sherry Peters,** Photo Editor

Science/Technology Page, Other Page ■ FEATURES

The Hartford Courant
Hartford, CT

Chris Moore, Designer; **Scott Johnson**, Assistant Art Director; **Christian P. Drury**, Art Director; **Sherry Peters**, Photo Editor

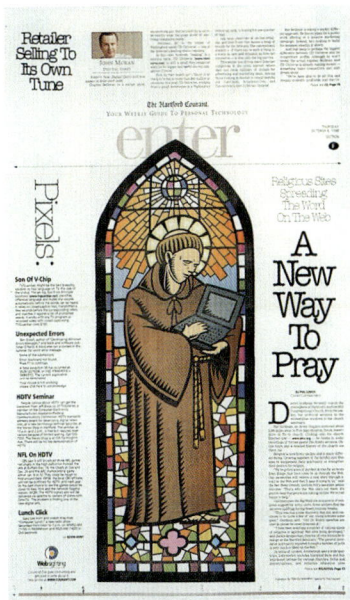

The San Diego Union-Tribune
San Diego, CA

Laurie Harker, Designer/Art Director; **Mark Nowlin**, Graphic Journalist

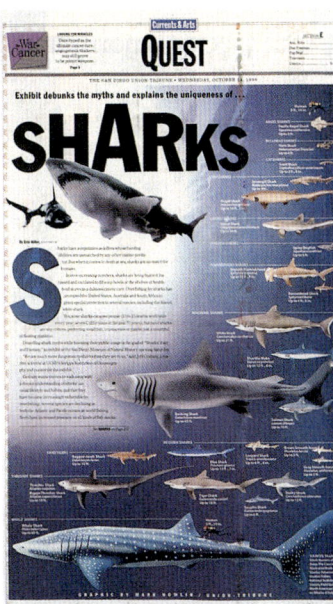

The San Diego Union-Tribune
San Diego, CA

Laurie Harker, Designer/Art Director/Illustrator

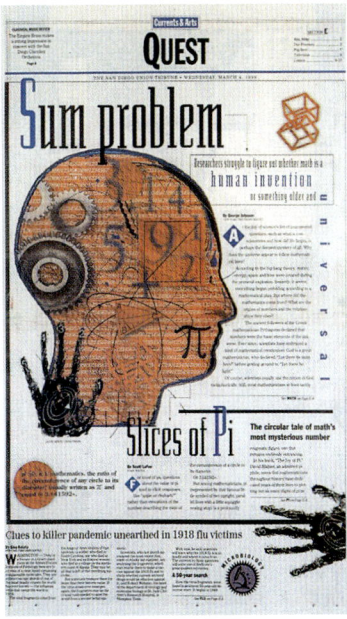

The Florida Times-Union
Jacksonville, FL

Tami Scholl, Features Designer; **Troy Oxford**, Illustrator

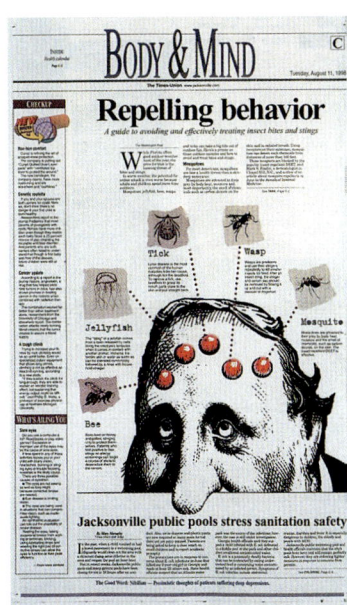

Silver
O Globo
Rio de Janeiro, Brasil

Cruz, Illustrator; **Helio Hara**, Editor

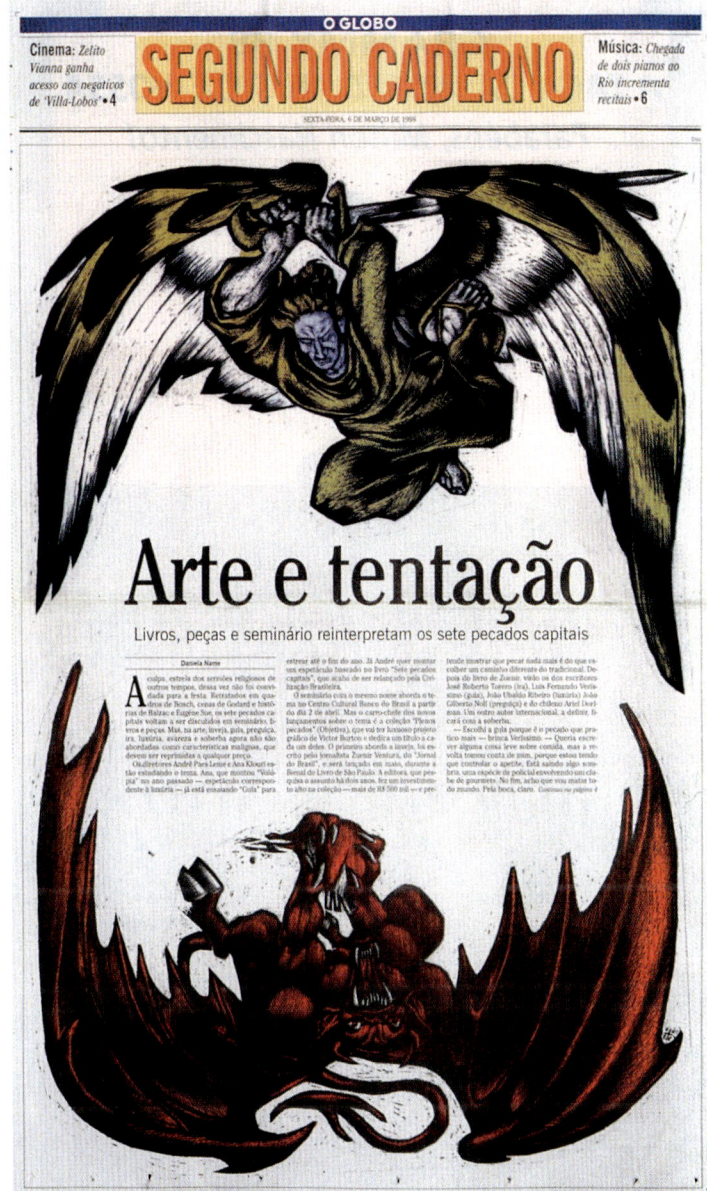

TWENTIETH EDITION ■ 133

FEATURES ■ Other Page

Gold
O Globo
Rio de Janeiro, Brasil
Luiz Noronha, Editor; **Télio Navega**, Designer

This is a daring and audacious page. It's a designer's defiance to editors and readers. It's an unusual cover story. The headline reads, "Who's afraid of white space?"

Es una página audaz y atrevida. Es un desafío lanzado por el diseñador a los redactores y lectores. Es una historia de portada poco común. La página blanca se utiliza a modo de contraste.

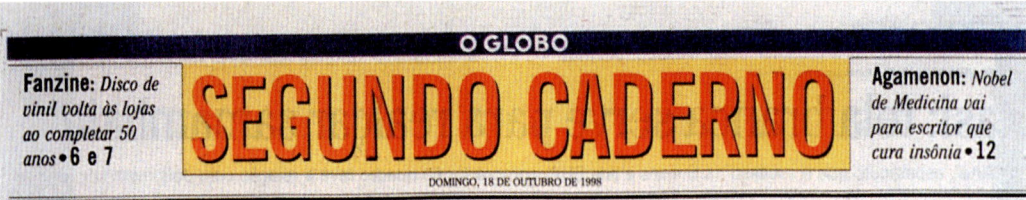

134 ■ THE BEST OF NEWSPAPER DESIGN

Science/Technology Page, Other Page ■ FEATURES

La Gaceta
San Miguel de Tucuman, Argentina
Falci Ruben, Designer; **Sergio Fernandez,** Art Director; **Mario García,** Design Consultant; **Daniel Fontanarrosa,** Photo Illustrator

The Boston Globe
Boston, MA
Jacqueline Berthet, Art Director & Designer; **Shirley Newsom,** Editor

La Gaceta
San Miguel de Tucuman, Argentina
Héctor Reinoso Gallo, Designer; **Sergio Fernandez,** Art Director; **Mario García,** Design Consultant

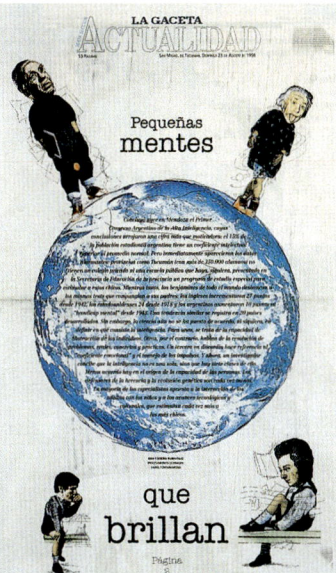

Dagbladet
Oslo, Norway
Eirik Vale Frogner, Designer

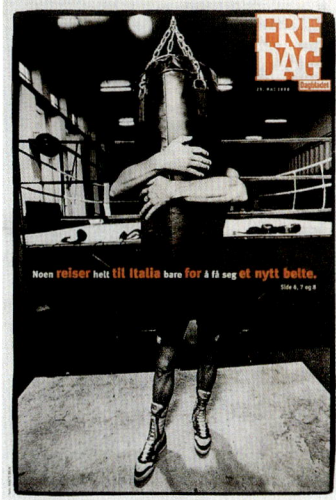

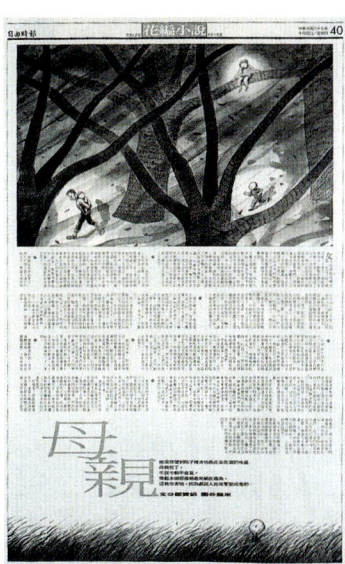

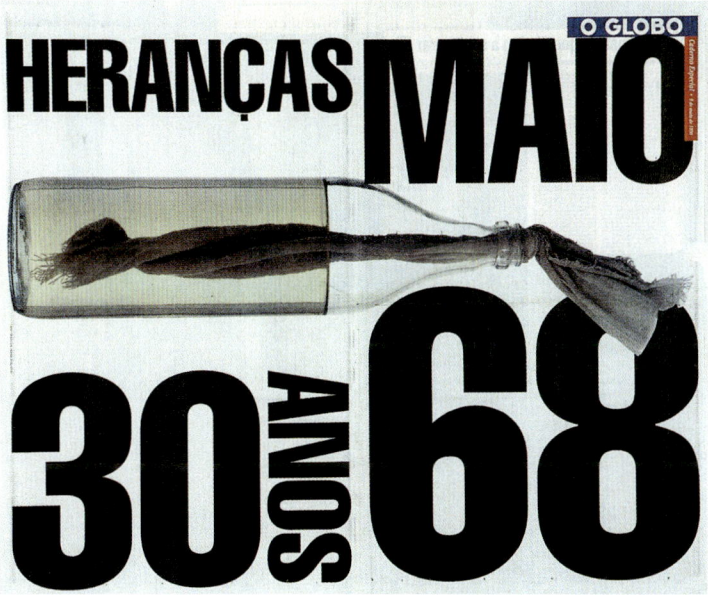

O Globo
Rio de Janeiro, Brasil
Felipe Taborda, Designer

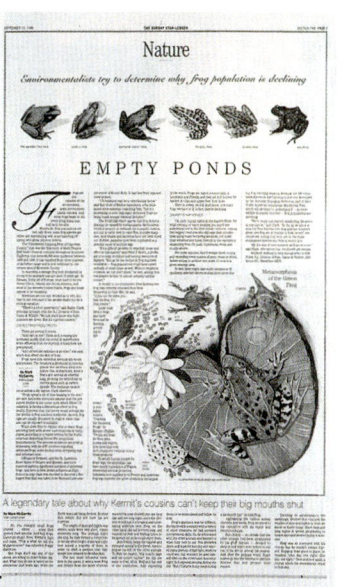

The Liberty Times
Taipei, R.O.C.
Tung Ku-Ying, Art Director & Designer

The Star-Ledger
Newark, NJ
Pablo Colon, Features Design Director/Designer; **Richard Bigelow,** Designer; **Andre Malok,** Graphic Artist; **Helen Driggs,** Graphic Artist

FEATURES ■ Other Page

Silver
El Norte
Monterrey, México
Perla Olmeda, Designer; **Arturo Rangel,** Design Editor & Illustrator; **Marcela García,** Section Editor; **Alexandro Medrano,** Design Manager Editor; **Raúl Braulio Martinez,** Art Director; **Martha Treviño,** Editor/Director; **Martin Pérez Martínez,** Editor/Director; **Ramón Alberto Garza,** General Editor Director; **Carlos Martínez,** Section Editor
• also an Award of Excellence for Illustration Black or Black and One Color

Silver
La Gaceta
San Miguel de Tucuman, Argentina
Sebastian Rosso, Designer; **Sergio Fernandez,** Art Director; **Mario García,** Design Consultant; **Raul Valverdi,** Photo Illustrator

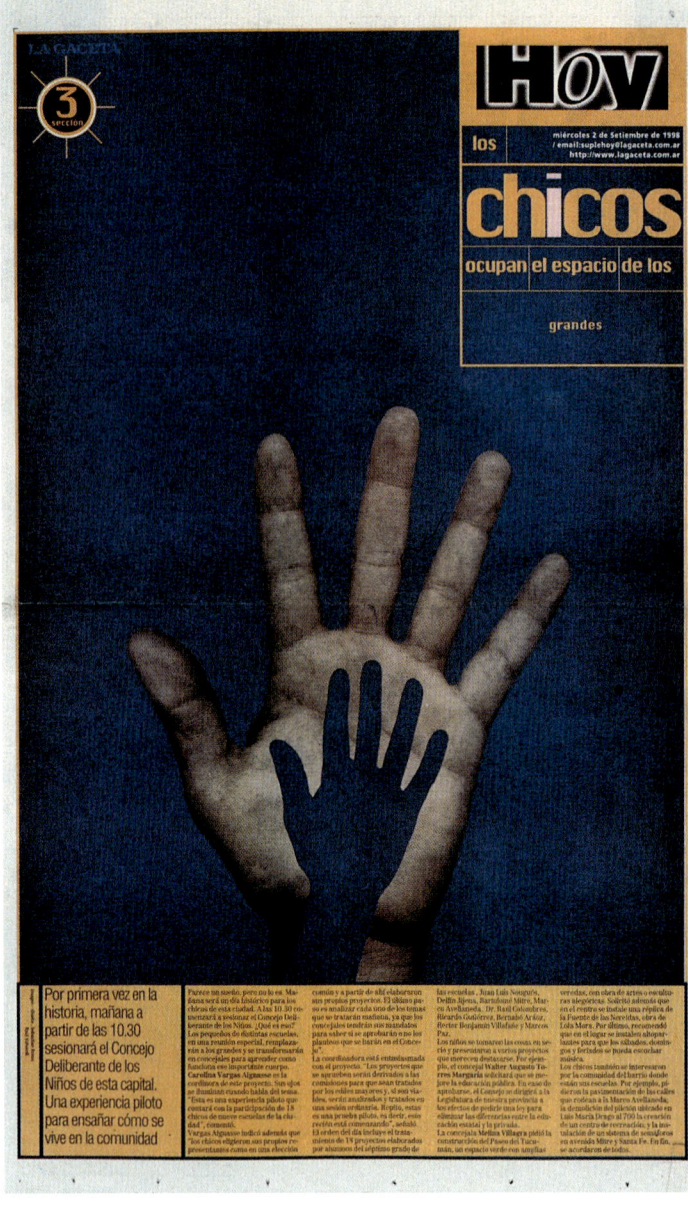

Silver
La Gaceta
San Miguel de Tucuman, Argentina
Sebastian Rosso, Designer; **Sergio Fernandez,** Art Director; **Mario García,** Design Consultant

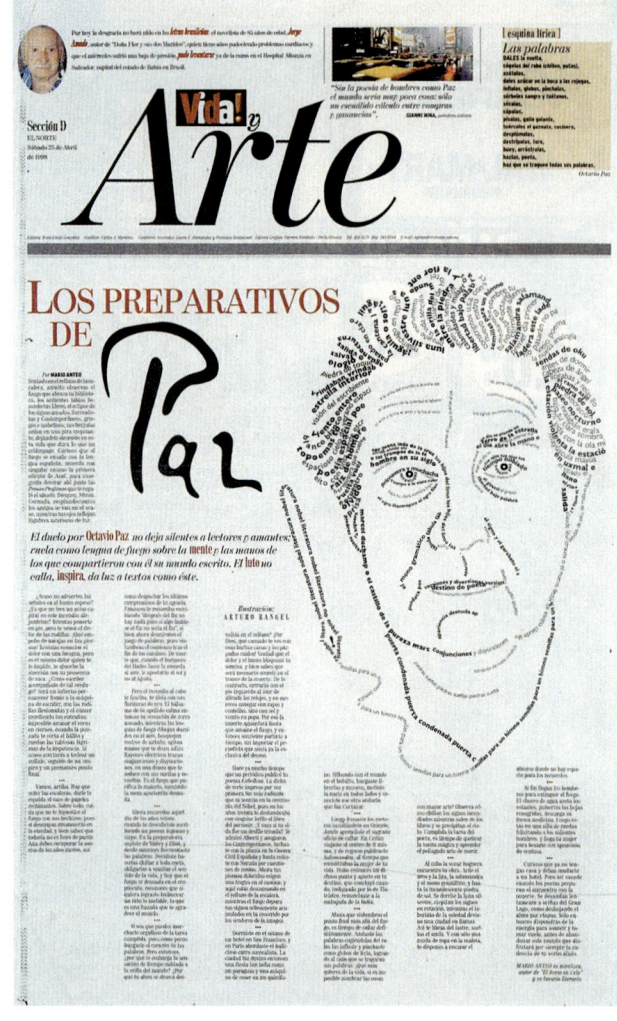

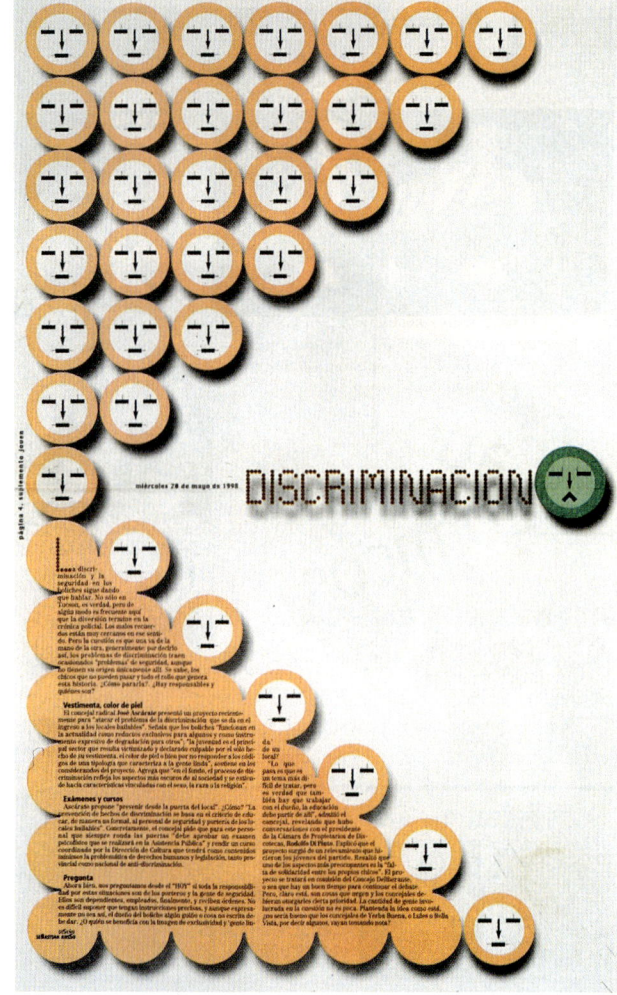

Other Page ■ FEATURES

Silver
Página/12
Buenos Aires, Argentina
Alejandro Ros, Art Director; **Florencia Helguera,** Graphic Designer

Silver
The Ottawa Citizen
Ottawa, Canada
Neil Reynolds, Editor; **Lynn McAuley,** Editor/Weekly; **Kit Collins,** Art Director & Designer; **Robert Cross,** Artist; **Russell Mills,** Publisher; **Hillary Mackenzie,** Photographer
• also an Award of Excellence for Other News Page

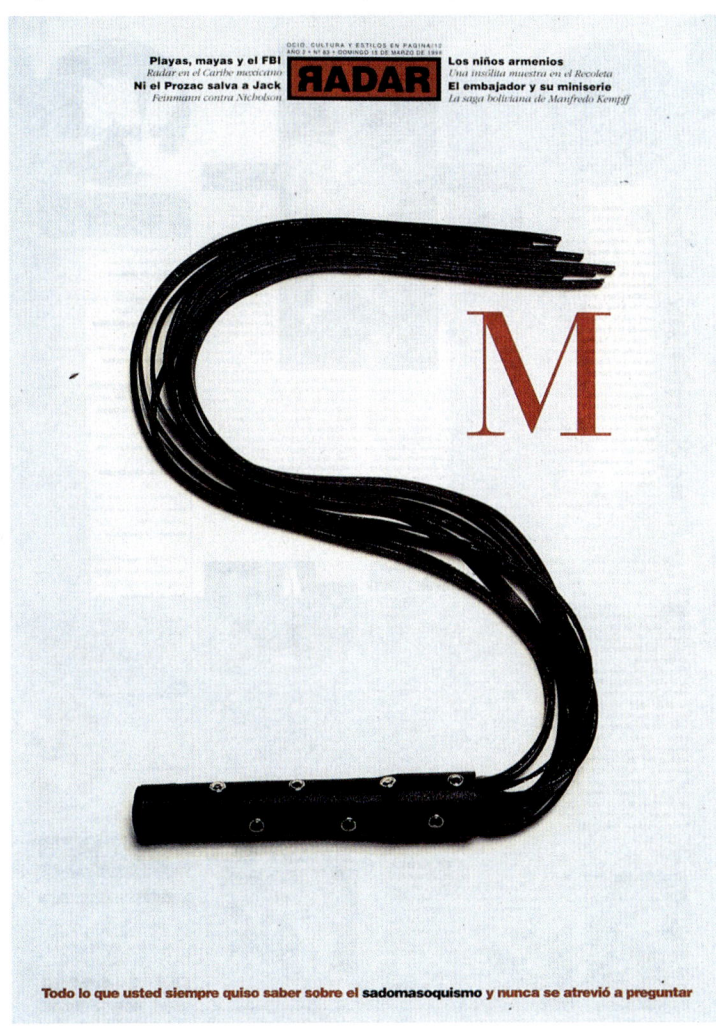

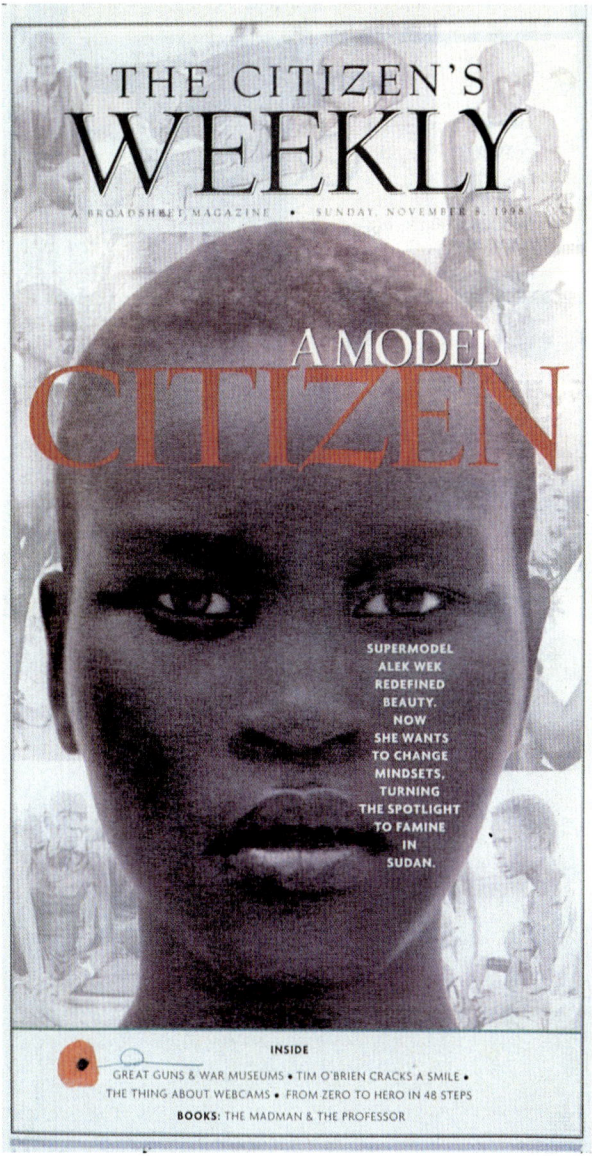

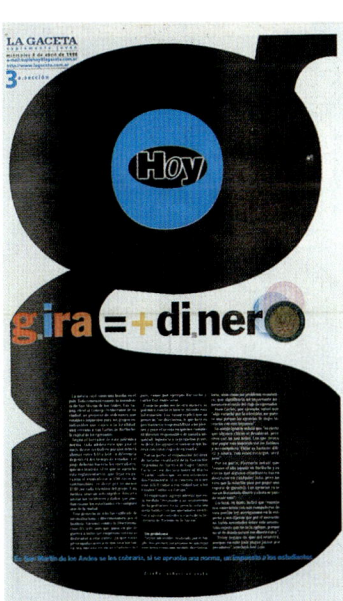

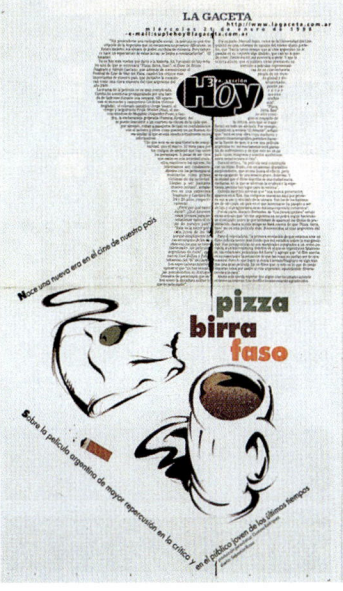

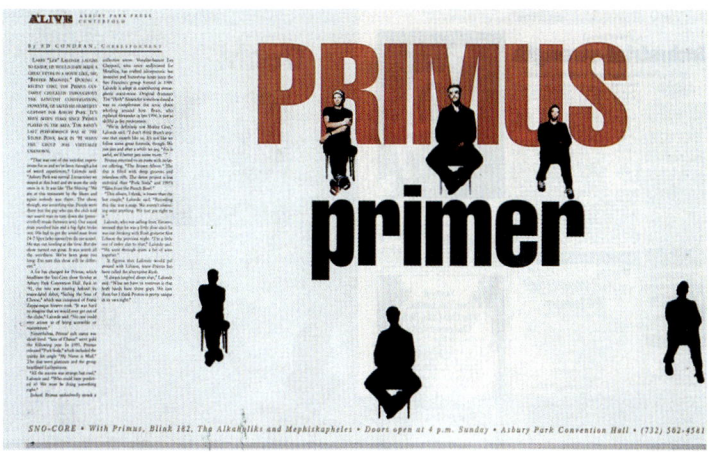

La Gaceta
San Miguel de Tucuman, Argentina
Sebastian Rosso, Designer; **Sergio Fernandez,** Art Director; **Mario García,** Design Consultant

La Gaceta
San Miguel de Tucuman, Argentina
Sebastian Rosso, Illustrator & Designer; **Sergio Fernandez,** Art Director; **Mario García,** Design Consultant

The Asbury Park Press
Neptune, NJ
Adriana Libreros, Designer; **Kathy Dzielak,** Editor; **Andrew Prendiamano,** Art & Photo Director; **Harris G. Siegel,** M.E./Design & Photography

FEATURES ■ Other Page

The Ottawa Citizen
Ottawa, Canada
Neil Reynolds, Editor; **Lynn McAuley,** Editor/Weekly; **Kit Collins,** Designer; **Mike Beedell,** Photographer

El Norte
Monterrey, México
Perla Olmeda, Designer; **Marcela García,** Section Editor; **Carlos Martínez,** Section Editor; **Alexandro Medrano,** Design Manager Editor; **Raúl Braulio Martinez,** Art Director; **Martha Treviño,** Editor/Director; **Ramón Alberto Garza,** General Editor Director

Página/12
Buenos Aires, Argentina
Alejandro Ros, Art Director; **Rubén Zerrizuela,** Graphic Designer

Página/12
Buenos Aires, Argentina
Alejandro Ros, Art Director; **Rubén Zerrizuela,** Graphic Designer

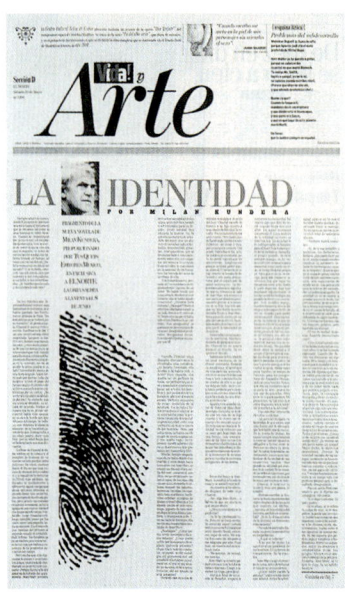
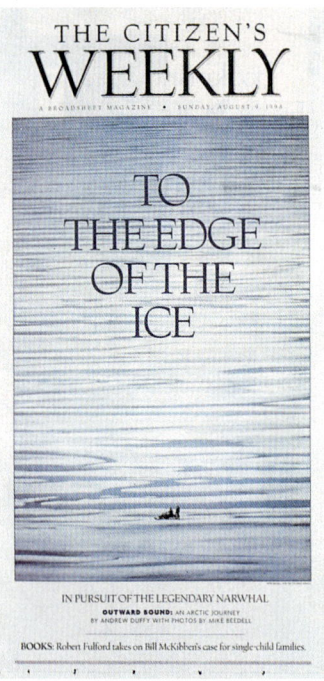
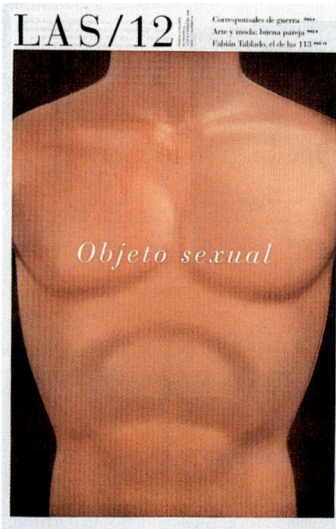
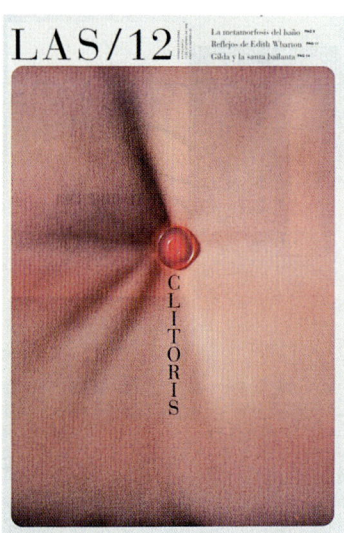

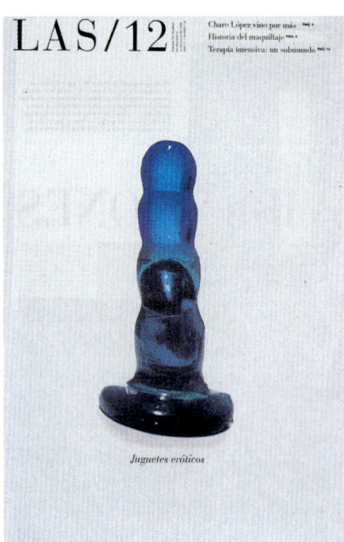
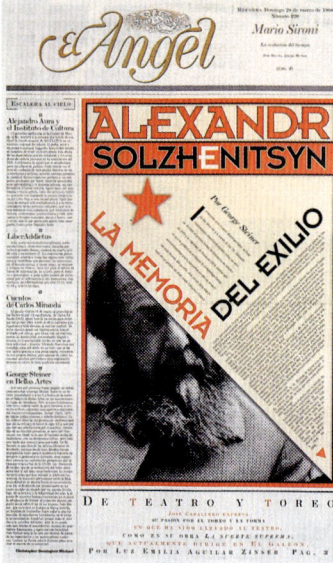
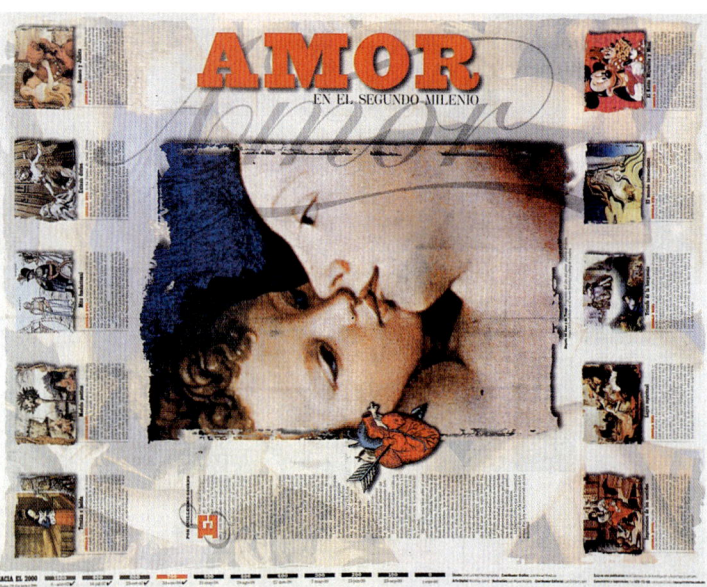

Reforma
México City, México
Efraín Folia, Photo Illustrator; **Eduardo Danilo,** Design Consultant; **Luzma Diaz de León Reyes,** Graphics Coordinator; **Emilio Deheza,** Art Director; **Beatriz de León,** Editor; **Marcela Rivas González,** Section Designer

Página/12
Buenos Aires, Argentina
Alejandro Ros, Art Director/Newspaper; **Ruben Zerrizuela,** Graphic Designer

Reforma
México City, México
José Luis Martinez, Designer; **Luis Enrique López,** Editor; **Marco Antonio Román,** Section Designer; **Emilio Deheza,** Art Director; **Moramay Juárez,** Photo Artist; **Luis Miguel Morales,** Illustrator; **Eduardo Danilo,** Design Consultant; **José Manuel Mendoza,** Graphics Coordinator

Other page ■ FEATURES

Reforma
México City, México

Marcela Rivas González, Section Designer; **Luzma Díaz de León Reyes,** Graphics Coordinator; **Beatriz de León,** Editor; **Emilio Deheza,** Art Director; **Eduardo Danilo,** Design Consultant

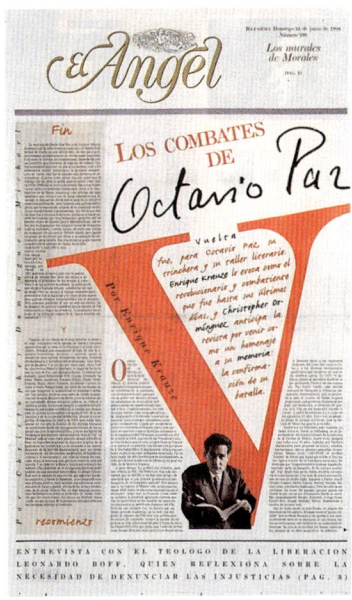

Reforma
México City, México

Beatriz de León, Editor; **Luzma Dias de León Reyes,** Graphics Coordinator; **Marcela Rivas González,** Section Designer/Photoartist; **Emilio Deheza,** Art Director; **Eduardo Danilo,** Design Consultant

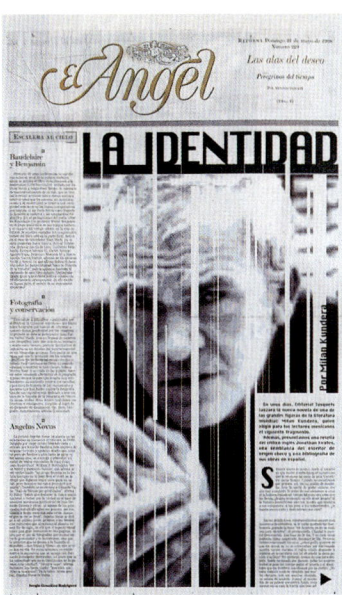

Silver
Jacksonville Journal-Courier
Jacksonville, IL

Mike Miner, Editor/Designer

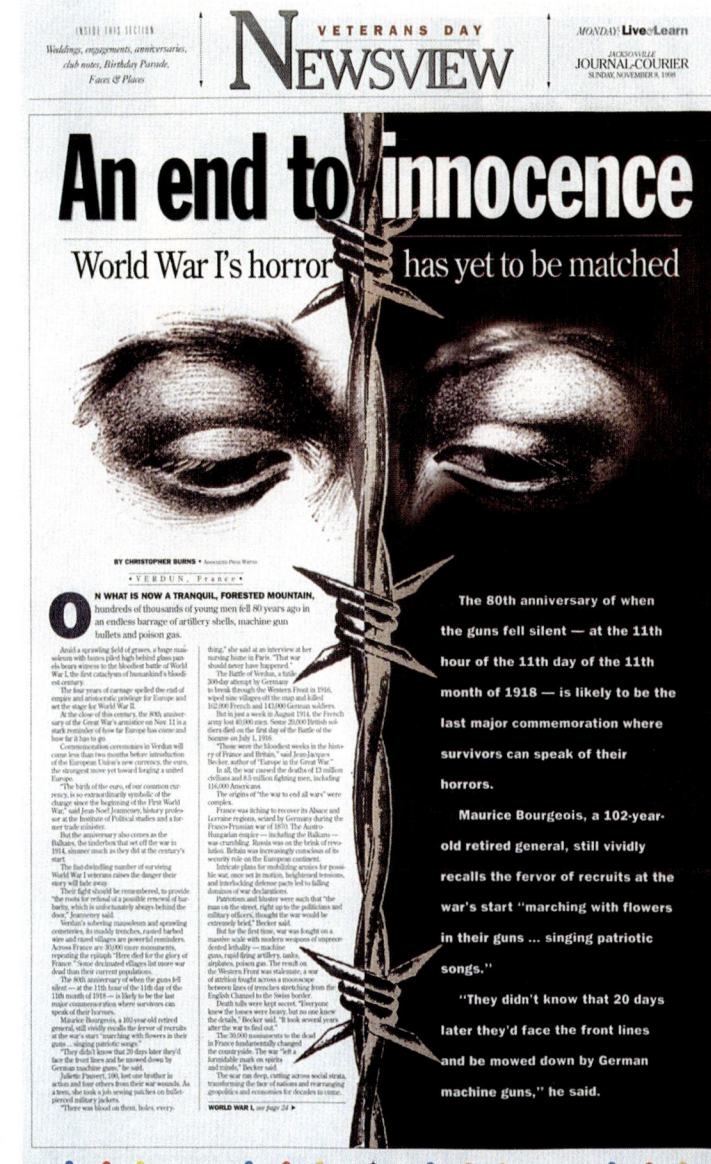

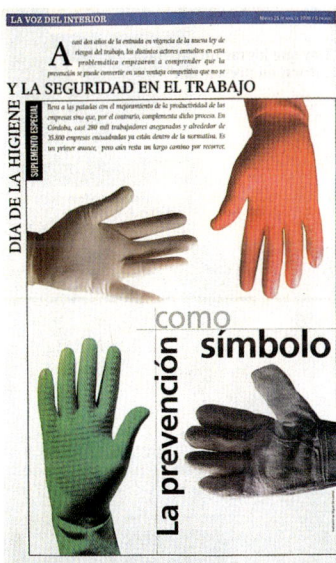

La Voz del Interior
Córdoba, Argentina

Miguel De Lorenzi, Designer/Illustrator/Art Director; **Oscar Beguán,** Photo Editor; **Javier Candellero,** Designer; **Carlos Jornet,** Publisher; **Mario García,** Design Consultant

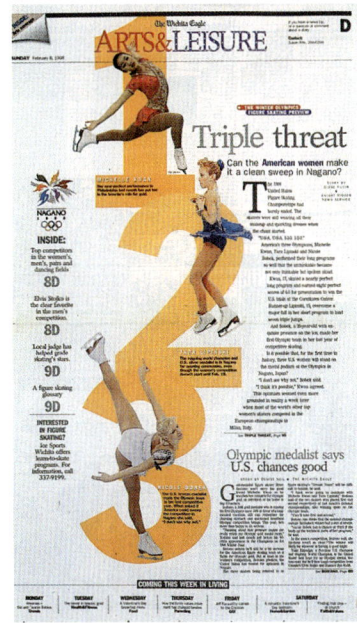

Wichita Eagle
Wichita, KS

Derek Simmons, Designer; **Sara Quinn,** Presentation Team Leader; **Susan Rife,** Living Team Leader

TWENTIETH EDITION ■ 139

FEATURES ■ Other Page, Inside Page

Cape Cod Times
Hyannis, MA
Patricia Cousins, Page Designer

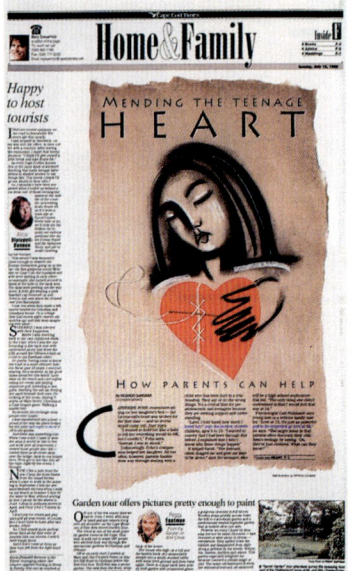

Le Devoir
Montréal, Canada
Christian Tiffet, Art Director

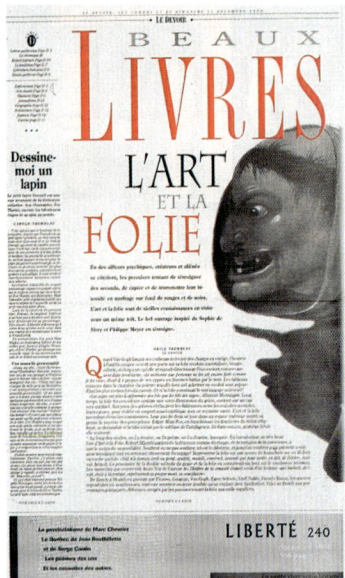

El Imparcial
Hermosillo, México
Zaida Cinco, Designer; **Ariel Medel**, Illustrator; **Sergio Serrano**, Art Director; **Margarita Oropeza**, Section Editor; **María Jesús Romero**, Section Coordinator

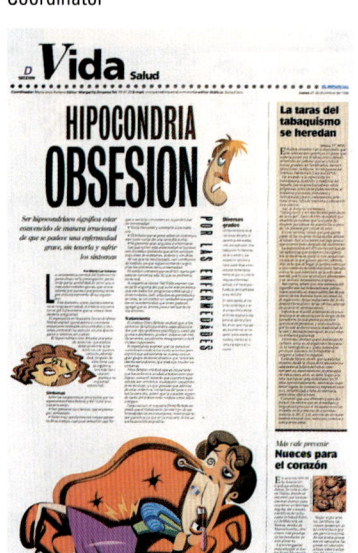

Jacksonville Journal-Courier
Jacksonville, IL
Mike Miner, Editor/Designer

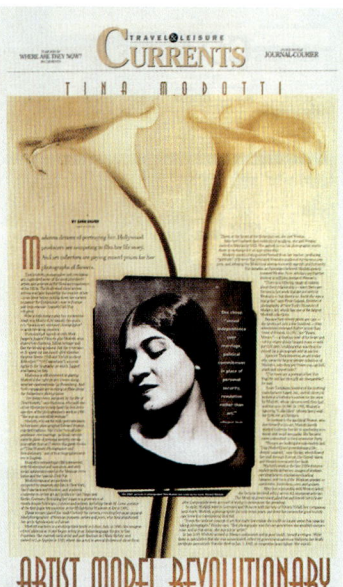

The Fox Valley Villages
Naperville, IL
Kerri Abrams, Designer; **Amanda Hamann**, Designer; **Sam Hundley**, Illustrator

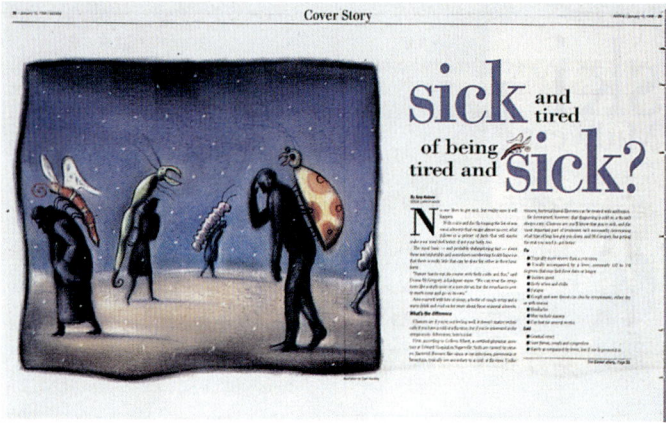

El Mundo
Madrid, Spain
Carmelo Caderot, Art Director & Designer

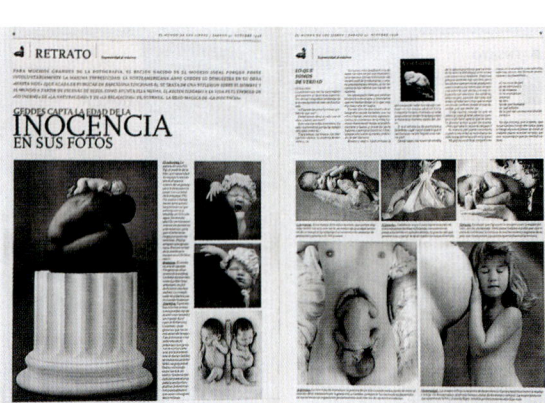

The National Post
Don Mills, Canada
Gayle Grin, Designer/Design Editor; **Karen Zagor**, Editor; **Lucie Lacava**, Design Consultant; **Kenneth Whyte**, Editor-in-Chief

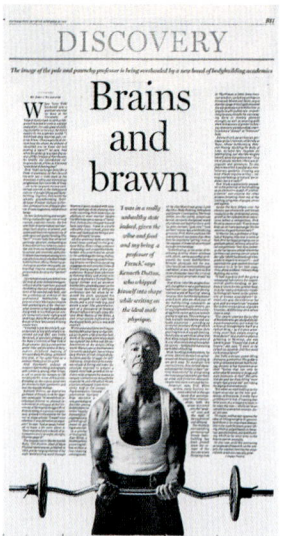

The National Post
Don Mills, Canada
Leanne Shapton, Designer & Editor; **Brian Hunt**, Copy Editor; **R.O. Blechman**, Illustrator; **Kenneth Whyte**, Editor-in-Chief; **Lucie Lacava**, Design Consultant

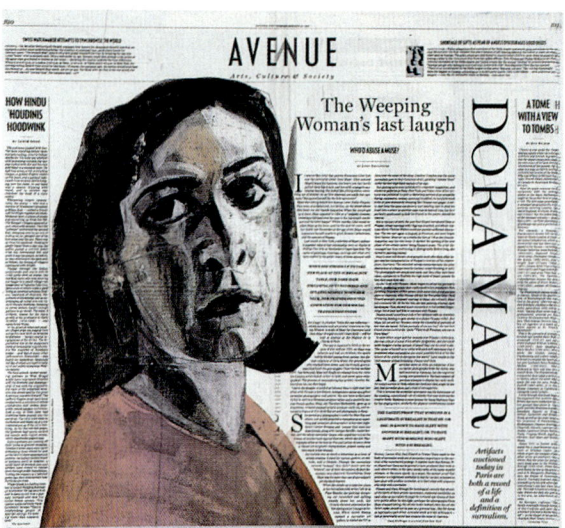

Inside Page ■ FEATURES

Gold
The National Post
Don Mills, Canada
Kenneth Whyte, Editor-in-Chief; **R.O. Blechman,** Illustrator; **Brian Hunt,** Copy Editor; **Leanne Shapton,** Designer/Editor; **Lucie Lacava,** Design Consultant

The page is delightful and refreshing. It is a joy. You want to spend a lot of time looking at it. Good use of spot color. Nice use of blending in the flag at the top.

Esta página causa deleite y es refrescante. Es una maravilla. Uno siente ganas de pasar mucho tiempo contemplándola. Buen uso de los colores premezclados. Buen uso de la combinación en la cabecera de la parte superior.

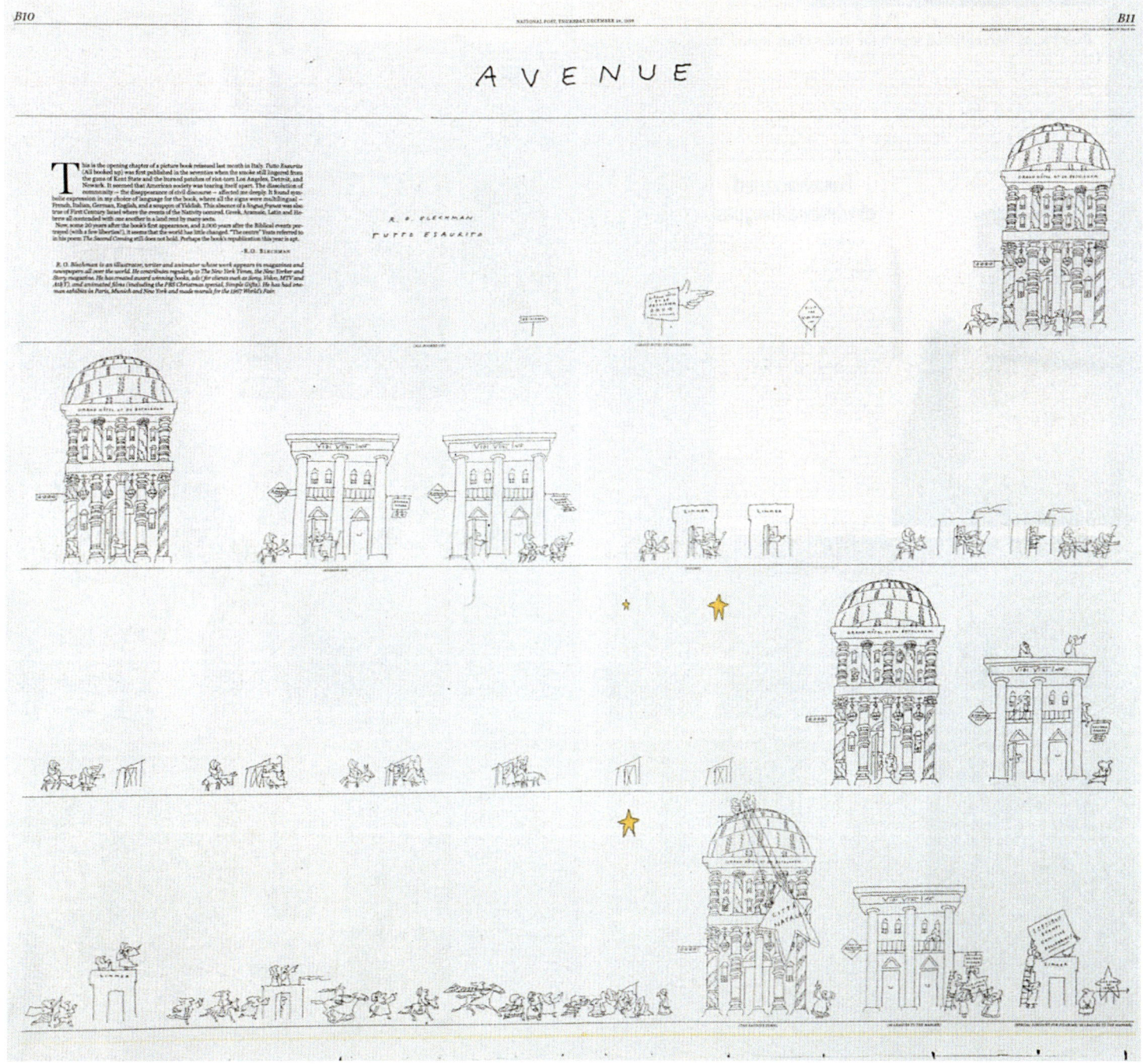

FEATURES ■ Inside Page

Silver
The Providence Journal
Providence, RI
Debra Page-Trim, Picture Editor/Designer; **Sandor Bodo,** Photographer

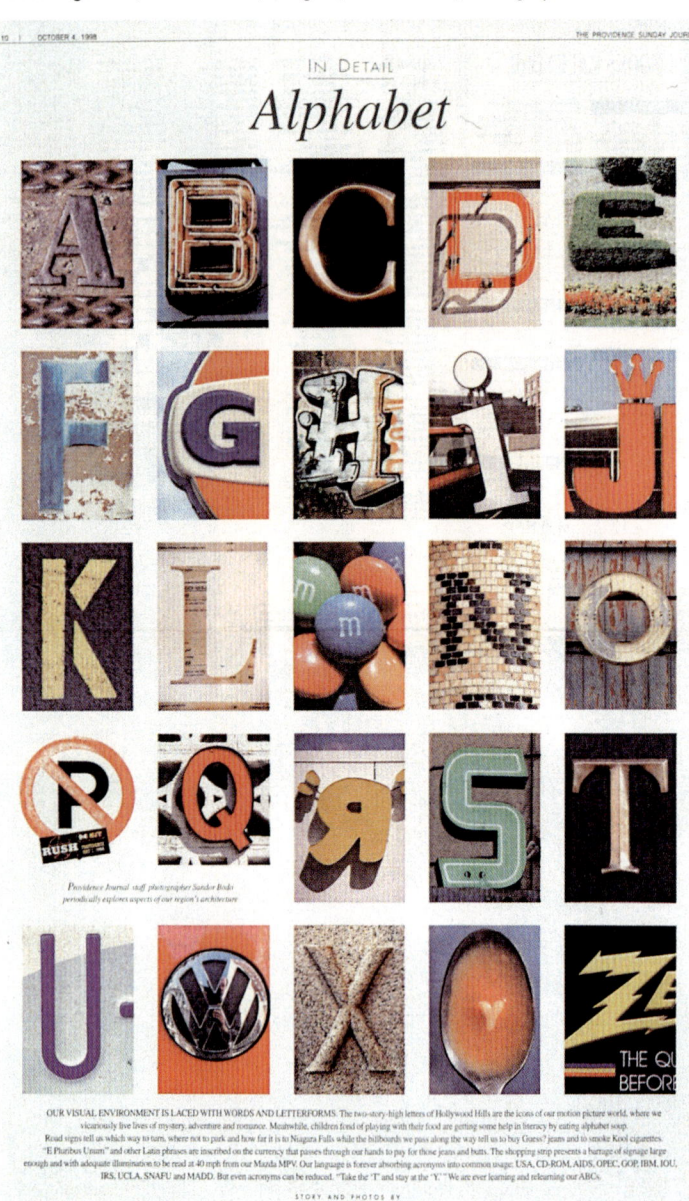

Göteborgs-Posten
Göteborg, Sweden
Mats Widebrant, Designer; **Greg Baker,** Photographer

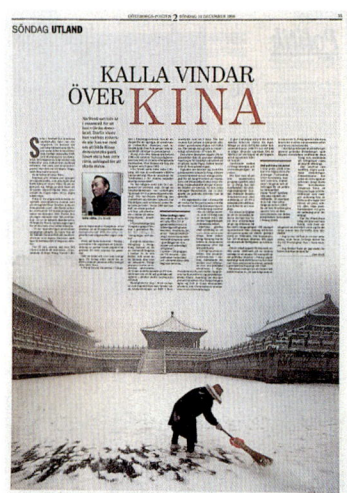

El Mundo
Madrid, Spain
Carmelo Caderot, Art Director & Designer; **Ulises Culebro,** Illustrator

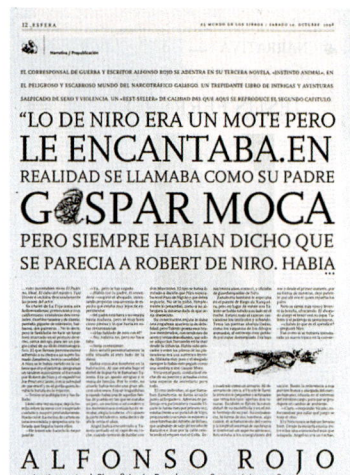

NRC Handelsblad
Rotterdam, The Netherlands
Wilfred Boom, Page Designer; **Marc Terstroet,** Illustration Artist

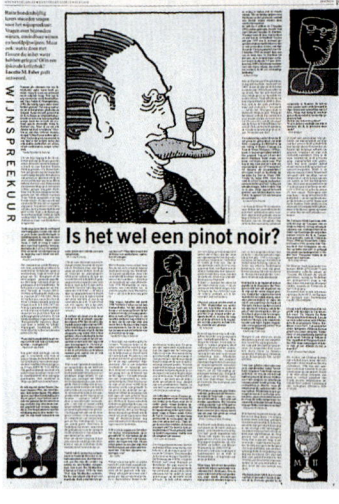

La Presse
Anjou, Canada
Steve Adams, Art Director & Designer; **Julien Chung,** Creative Director; **Marc-André Lussier,** Staff Writer; **Jocelyne LePage,** Page Editor

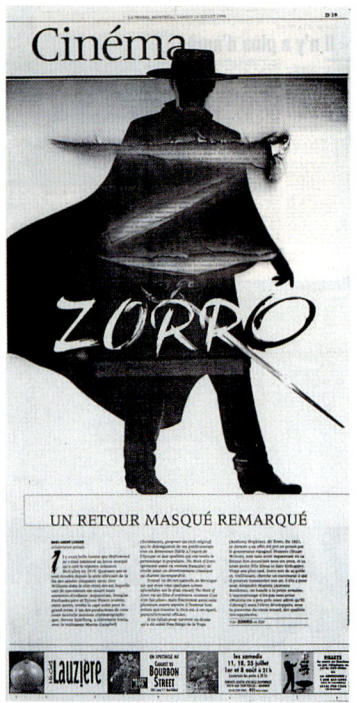

142 ■ THE BEST OF NEWSPAPER DESIGN

MAGAZINE

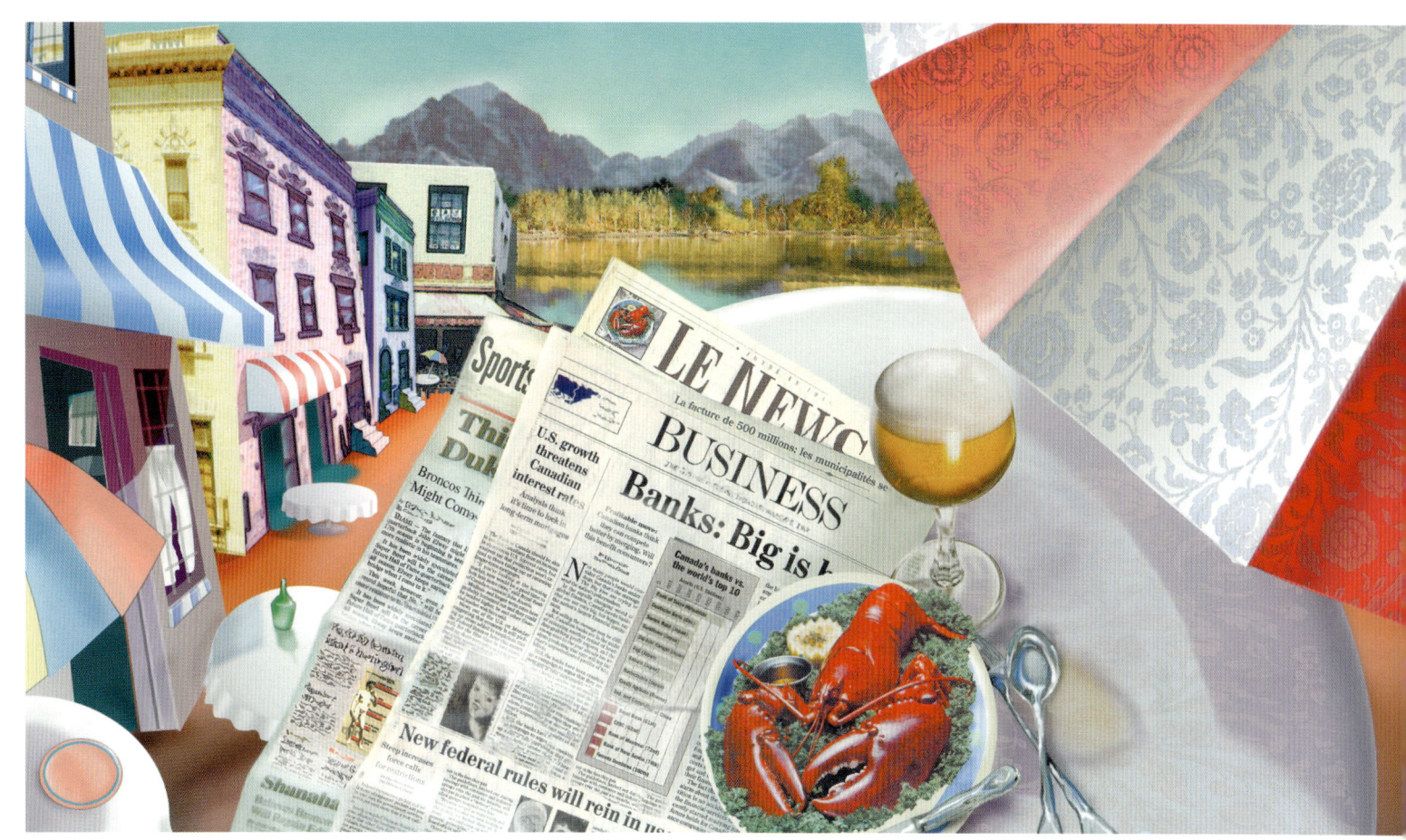

CHAPTER FOUR

OVERALL DESIGN

SPECIAL SECTIONS

COVERS

PAGE DESIGN

MAGAZINE — Overall Design

Gold
Diario de Noticias / DNA
Lisbon, Portugal
Mário B. Resendes, Editor-in-Chief; **José Maria Ribeirinho,** Art Director; **Pedro Rolo Duarte,** Editor; **Luís Silva Dias,** Design Editor; **Miguel Pedroso,** Designer

"Es preciosa, maravillosa y espectacular." The photography is big and displayed well. The typography is extraordinary and with full bleed. This could be the best of the century. The spot color and color palette is stunning and the flag is wonderful.

"Es preciosa, maravillosa y espectacular". La fotografía es grande y está bien desplegada. La tipografía, por su parte, es extraordinaria y llega hasta los bordes. Podría ser lo mejor del siglo. Los colores premezclados ("spot colors") y la gama de colores son impresionantes y la cabecera es estupenda.

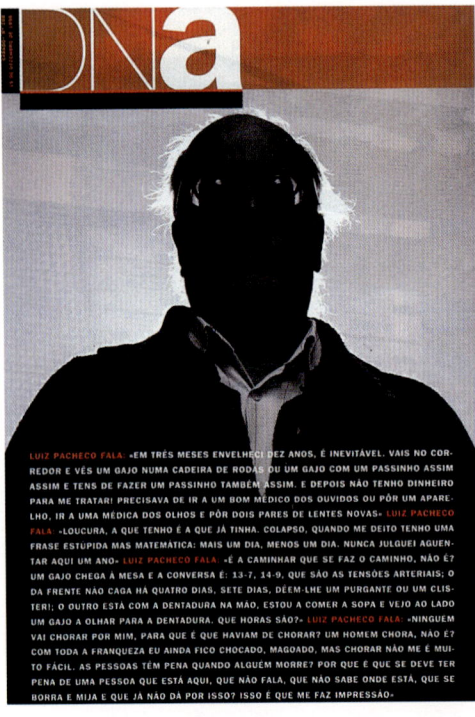 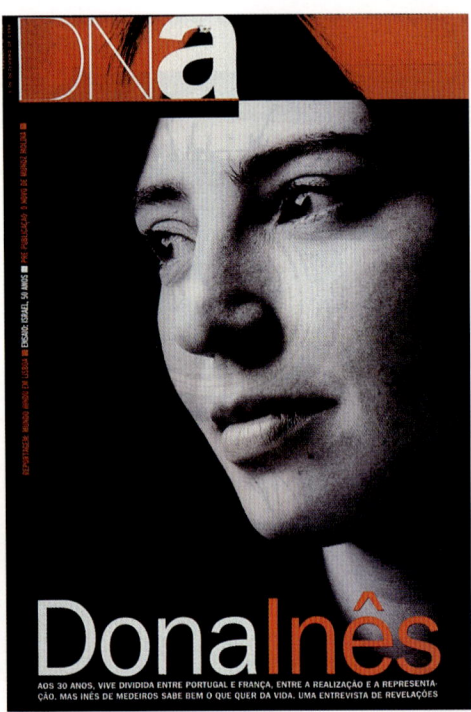 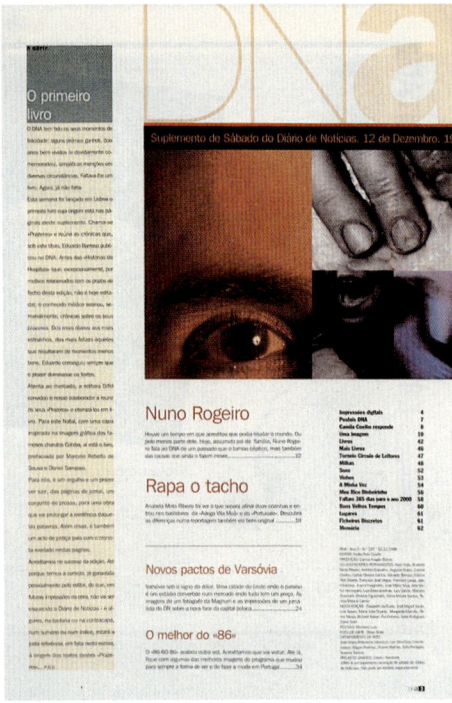

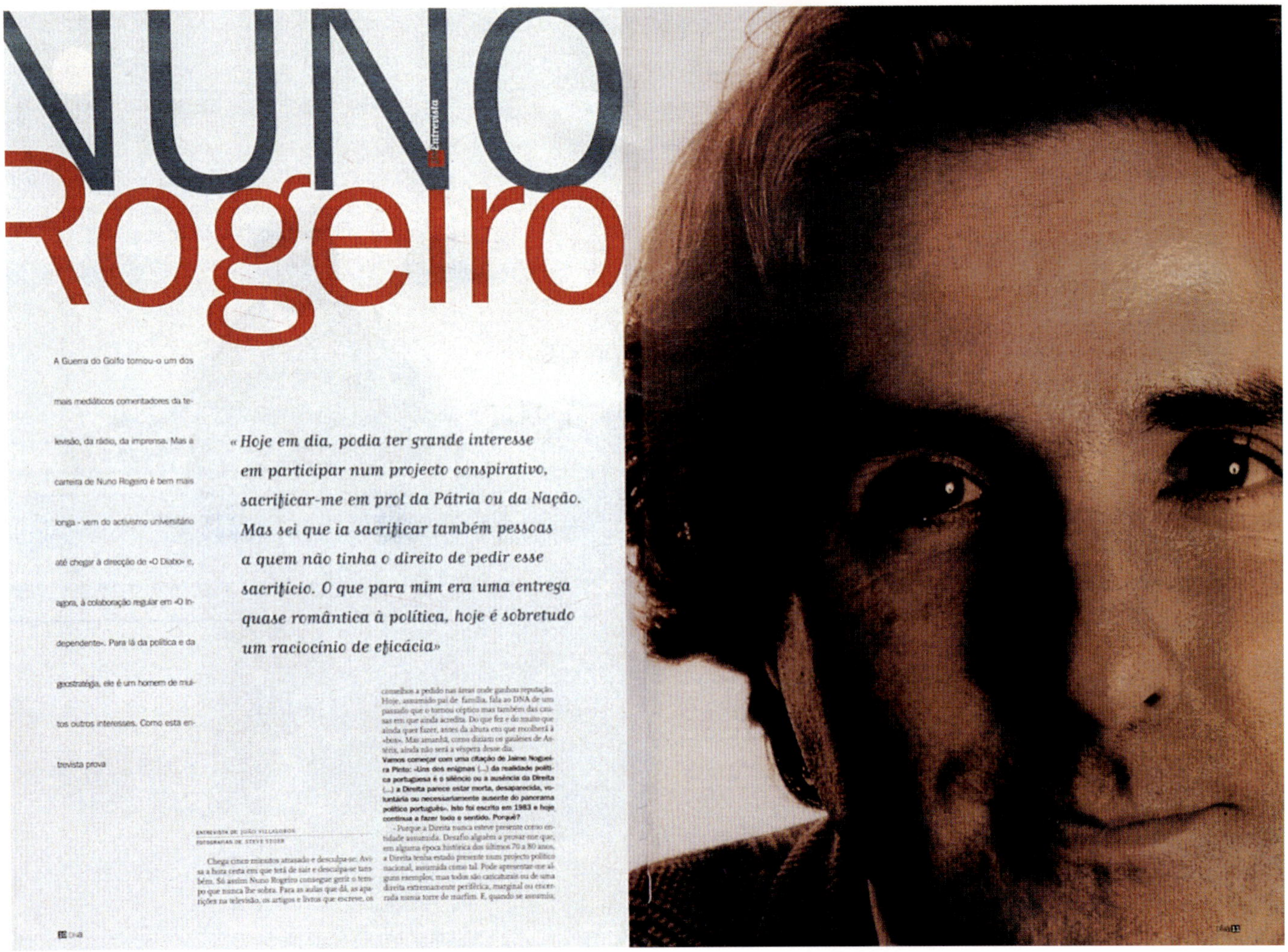

144 ■ THE BEST OF NEWSPAPER DESIGN

Silver
El Mundo Siete Leguas
Madrid, Spain

Carmelo Caderot, Art Director & Designer; **Manuel de Miguel,** Assistant Art Director & Designer; **Toño Benavides,** Illustrator
• also an Award of Excellence for Illustration and Magazine Cover

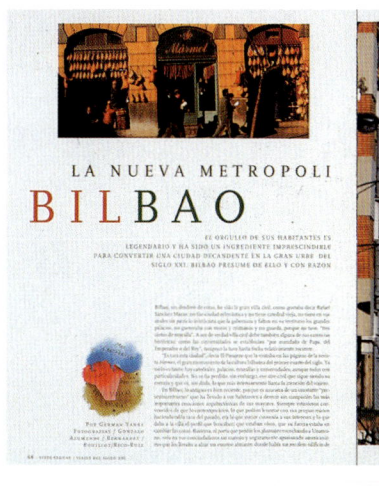
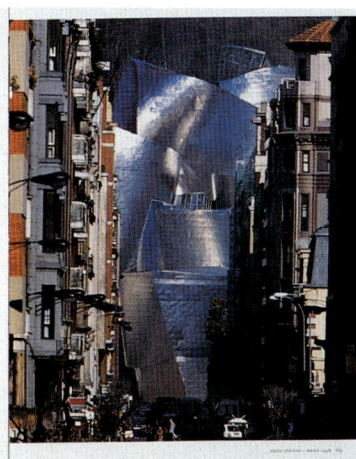
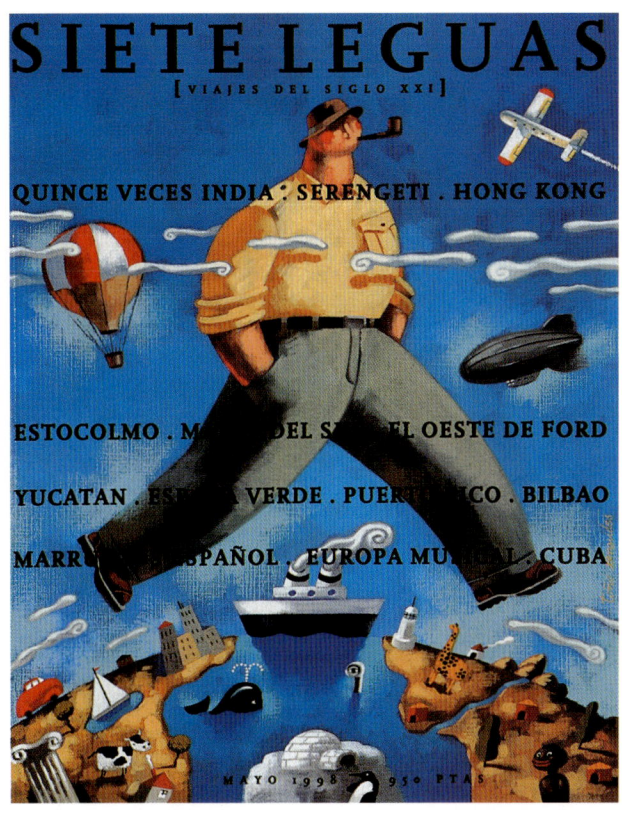
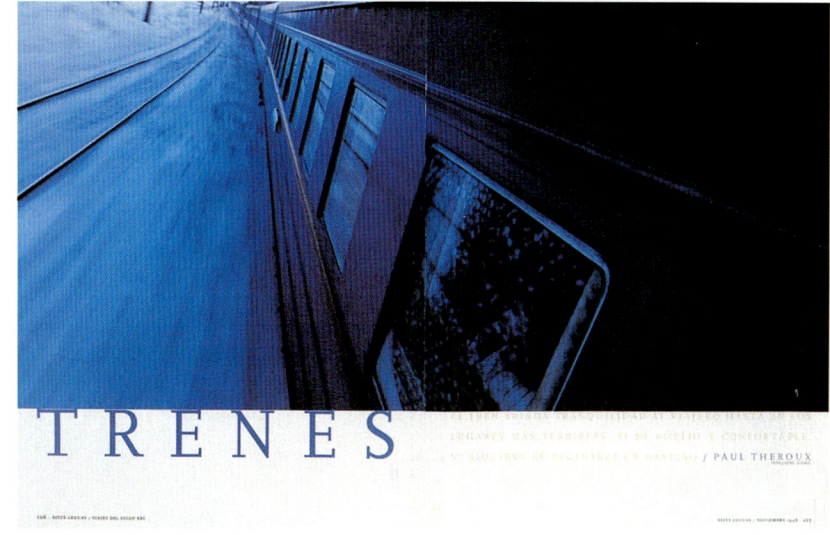

• also an Award of Excellence for Magazine Page Design

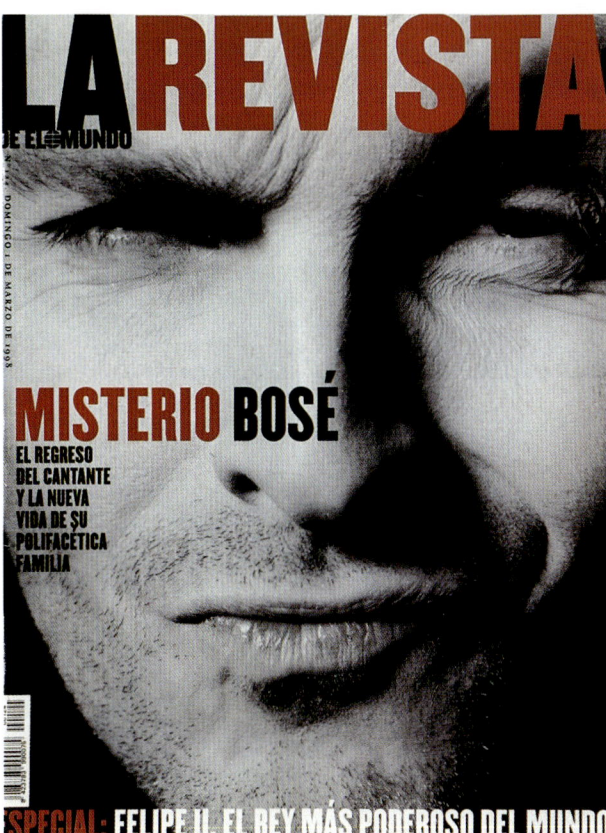
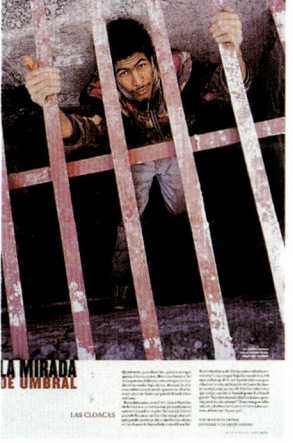
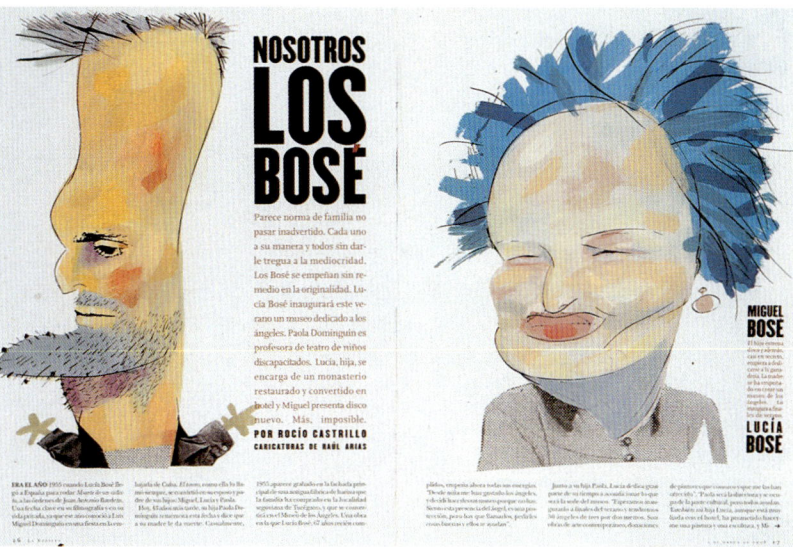

Silver
La Revista de El Mundo
Madrid, Spain

Rodrigo Sánchez, Art Director; **María González,** Designer; **Amparo Redondo,** Designer; **Carmelo Caderot,** Design Director

MAGAZINE | Overall Design

La Nacion
Buenos Aires, Argentina
Jesica Rizzo, Graphic Design; **Daniel Hergott,** Graphic Design; **Nariano Enriquez,** Graphic Design

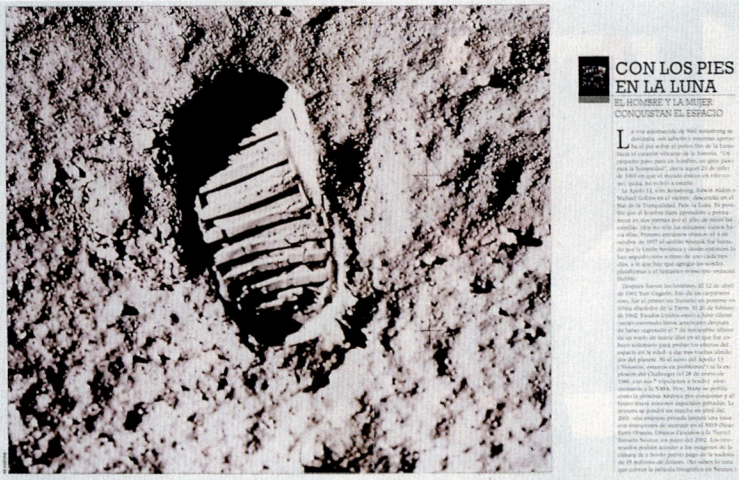
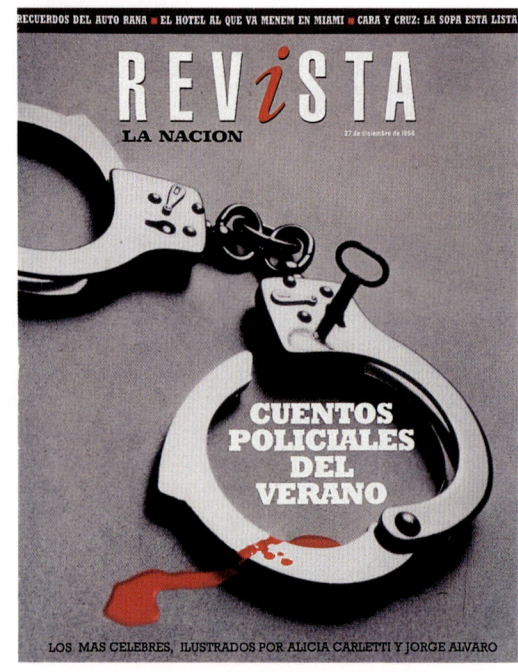

The National Post
Don Mills, Canada
Karen Simpson, Design Consultant; **Fredericke Gauss,** Designer; **Thea Partridge,** Production; **Kate Fillion,** Editor

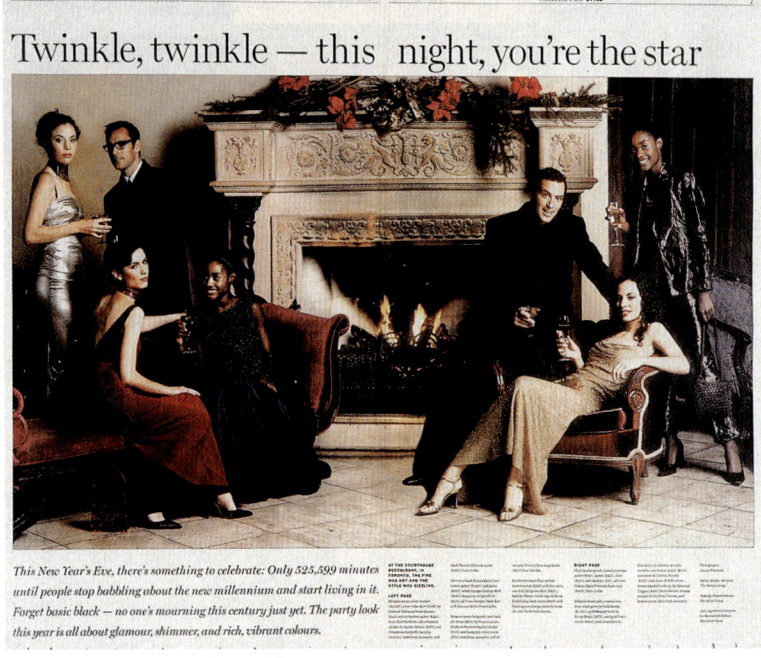
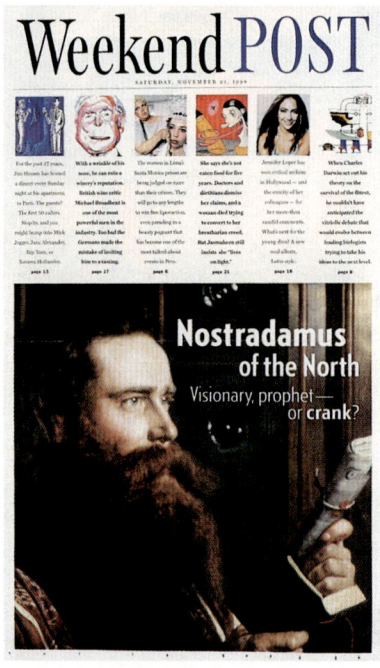

El País
Madrid, Spain
David García, Art Director; **Fernando Gutiérrez,** Original Design; **Nuria Muiña,** Art Editor; **Tori Alimbau,** Art Editor; **Guillermo Trigo,** Assistant Designer; **José Guillermo Abad,** Assistant Designer

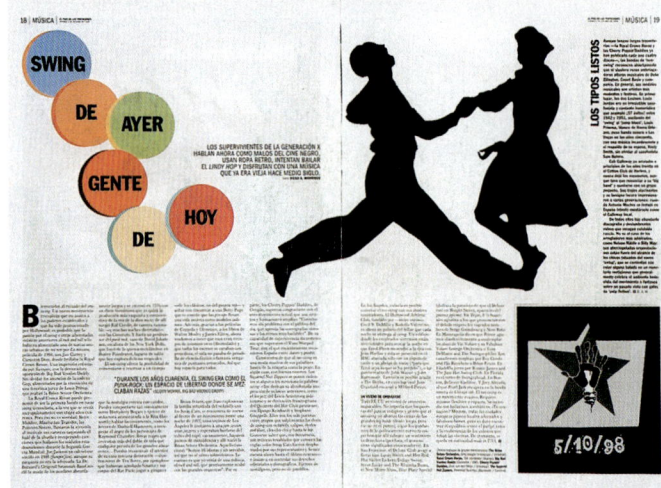
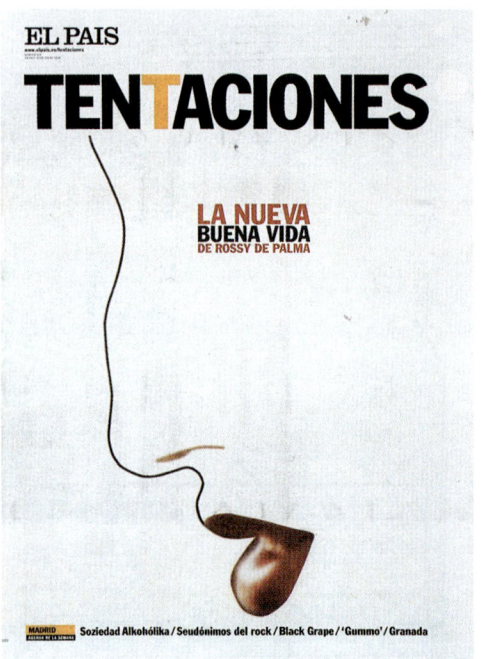

Overall Design, Special Section ■ MAGAZINE

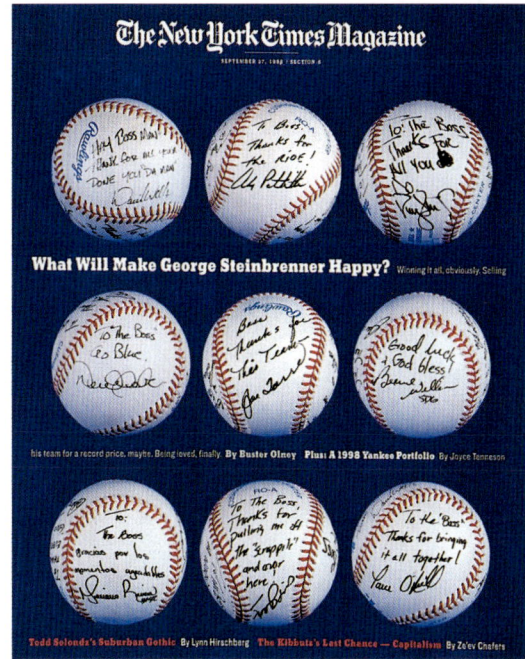

The New York Times Magazine
New York, NY
Janet Froelich, Art Director; **Kathy Ryan,** Photo Editor

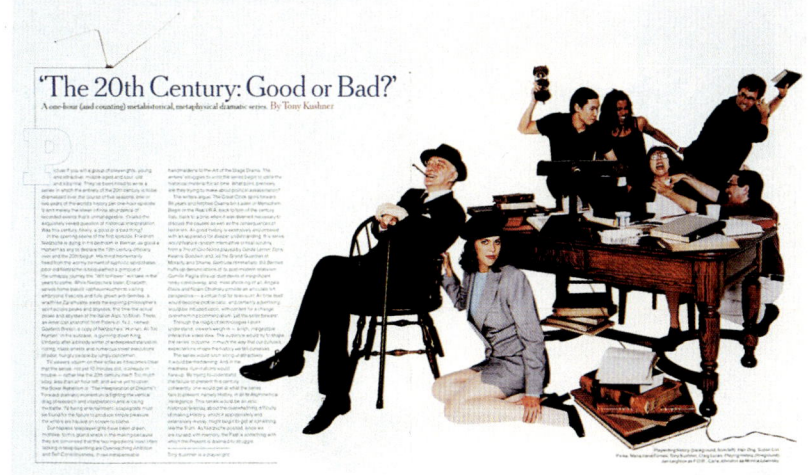

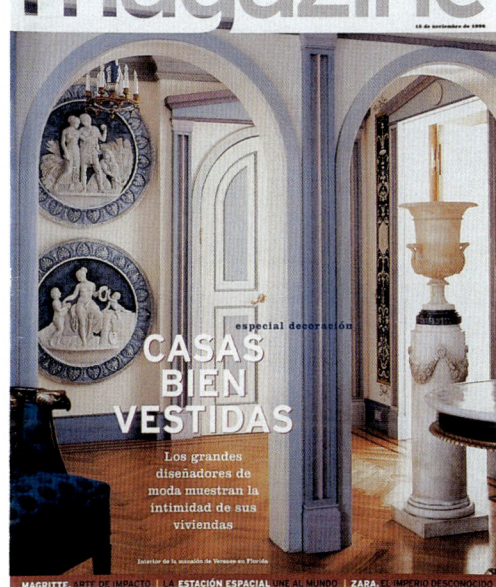

La Vanguardia Magazine
Barcelona, Spain
Carlos Pérez de Rozas, Art Director; **Rosa Mundet Poch,** Editor-in-Chief/Design & Infographics; **Emilio Álvarez Ramallo,** Jefe de Sección; **Antonio Soto,** Jefe de Sección; **Mª José Oriol Roca,** Designer; **Mònica Caparrós,** Designer

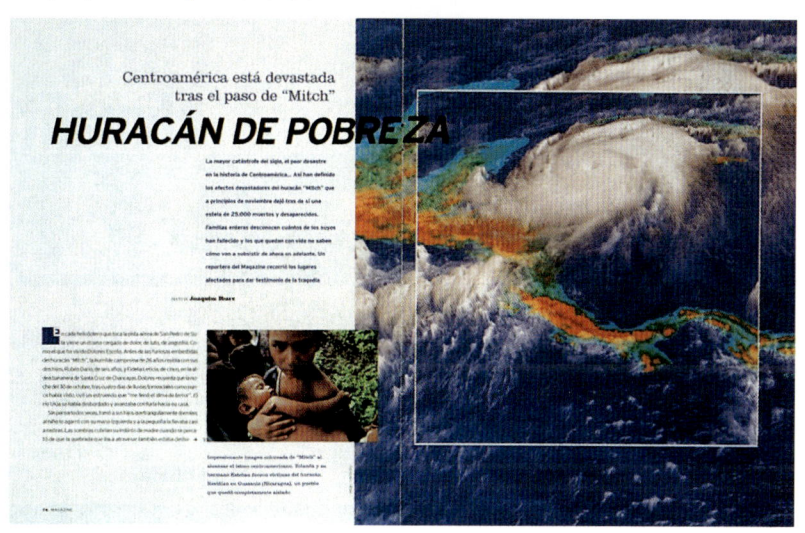

The New York Times Magazine
New York, NY
Janet Froelich, Art Director

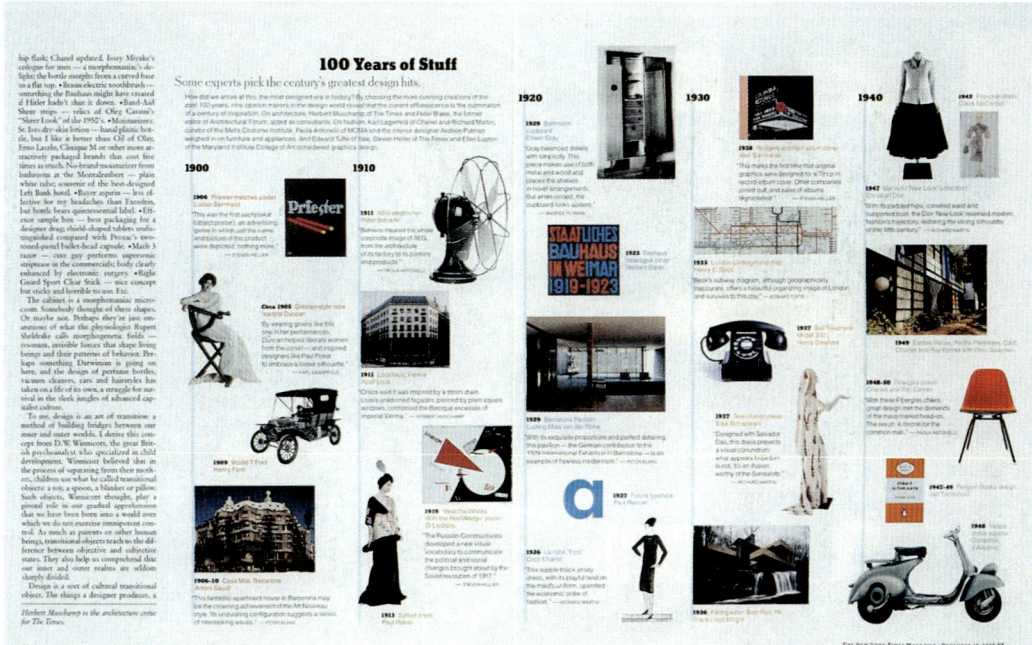

TWENTIETH EDITION ■ 147

MAGAZINE ■ Special Section

Marcelo's work is one of the most transporting bodies of photographic work about the Indian in recent time. This is a work that will be of great influence. Viewing his photos moved us beyond the exterior and afforded a personal glimpse into the stereotypical masses of this region. The presentation is artistic, and the images are compelling.

La obra de Marcelo es uno de los conjuntos de trabajo fotográfico más conmovedores que se han realizado acerca de los pueblos indios en tiempos recientes. Es una obra que tendrá una gran influencia. Contemplar sus fotos nos llevó más allá de la superficie exterior y nos ofreció una visión personal de las masas de la región, objeto de estereotipos. La presentación es artística y las imágenes son persuasivas.

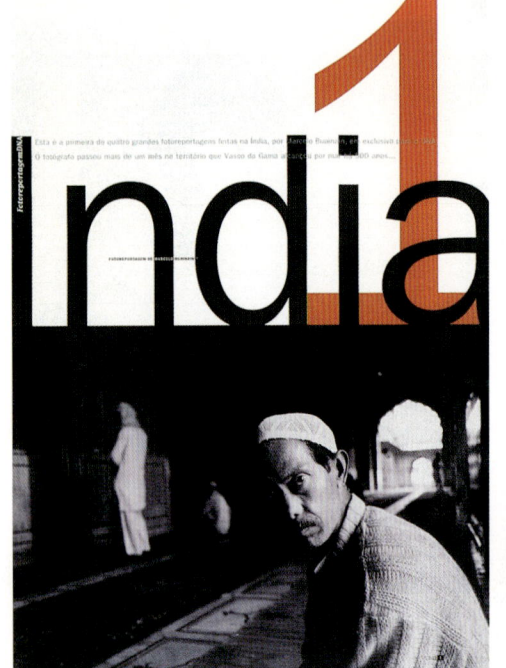
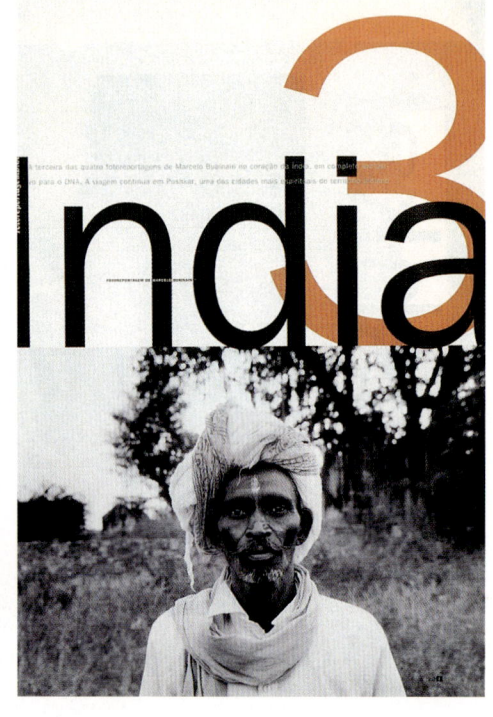

Gold
Diario de Noticias / DNA
Lisbon, Portugal
Mário B. Resendes, Editor-in-Chief; **José Maria Ribeirinho,** Art Director; **Pedro Rolo Duarte,** Editor; **Luís Silva Dias,** Design Editor; **Miguel Pedroso,** Designer; **Marcelo Buainain,** Photographer
• also Gold for Photo Series

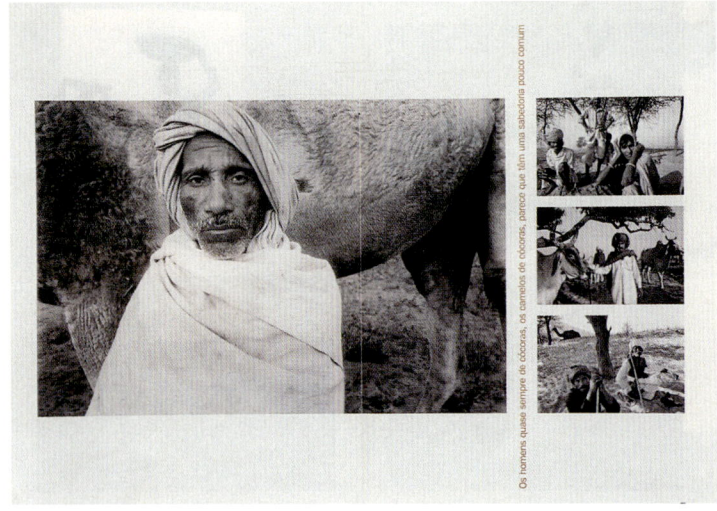
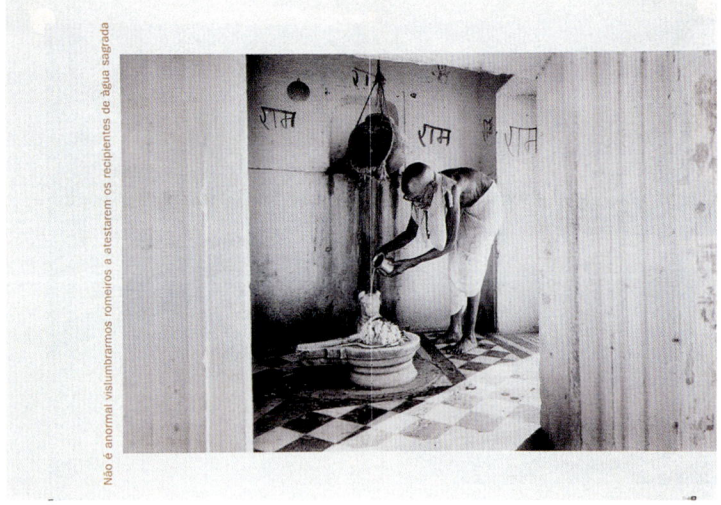
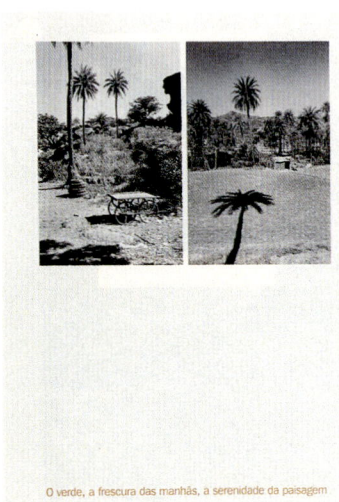
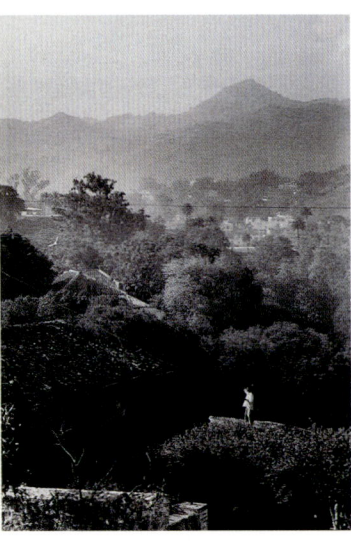
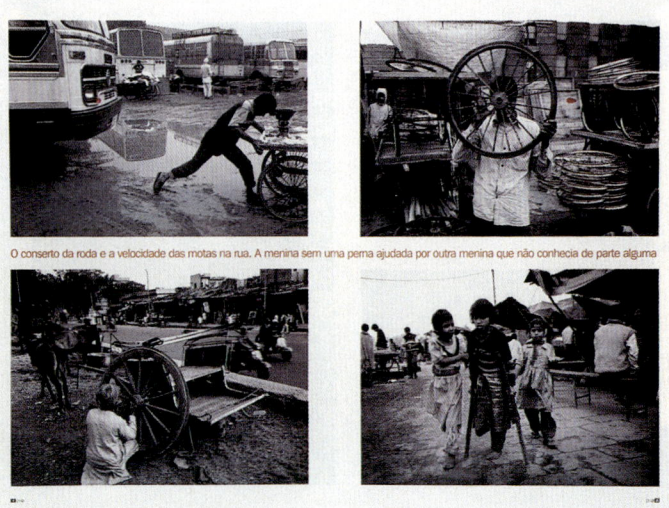

148 ■ THE BEST OF NEWSPAPER DESIGN

Special Section ■ MAGAZINE

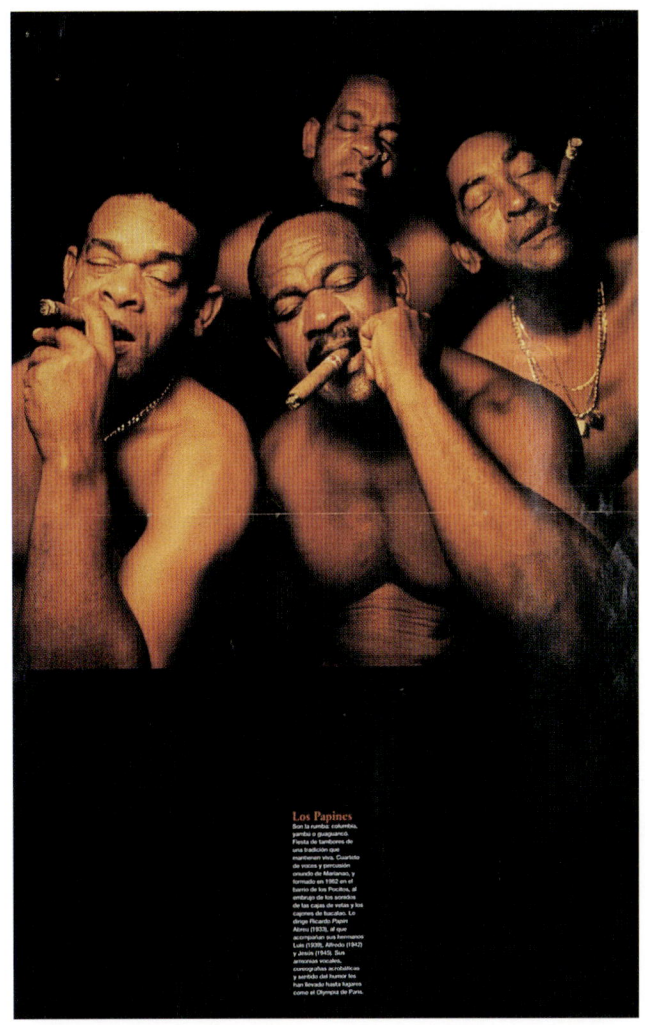

Gold
El País Semanal
Madrid, Spain

David García, Art Director; **Eugenio González**, Design Director; **Maripaz Domingo**, Designer; **Gustavo Sánchez**, Designer; **Patricia Álvarez**, Designer; **Alex M. Roig**, Editor-in-Chief; **Francis Giacobetti**, Photographer
• also Gold for Photo Series

In this package on Cuba, the warm glow of the photography and the stories are just like that part of the world. The design that it is done vertically draws you down. Great storytelling through design and photography.

El cálido brillo de la fotografía y las historias que nacen de ella son justo como esa parte del mundo. El diseño vertical lo atrae a uno. El diseño y la fotografía narran la historia con gran eficacia.

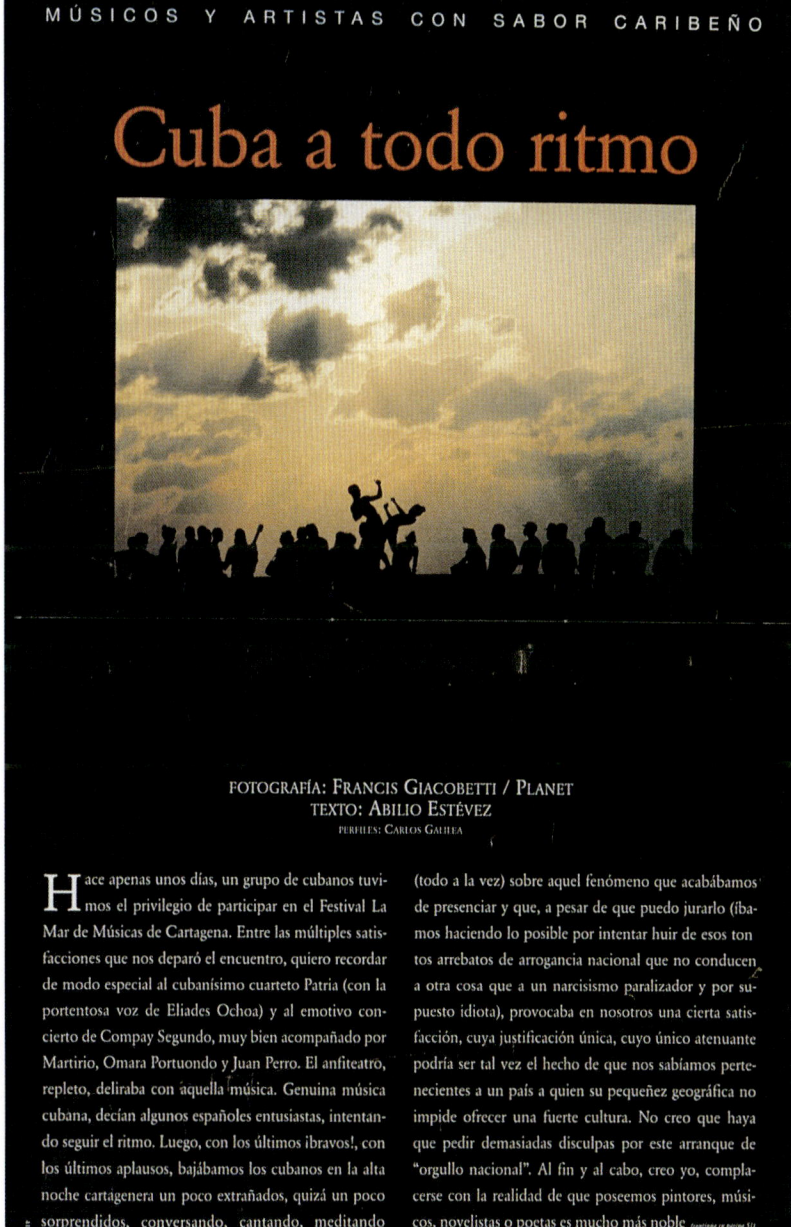

MAGAZINE ■ Special Section

Silver
La Revista de El Mundo
Madrid, Spain

Rodrigo Sánchez, Art Director; **María González,** Designer; **Amparo Redondo,** Designer; **Carmelo Caderot,** Design Director; **Sean Makaoui,** Illustrator

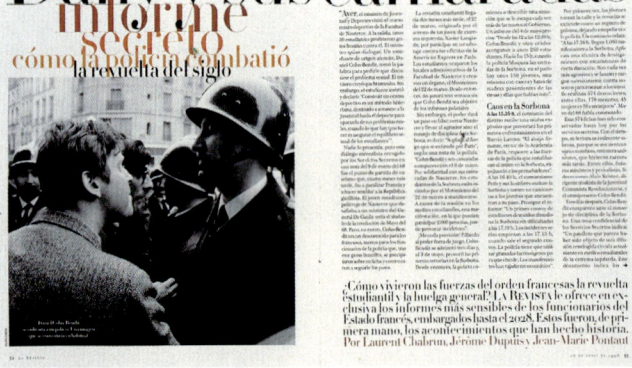
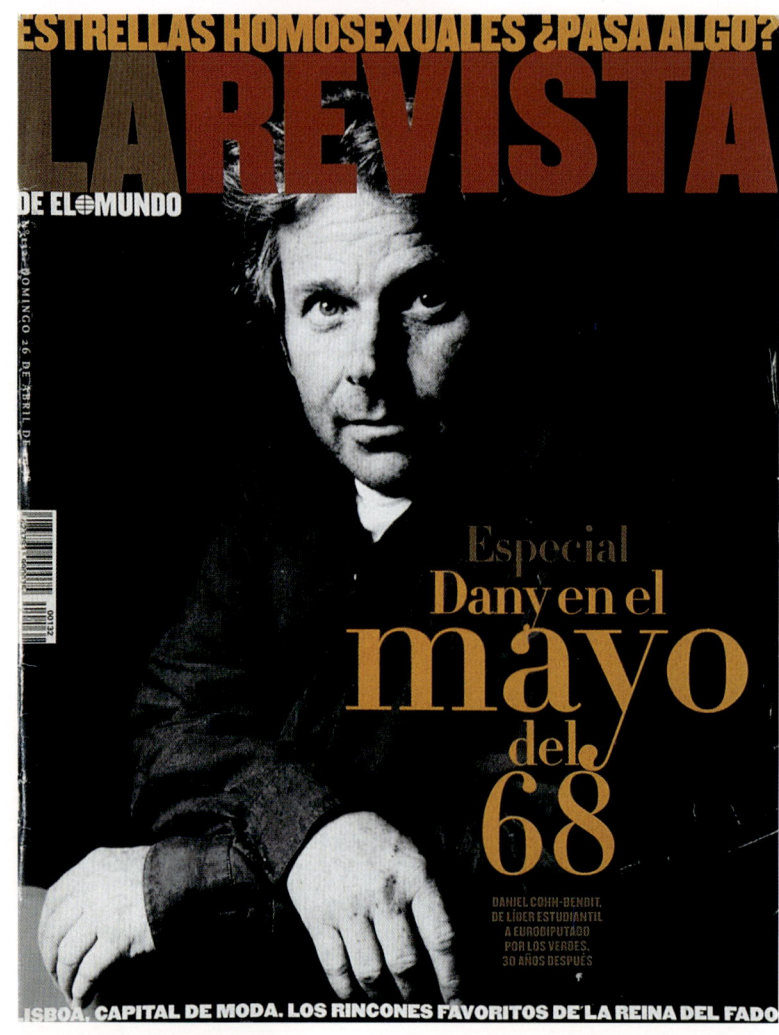

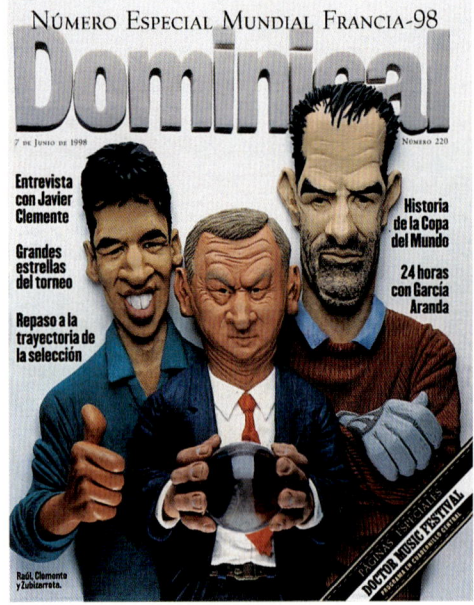

El Periodíco de Catalunya/El Dominical
Barcelona, Spain

Ferran Sendra, Designer; **Núria Miquel,** Designer; **Alejandro Yofre,** Photo Editor; **Albert Bertran,** Photo Editor; **Héctor Chimirri,** News Editor; **Maria Ràfols,** Vice Editor

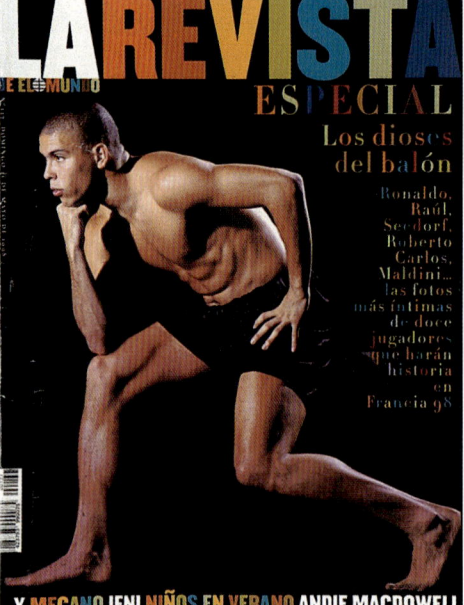

La Revista de El Mundo
Madrid, Spain

Rodrigo Sánchez, Art Director; **María González,** Designer; **Amparo Redondo,** Designer; **Carmelo Caderot,** Design Director

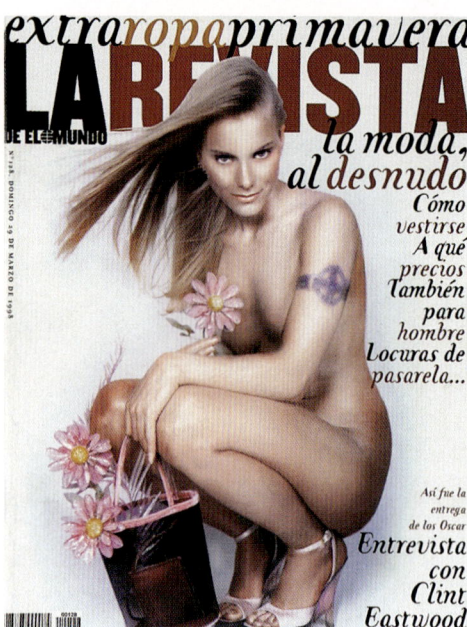

La Revista de El Mundo
Madrid, Spain

Rodrigo Sánchez, Art Director; **María González,** Designer; **Amparo Redondo,** Designer; **Carmelo Caderot,** Design Director

Gold
El Mundo Metropoli
Madrid, Spain
Rodrigo Sánchez, Art Director; **Maria Gonzalez,** Designer; **Carmelo Caderot,** Design Director; **Raul Arias,** Illustrator
• also Gold for Illustration

This cover is editorially sharp and clever. It's visually compelling and an unorthodox way to deal with Woody Allen. Even Woody would like the cover.

Esta portada tiene agudeza e ingenio desde el punto de vista editorial. Es visualmente contundente y una manera poco ortodoxa de abordar a Woody Allen. Hasta el propio Woody disfrutaría de la portada.

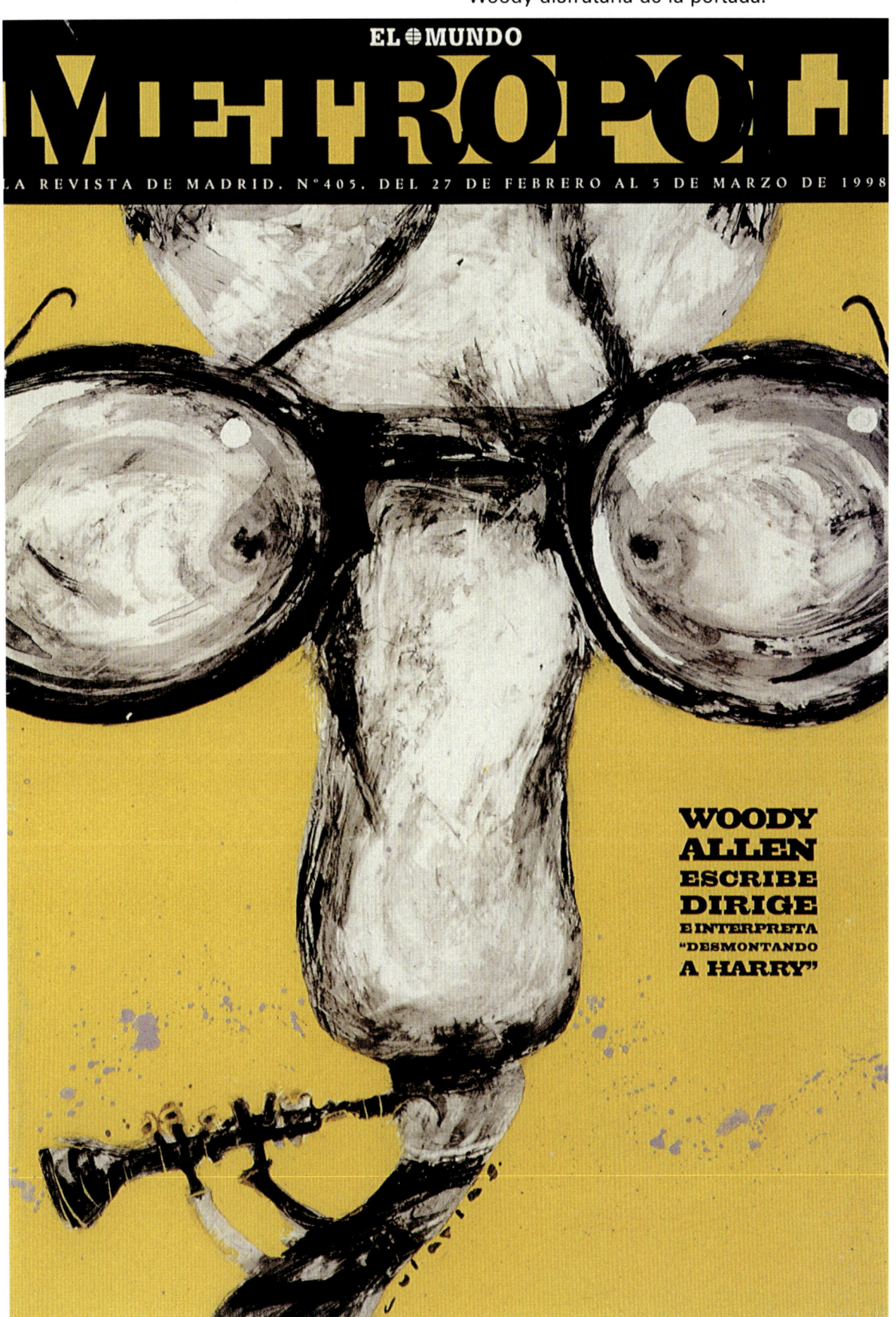

Gold
El Mundo Metropoli
Madrid, Spain
Rodrigo Sánchez, Art Director; **María González**, Designer; **Carmelo Caderot**, Design Director

This illustration must have a computer chip or battery in it somewhere. You can't stop it. It moves. It's so kinetic, there is no way to avoid it. It's the best of the group.

Esta ilustración debe tener algún chip de computadora o batería en algún lugar de su interior. Es imparable, se mueve. Tiene tanto movimiento que no se puede evitar. Es lo mejor del grupo.

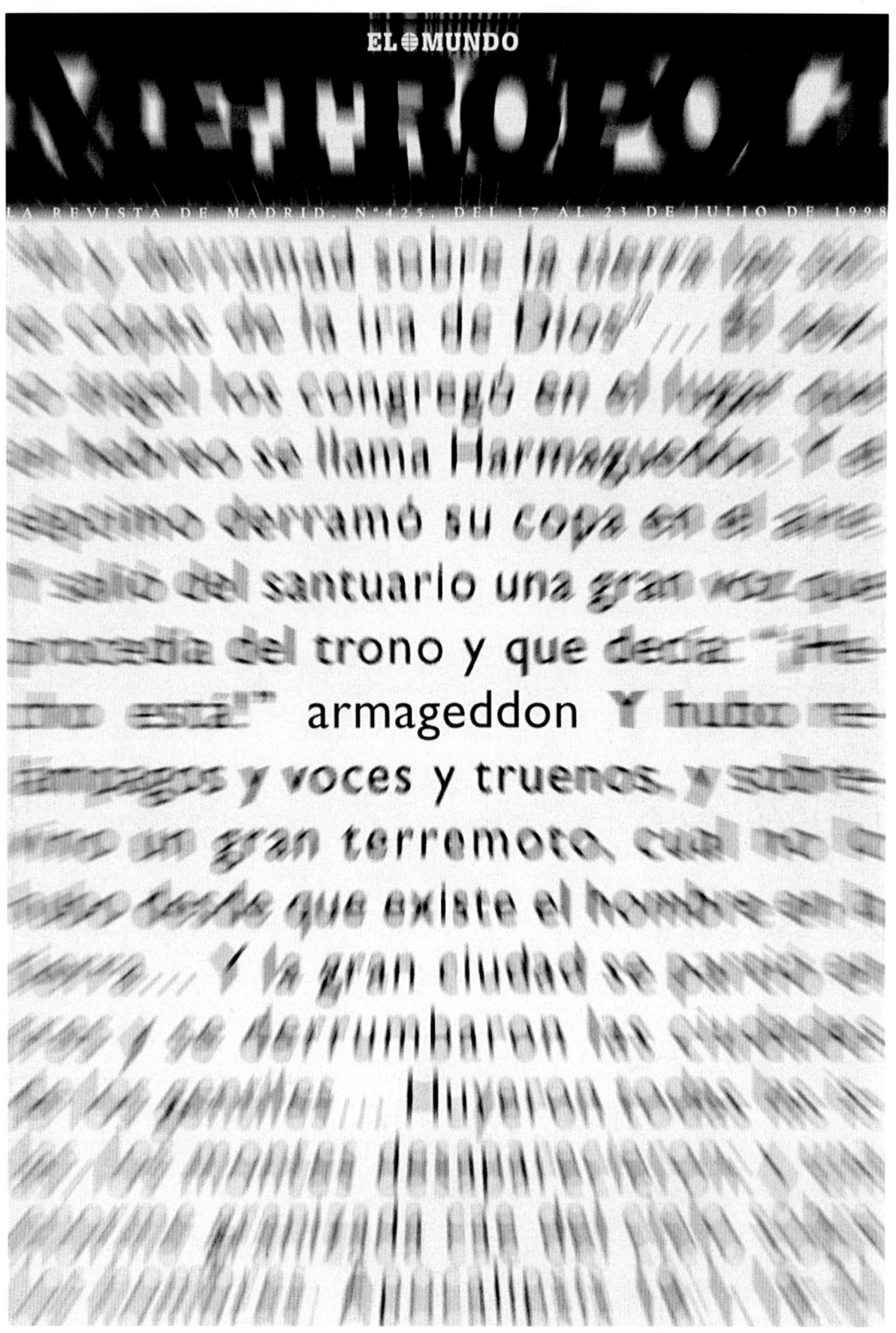

Gold
El Mundo Metropoli
Madrid, Spain
Rodrigo Sánchez, Art Director; **Maria Gonzalez,** Designer; **Carmelo Caderot,** Design Director; **Jose Latova,** Photographer

We loved the interplay with the nameplate. Can you imagine being allowed to do this? No one at Metropoli is saying you can't; they just make the covers as exciting and compelling as possible. They make their own rules based on a good sense of what design is supposed to do.

Nos encantó la interacción con la placa de nombre. ¿Se pudieran imaginar tener libertad para hacer esto? En Metropoli nadie dice que no se puede; simplemente hacen que las portadas sean tan emocionantes y convincentes como sea posible. Ellos ponen sus propias reglas tomando en cuenta un buen sentido del diseño y de lo que éste debería ser.

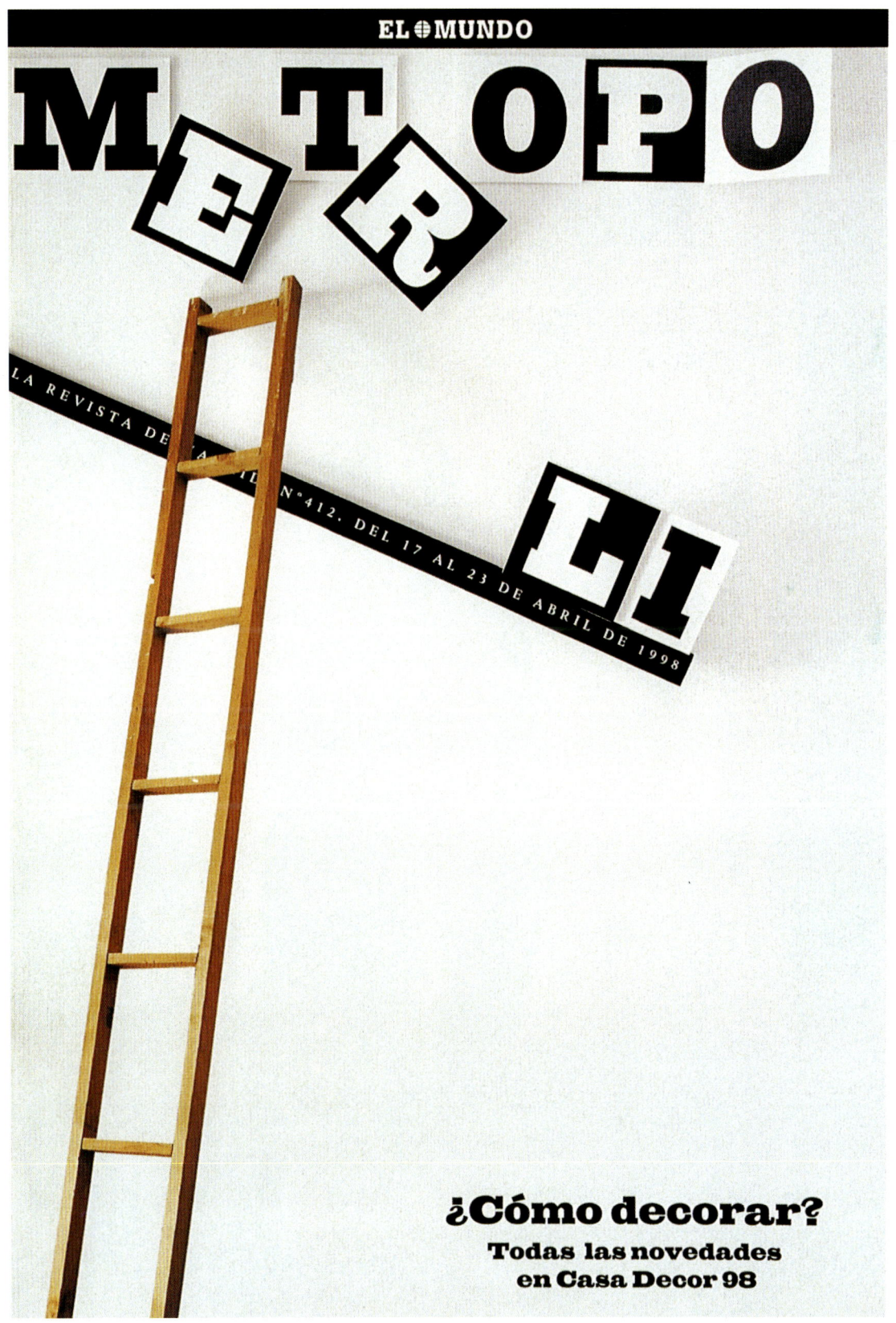

MAGAZINE ■ Cover Black or Black and One Color

Gold
The New York Times Magazine
New York, NY
Janet Froelich, Art Director; **Jennifer Morla,** Designer

Even to its most conservative readers there is a value in turning this cover upside down. The concept is very clever. Its technique is minimal, but it achieved the maximum results.

Incluso para sus lectores más conservadores, hay un valor en virar esta portada de abajo hacia arriba. Es un concepto muy hábil. La técnica empleada es mínima pero alcanza los máximos resultados.

the shock of the
familiar

The objects of ordinary life are, as never before, designed to manipulate taste and desire. There is a design explosion under way — and it is forcing us to see everyday things in entirely new ways.

From toothbrushes to Web pages, a guided tour.

The New York Times Magazine
DECEMBER 13, 1998 / SECTION 6

154 ■ THE BEST OF NEWSPAPER DESIGN

Cover Black or Black and One Color ■ MAGAZINE

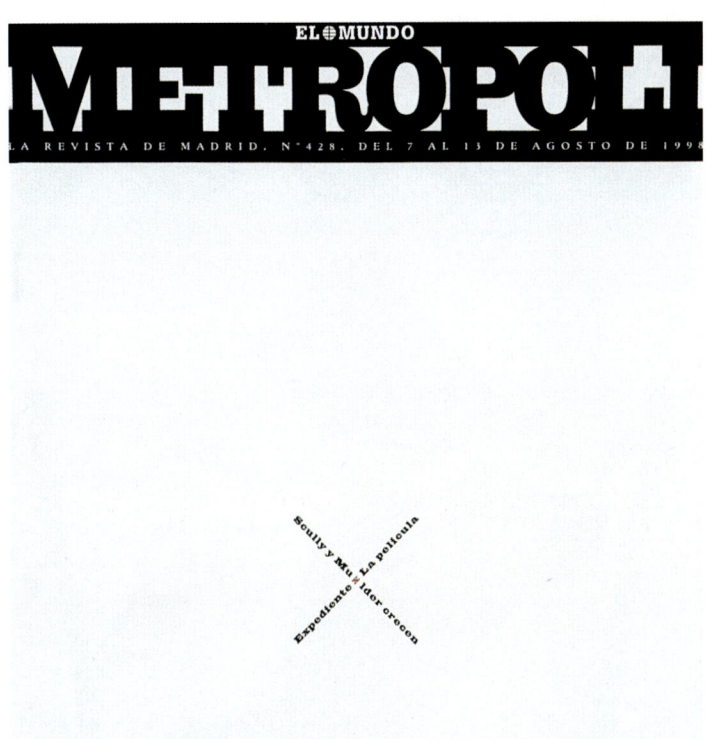

Silver
El Mundo Metropoli
Madrid, Spain
Rodrigo Sánchez, Art Director; **María González,** Designer; **Carmelo Caderot,** Design Director

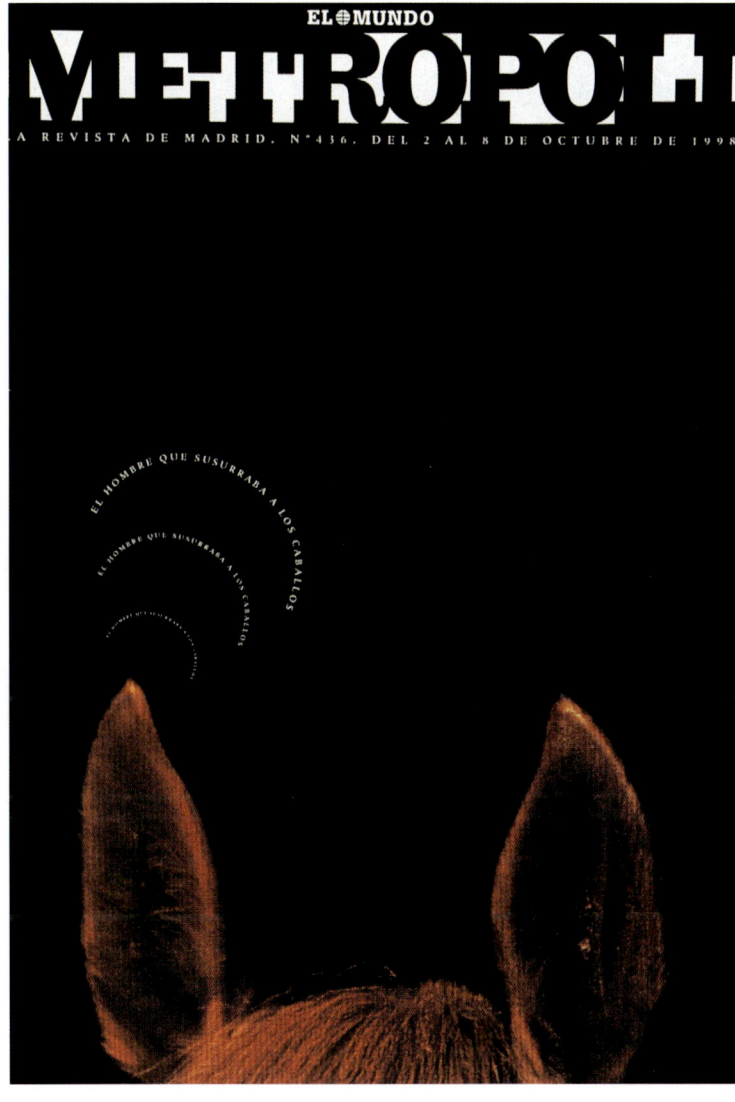

Silver
El Mundo Metropoli
Madrid, Spain
Rodrigo Sánchez, Art Director; **María González,** Designer; **Carmelo Caderot,** Design Director

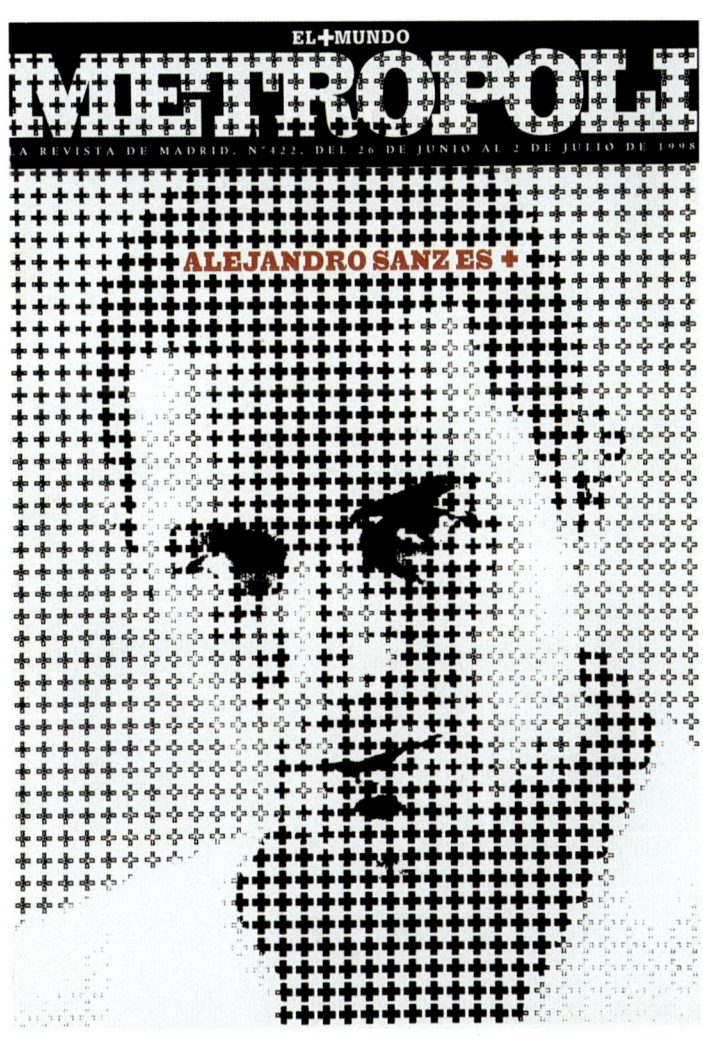

Silver
El Mundo Metropoli
Madrid, Spain
Rodrigo Sánchez, Art Director; **María González,** Designer; **Carmelo Caderot,** Design Director

MAGAZINE — Cover Black or Black and One Color

Silver
El Mundo Metropoli
Madrid, Spain
Rodrigo Sánchez, Art Director; **María González,** Designer; **Carmelo Caderot,** Design Director

Silver
El Mundo Metropoli
Madrid, Spain
Rodrigo Sánchez, Art Director; **María González,** Designer; **Carmelo Caderot,** Design Director

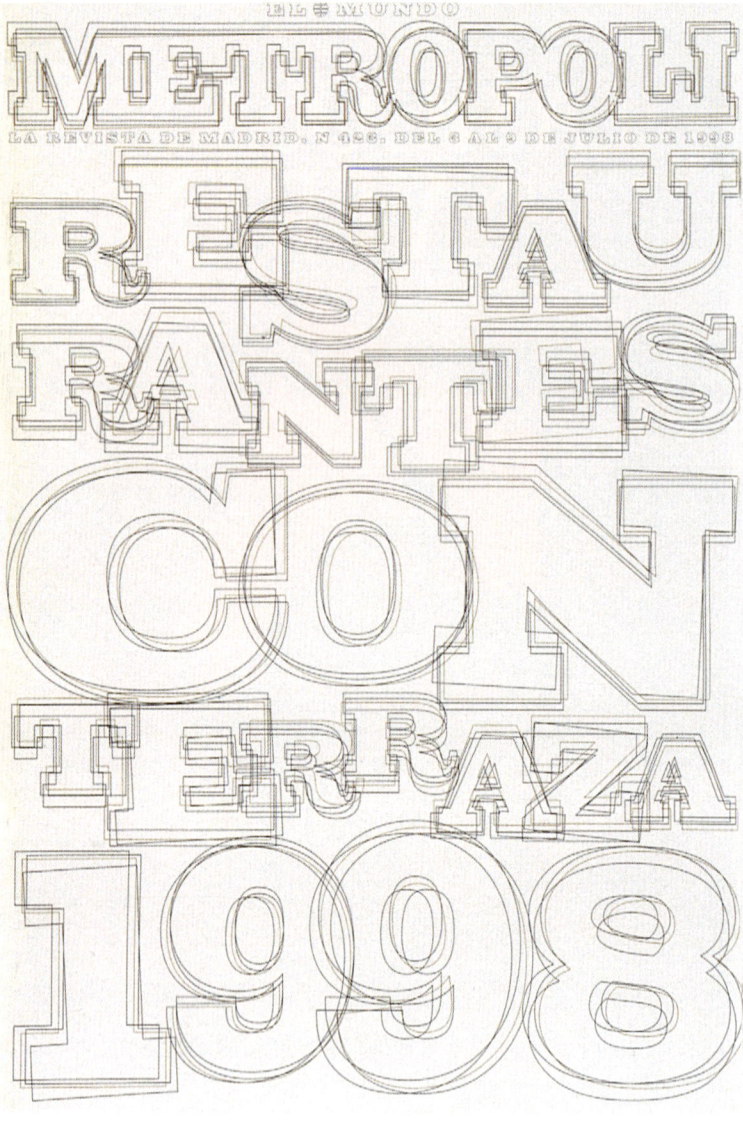

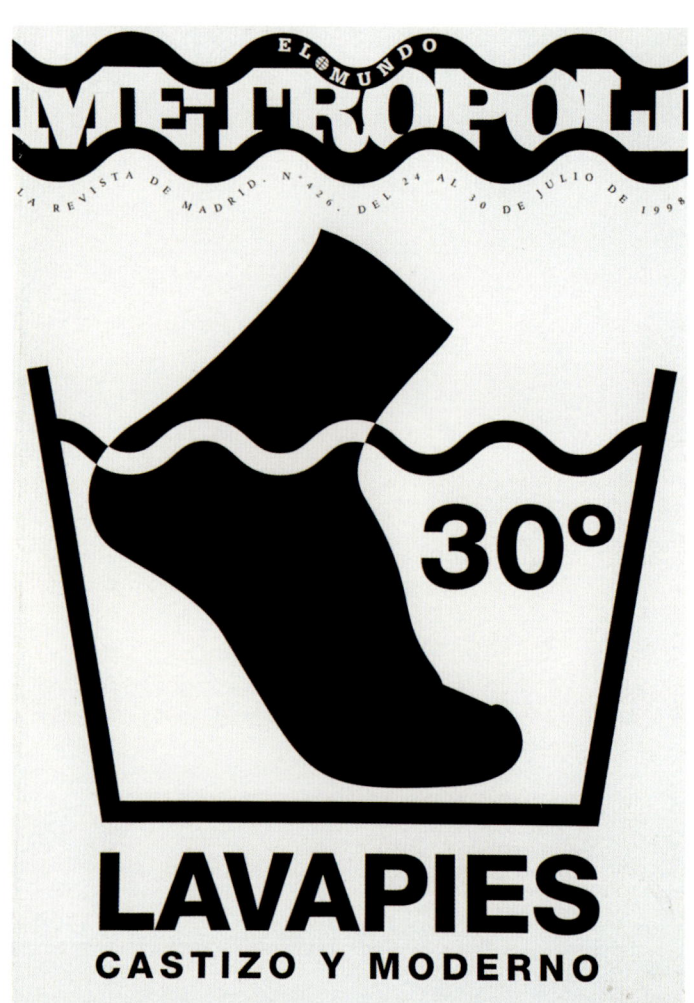

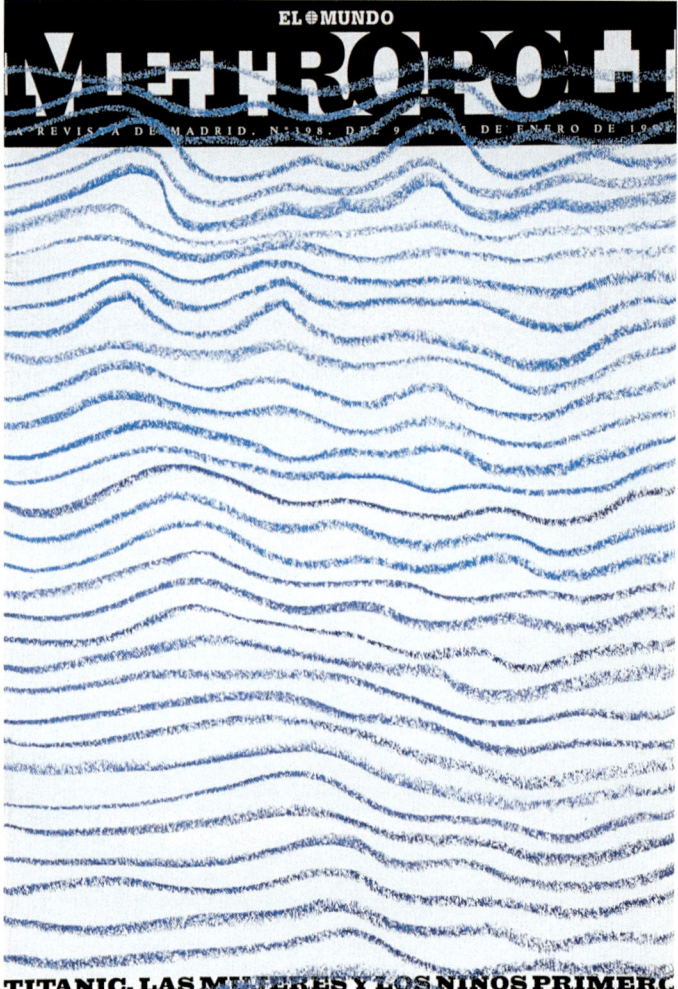

Silver
El Mundo Metropoli
Madrid, Spain
Rodrigo Sánchez, Art Director; **María González,** Designer; **Carmelo Caderot,** Design Director

Cover Black or Black and One Color, Cover Color ■ MAGAZINE

El Mundo Metropoli
Madrid, Spain
Rodrigo Sánchez, Art Director; **Maria Gonzalez**, Designer; **Carmelo Caderot**, Design Director

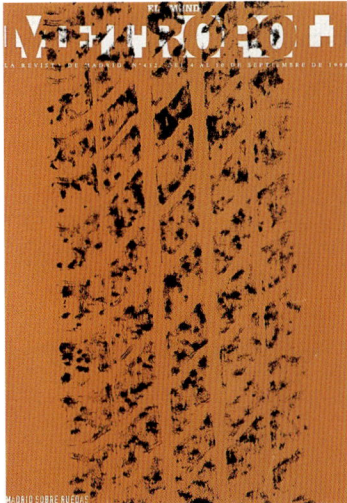

El Mundo Metropoli
Madrid, Spain
Rodrigo Sánchez, Art Director; **Maria Gonzalez**, Designer; **Carmelo Caderot**, Design Director; **Gonzalo Gonzalez**, Illustrator

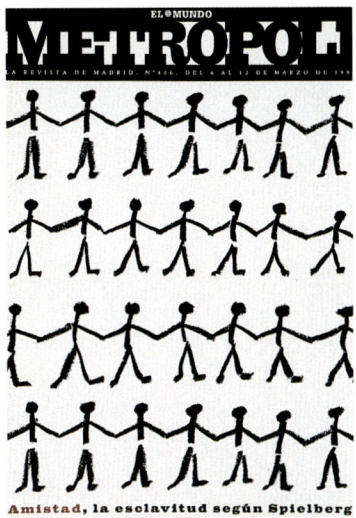

El Norte
Monterrey, México
Rosalinda Rodríguez Peña, Designer; **Luis Vázquez**, Illustrator; **Miguel Rodríguez**, Photographer; **Juan F. Araujo**, Photographer; **Carlos Benítez**, Section Editor; **Granada Ramírez**, Design Editor; **Alejandro Banuet**, Design Manager Editor; **Raúl Braulio Martínez**, Art Director; **Martín Pérez Cerda**, Editor Director; **Ramón Alberto Garza**, General Editor Director

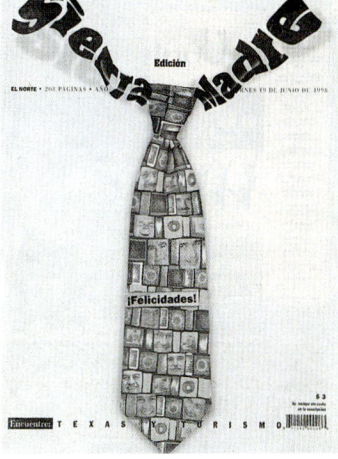

Anchorage Daily News
Anchorage, AK
Pamela Dunlap-Shohl, Illustrator & Designer

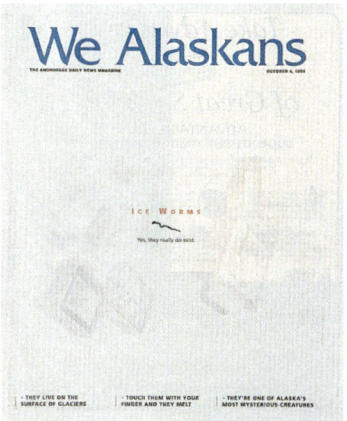

The Boston Globe
Boston, MA
Catherine Aldrich, Art Director & Designer

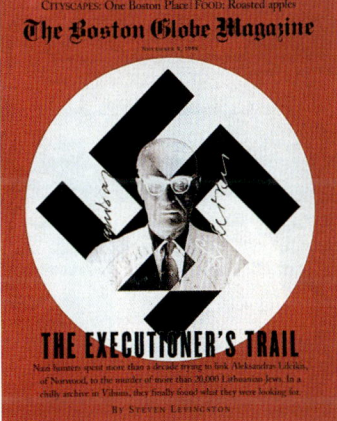

Diario de Noticias / DNA
Lisbon, Portugal
Mário B. Resendes, Editor-in-Chief; **José Maria Ribeirinho**, Art Director; **Pedro Rolo Duarte**, Editor; **Luís Silva Dias**, Design Editor; **Miguel Pedroso**, Designer

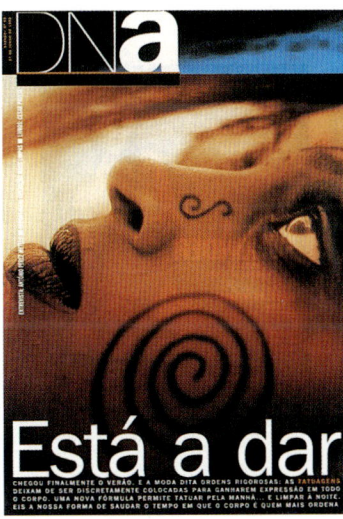

Diario de Noticias / DNA
Lisbon, Portugal
Mário B. Resendes, Editor-in-Chief; **José Maria Ribeirinho**, Art Director; **Pedro Rolo Duarte**, Editor; **Luís Silva Dias**, Design Editor; **Miguel Pedroso**, Designer

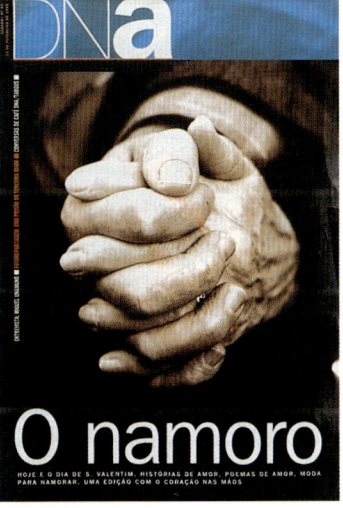

Diario de Noticias / DNA
Lisbon, Portugal
Mário B. Resendes, Editor-in-Chief; **José Maria Ribeirinho**, Art Director; **Pedro Rolo Duarte**, Editor; **Luís Silva Dias**, Design Editor; **Miguel Pedroso**, Designer

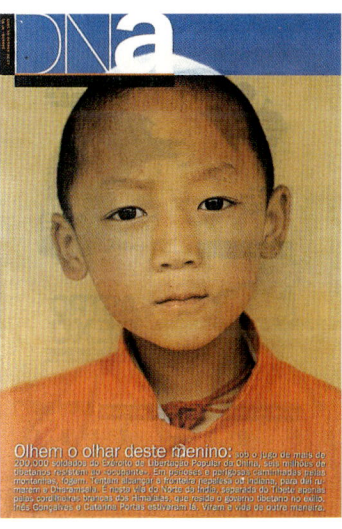

MAGAZINE — Cover Color

Gold
El Mundo Metropoli
Madrid, Spain
Rodrigo Sánchez, Art Director; **María González**, Designer; **Carmelo Caderot**, Design Director

This cover is obviously simple but still innovative. The imagination that goes into this publication's covers is outstanding. They are constantly producing work of this kind of energy and imagery. It's near-genius how they change the flag each time to go with the artwork to help illustrate the idea.

Esta portada es obviamente simple y, no obstante, innovadora. Es increíble el derroche de imaginación del cual hacen gala las portadas de esta publicación. Ellos producen de modo sistemático obras con este tipo de energía e imágenes. Es casi genial cómo logran cambiar la cabecera según la ocasión para que armonice con las imágenes de arte, de tal modo que contribuya a ilustrar la idea.

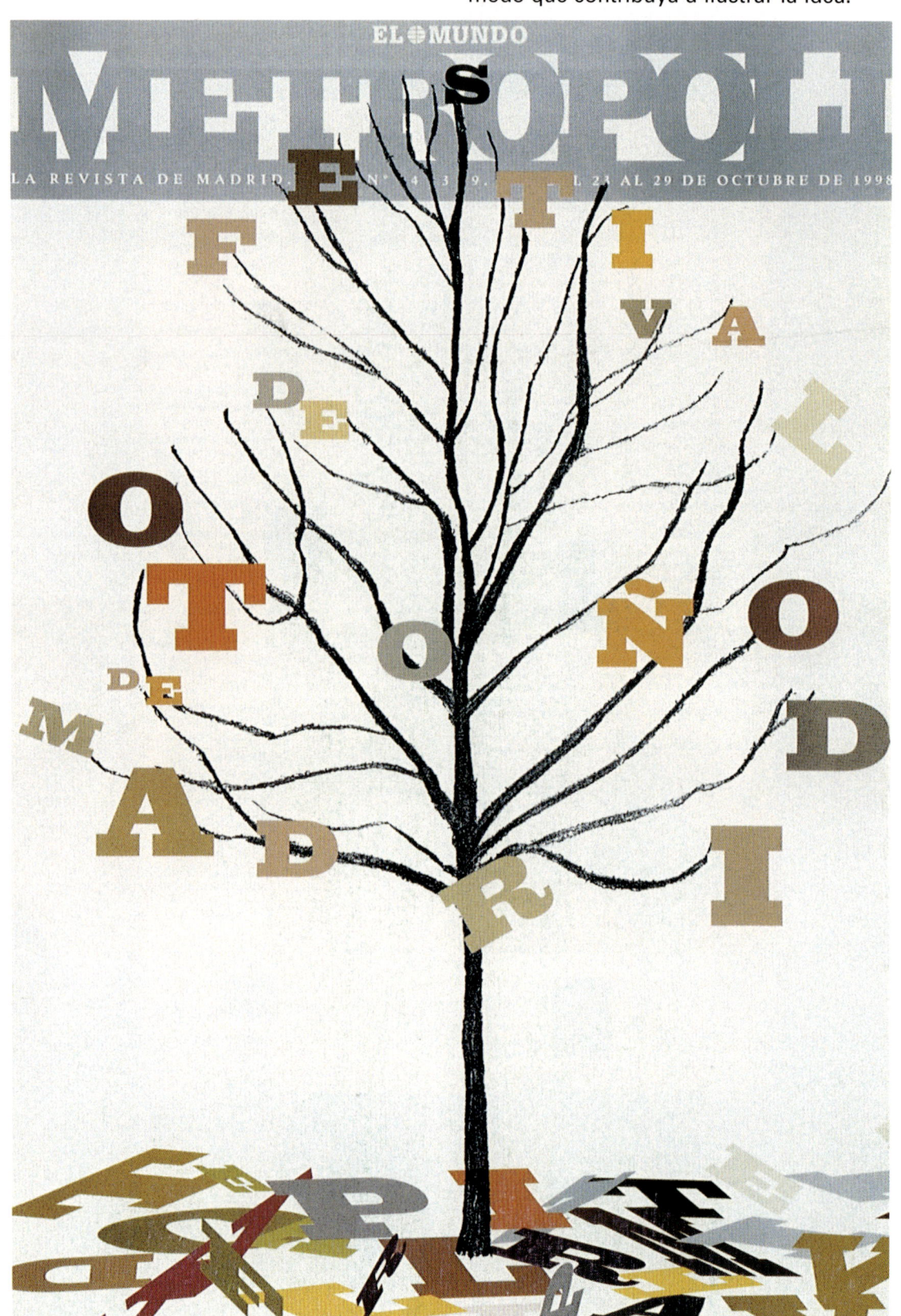

Cover Color ■ MAGAZINE

Gold
The New York Times Magazine
New York, NY
Janet Froelich, Art Director; **Joele Cuyler,** Designer;
Karen Kuehn, Photographer; **Kathy Ryan,** Photo Editor

It's striking. It's perfect. It's clever and beautiful. Their covers are excellent introductions to the content inside.

Es impactante y perfecto. Ingenioso y bello. Sus portadas dejan entrever el atractivo del contenido interior.

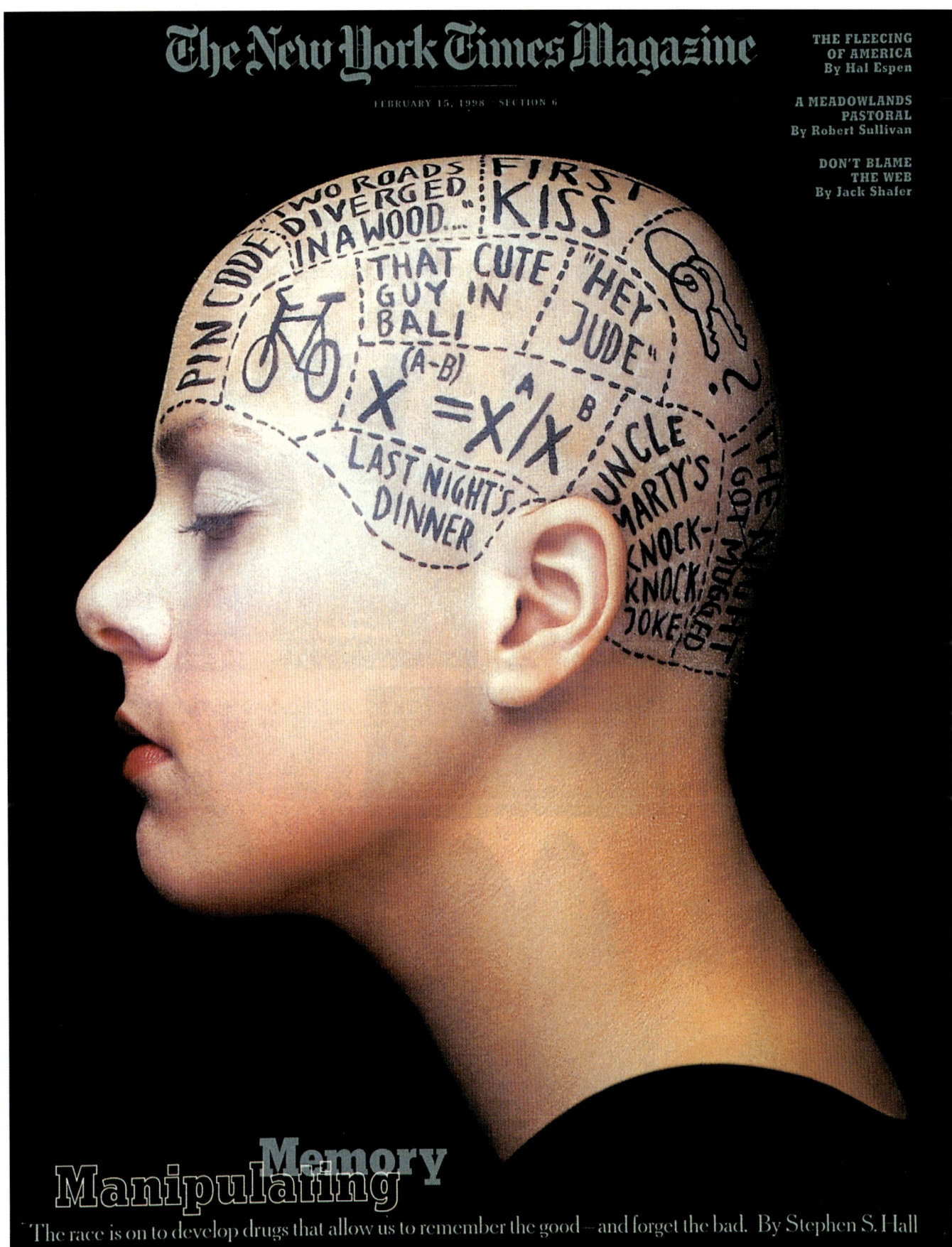

TWENTIETH EDITION ■ 159

MAGAZINE ■ Cover Color

Gold
The New York Times Magazine
New York, NY
Janet Froelich, Art Director; **Andrea Fella,** Designer; **Christoph Niemann,** Illustrator

It's amazing the artist could render Starr out of a few brush strokes. It's such a bold use of color, and the green is so catchy, that it works.

Es increíble que el artista pudiera reproducir a Starr con sólo unas pinceladas. Es un uso tan atrevido del color y el verde llama tanto la atención que surte un gran efecto.

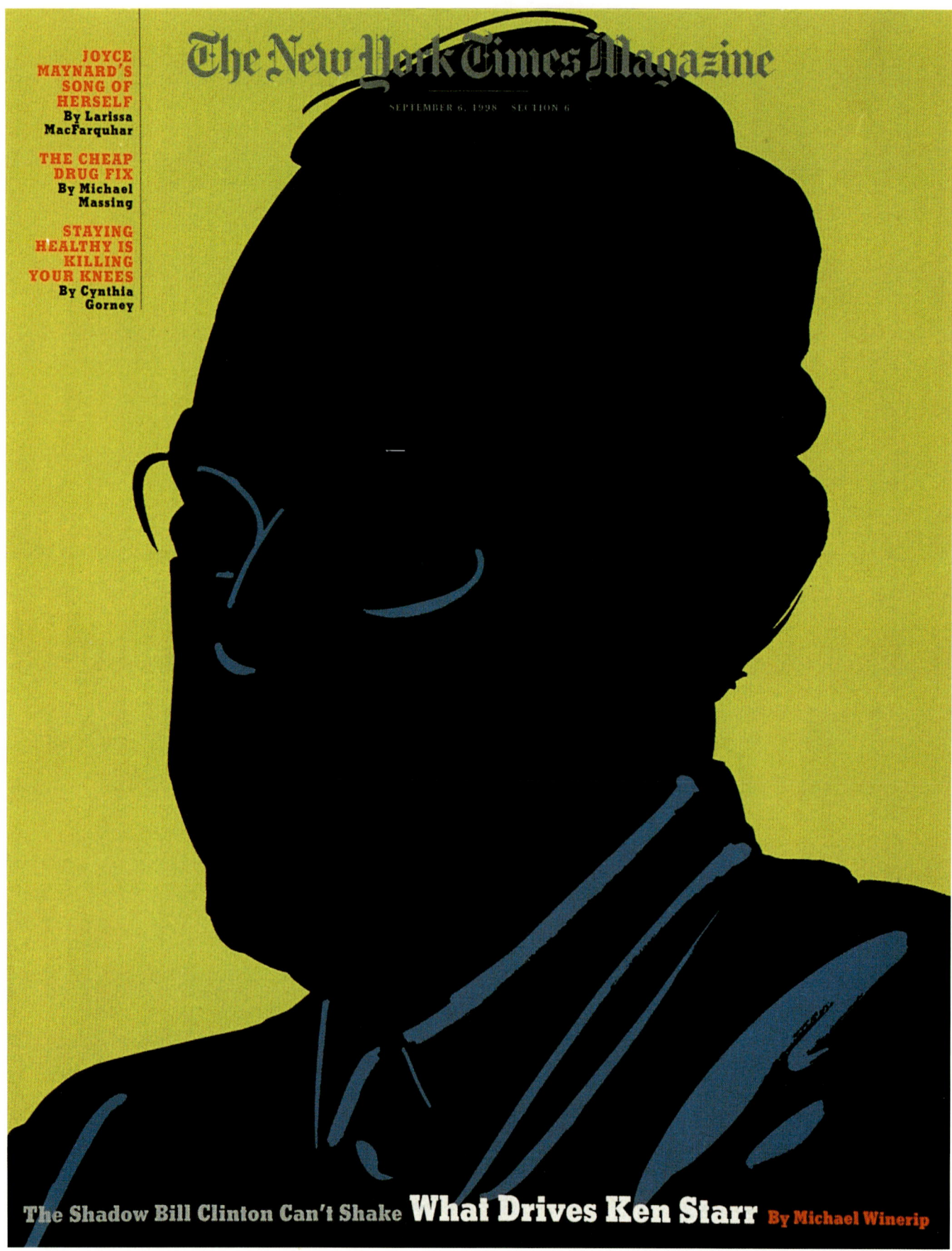

Silver
El Mundo Metropoli
Madrid, Spain

Rodrigo Sánchez, Art Director; **María González,** Designer; **Ulises Culebro,** Illustrator; **Carmelo Caderot,** Design Director

Silver
Diario de Noticias / DNA
Lisbon, Portugal

Mário B. Resendes, Editor-in-Chief; **José Maria Ribeirinho,** Art Director; **Pedro Rolo Duarte,** Editor; **Luís Silva Dias,** Design Editor; **Miguel Pedroso,** Designer

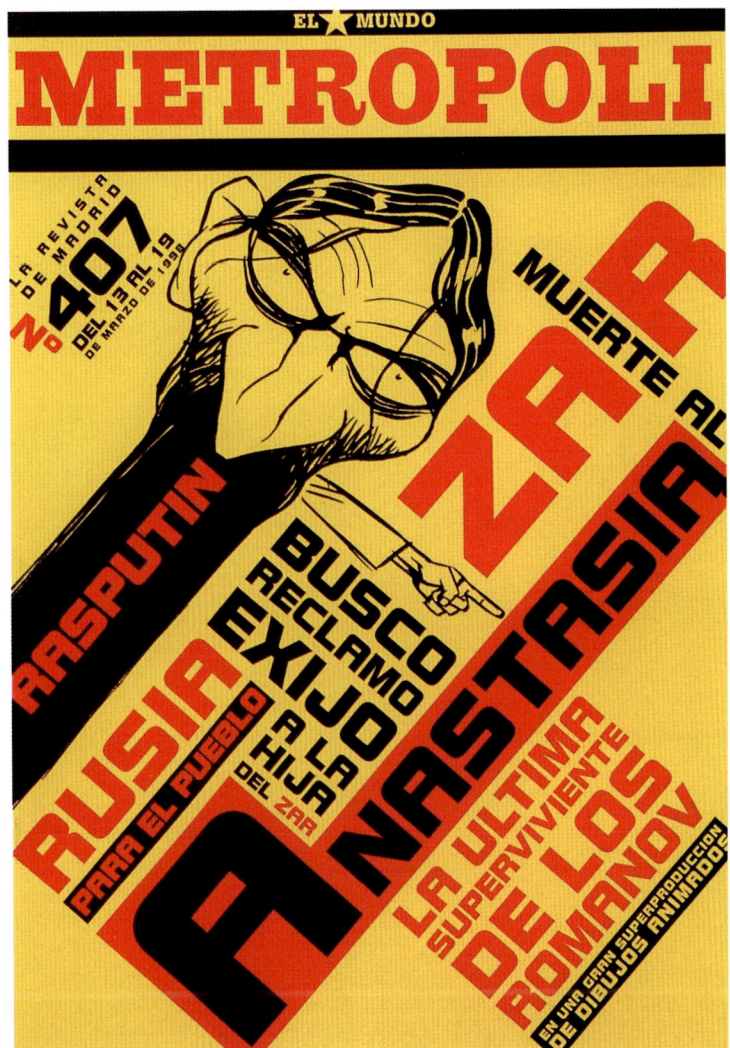

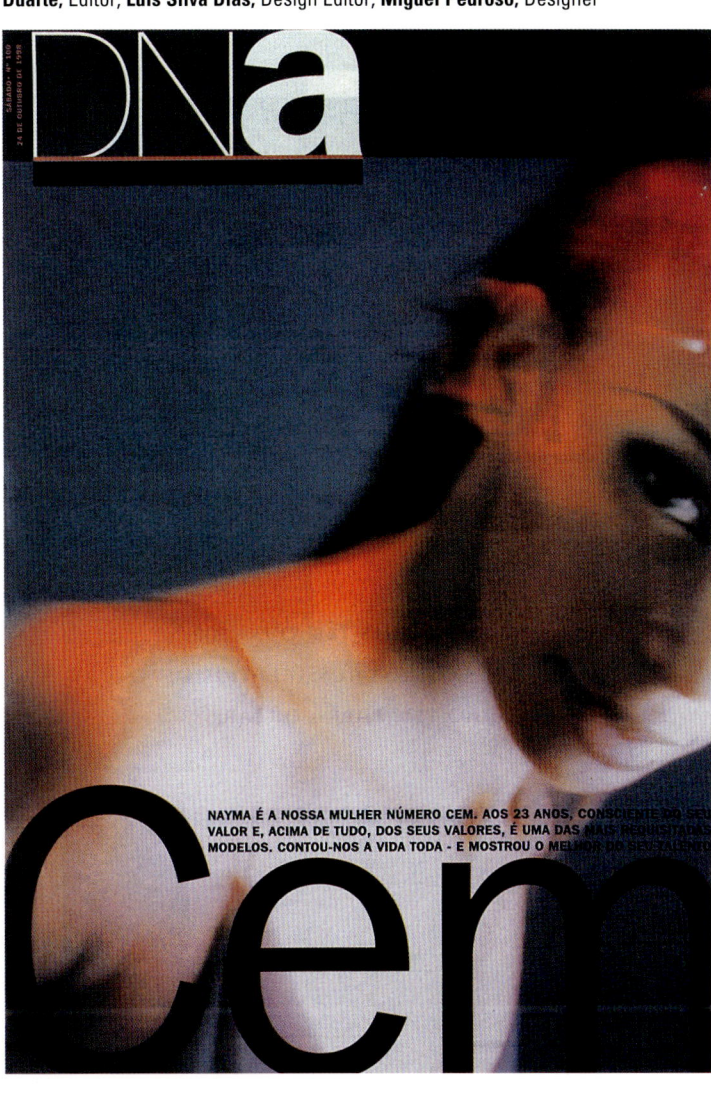

Silver
Diario de Noticias / DNA
Lisbon, Portugal

Mário B. Resendes, Editor-in-Chief; **José Maria Ribeirinho,** Art Director; **Pedro Rolo Duarte,** Editor; **Luís Silva Dias,** Design Editor; **Miguel Pedroso,** Designer

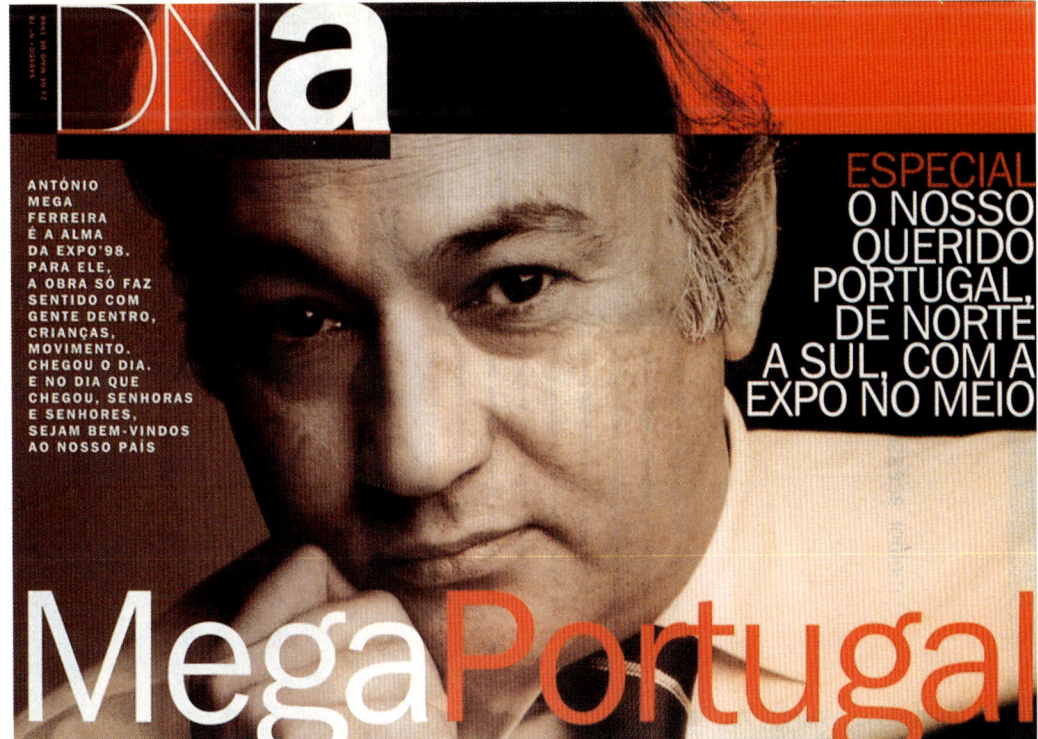

MAGAZINE — Cover Color

El Mundo Metropoli
Madrid, Spain
Rodrigo Sánchez, Art Director; **Maria Gonzalez,** Designer; **Carmelo Caderot,** Design Director

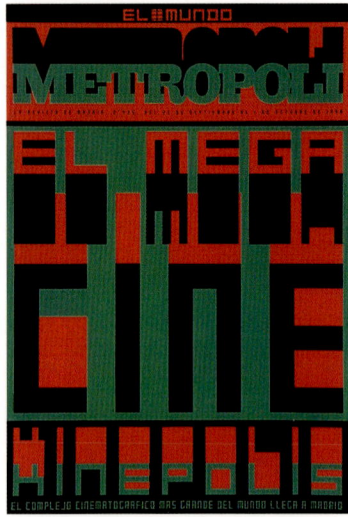

El Mundo Metropoli
Madrid, Spain
Rodrigo Sánchez, Art Director; **Maria Gonzalez,** Designer; **Carmelo Caderot,** Design Director

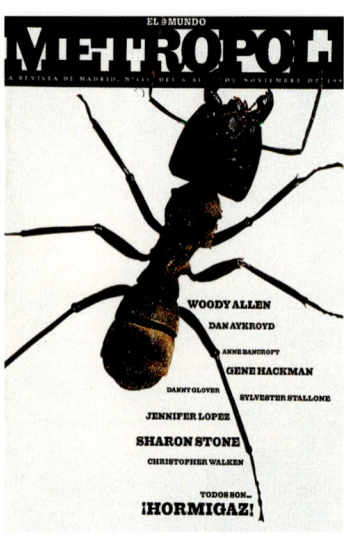

El Mundo Metropoli
Madrid, Spain
Rodrigo Sánchez, Art Director; **Maria Gonzalez,** Designer; **Carmelo Caderot,** Design Director

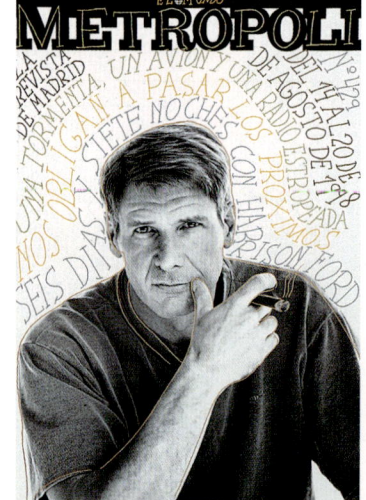

The New York Times
New York, NY
Janet Froelich, Art Director; **Lisa Naftolin,** Designer; **Timothy Greenfield-Sanders,** Photographer; **Kathy Ryan,** Photo Editor

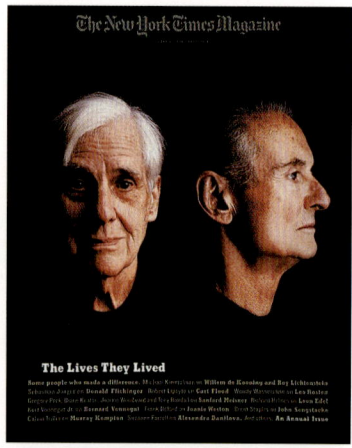

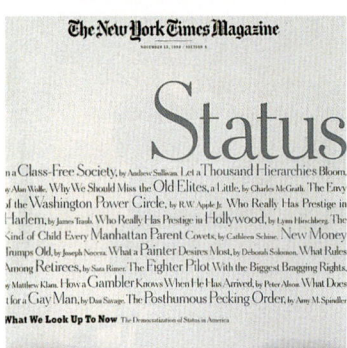

The New York Times Magazine
New York, NY
Janet Froelich, Art Director; **Nancy Harris,** Designer; **James Wojcik,** Photographer; **Kathy Ryan,** Photo Editor

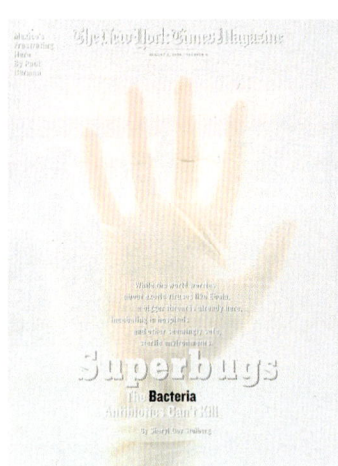

The New York Times Magazine
New York, NY
Janet Froelich, Art Director; **Joele Cuyler,** Designer; **Tom Schierlitz,** Photographer; **Kathy Ryan,** Photo Editor

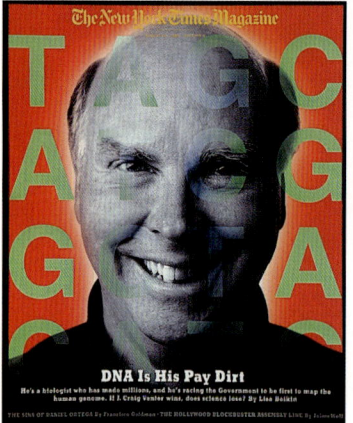

The New York Times Magazine
New York, NY
Janet Froelich, Art Director; **Joele Cuyler,** Designer; **Gene Pierce,** Photographer; **Kathy Ryan,** Photo Editor; **Ignacio Rodriguez,** Digital Imaging

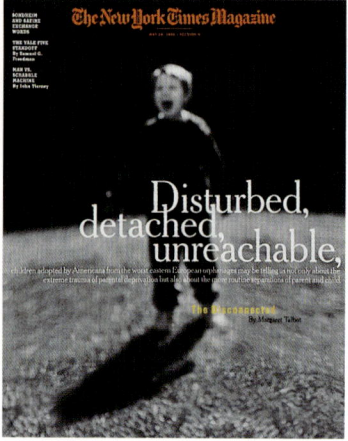

The New York Times Magazine
New York, NY
Janet Froelich, Art Director; **Claude Martel,** Designer; **Gerald Slota,** Photographer; **Kathy Ryan,** Photo Editor

Cover Color, Page Design ■ MAGAZINE

La Revista
Buenos Aires, Argentina
Jorge Piñeyro, Art Director

The Washington Post Magazine
Washington, DC
Kelly Doe, Art Director; **Crary Pullen,** Photo Editor; **D.A. Peterson,** Photographer

Diario de Noticias / DNA
Lisbon, Portugal
Mário B. Resendes, Editor-in-Chief; **José Maria Ribeirinho,** Art Director; **Pedro Rolo Duarte,** Editor; **Luís Silva Dias,** Design Editor; **Miguel Pedroso,** Designer

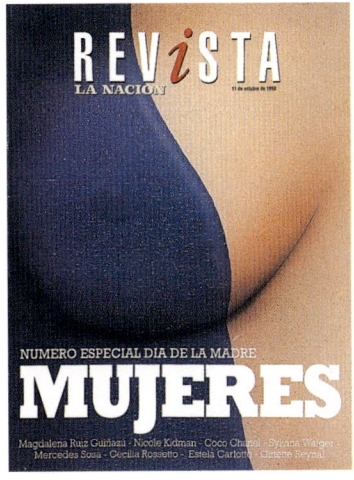
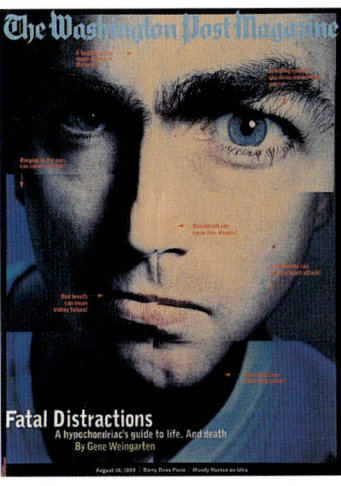
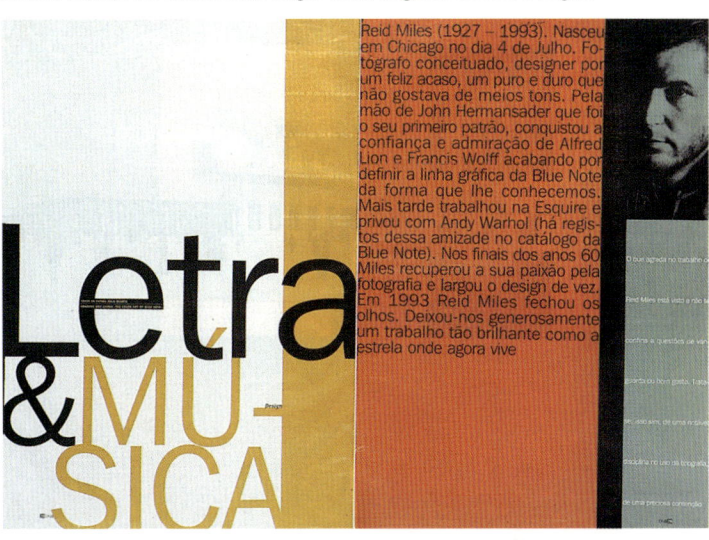

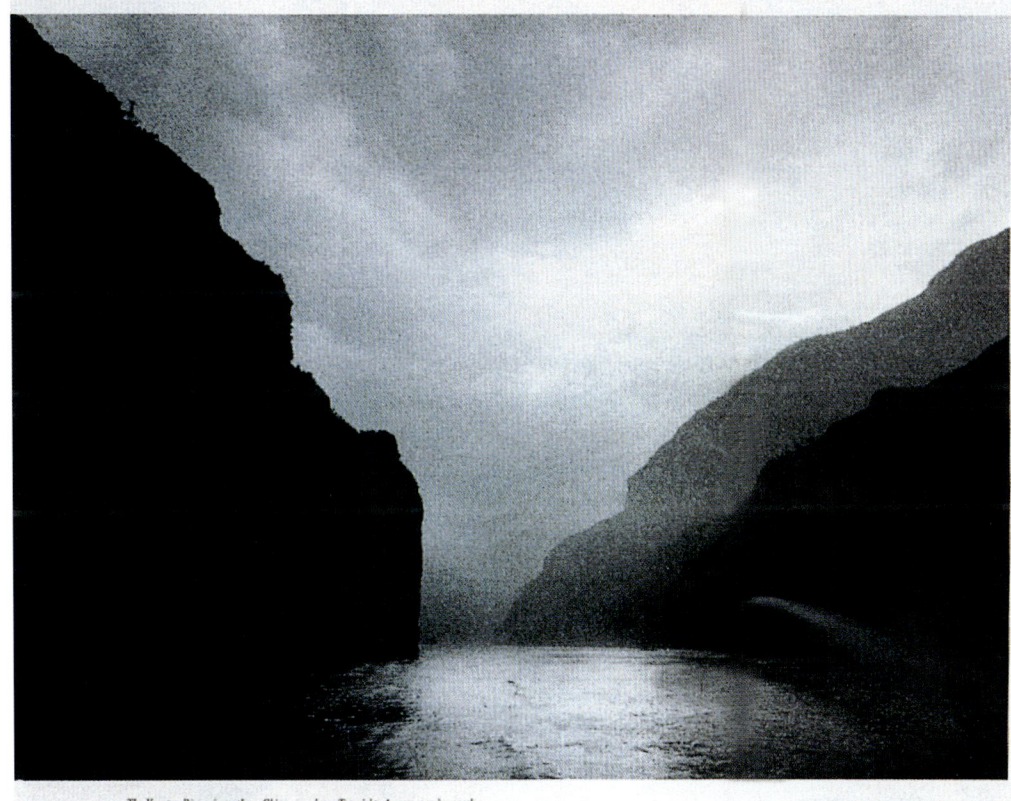
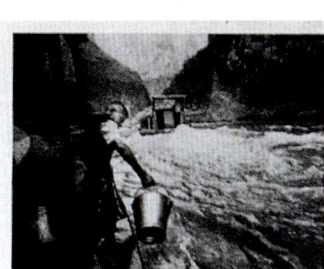

Silver
The Boston Globe
Boston, MA
Catherine Aldrich, Art Director & Designer; **Lane Turner,** Photographer

MAGAZINE ■ Page Design

Silver
Diario de Noticias / DNA
Lisbon, Portugal
Mário B. Resendes, Editor-in-Chief; **José Maria Ribeirinho,** Art Director; **Pedro Rolo Duarte,** Editor; **Luís Silva Dias,** Design Editor; **Miguel Pedroso,** Designer

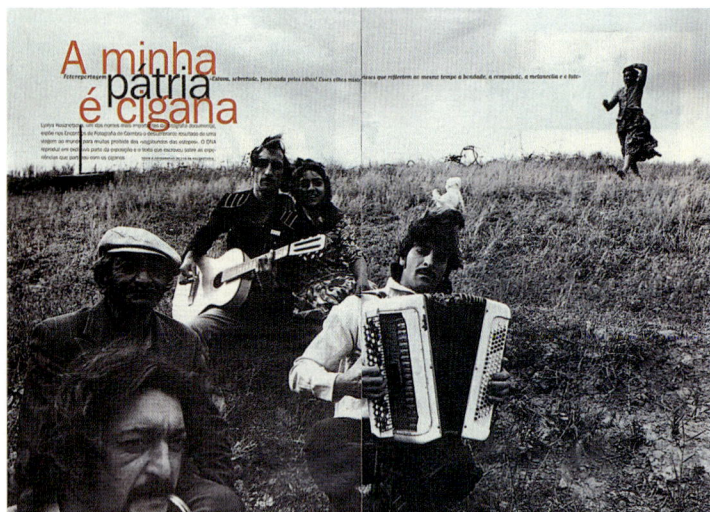
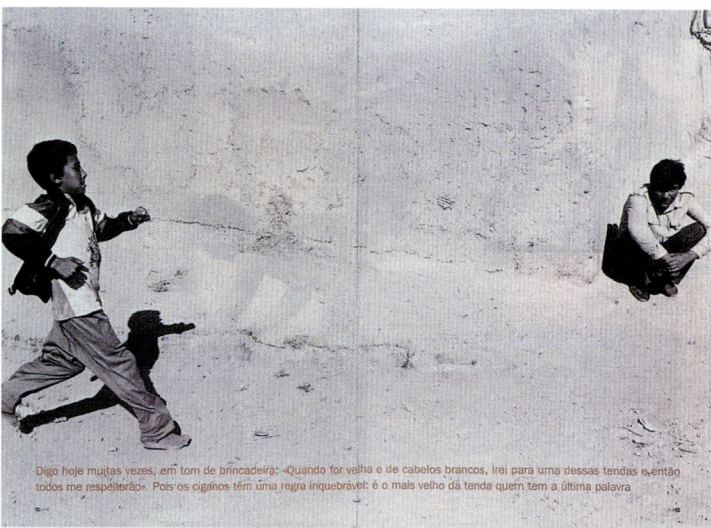

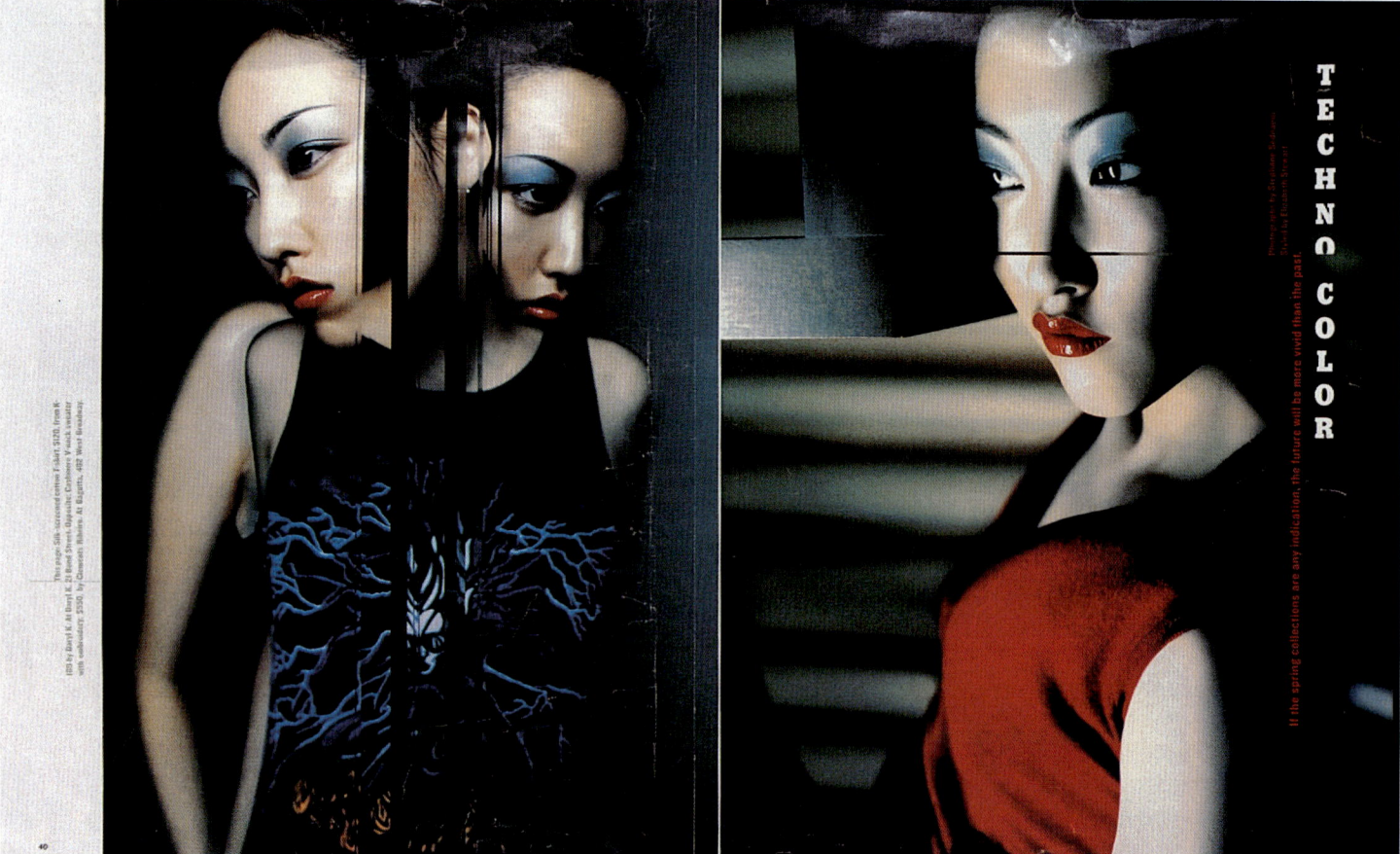

Silver
The New York Times Magazine
New York, NY
Janet Froelich, Art Director; **Claude Martel,** Designer; **Stephane Sednaoui,** Photographer; **Kathy Ryan,** Photo Editor

164 ■ THE BEST OF NEWSPAPER DESIGN

Silver
La Revista de El Mundo
Madrid, Spain
Rodrigo Sánchez, Art Director; **María González**, Designer; **Amparo Redondo**, Designer; **Carmelo Caderot**, Design Director

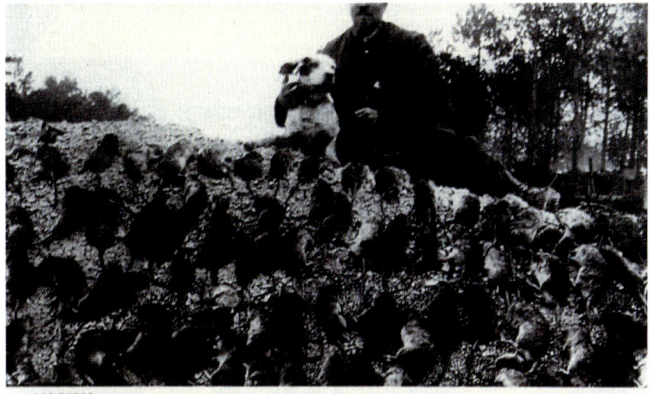

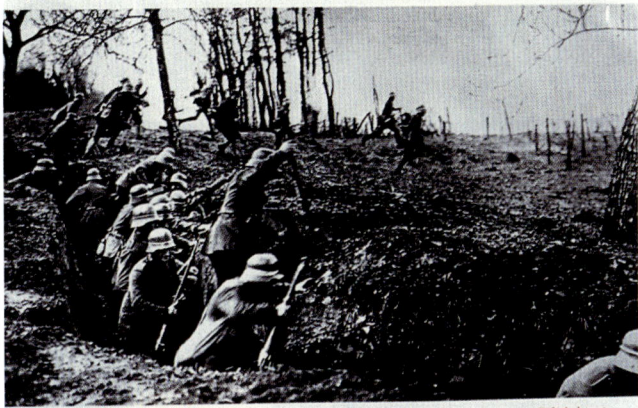

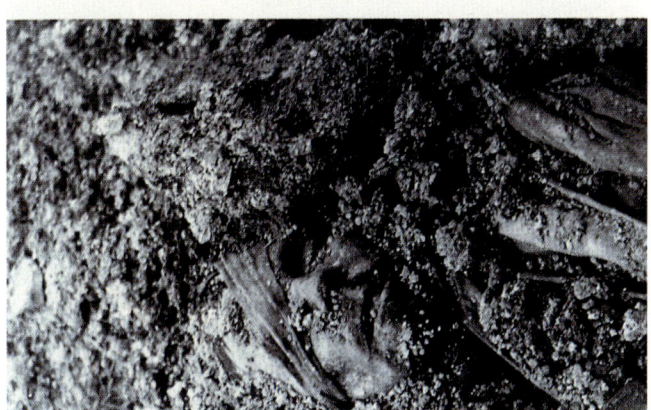

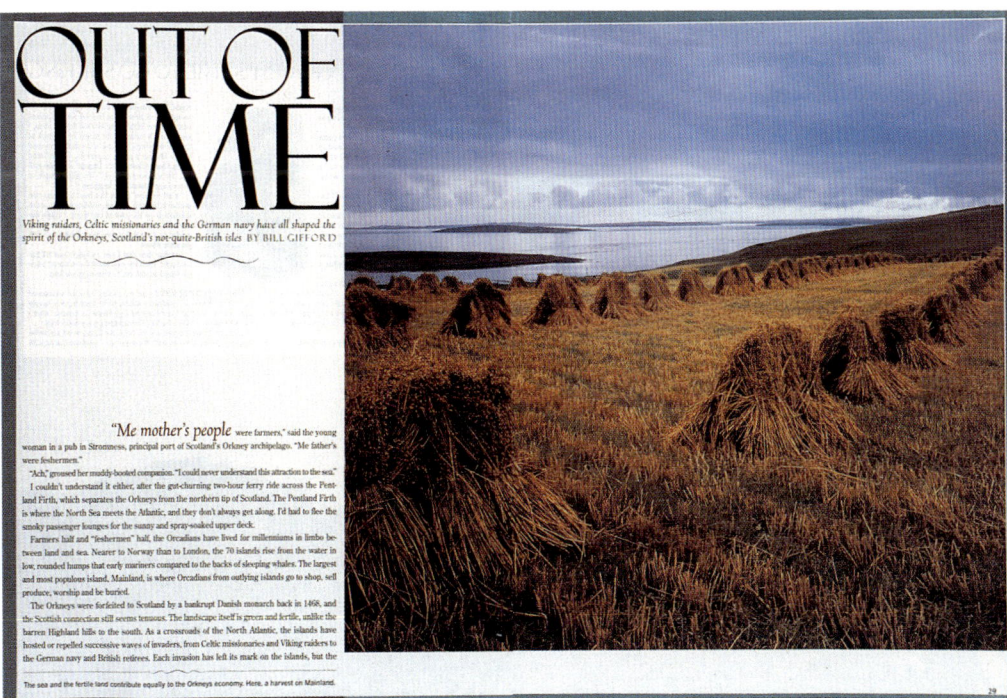

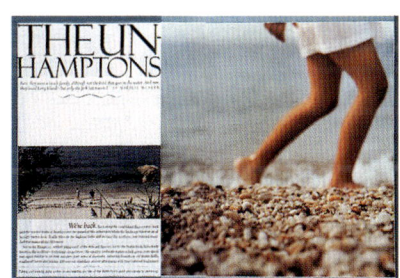

Silver
The Washington Post Magazine
Washington, DC
Kelly Doe, Art Director; **Lisa Schreiber**, Associate Art Director; **Karen Tanaka**, Photo Editor; **Beatriz Da Costa**, Photographer

MAGAZINE ■ Page Design

Diario de Noticias / DNA
Lisbon, Portugal

Mário B. Resendes, Editor-in-Chief; **José Maria Ribeirinho,** Art Director; **Pedro Rolo Duarte,** Editor; **Luís Silva Dias,** Design Editor; **Miguel Pedroso,** Designer

Diario de Noticias / DNA
Lisbon, Portugal

Mário B. Resendes, Editor-in-Chief; **José Maria Ribeirinho,** Art Director; **Pedro Rolo Duarte,** Editor; **Luís Silva Dias,** Design Editor; **Miguel Pedroso,** Designer

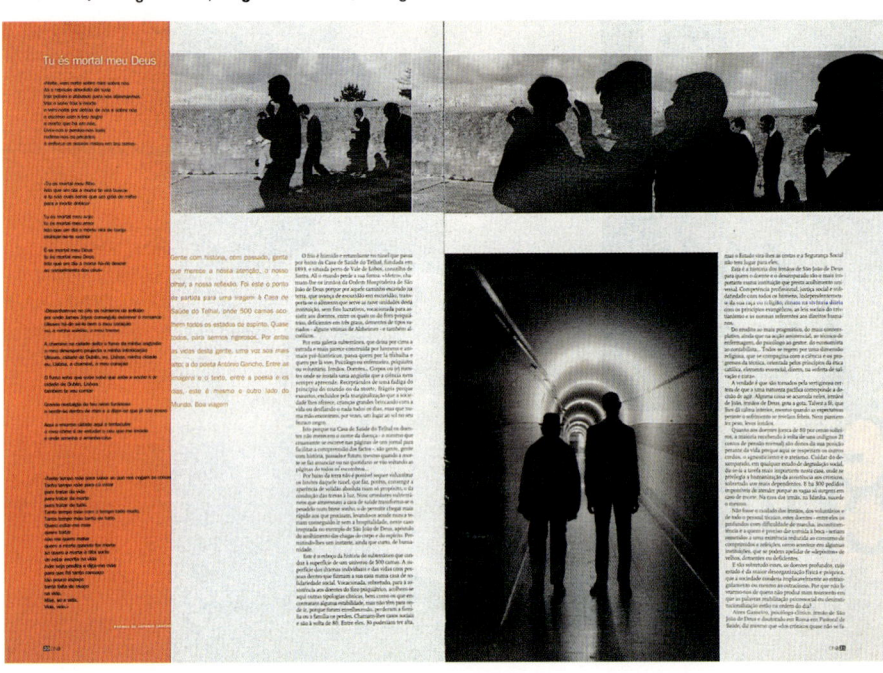

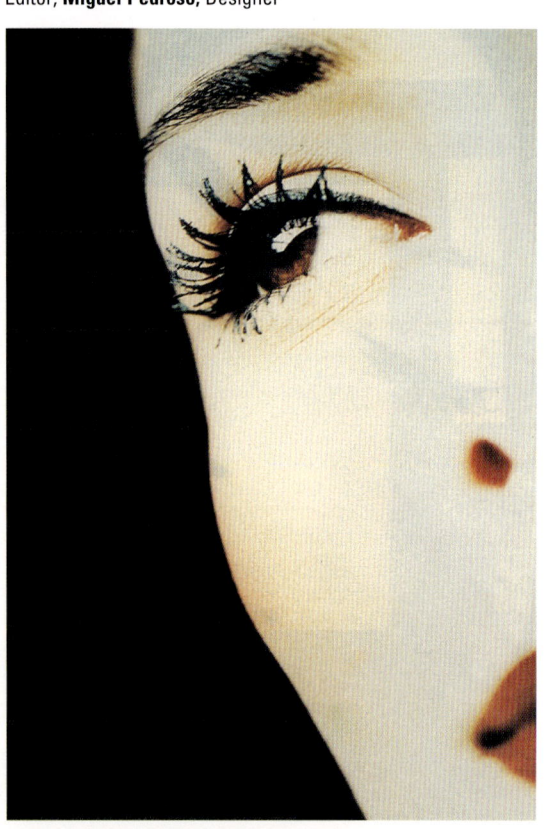

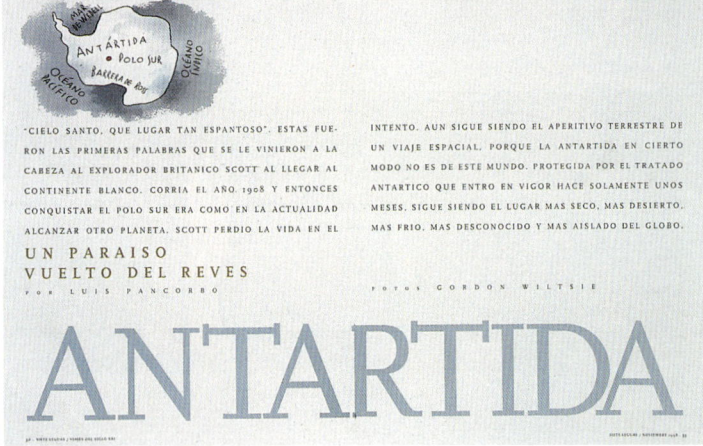

El Mundo Del Siglo XXI
Madrid, Spain

Carmelo Caderot, Art Director & Designer; **Manuel de Miguel,** Assistant Art Director & Designer

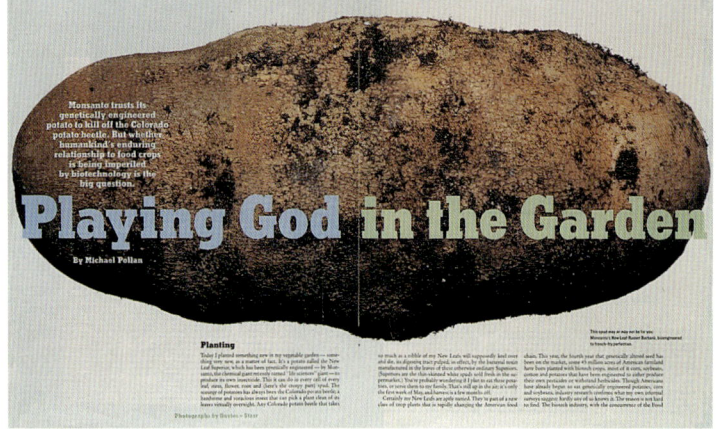

The New York Times Magazine
New York, NY

Janet Froelich, Art Director; **Claude Martel,** Designer; **Davies & Starr,** Photographer; **Kathy Ryan,** Photo Editor

Page Design ■ MAGAZINE

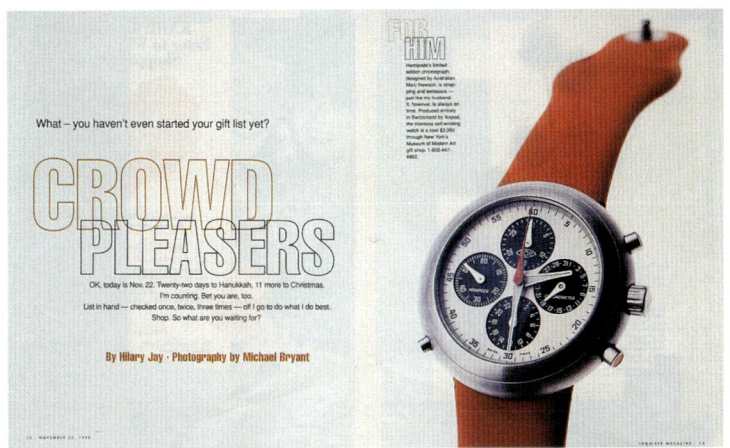

The Philadelphia Inquirer Magazine
Philadelphia, PA
Christine Dunleavy, Art Director; **Susan Syrnick,** Assistant Art Director & Designer; **Michael Bryant,** Photographer

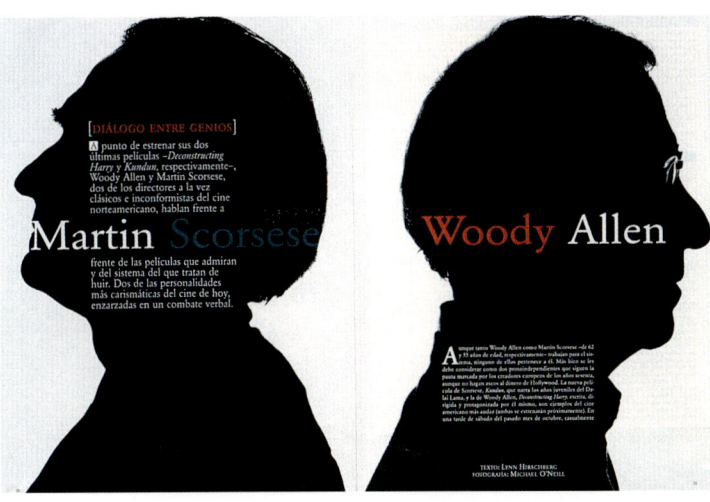

El País Semanal
Madrid, Spain
David García, Art Director; **Eugenio González,** Design Director; **Maripaz Domingo,** Designer; **Gustavo Sánchez,** Designer; **Patricia Álverez,** Designer; **Alex M. Roig,** Editor-in-Chief; **Michael O'Neill,** Photographer

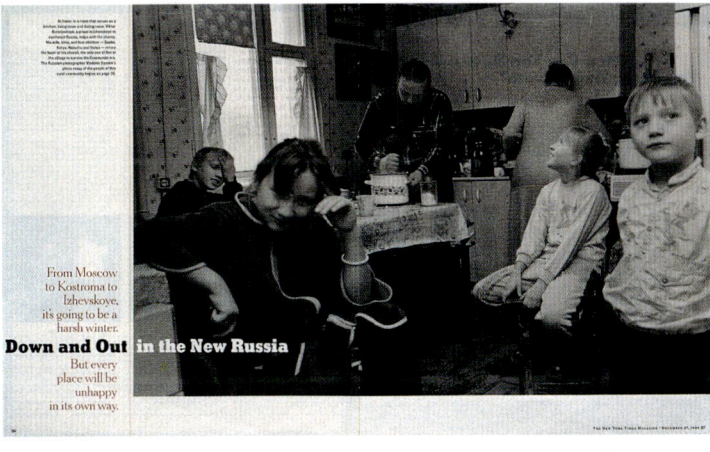

The New York Times Magazine
New York, NY
Janet Froelich, Art Director; **Catherine Gilmore-Barnes,** Designer; **Vladimir Syomin,** Photographer; **Kathy Ryan,** Photo Editor
• also for Photo Series

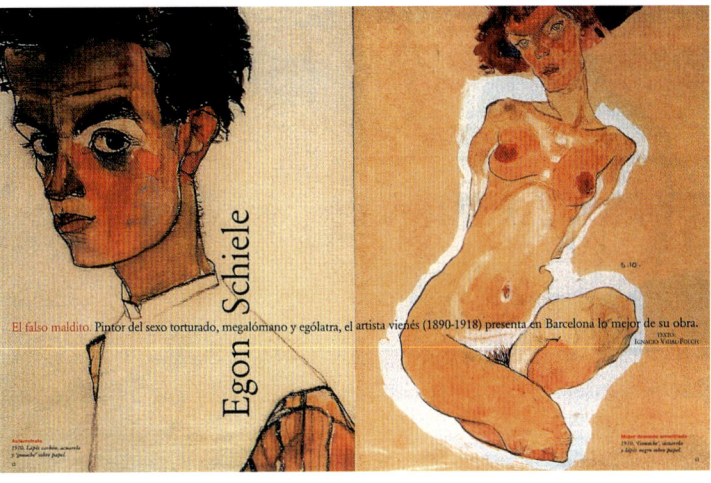

El País Semanal
Madrid, Spain
David García, Art Director; **Eugenio González,** Design Director; **Maripaz Domingo,** Designer; **Gustavo Sánchez,** Designer; **Patricia Álvarez,** Designer; **Alex M. Roig,** Editor-in-Chief

MAGAZINE ■ Page Design

Report on Business Magazine
Toronto, Canada
Bryce Duffy, Photographer; **Domenic Macri**, Acting Art Director

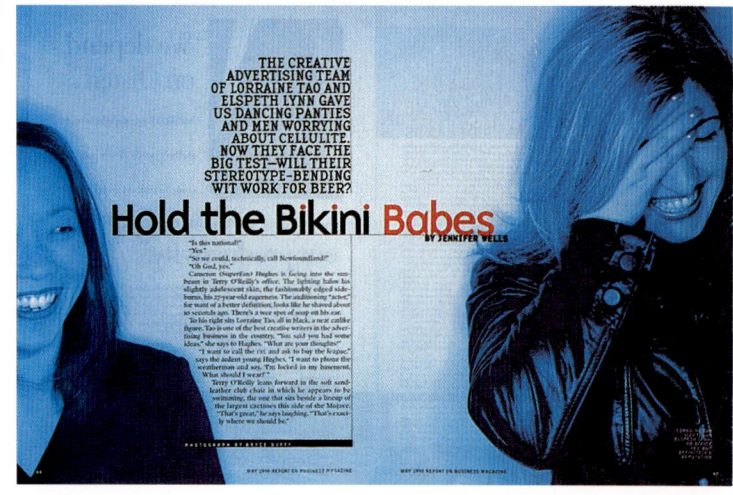

La Revista de El Mundo
Madrid, Spain
Rodrigo Sánchez, Art Director; **María González**, Designer; **Amparo Redondo**, Designer; **Carmelo Caderot**, Design Director; **Michel Haddi**, Photographer

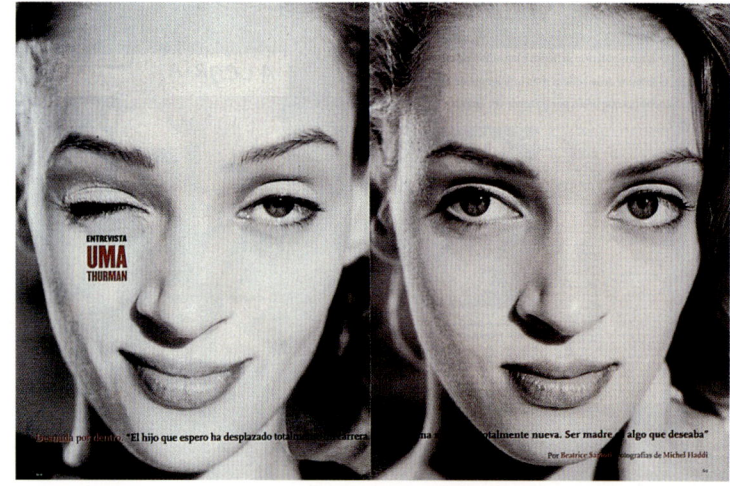

The Washington Post Magazine
Washington, DC
Kelly Doe, Art Director; **Lisa Schreiber**, Designer; **Crary Pullen**, Photo Editor; **Michael Williamson**, Photographer

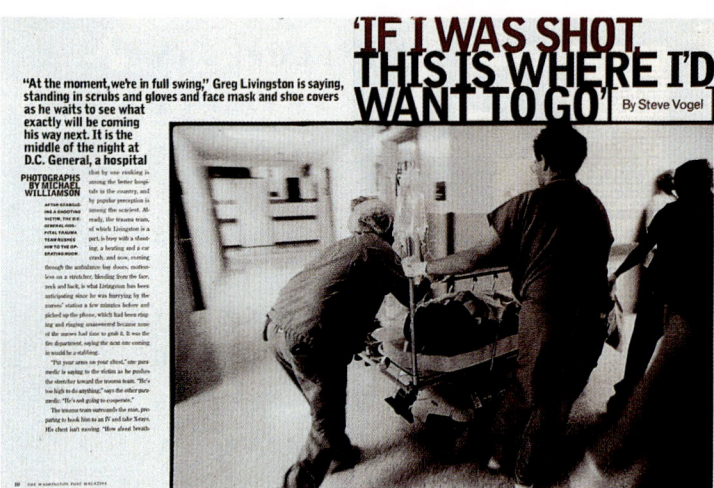

The Washington Post Magazine
Washington, DC
Kelly Doe, Art Director; **Lisa Schreiber**, Designer; **Crary Pullen**, Photo Editor

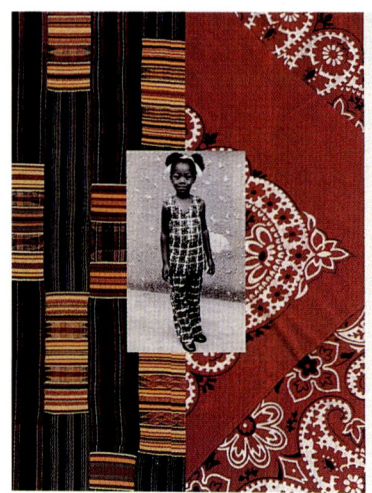 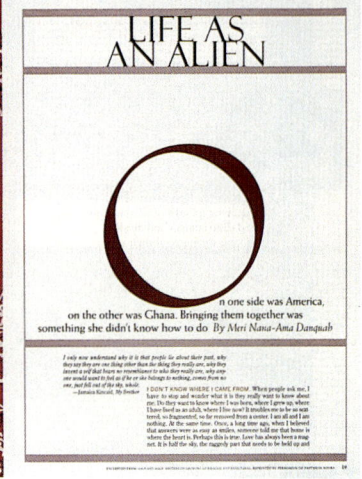

SPECIAL SECTIONS

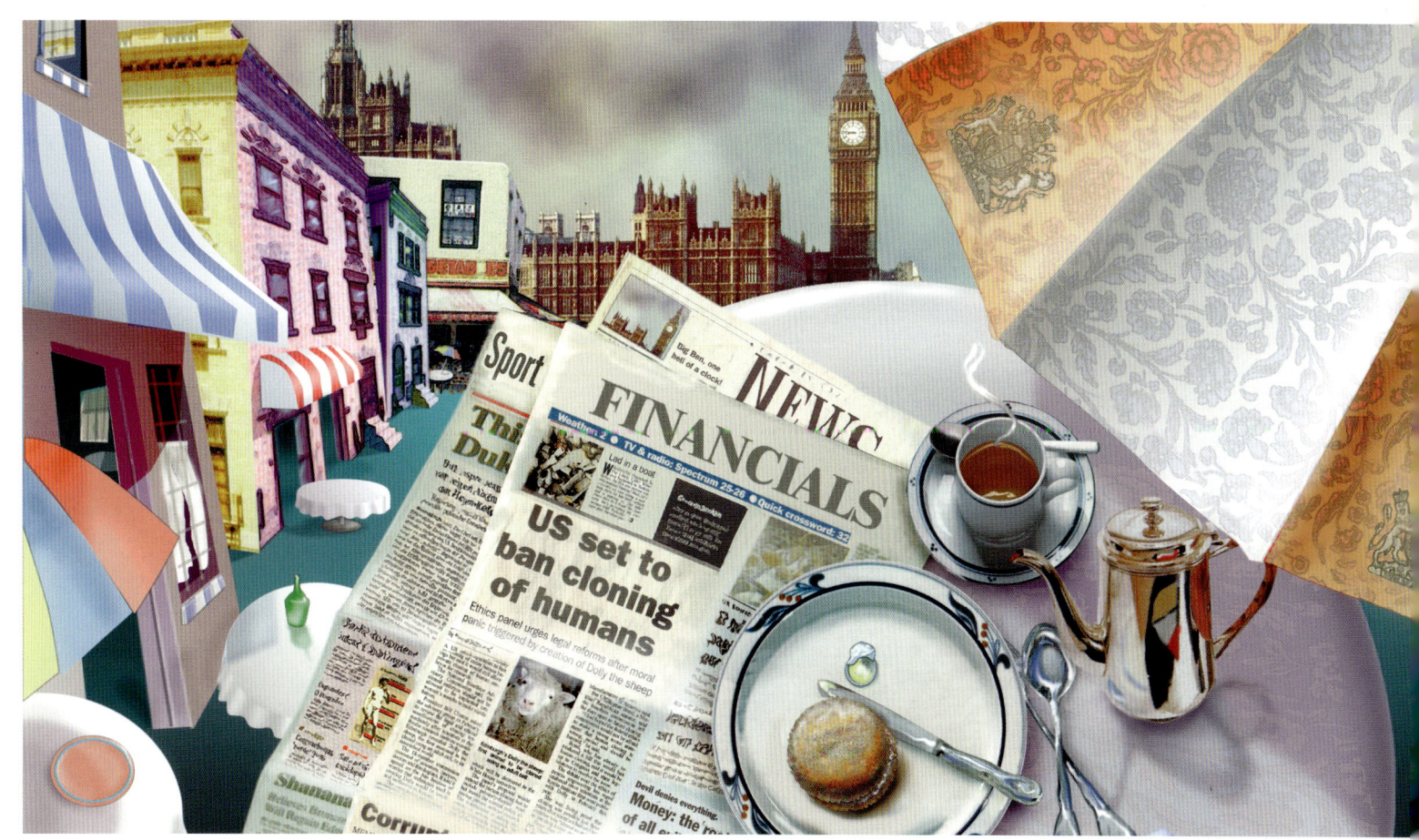

CHAPTER FIVE

SINGLE-SUBJECT SERIES

COVER PAGE

INSIDE PAGES

TWENTIETH EDITION ■ 169

SPECIAL SECTIONS — Single-Subject Series

Silver
The Times-Picayune
New Orleans, LA
Susan Koenig, News Design Editor; **Daniel Swenson,** Graphic Artist; **G. Andrew Boyd,** Photographer; **Scott Threlkeld,** Photographer; **Angela Hill,** Graphics Editor; **Tim Morris,** Project Editor; **James O'Byrne,** Sunday Editor; **George Berke,** Design Director; **Doug Parker,** Photo Editor; **Staff**
• also Silver for Photo Series

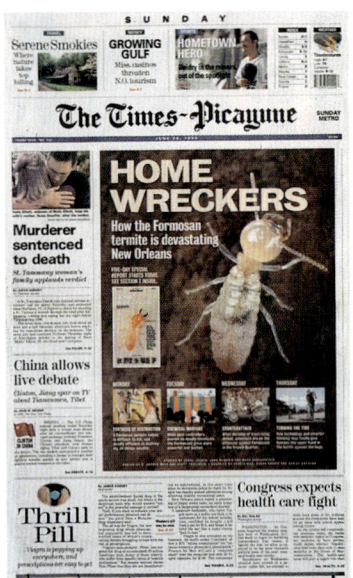
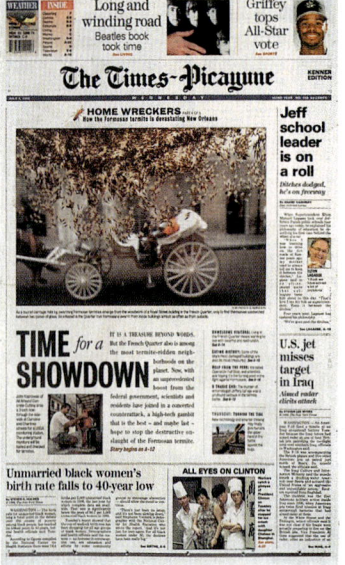
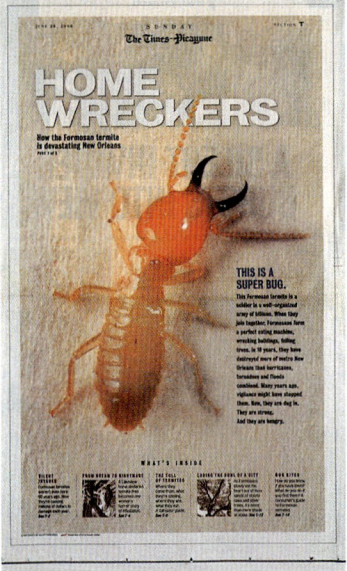
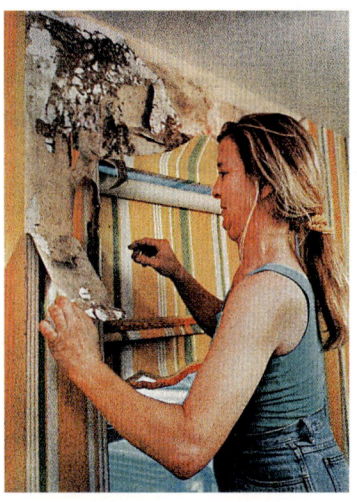

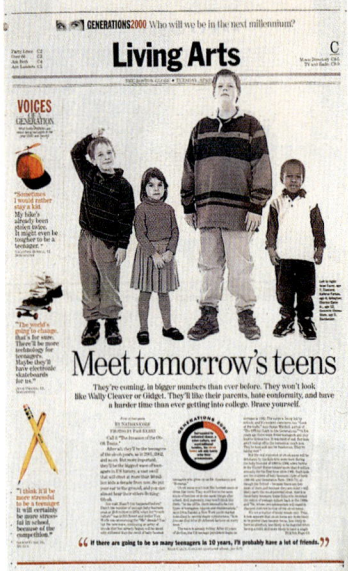
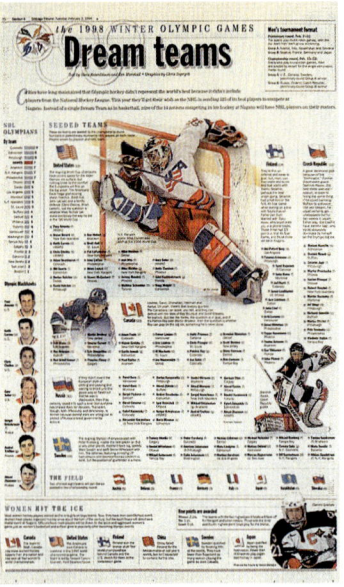
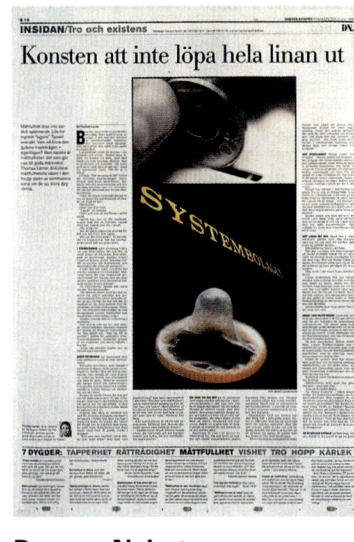
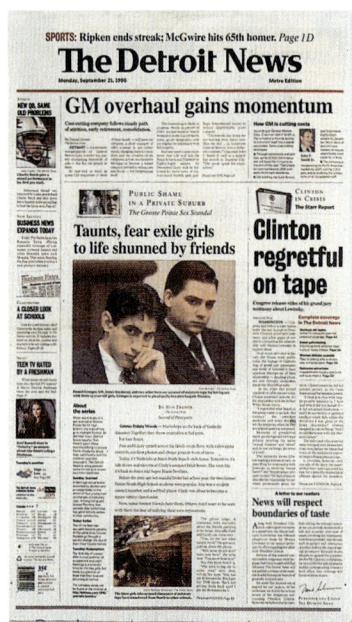

The Boston Globe
Boston, MA
Jane Martin, Art Director, Designer & Illustrator; **Pam Berry,** Photographer; **Linda Matchan,** Editor; **Nick King,** Editor; **Deb Jacobs,** Copy Editor; **Nathan Cobb,** Staff Writer
• also for Lifestyle Page

The Chicago Tribune
Chicago, IL
Steve Layton, Assistant Graphics Editor; **Lara Weber,** Reporter; **Ken Marshall,** Reporter; **Melissa Nagy,** Reporter; **Charles Apple,** Graphic Artist; **Kevin Hand,** Graphic Artist; **Rick Tuma,** Graphic Artist; **Steve Rosenbloom,** Reporter; **Chris Soprych,** Graphic Artist; **Phil Geib,** Graphic Artist

Dagens Nyheter
Stockholm, Sweden
Anneli Steen, Designer; **Marco Gustafsson,** Photographer

The Detroit News
Detroit, MI
David Kordalski, A.M.E./Presentation; **Brian Shellito,** Illustrator; **Tim Summers,** Assistant Graphic Editor; **Steve Fecht,** Photo Director; **Shanna Flowers,** City Editor; **Marty Fischhoff,** A.M.E.

Single-Subject Series, Without Ads ■ SPECIAL SECTIONS

The Hartford Courant
Hartford, CT

Cloe Poisson, Photographer; **Christopher Moore**, Graphic Artist; **Cecilia Prestamo**, Photo Editor/Designer

Philadelphia Daily News
Philadelphia, PA

Jon Snyder, Designer; **John Sherlock**, Graphics Editor

The Seattle Times
Seattle, WA

Carol Nakagaw, Designer; **Steve Ringman**, Photographer; **David Miller**, Art Director & Designer; **Betty Udesen**, Photographer; **Tom Reese**, Photographer; **Dean Rutz**, Photographer; **Liz McClure**, Designer

The Seattle Times
Seattle, WA

Michael Kellams, Designer; **Mark Harrison**, Photographer; **Steve Ringman**, Photographer; **David Miller**, Designer

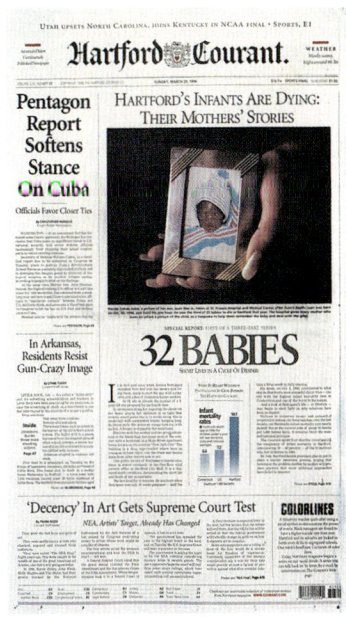
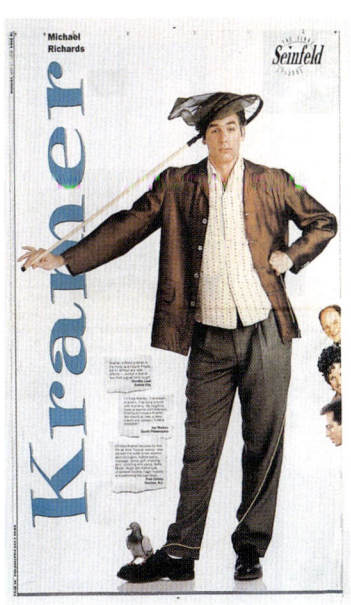
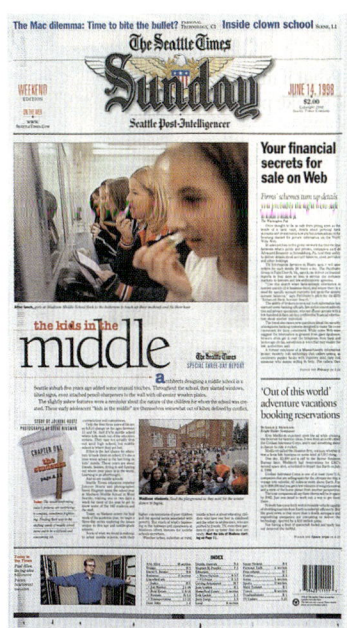
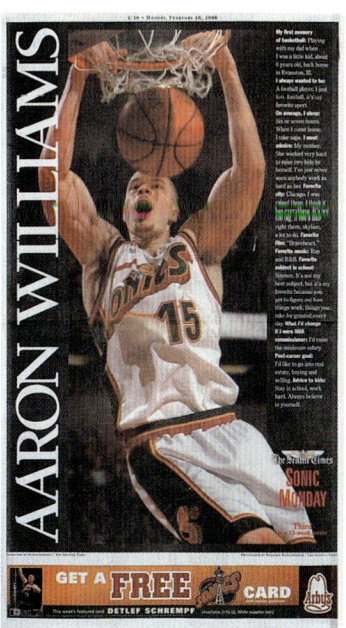

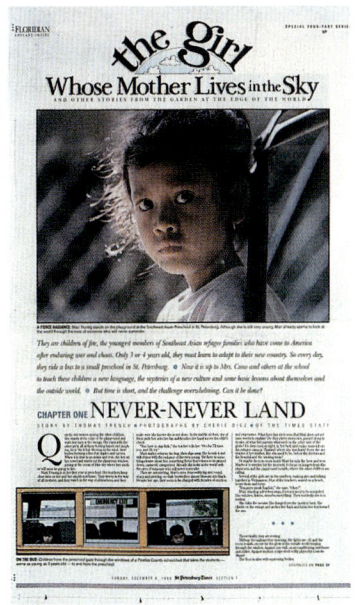

The St. Petersburg Times
St. Petersburg, FL

Audra Buck Spears, Designer; **Cherie Diez**, Photographer; **Don Morris**, Art Director; **Neville Green**, Editor; **Thomas French**, Reporter; **Sonya Doctorian**, Photo/Graphics Editor

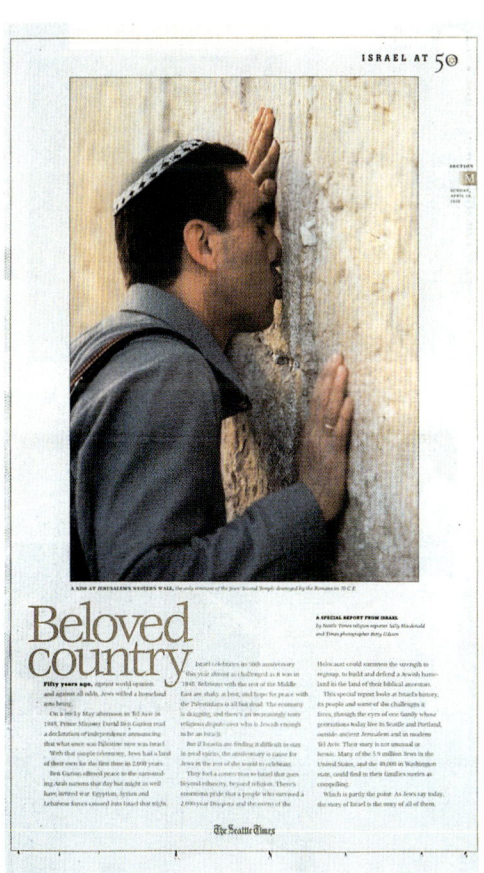
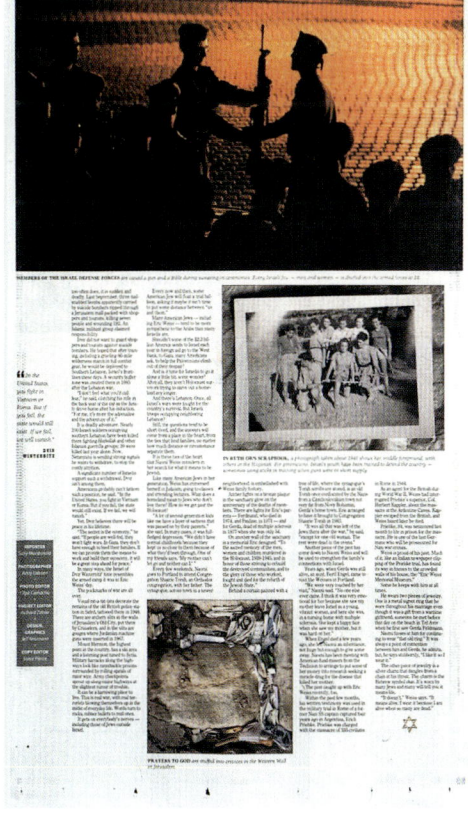

Silver
The Seattle Times
Seattle, WA

Jeff Neumann, Designer & Infographics Artist; **David Miller**, Art Director; **Betty Udesen**, Photographer; **Sally Macdonald**, Staff Writer; **Olga Camacho**, Photo Editor

SPECIAL SECTIONS — Without Ads

Silver
Östgöta Correspondenten
Linkoping, Sweden
Christer Berg, Designer

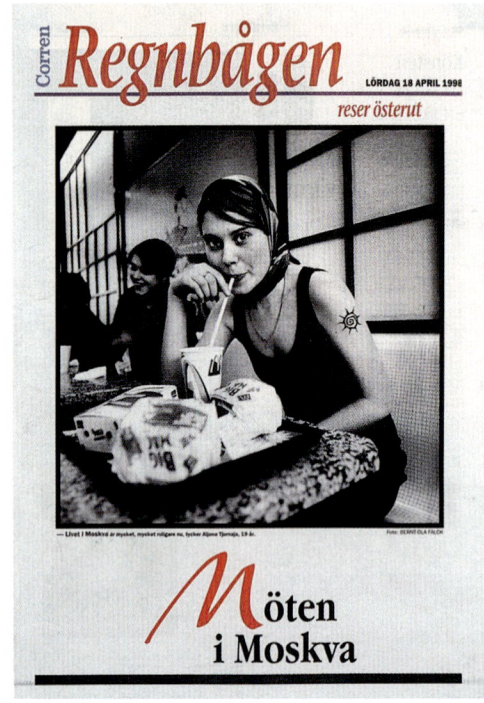

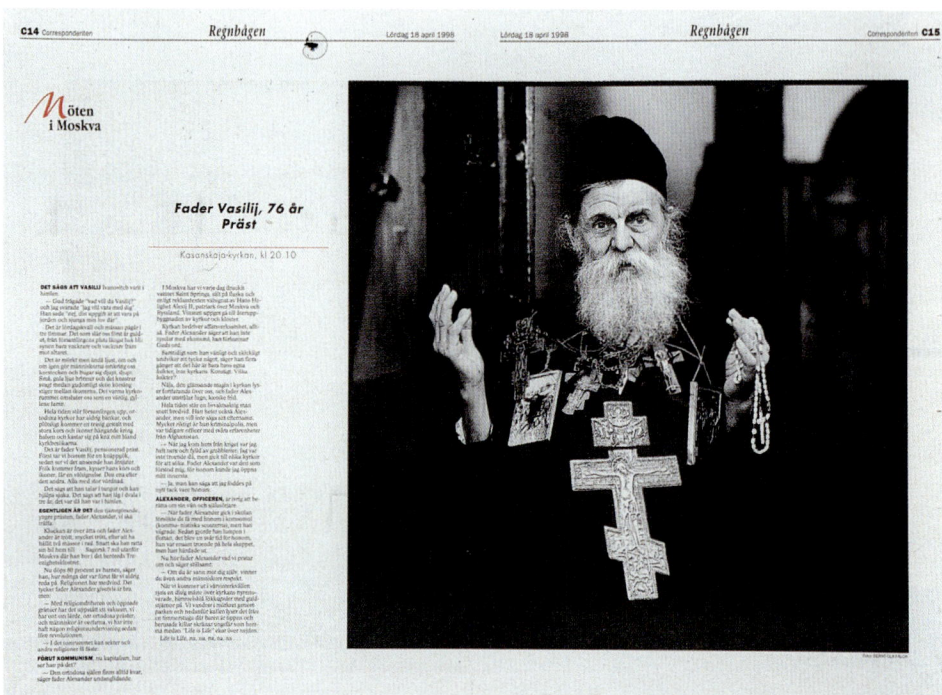

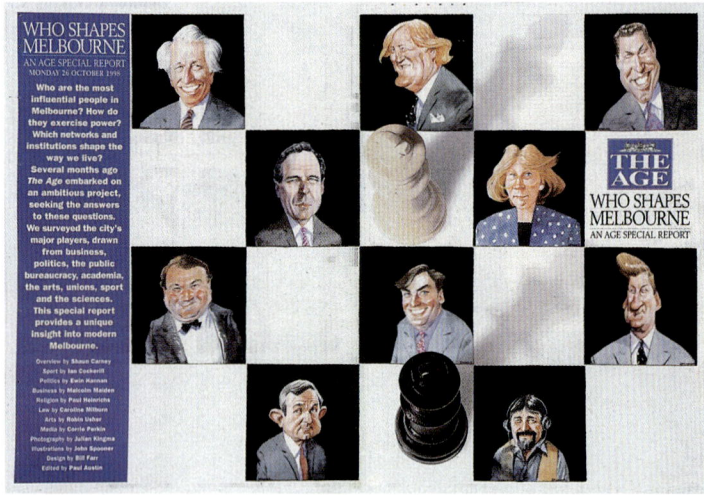

The Age
Melbourne, Australia
Bill Farr, Art Director

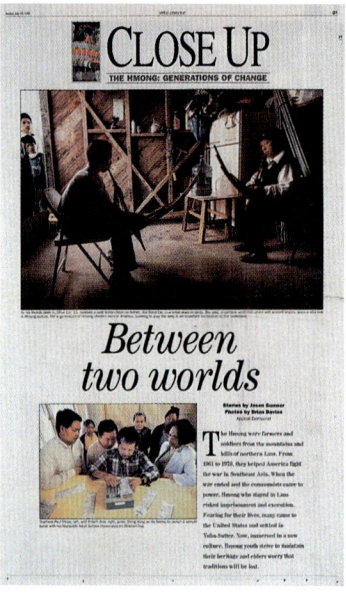

Appeal-Democrat
Marysville, CA
Julie Shirley, Editor & Designer; **Brian Davies,** Photographer

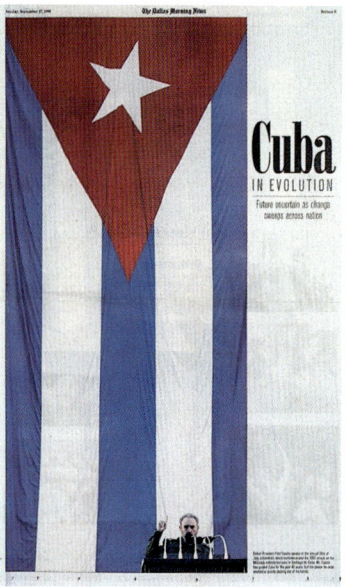

The Dallas Morning News
Dallas, TX
Lesley Becker, Designer; **Erich Schlegel,** Photographer; **Jeff Goertzen,** Illustrator

Without Ads ■ SPECIAL SECTIONS

The Montreal Gazette
Montreal, Canada
Jack Romanelli, A.M.E.; **Eva Friede,** Review Editor; **Louise Vincent,** Design Editor & Designer; **Dean Tweed,** Graphics

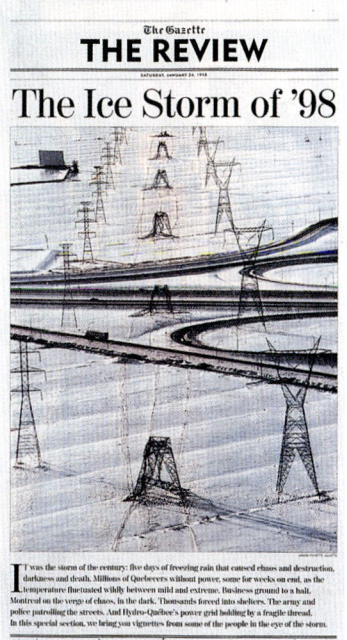

The Detroit News
Detroit, MI
Ray Stanczak, Art Director; **Kris Karnopp,** Designer; **James Borchuck,** Photographer; **Steve Fecht,** Photo Director; **Marty Fischhoff,** A.M.E.

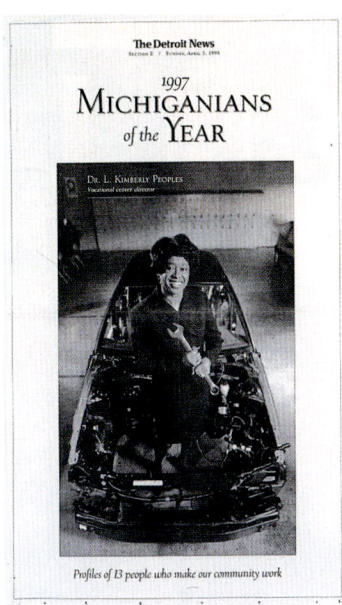

El Mundo
Madrid, Spain
Carmelo Caderot, Art Director & Designer; **Manuel de Miguel,** Assistant Art Director & Designer

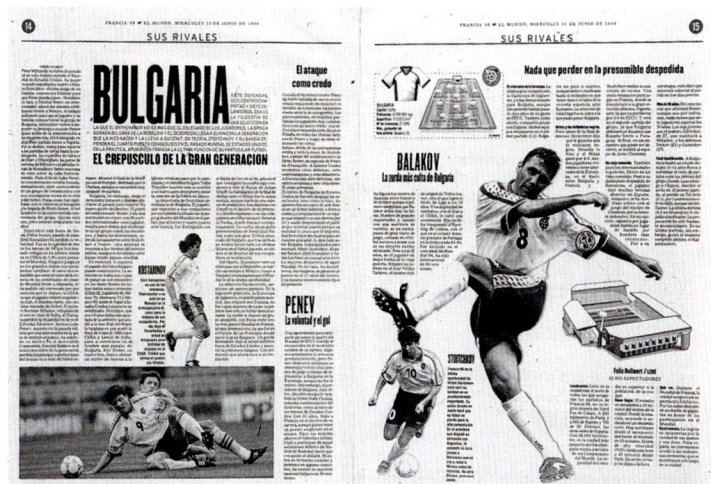

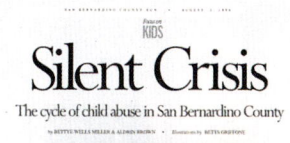

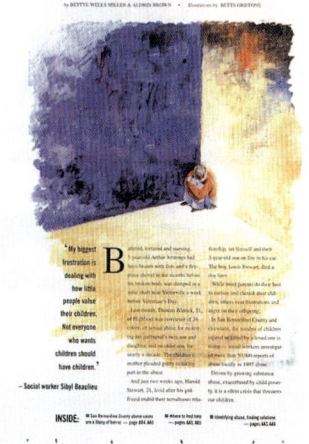

The San Bernardino County Sun
San Bernardino, CA
Betts Griffone, Graphics Editor

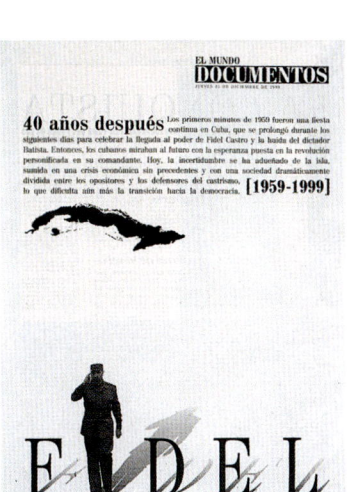

El Mundo
Madrid, Spain
Carmelo Caderot, Art Director & Designer; **Manuel de Miguel,** Assistant Art Director & Designer
• also for Special Section Cover Page

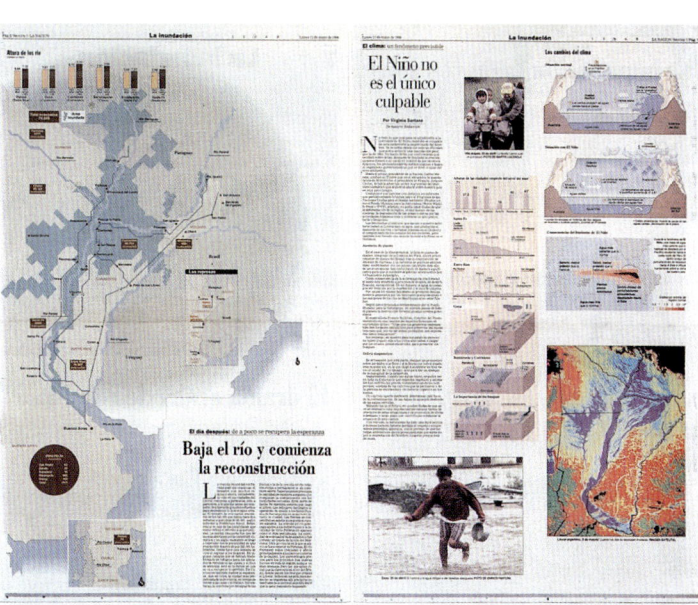

La Nacion
Buenos Aires, Argentina
Carmen Piaggio, Art Director

TWENTIETH EDITION ■ 173

SPECIAL SECTIONS — Without Ads, With Ads

The Spokesman-Review
Spokane, WA

John Nelson, Design Editor; **John Sale,** Photo Editor; **Colin Mulvany,** Photographer; **Vince Grippi,** Graphics

The Spokesman-Review
Spokane, WA

John Nelson, Design Editor; **John Sale,** Photo Editor; **Colin Mulvany,** Photographer; **Vince Grippi,** Graphics

The Orange County Register
Santa Ana, CA

Karen Kelso, Designer; **Cathy Armstrong,** Section Editor; **Robin Doussard,** Deputy Editor; **Dan Anderson,** Photographer; **Mike Pilgrim,** Photo Editor; **Laura Saari,** Staff Writer; **Brenda Shoun,** Deputy Editor/Visuals

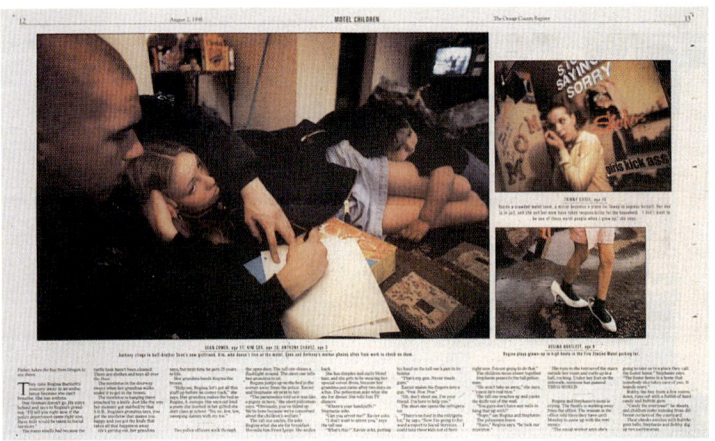

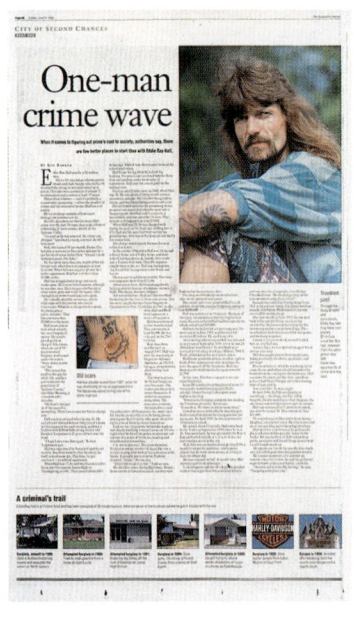

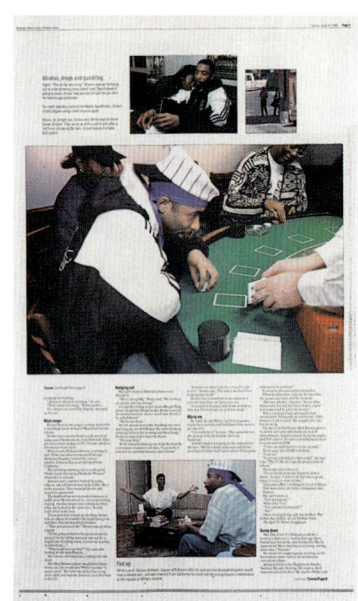

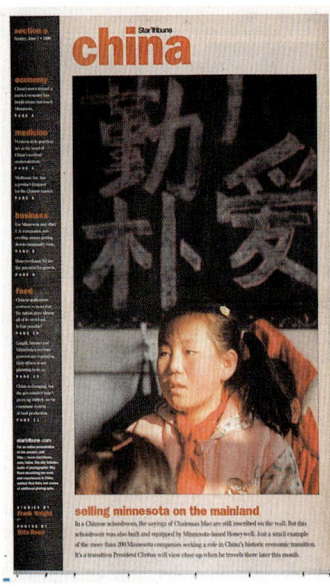

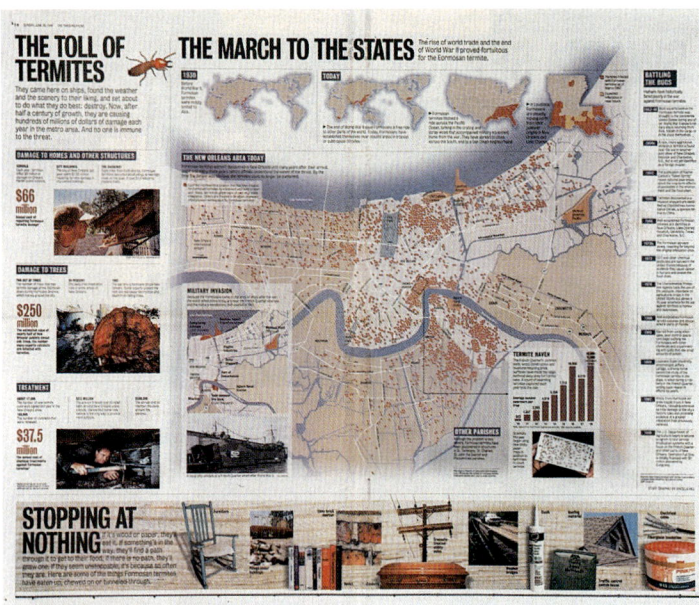

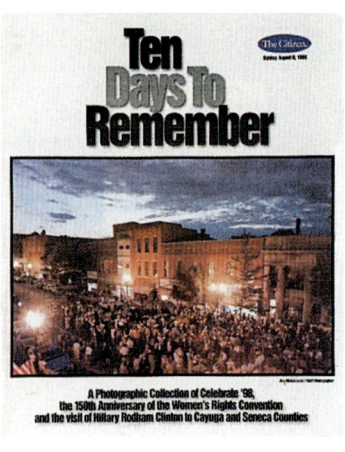

Star Tribune
Minneapolis, MN

Denise M. Reagan, Designer/Art Director; **Rita Reed,** Photographer; **Dave Denney,** Photo Editor; **Gerard Cagayat,** Graphic Artist; **Michael Godfrey,** Graphic Artist

The Times-Picayune
New Orleans, LA

Susan Koenig, News Design Editor; **Daniel Swenson,** Graphic Artist; **G. Andrew Boyd,** Photographer; **Scott Threlkeld,** Photographer; **Angela Hill,** Graphics Editor; **Tim Morris,** Project Editor; **James O'Byrne,** Sunday Editor; **George Berke,** Design Director; **Doug Parker,** Photo Editor; **Staff**

The Citizen
Auburn, NY

Jim Michalowski, Director of Photography & Designer

With Ads ■ SPECIAL SECTIONS

Democrat and Chronicle
Rochester, NY

Dennis R. Floss, A.M.E./Presentation/Graphics; **Steve Boerner,** Assistant Presentation Editor; **Herm Auch,** Artist; **Yvonne Lin,** Artist

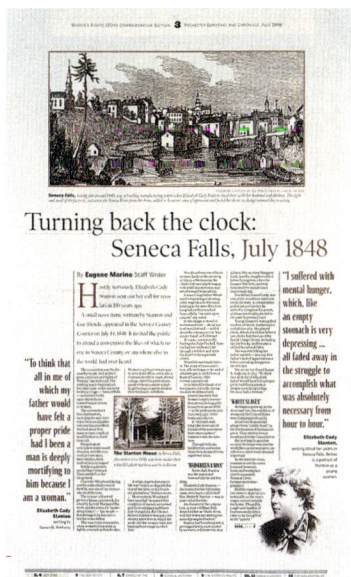

Diario de Noticias
Lisbon, Portugal

Mário B. Resendes, Editor-in-Chief; **José Maria Ribeirinho,** Art Director; **Francisco Azevedo e Silva,** Editor; **Carlos Jorge,** Designer; **Albano Matos,** Editor

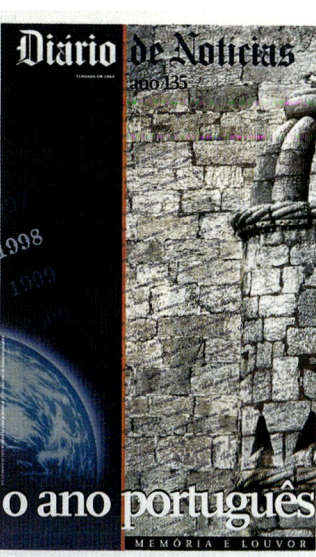

La Luna
Madrid, Spain

Rodrigo Sánchez, Art Director; **Francisco Dorado,** Designer; **Chano del Río,** Designer; **Carmelo Caderot,** Design Director

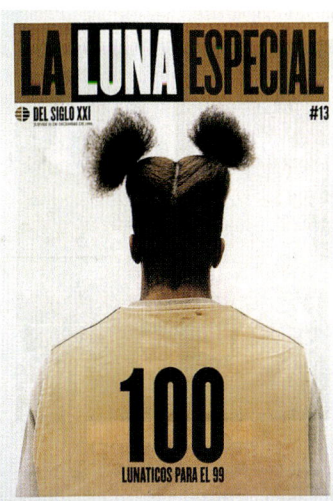

Morgenavisen Jyllands-Posten
Viby J., Denmark

Anne Marie Dohm, Reporter; **Finn Koch,** Editor; **Lone Ryg Olsen,** Reporter; **Annette Juul Steen,** News Graphic Artist; **Lotte Overgaard,** News Graphic Artist

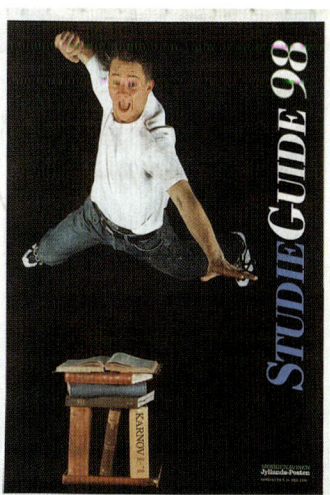

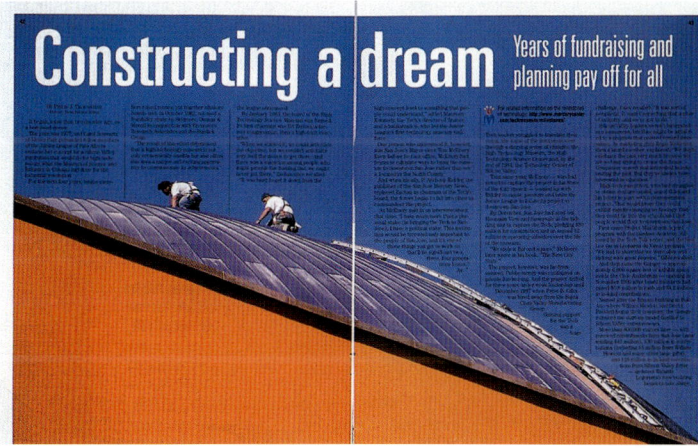

San Jose Mercury News
San Jose, CA

Howard Davy, Designer; **David Pollak,** Section Editor; **Pai Ching Wei,** Artist; **Anne Marie Dos Remedios,** Photographer; **Patricia Yablonski,** Photo Editor; **Bryan Monroe,** A.M.E./News, Visuals & Technology

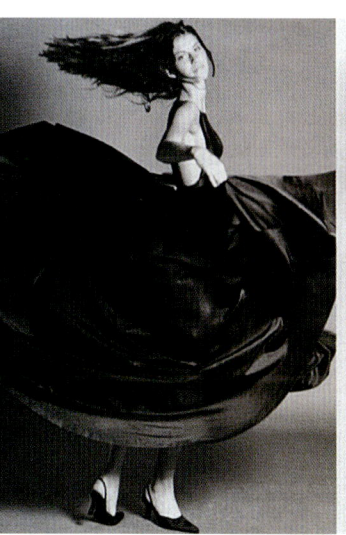

Women's Wear Daily
New York, NY

Edward Leida, Design Director; **Jean Griffin,** Design Director; **Janice Carpentier,** Art Director

SPECIAL SECTIONS — With Ads, Cover, Inside Page

The Boston Globe
Boston, MA
Rena Anderson Sokolow, Art Director & Designer; Janet L. Michaud, Art Director & Designer

The Columbus Dispatch
Columbus, OH
Scott Minister, Art Director & Designer; Becky Kover, Section Coordinator

The Toronto Star
Toronto, Canada
Mark Atchison, Designer & Editor; Steve Tustin, Sports Editor

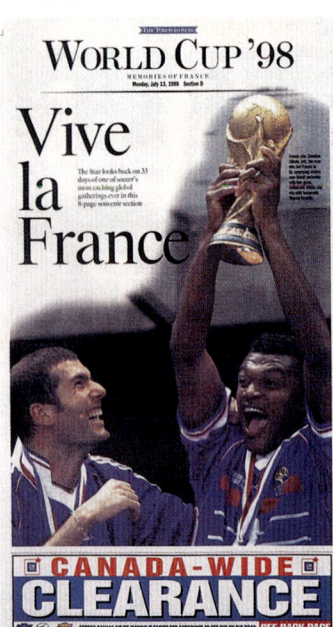

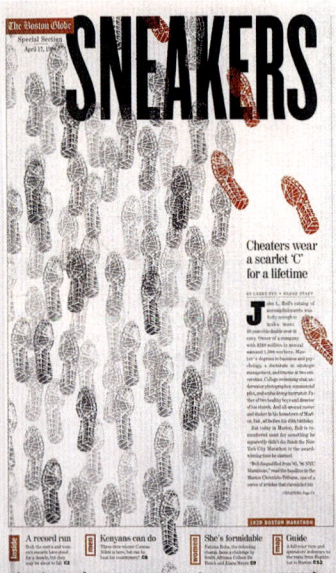

The Columbus Dispatch
Columbus, OH
Scott Minister, Art Director & Designer; Richard Lillash, Illustrator; Becky Kover, Section Coordinator

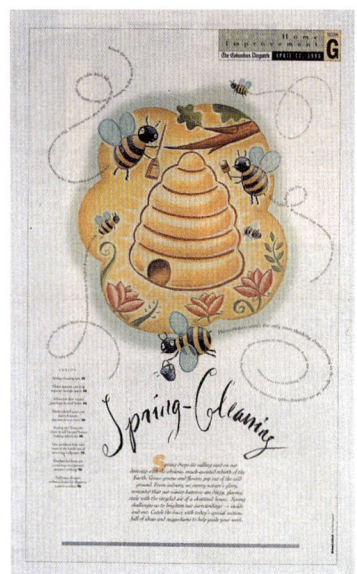

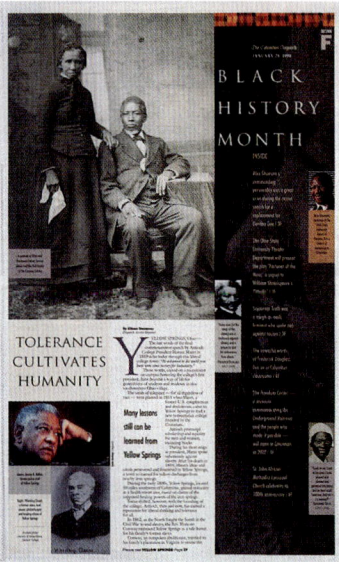

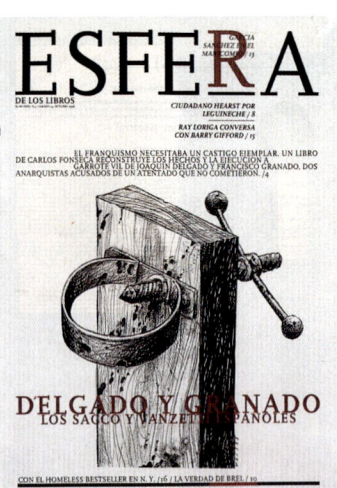

El Mundo
Madrid, Spain
Carmelo Caderot, Art Director & Designer; Ulises Culebro, Illustrator

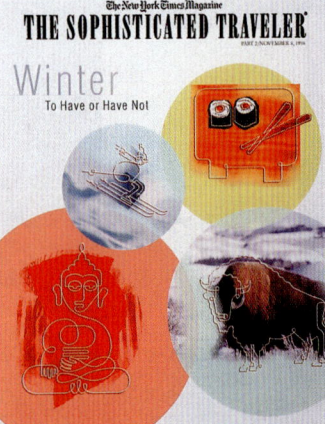

The New York Times Magazine
New York, NY
Ken McFarlin, Art Director; Otto Steininger, Illustrator

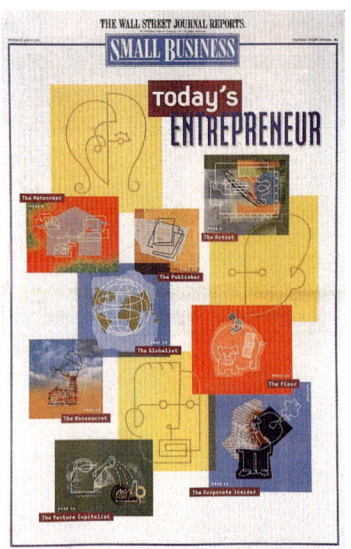

The Wall Street Journal Reports
New York, NY
Greg Leeds, Design Director; Orlie Kraus, Art Director & Designer; Otto Steininger, Illustrator

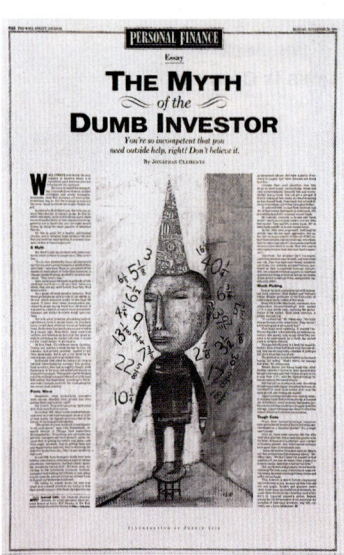

The Wall Street Journal Reports
New York, NY
Greg Leeds, Design Director; Orlie Kraus, Art Director & Designer; Jordin Isip, Illustrator

Star Tribune
Minneapolis, MN
Denise M. Reagan, Designer/Art Director; **Rita Reed,** Photographer; **Dave Denney,** Photo Editor

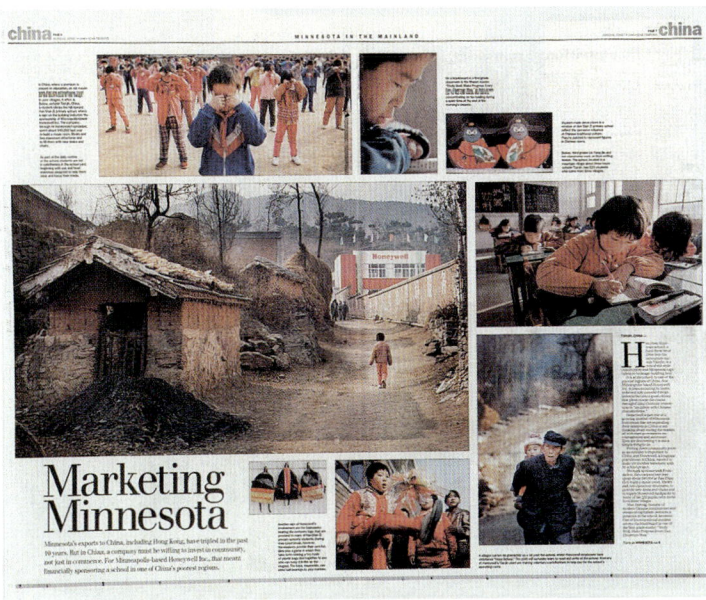

The Wall Street Journal Reports
New York, NY
Greg Leeds, Design Director; **Vera Naughton,** Art Director & Designer; **Jordin Isip,** Illustrator
• also Silver for Illustration

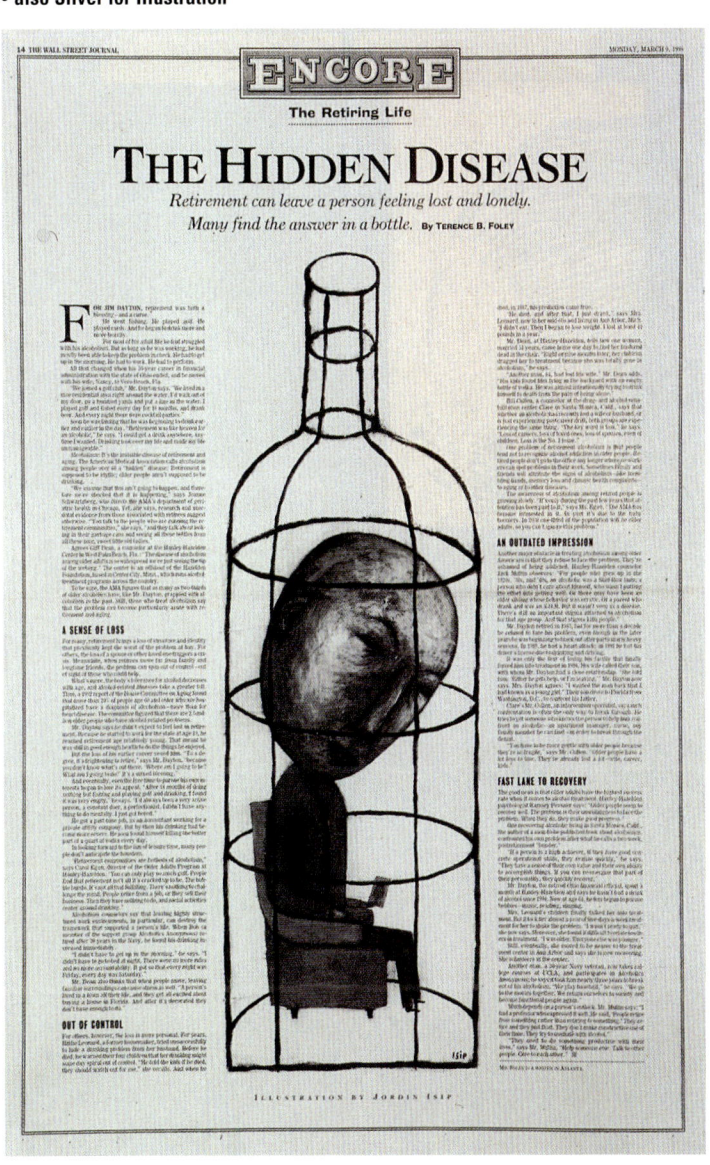

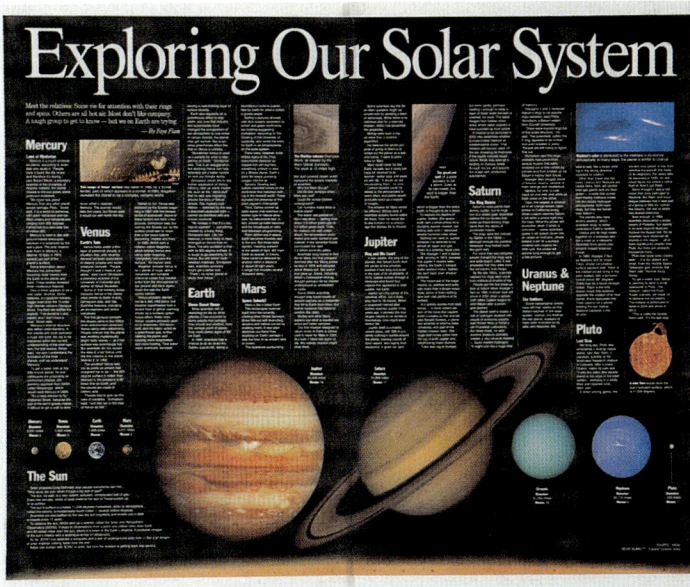

The Philadelphia Inquirer
Philadelphia, PA
Kevin Burkett, Graphic Artist

SPECIAL SECTIONS ▪ Inside Page

The Wall Street Journal Reports
New York, NY
Greg Leeds, Design Director; **Vera Naughton,** Art Director & Designer; **John Nickle,** Illustrator

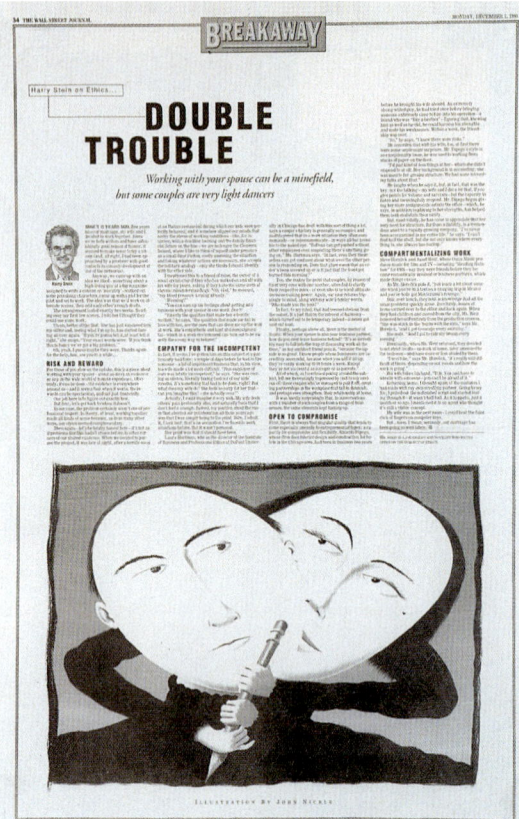

Women's Wear Daily
New York, NY
Edward Leida, Design Director; **Janice Carpentier,** Art Director

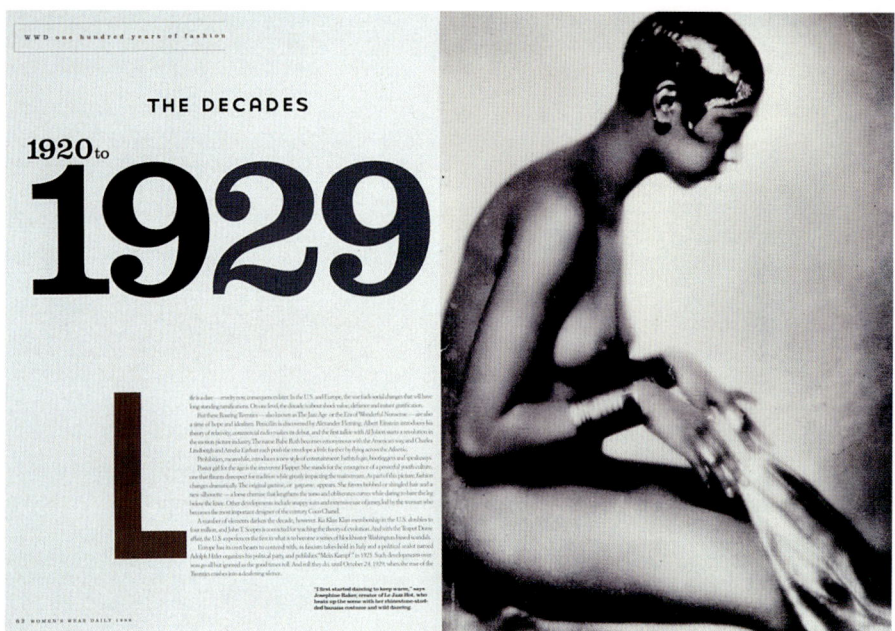

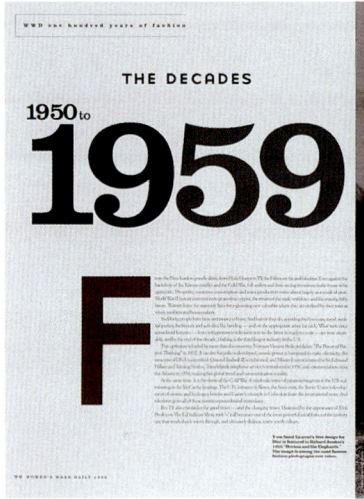
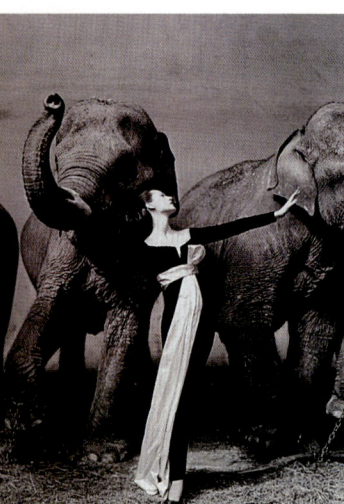

Women's Wear Daily
New York, NY
Edward Leida, Design Director; **Janice Carpentier,** Art Director

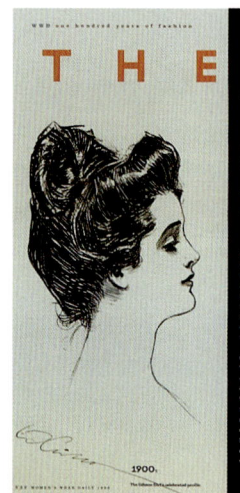
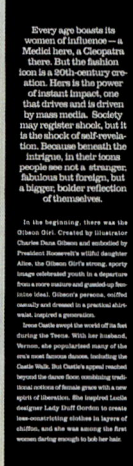
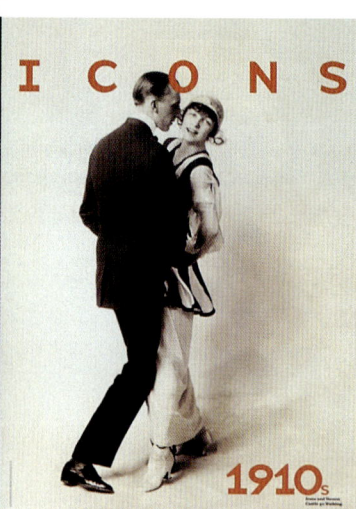

Women's Wear Daily
New York, NY
Edward Leida, Design Director; **Janice Carpentier,** Art Director

178 ▪ THE BEST OF NEWSPAPER DESIGN

DESIGN PORTFOLIO

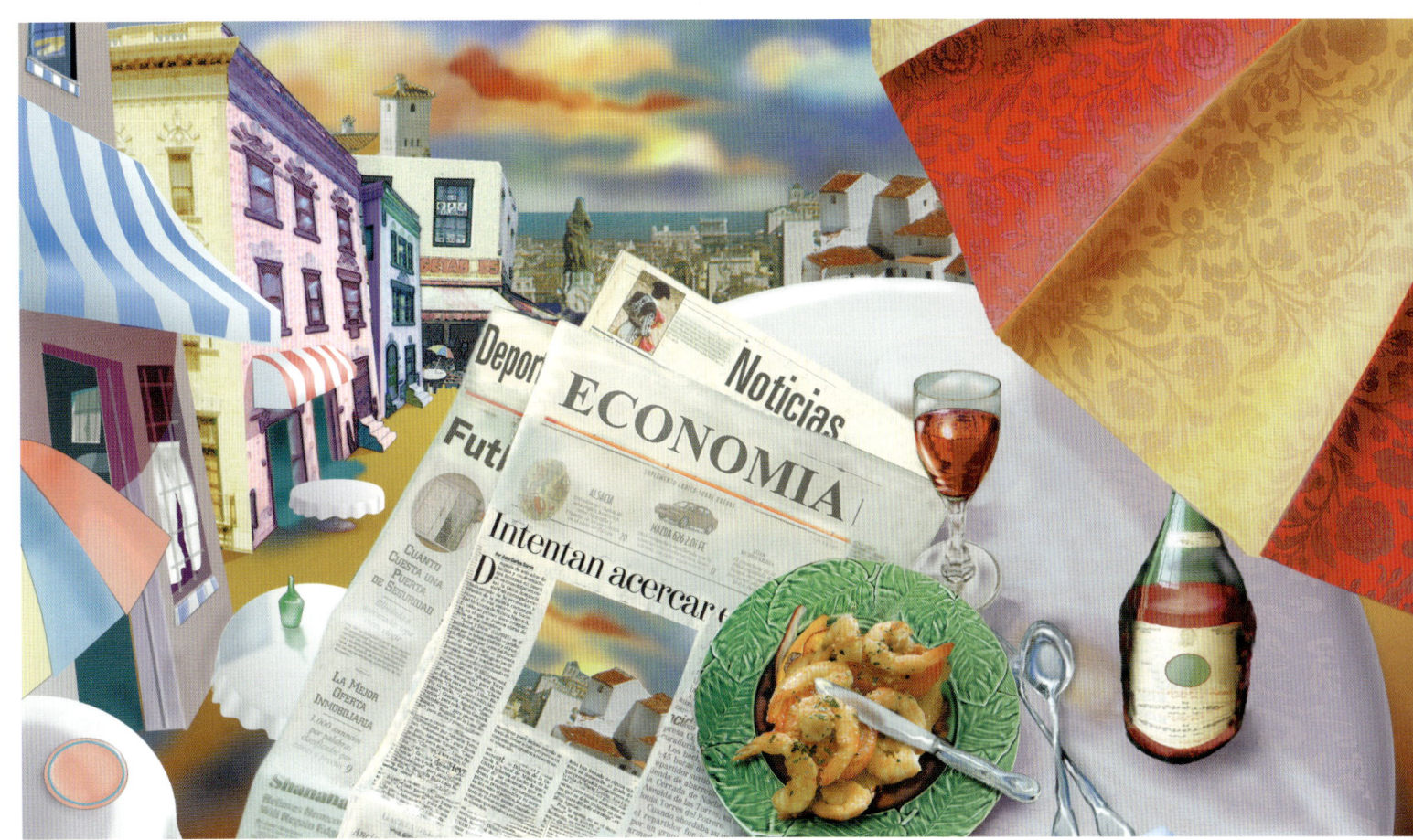

CHAPTER SIX

NEWS

FEATURES

MAGAZINE

COMBINATION

TWENTIETH EDITION ■ 179

DESIGN PORTFOLIO ■ News

The Boston Globe
Boston, MA
Janet L. Michaud, Art Director & Designer

The Boston Globe
Boston, MA
Janet L. Michaud, Art Director & Designer

The Hartford Courant
Hartford, CT
Ingrid Muller, Designer

The National Post
Don Mills, Canada
Roland-Yves Carignan, Designer/Design Editor

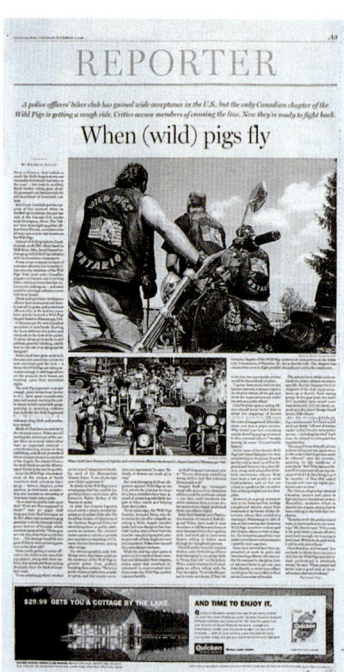

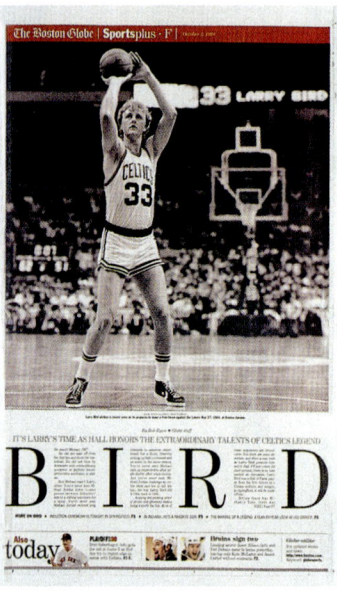

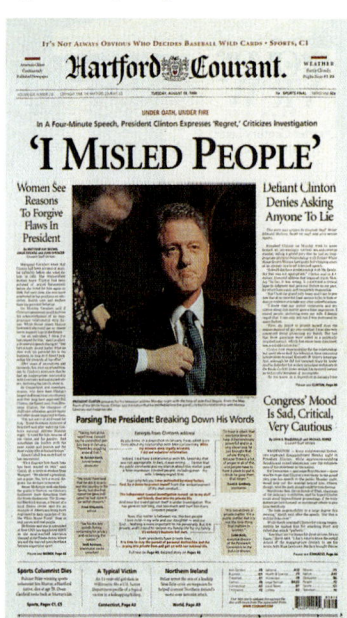

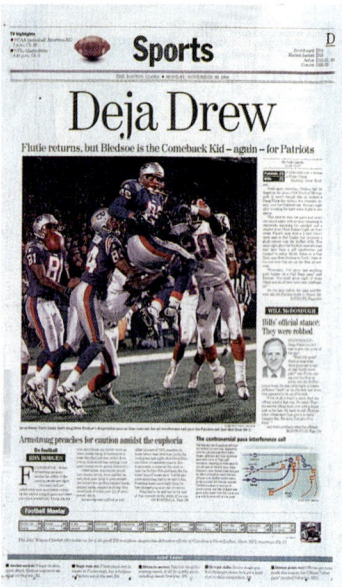

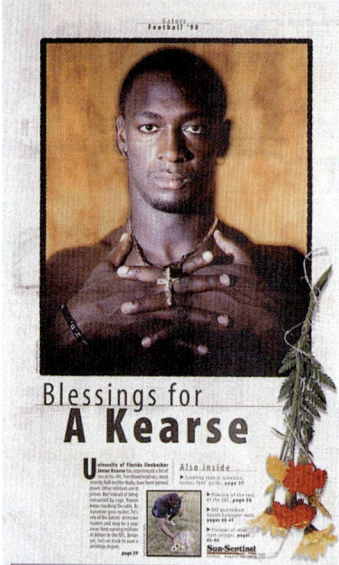

Sun-Sentinel
Ft. Lauderdale, FL
Chris Kirkman, Graphics Reporter

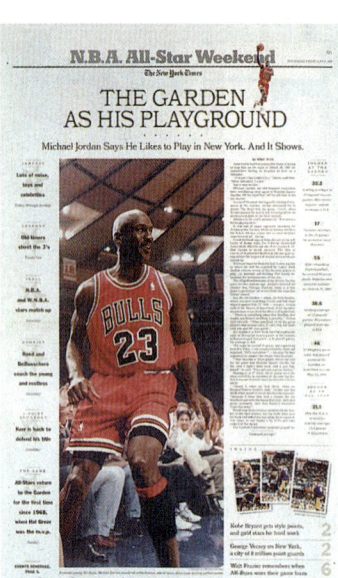

The New York Times
New York, NY
Wayne Kamidoi, Designer

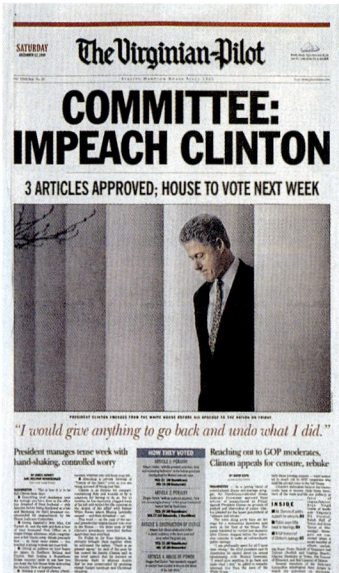

The Virginian-Pilot
Norfolk, VA
Julie Elman, Designer

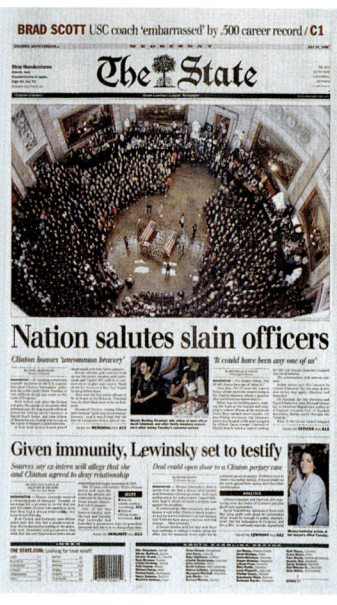

The State
Columbia, SC
William Castronuovo, Associate Editor

180 ■ THE BEST OF NEWSPAPER DESIGN

News, Features ■ DESIGN PORTFOLIO

The Times
Munster, IN
Kevin Poortinga, Design Director

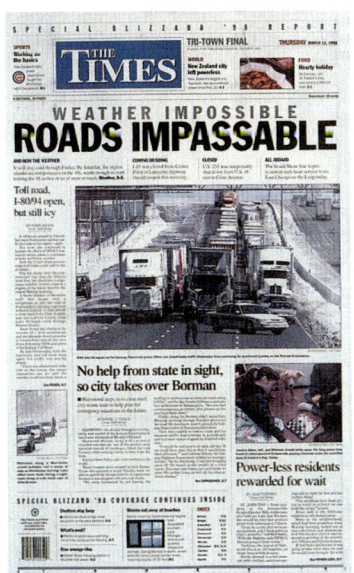

Expansión
Madrid, Spain
Pablo Mª Ramírez, Designer

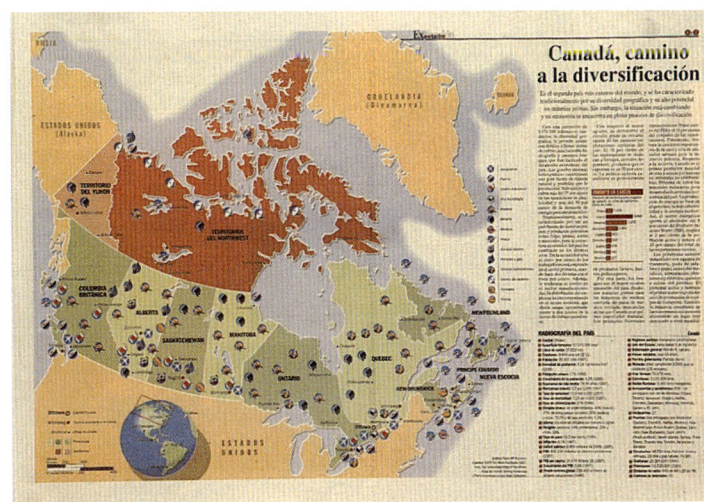

Austin American-Statesman
Austin, TX
Mike Sutter, Designer

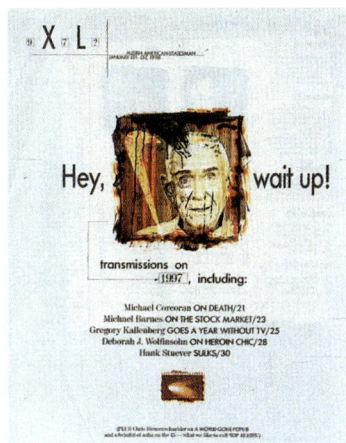

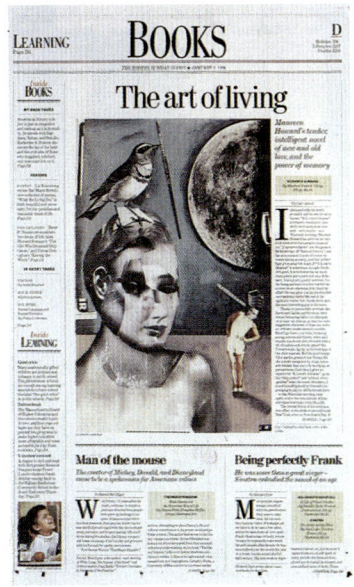

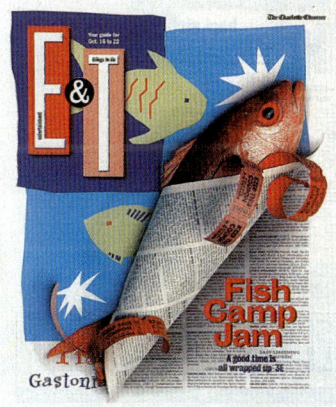

The Charlotte Observer
Charlotte, NC
Kristen Powell, Designer; **Monica Moses,** Design Director; **Brenda Pinnell,** Artist; **Joanne Miller,** Art Director; **Todd Sumlin,** Photographer
• also for Entertainment Page

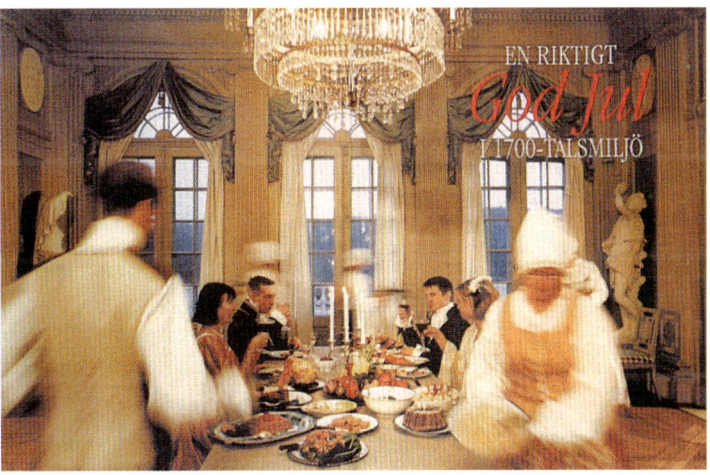

Göteborgs-Posten
Göteborg, Sweden
Gunilla Wernhamn, Designer

The Boston Globe
Boston, MA
Aldona Charlon, Art Director

TWENTIETH EDITION ■ 181

DESIGN PORTFOLIO ■ Features

Gold
La Luna
Madrid, Spain
Rodrigo Sánchez, Art Director

These are top-of-the-line caricatures and illustrations. They have a great use of subdued color and an interesting contrast between the typography and the illustrations. These are very bold presentations that exude confidence in their ability to communicate ideas to readers in a forceful way. The Illustrations are extremely well done with simple line work strokes of the brush.

Estas son caricaturas e ilustraciones de primera, hacen un excelente uso del color tenue y logran un interesante contraste entre la tipografía y las ilustraciones. Son presentaciones muy atrevidas que desprenden confianza en su capacidad de trasmitir ideas a los lectores de modo contundente. Las ilustraciones están muy bien realizadas con sencillas pinceladas en sus líneas.

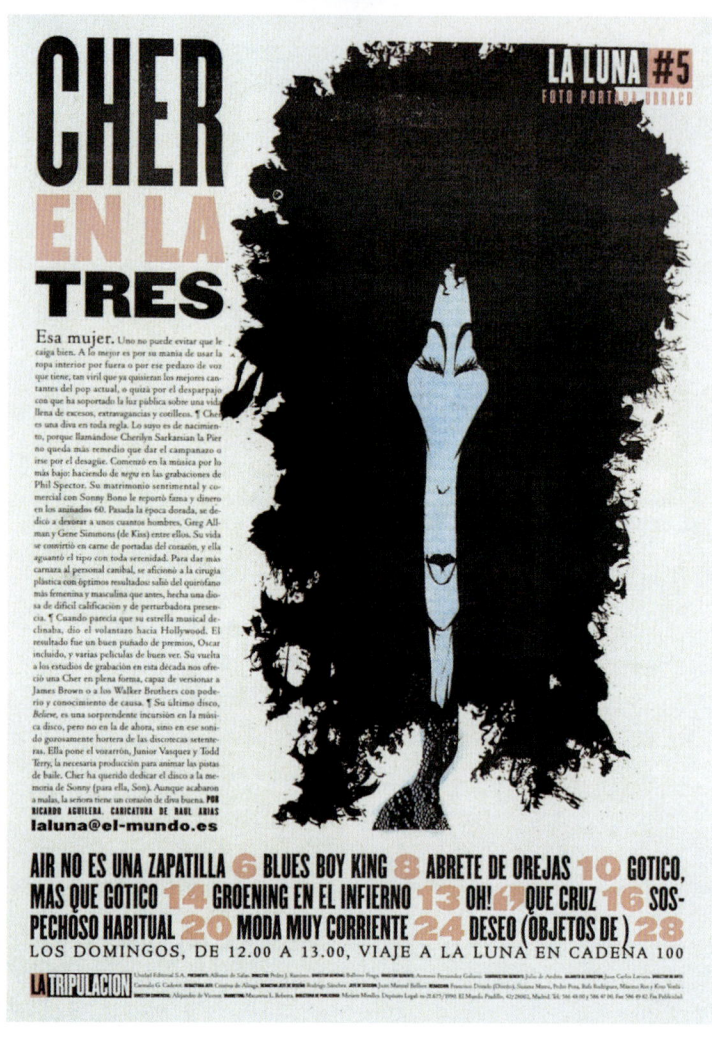

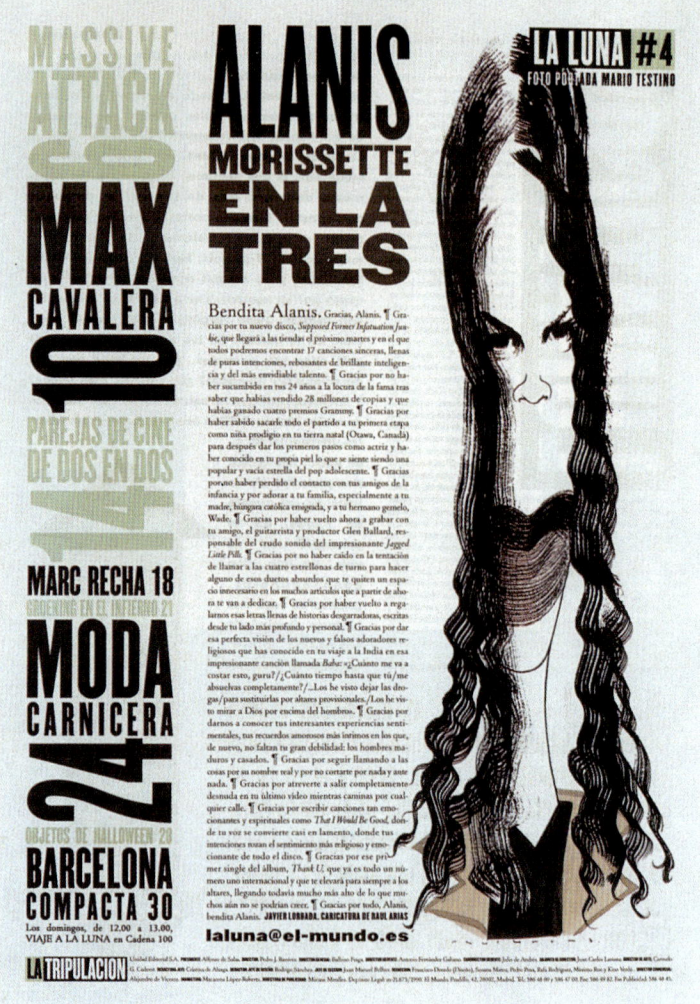

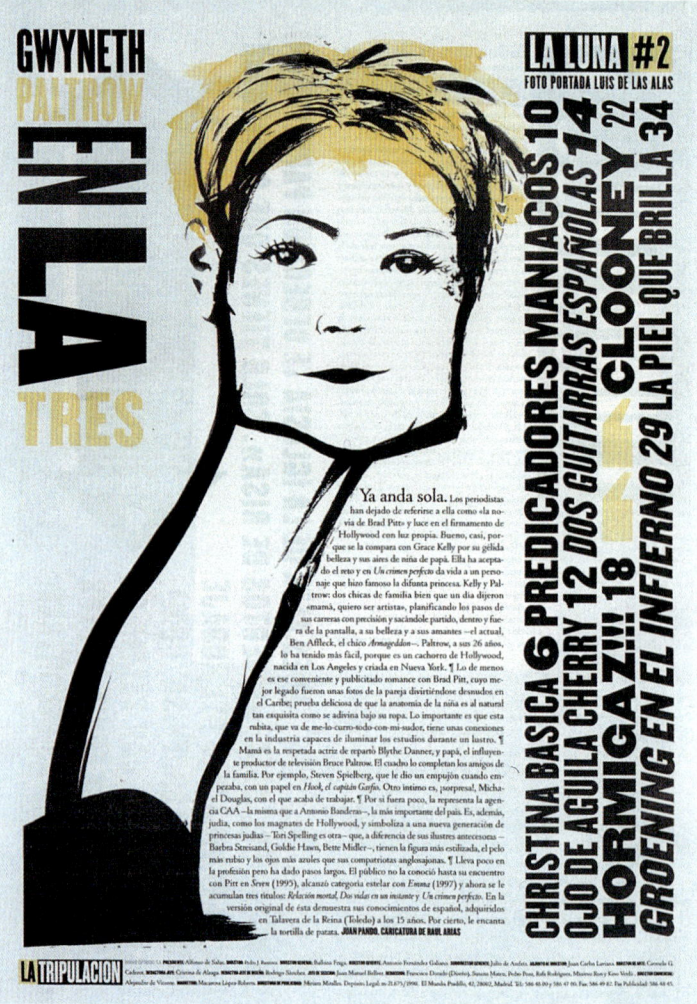

Features ■ DESIGN PORTFOLIO

Gold
La Luna
Madrid, Spain
Rodrigo Sánchez, Art Director

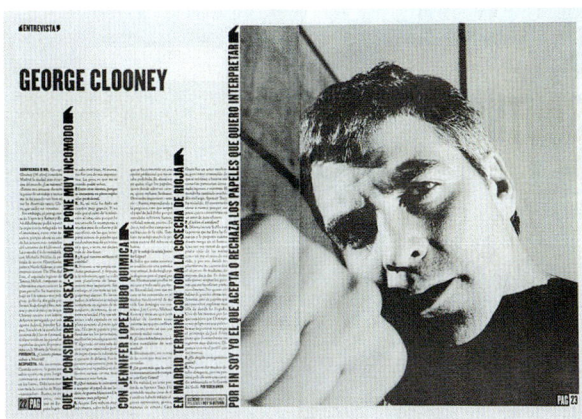

• also an Award of Excellence for Entertainment Page
Rodrigo Sánchez, Art Director; **Francisco Dorado,** Designer; **Chano del Río,** Designer; **Carmelo Caderot,** Design Director; **Herb Ritts,** Photographer

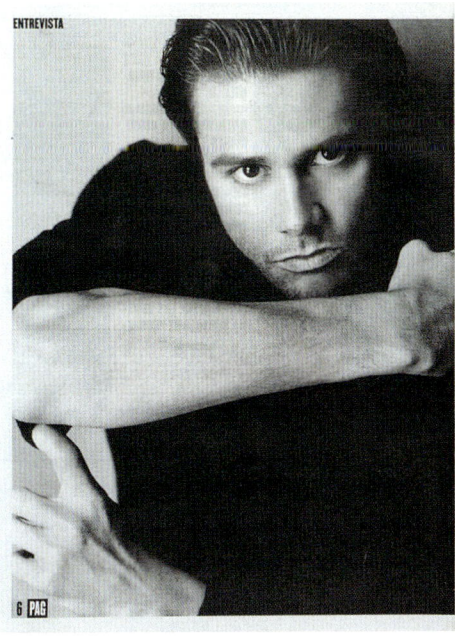 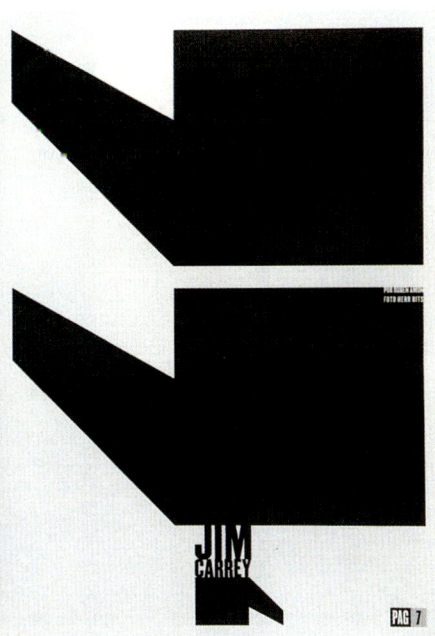

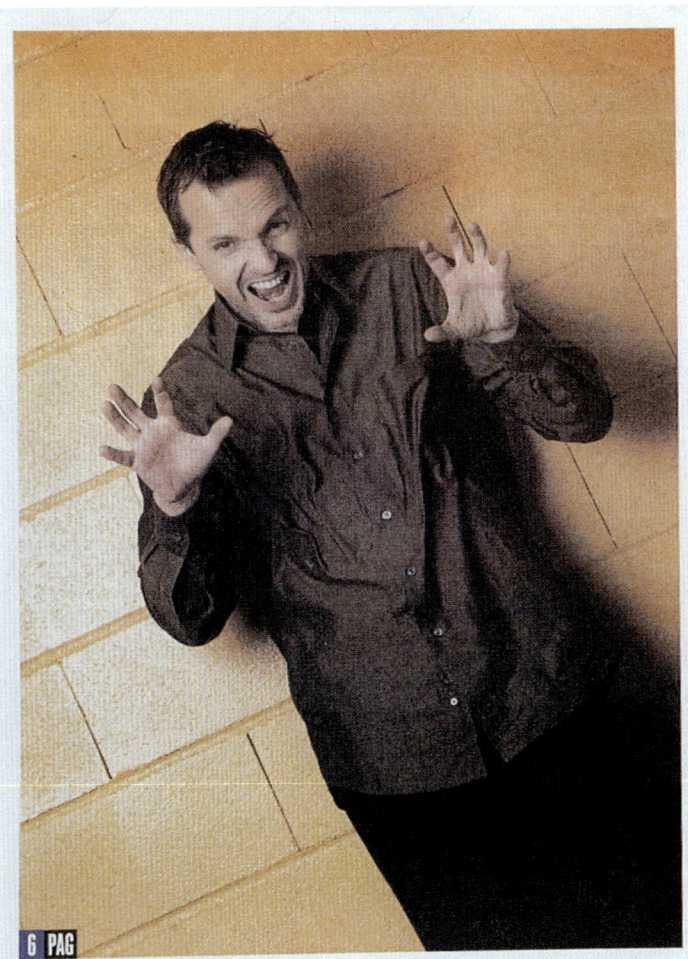

DESIGN PORTFOLIO — Features

Silver
The Boston Globe
Boston, MA
Cindy Daniels, Designer

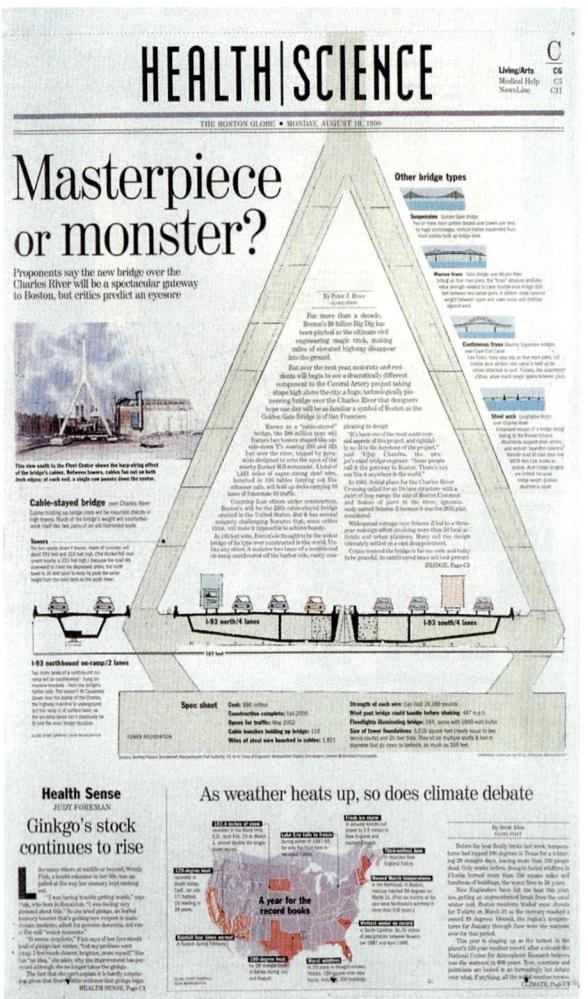
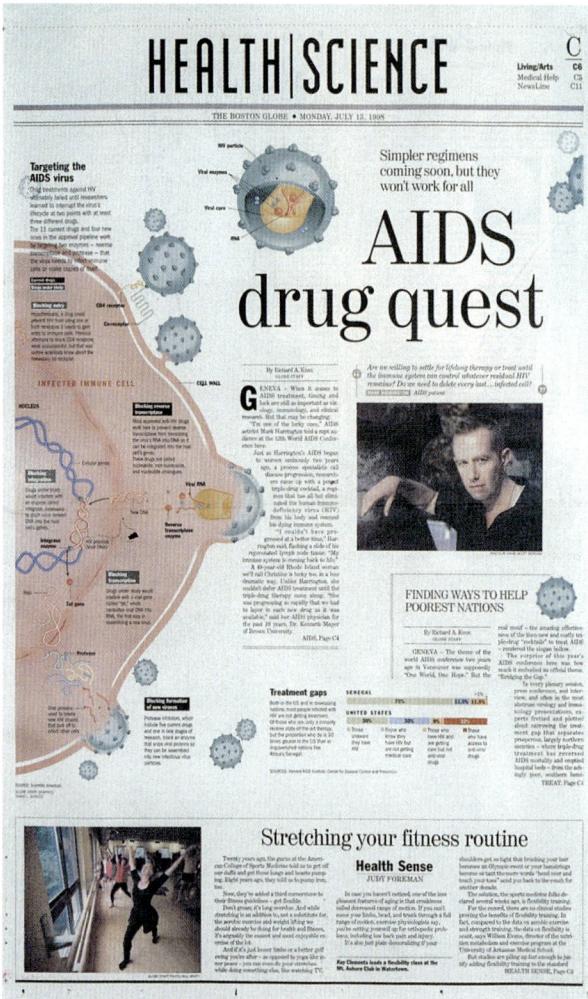

Silver
The Boston Globe
Boston, MA
Keith A. Webb, Art Director & Designer

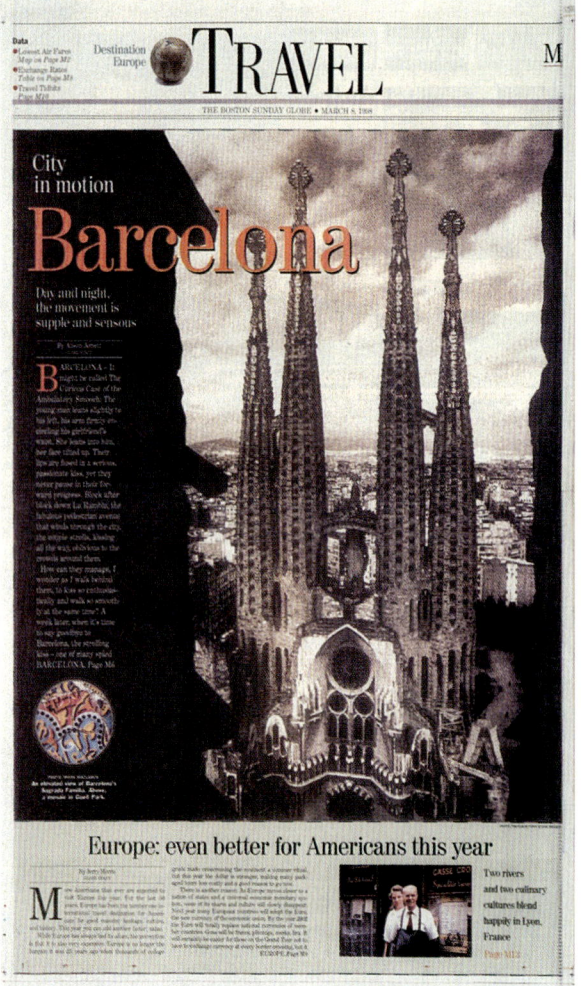
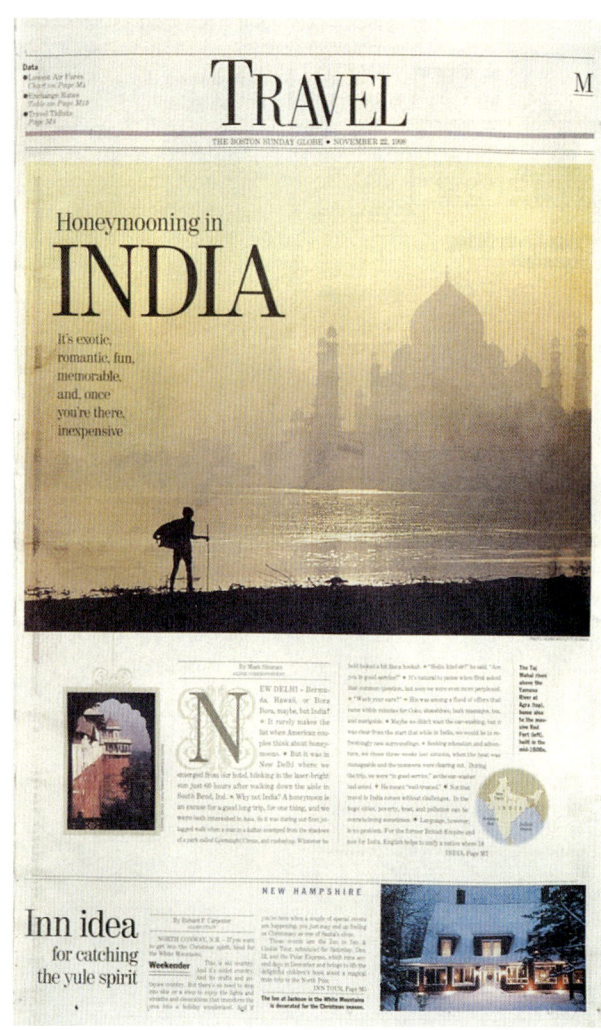

184 ■ THE BEST OF NEWSPAPER DESIGN

Features ■ DESIGN PORTFOLIO

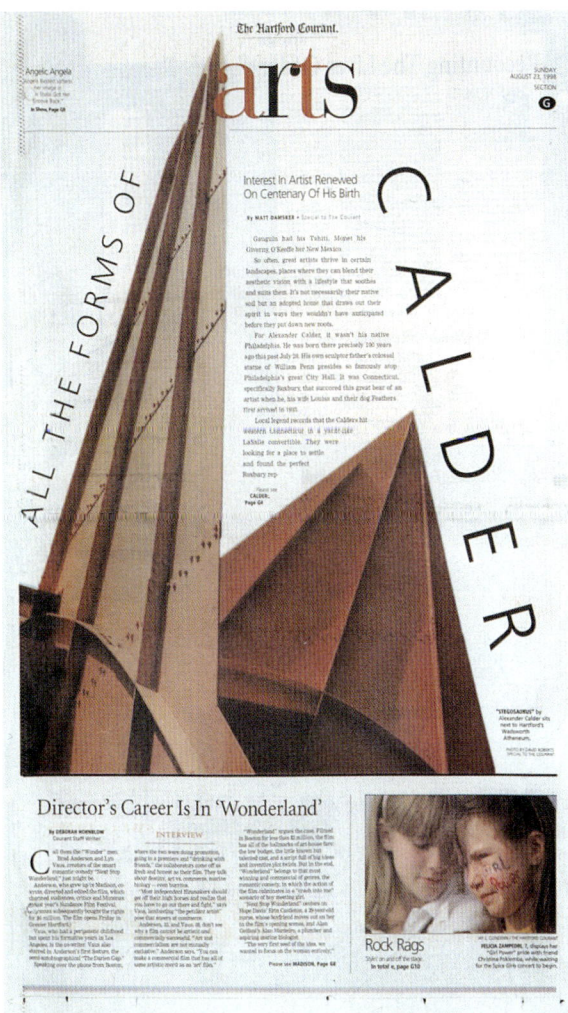

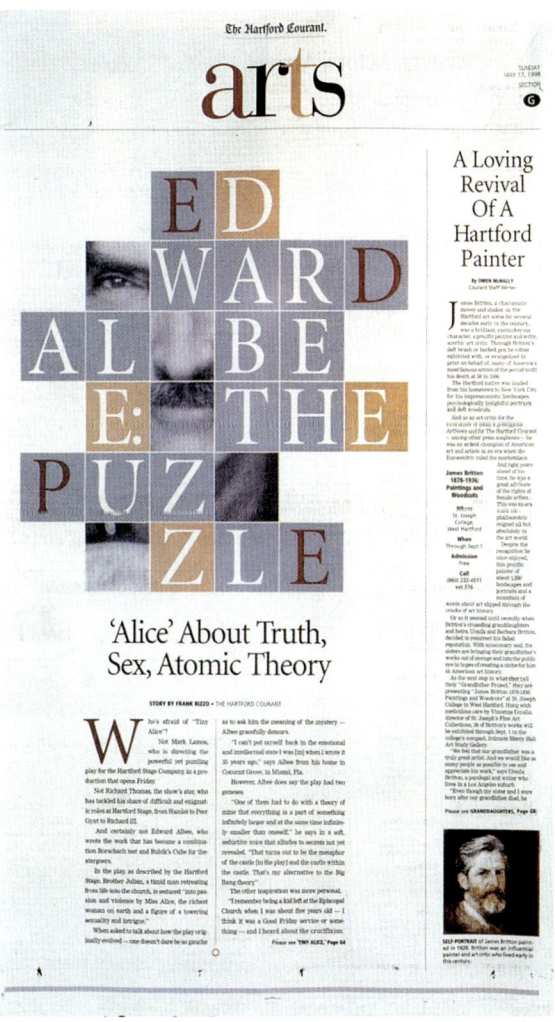

Silver
The Hartford Courant
Hartford, CT
Melanie Shaffer, Designer

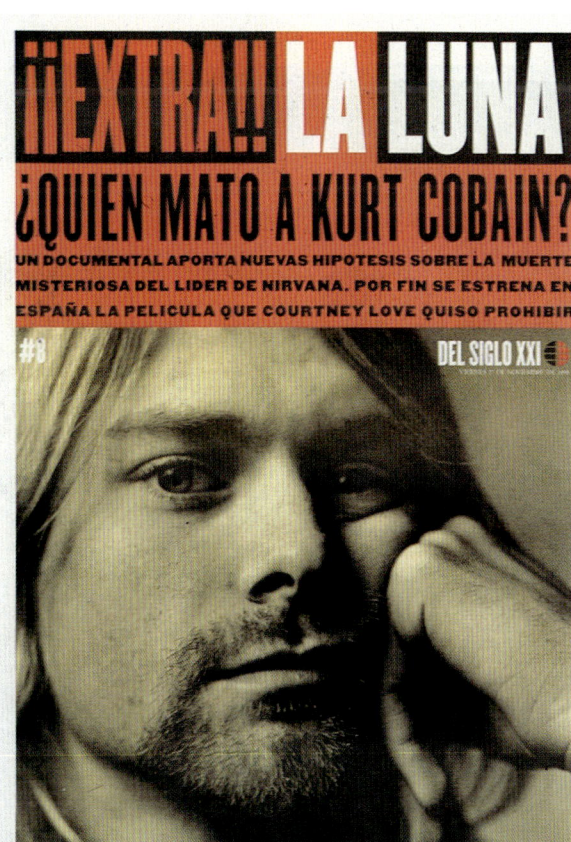

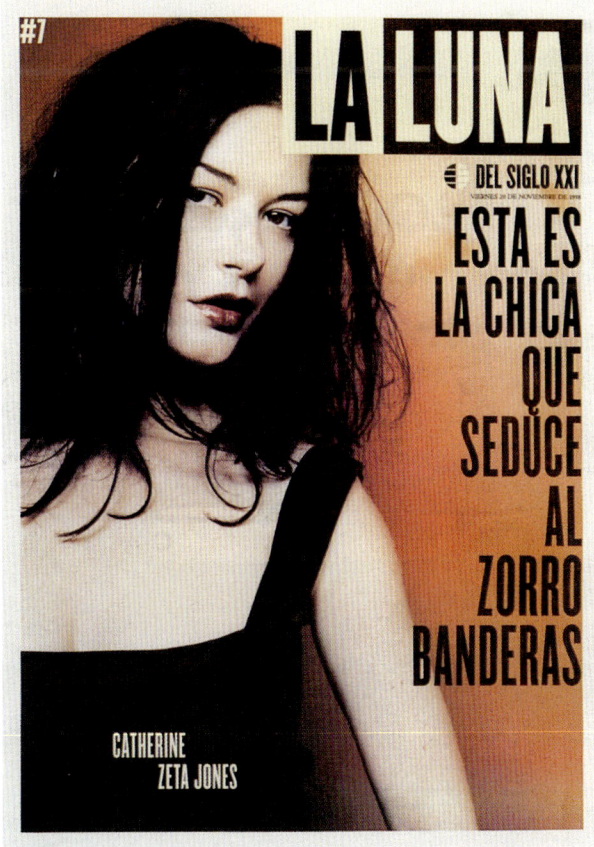

Silver
La Luna
Madrid, Spain
Rodrigo Sánchez, Art Director

DESIGN PORTFOLIO ■ Features

Silver
The National Post
Don Mills, Canada
Gayle Grin, Designer/Design Editor

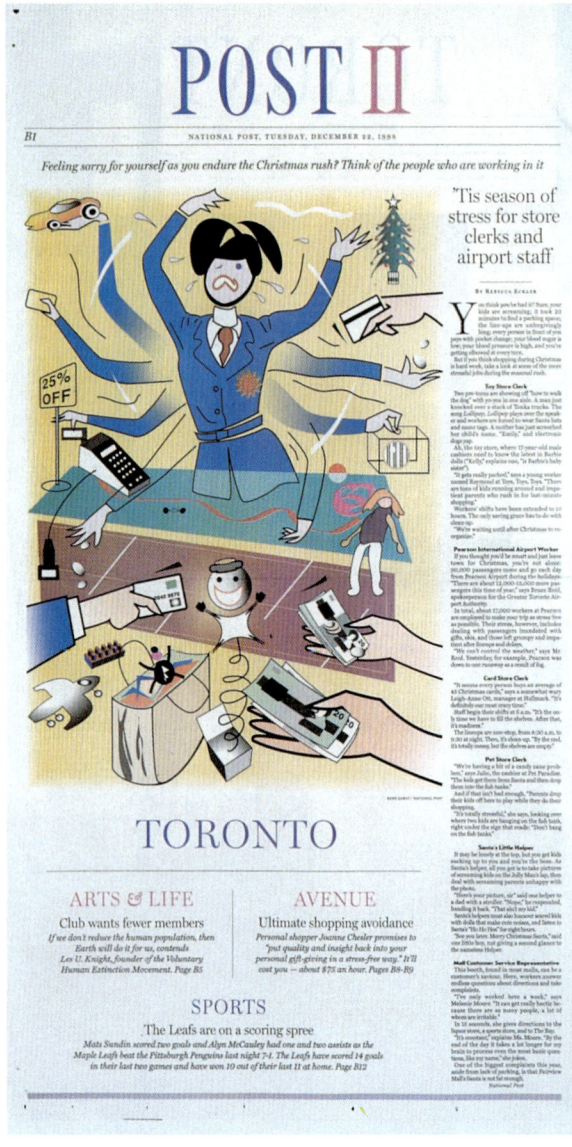
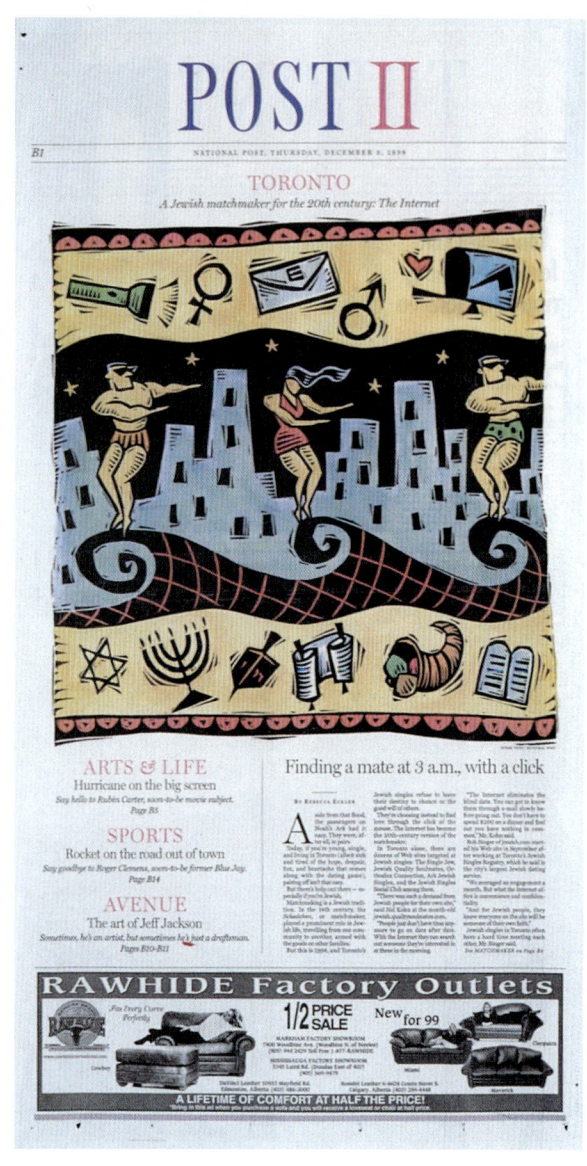

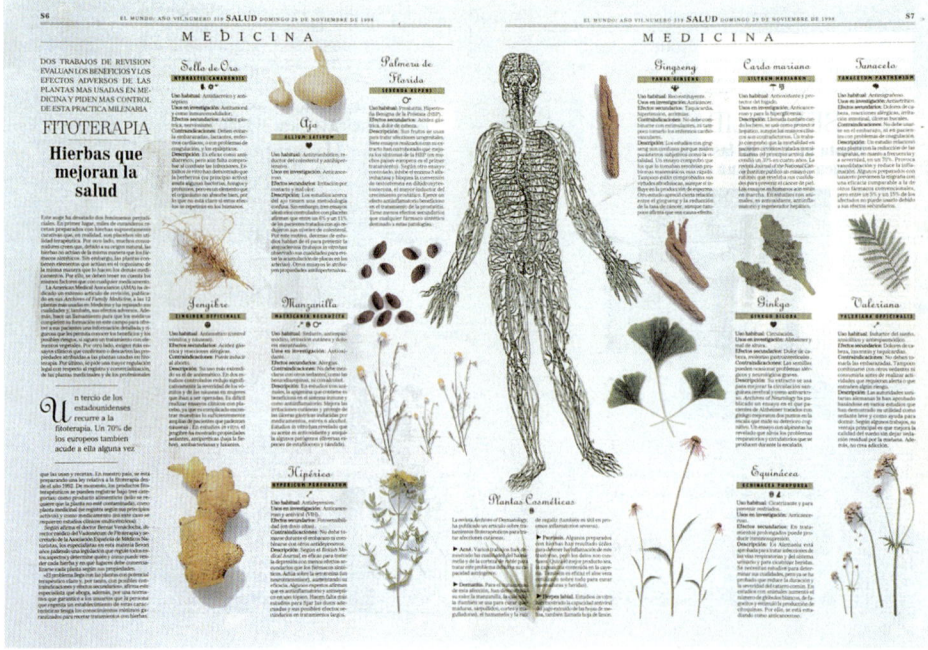
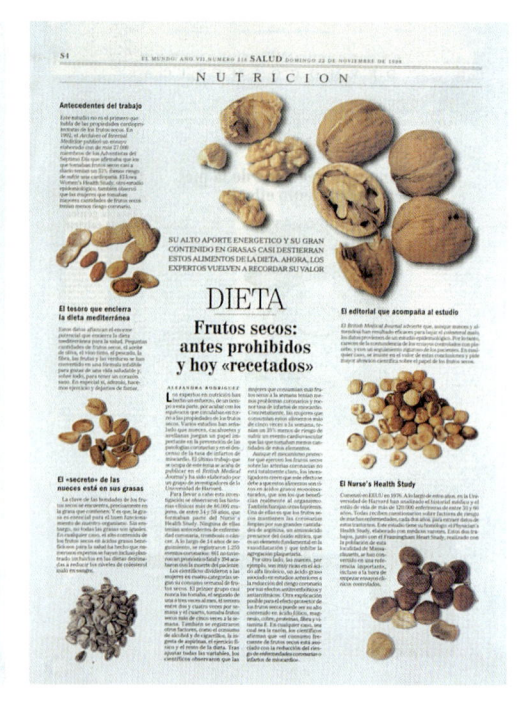

Silver
El Mundo
Madrid, Spain
Carmelo Caderot, Art Director & Designer

Features ■ **DESIGN PORTFOLIO**

La Luna
Madrid, Spain
Rodrigo Sánchez, Art Director

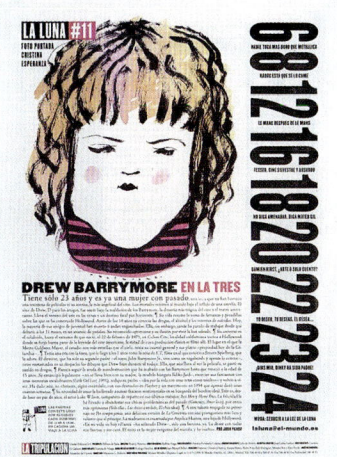

La Luna
Madrid, Spain
Rodrigo Sánchez, Art Director

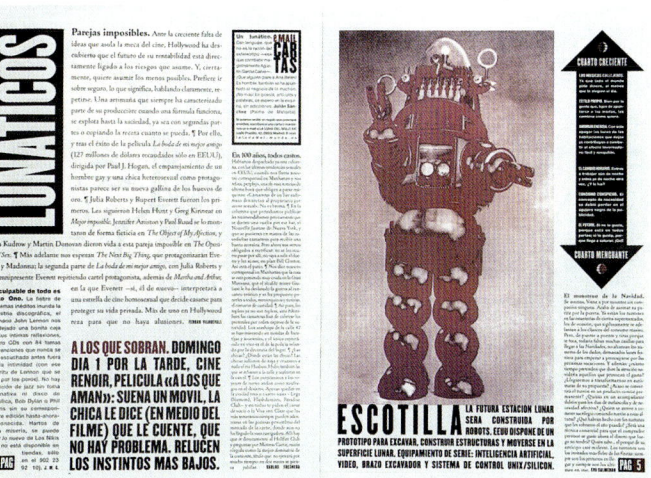

La Luna
Madrid, Spain
Rodrigo Sánchez, Art Director; **Francisco Dorado,** Designer; **Chano del Río,** Designer; **Carmelo Caderot,** Design Director; **Luis de las Alas,** Photographer
• also for Entertainment Page

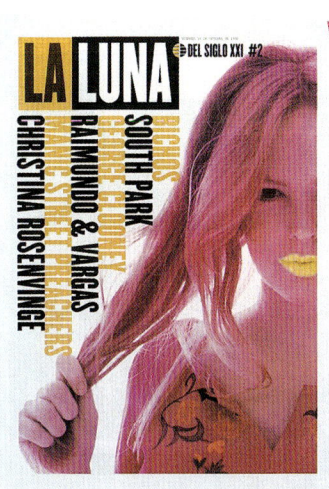

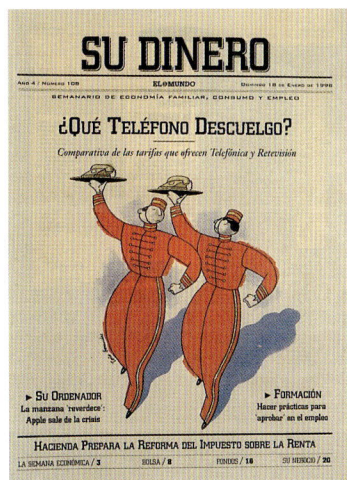

El Mundo
Madrid, Spain
Carmelo Caderot, Art Director & Designer

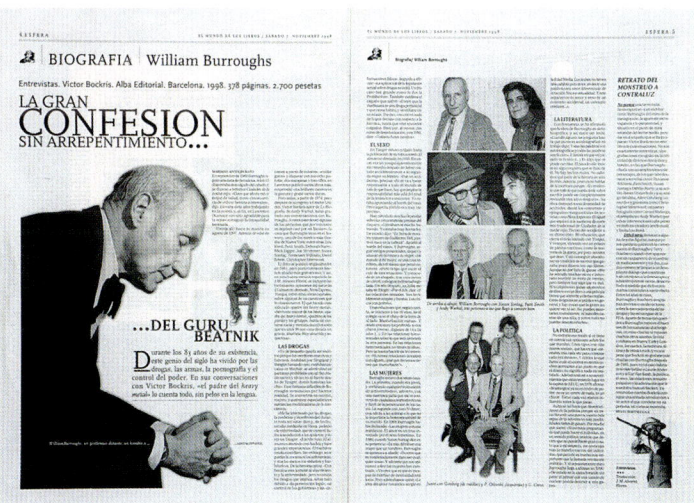

El Mundo
Madrid, Spain
Carmelo Caderot, Art Director & Designer

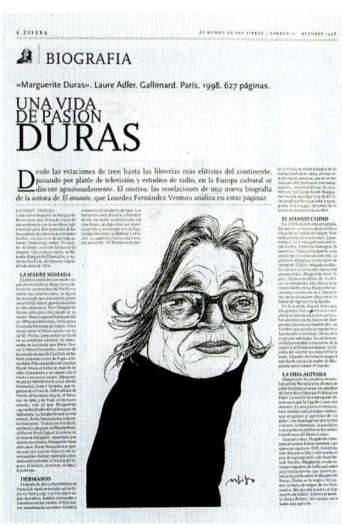

El Mundo
Madrid, Spain
Carmelo Caderot, Art Director & Designer

TWENTIETH EDITION ■ 187

DESIGN PORTFOLIO ■ Features

El Mundo
Madrid, Spain
Carmelo Caderot, Art Director & Designer

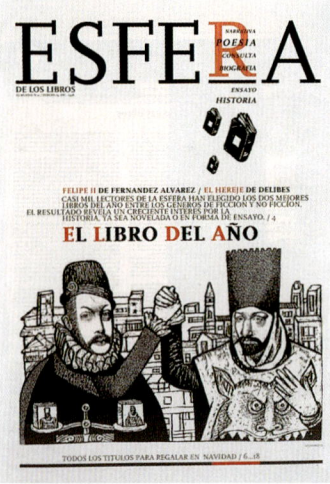

El Mundo
Madrid, Spain
Carmelo Caderot, Art Director & Designer

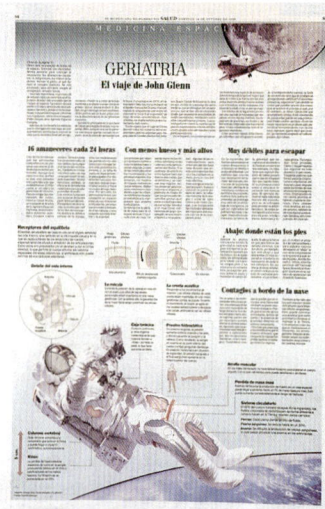

El Mundo
Madrid, Spain
Carmelo Caderot, Art Director & Designer; **Manuel de Miguel,** Assistant Art Director & Designer
• also for Special Section Without Ads and Cover Page

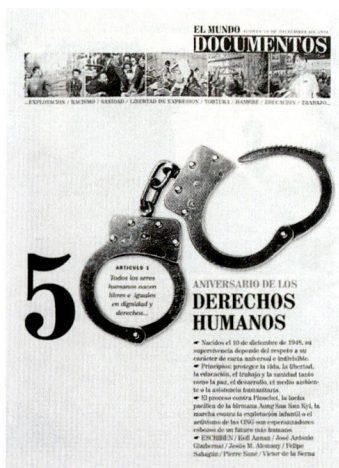

The National Post
Don Mills, Canada
Gayle Grin, Designer/Design Editor; **Tim Rostrum,** Arts Editor; **Peter Scowen,** Toronto Editor; **Kenneth Whyte,** Editor-in-Chief; **Diane de Fenoyl,** Living Editor
• also for Lifestyle Page

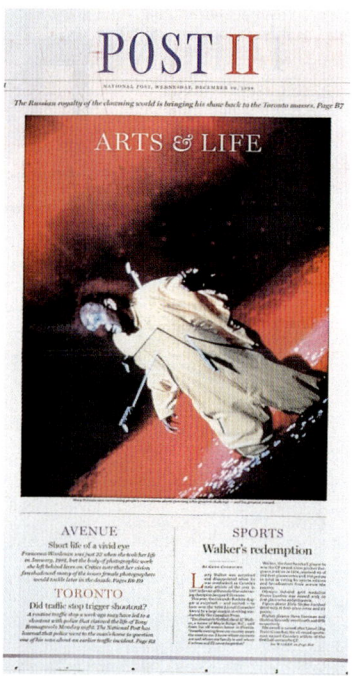

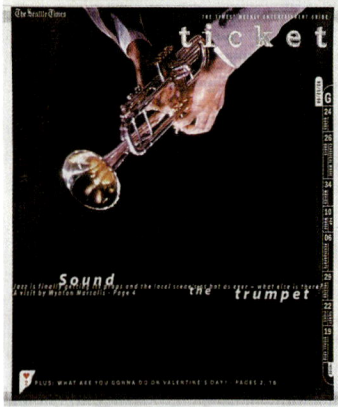

The Seattle Times
Seattle, WA
Jeff Neumann, Designer/Illustrator

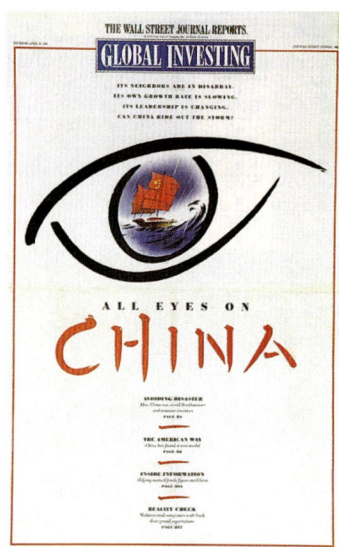

The Wall Street Journal Reports
New York, NY
Greg Leeds, Design Director; **Orlie Kraus,** Art Director & Designer; **Min Jae Hong,** Illustrator
• also for Special Section Cover

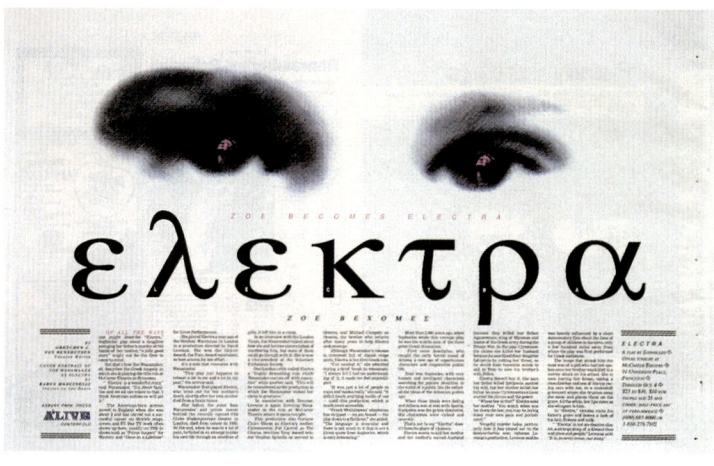

The Asbury Park Press
Neptune, NJ
Adriana Libreros, Designer

Features ■ DESIGN PORTFOLIO

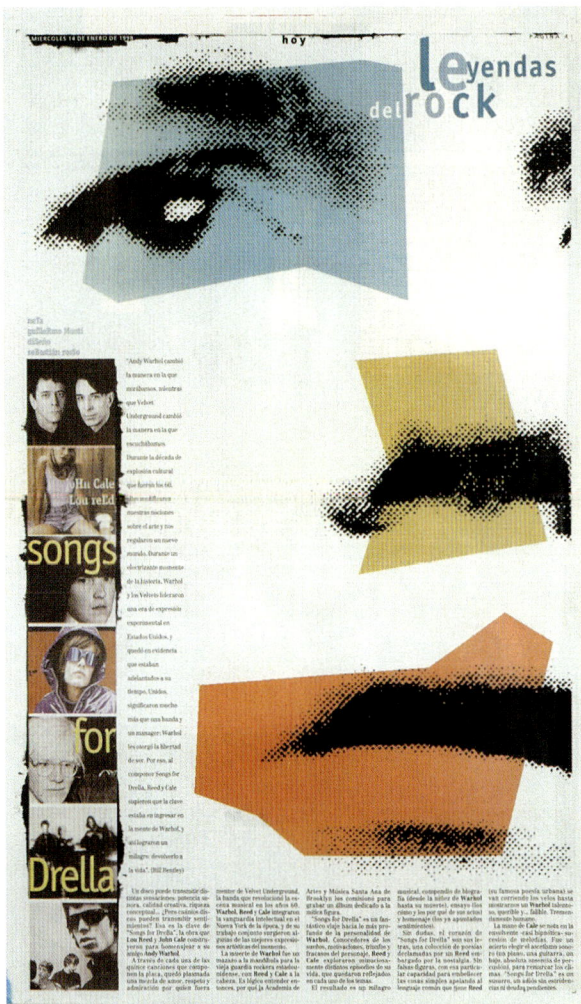

Gold
La Gaceta
San Miguel de Tucuman, Argentina
Sebastian Rosso, Illustrator & Designer

This tribute is daring and balanced. It is cutting edge, yet readable and legible. The color palette is interesting and appealing. This paper takes everything to the edge and is not over designed. The section header blends in, yet stands out as part of the design. The headers don't overpower the page and lets the art shine through in a variety of ways so it is still recognizable.

Este tributo es atrevido y bien equilibrado. Es muy moderno y, no obstante, legible y fácil de leer. La gama de colores es interesante y atractiva. Este diario gusta de innovar y nunca tiene más diseño del necesario. El titular de la sección combina con el diseño y, sin embargo, sobresale. Sus titulares no sobrecargan la página y deja destacar el arte de diversas maneras de modo tal que se le pueda reconocer.

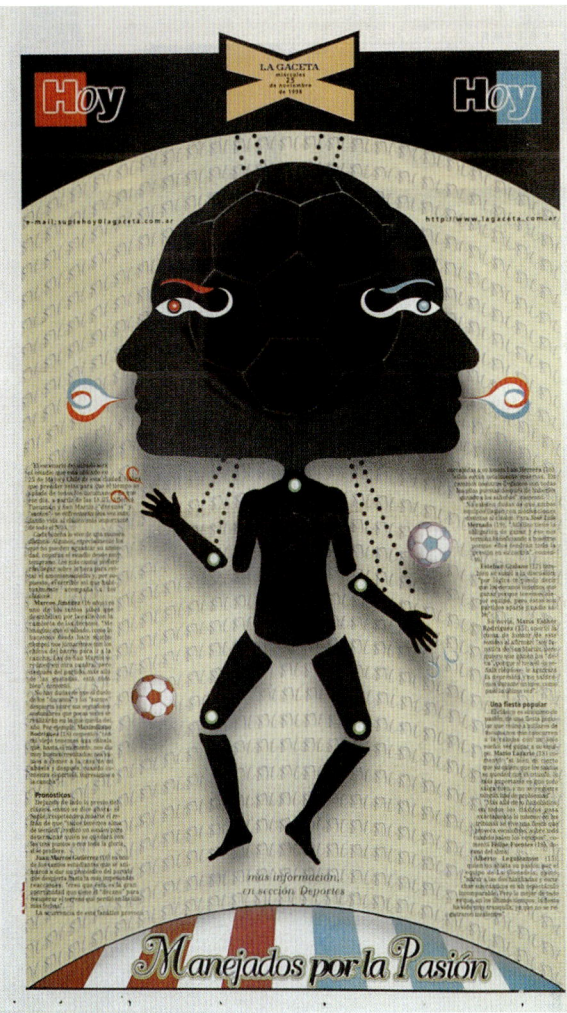

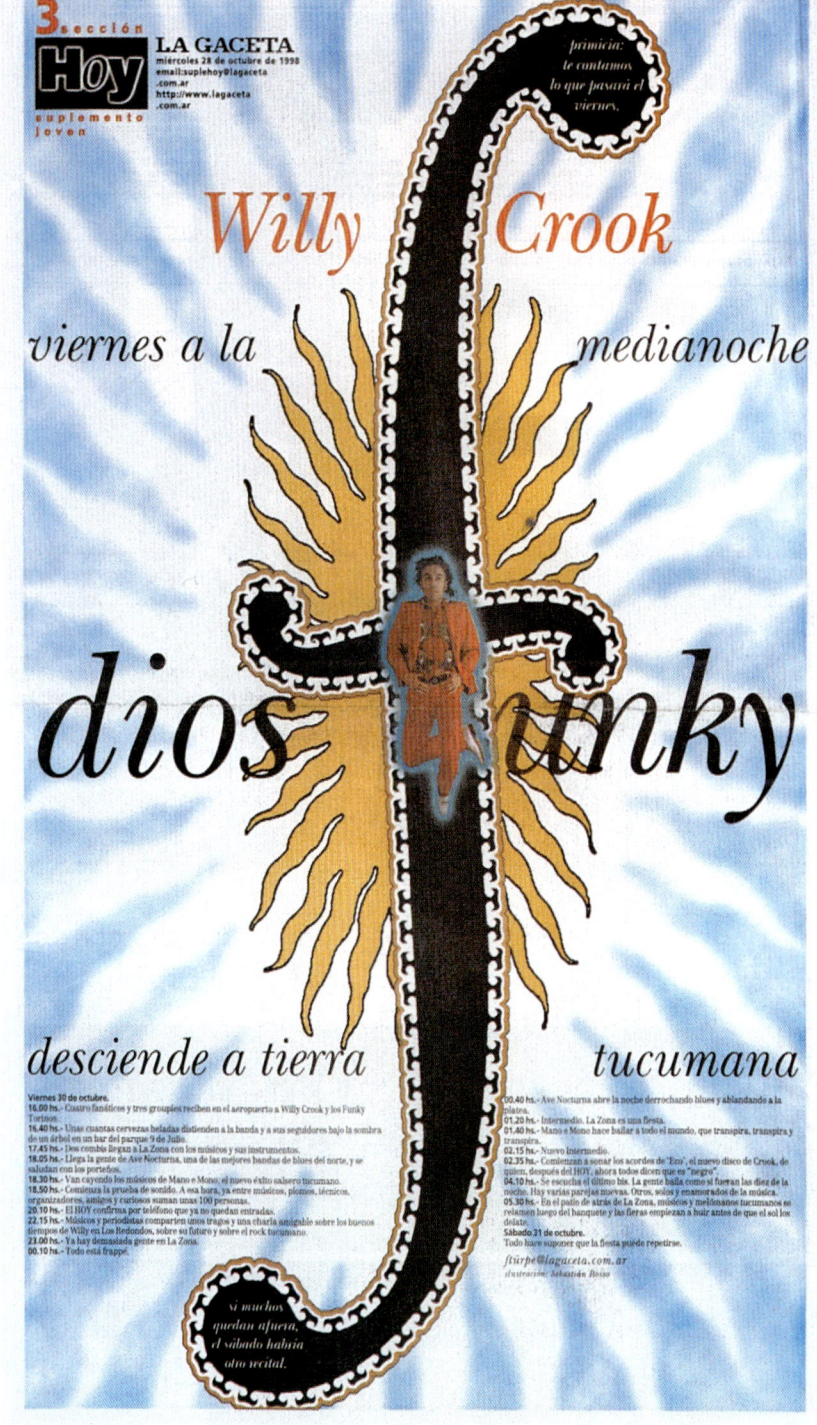

DESIGN PORTFOLIO ■ Features

**Silver
Anchorage Daily News**
Anchorage, AK
Lance Lekander, Designer;
Len Irish, Photographer
• also an Award of Excellence for Entertainment Page

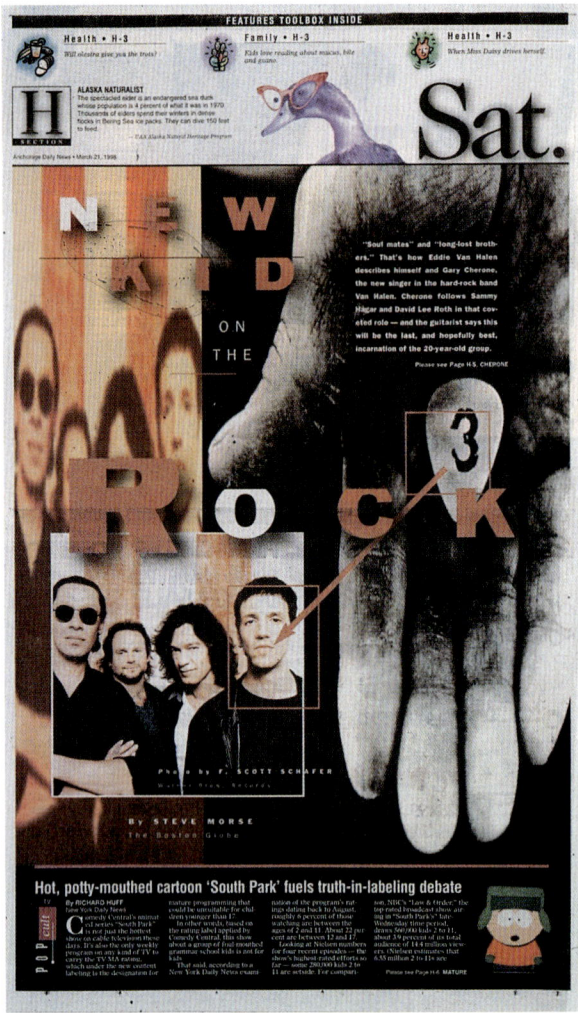
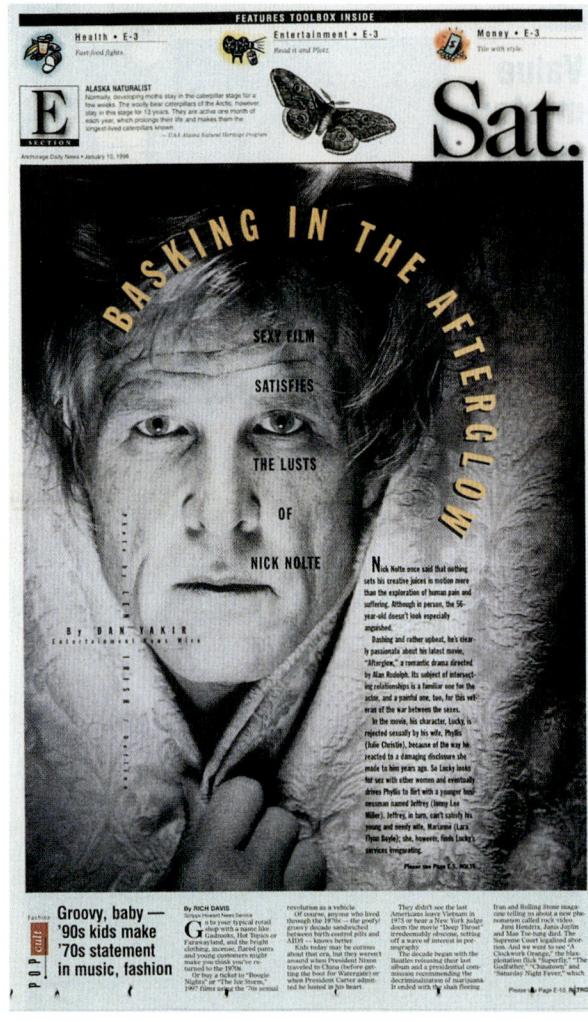

**Silver
Berlingske Tidende**
Copenhagen, Denmark
Bettina Kofmann, Page Designer
• also an Award of Excellence for Lifestyle Page

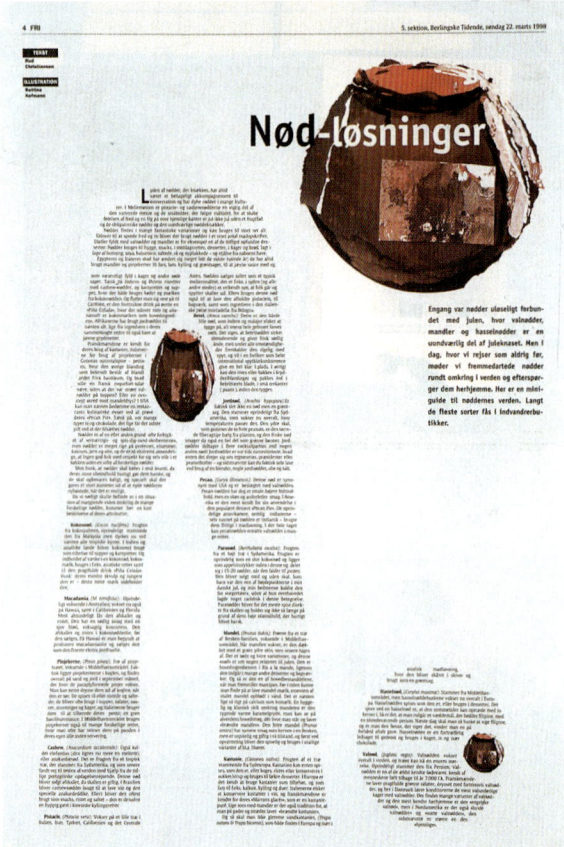
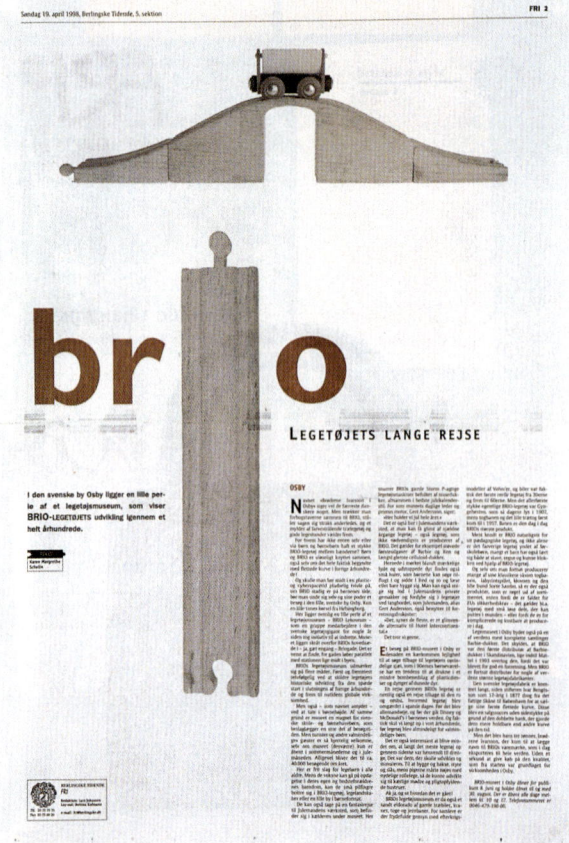

Features ■ DESIGN PORTFOLIO

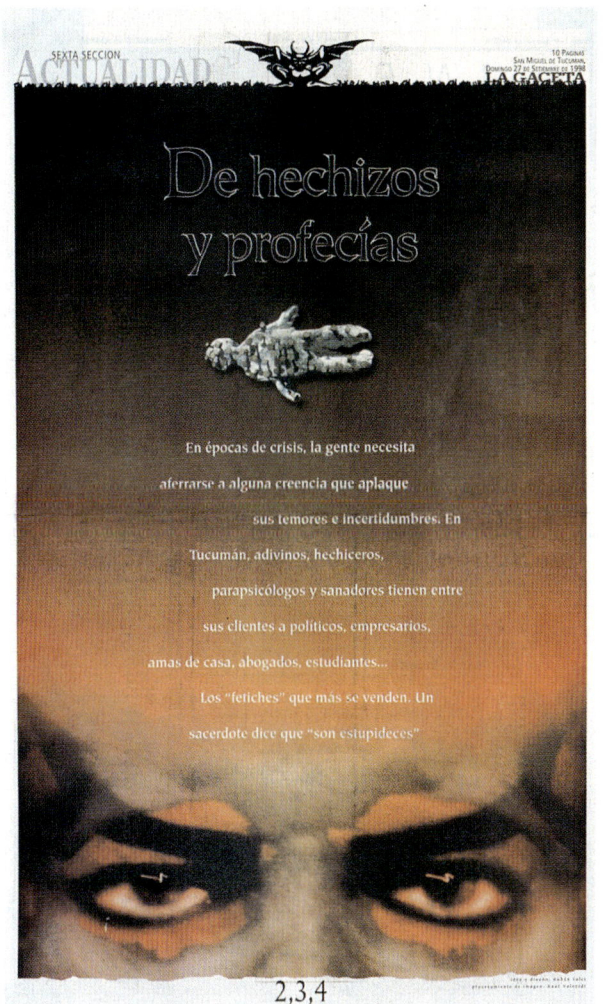
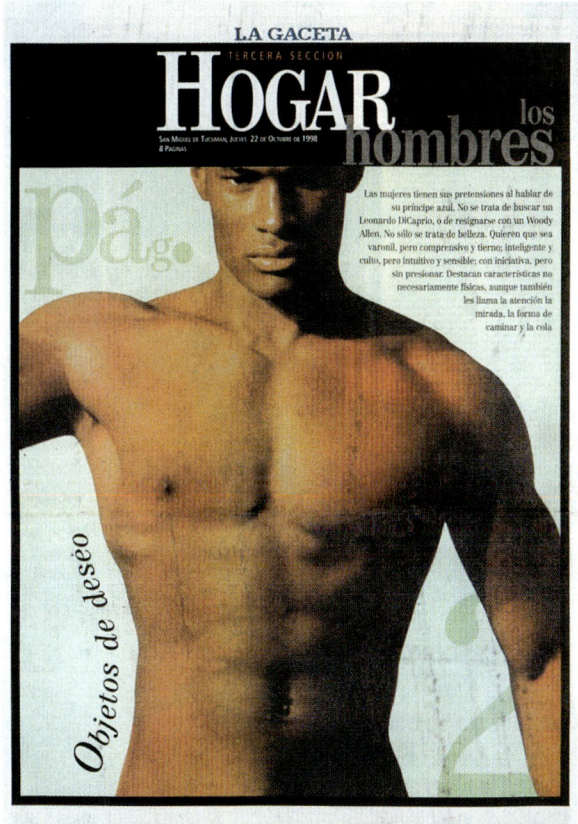

**Silver
La Gaceta**
San Miguel de Tucuman, Argentina
Falci Ruben, Designer; **Sergio Fernandez,** Art Director; **Mario García,** Design Consultant; **Raul Valverdi,** Photo Illustrator
• also an Award of Excellence for Features Other Page

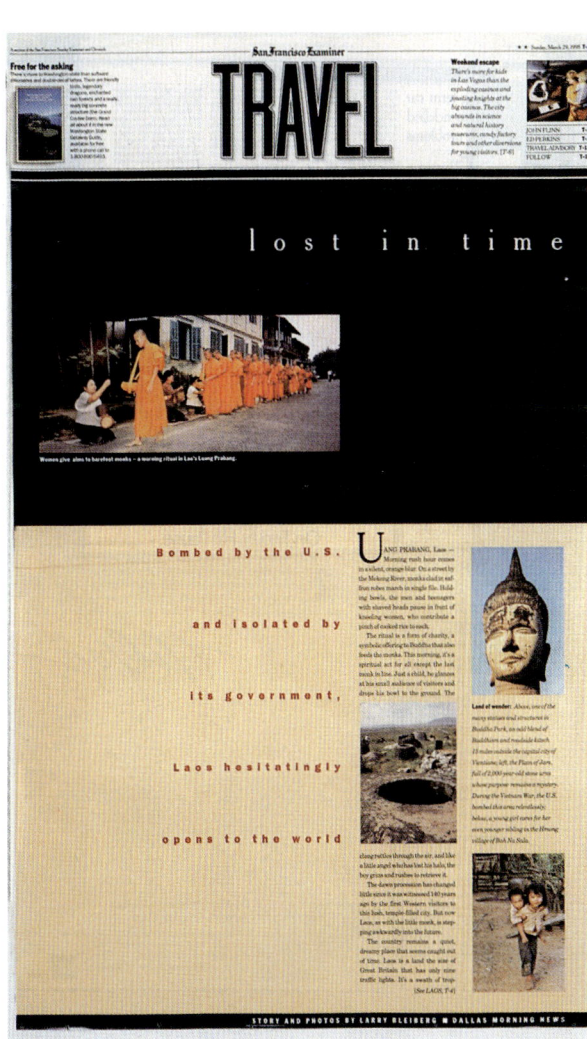
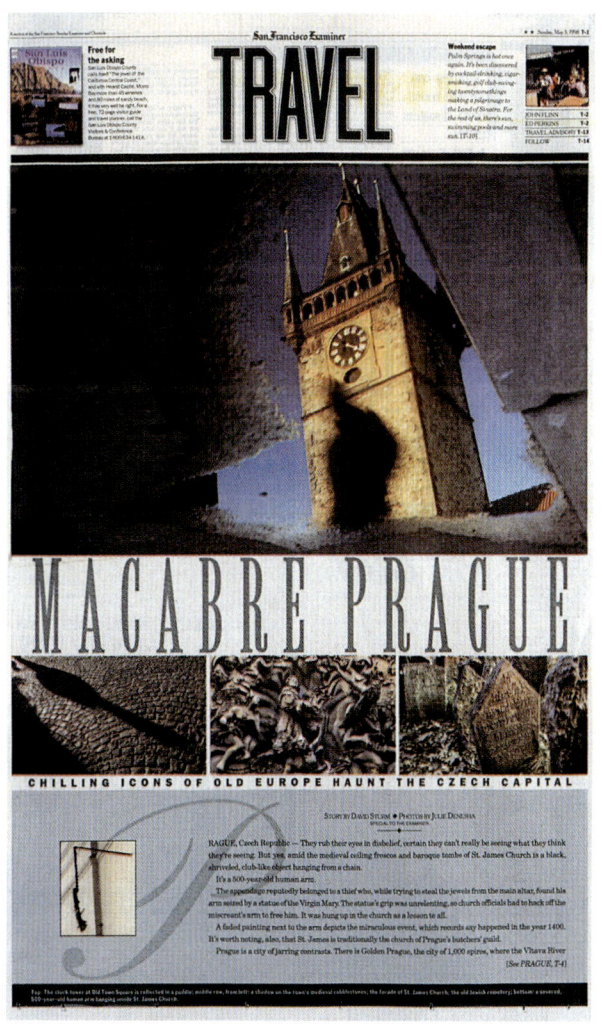

**Silver
San Francisco Examiner**
San Francisco, CA
Andrew Skwish, Designer; **Kelly Frankeny,** A.M.E. Design; **Don McCartney,** Design Director; **John Flinn,** Travel Editor
• also an Award of Excellence for Travel Page

TWENTIETH EDITION ■ 191

DESIGN PORTFOLIO ■ Features

The News & Observer
Raleigh, NC
Robin Johnston, Features Design Director

Le Devoir
Montréal, Canada
Christian Vien, Graphic Designer

San Francisco Examiner
San Francisco, CA
Andrew Skwish, Designer; **Kelly Frankeny,** A.M.E. Design; **Don McCartney,** Design Director; **Jo Mancuso,** Habitat Editor; **Richard Paoli,** Director/Photography; **Liz Mangelsdorf,** Photo Editor; **John Storey,** Photographer
• also for Food Page

San Francisco Examiner
San Francisco, CA
Don McCartney, Design Director/Designer

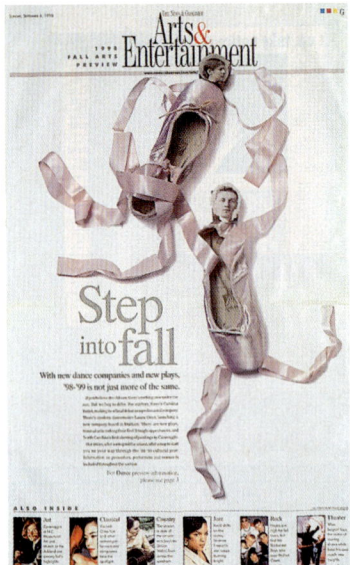
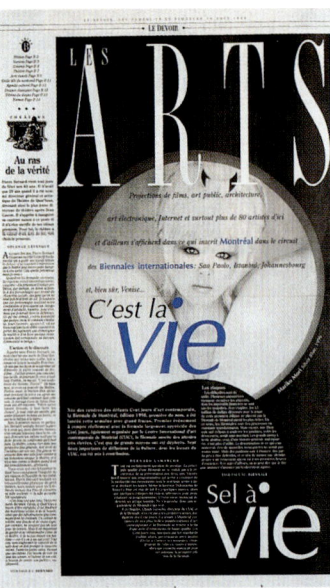
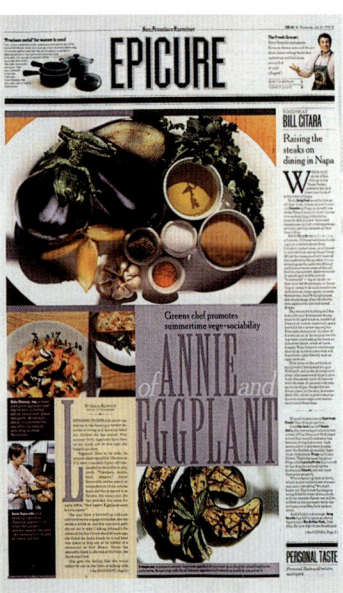
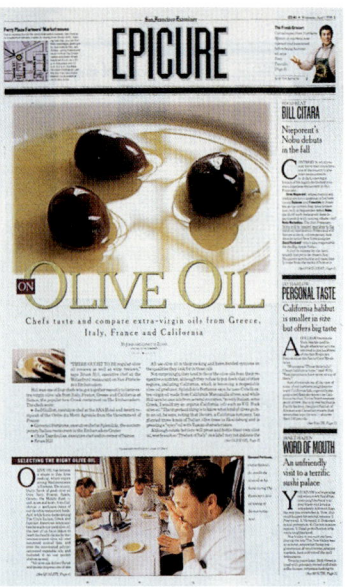

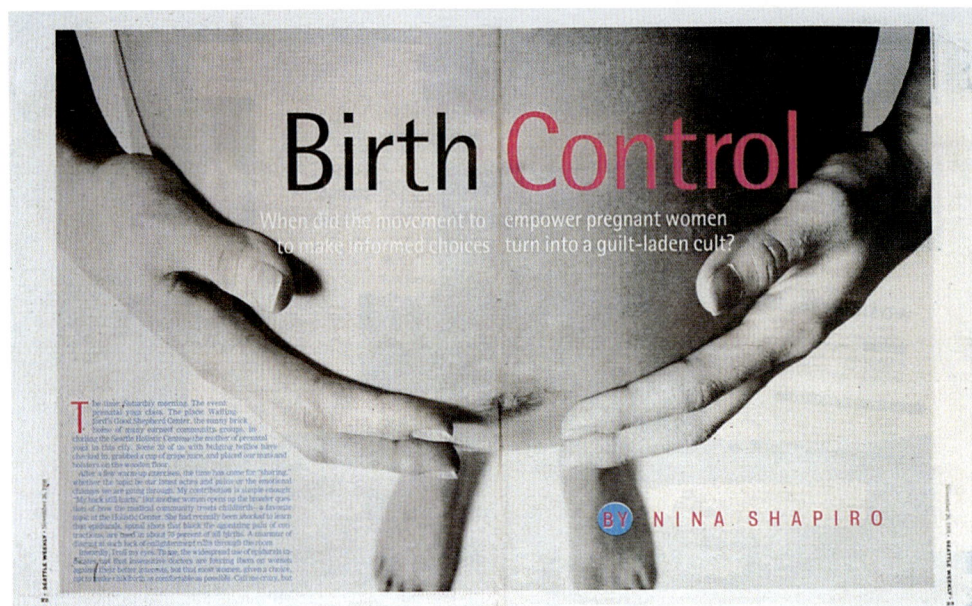

Seattle Weekly
Seattle, WA
Barbara Dow, Art Director & Designer

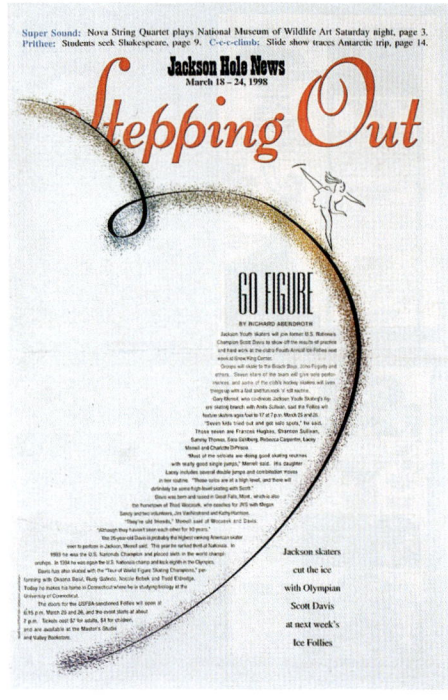

Jackson Hole News
Jackson, WY
Dorothy Jankowsky, Illustrator & Designer

Silver
Le Devoir
Don Mills, Canada
Roland-Yves Carignan, Deputy Editor-in-Chief

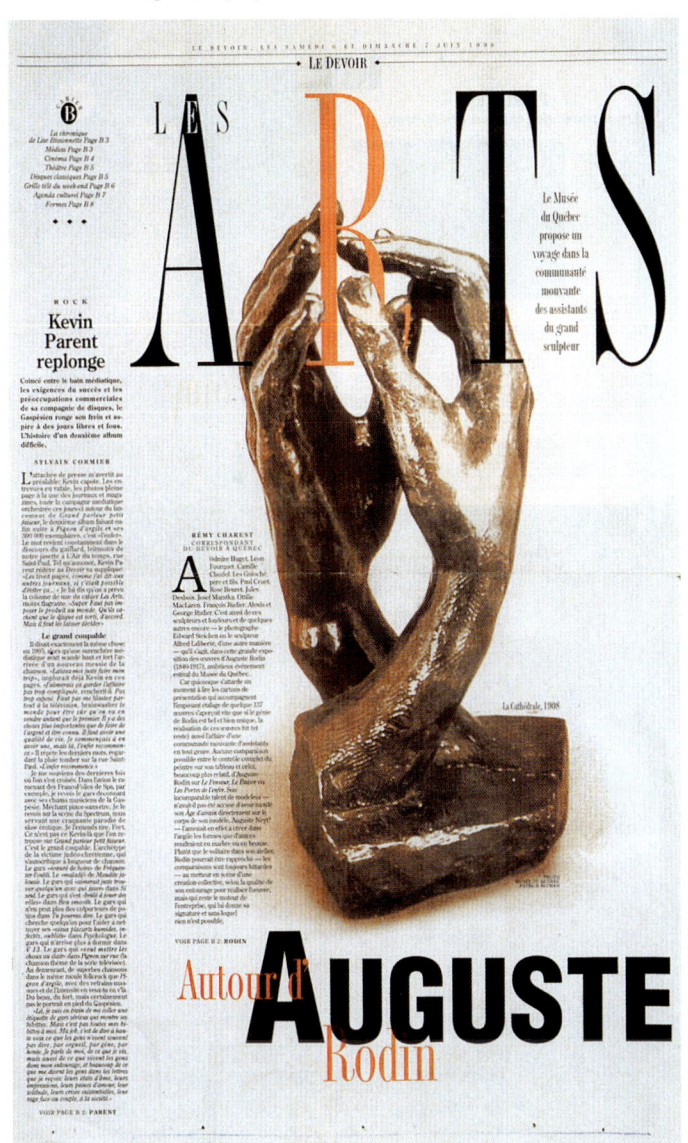
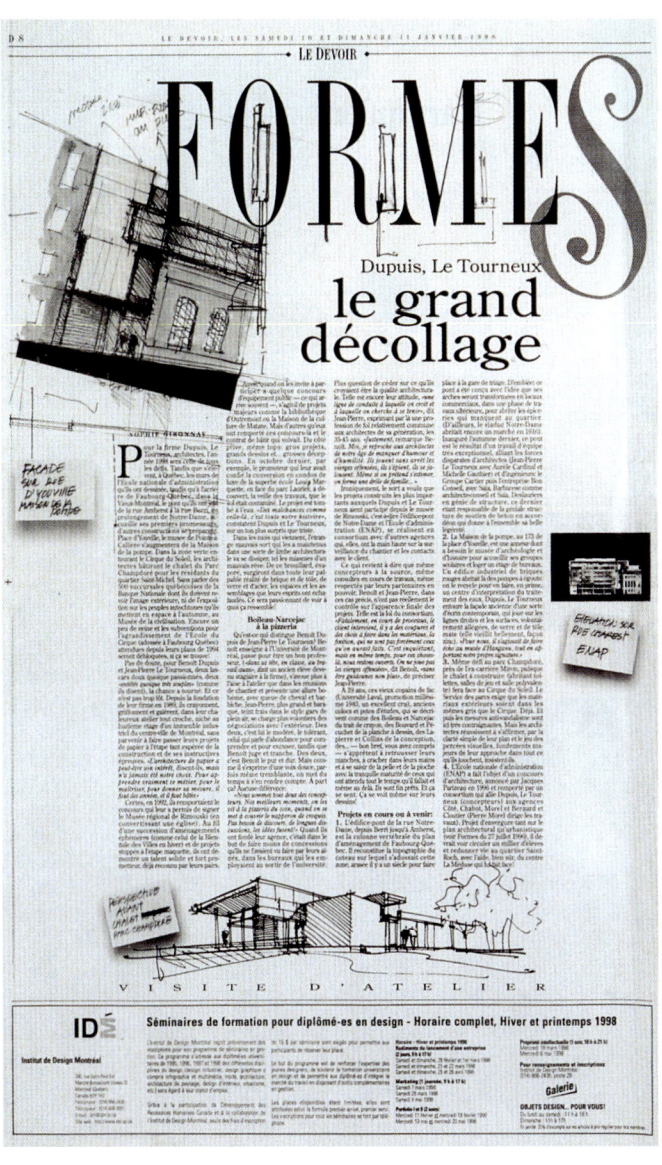

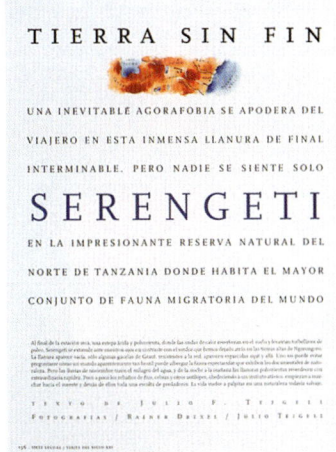
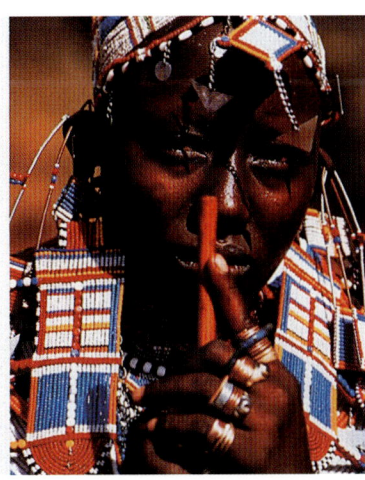
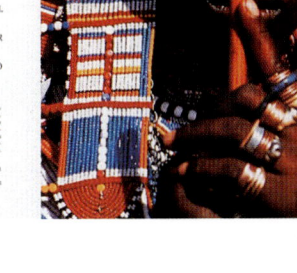
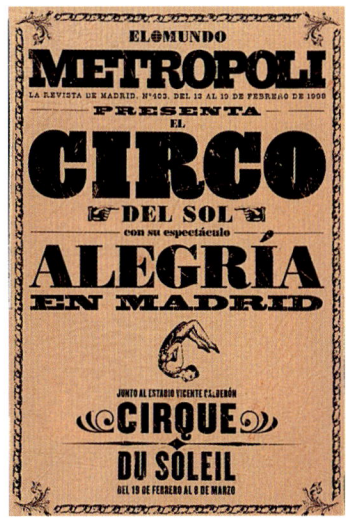

El Mundo
Madrid, Spain
Carmelo Caderot, Art Director & Designer

El Mundo Metropoli
Madrid, Spain
Rodrigo Sánchez, Art Director

El Mundo Metropoli
Madrid, Spain
Rodrigo Sánchez, Art Director

DESIGN PORTFOLIO ■ Magazine

Gold
La Revista de El Mundo
Madrid, Spain
Maria González, Designer

Very clever ways to use name of magazine; it doesn't overpower the page. Some of the most tasteful, sexy pictures we have seen. The type integrates and blends into the picture.

Tiene modos muy ingeniosos de utilizar el nombre de la revista; no sobrecarga la página. Algunas de las fotos de mejor gusto y mayor sensualidad que hemos visto. El tipo se integra y combina con la figura.

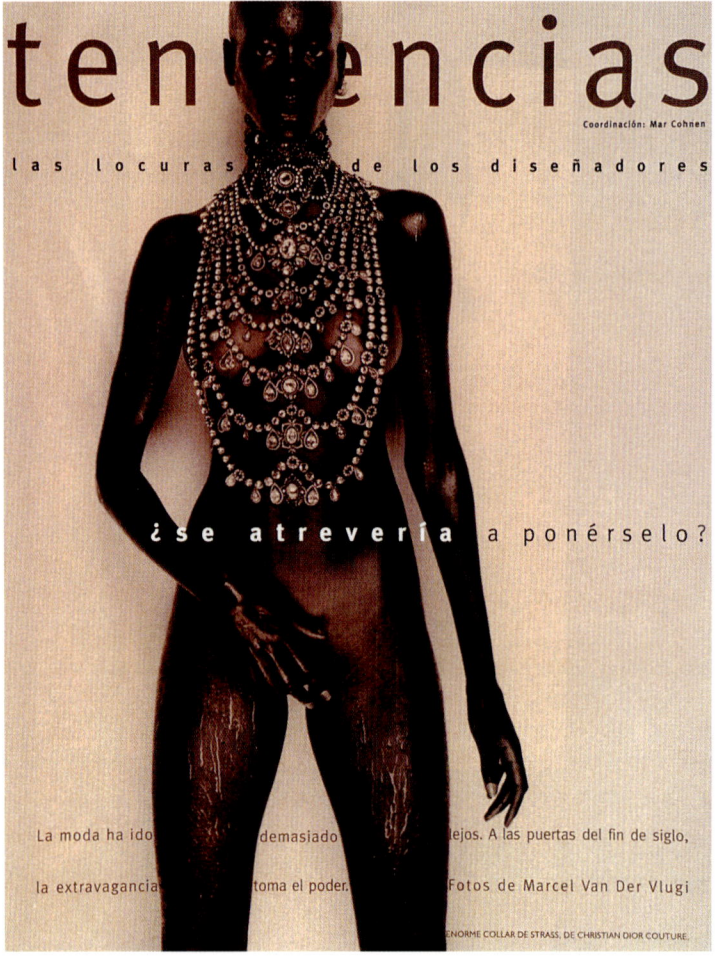

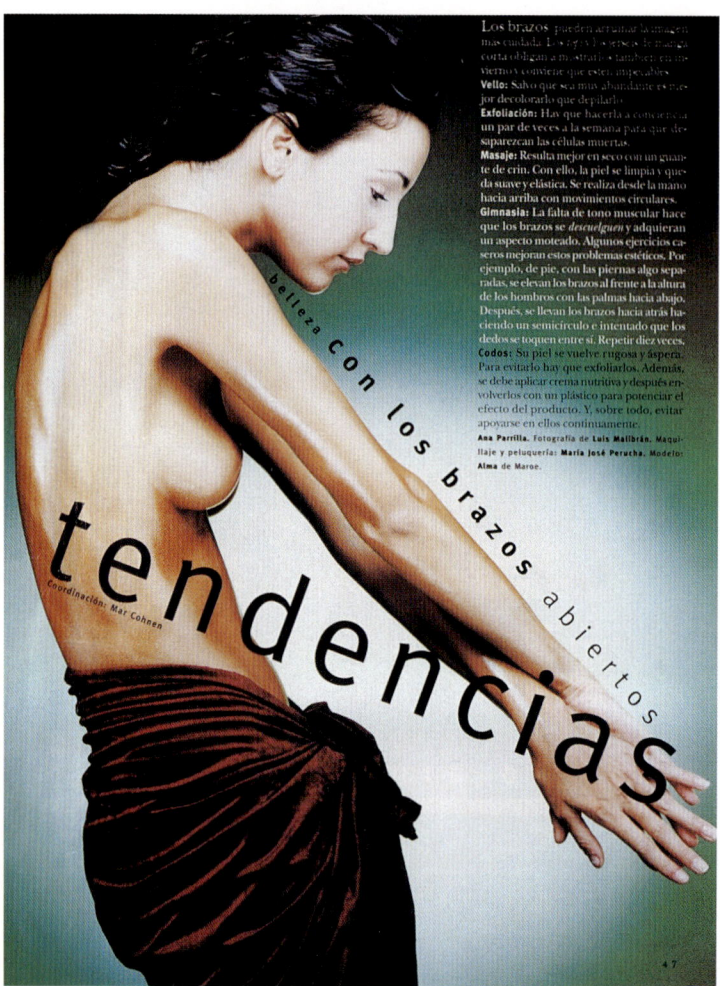

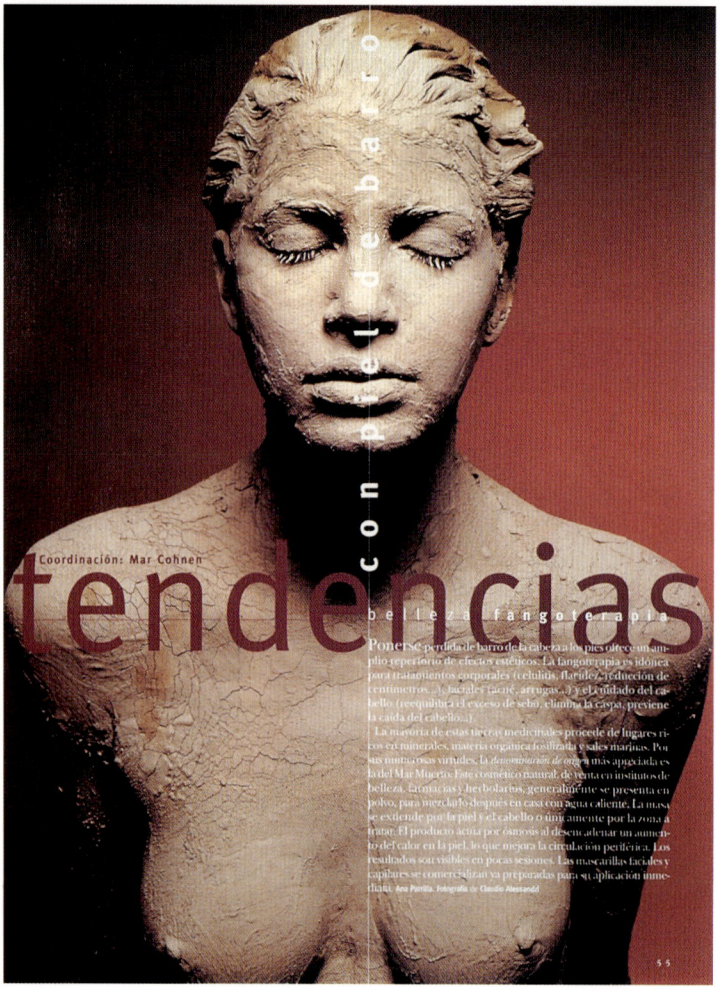

Magazine ■ DESIGN PORTFOLIO

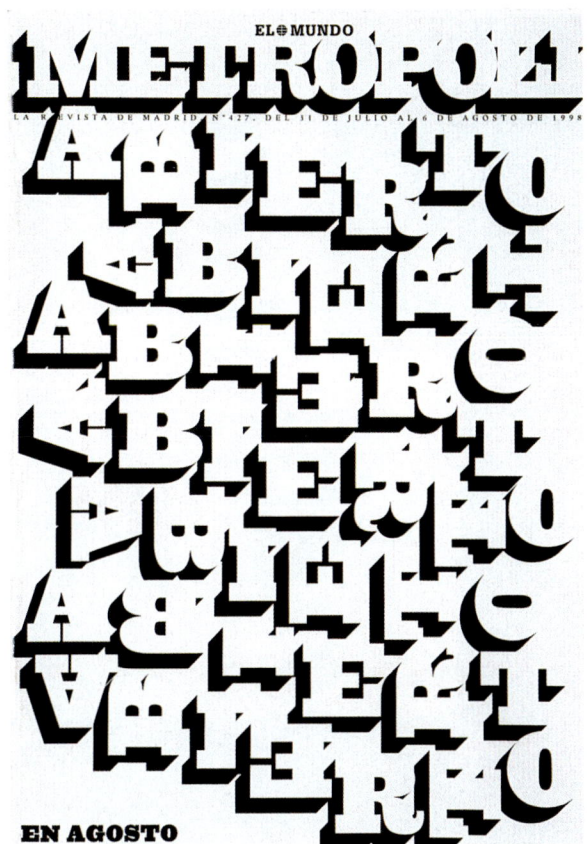
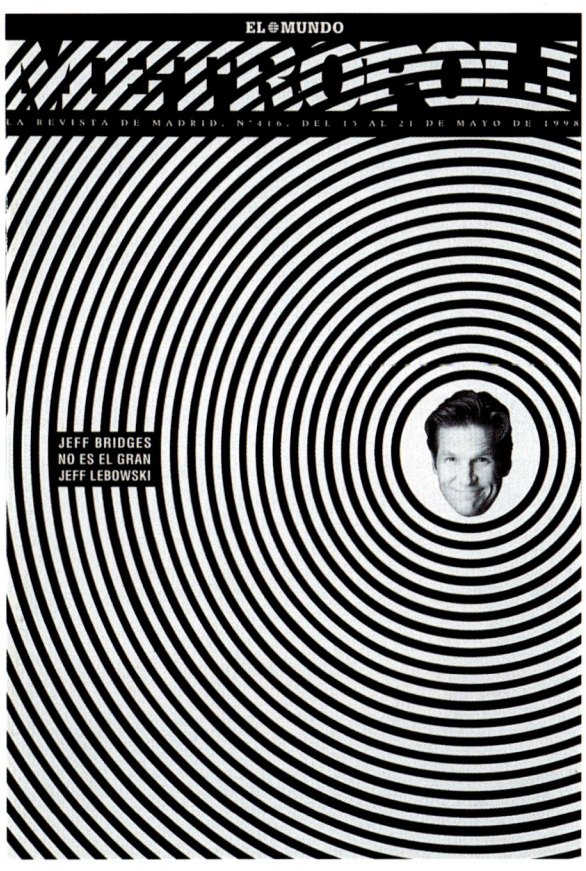

Silver
El Mundo Metropoli
Madrid, Spain
Rodrigo Sánchez, Designer

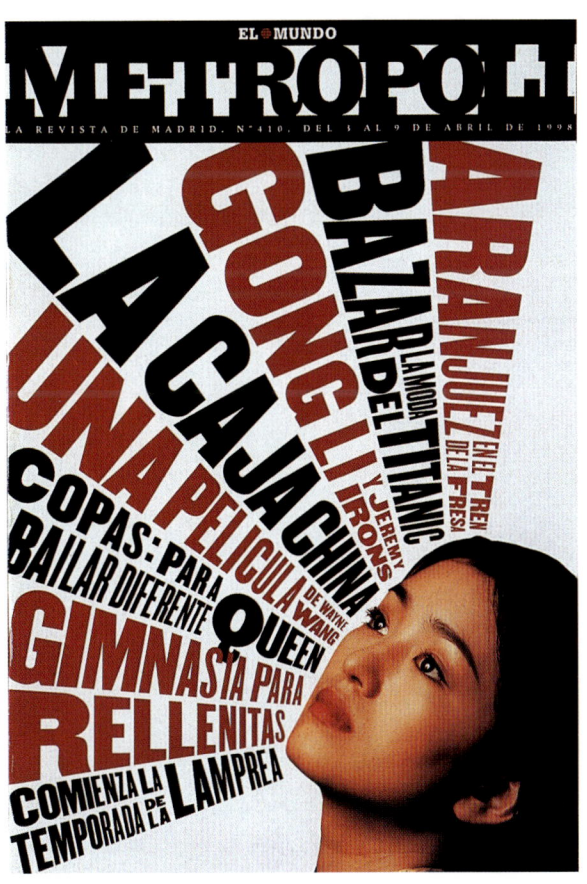
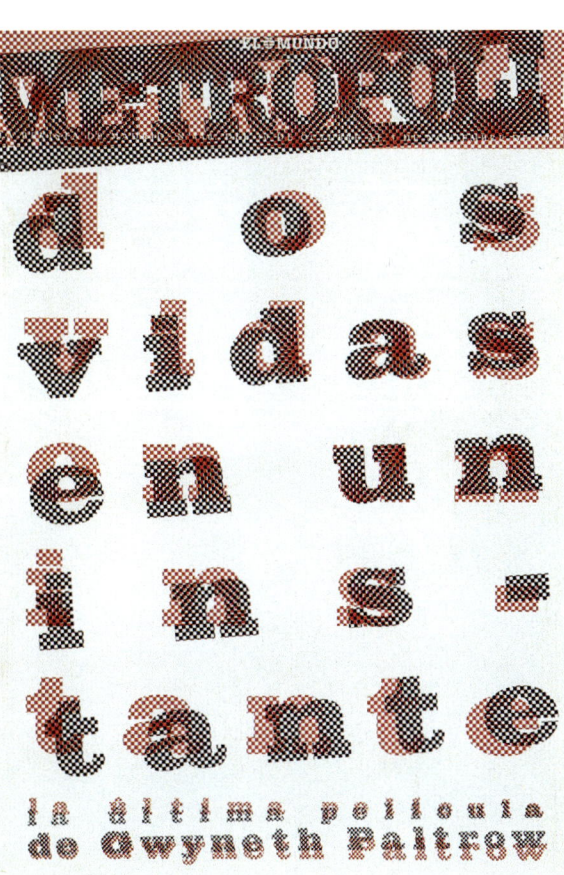

Silver
El Mundo Metropoli
Madrid, Spain
Rodrigo Sánchez, Designer

DESIGN PORTFOLIO ■ Magazine

Silver
El Mundo Metropoli
Madrid, Spain
Rodrigo Sánchez, Designer, Art Director; **Maria Gonzalez**, Designer; **Carmelo Caderot**, Design Director
• also an Award of Excellence for Magazine cover

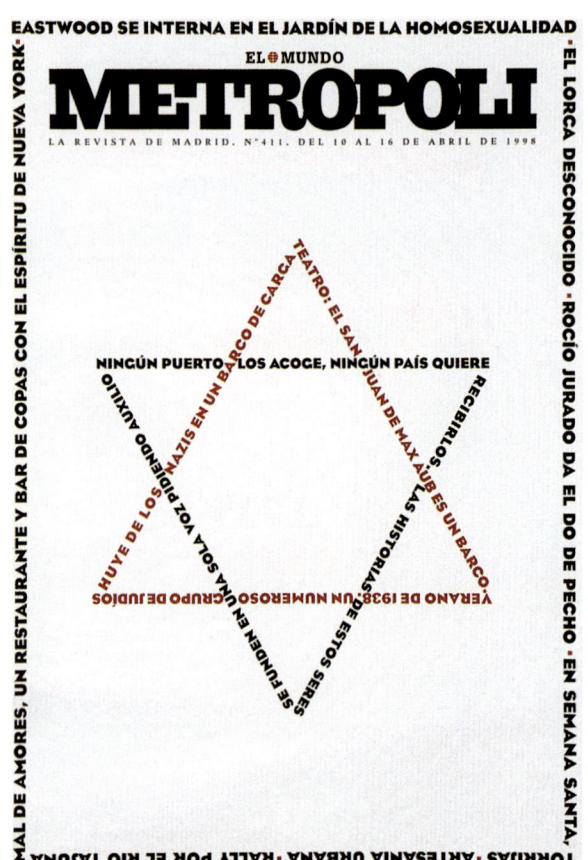
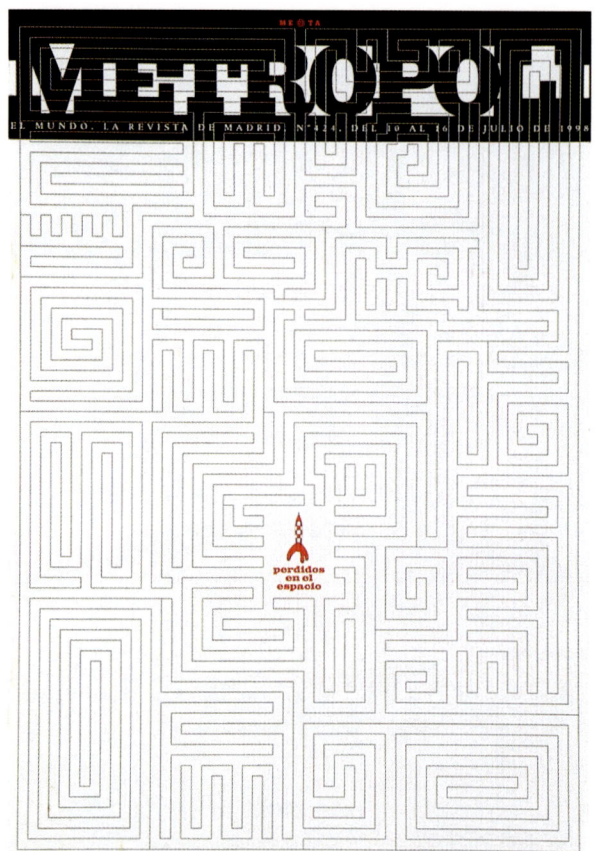

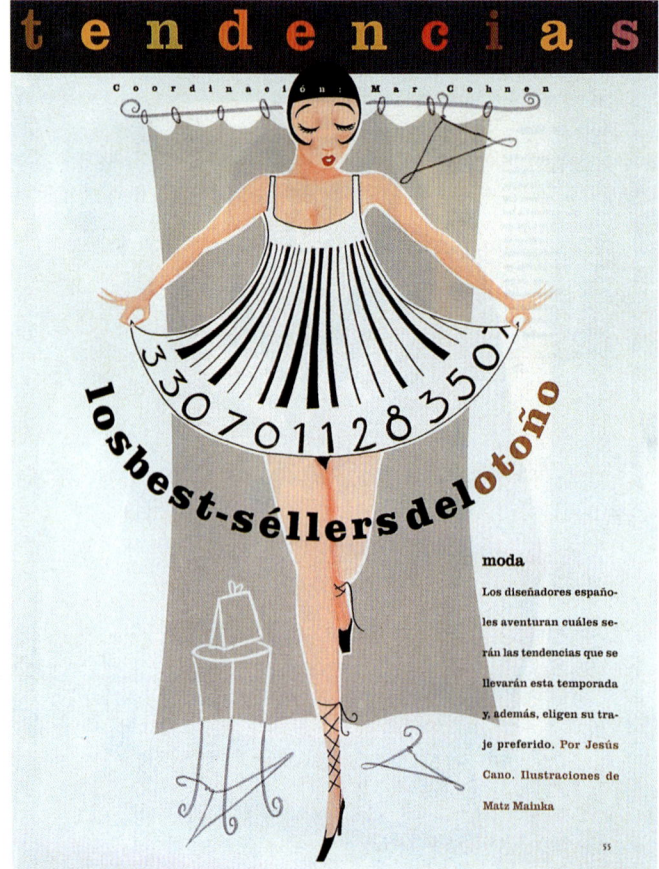
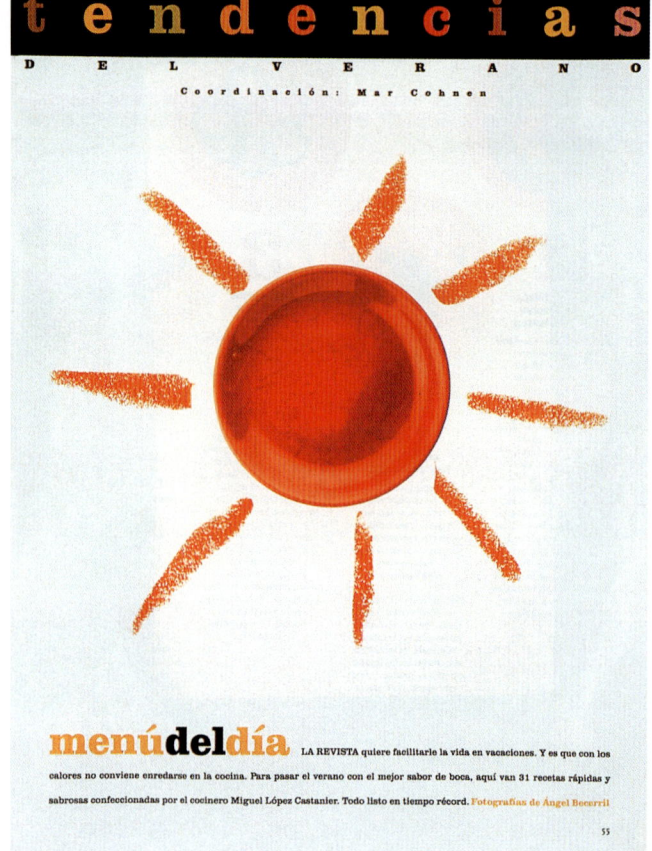

Silver
La Revista de El Mundo
Madrid, Spain
Amparo Redondo, Designer

Magazine ■ DESIGN PORTFOLIO

Silver
La Revista de El Mundo
Madrid, Spain
María González, Designer

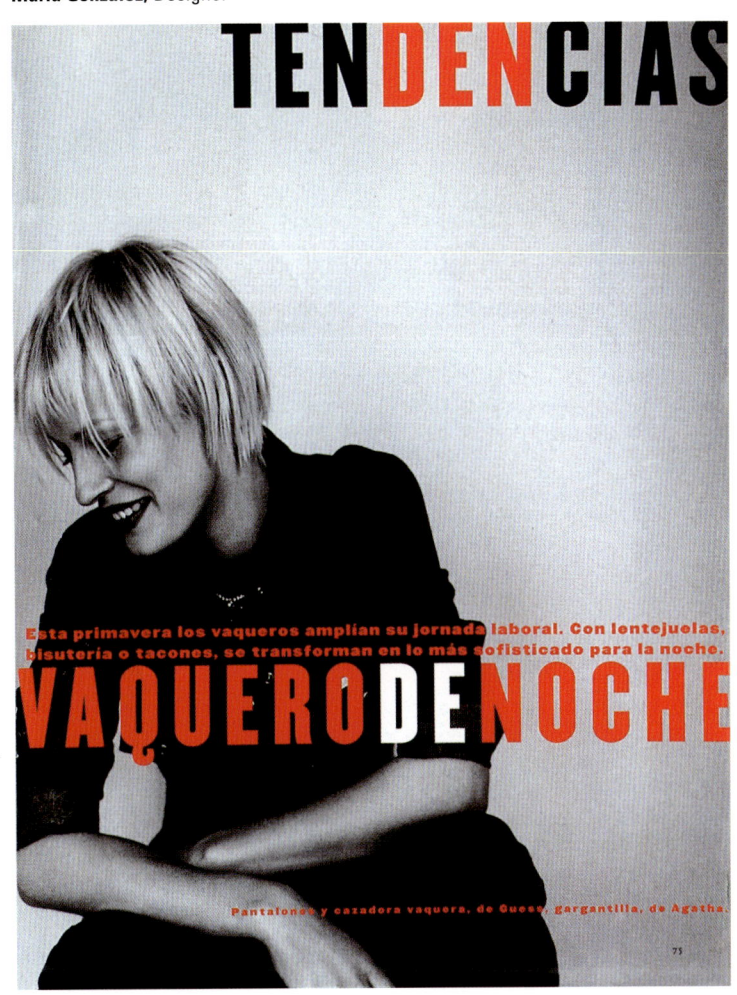
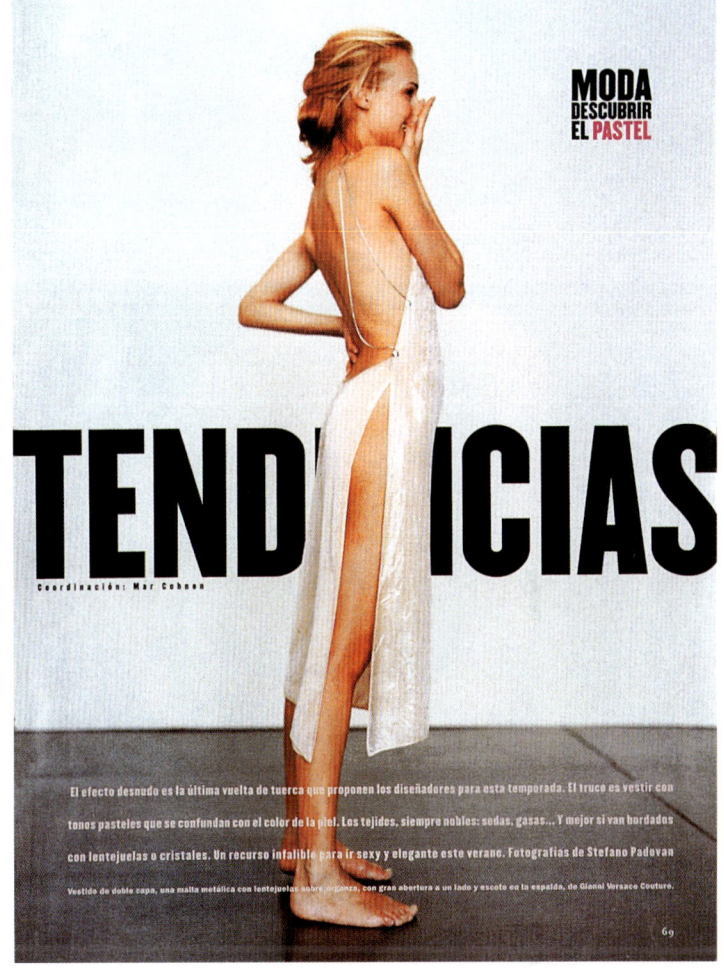

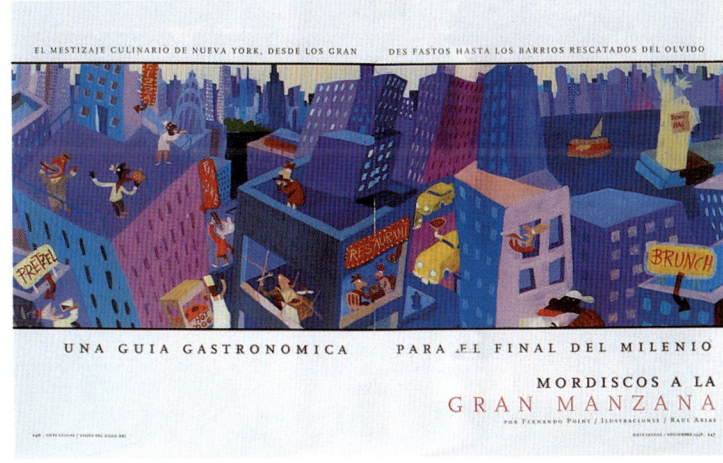

El Mundo Siete Leguas
Madrid, Spain
Carmelo Caderot, Art Director & Designer

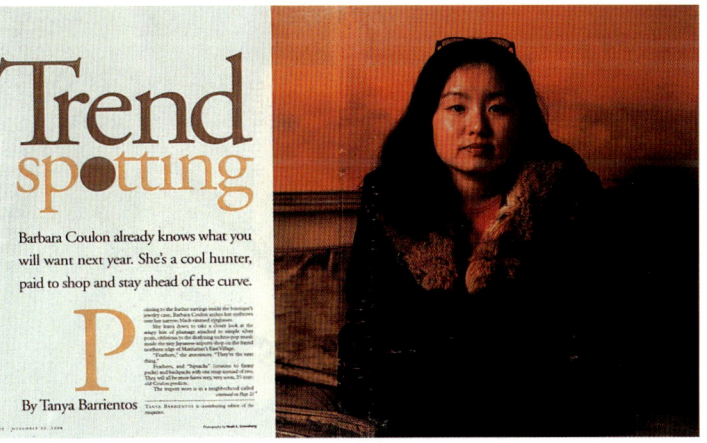

The Philadelphia Inquirer Magazine
Philadelphia, PA
Christine Dunleavy, Art Director

DESIGN PORTFOLIO ■ Magazine, Combination

La Revista de El Mundo
Madrid, Spain
Amparo Redondo, Designer

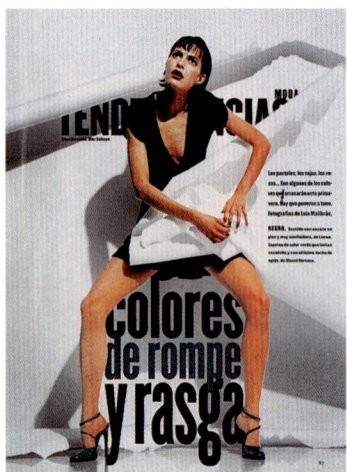

La Revista de El Mundo
Madrid, Spain
Rodrigo Sánchez, Art Director

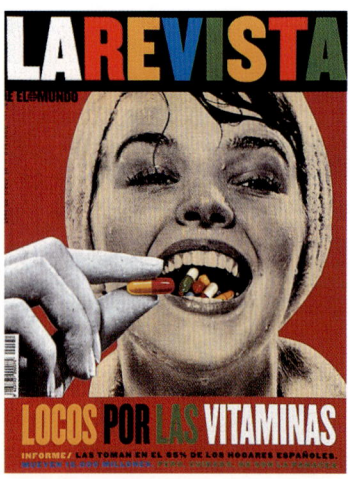

The Washington Post Magazine
Washington, DC
Kelly Doe, Art Director

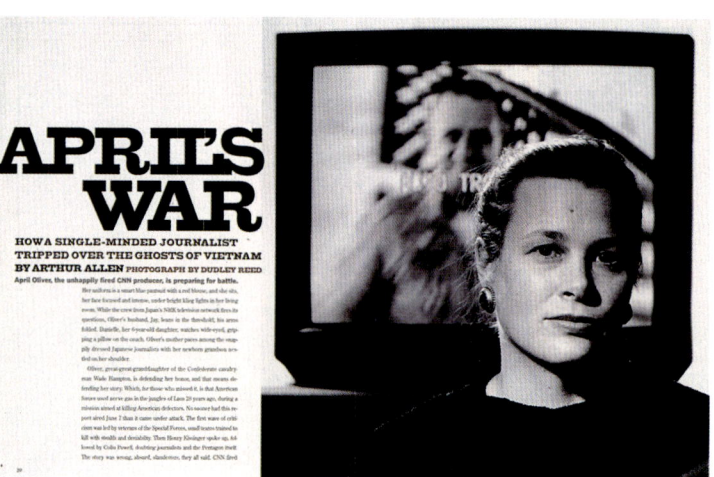

The Washington Post Magazine
Washington, DC
Kelly Doe, Art Director

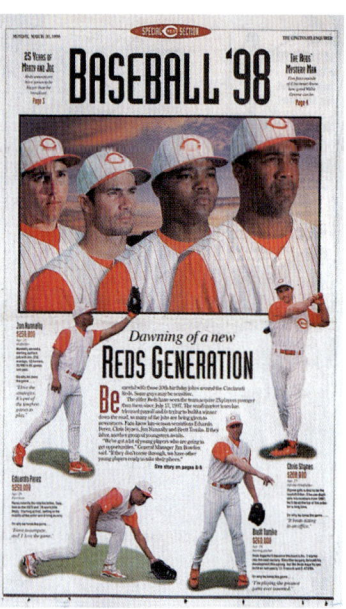

The Cincinnati Enquirer
Cincinnati, OH
Ron Huff, Designer

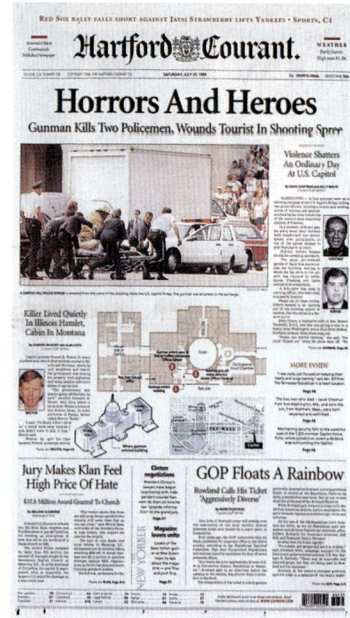

The Hartford Courant
Hartford, CT
Jim Kuykendall, Designer

198 ■ THE BEST OF NEWSPAPER DESIGN

Combination ■ DESIGN PORTFOLIO

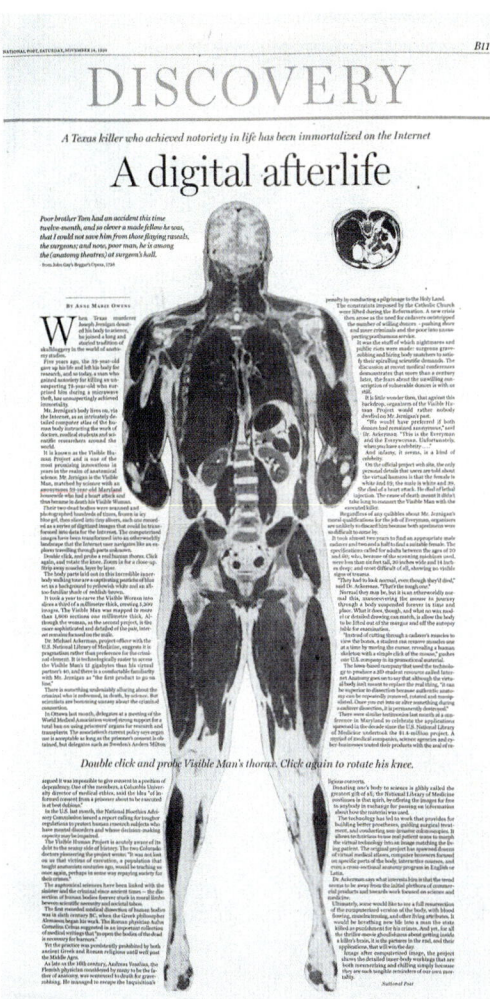
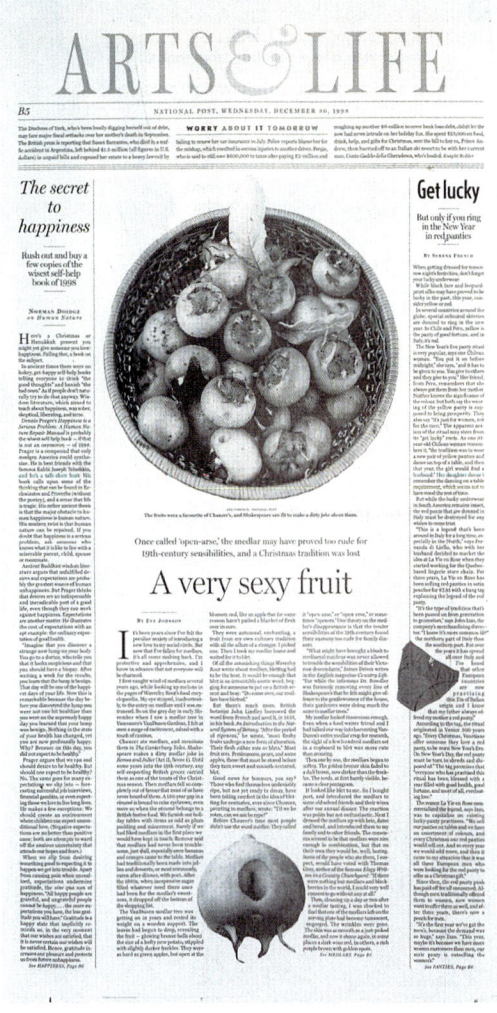

Silver
The National Post
Don Mills, Canada
Gayle Grin, Designer/Design Editor

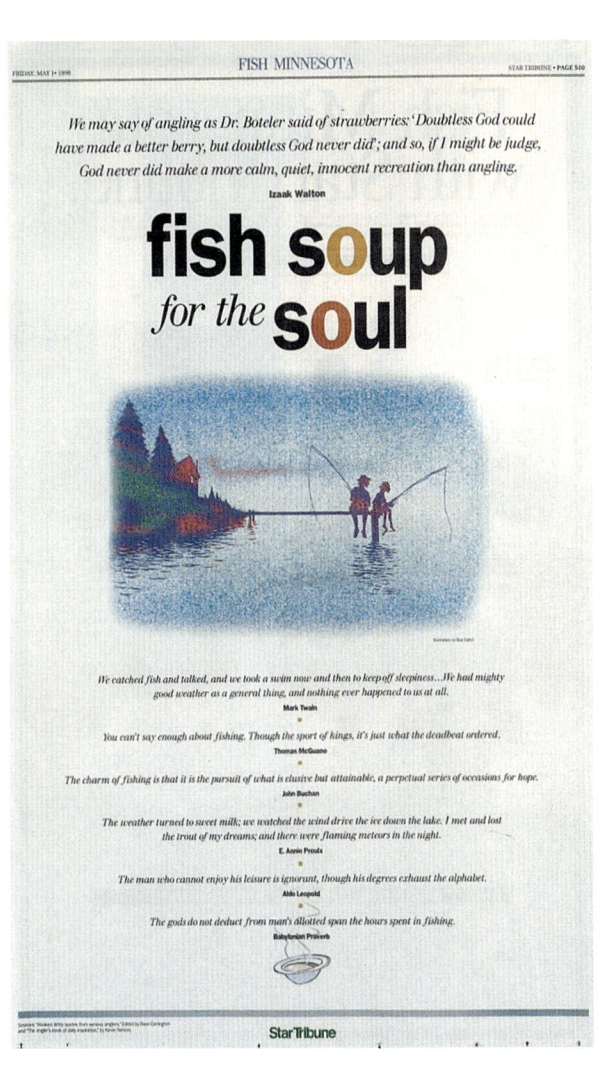
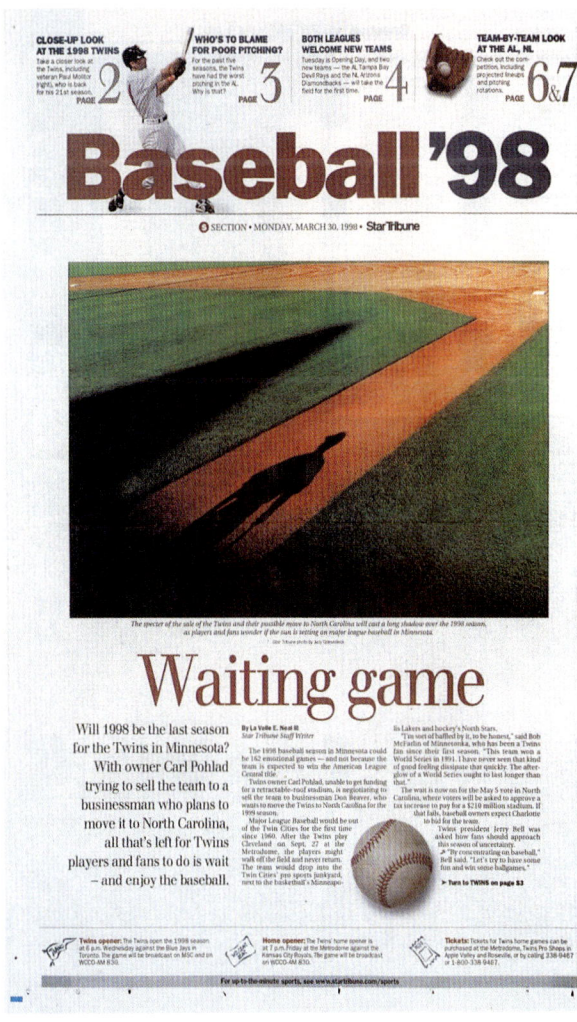

Silver
Star Tribune
Minneapolis, MN
Anders Ramberg, Design Director/Designer; **Dennis Anderson,** Sports Outdoors Team Leader; **Bob Dahm,** Illustrator
• also Silver for Inside News Page
• also an Award of Excellence for News Portfolio and Sports Page

DESIGN PORTFOLIO ◼ Combination

Le Soleil
Québec, Canada
Marc Duplain, Designer
• also Silver for Entertainment Page

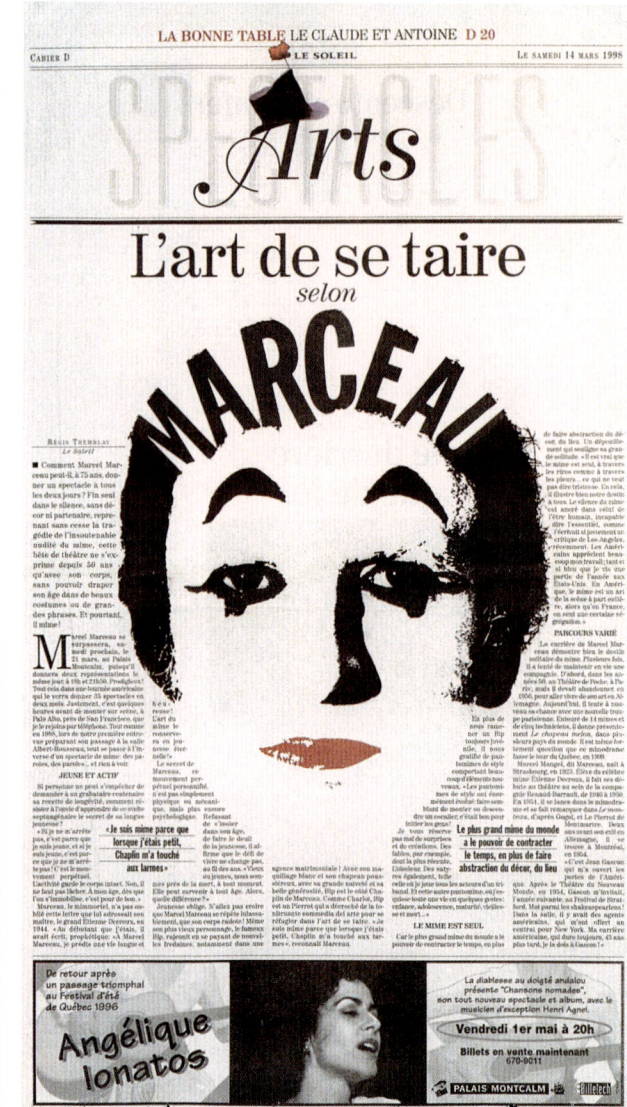

The Albuquerque Tribune
Albuquerque, NM
David Carrillo, News Editor

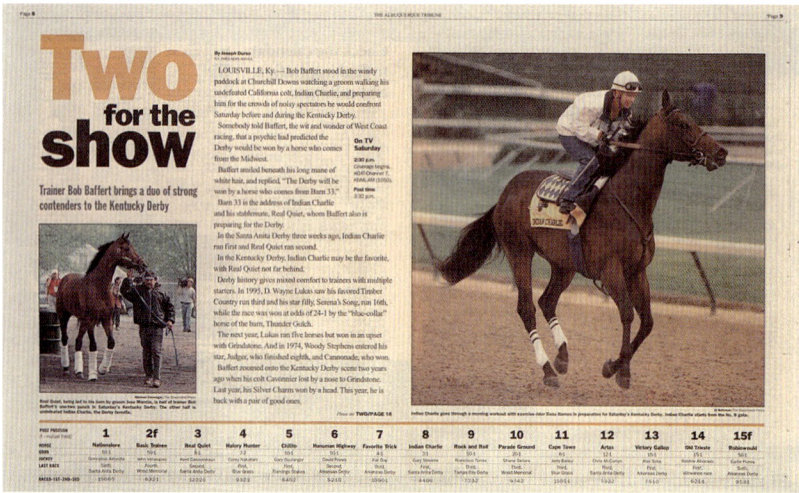

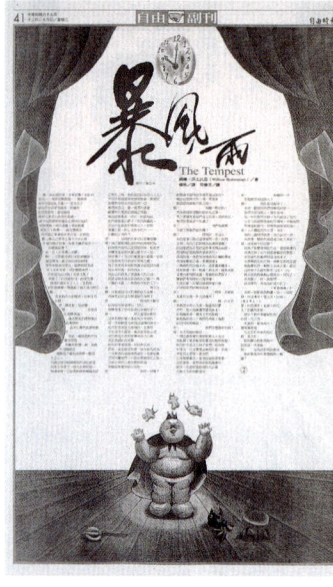

The Liberty Times
Taipei, R.O.C.
Tung Ku-Ying, Art Director & Designer

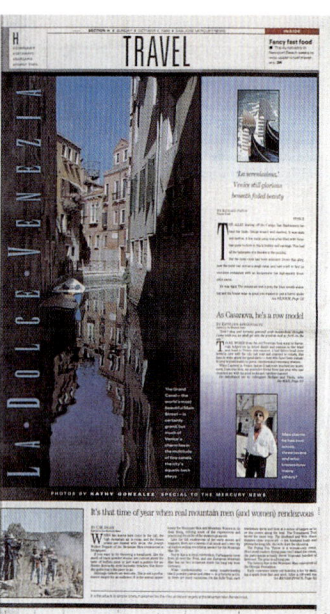

San Jose Mercury News
San Jose, CA
Rebecca Hall, Features Designer

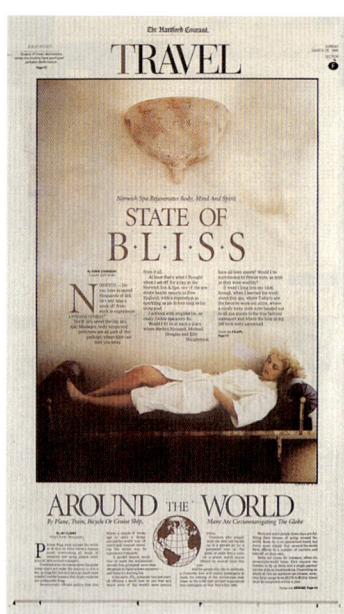

The Providence Journal
Providence, RI
Cecilia Prestamo, Editor/Page Designer

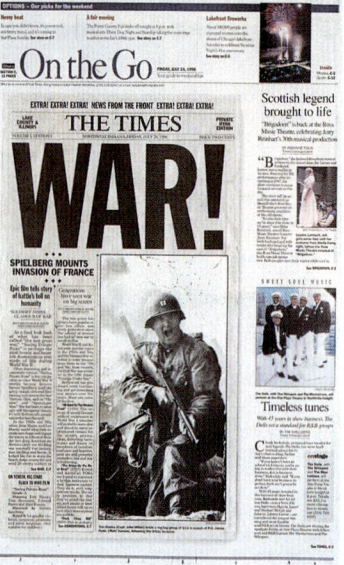

The Times
Munster, IN
Craig Newman, Design Team Leader & Designer

ILLUSTRATION

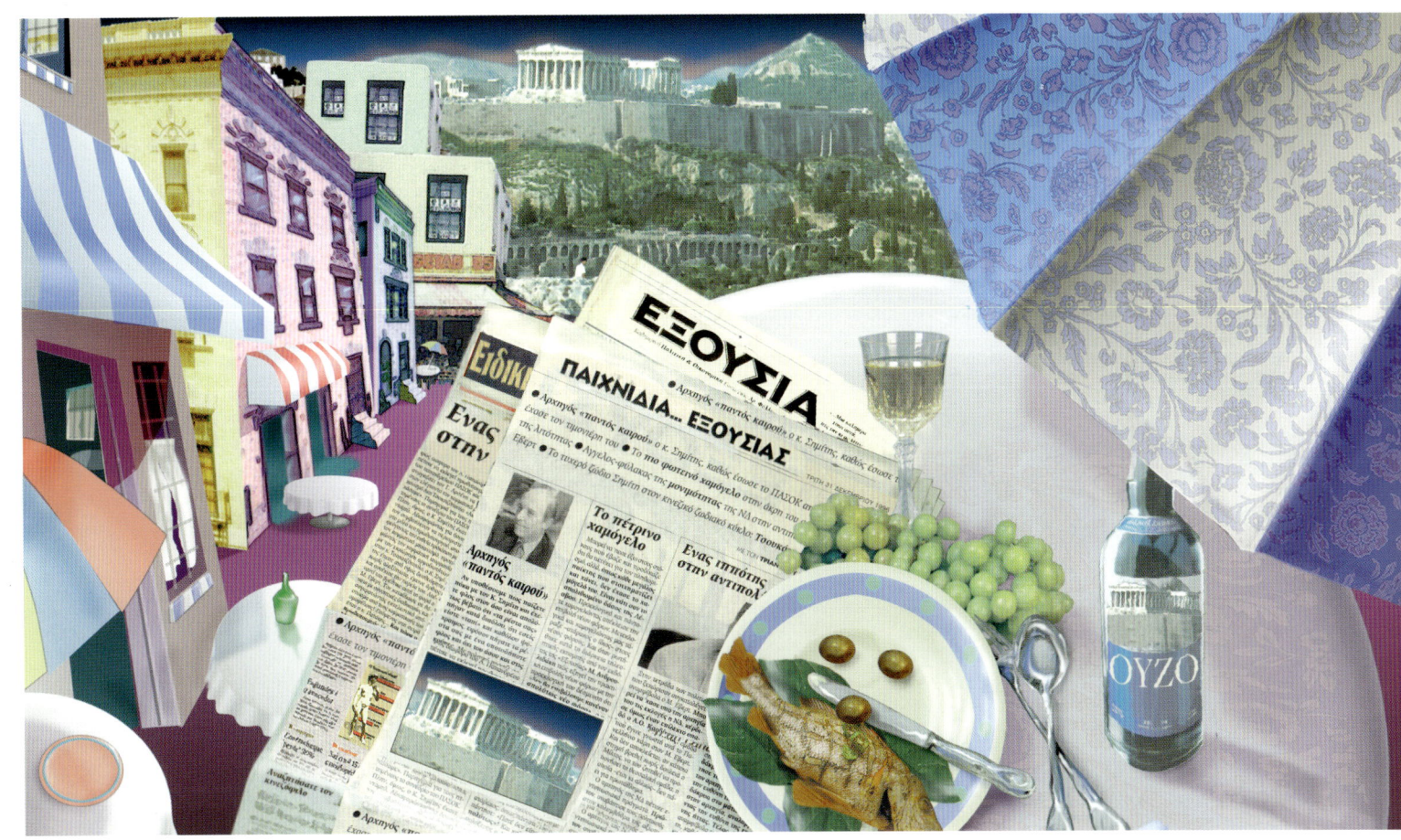

CHAPTER SEVEN

BLACK & WHITE AND/OR ONE COLOR

TWO OR MORE COLORS

PORTFOLIO BY ONE ARTIST

PORTFOLIO BY MORE THAN ONE ARTIST

ILLUSTRATION ■ Black or Black and One Color

Gold
El Mundo Del Siglo XXI
Madrid, Spain
Ricardo Martinez, Illustrator

The artist is a master at illustrating concepts in a simple manner. An intriguing concept, viewing the world as a prison for Pinochet, is great.

El artista es un maestro en ilustrar conceptos de un modo sencillo. Un concepto fascinante, ver el mundo como una prisión para Pinochet, es muy eficaz

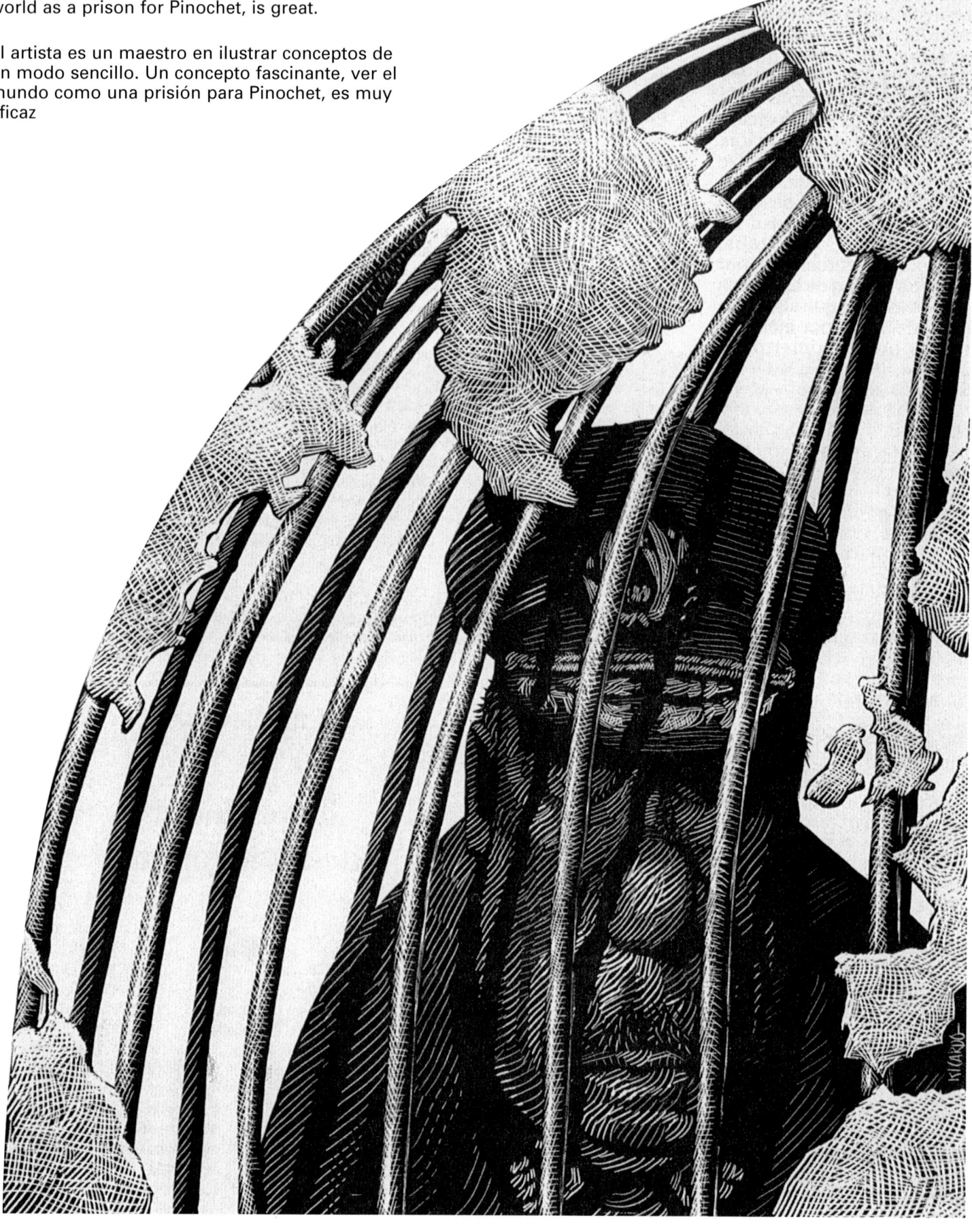

202 ■ THE BEST OF NEWSPAPER DESIGN

Silver
El Mundo Del Siglo XXI
Madrid, Spain
Ricardo Martinez, Illustrator

Silver
El Mundo Del Siglo XXI
Madrid, Spain
Ricardo Martinez, Illustrator

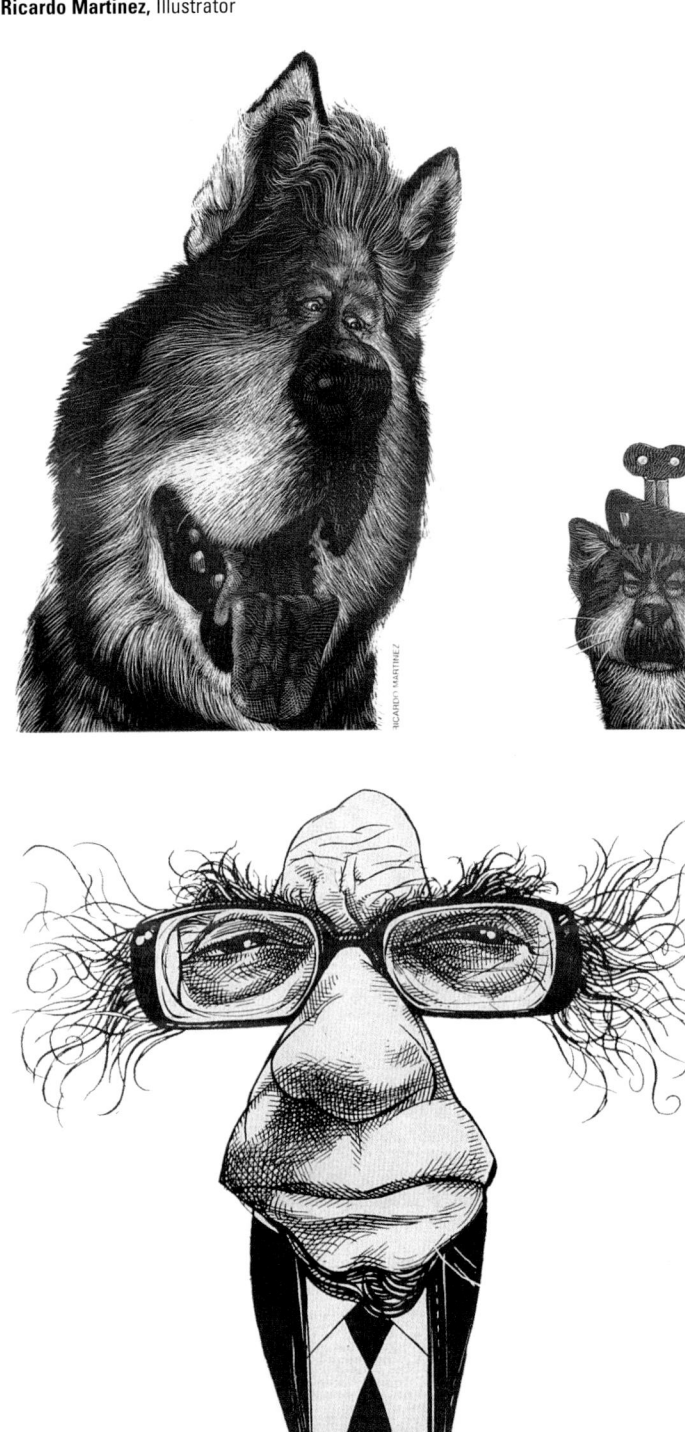
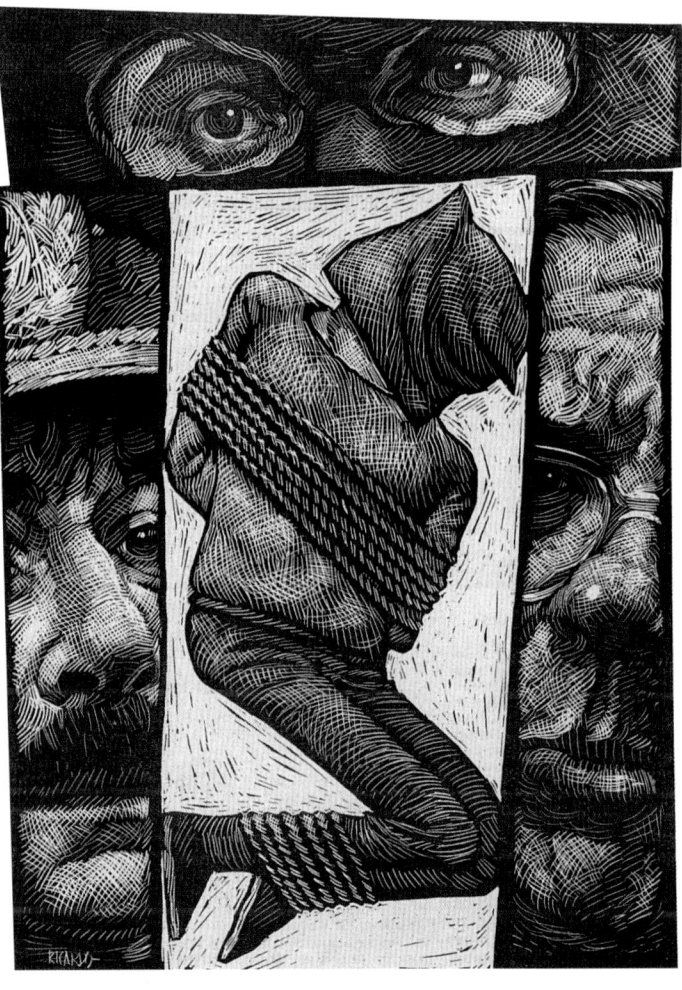

Silver
El Mundo Del Siglo XXI
Madrid, Spain
Ulises Culebro, Illustration Editor

ILLUSTRATION ■ Black or Black and One Color

Silver
Reforma
México City, México

Fabricio Vanden Broeck, Illustrator; **Guilermo Larios,** Section Designer; **Réne Delgado,** Editor; **Emilio Deheza,** Art Director; **Eduardo Danilo,** Design Consultant; **Ricardo del Castillo,** Graphic Editor

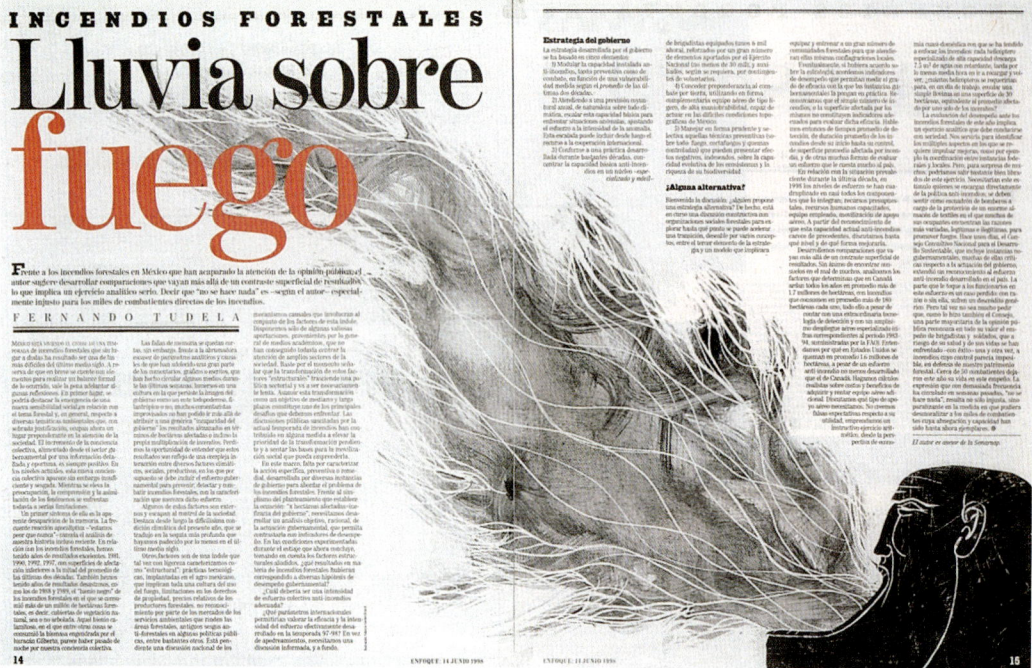

Silver
Reforma
México City, México

Fabricio Vanden Broeck, Illustrator; **Guilermo Larios,** Section Designer; **Réne Delgado,** Editor; **Emilio Deheza,** Art Director; **Eduardo Danilo,** Design Consultant; **Ricardo del Castillo,** Graphic Editor

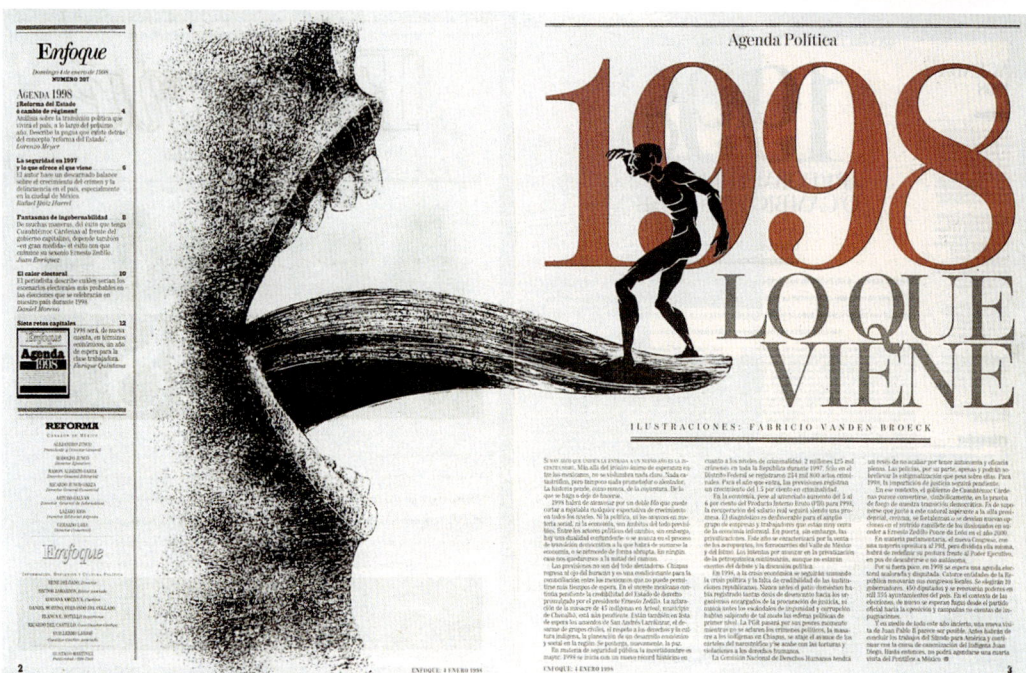

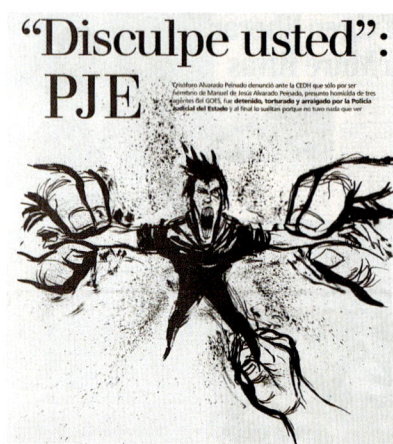

El Imparcial
Hermosillo, México

Ariel Medel, Illustrator; **José de Jesús Arce,** Designer; **Sergio Serrano,** Art Director

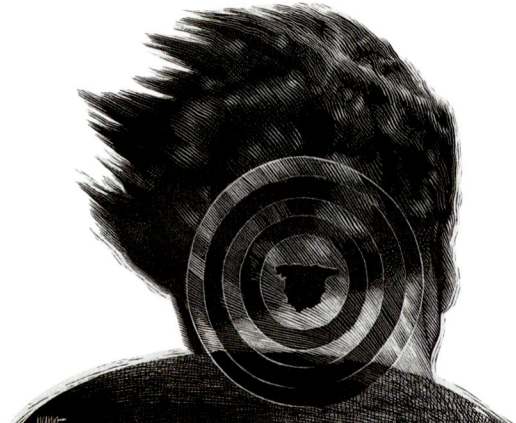

El Mundo Del Siglo XXI
Madrid, Spain

Ricardo Martinez, Illustrator

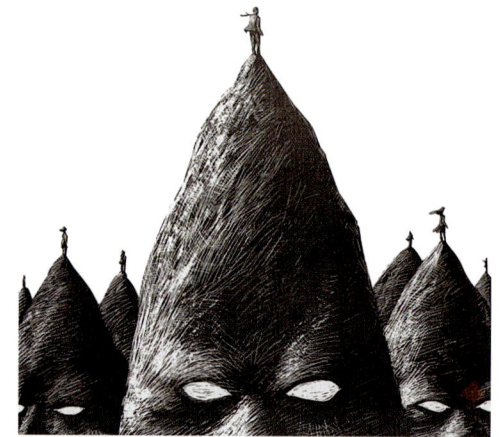

El Mundo Del Siglo XXI
Madrid, Spain

Ricardo Martinez, Illustrator

Black or Black and One Color — ILLUSTRATION

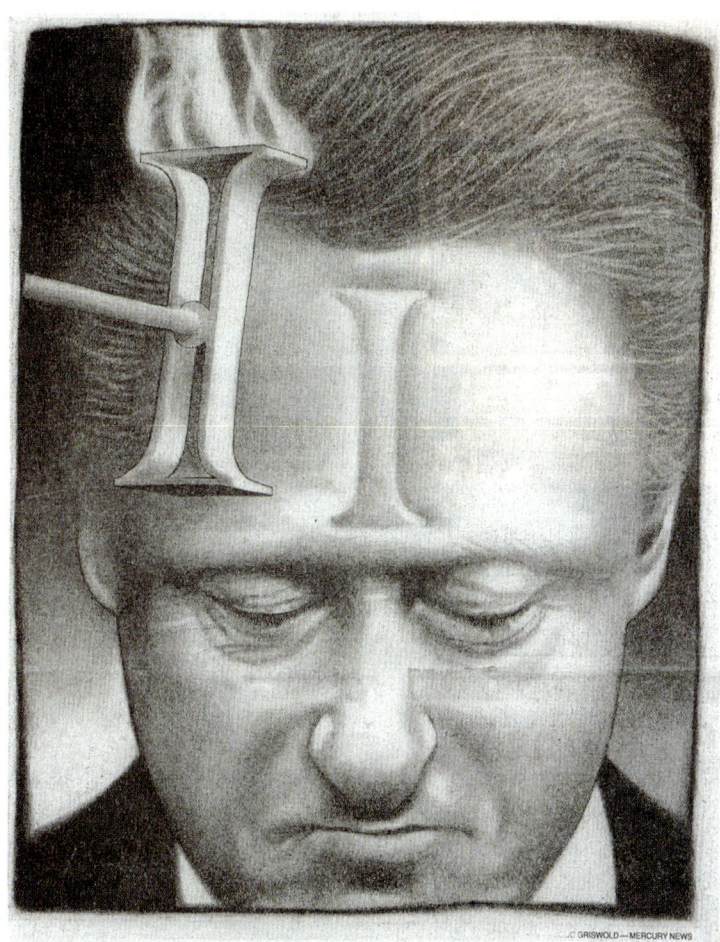

Silver
San Jose Mercury News
San Jose, CA
Doug Griswold, Artist; **Minal Hajratwala,** Perspective Editor; **Kevin Boyd,** Art Director

El Mundo Del Siglo XXI
Madrid, Spain
Ricardo Martinez, Illustrator

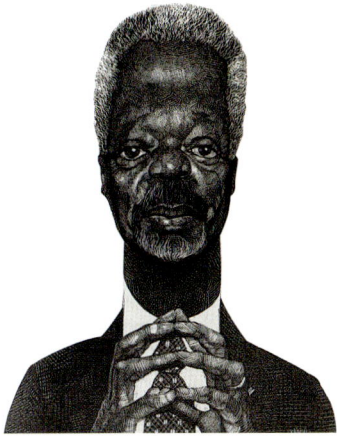

El Mundo Del Siglo XXI
Madrid, Spain
Ulises Culebro, Illustration Editor

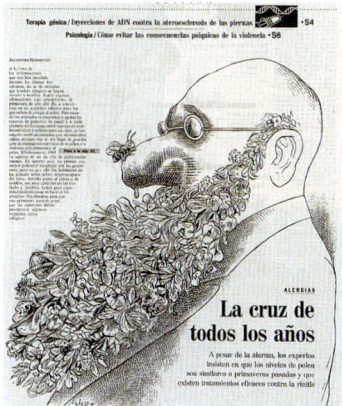

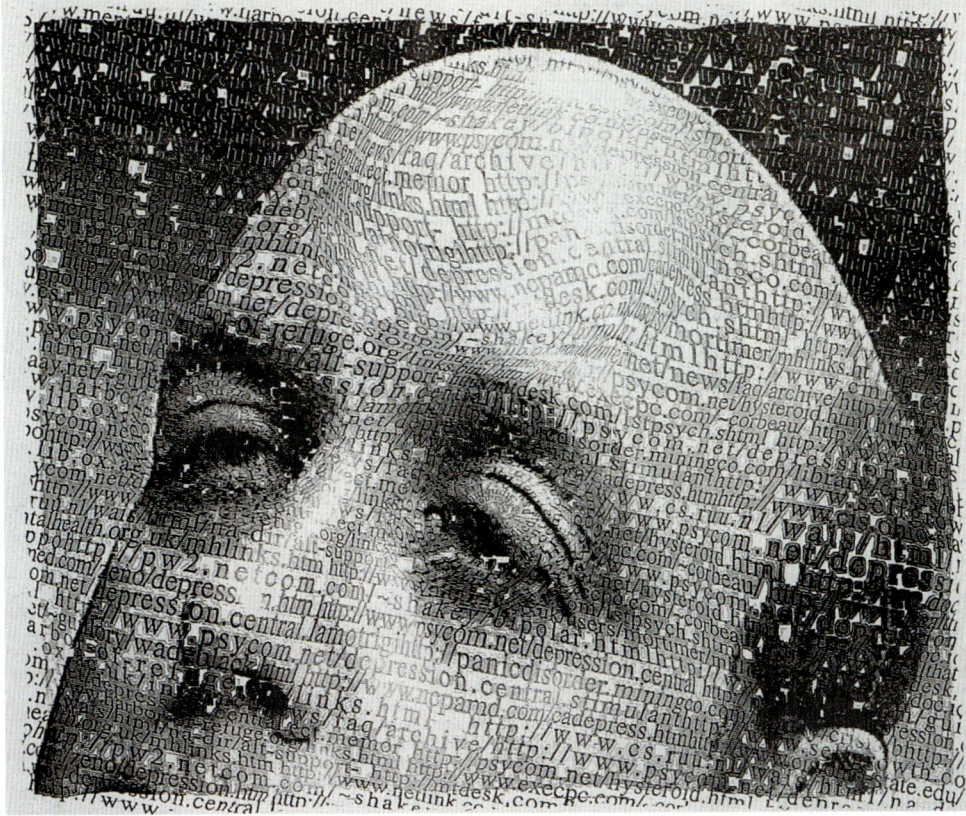

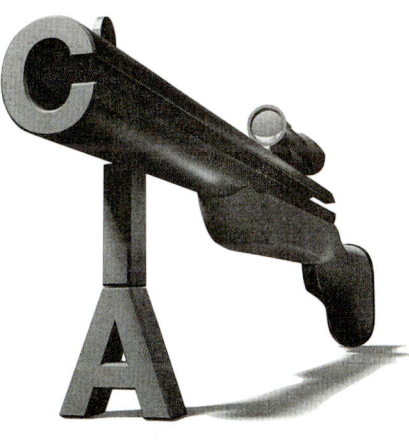

The New York Times
New York, NY
Mirko Ilic, Illustrator; **Nicholas Blechman,** Art Director

Silver
The Washington Post
Washington, DC
Patterson Clark, Artist

TWENTIETH EDITION ■ 205

ILLUSTRATION ▪ Black or Black and One Color, Three or More Colors

Silver
The Globe and Mail
Toronto, Canada
Tony Jenkins, Illustrator;
Deborah Pang, Art Director

Svenska Dagbladet
Stockholm, Sweden
Riber Hansson, Artist

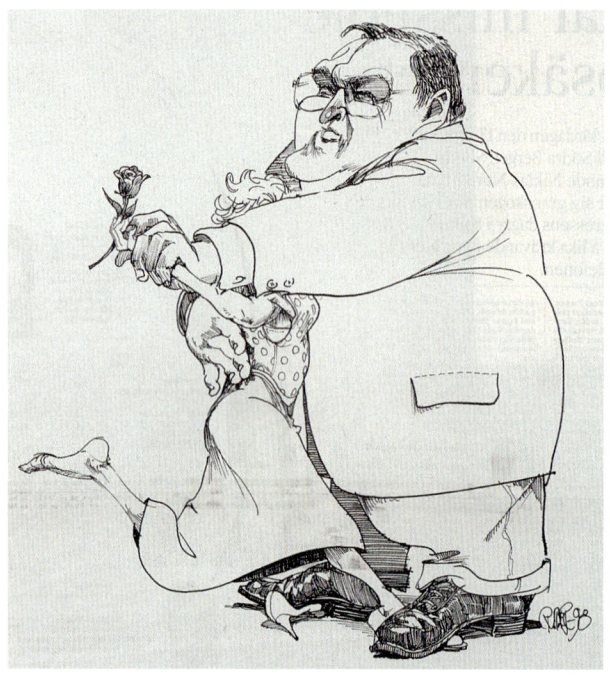

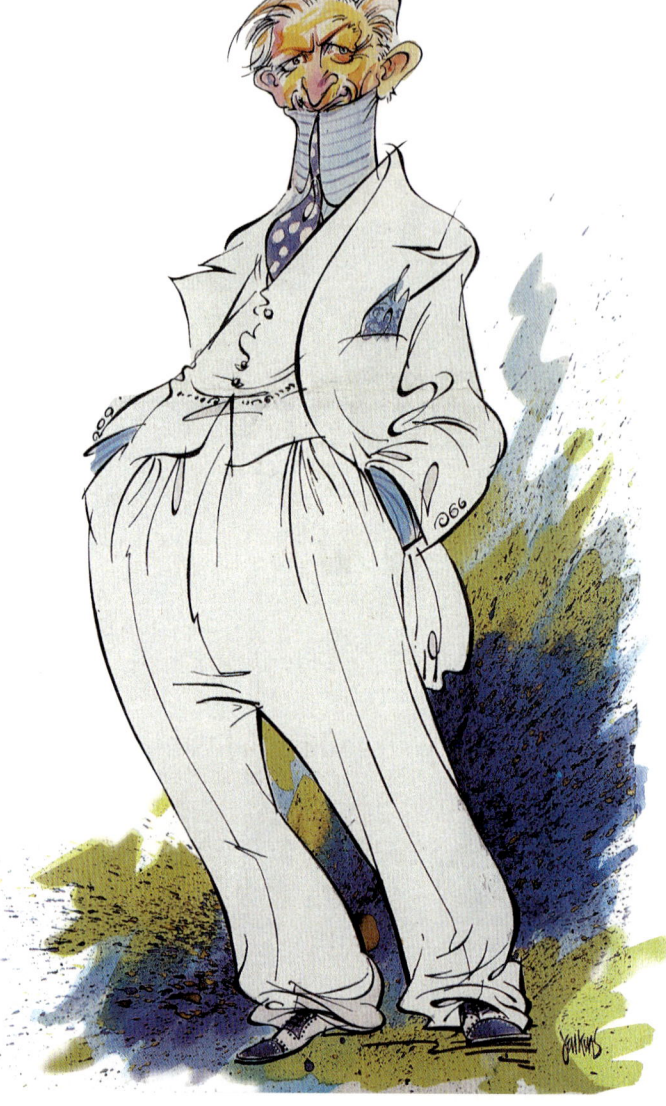

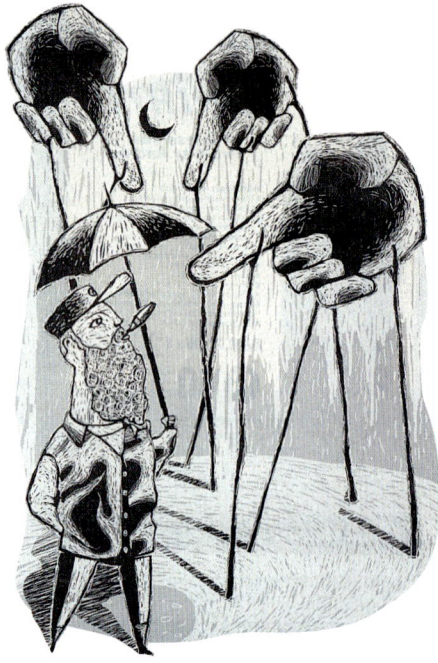

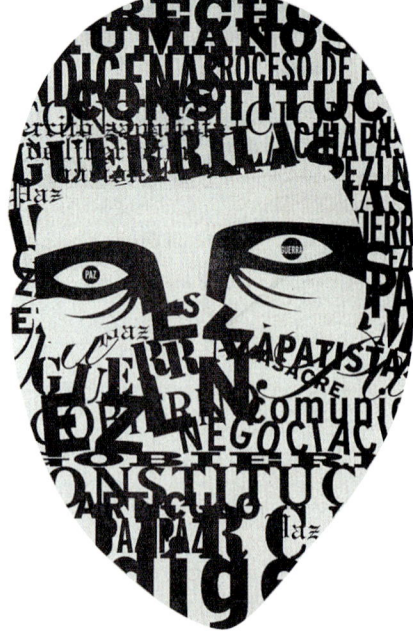

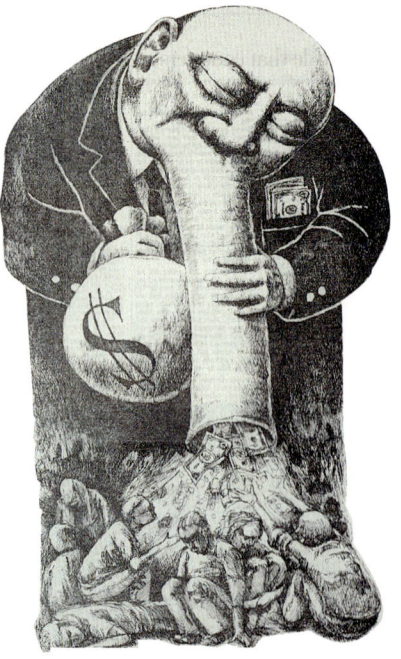

El Norte
Monterrey, México
Isaac de Coss, Illustrator; **Verónica Alvarez,** Designer; **Arturo Rangel,** Design Editor; **Alexandro Medrano,** Design Manager Editor; **Raúl Braulio Martínez,** Art Director; **Martín Pérez Martínez,** Editor/Director; **Ramón Alberto Garza,** General Editor Director

El Norte
Monterrey, México
Arturo Rangel, Design Editor & Illustrator; **Martin Alvarado,** Designer; **Alexandro Medrano,** Design Manager Editor; **Ramón Alberto Garza,** General Editor Director; **Raúl Braulio Martínez,** Art Director; **Martín Pérez Martínez,** Editor/Director

Pittsburgh Post-Gazette
Pittsburgh, PA
Daniel Marsula, Illustrator

206 ▪ THE BEST OF NEWSPAPER DESIGN

Three or More Colors ■ ILLUSTRATION

Silver
O Globo
Rio de Janeiro, Brasil
Lula, Illustrator

Silver
El Mundo Metropoli
Madrid, Spain
Jose Belmonte, Illustrator
• also an Award of Excellence for Magazine Cover

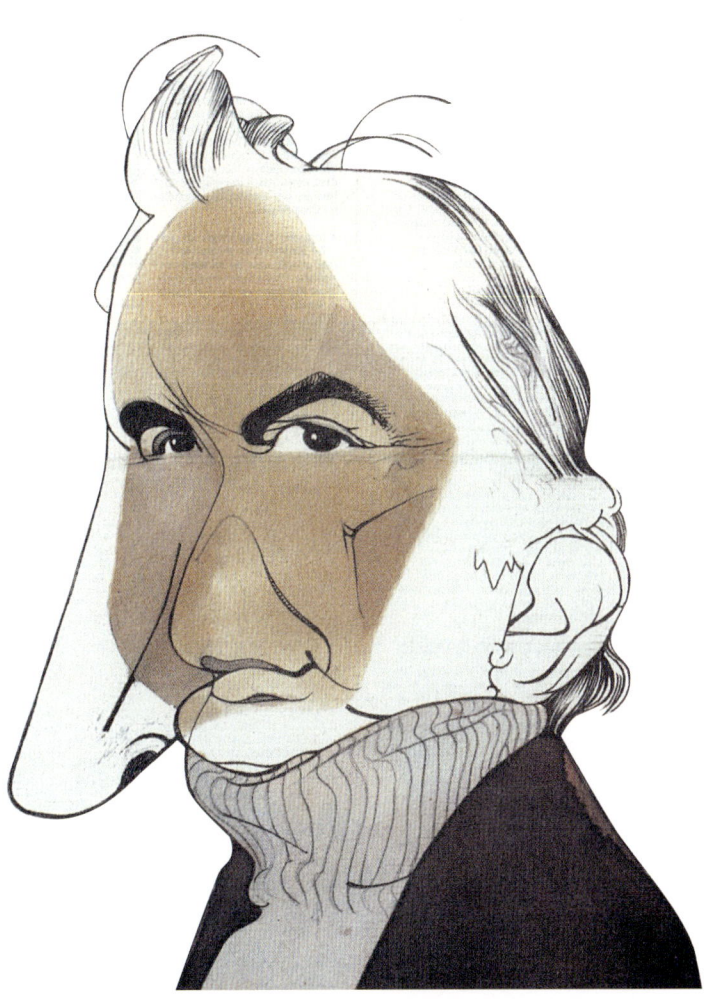

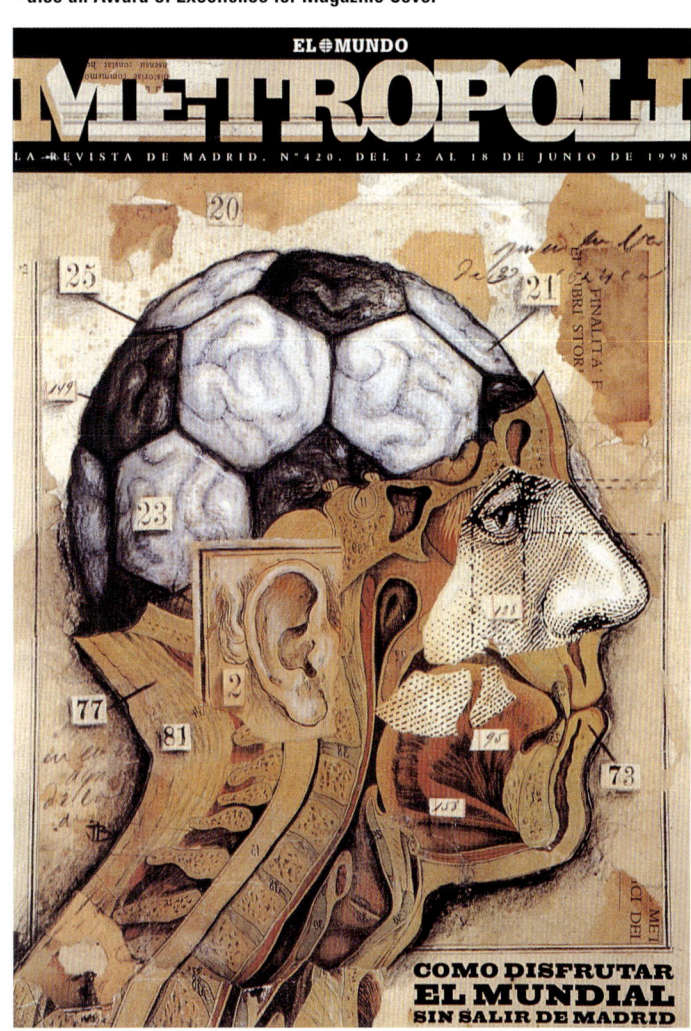

Silver
El Mundo Del Siglo XXI
Madrid, Spain
Raul Arias, Illustrator

TWENTIETH EDITION ■ 207

ILLUSTRATION ■ Three or More Colors

Silver
The National Post
Don Mills, Canada
James O'Donall, Illustrator; **Karen Simpson,** Design Consultant; **Fredericke Gauss,** Designer; **Kate Fillion,** Editor

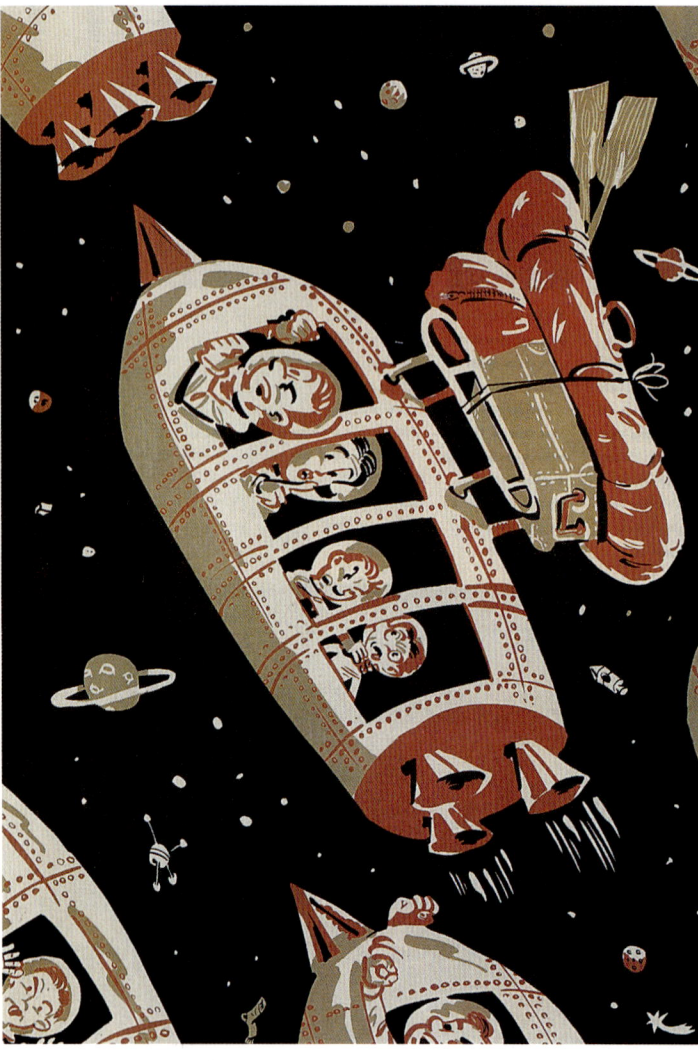

Silver
The New York Times
New York, NY
Deborah Barret, Illustrator; **Steven Heller,** Art Director

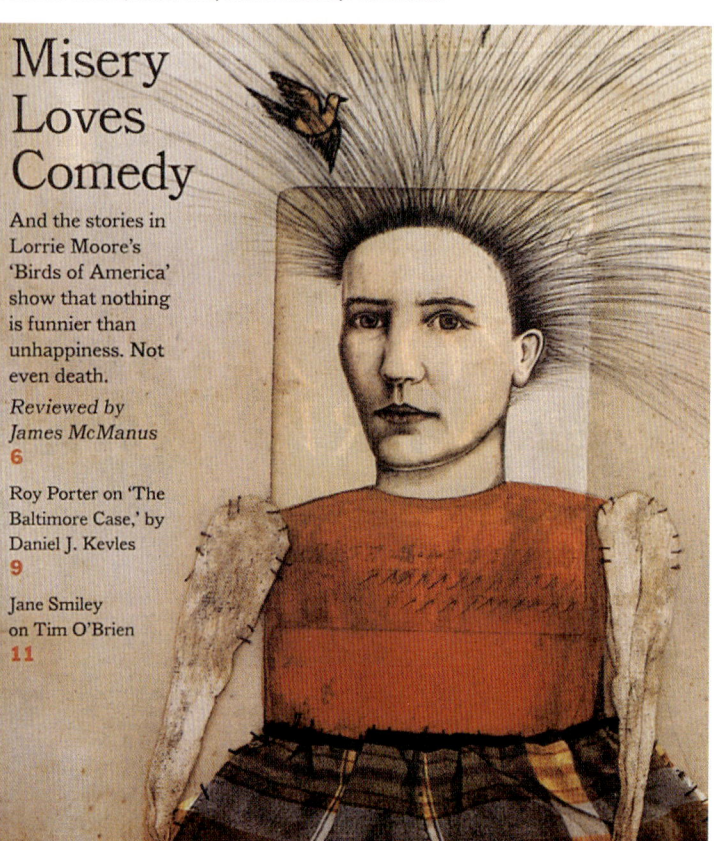

Silver
The New York Times Magazine
New York, NY
Philip Burke, Illustrator; **Janet Froelich,** Art Director; **Claudia Brandenburg,** Designer

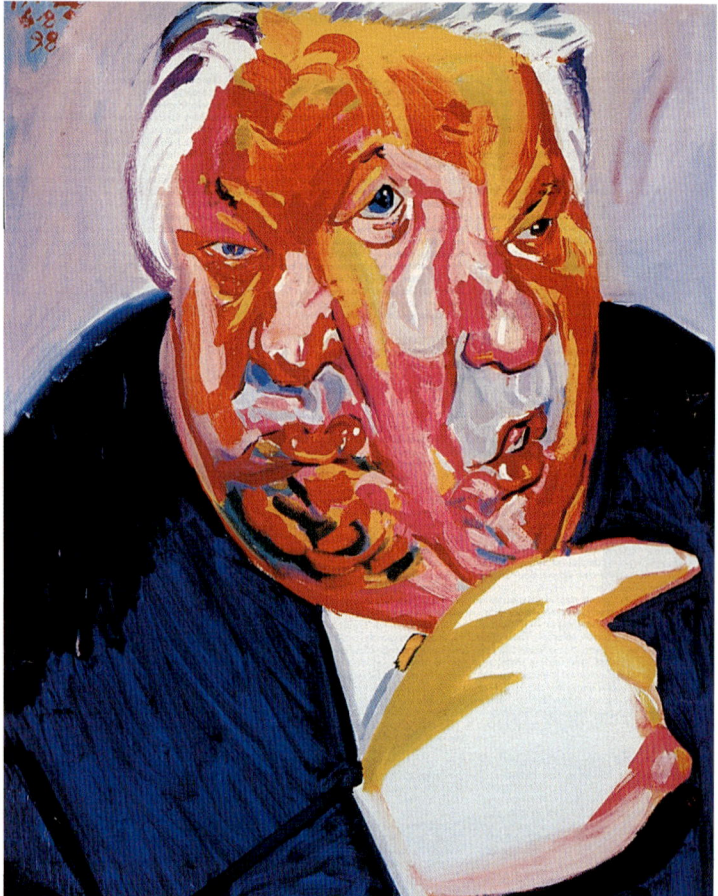

Three or More Colors ■ ILLUSTRATION

Silver
La Revista de El Mundo
Madrid, Spain
Ana Juan, Illustrator

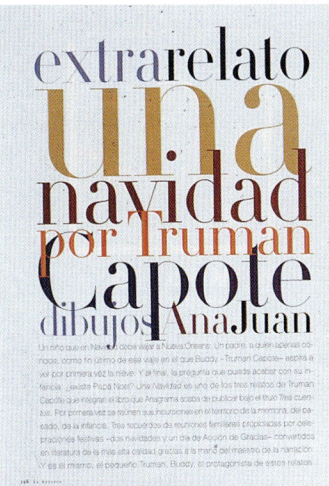
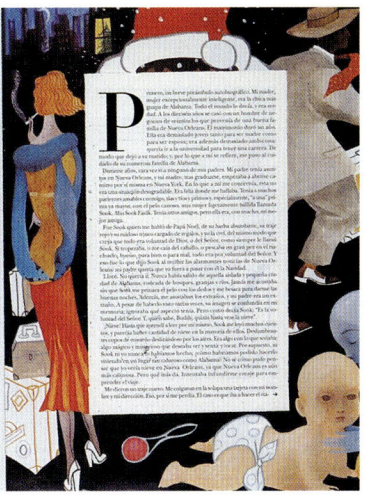
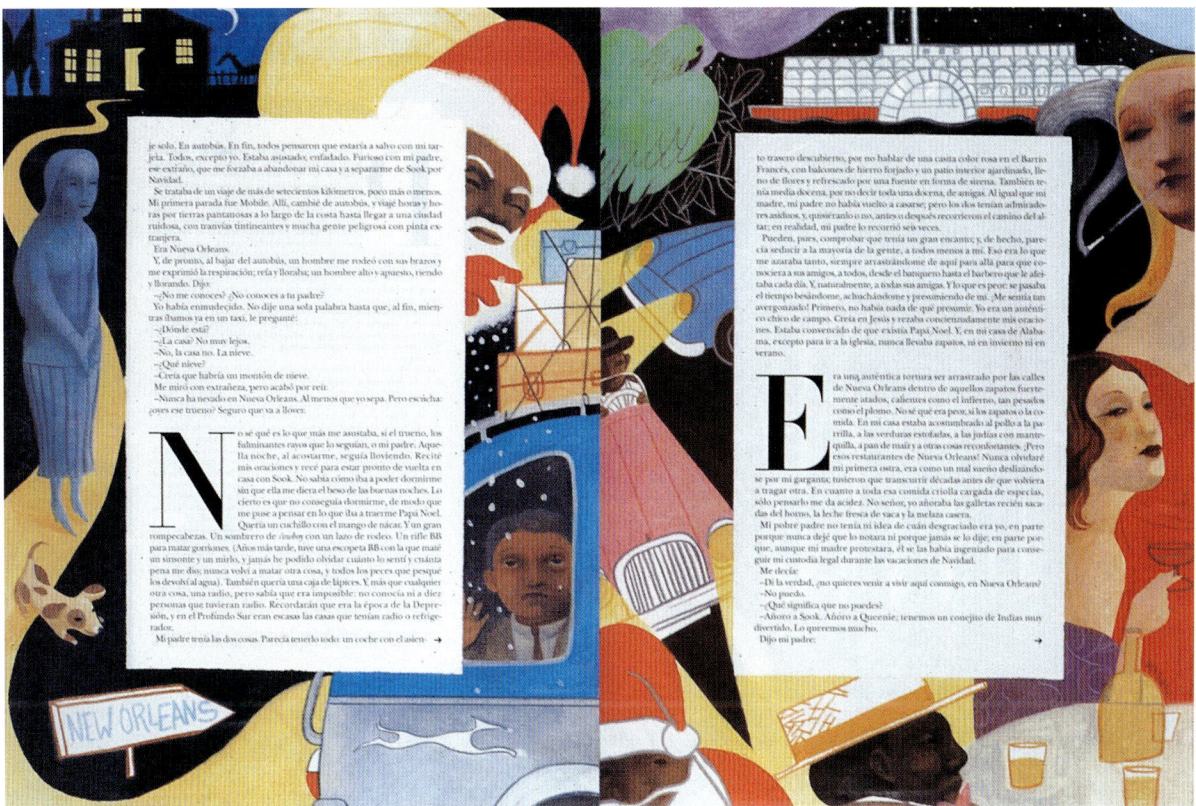

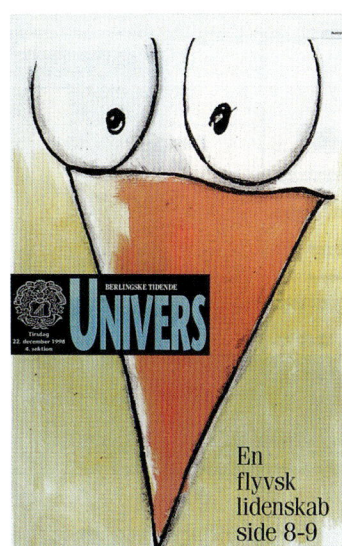

Berlingske Tidende
Copenhagen, Denmark
Lise Roennebaek, Illustrator

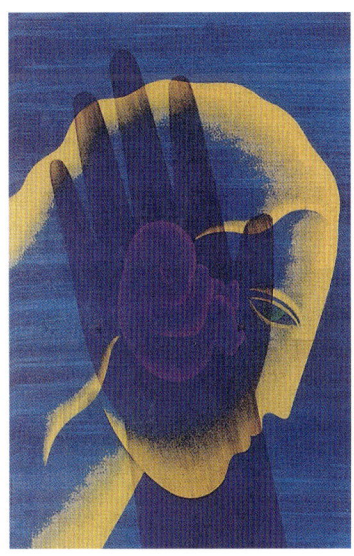

The Boston Globe
Boston, MA
Sandra Dionisi, Illustrator/Photographer; Susan Levin, Art Director & Designer; David Mehegan, Editor; Julie Dalton, Copy Editor

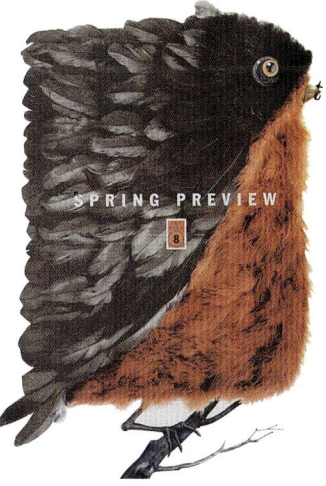

The Chicago Tribune
Chicago, IL
Jack Graham, Illustrator; Stephen Ravenscraft, Designer; Tim Bannon, Editor

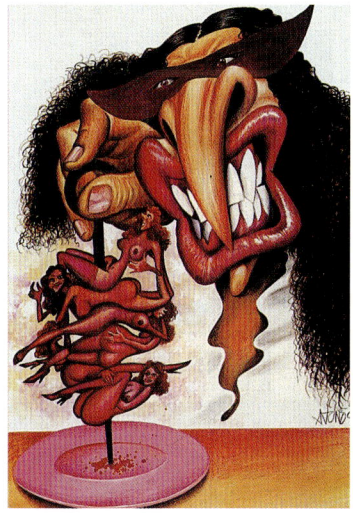

Expresso
Lisbon, Portugal
António Antunes, Illustrator

ILLUSTRATION ■ Three or More Colors

Arkansas Democrat-Gazette
Little Rock, AR
Al Cameron, Illustrator

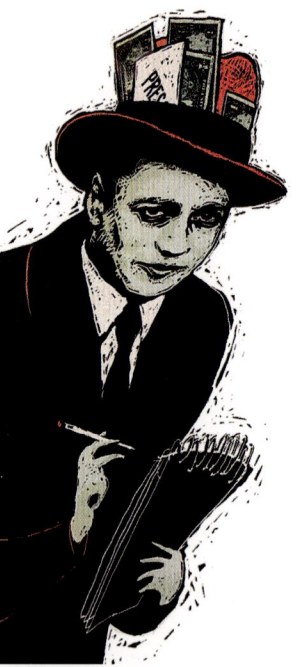

Cape Cod Times
Hyannis, MA
Patricia Cousins, Page Designer

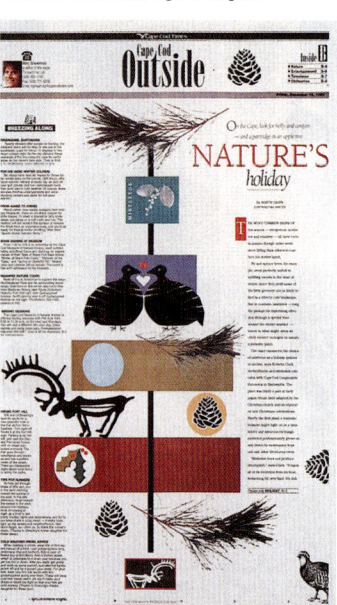

La Gaceta
San Miguel de Tucuman, Argentina
Sebastian Rosso, Illustrator & Designer

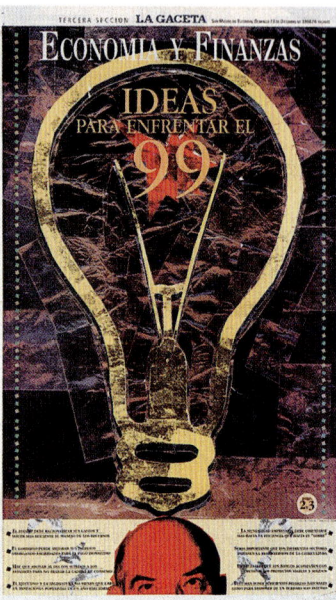

Arkansas Democrat-Gazette
Little Rock, AR
Al Cameron, Illustrator

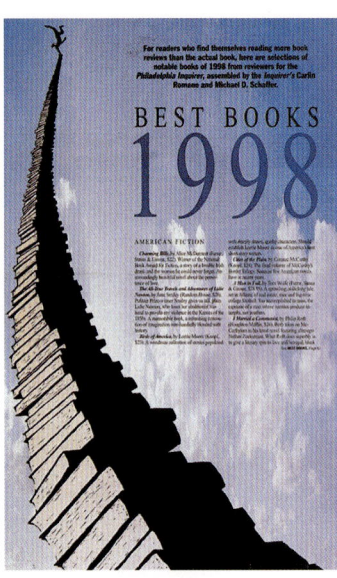

The National Post
Don Mills, Canada
Alain Pilon, Illustrator; **Karen Simpson,** Design Consultant; **Kate Fillion,** Editor; **Fredericke Gauss,** Designer

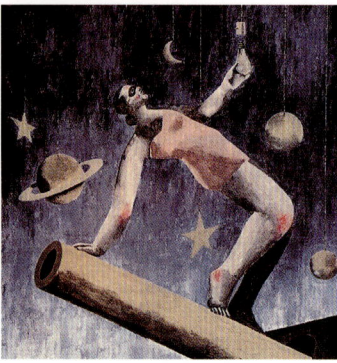

The New York Times
New York, NY
Michael Schwab Studio, Illustrator; **Anne Leigh,** Art Director

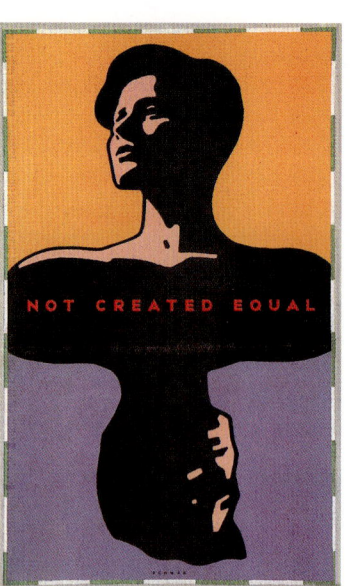

The News Tribune
Tacoma, WA
Reggie Myers, Illustrator

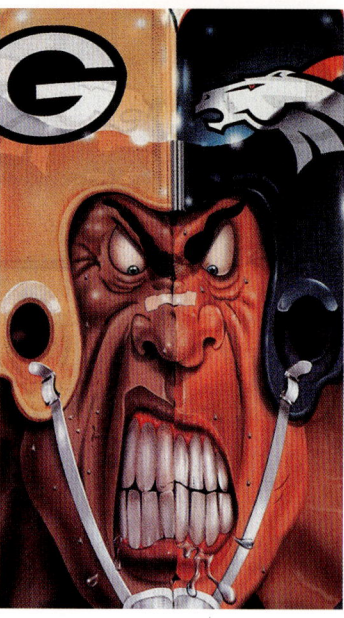

O Globo
Rio de Janeiro, Brasil
Cavalcante, Illustrator

Three or More Colors ■ ILLUSTRATION

The National Post
Don Mills, Canada
Depuy-Barbanian, Illustrator; **Karen Simpson,** Design Consultant; **Fredericke Gauss,** Designer; **Kate Fillion,** Editor

The New York Times
New York, NY
C.F. Payne, Illustrator; **Steven Heller,** Art Director

The New York Times
New York, NY
Cathie Bleck, Illustrator; **Ken McFarlin,** Art Director

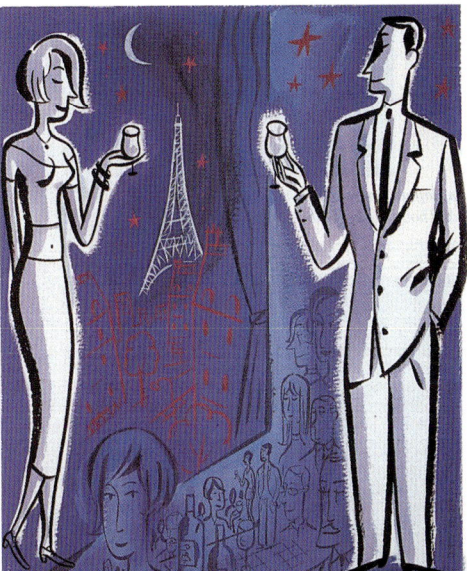
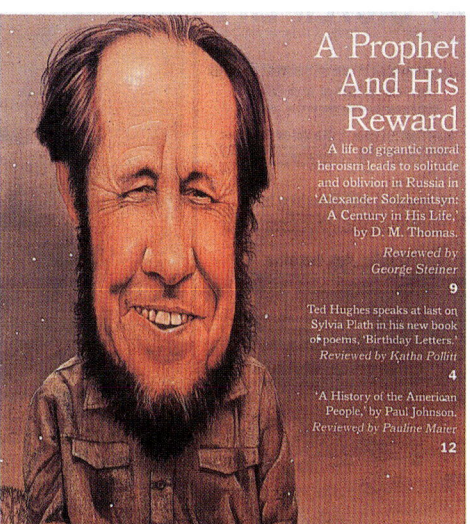
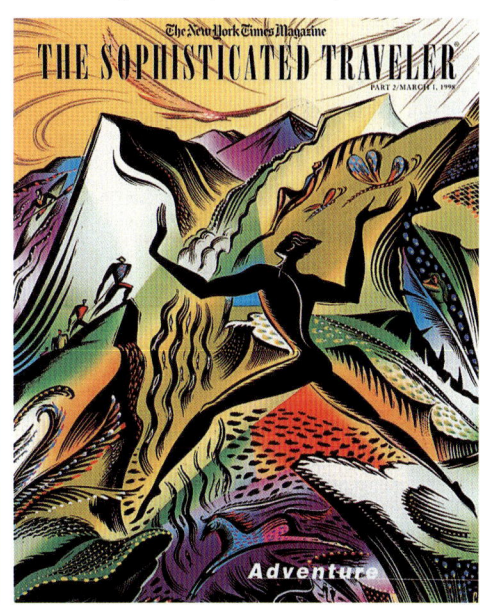

The Globe and Mail/Report on Business
Toronto, Canada
Steve Adams, Illustrator; **Marcello Biagioni,** Senior Art Director; **Fernanda Pisani,** Associate Art Director; **Dominic Macri,** Senior Designer; **Patricia Best,** Editor; **Jo-Anne Martin Grier,** Designer

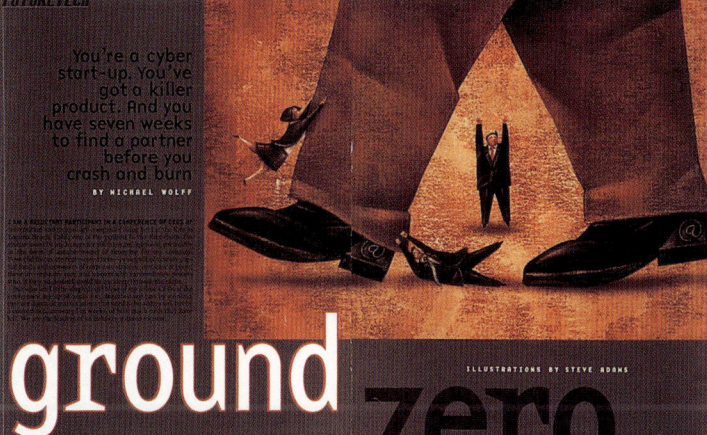

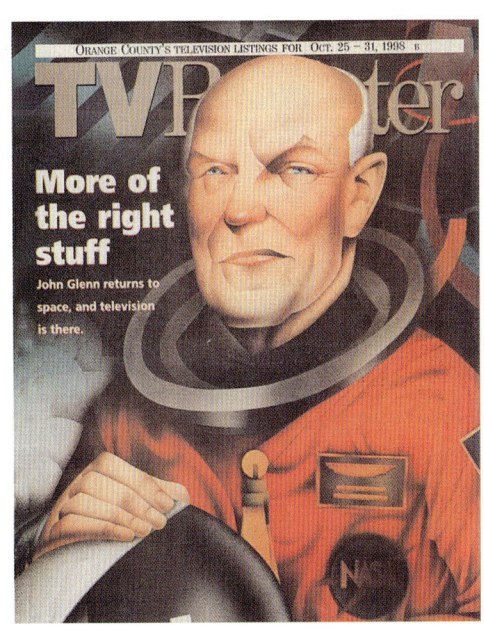

The Orange County Register
Santa Ana, CA
Amy Ning, Artist; **Jennifer Madrid,** Designer; **Kris Viesselman Onuigbo,** Art Director

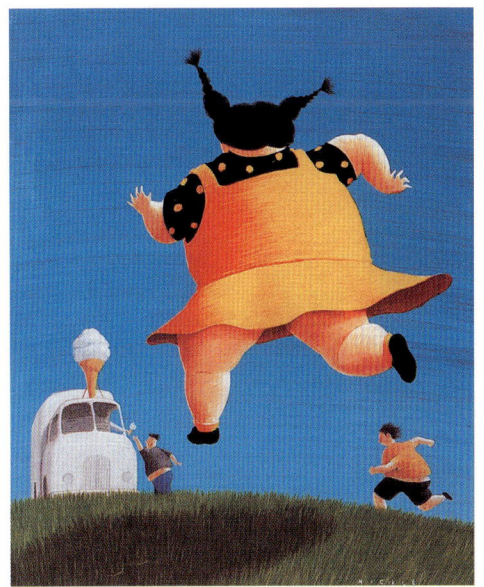

The Philadelphia Inquirer Magazine
Philadelphia, PA
John Nickle, Illustrator; **Christine Dunleavy,** Art Director; **Susan Syrnick,** Assistant Art Director & Designer

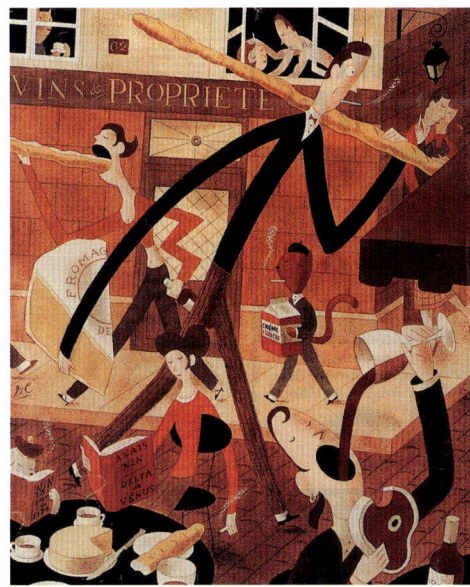

The Philadelphia Inquirer Magazine
Philadelphia, PA
Greg Clarke, Illustrator; **Christine Dunleavy,** Art Director; **Susan Syrnick,** Assistant Art Director & Designer

TWENTIETH EDITION ■ 211

ILLUSTRATION ■ Three or More Colors

Pittsburgh Post-Gazette
Pittsburgh, PA
Anita Dufalla, Art Director & Illustrator

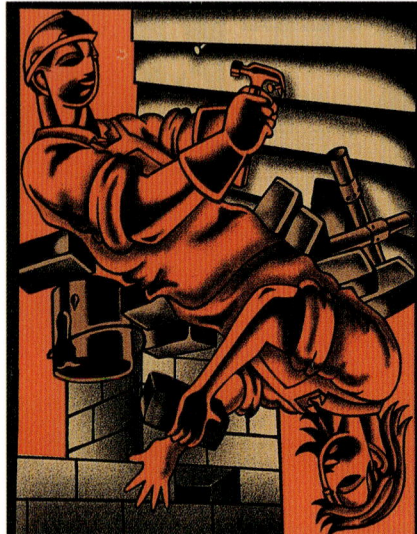

Reforma
México City, México
Rodrigo Tovar, Illustrator; **Guilermo Larios**, Section Designer; **Réne Delgado**, Editor; **Emilio Deheza**, Art Director; **Eduardo Danilo**, Design Consultant; **Ricardo del Castillo**, Graphic Editor

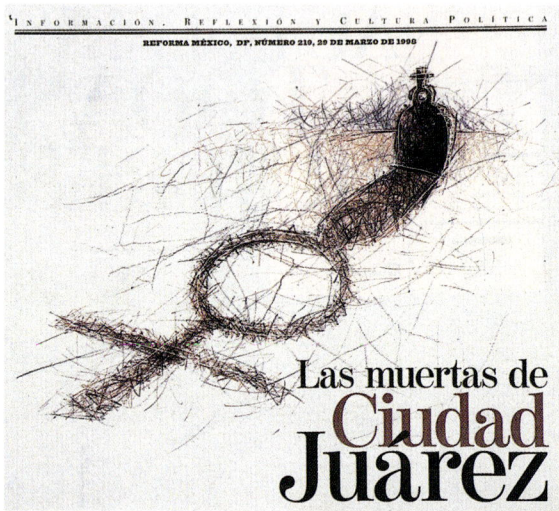

La Revista de El Mundo
Madrid, Spain
Toño Benavides, Illustrator

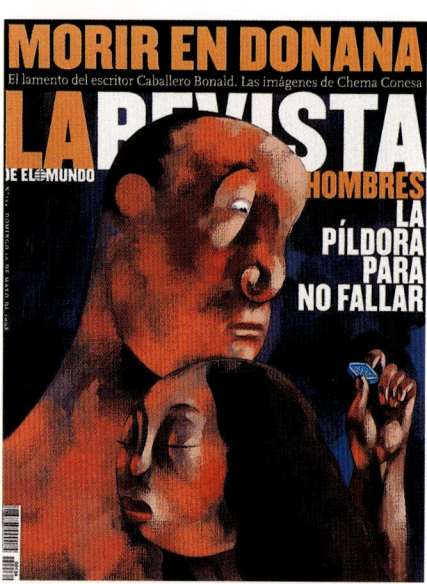

La Revista de El Mundo
Madrid, Spain
Ana Juan, Illustrator

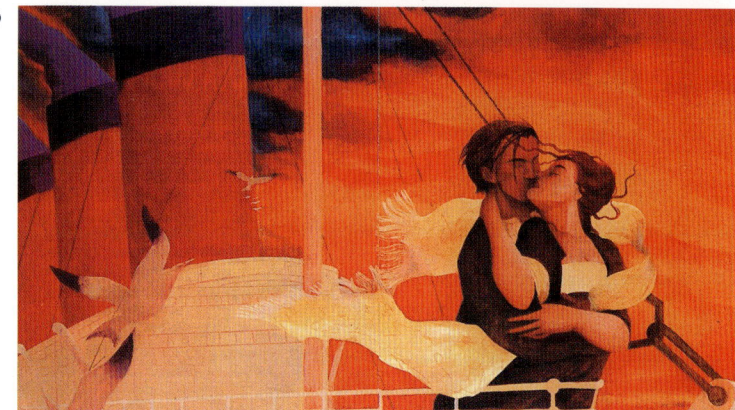

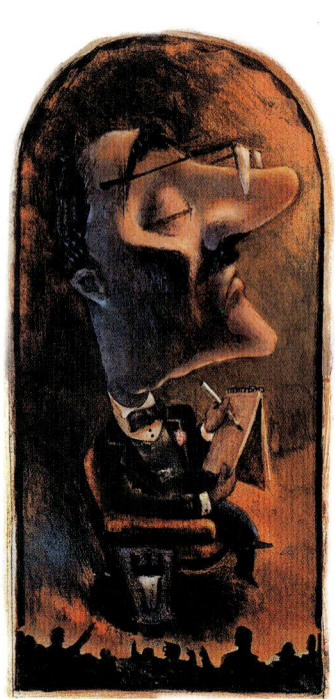

Pittsburgh Post-Gazette
Pittsburgh, PA
Daniel Marsula, Illustrator

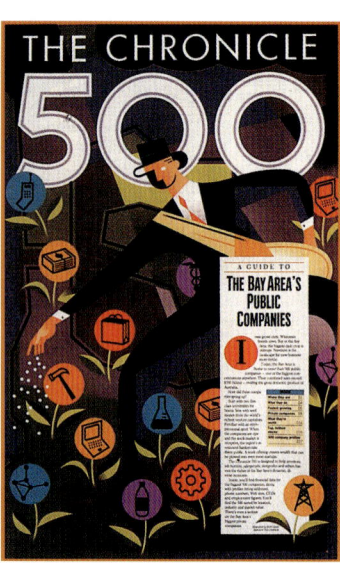

The San Francisco Chronicle
San Francisco, CA
Ron Chan, Illustrator; **Hulda Nelson**, Art Director

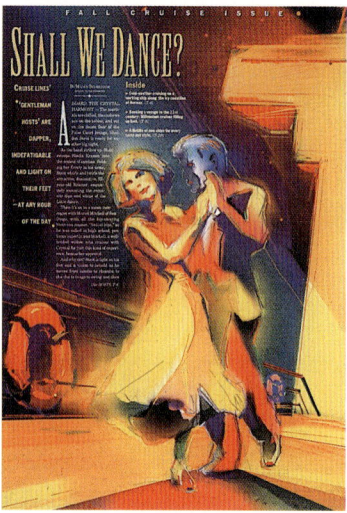

San Francisco Examiner
San Francisco, CA
Lance Jackson, Illustrator; **Kelly Frankeny**, A.M.E. Design; **Don McCartney**, Design Director; **John Flinn**, Travel Editor; **Andrew Skwish**, Designer

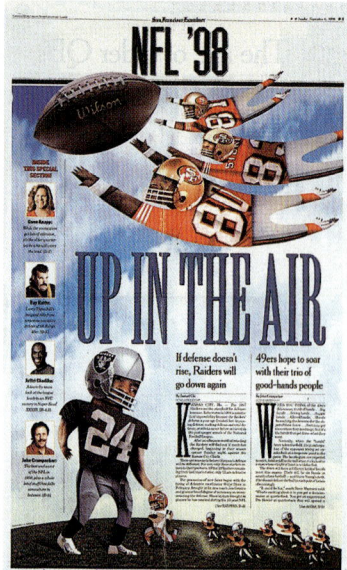

San Francisco Examiner
San Francisco, CA
Andrew Skwish, Illustrator & Designer; **Kelly Frankeny**, A.M.E. Design; **Don McCartney**, Design Director; **Glenn Schwarz**, Sports Editor

212 ■ THE BEST OF NEWSPAPER DESIGN

Three or More Colors ■ ILLUSTRATION

Seattle Post-Intelligencer
Seattle, WA
Stacy Innerst, Artist

St. Louis Post-Dispatch
St. Louis, MO
Gary Kelley, Illustrator; **Dan Martin,** Art Director; **Norma Klingsick,** Designer

Sunday Magazine
Melbourne, Australia
Matthew Davidson, Illustrator

The Wall Street Journal Reports
New York, NY
Brian Cronin, Illustrator; **Greg Leeds,** Design Director; **Orlie Kraus,** Art Director & Designer

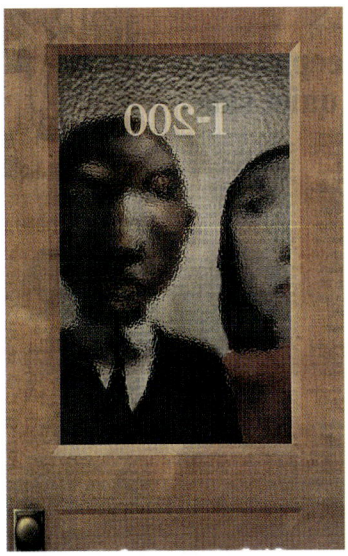
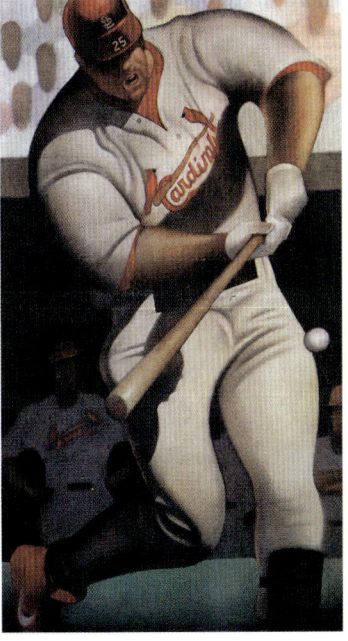
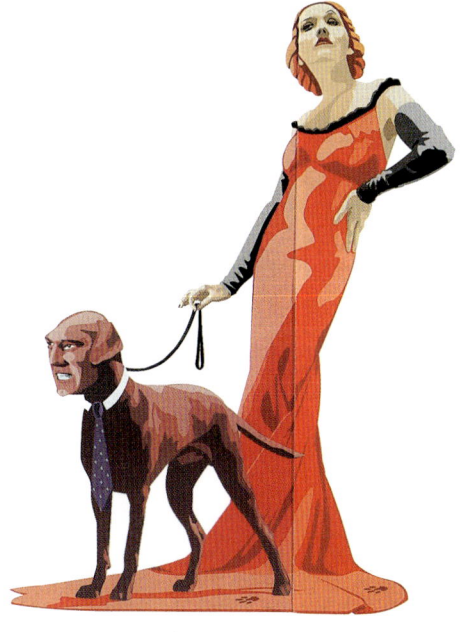
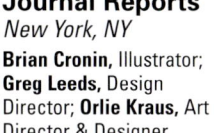

Zero Hora
Porto Alegre, Brasil
Eduardo Oliveira, Illustrator; **Luiz Adolfo,** Art Director

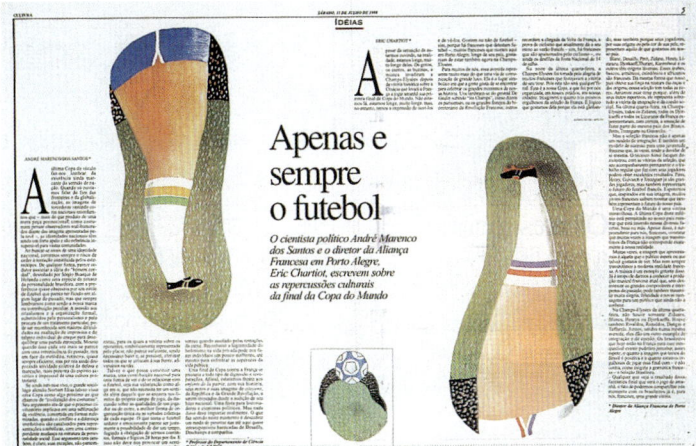

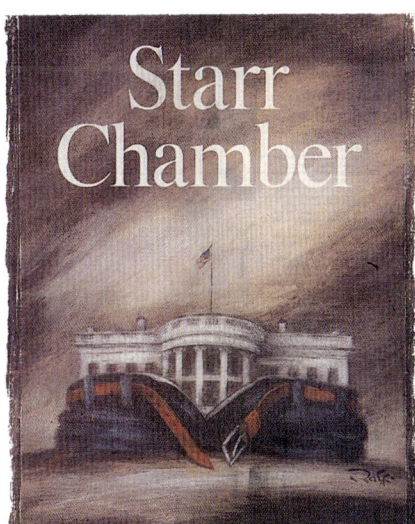
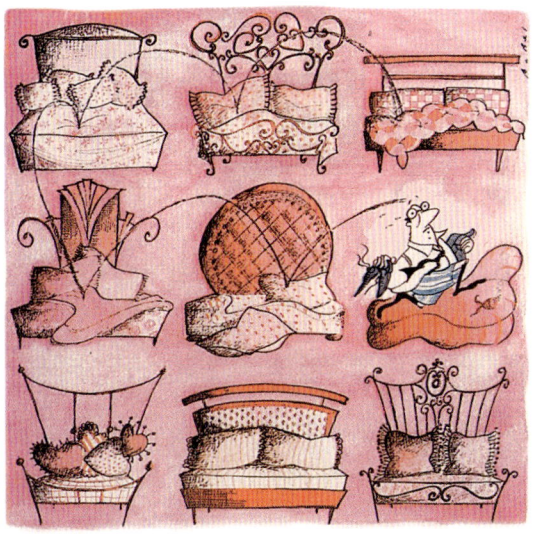
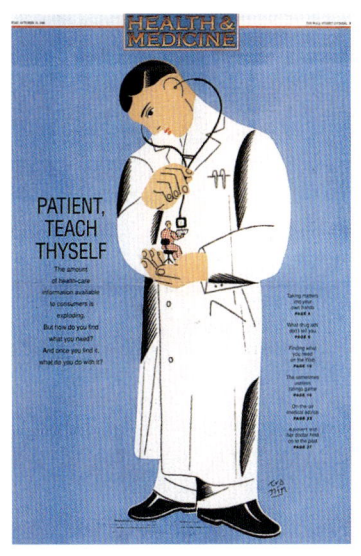

The Toronto Star
Toronto, Canada
Raffi Anderian, Illustrator; **Ian Somerville,** Art Director; **James Harrison,** Designer; **Peter Gorrie,** Editor

Zero Hora
Porto Alegre, Brasil
Isabel Callage, Illustrator; **Silvia Braccio,** Editor; **Luiz Adolfo,** Art Director; **Mario García,** Design Consultant

The Wall Street Journal Reports
New York, NY
Brian Cronin, Illustrator; **Greg Leeds,** Design Director; **Orlie Kraus,** Art Director & Designer

TWENTIETH EDITION ■ 213

ILLUSTRATION ■ Portfolio One Artist

The artist shows an emotional connection between the illustration and the story. The intensity of detail is amazing. It has a strong point of view that many others do not. There's no mistake the artist contributed: his fingerprints are all over the story. The refinement and clarity are outstanding.

El artista muestra una conexión emotiva entre la ilustración y la historia. La intensidad de los detalles es impresionante. Tiene un punto de vista muy firme del que carecen muchos otros. La contribución del artista es evidente: sus huellas están en toda la historia. El refinamiento y la claridad son sobresalientes.

Gold
El Mundo Del Siglo XXI
Madrid, Spain
Ricardo Martinez, Illustrator

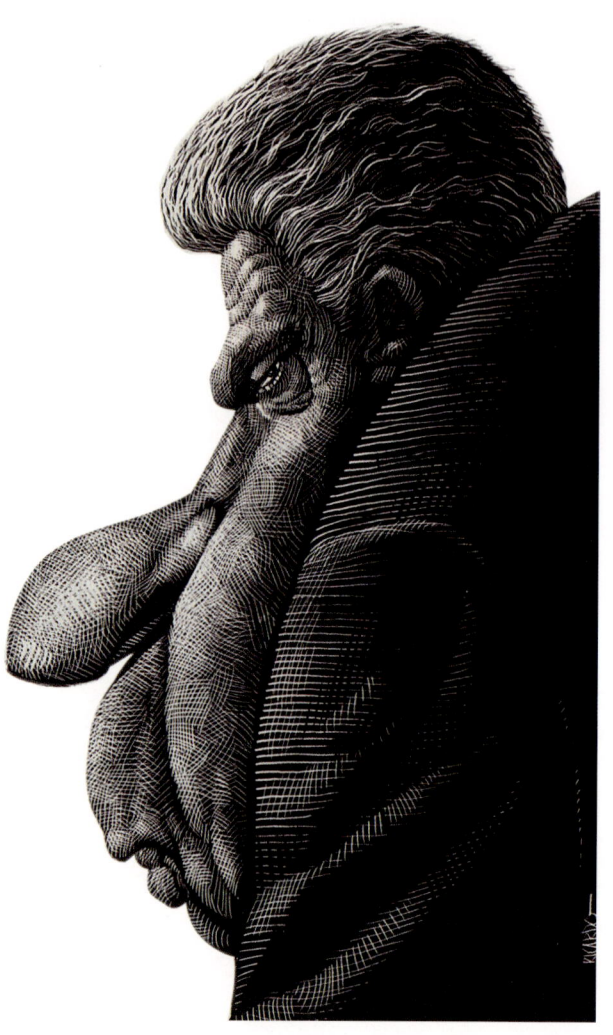
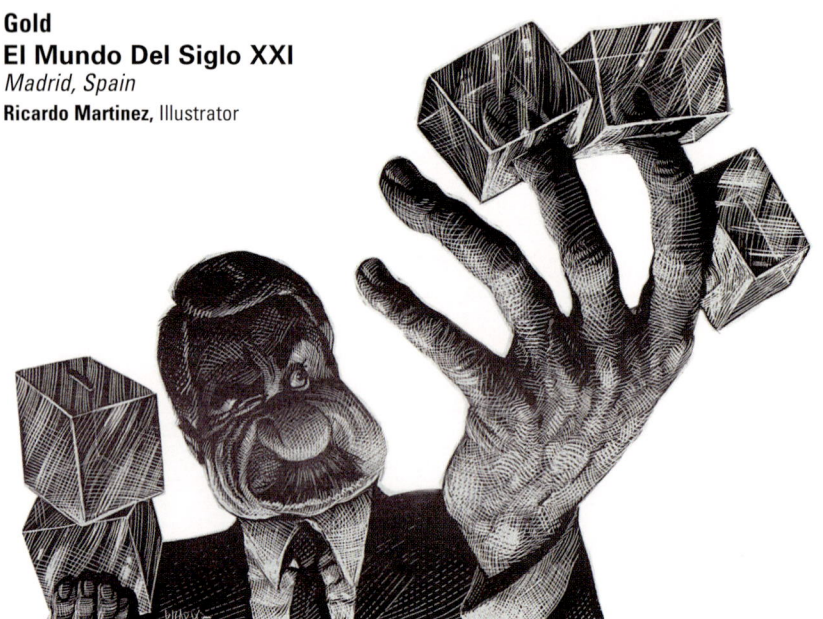
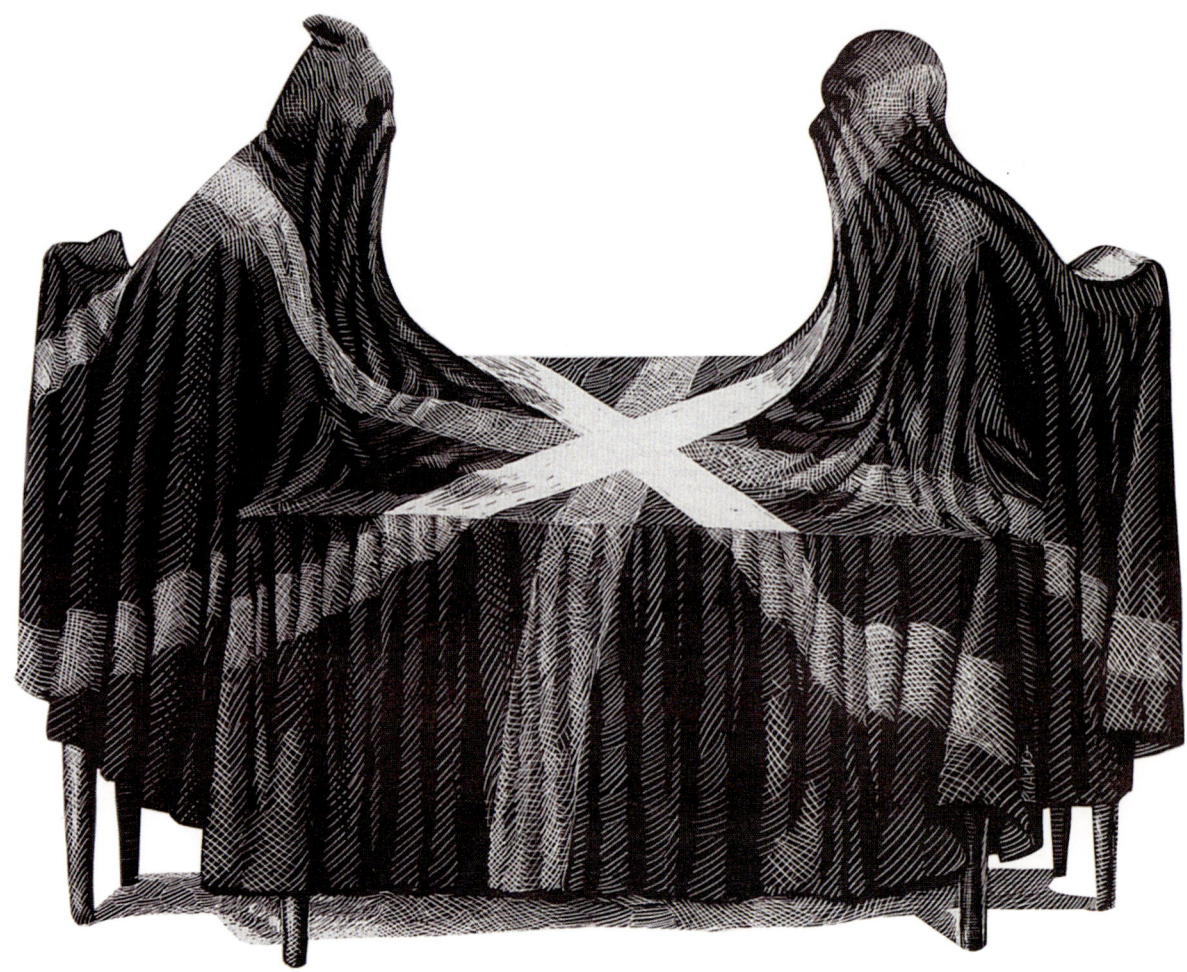

Portfolio One Artist ■ ILLUSTRATION

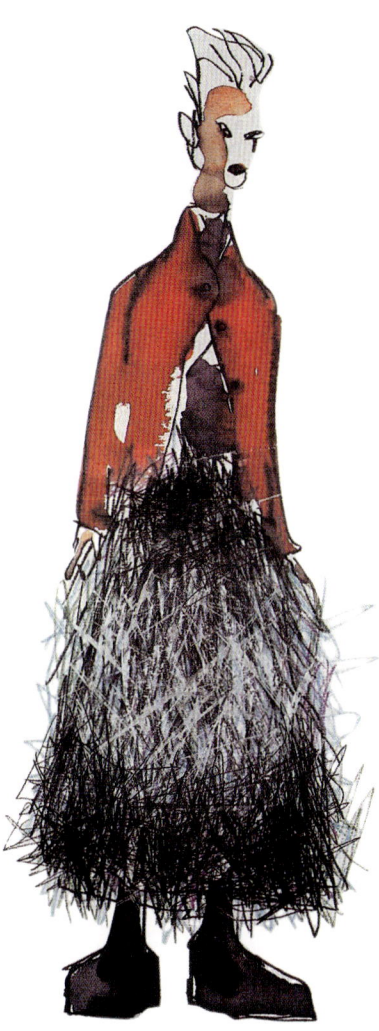

Gold
Dagens Nyheter
Stockholm, Sweden
Stina Wirsén, Illustrator

This illustration is totally different from what we normally see in newspapers. The material is well laid out with excellent use of color over basic lines. It's stylish with lots of humor in the background. The drawing gives you a feeling of texture. Poses are so casual, elegantly framed in their own white space.

Su ilustración no se asemeja en nada a lo que vemos normalmente en los periódicos. El material tiene una gran composición gráfica y se hace un uso excelente del color sobre líneas básicas. Es elegante, con mucho humor de trasfondo. Los dibujos dan la sensación de textura. Los poses tienen un aire informal y están enmarcados elegantemente en su propio espacio blanco.

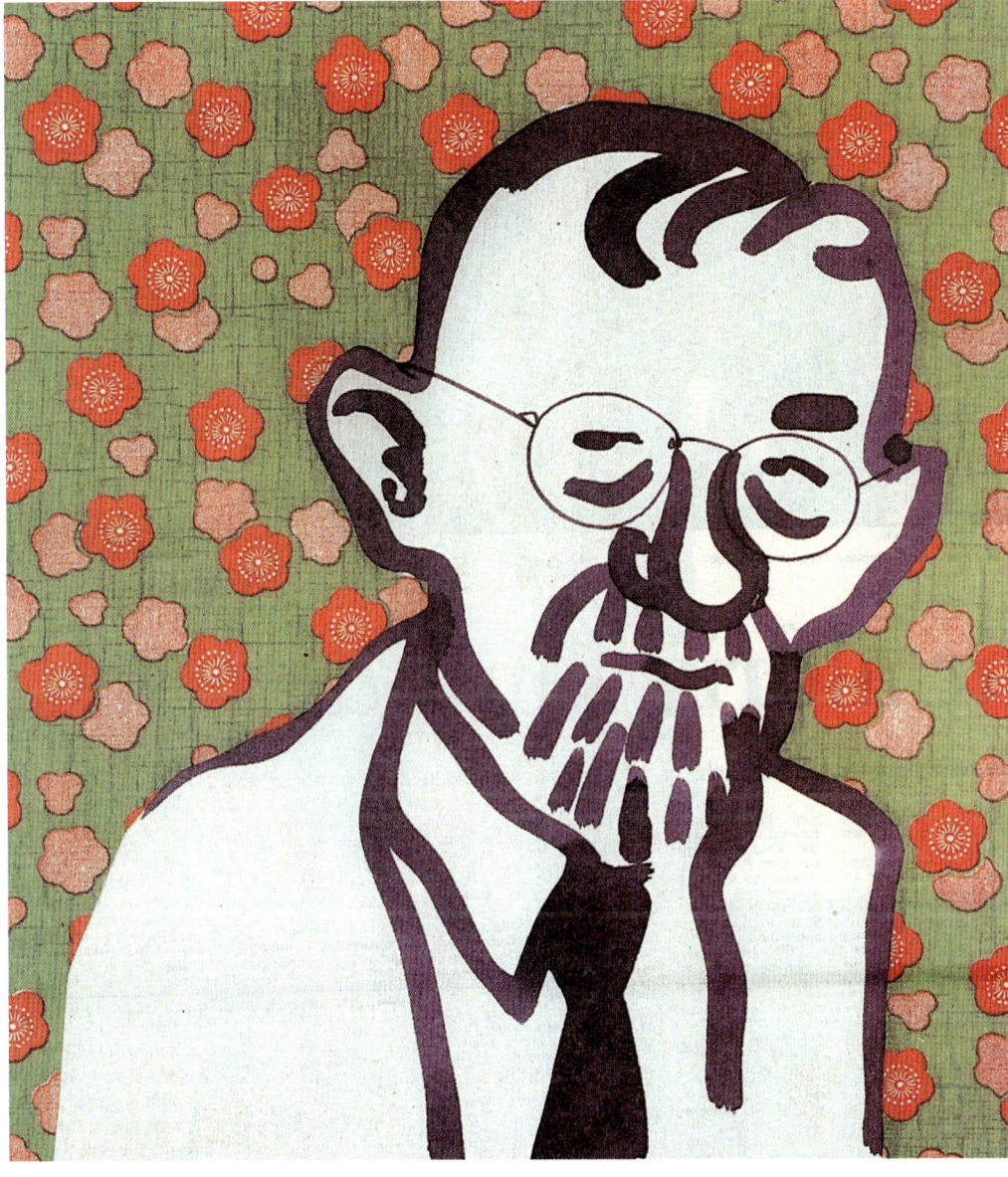

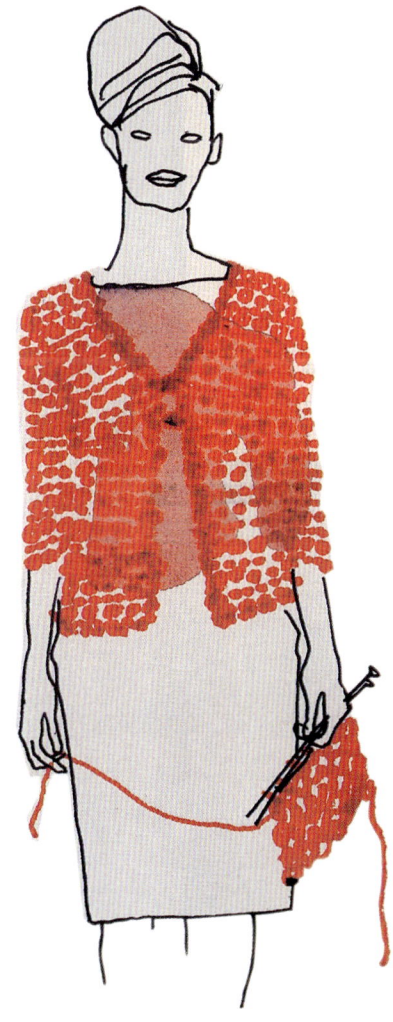

ILLUSTRATION ■ Portfolio One Artist

Gold
The New York Times
New York, NY
Christoph Niemann, Illustrator

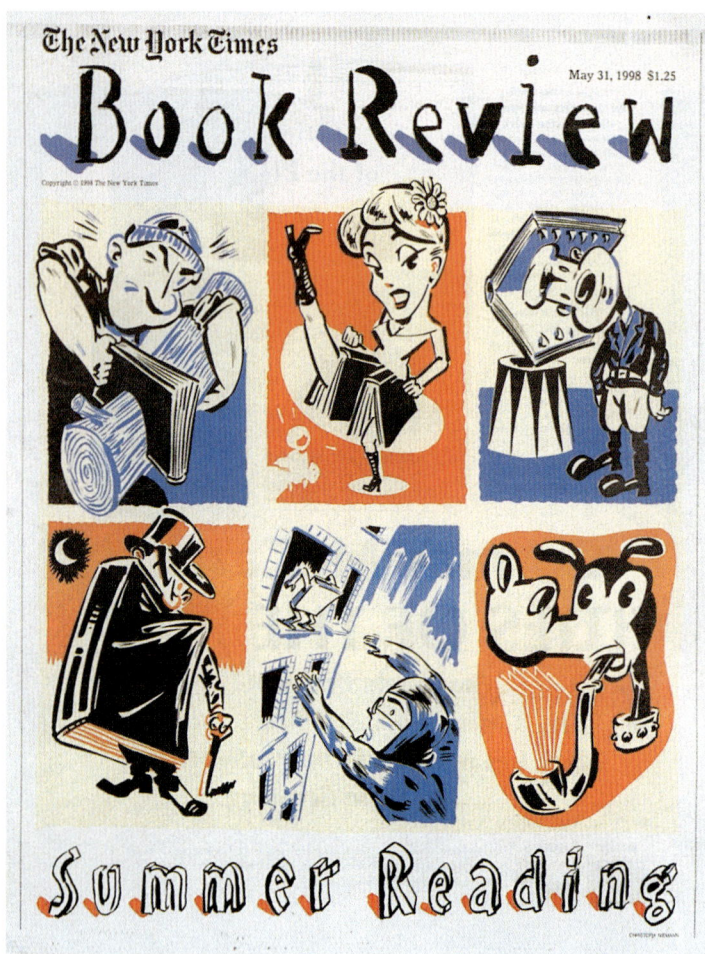

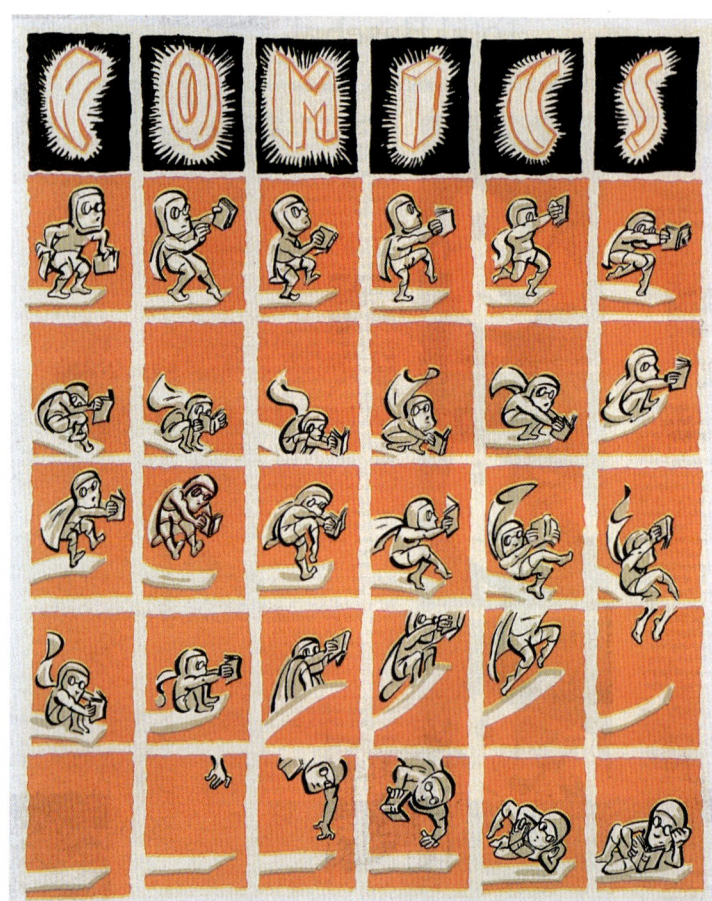

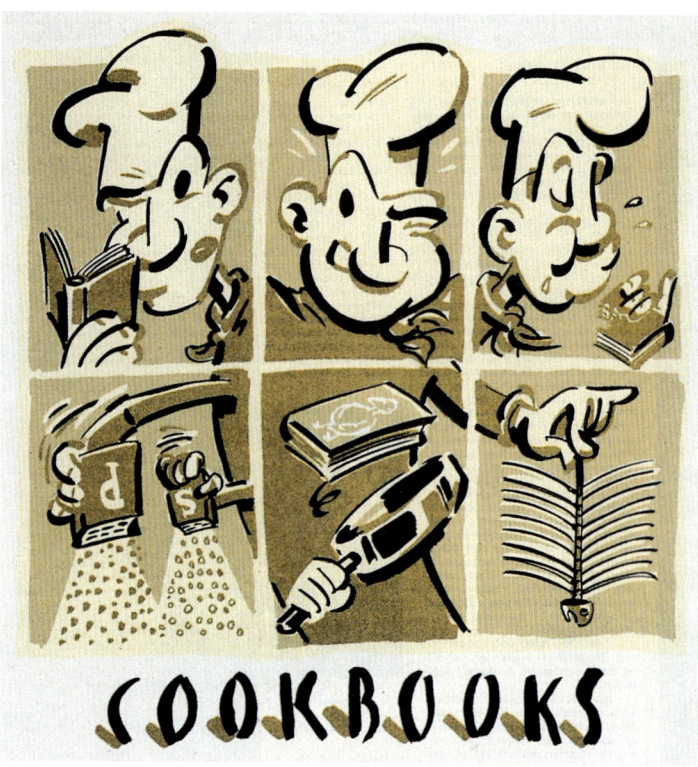

Awesome work. Unusual departure from the normal section. The illustrations flow from the corner to inside pages using full color to surprise the readers. The illustrations move and make the books talk — King Kong, Waterfalls and parachutes — to grab the reader's attention.

Imponente labor. Una desviación inusual de la sección normal. Las ilustraciones fluyen desde la esquina hasta las páginas interiores a todo color para sorprender a los lectores. Las ilustraciones se mueven y hacen hablar a los libros —King Kong, Waterfalls y paracaídas— para atrapar la atención del lector.

Portfolio One Artist ■ ILLUSTRATION

Gold
La Revista de El Mundo
Madrid, Spain
Ana Juan, Illustrator

The way this artist uses contrasting colors is different from other illustrators and fits the audience because of the bright colors. It has a certain whimsy. It's outspoken, yet refined. It has subtle irony to it with lots of little touches appearing throughout. It goes far beyond being just a good drawing.

El modo en que este artista emplea el contraste de colores no se asemeja al de otros ilustradores y se ajusta al público debido a los brillantes colores. Tiene un aire enigmático que divierte. Es franco sin dejar de ser refinado. Tiene una ironía sutil con muchos pequeños retoques que aparecen en diferentes partes. Es mucho más que un buen dibujo.

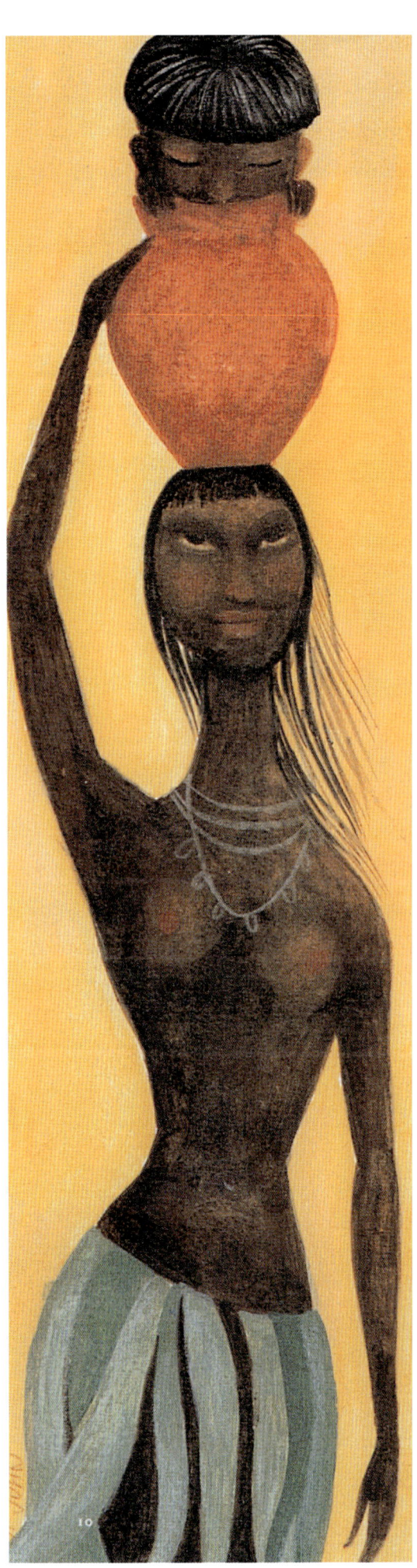
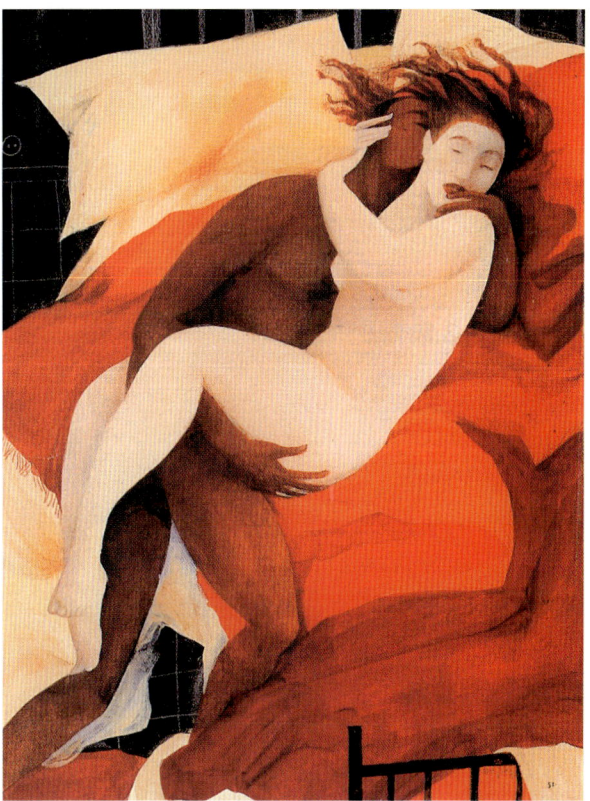
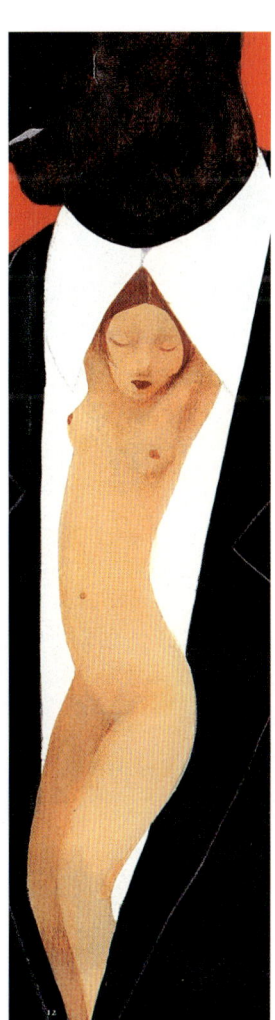
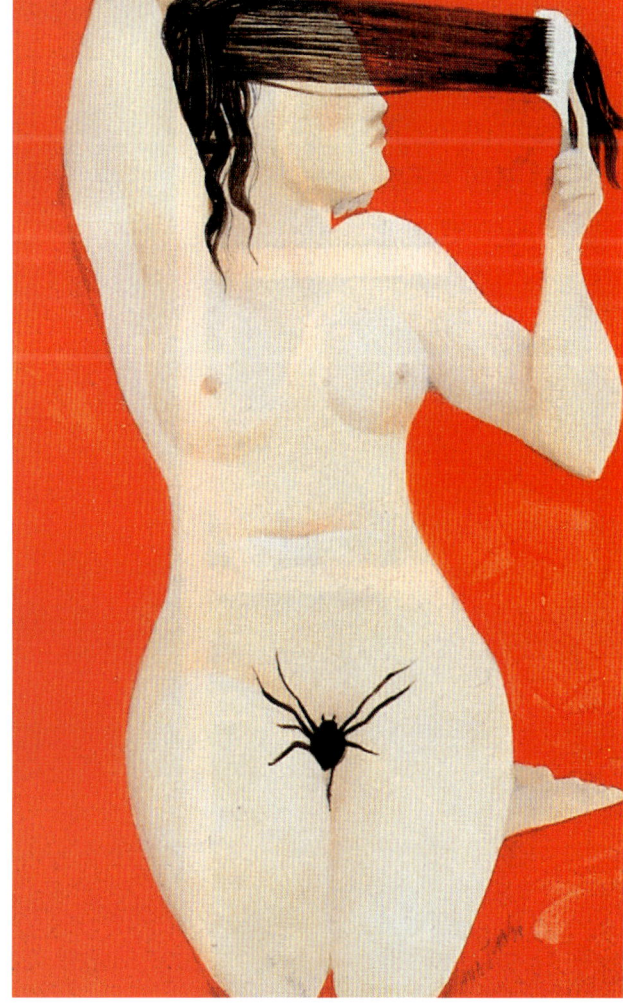

TWENTIETH EDITION

ILLUSTRATION ■ Portfolio One Artist

Silver
Berlingske Tidende
Copenhagen, Denmark
Lise Roennebaek, Illustrator
• also an Award of Excellence for Illustration Three or More Colors

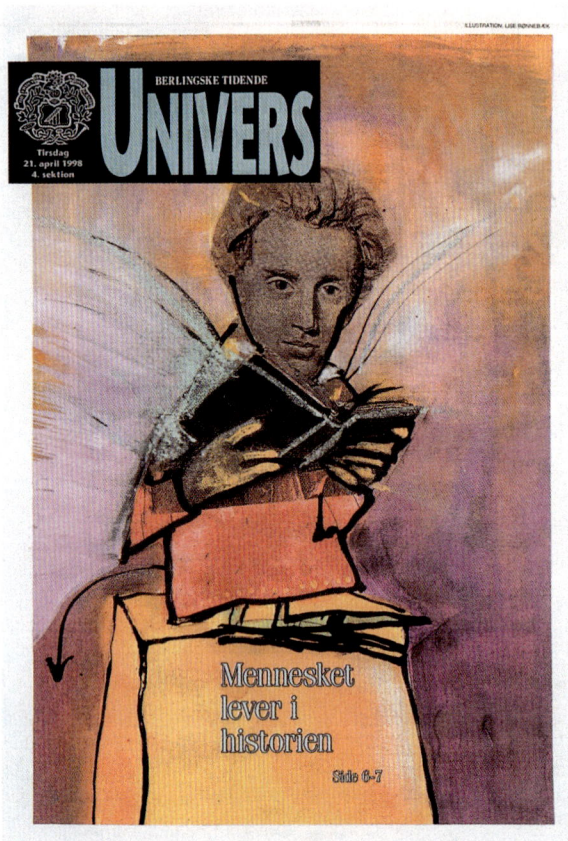

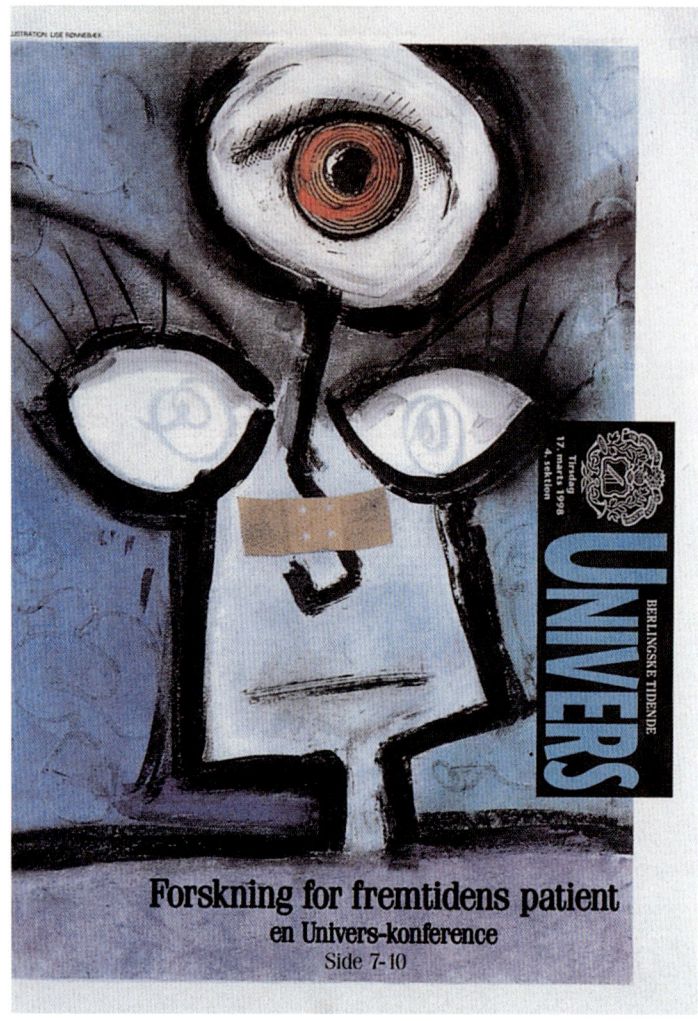

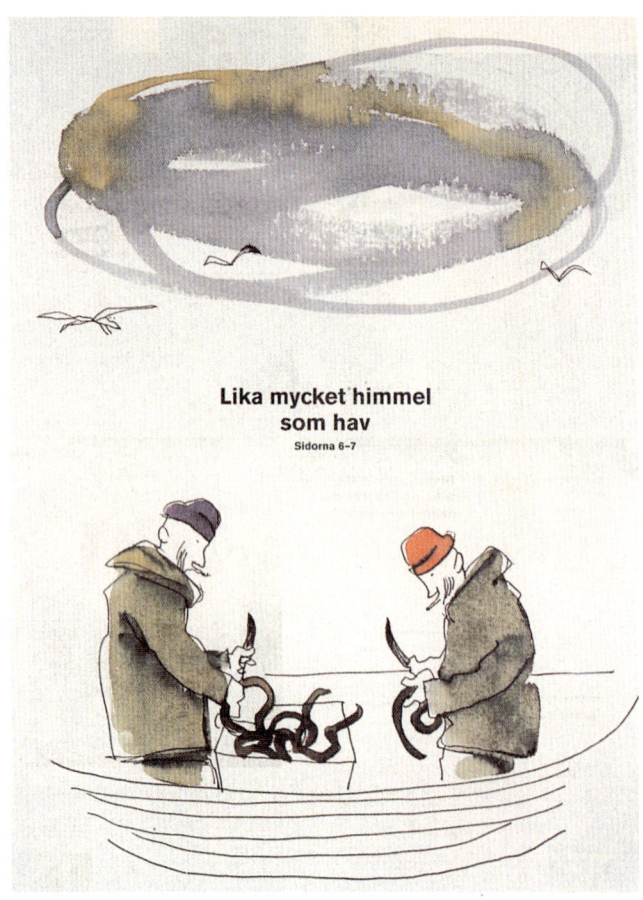

Silver
Dagens Nyheter
Stockholm, Sweden
Stina Wirsén, Illustrator

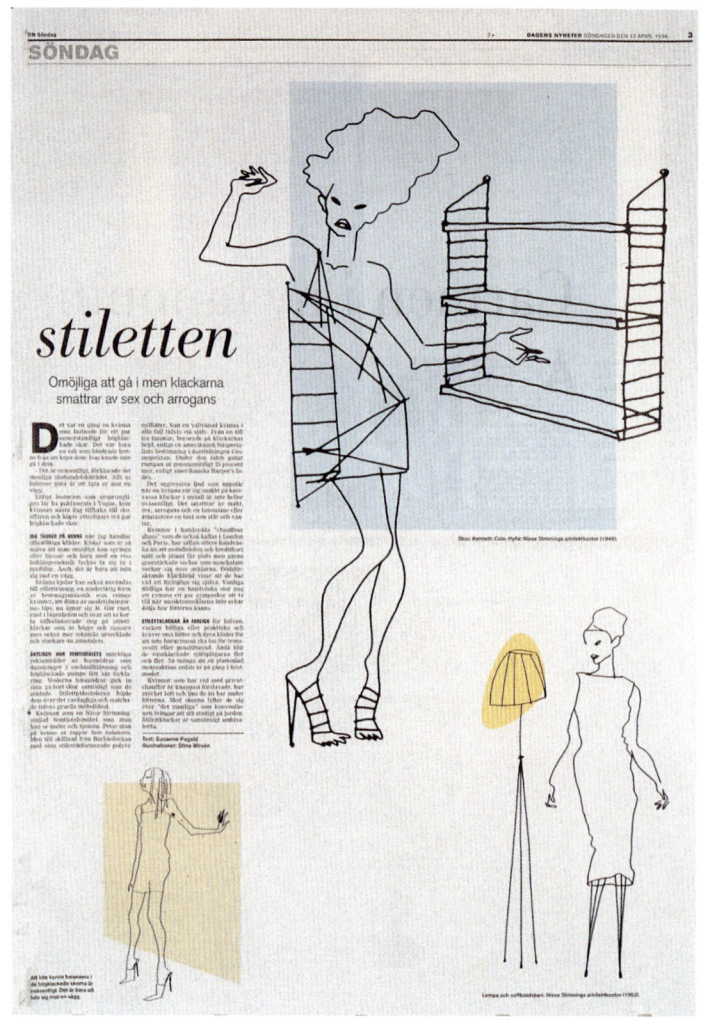

Portfolio One Artist ■ ILLUSTRATION

Silver
El Mundo Del Siglo XXI
Madrid, Spain
Raul Arias, Illustrator

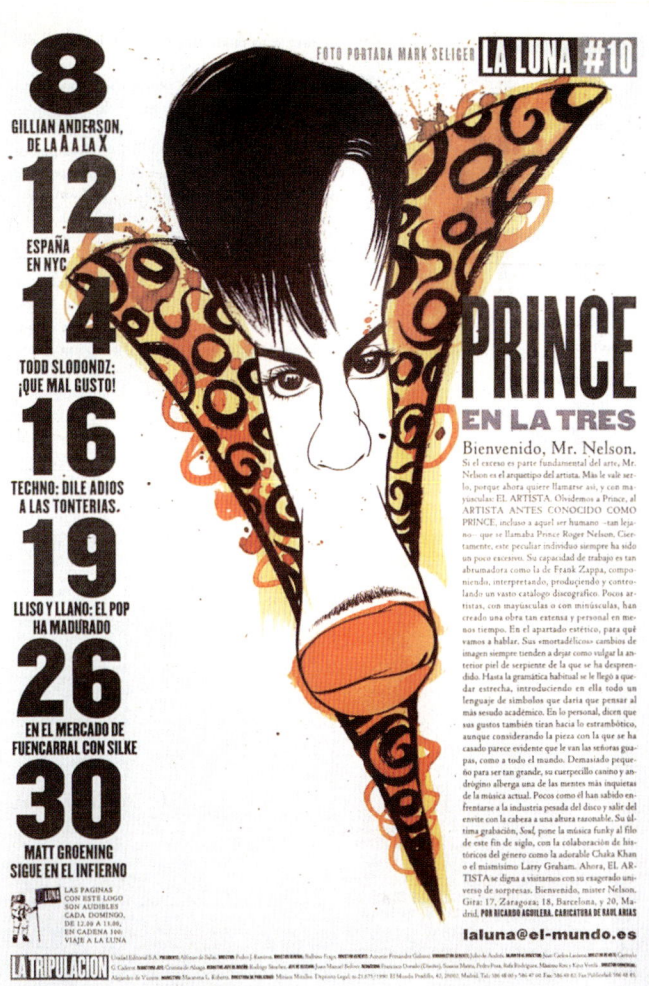
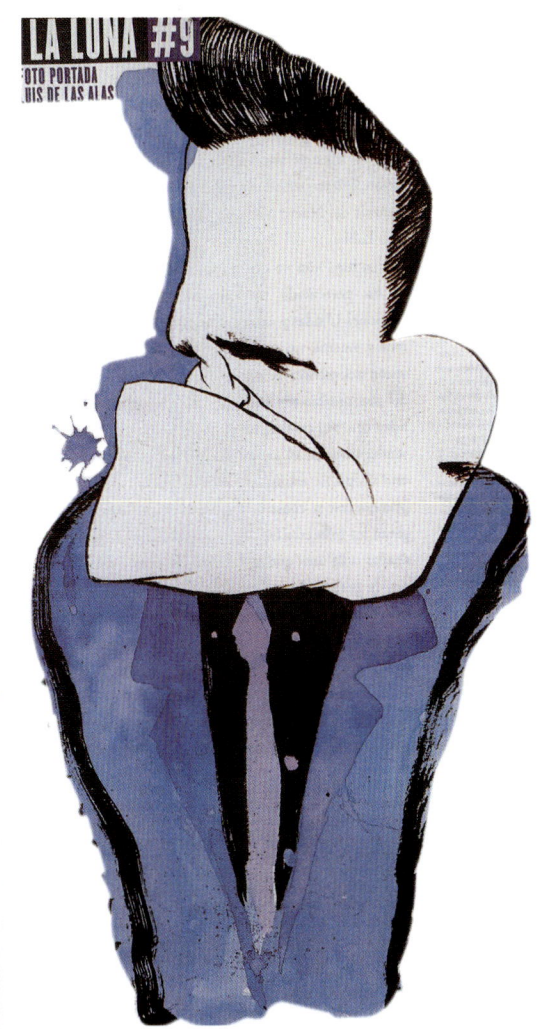

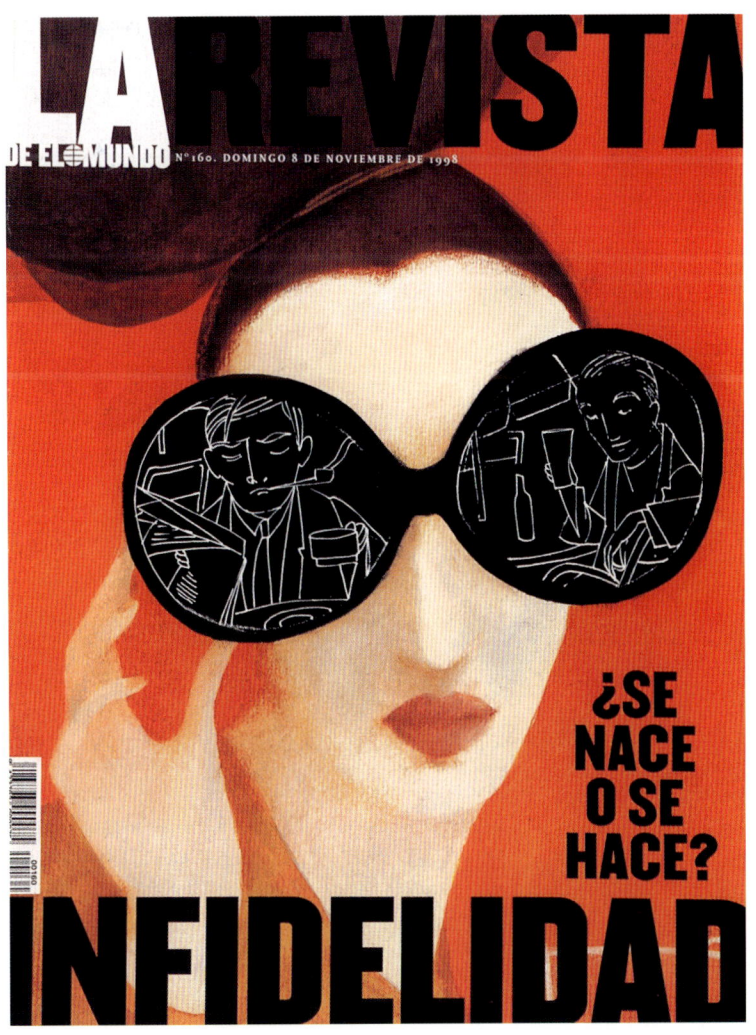
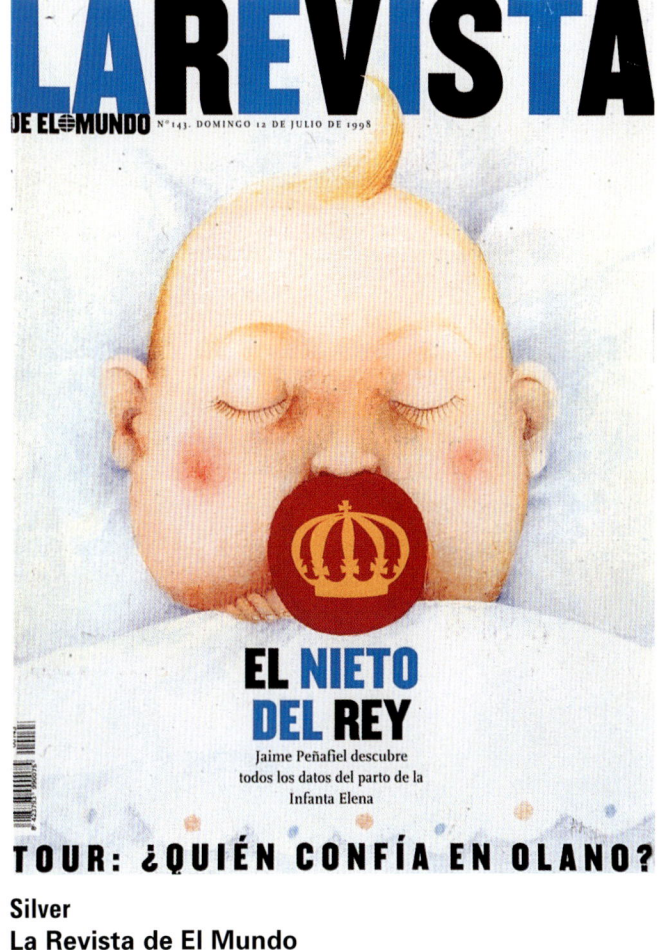

Silver
La Revista de El Mundo
Madrid, Spain
Ana Juan, Illustrator

ILLUSTRATION ■ Portfolio One Artist

Dagens Nyheter
Stockholm, Sweden
Stina Wirsén, Illustrator

Dagens Nyheter
Stockholm, Sweden
Stina Wirsén, Illustrator

Estado de Minas
Belo Horizonte, Brasil
Alexandre Coelho, Illustrator

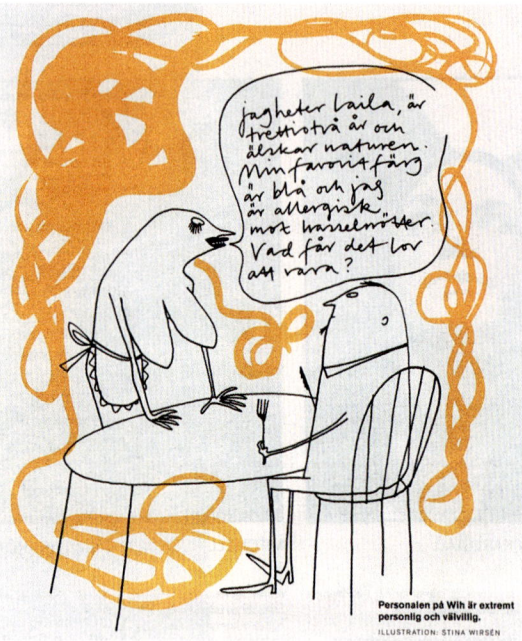
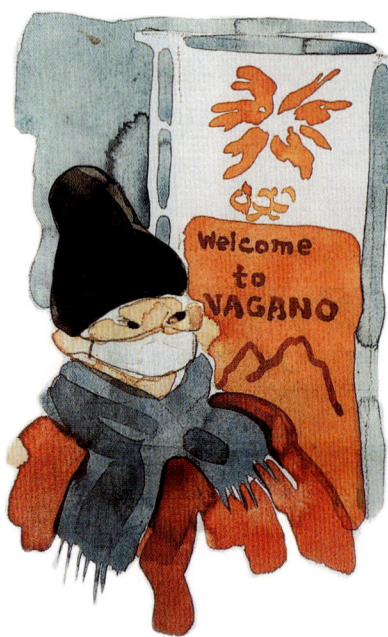
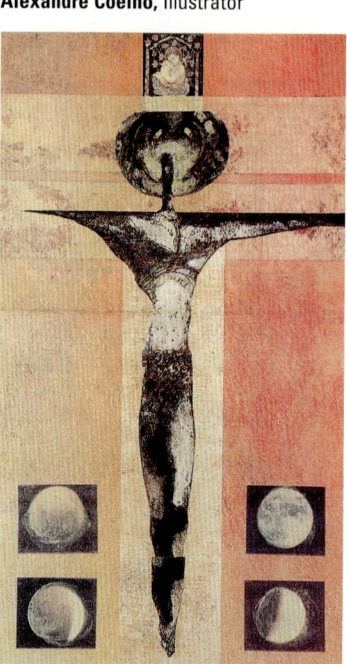

Dagens Nyheter
Stockholm, Sweden
Jockum Nordström, Illustrator

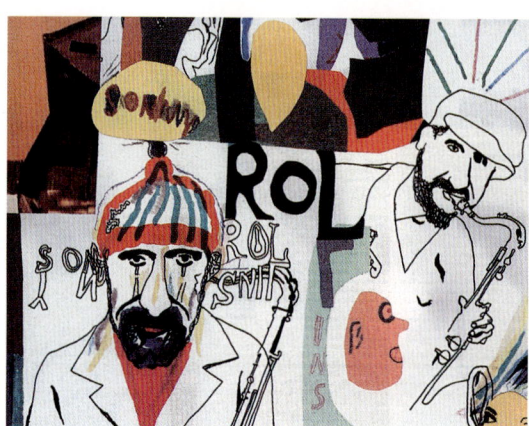

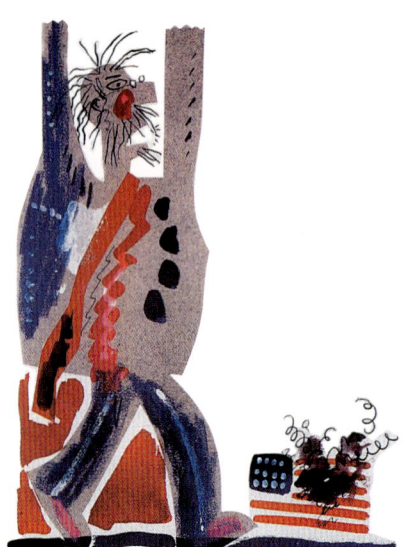
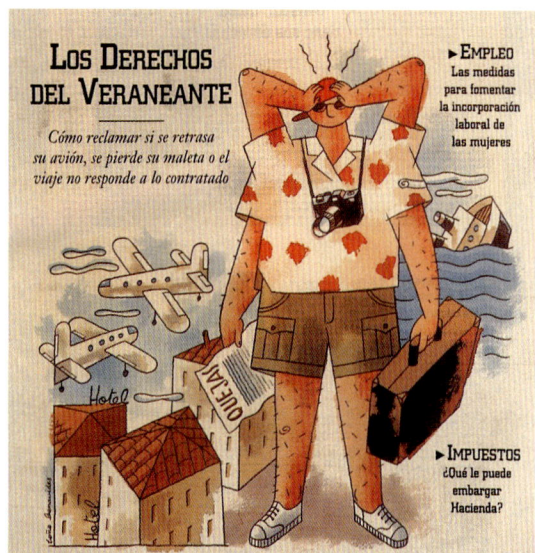
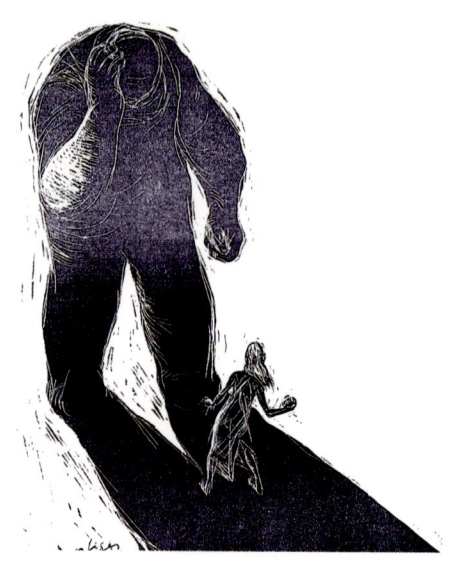

Göteborgs-Posten
Göteborg, Sweden
Ulf Sveningson, Illustrator

El Mundo Del Siglo XXI
Madrid, Spain
Toño Benavides, Illustrator

El Mundo Del Siglo XXI
Madrid, Spain
Ulises Culebro, Illustration Editor

220 ■ THE BEST OF NEWSPAPER DESIGN

Portfolio One Artist, More than One Artist ■ ILLUSTRATION

El Mundo Del Siglo XXI
Madrid, Spain
Ulises Culebro, Illustration Editor
• also for Illustration Black or Black and One Color

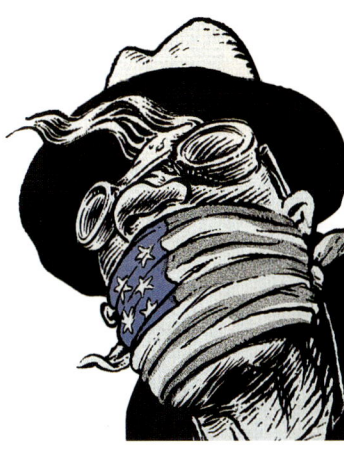

El Mundo SU Dinero
Madrid, Spain
Ramón Rodríguez Ramos, Illustrator

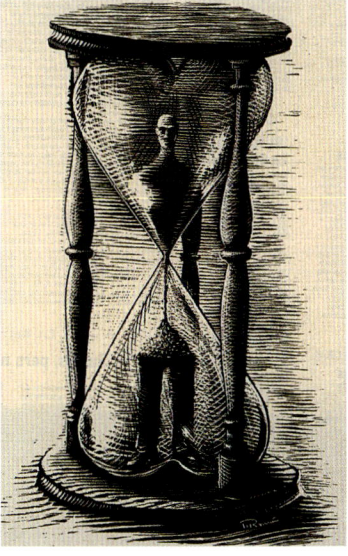

The Orange County Register
Santa Ana, CA
Amy Ning, Illustrator
• also for Illustration Three or More colors

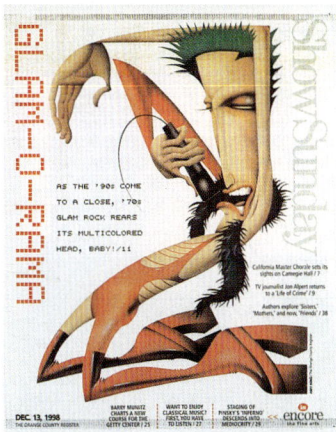

Seattle Post-Intelligencer
Seattle, WA
Stacy Innerst, Artist

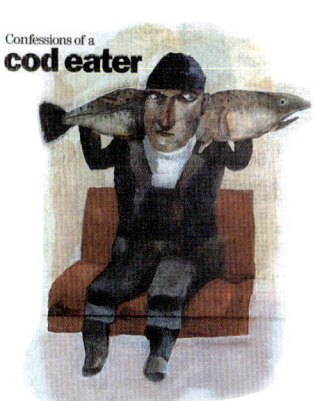

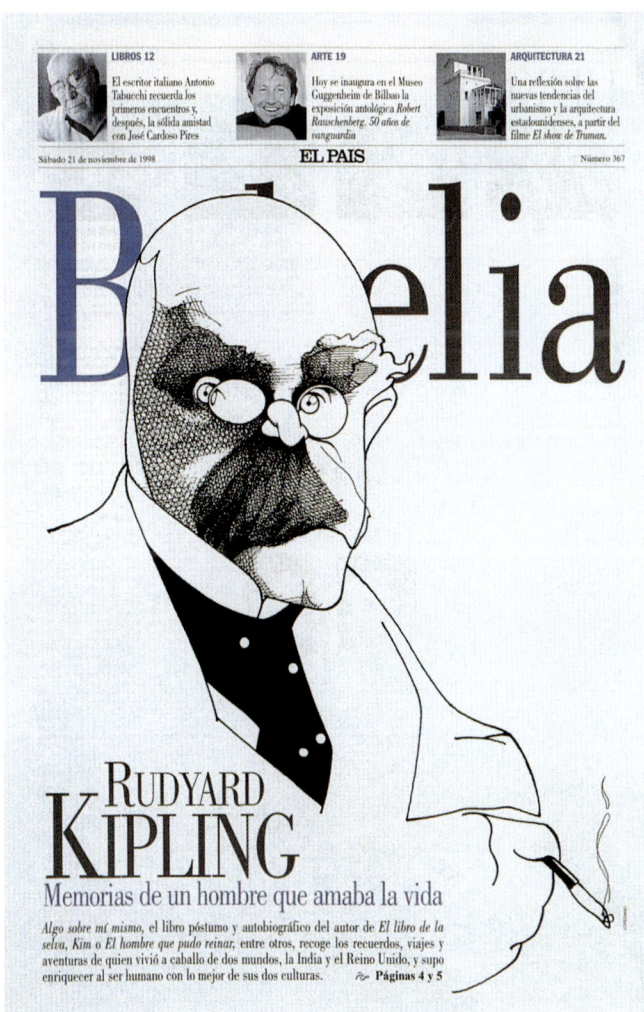

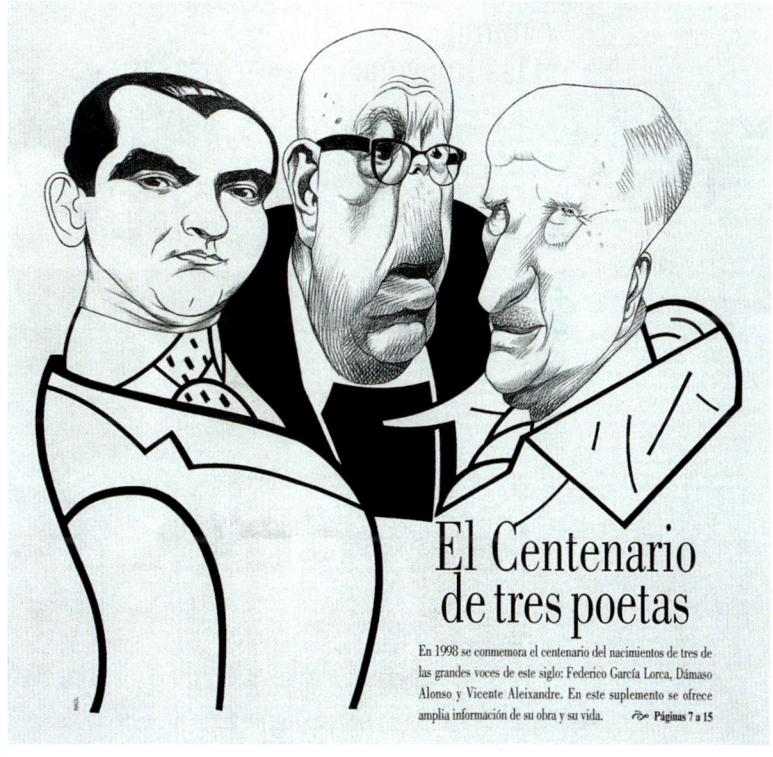

Silver
El País
Madrid, Spain
Raul F. Calleja, Artist; **Loredanto,** Artist; **Jesus Martines,** Designer; **Luis Galán,** Designer

ILLUSTRATION ■ Portfolio More than One Artist

Silver
The Philadelphia Inquirer Magazine
Philadelphia, PA

Stacy Innerst, Illustrator; **Anja Kroencke**, Illustrator; **Frederique Bertrand**, Illustrator; **Gregory Manchess**, Illustrator; **Olaf Hajek**, Illustrator; **Angela Moore**, Illustrator; **Christine Dunleavy**, Art Director; **Susan Syrnick**, Assistant Art Director

• also Silver for Illusrtration Three or More Colors
• also an Award of Excellence for Magazine Portfolio

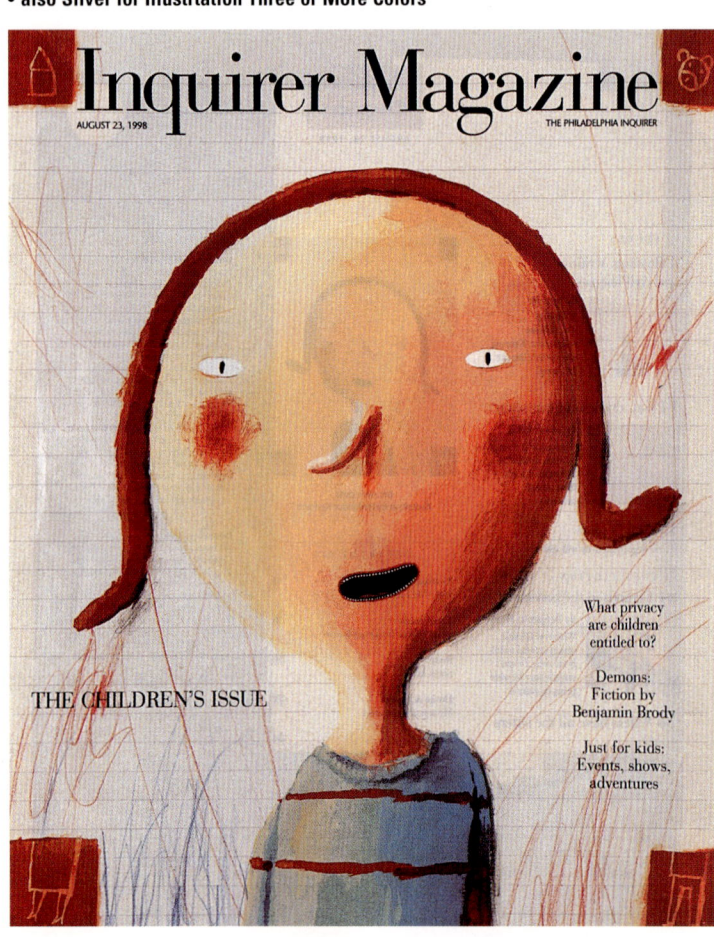
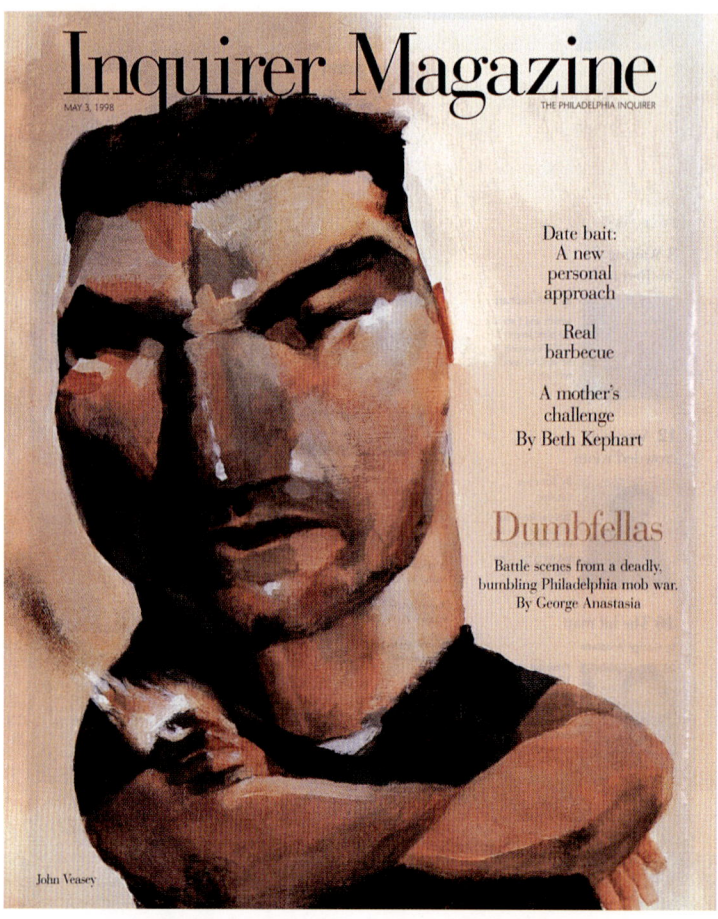

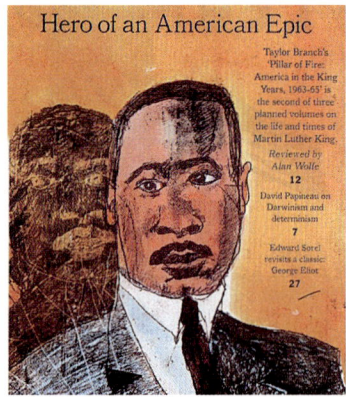

The New York Times
New York, NY

Robert Andrew Parker, Illustrator; **Marshall Arisman**, Illustrator; **Brad Holland**, Illustrator; **Thomas Fuchs**, Illustrator; **Etienne Delessert**, Illustrator; **Dugald Stermer**, Illustrator; **Steven Heller**, Art Director

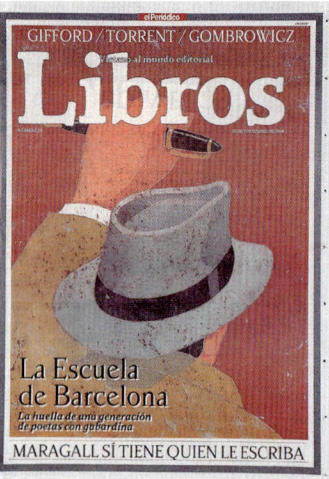

El Períodico de Catalunya
Barcelona, Spain

Feriche Ricardo, Designer; **Ismael Carrillo**, Illustrator; **Rafael Tapounet**, News Editor

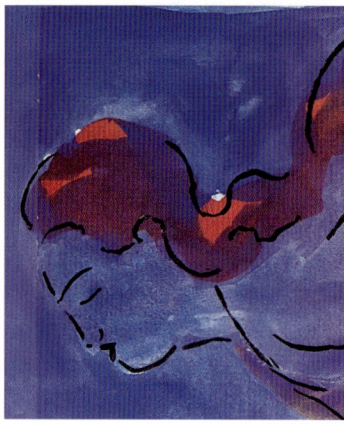

The Washington Post Magazine
Washington, DC

Kelly Doe, Art Director & Designer; **Brad Holland**, Illustrator; **Carol Benioff**, Illustrator; **Tim Bower**, Illustrator; **Kari Alberg**, Illustrator

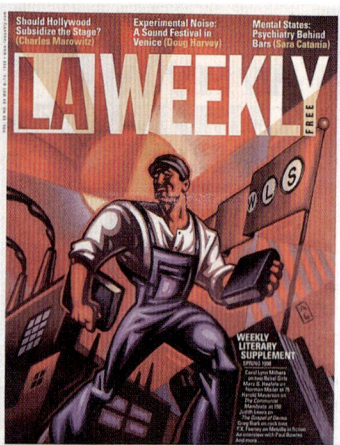

L.A. Weekly
Los Angeles, CA

Geoff Grahn, Illustrator; **Bill Smith**, Art Director

PHOTOJOURNALISM

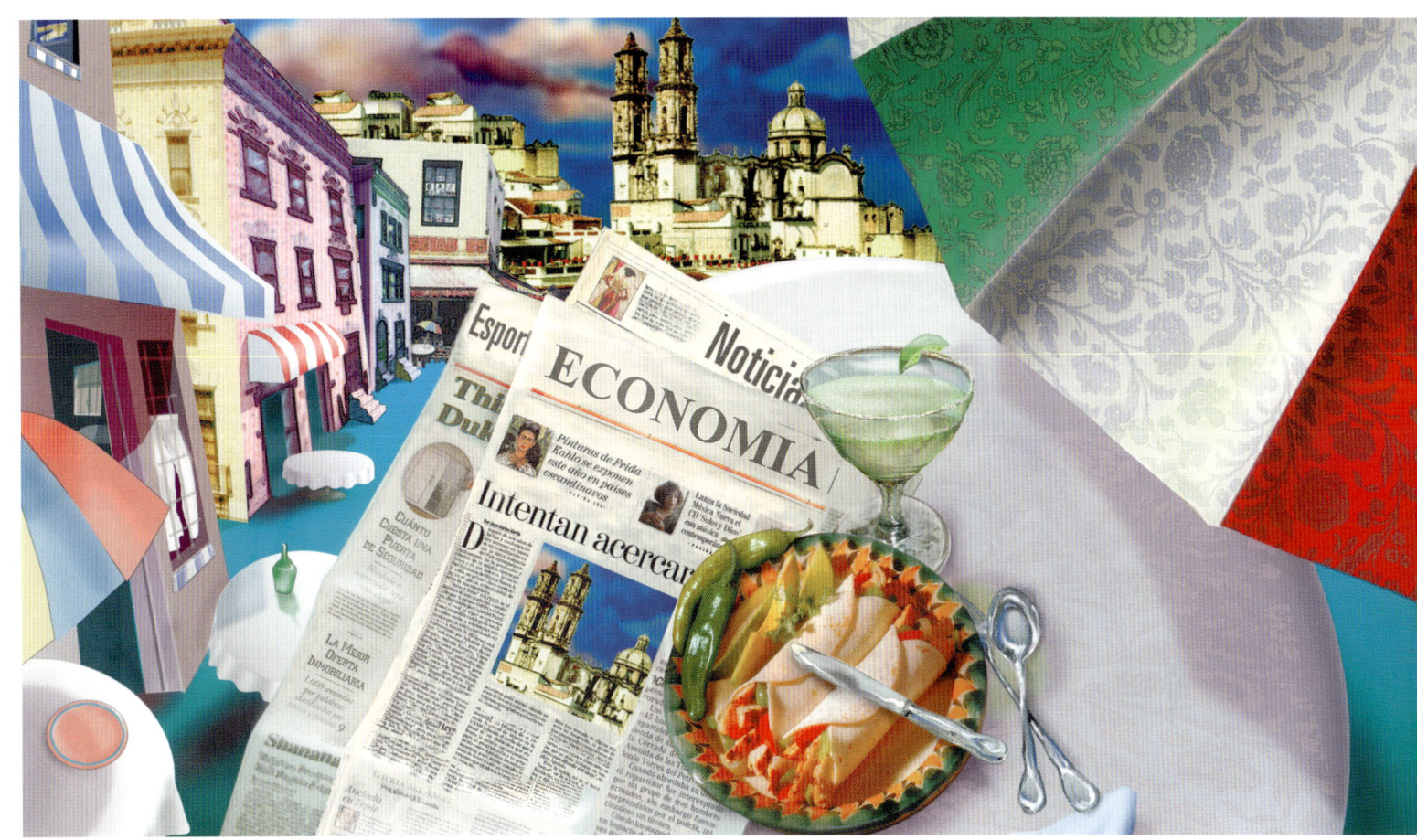

CHAPTER EIGHT

SPOT NEWS

FEATURE

PHOTO STORY

PHOTO ILLUSTRATION

PORTFOLIO

PHOTOJOURNALISM ■ Spot News

Silver
B.T.
Copenhagen, Denmark
Nils Meilvang, Photographer; **Michael Olsen,** Sub-Editor

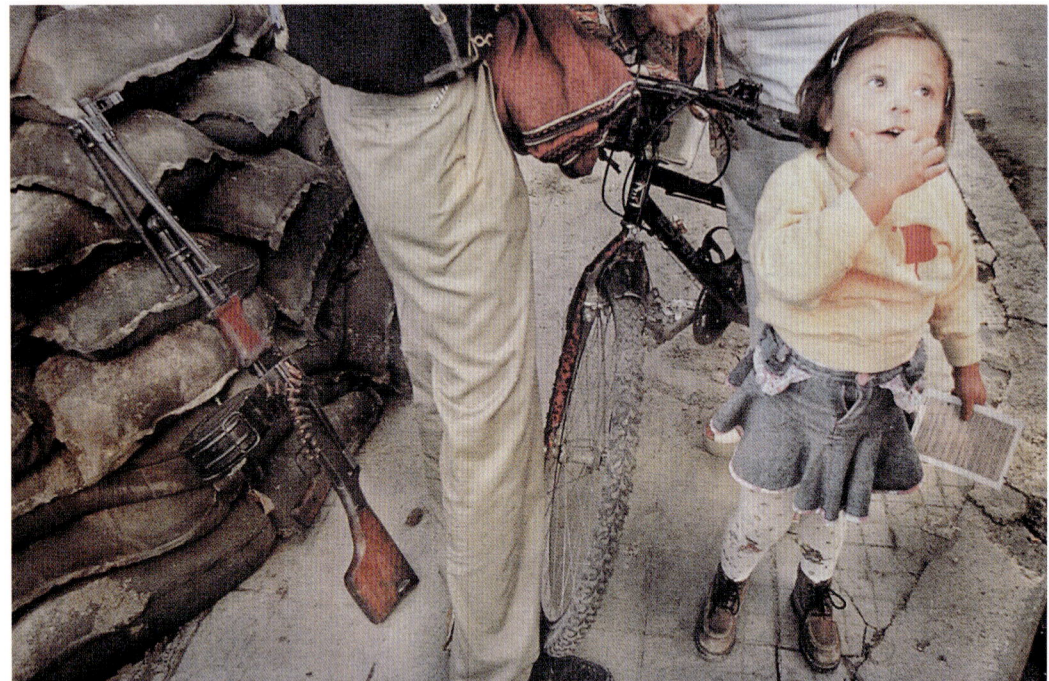

The Los Angeles Times
Costa Mesa, CA
Al Schaben, Photographer; **Mark Boster,** Photo Editor; **Kim Dryer,** Designer

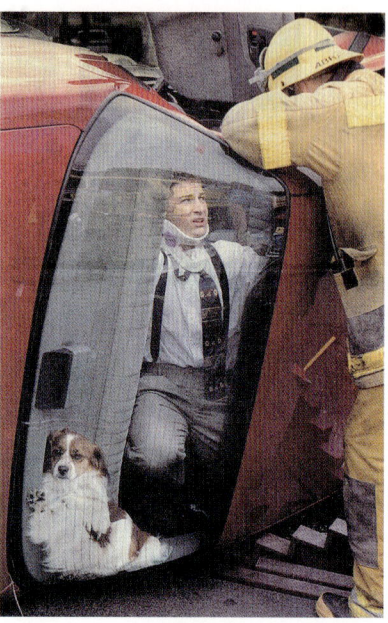

El Nuevo Día
San Juan, PR
Jose Ismael Fernandez, Photographer; **Jose L. Diaz de Villegas, Jr.,** Art Director; **Claudia Robiou,** Designer

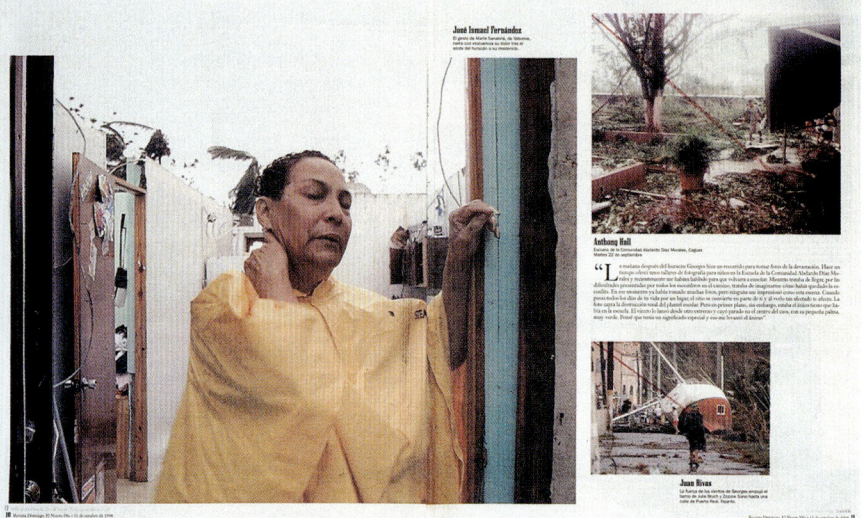

The Fresno Bee
Fresno, CA
John Walker, Photographer

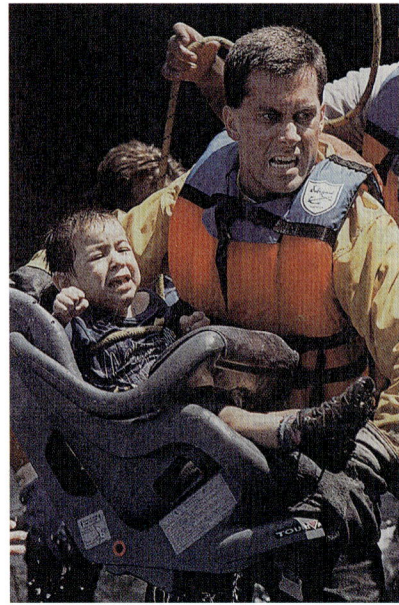

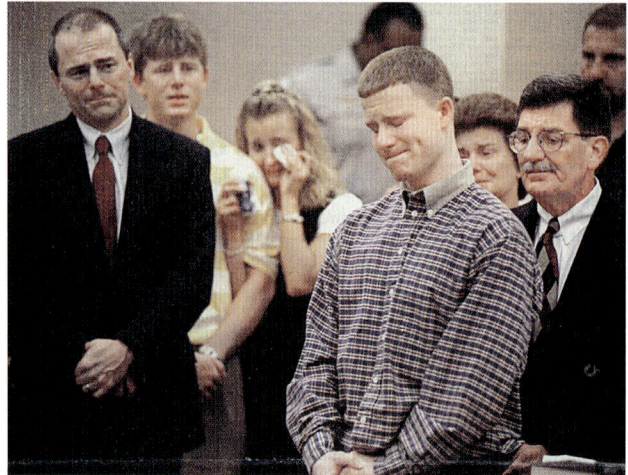

The Charlotte Observer
Charlotte, NC
Diedra Laird, Photographer; **Monica Moses,** Design Director; **Crystal Dempsey,** Designer; **The' Pham,** Photo Editor

Spot News ■ **PHOTOJOURNALISM**

El Nuevo Día
San Juan, PR
Jose Ismael Fernandez, Photographer; **Jose L. Diaz de Villegas, Jr.**, Art Director; **Claudia Robiou**, Designer

The Spokesman-Review
Spokane, WA
Christopher Anderson, Photographer

Pittsburgh Post-Gazette
Pittsburgh, PA
Steve Mellon, Photographer

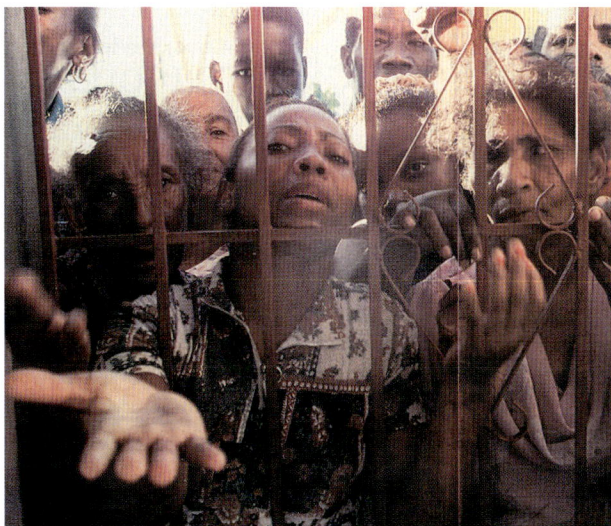
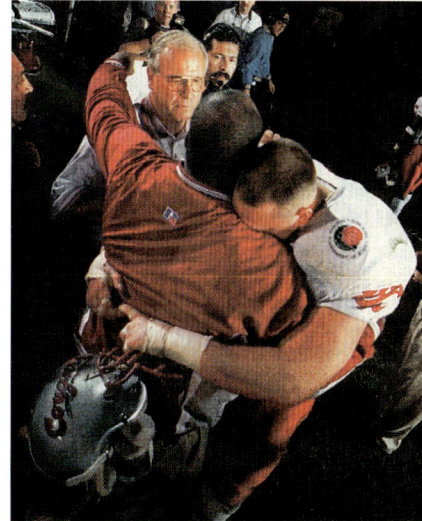
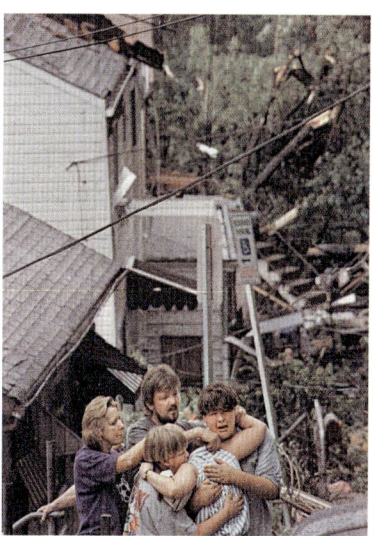

The Spokesman-Review
Spokane, WA
Christopher Anderson, Photographer

St. Louis Post-Dispatch
St. Louis, MO
Jane Rudolph, Photographer

The Oregonian
Portland, OR
Paul Kitagaki, Jr., Photographer

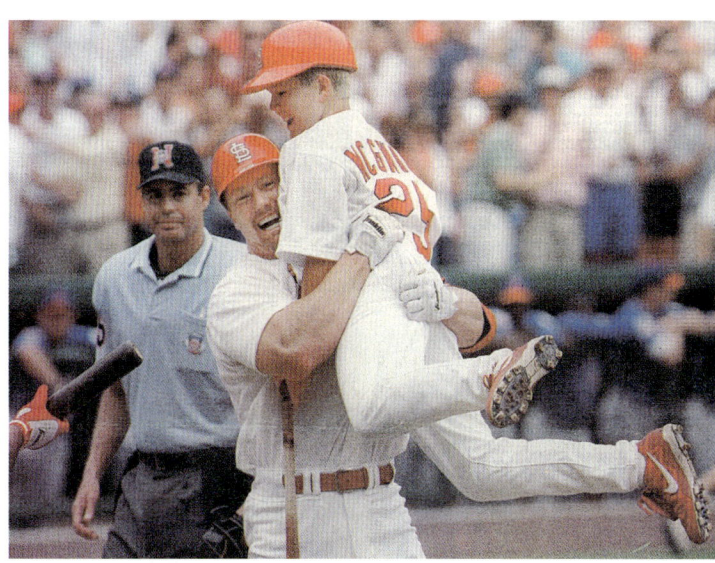
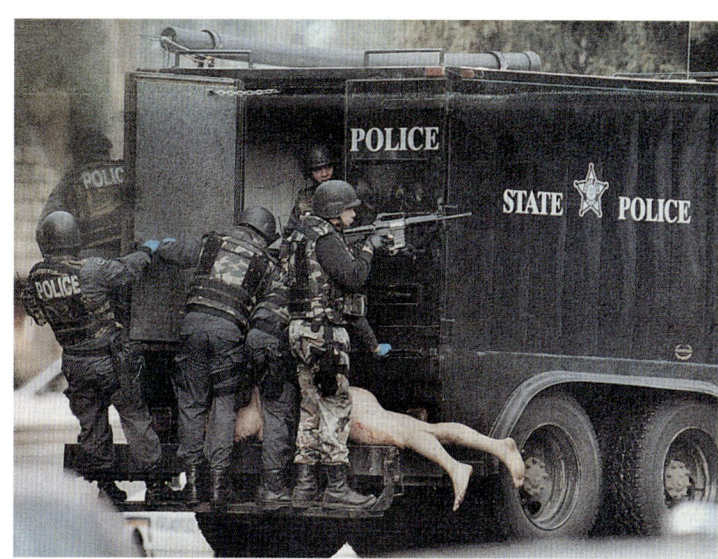

TWENTIETH EDITION ■ **225**

PHOTOJOURNALISM ■ Spot News, Feature

Silver
Göteborgs-Posten
Göteborg, Sweden
Jonny Mattsson, Photographer; **Thomas Andersson,** Designer

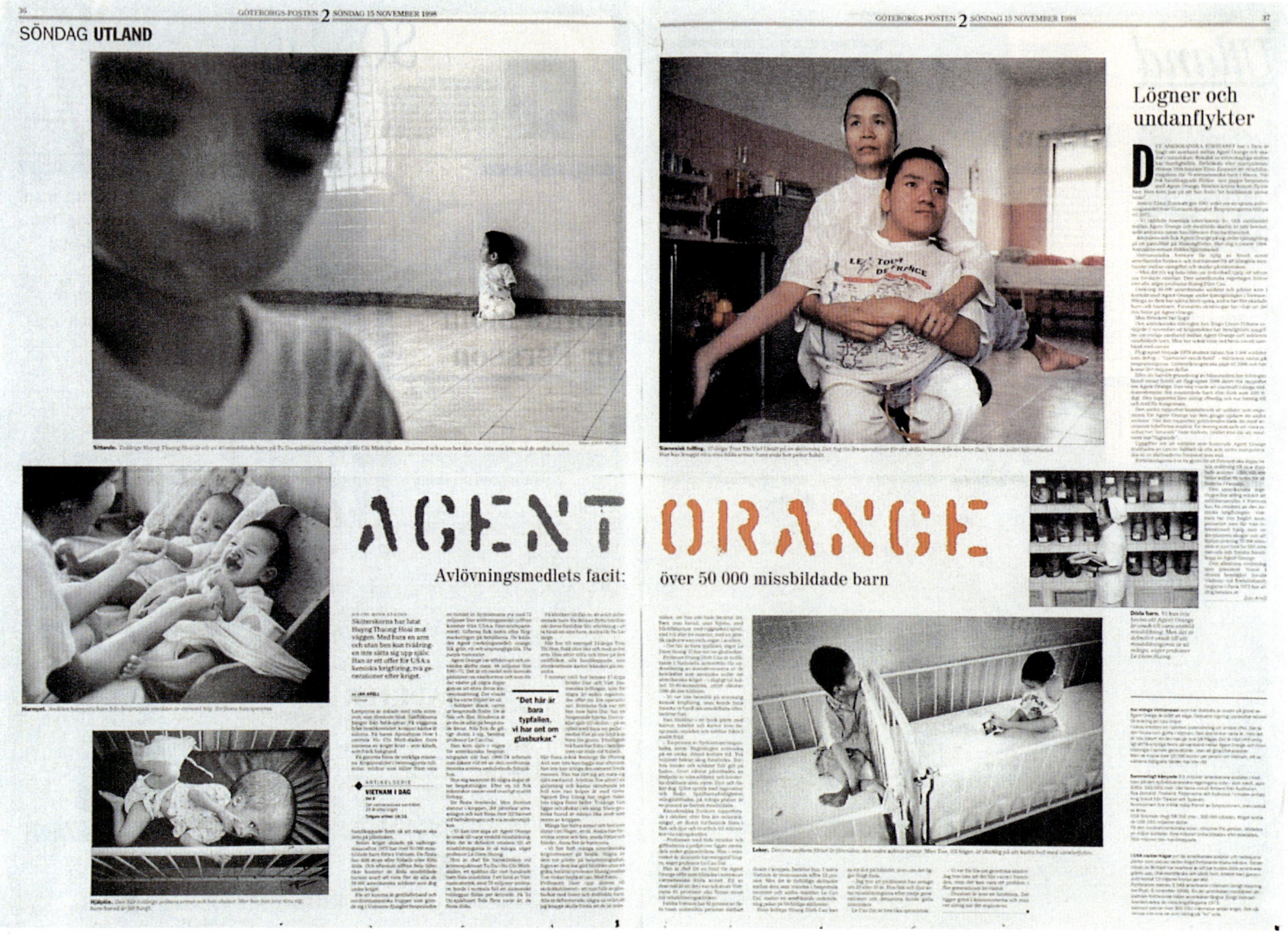

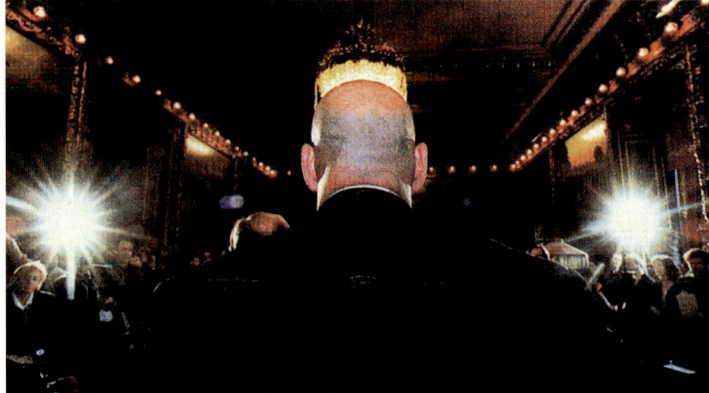

St. Paul Pioneer Press
St. Paul, MN
Richard Marshall, Photographer

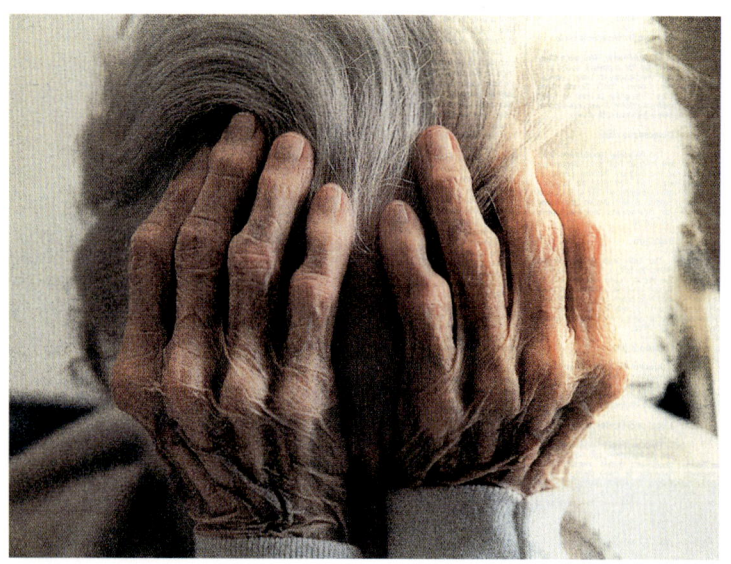

Las Vegas Review-Journal
Las Vegas, NV
John Gurzinski, Photographer

Feature ■ PHOTOJOURNALISM

The National Post
Don Mills, Canada
John Lehmann, Photographer; **Gayle Grin,** Design Editor; **Denis Paquin,** Photo Editor; **Kenneth Whyte,** Editor-in-Chief; **Diane de Fenoyl,** Living Editor; **Tim Rostrum,** Arts Editor; **Lucie Lacava,** Design Consultant

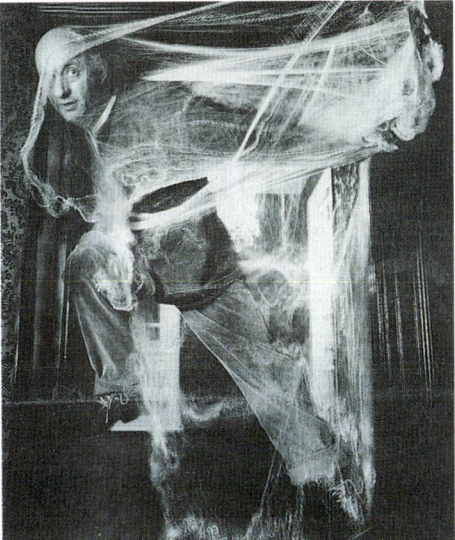

Pittsburgh Post-Gazette
Pittsburgh, PA
Robin Rombach, Photographer

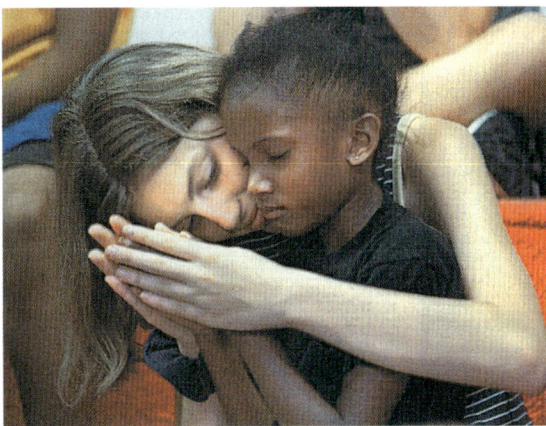

The Toronto Star
Toronto, Canada
Dick Loek, Photographer

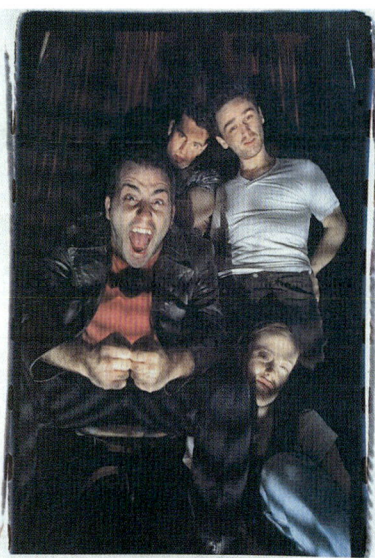

The New York Times Magazine
New York, NY
Michael O'Neill, Photographer; **Janet Froelich,** Art Director; **Joele Cuyler,** Designer; **Kathy Ryan,** Photo Editor

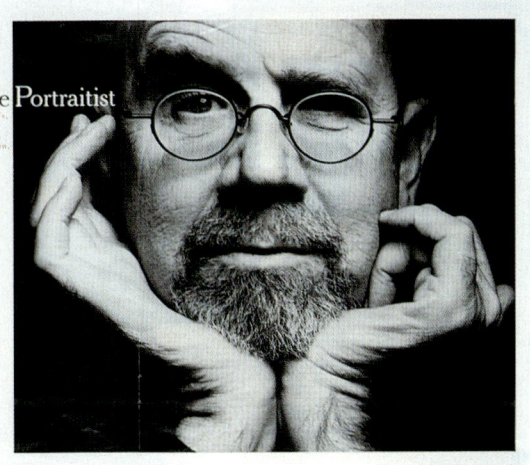

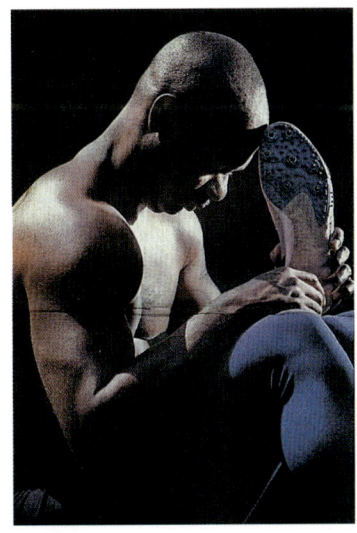

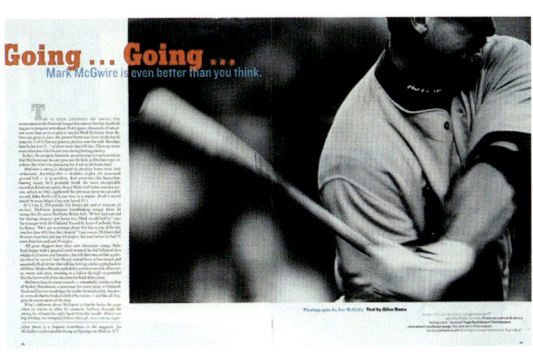

The New York Times Magazine
New York, NY
McNally, Photographer; **Janet Froelich,** Art Director; **Andrea Fella,** Designer; **Joe Kathy Ryan,** Photo/Graphics Editor

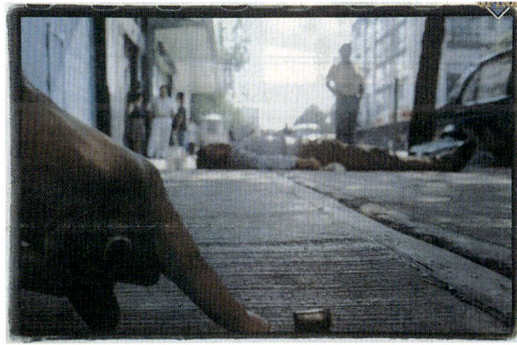

Reforma
México City, México
Augustin Marquez, Photographer; **Eduardo Danilo,** Design Consultant; **Oscar Yanez,** Section Designer; **Emilio Deheza,** Art Director; **Victor Hugo Arteaga,** Photo Coeditor; **Ricardo Del Castillo,** Graphic Editor; **Hector Zamarron,** Section Editor

The Toronto Star
Toronto, Canada
Richard Lautens, Photographer

TWENTIETH EDITION ■ 227

PHOTOJOURNALISM ■ Photo Illustration

Lexington Herald-Leader
Lexington, KY
David Stephenson, Photographer; **Ron Garrison,** Photo Director; **Marilyn S. Kitchens,** Features Designer; **Steve Dorsey,** Presentation Director & Designer

The Charlotte Observer
Charlotte, NC
Stephanie Grace Lim, Photographer; **Susan Gilbert,** Director/Photography; **The' Pham,** Editor; **Susan Knapp,** Designer

The New York Times
New York, NY
Gerald Slota, Photographer; **Janet Froelich,** Art Director; **Claude Martell,** Designer; **Kathy Ryan,** Photo/Graphics Editor

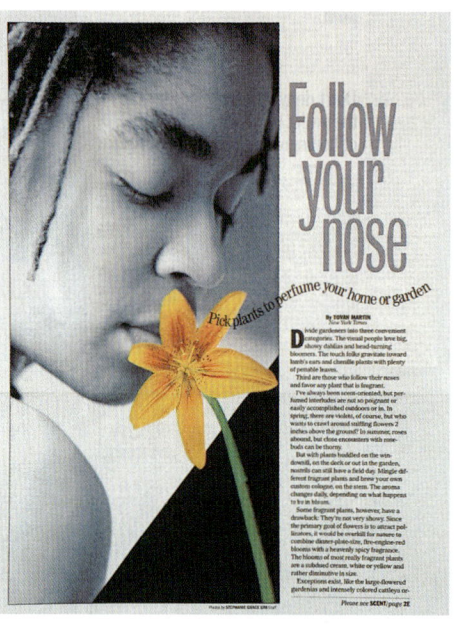
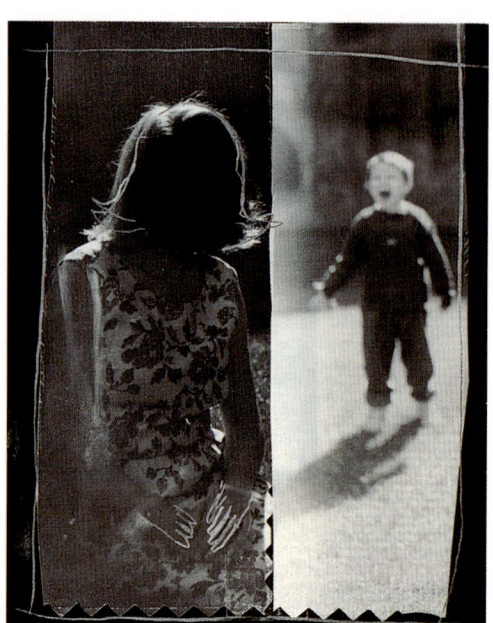

The Oregonian
Portland, OR
Dana E. Olsen, Photographer

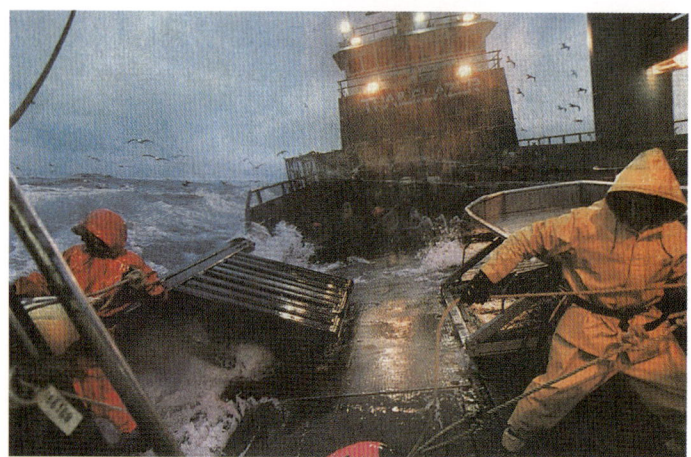

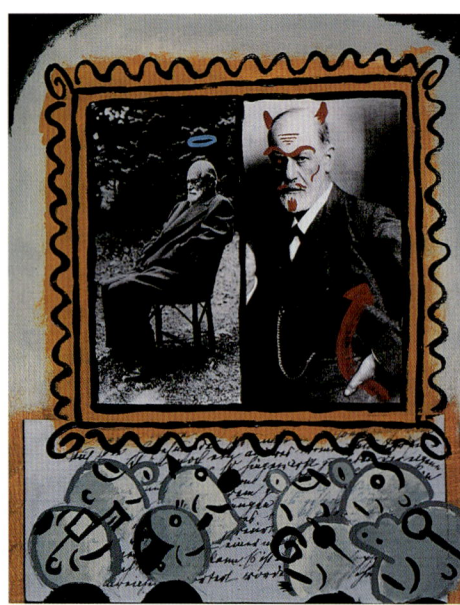

The New York Times Magazine
New York, NY
Gary Baseman, Illustrator; **Janet Froelich,** Art Director; **Claudia Brandenburg,** Designer

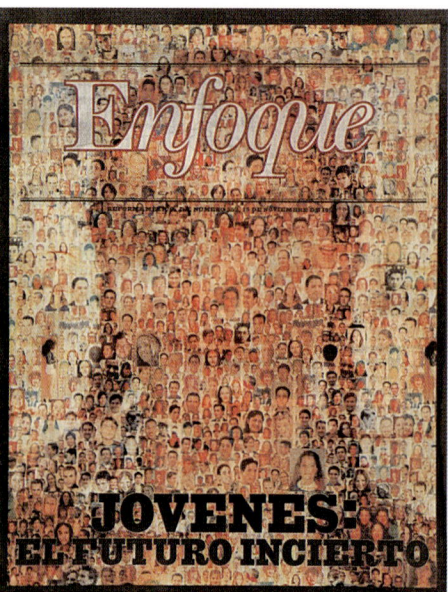

Reforma
México City, México
Efraín Folia, Photo Illustrator; **Ernesto Montes de oca,** Designer; **José Manuel Mendoza,** Graphics Coordinator; **Emilio Deheza,** Art Director; **Eduardo Danilo,** Design Consultant

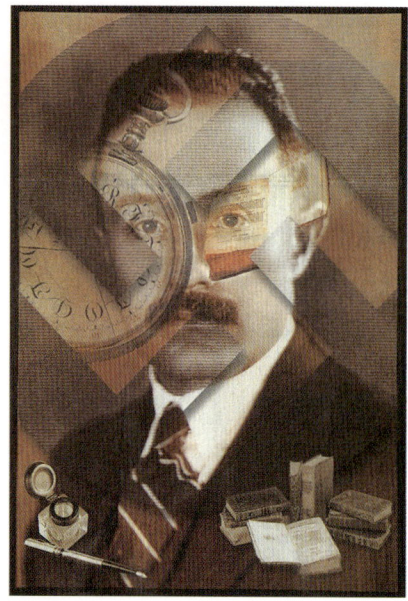

Reforma
México City, México
Efraín Foglia, Photo Illustrator; **Eduardo Danilo,** Design Consultant; **José Manuel Mendoza,** Graphics Coordinator; **Emilio Deheza,** Art Director

Photo Series ■ PHOTOJOURNALISM

Gold
Denver Rocky Mountain News
Denver, CO

Paul Keebler, Designer; **Randall K. Roberts**, Design Director; **Pat Davison**, Photographer; **Janet Reeves**, Director/Photography • also an Award of Excellence for Special Section Without Ads

The more you study this story, the more drawn to it you become. Davison's mother's struggle with Alzheimer's disease embraces you. The photographer's powerful story telling is gripping. Every image preserves his mother's dignity and builds the reader's understanding about life.

Mientras más se examina esta historia, más lo atrae a uno. La lucha de la madre de Davison contra la enfermedad de Alzheimer lo toca a uno. Las impresionantes imágenes de la historia tomadas por el fotógrafo atrapan al lector. Cada imagen conserva la dignidad de su madre y contribuye a que el lector comprenda mejor la vida.

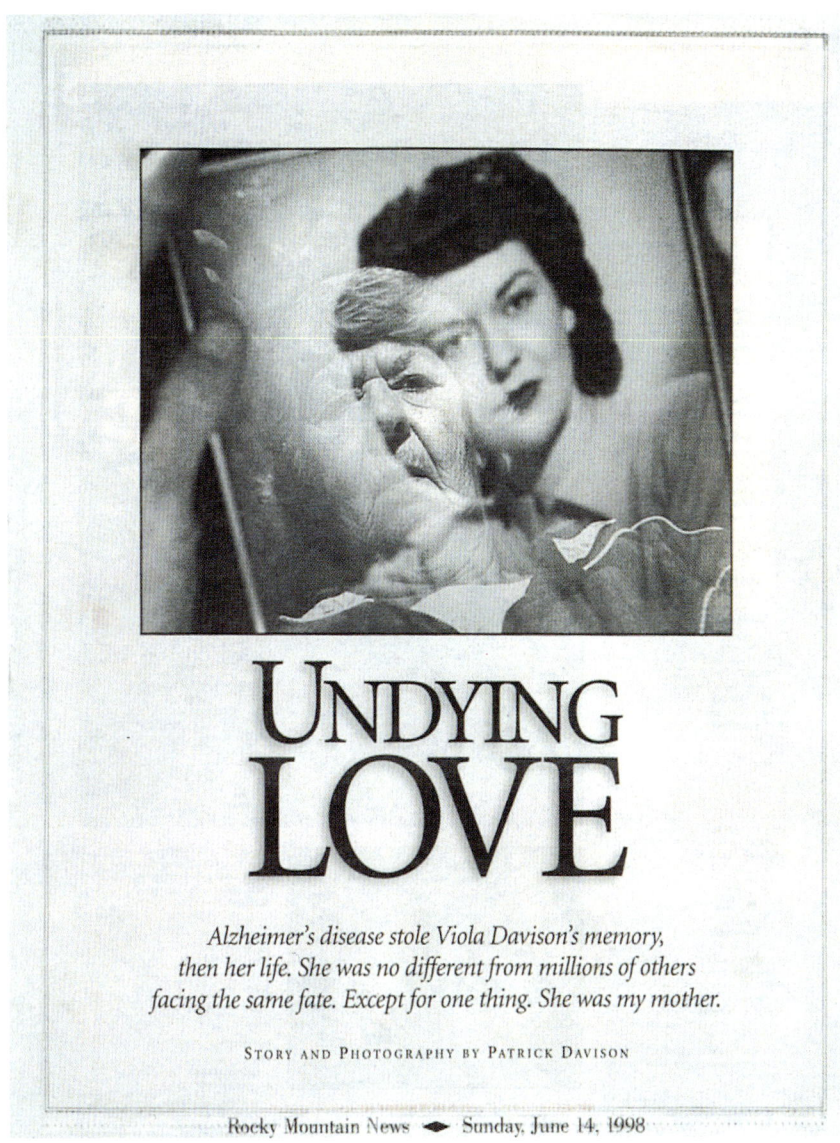
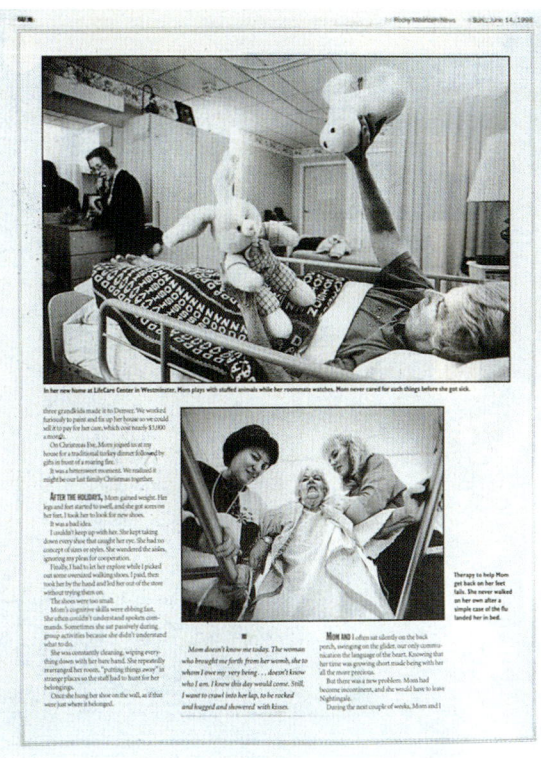
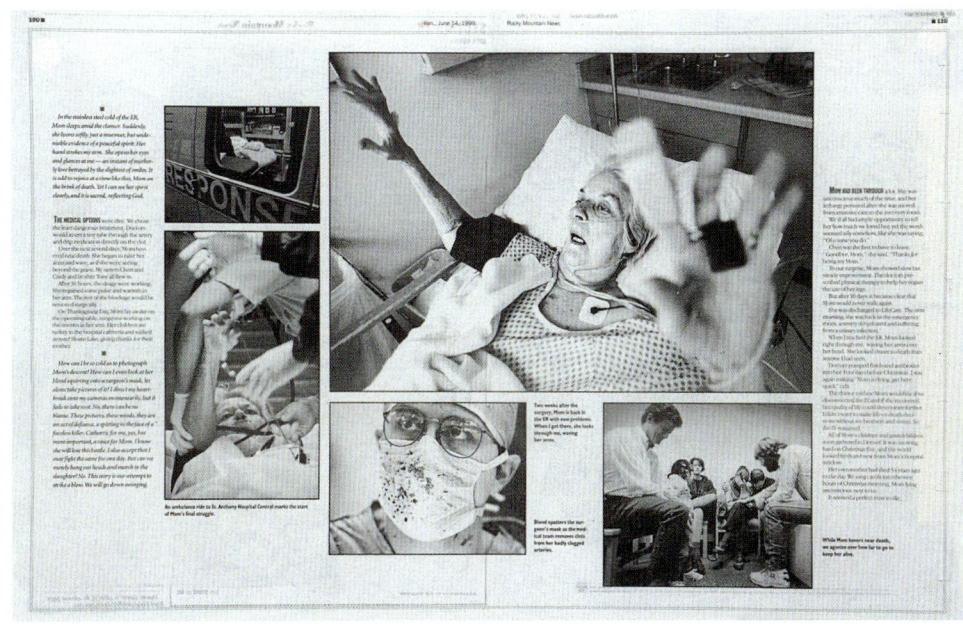
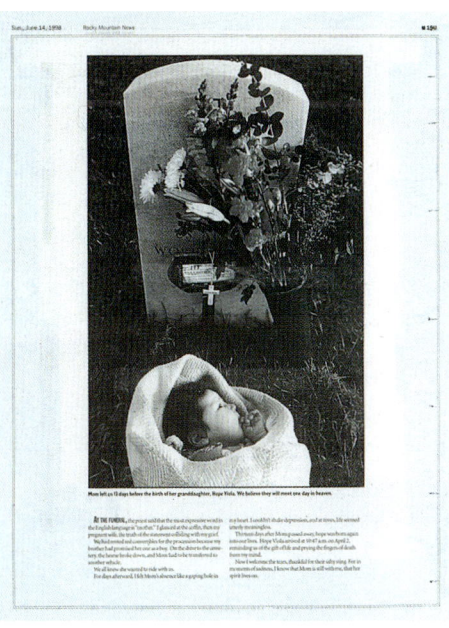

PHOTOJOURNALISM ■ Photo Series

Silver
Diario de Noticias / DNA
Lisbon, Portugal

Mário B. Resendes, Editor-in-Chief; **José Maria Ribeirinho,** Art Director; **Pedro Rolo Duarte,** Editor; **Luís Silva Dias,** Design Editor; **Miguel Pedroso,** Designer

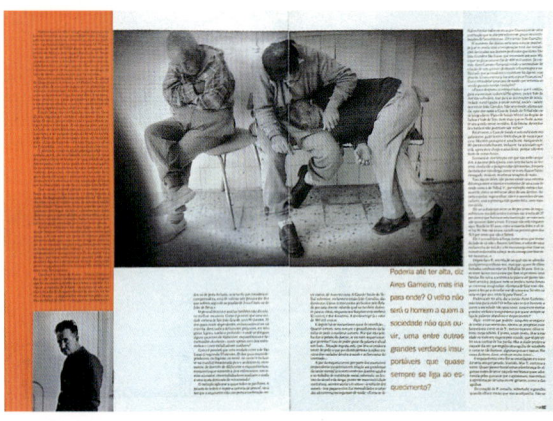
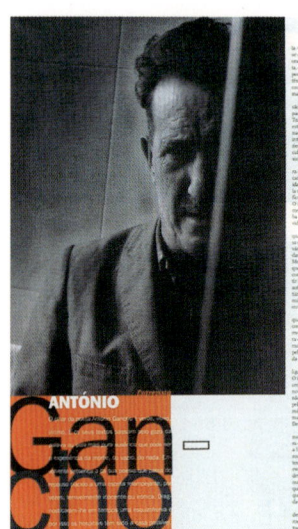
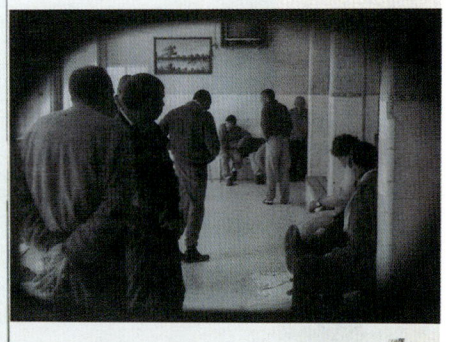

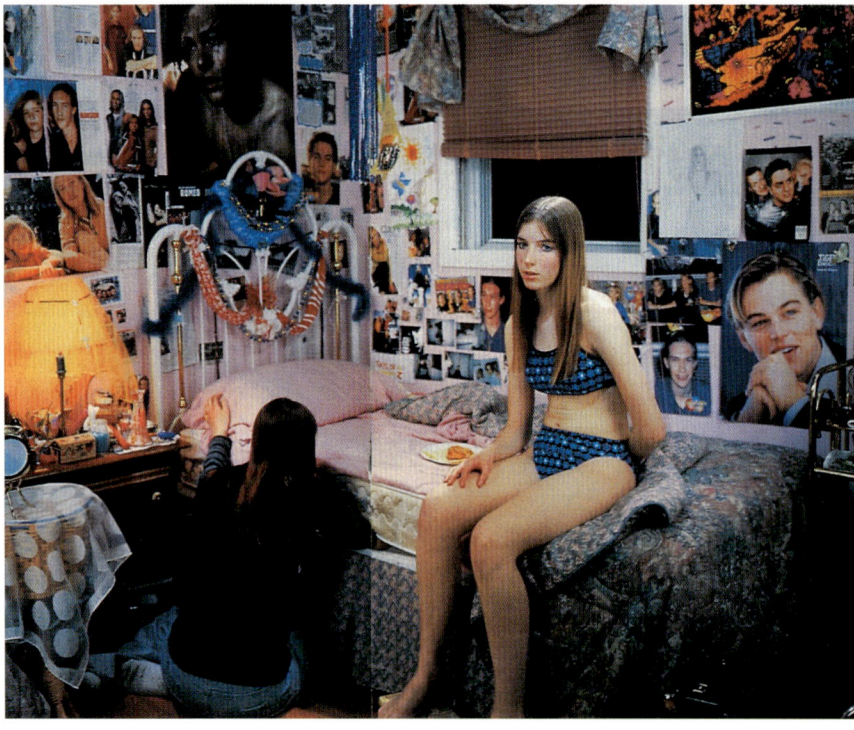
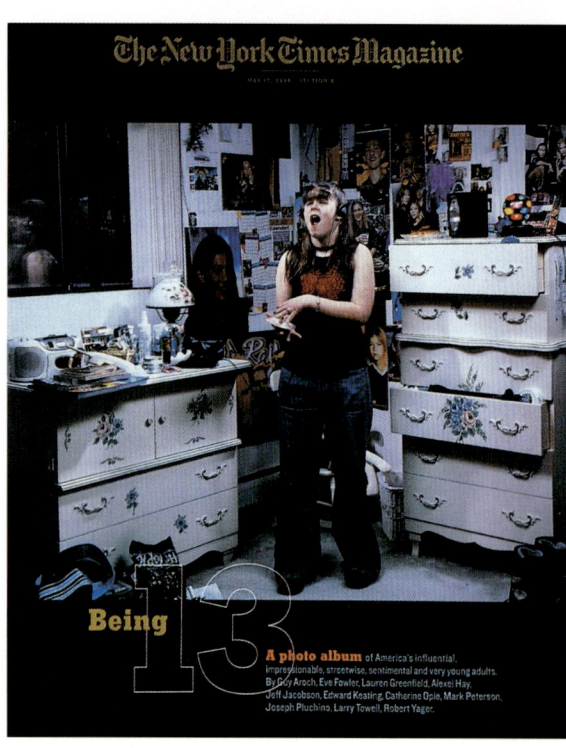

Silver
The New York Times Magazine
New York, NY

Kathy Ryan, Photo Editor; **Janet Froelich,** Art Director

Photo Series ■ PHOTOJOURNALISM

Silver
The Orange County Register
Santa Ana, CA

Daniel A. Anderson, Photographer; **Mike Goulding,** Photographer; **Bruce Chambers,** Photographer; **Paul E. Rodriguez,** Photographer; **Jeff Gritchen,** Photographer; **Michele Cardon,** Photo Editor; **Mike Pilgrim,** Photo Editor; **Chris Carlson,** Photographer/Photo Editor; **Marcia Joy Prouse,** Director/Photography; **Michael Kitada,** Photo Editor

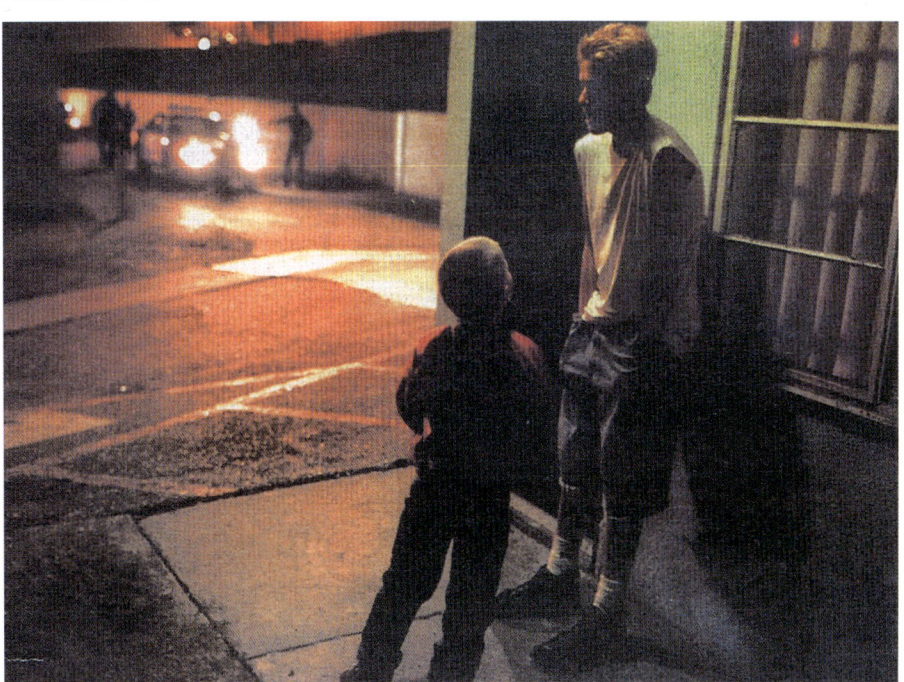

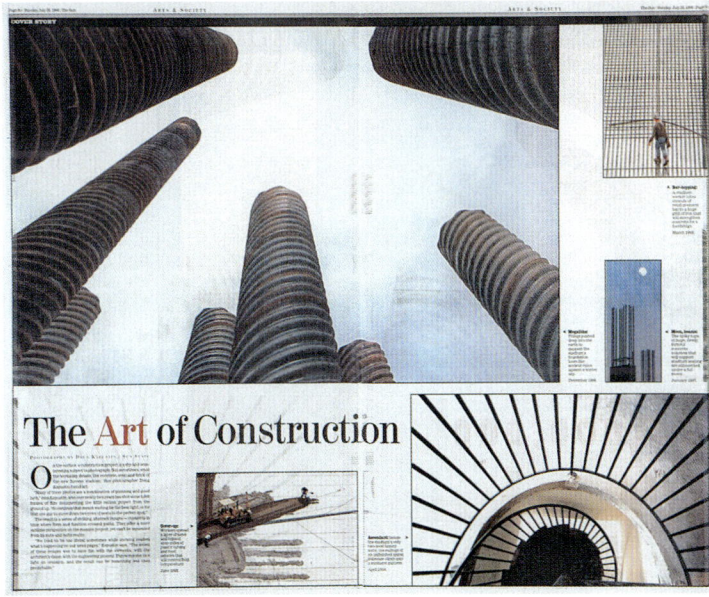

The Sun
Baltimore, MD
Doug Kapustin, Photographer; **Victor Panichkul,** Features Design Director; **Joseph Hutchinson,** A.M.E. Graphics/Design
• also for Entertainment Page

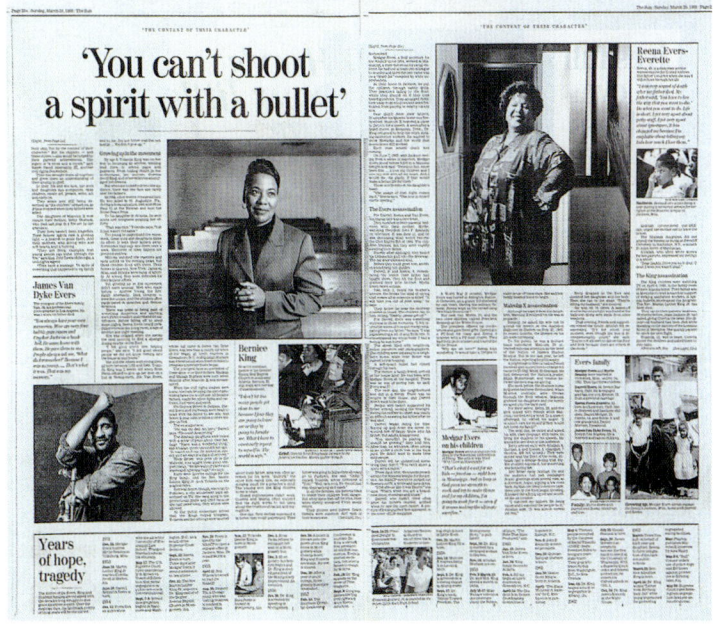

The Sun
Baltimore, MD
Andre Chung, Photographer

PHOTOJOURNALISM ■ Photo Series

The Boston Globe Magazine
Boston, MA

Michael Robinson-Chavez, Photographer; **Catherine Aldrich,** Art Director

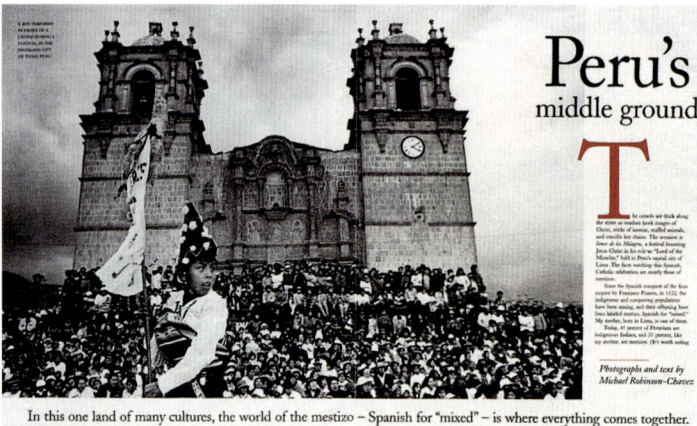

The Charlotte Observer
Charlotte, NC

Patrick Schneider, Photographer; **Susan Gilbert,** Director/Photography; **Monica Moses,** Designer

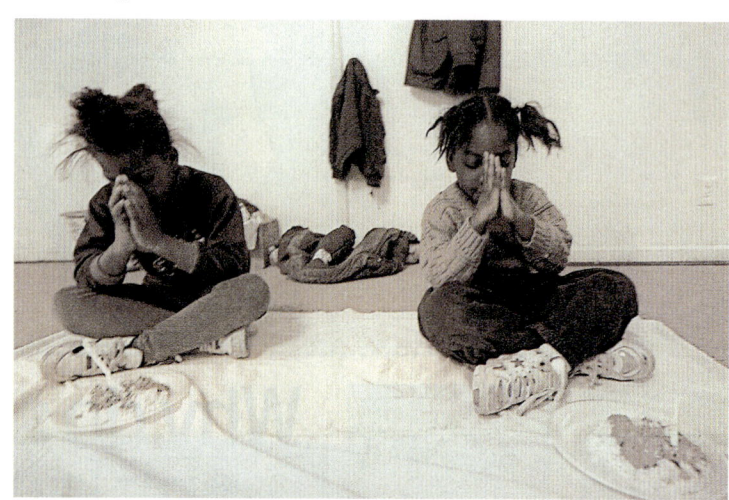

The Boston Globe Magazine
Boston, MA

Mark Wilson, Photographer; **Catherine Aldrich,** Art Director

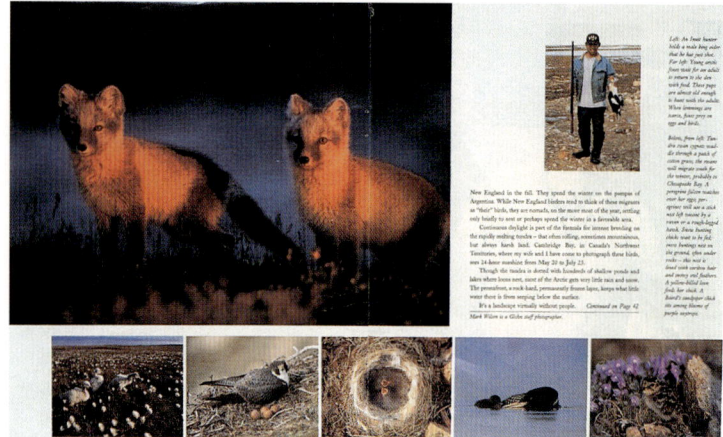

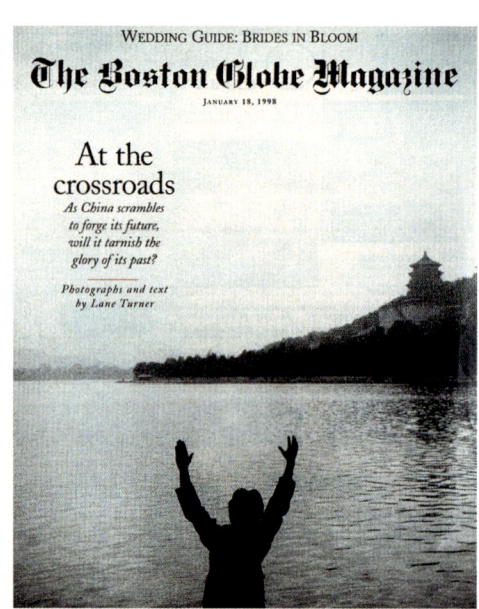

The Boston Globe Magazine
Boston, MA

Catherine Aldrich, Art Director; **Lane Turner,** Photographer

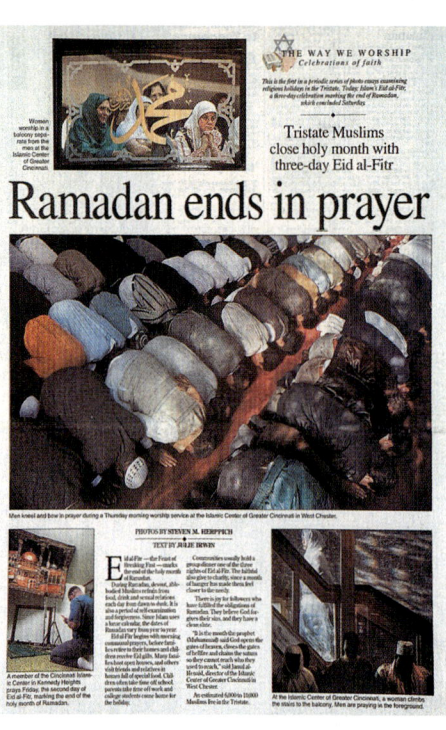

The Cincinnati Enquirer
Cincinnati, OH

Steven M. Herppich, Photographer; **Liz Dufour,** Director/Photography; **Sara Pearce,** Features Editor; **Bill Cieslewicz,** Deputy Features Editor

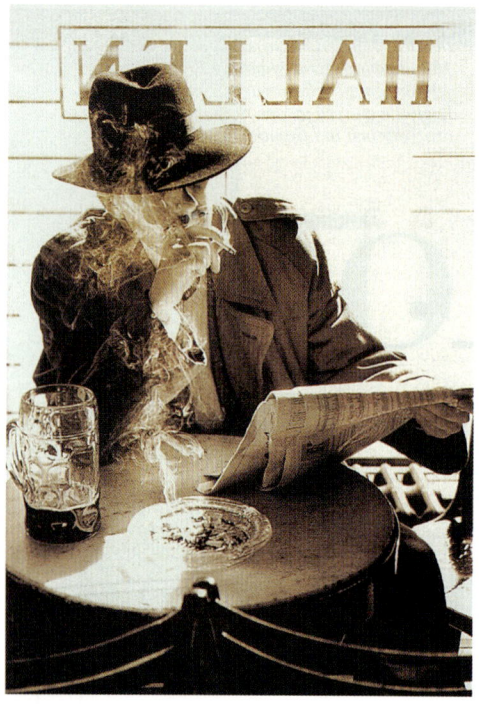

Göteborgs-Posten
Göteborg, Sweden

Lisa Thanner, Photographer; **Henrik Stromberg,** Designer

Photo Series ■ PHOTOJOURNALISM

Expresso
Lisbon, Portugal
Rui Ochoa, Photo Director

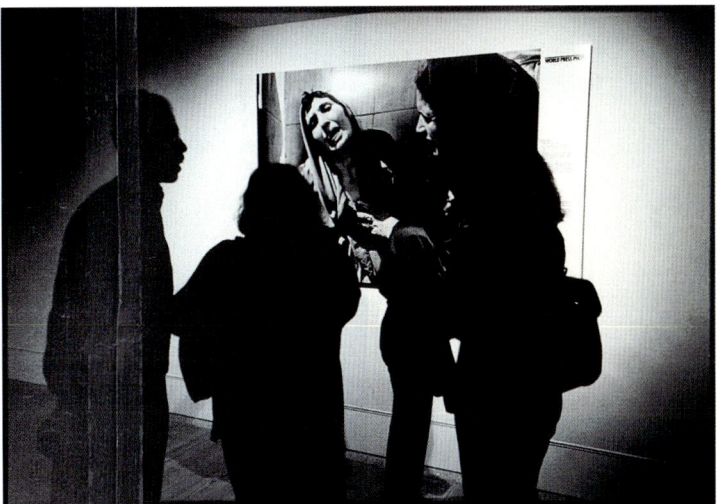

Expresso
Lisbon, Portugal
Rui Ochoa, Photo Director

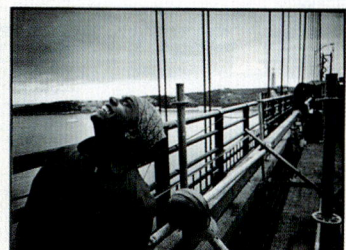
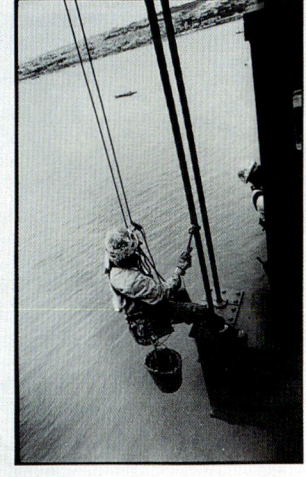
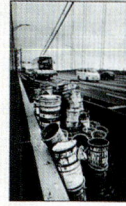

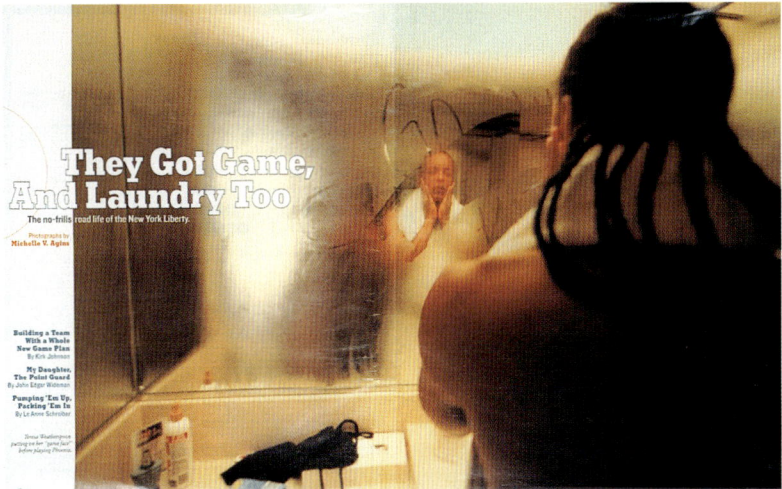

The New York Times Magazine
New York, NY
Michele V. Agins, Photographer; **Janet Froelich,** Art Director; **Nancy Harris,** Designer; **Kathy Ryan,** Photo Editor

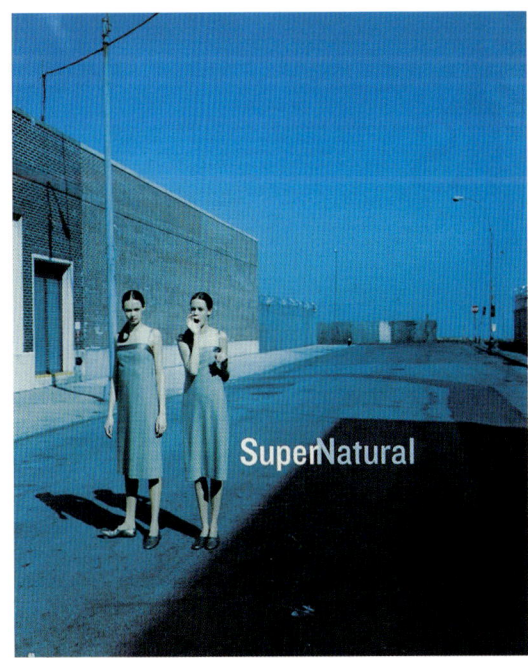

The New York Times Magazine
New York, NY
Cleo Sullivan, Photographer; **Janet Froelich,** Art Director; **Claudia Brandenburg,** Designer; **Kathy Ryan,** Photo Editor

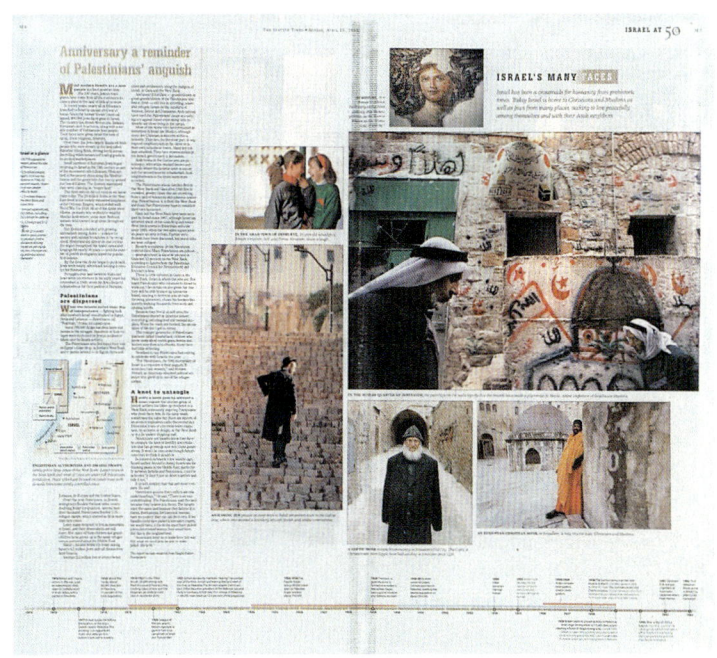

The Seattle Times
Seattle, WA
Betty Udesen, Photographer

TWENTIETH EDITION ■ 233

PHOTOJOURNALISM ■ Photo Series

The San Francisco Chronicle
San Francisco, CA
Fredic Larson, Photographer; **Kathleen Hennessy,** Photo Editor; **Frank Mina,** Page Designer

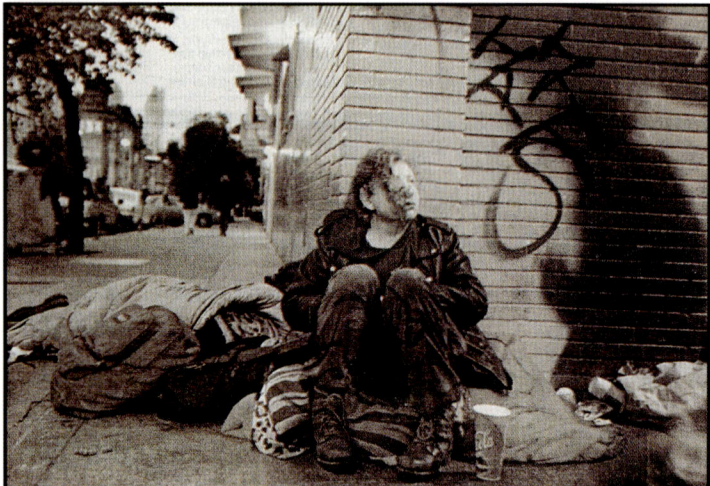

The New York Times Magazine
New York, NY
Vladimir Syomin, Photographer; **Janet Froelich,** Art Director; **Catherine Gilmore-Barnes,** Designer; **Kathy Ryan,** Photo Editor

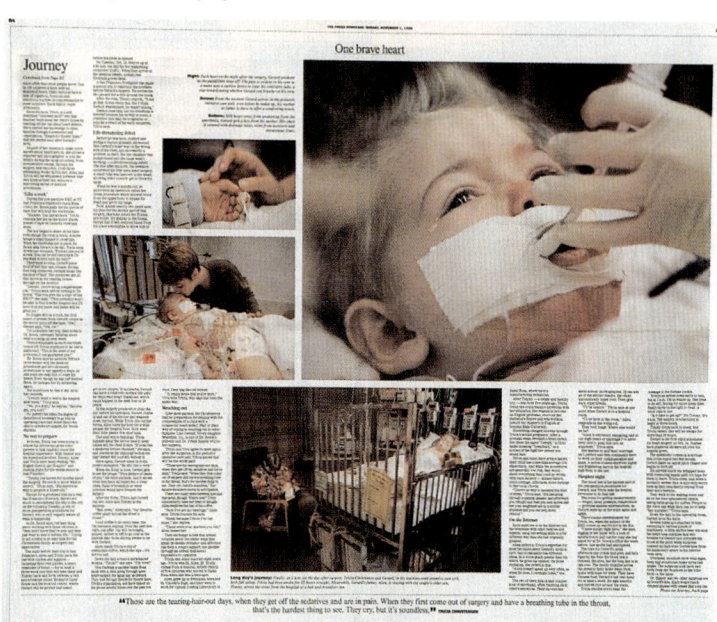

The Times
Munster, IN
Zbigniew Bzdak, Assistant Photo Editor

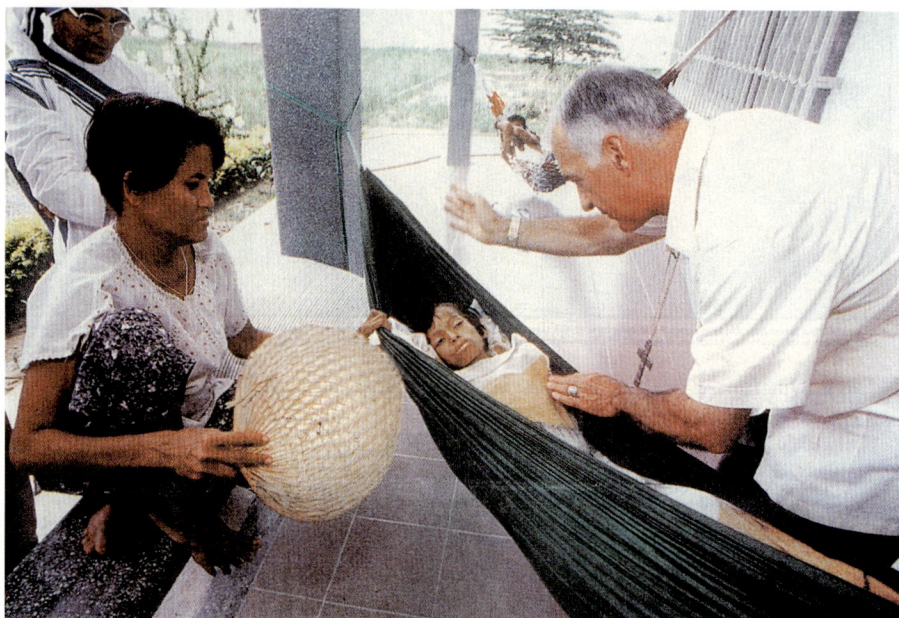

The Seattle Times
Seattle, WA
Harley Stoles, Photographer; **Rhonda Prast,** Designer/Photo Editor/Art Director

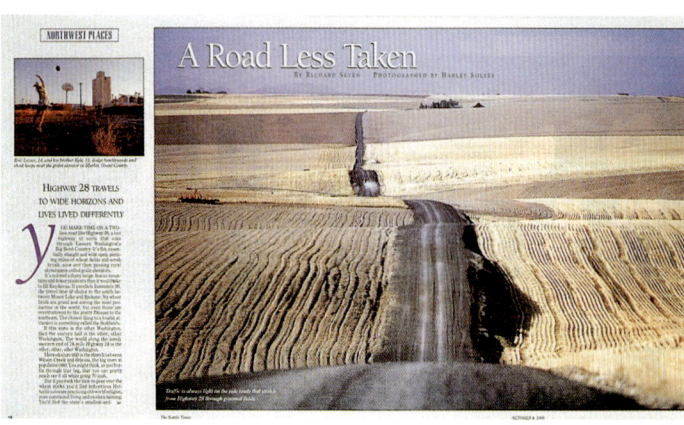

Texas, Houston Chronicle Magazine
Houston, TX
O. Rufus Lovett, Photographer; **Catherine McIntosh,** Art Director

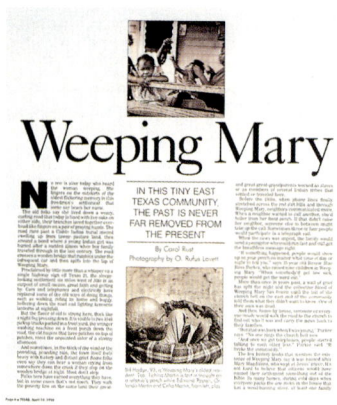
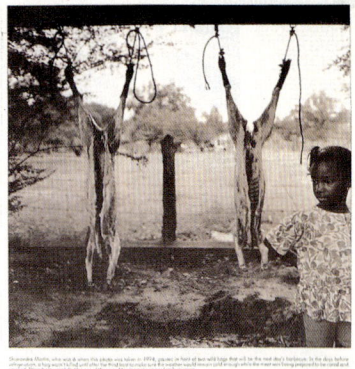

Portfolio One Photographer, More than One ■ PHOTOJOURNALISM

Detroit Free Press
Detroit, MI
J. Kyle Keener, Features Photography

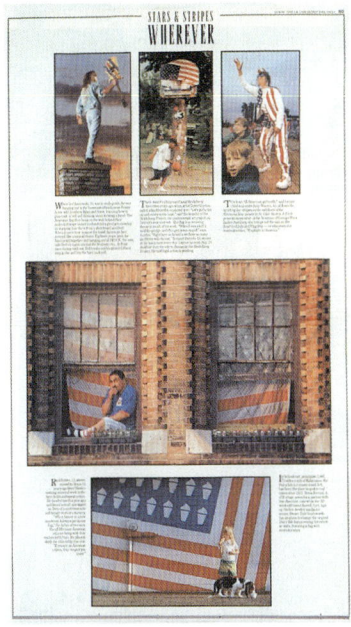

San Jose Mercury News
San Jose, CA
Tom Van Dyke, Photojournalist

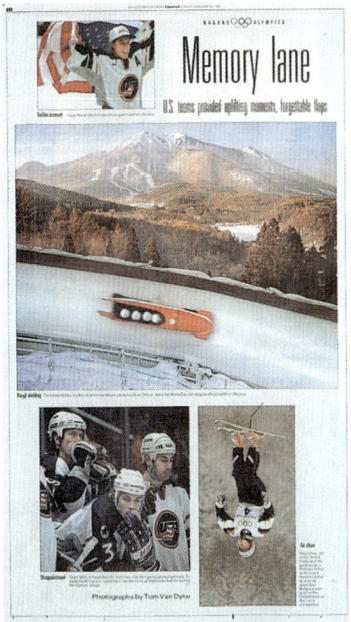

The Seattle Times
Seattle, WA
Steve Ringman, Photographer

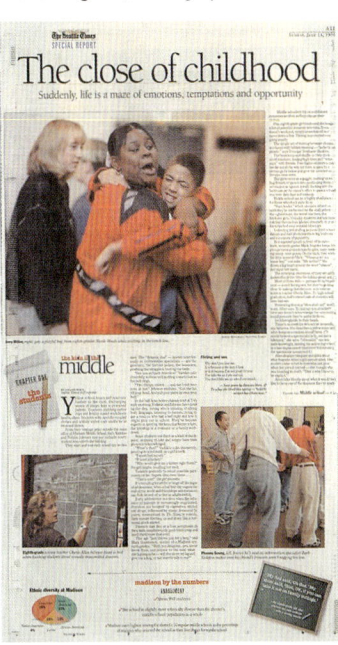

The Palm Beach Post
W. Palm Beach, FL
Greg Lovett, Photographer; **Paul J. Milette,** Photographer; **Mark Mirko,** Photographer; **Bob Shanley,** Photographer; **Lannis Waters,** Photographer; **Liu Xin,** Photographer; **Mark Edelson,** Photo Editor

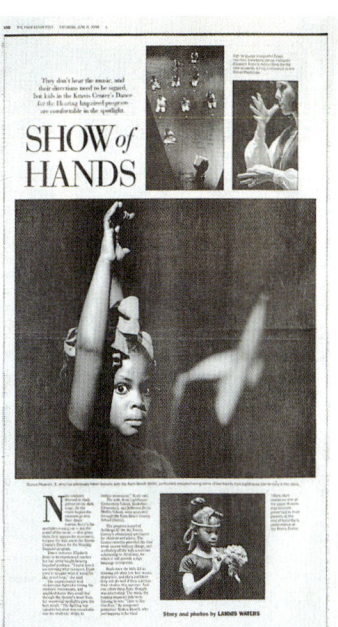

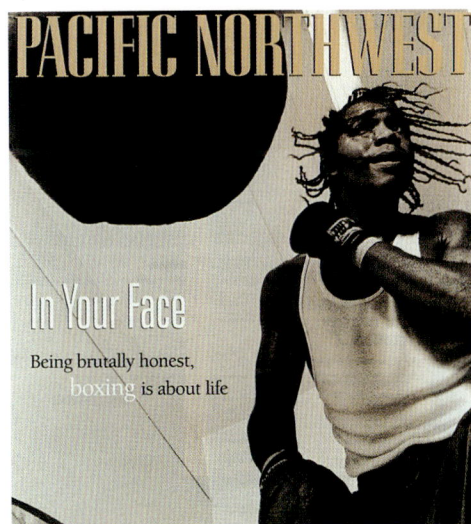

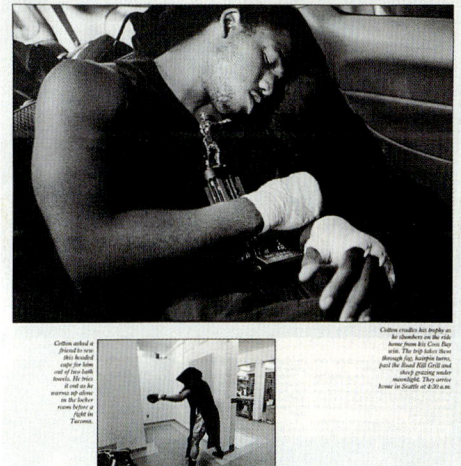

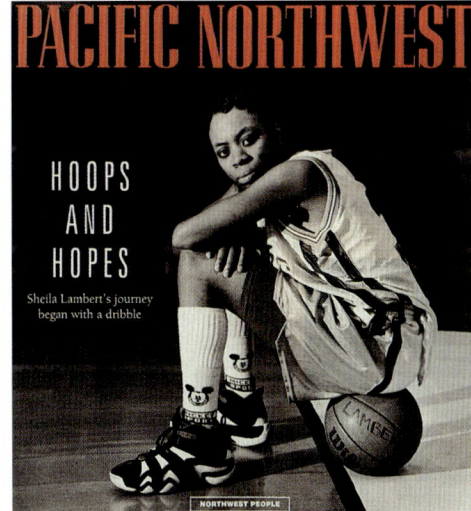

Silver
The Seattle Times
Seattle, WA
Betty Udesen, Photographer

The Seattle Times
Seattle, WA
Harley Soltes, Photographer

TWENTIETH EDITION ■ 235

PHOTOJOURNALISM ■ Portfolio More than One Photographer

Silver
San Jose Mercury News
San Jose, CA

Karen T. Borchers, Photographer; **Patrick Tehan**, Photographer; **Richard Koci Hernandez**, Photographer; **Geri Migielicz**, Director/Photography
• also an Award of Excellence for Photo Series

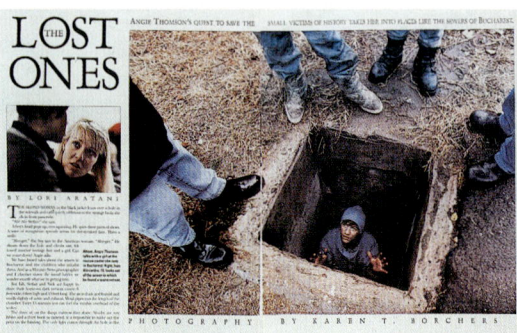
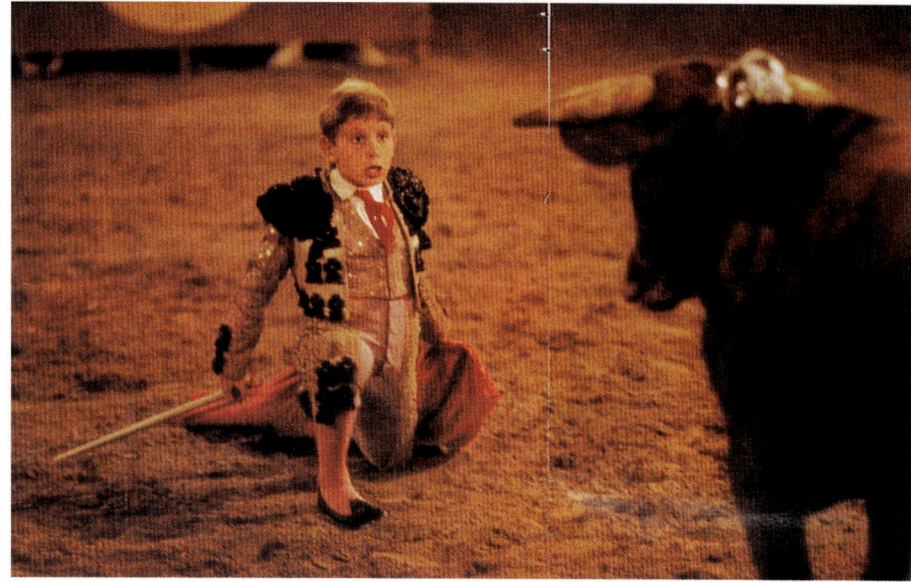

Silver
The Times-Picayune
New Orleans, LA

G. Andrew Boyd, Photographer; **Scott Threlkeld**, Photographer; **Doug Parker**, Photo/Graphics Editor; **Susan Koenig**, Designer

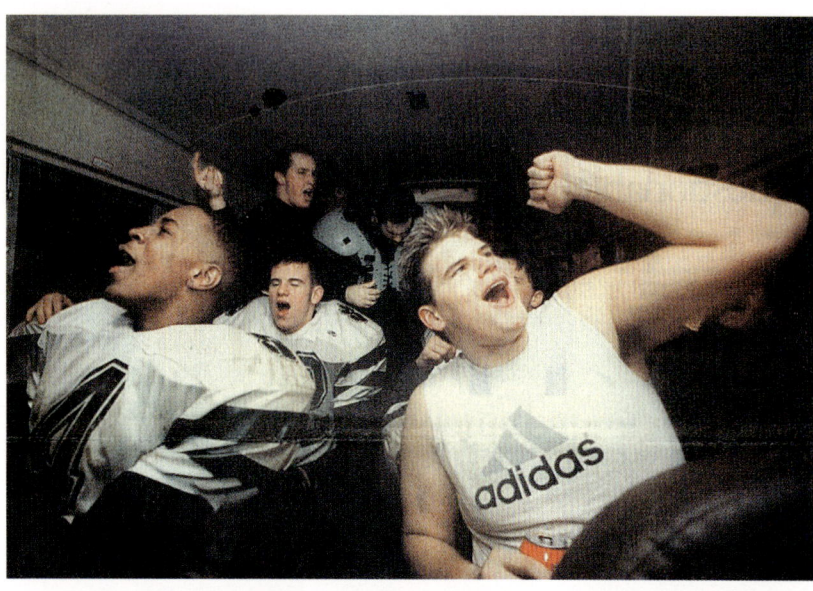
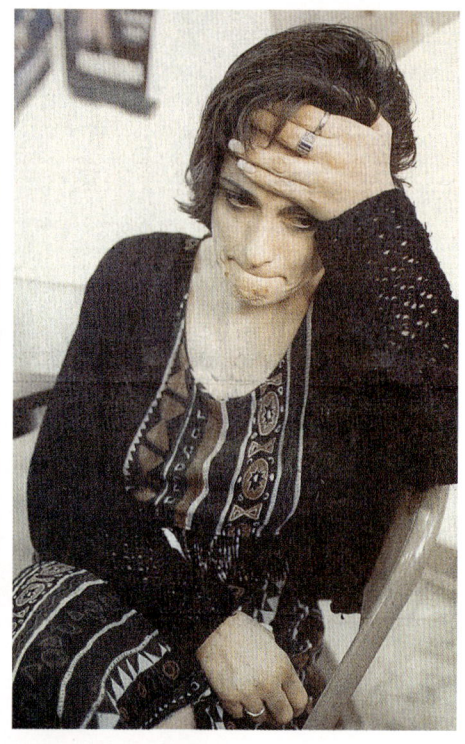
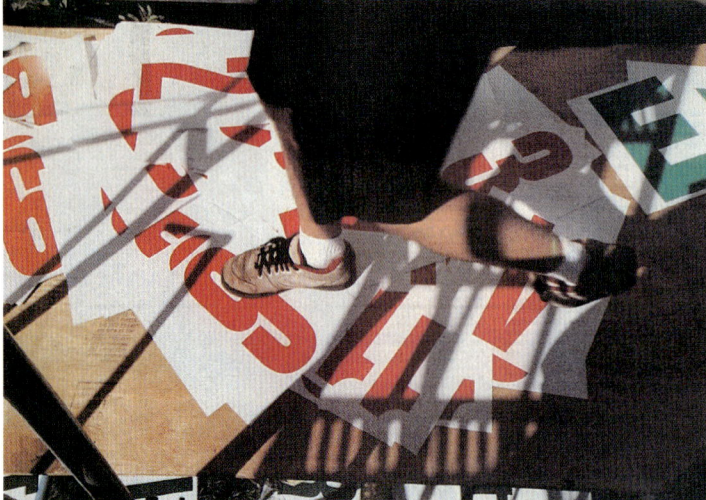
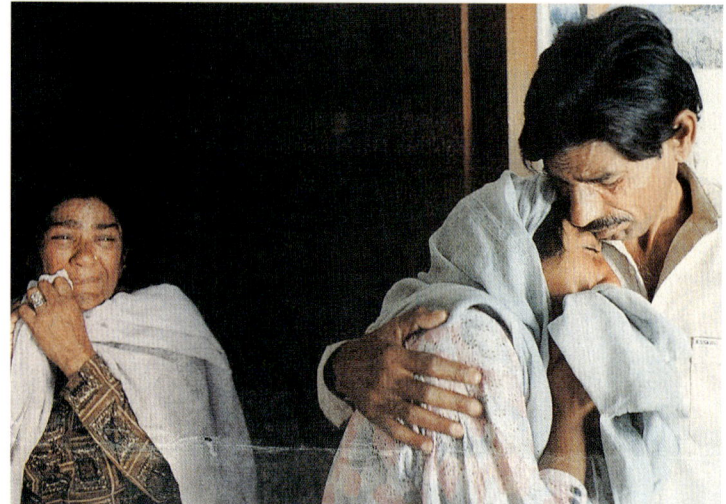

The Hartford Courant
Hartford, CT
Thom McGuire, Director/Photography

The Oregonian
Portland, OR
Staff, Photographers

INFOGRAPHICS

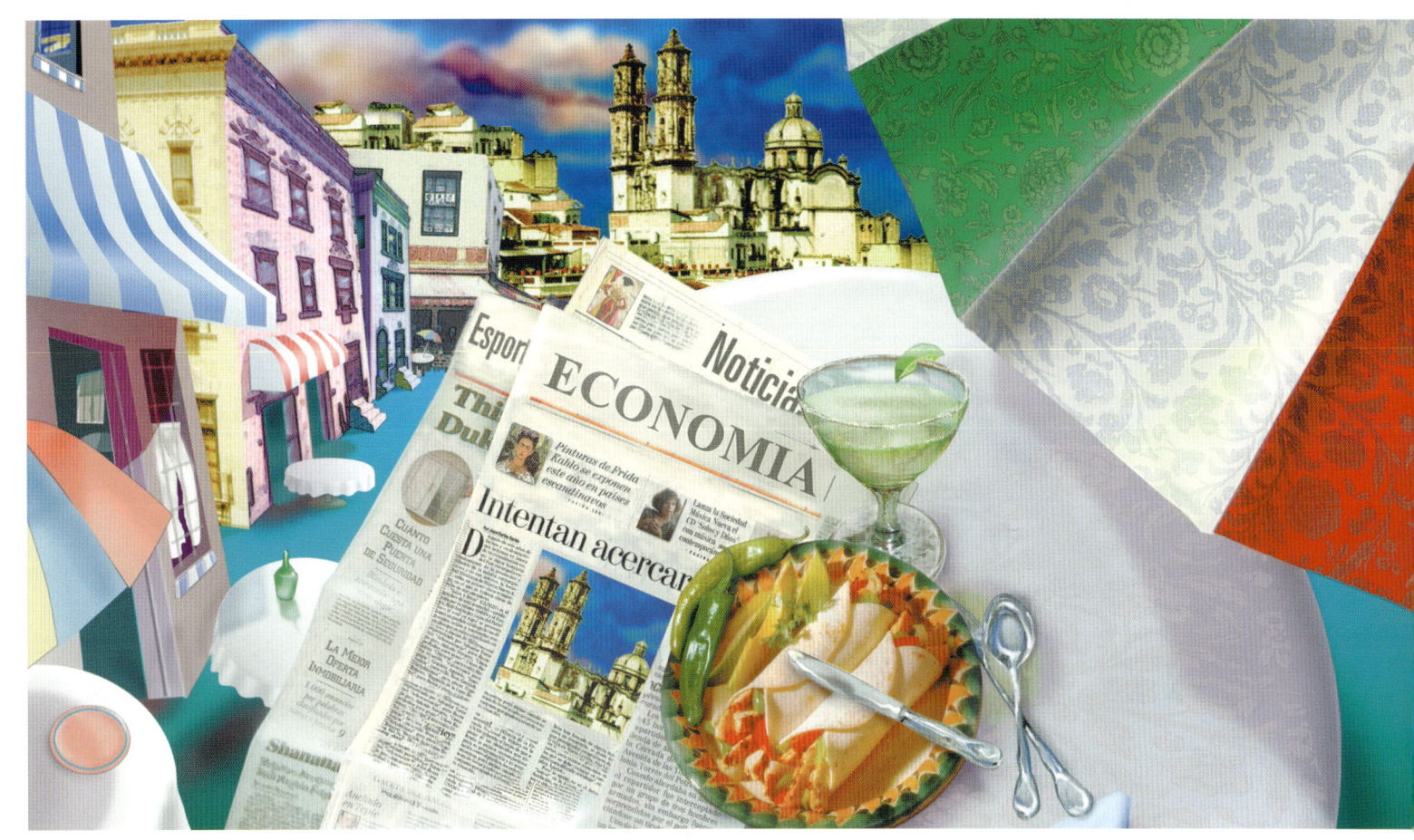

CHAPTER NINE

BREAKING NEWS

**BLACK & WHITE
AND/OR ONE COLOR**

**TWO OR MORE
COLORS**

PORTFOLIO

INFOGRAPHICS ■ Breaking News, Black or Black and One Color

The Sun
Baltimore, MD
Charles Jones, News Artist; **Lamont W. Harvey,** News Artist; **Emily Holmes,** Graphics Editor; **Jerold Council,** Graphics Director; **Joseph Hutchinson,** A.M.E. Graphics/Design

O Globo
Rio de Janeiro, Brasil
Fernando Alvarus, Infographic Artist; **Alvim,** Infographic Artist; **Renato Carvalho,** Infographic Artist

The Orange County Register
Santa Ana, CA
George Turney; Kris Viesselman Onuigbo, Art Director

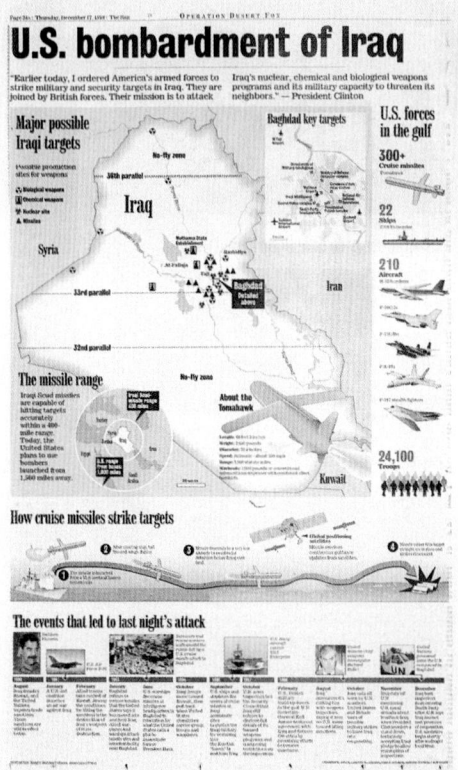 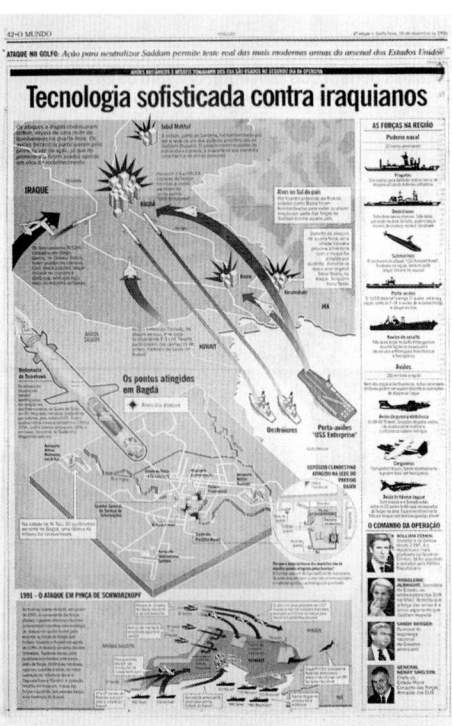 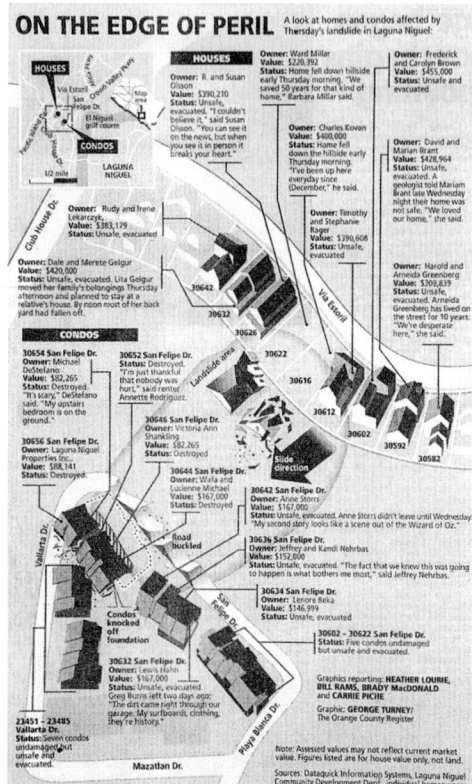

Clarín
Buenos Aires, Argentina
Iñaki Palacios, Art Director; **Jaime Serra,** Graphic Director; **Gerardo Morel,** Artist

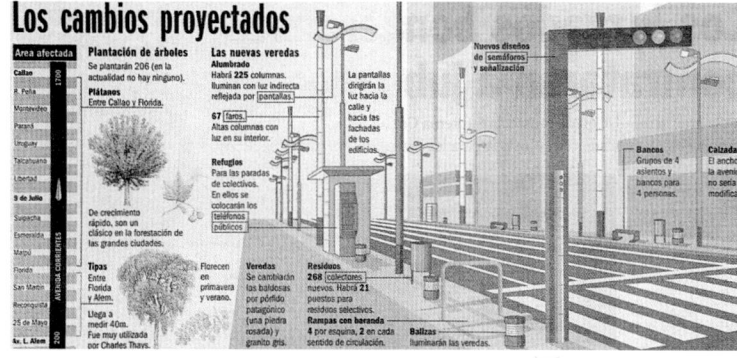

Clarín
Buenos Aires, Argentina
Iñaki Palacios, Art Director; **Jaime Serra,** Graphics Director/Artist; **Stella Bin,** Researcher

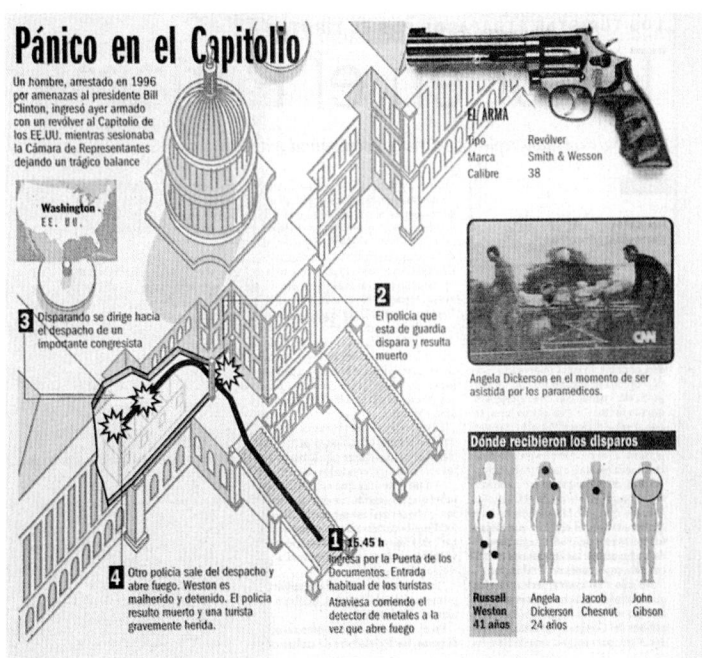 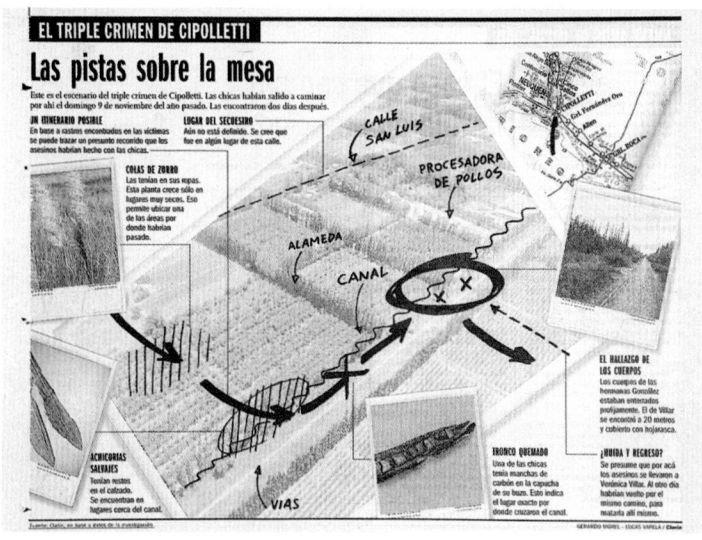

Clarín
Buenos Aires, Argentina
Iñaki Palacios, Art Director; **Jaime Serra,** Graphics Director/Artist; **Lucas Varela,** Artist; **Gerardo Morel,** Artist; **Stella Bin,** Researcher

Breaking News, Black or Black and One Color ■ INFOGRAPHICS

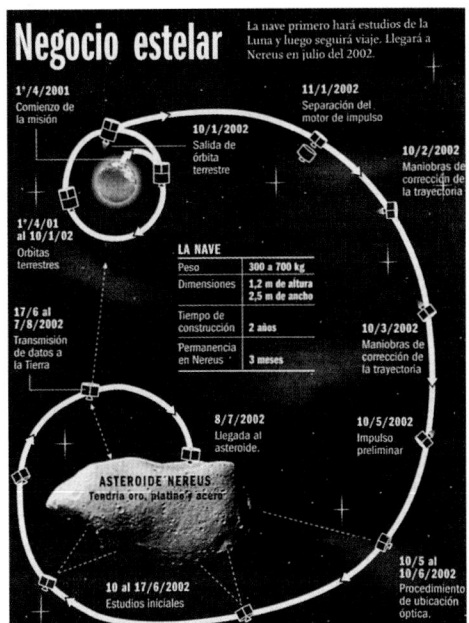

Clarín
Buenos Aires, Argentina
Iñaki Palacios, Art Director; Jaime Serra, Graphic Director

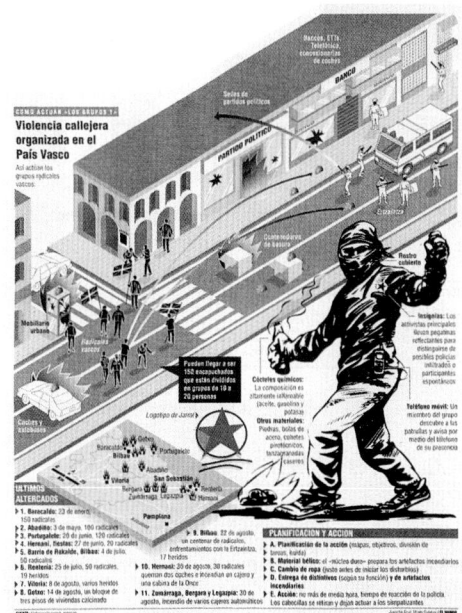

El Mundo Del Siglo XXI
Madrid, Spain
Juancho Cruz, Graphic Journalist; Ulises Culebro, Illustrator

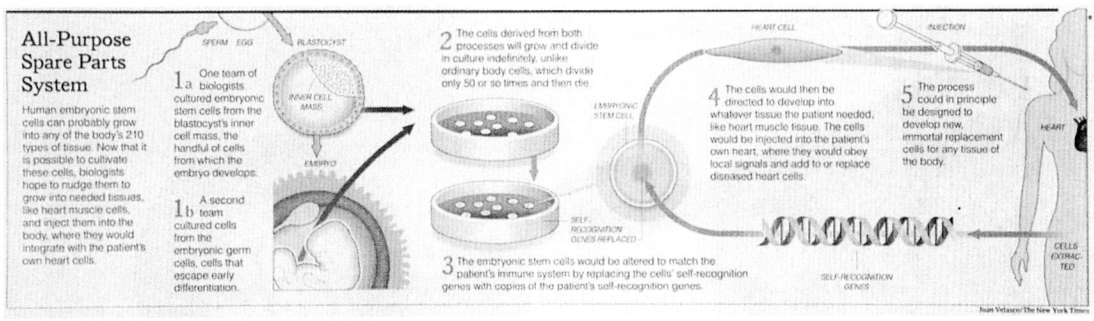

The New York Times
New York, NY
Juan Velasco, Graphics Editor

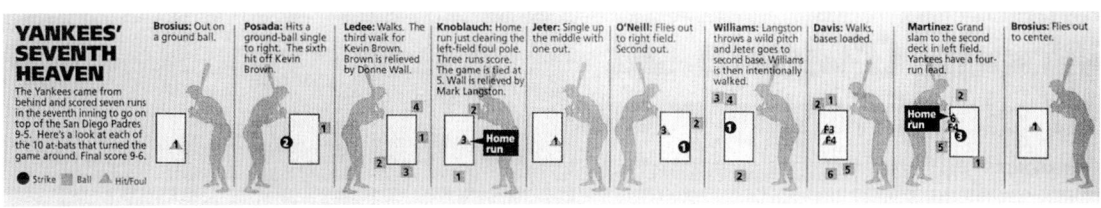

The Orange County Register
Santa Ana, CA
Kurt Snibbe, Artist; Kris Viesselman Onuigbo, Art Director

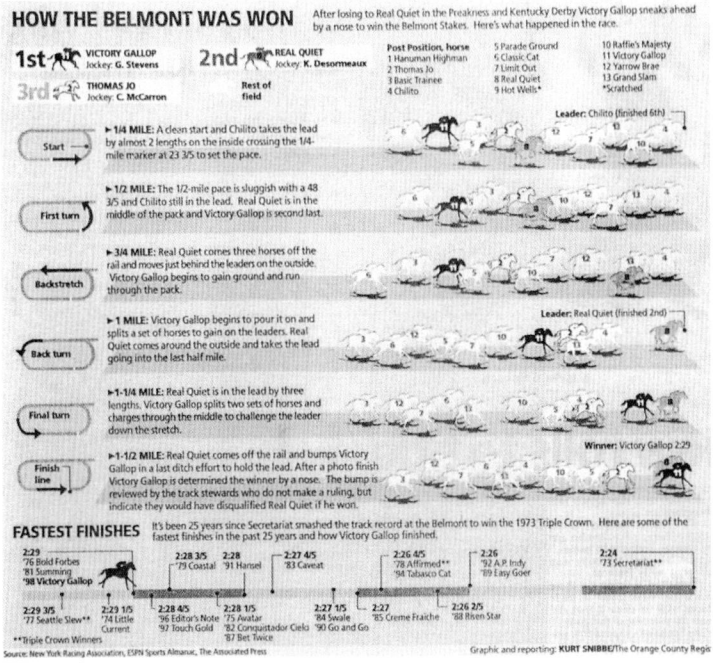

The Orange County Register
Santa Ana, CA
Kurt Snibbe, Artist; Kris Viesselman Onuigbo, Art Director

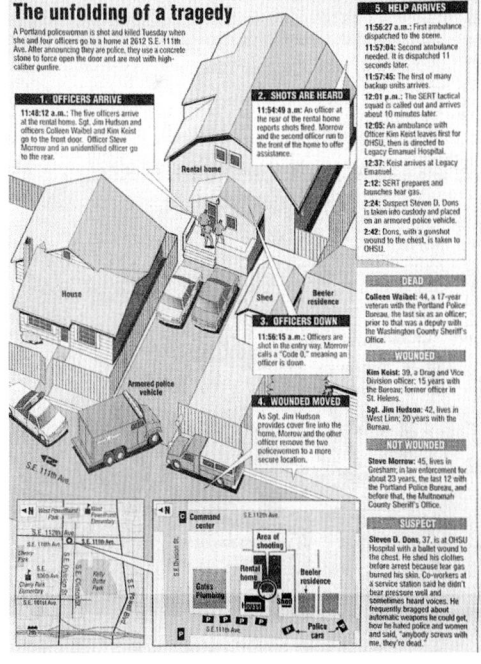

The Oregonian
Portland, OR
Michael Mode, Graphic Artist; Steve Cowden, Graphic Artist; Molly Swisher, Graphic Artist; Linda Shankweiler, Art Director; Steve McKinstry, Assistant Art Director

TWENTIETH EDITION ■ 239

INFOGRAPHICS ■ Breaking News, Black or Black and One Color

El País
Madrid, Spain
Staff

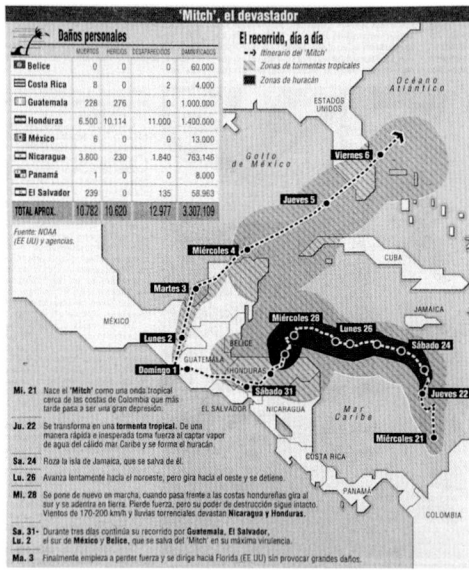

El País
Madrid, Spain
Nacho Catalan, Infographic Artist; **Carmen Treio,** Infographic Artist

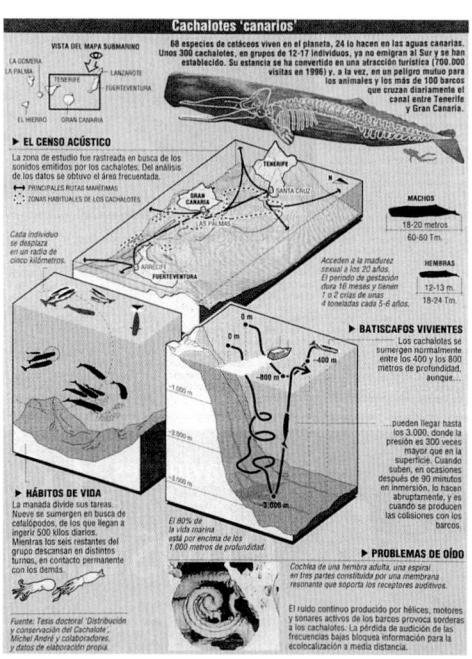

El País
Madrid, Spain
Gustavo Hermoso, Infographic Artist

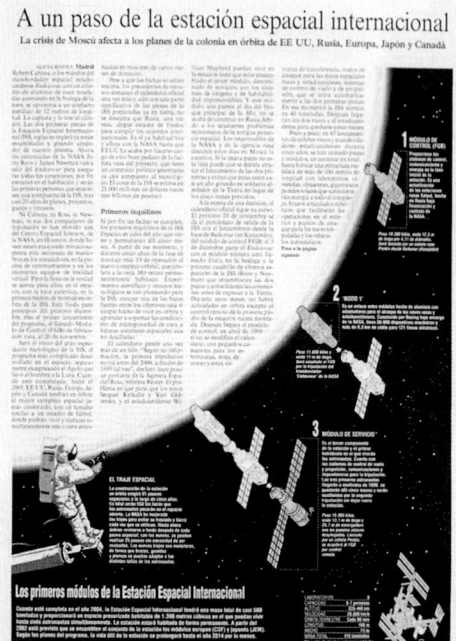

The Sunday Times
London, England
John Smith, Graphics Editor; **Ian Moores,** Graphic Artist; **Jenny Preece,** Graphic Artist; **Matthew Cornick,** Graphic Artist

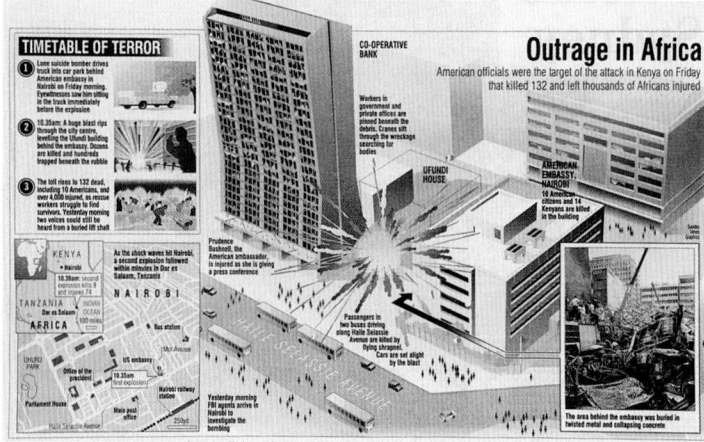

The Sunday Telegraph
London, England
Phillip J. Green, Graphics Editor

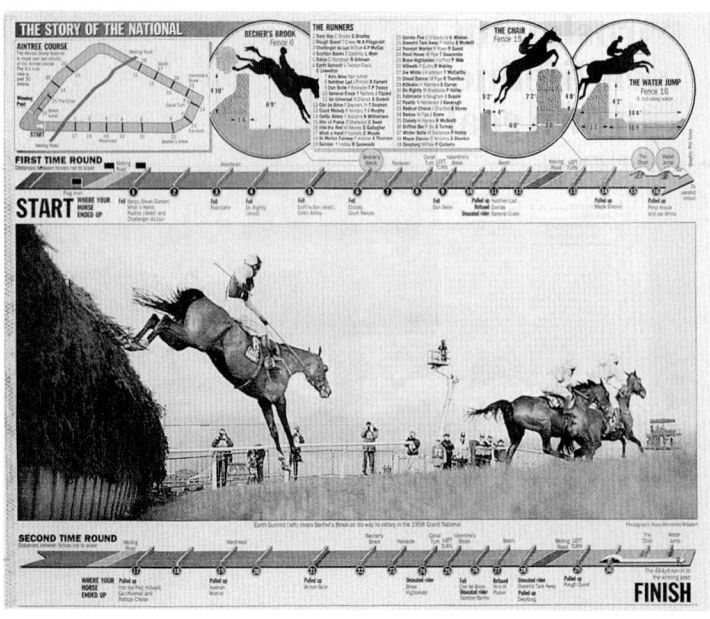

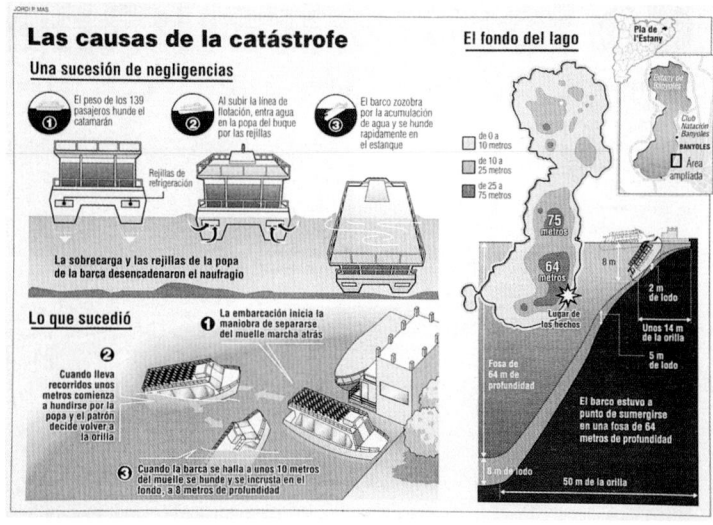

El Periódico de Catalunya
Barcelona, Spain
Jordi Pernau, Designer; **Jordi Català,** Graphics Editor; **Ricard Gràcia,** Graphics Editor; **Ernest Alós,** Information; **Iosu de la Torre,** News Editor

240 ■ THE BEST OF NEWSPAPER DESIGN

Breaking News, Three or More Colors ■ INFOGRAPHICS

Silver
The News Tribune
Tacoma, WA
Derrik Quenzer, Graphic Artist; **Roy Gallopo,** Graphic Artist; **Lisa Kremer,** Researcher; **Reggie Myers,** Art Director

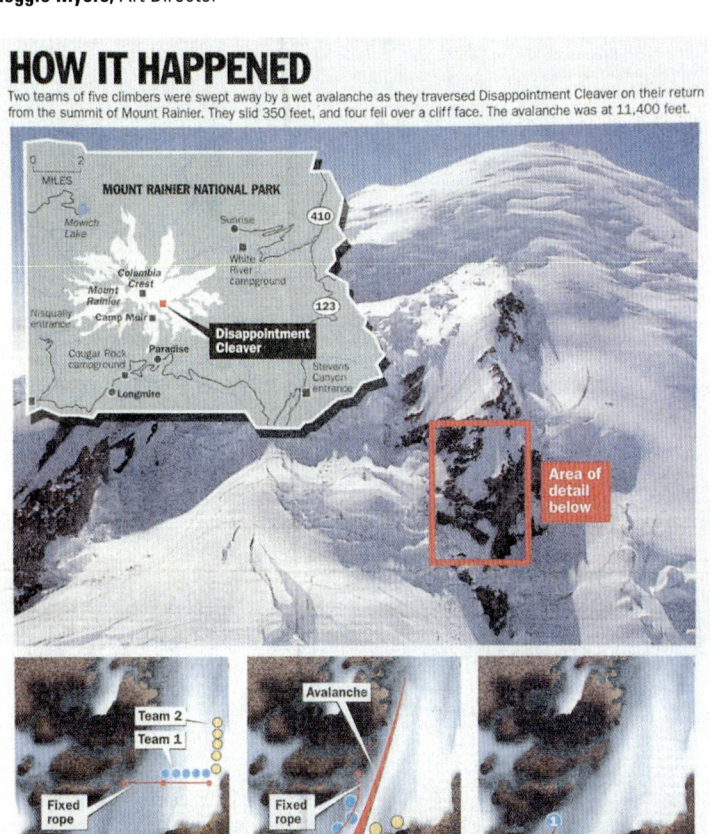
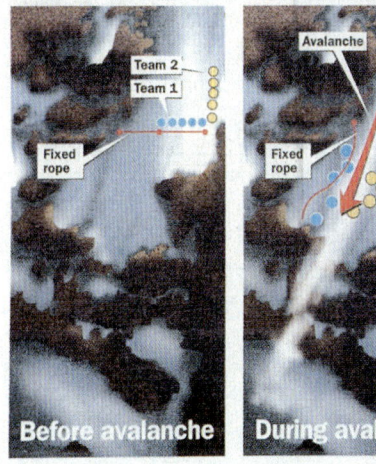
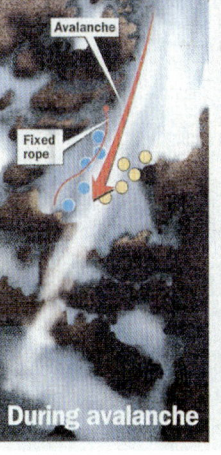
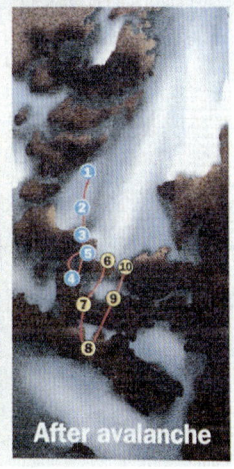

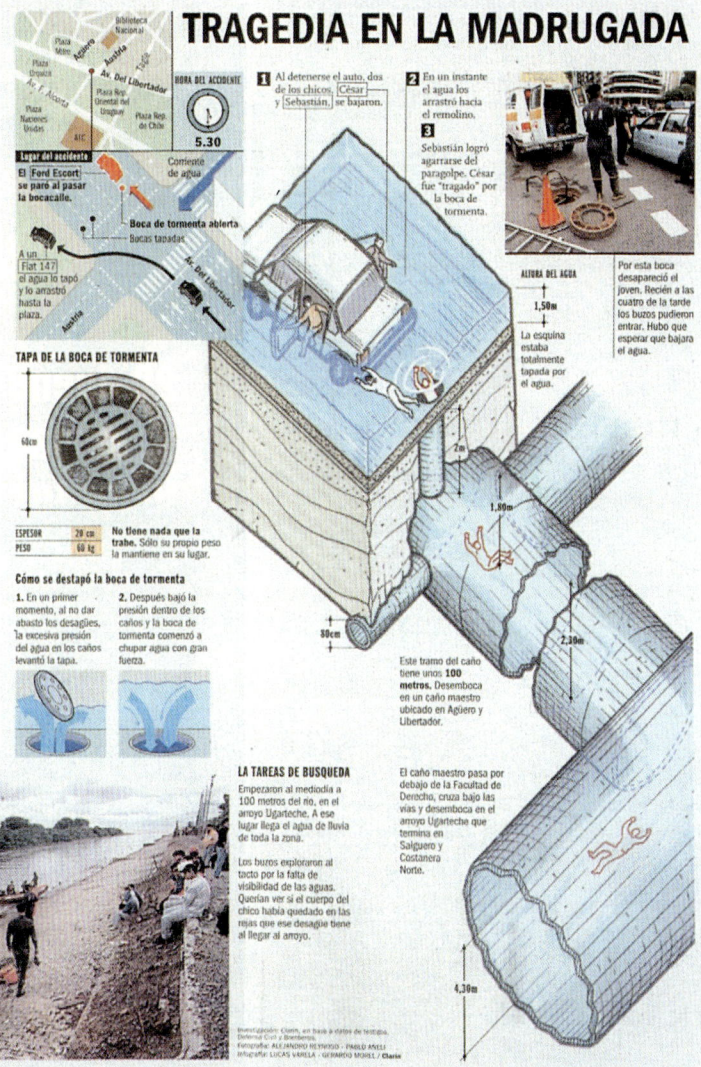

Silver
Clarín
Buenos Aires, Argentina
Iñaki Palacios, Art Director; **Jaime Serra,** Graphics Director; **Lucas Varela,** Artist; **Gerardo Morel,** Artist; **Alejandro Reynoso,** Photographer; **Pablo Añeli,** Photographer

TWENTIETH EDITION ■ 241

INFOGRAPHICS ■ Breaking News, Three or More Colors

Clarín
Buenos Aires, Argentina
Iñaki Palacios, Art Director; **Jaime Serra**, Graphics Director; **Alejandro Tumas**, Artist; **Luis Yong**, Artist/Researcher

Clarín
Buenos Aires, Argentina
Iñaki Palacios, Art Director; **Jaime Serra**, Graphics Director; **Alejandro Tumas**, Artist; **Luis Yong**, Artist; **Gerardo Morel**, Artist; **Pablo Loscri**, Artist; **Stella Bin**, Researcher

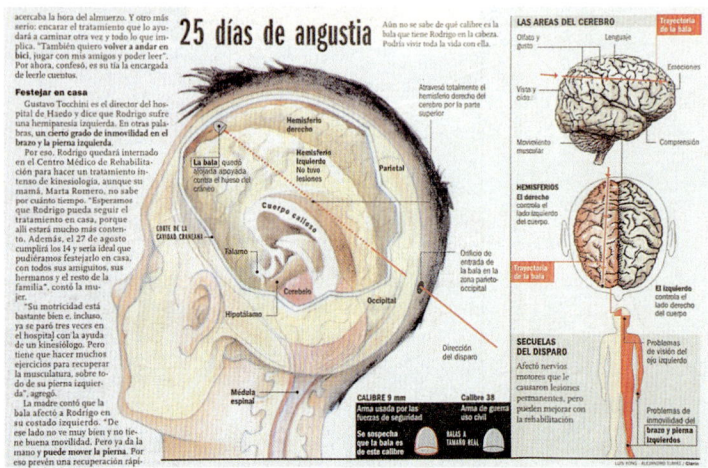
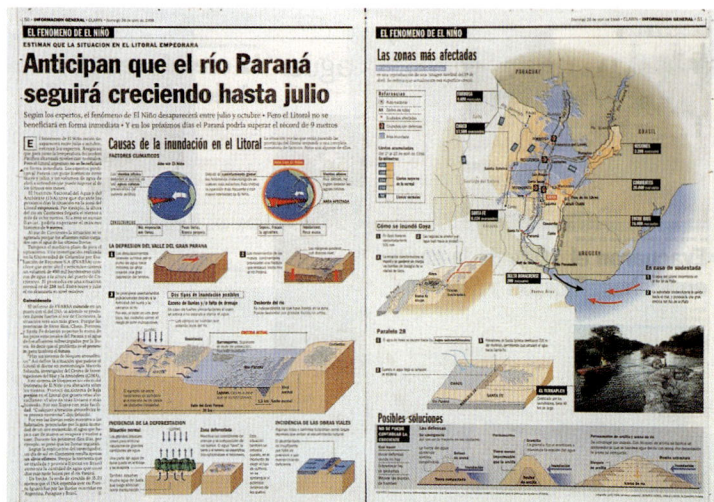

Detroit Free Press
Detroit, MI
Martha Thiery, Assistant Graphics Editor; **Rick Nease**, Assistant Graphics Editor; **Brian James**, Designer

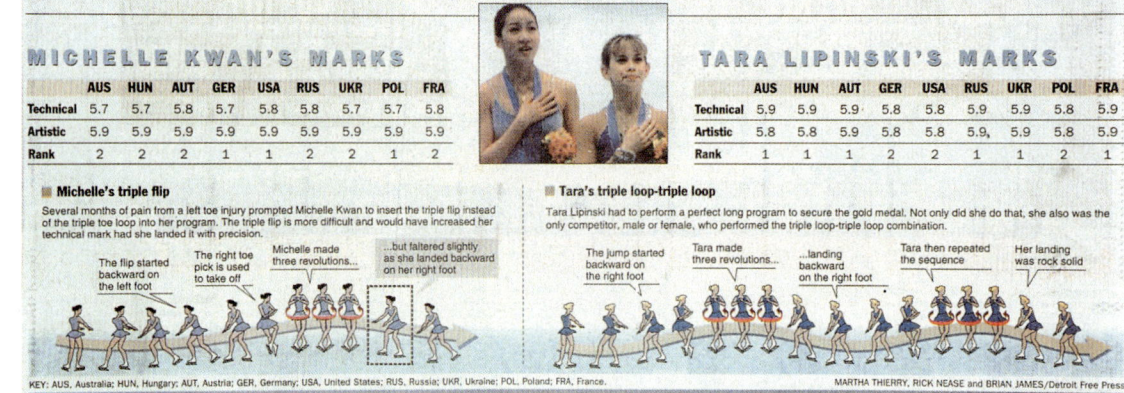

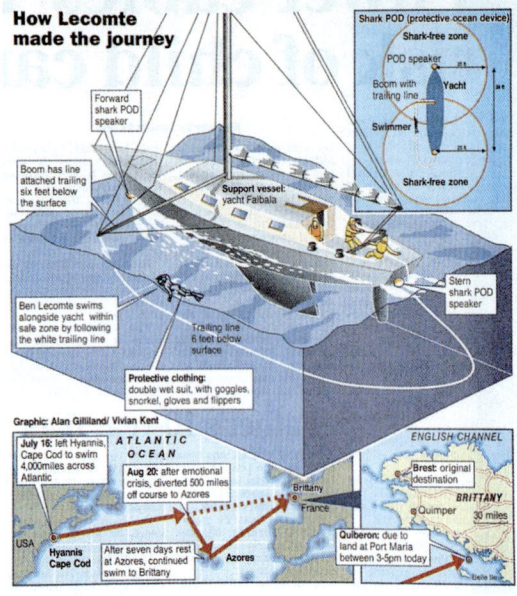

The Daily Telegraph
London, England
Alan Gilliland, Graphics Editor/Artist; **Vivian Kent**, Deputy Graphics Editor/Artist

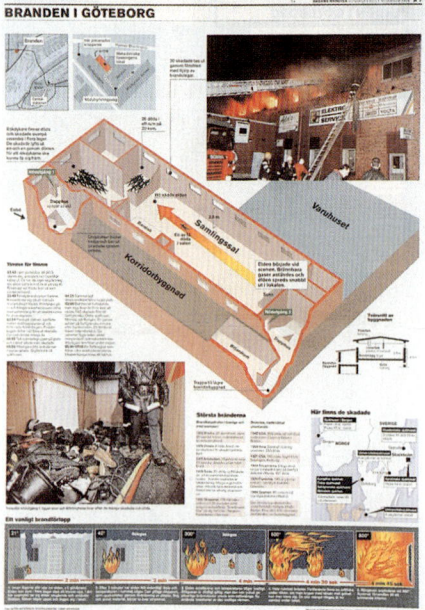

Dagens Nyheter
Stockholm, Sweden
Kerstin Wigstrand, News Graphic Editor; **Alexander Rauscher**, News Graphic Artist; **Johan Jarnestad**, News Graphic Artist; **Lennart Lindgren**, News Graphic Artist

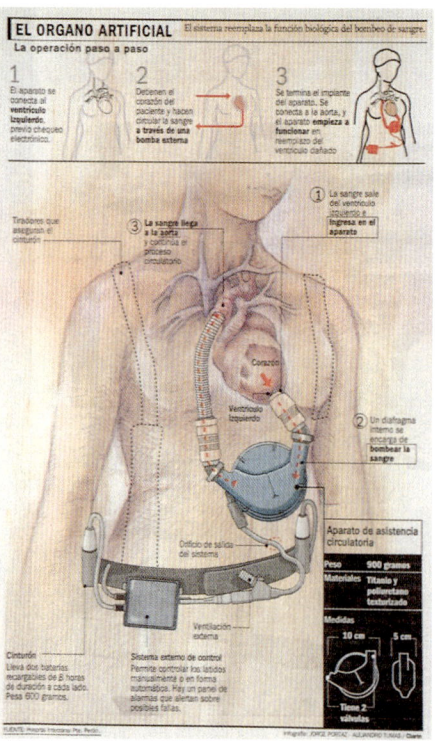

Clarín
Buenos Aires, Argentina
Iñaki Palacios, Art Director; **Jaime Serra**, Graphics Director; **Alejandro Tumas**, Artist; **Jorge Portaz**, Artist; **Stella Bin**, Researcher

Breaking News, Three or More Colors ■ INFOGRAPHICS

Marca
Madrid, Spain
José Juan Gámez, Graphics Editor; **César Galera**, Graphics Editor

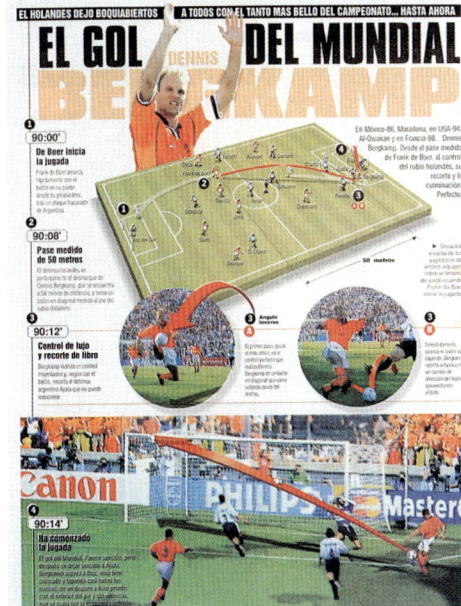

Marca
Madrid, Spain
José Juan Gámez, Graphics Editor; **César Galera**, Graphics Editor; **Juan de Dios Ferreira**, Graphic Designer

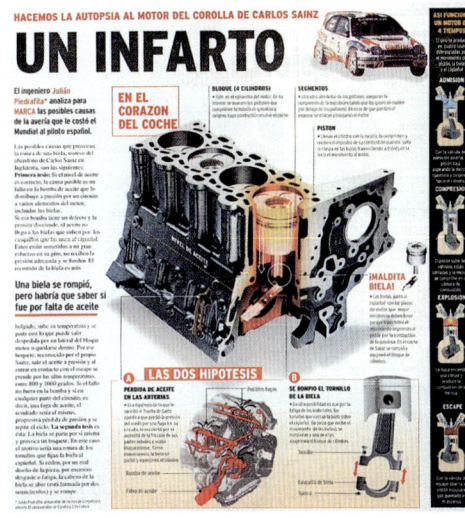

Marca
Madrid, Spain
José Juan Gámez, Graphics Editor/Designer

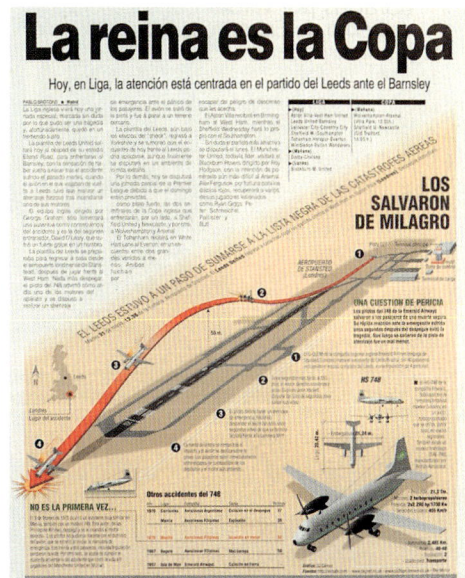

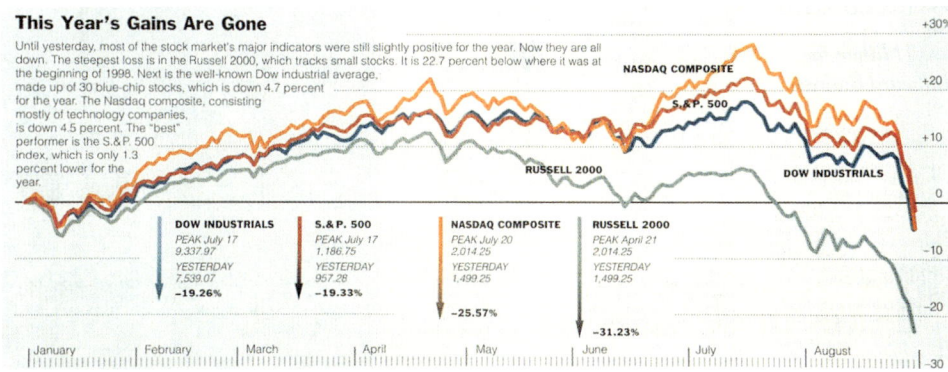

The New York Times
New York, NY
Karl Russell, Graphics Editor

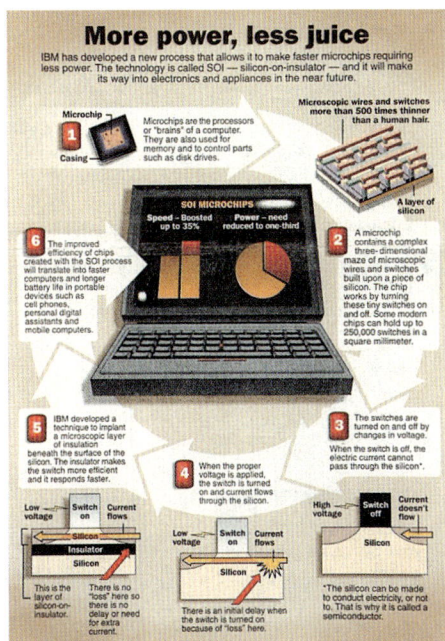

Poughkeepsie Journal
Poughkeepsie, NY
Dean DiMarzo, Art Director

Star Tribune
Minneapolis, MN
John Liu, Graphic Artist; **Mark Boswell**, Graphic Artist; **Greg Branson**, Assistant Graphics Editor; **Ray Grumney**, Graphics Director; **Anders Ramberg**, Design Director; **Bill Dunn**, Visual Content Editor

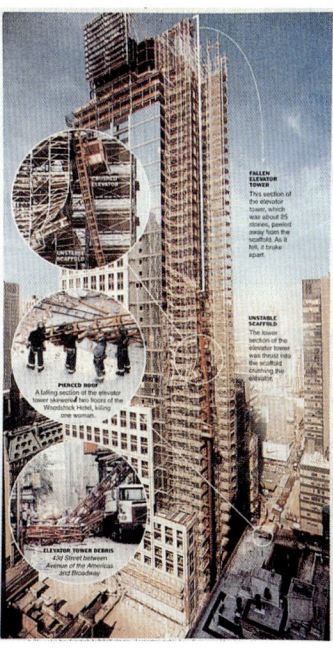

The New York Times
New York, NY
Tom Bodkin, Design Director; **Charles M. Blow**, Graphics Director; **Kris Goodfellow**, Graphics Editor; **Ruby Washington**, Photographer; **James Estrin**, Photographer; **Jack Manning**, Photographer

INFOGRAPHICS ■ Breaking News, Three or More Colors, Portfolio One Artist

The Times-Picayune
New Orleans, LA
Elizabeth Carmody, Designer; **Angela Hill,** Graphics Editor; **Daniel Swenson,** Graphic Artist

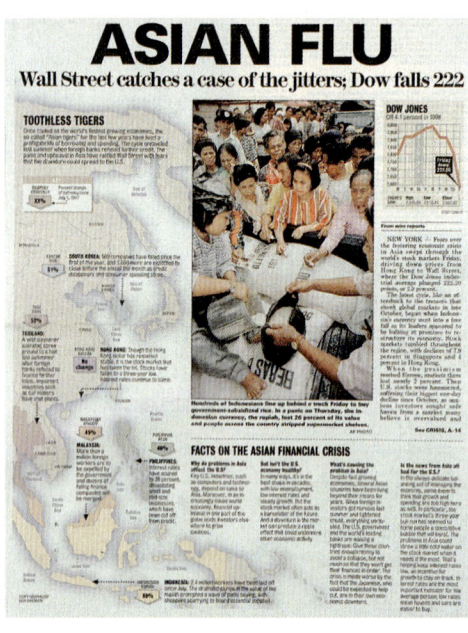

Svenska Dagbladet
Stockholm, Sweden
Arm Dahl, Researcher; **Mats Svegfors,** Researcher; **Rickard Frank,** Artist; **Bengt Salomonson,** Artist; **Bjorn Larsson Ask,** Photographe

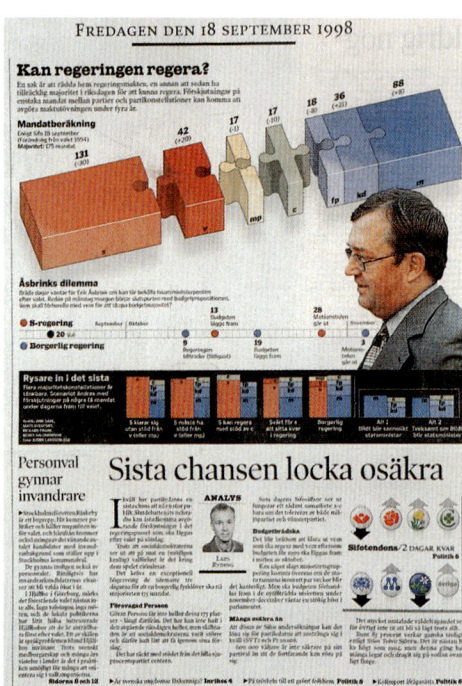

Svenska Dagbladet
Stockholm, Sweden
Jonas Askergren, Artist; **Bengt Salomonson,** Artist; **Ann Dahl,** Researcher; **Birgitta Haglund,** Researcher; **Bengt Jonsson,** Researcher

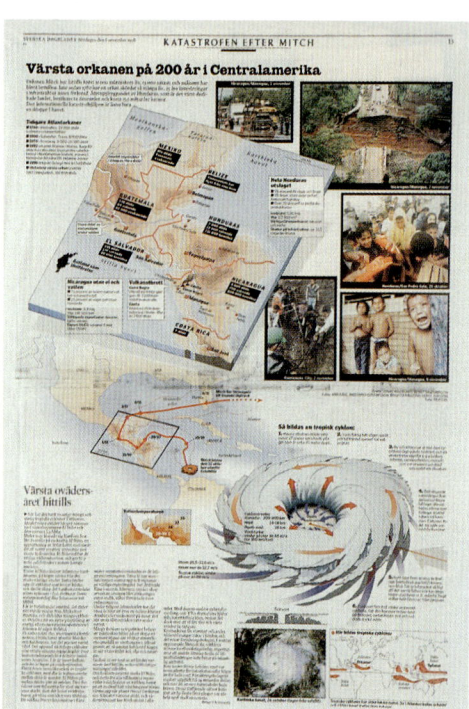

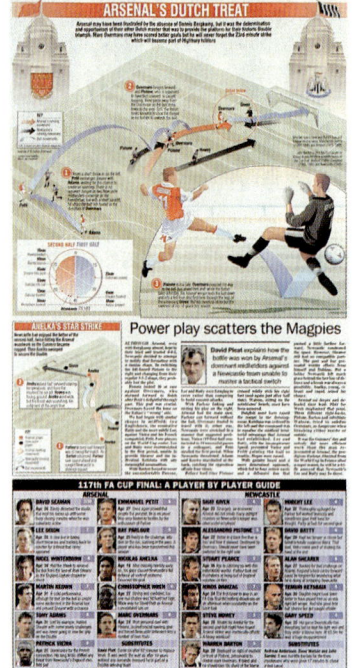

The Sunday Times
London, England
John Smith, Graphics Editor; **Gary Cook,** Associate Graphics Editor; **Chris Sargent,** Associate Graphics Editor

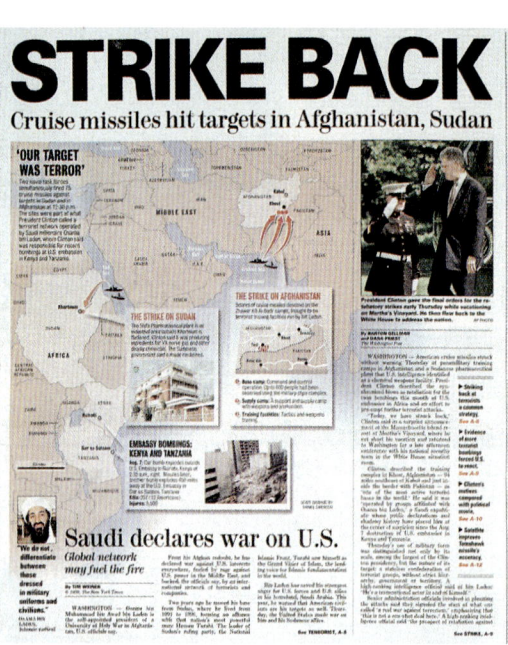

The Times-Picayune
New Orleans, LA
Daniel Swenson, Graphic Artist; **Grant Staublin,** Designer

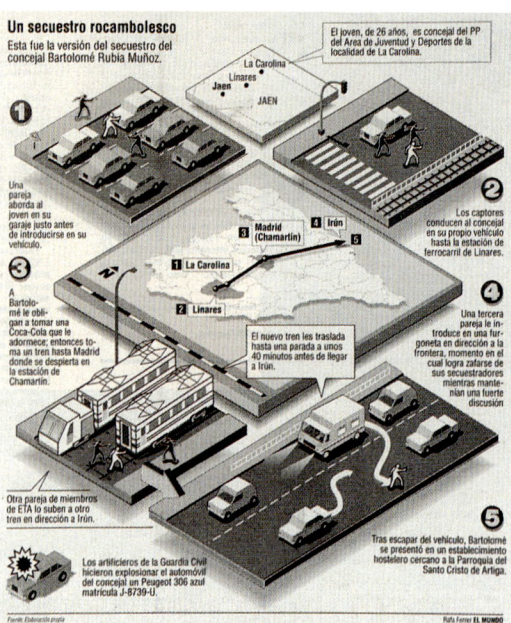

El Mundo Del Siglo XXI
Madrid, Spain
Rafael Ferrer, Graphic Journalist

Breaking News, Portfolio More than One Artist ■ INFOGRAPHICS

Clarín
Buenos Aires, Argentina

Iñaki Palacios, Art Director; **Jaime Serra**, Graphics Director/Artist; **Gerardo Morel**, Artist; **Luis Yong**, Artist; **Alejandro Tumas**, Artist; **Pablo Loscri**, Artist; **Stella Bin**, Researcher; **Hector Ceballos**, Artist; **Jorge Portaz**, Artist
• also for Breaking News Graphics Three or More Colors

El Mundo Del Siglo XXI
Madrid, Spain

Juancho Cruz, Graphic Journalist; **Ulises Culebro**, Illustrator; **Modesto J. Carrasco**, Infographic Editor; **Rafael Ferrer**, Graphic Journalist; **Chema Matia**, Graphic Journalist; **Rafael Estrada**, Graphic Journalist; **Emilio Amade**, Graphic Journalist; **Isabel González**, Graphic Journalist; **Rodrigo Silva**, Graphic Journalist; **Dina Sánchez**, Graphic Journalist

El País
Madrid, Spain

Antonio Alonso, Infographic Artist; **Angel Naja**, Infographic Artist; **Gustavo Hermoso**, Infographic Artist; **Nacho Catalan**, Infographic Artist; **Carmen Treio**, Infographic Artist

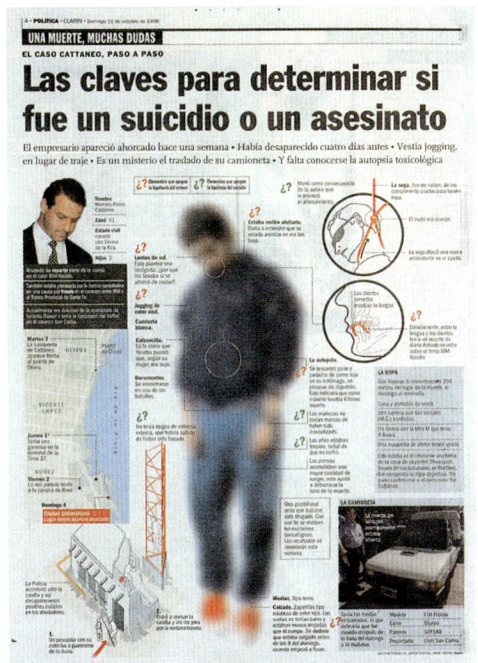
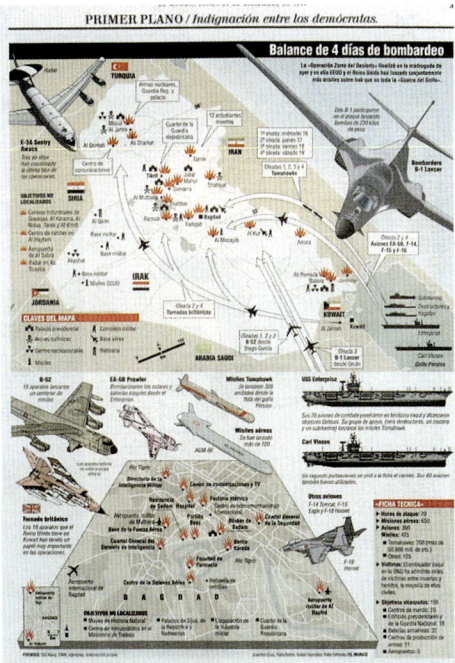
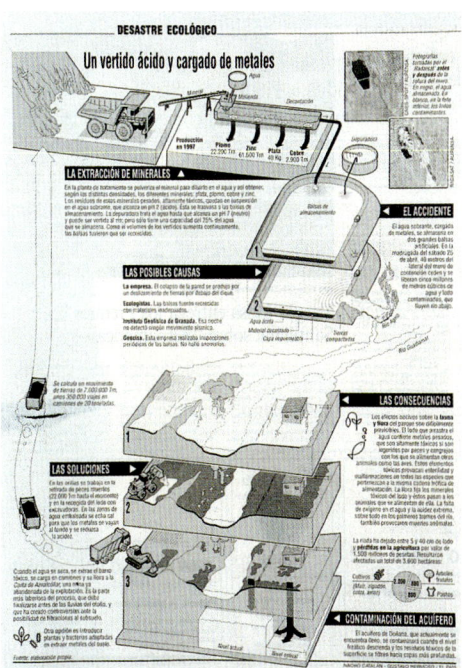

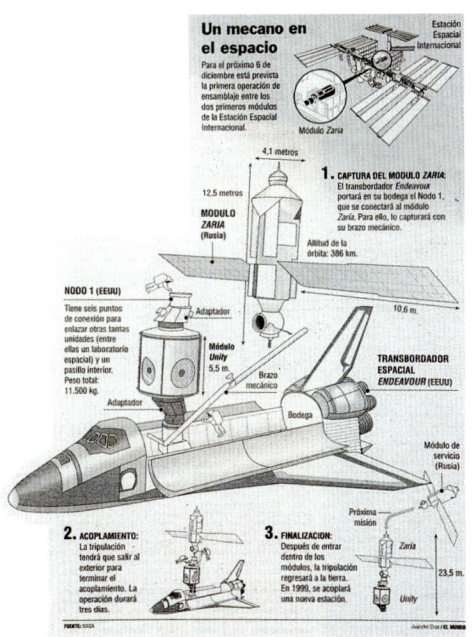
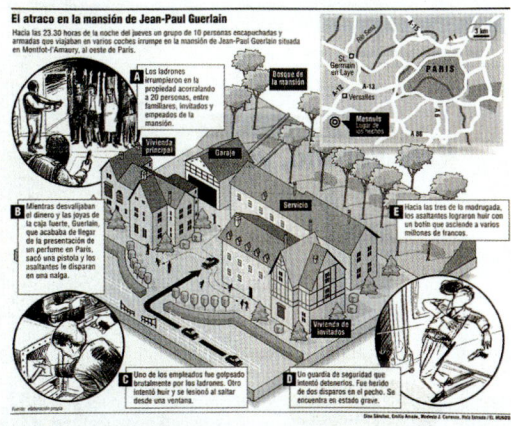
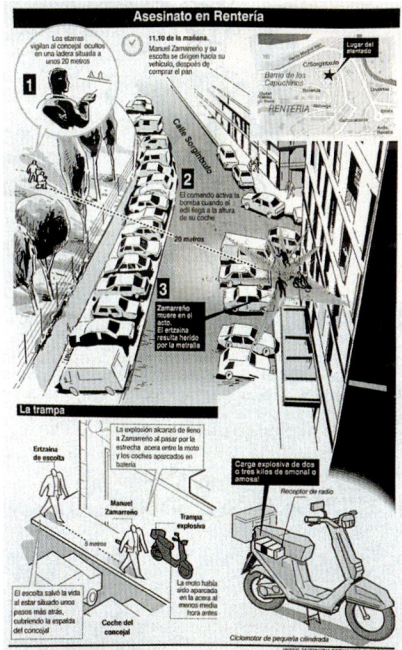

El Mundo Del Siglo XXI
Madrid, Spain

Modesto J. Carrasco, Infographic Artist; **Juancho Cruz**, Graphic Journalist; **Rafael Ferrer**, Graphic Journalist; **Chema Matiá**, Graphic Journalist; **Rafael Estrada**, Graphic Journalist; **Ulises Culebro**, Illustrator; **Isabel González**, Graphic Journalist; **Rodrigo Silva**, Graphic Journalist; **Dina Sánchez**, Graphic Journalist; **Emilio Amade**, Graphic Journalist

El Mundo Del Siglo XXI
Madrid, Spain

Juancho Cruz, Graphic Journalist; **Ulises Culebro**, Illustrator; **Modesto J. Carrasco**, Infographic Editor; **Rafael Ferrer**, Graphic Journalist; **Chema Matia**, Graphic Journalist; **Rafael Estrada**, Graphic Journalist; **Emilio Amade**, Graphic Journalist; **Isabel González**, Graphic Journalist; **Rodrigo Silva**, Graphic Journalist; **Dina Sánchez**, Graphic Journalist

El Correo
Bilbao, Spain

Javier Zarracina, Infographic Editor; **Fernando G. Baptista**, Infographic Artist

INFOGRAPHICS ■ Black or Black and One Color

Silver
Clarín
Buenos Aires, Argentina
Iñaki Palacios, Art Director; **Jaime Serra**, Graphic Director; **Lucas Varela**, Artist; **Alejandro Tumas**, Artist

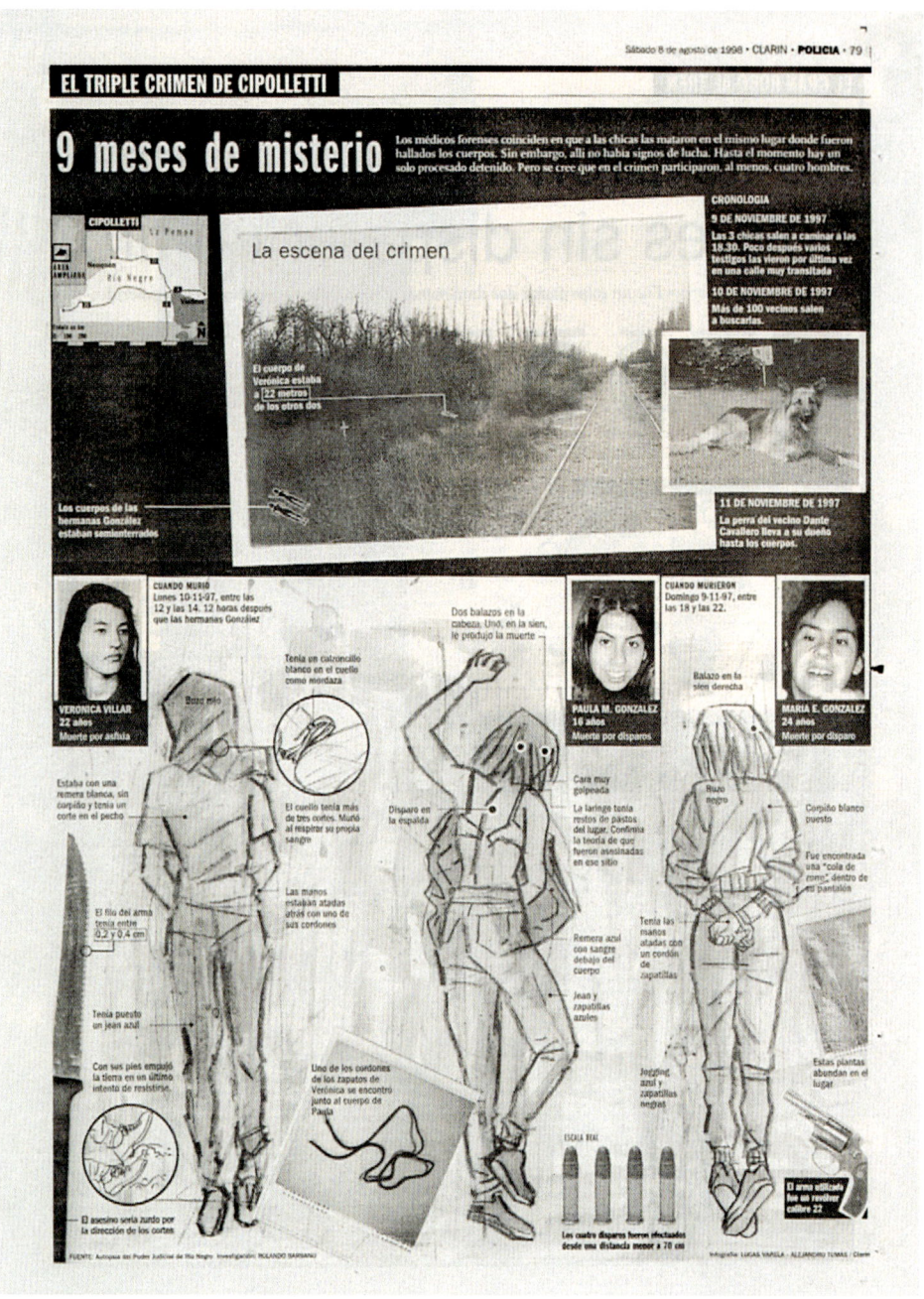

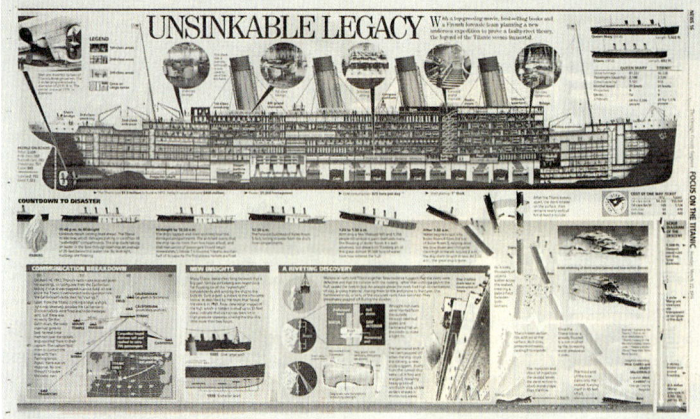

The Orange County Register
Santa Ana, CA
Paul Carbo, Artist; **Brady MacDonald**, Graphics Reporter; **Tia Lai**, Art Director

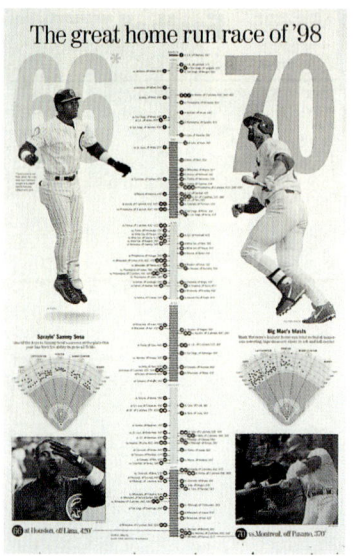

The Boston Globe
Boston, MA
Ed Wiederer, Graphic Artist; **Janet L. Michaud**, Sports Designer; **David Schutz**, Graphic Artist; **Lucy Bartholomay**, Deputy M.E./Design

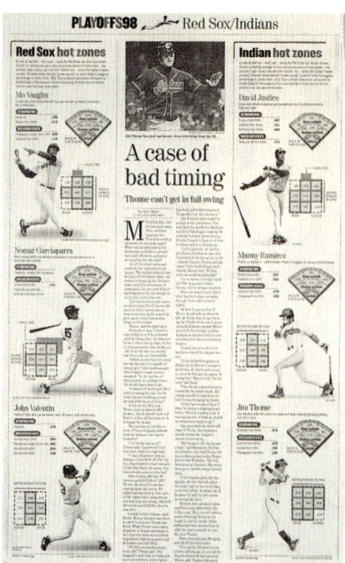

The Boston Globe
Boston, MA
Richard R. Sanchez, Graphic Designer; **Janet L. Michaud**, Art Director

Black or Black and One Color, Three or More Colors ■ INFOGRAPHICS

The Washington Post
Washington, DC

Lon Tweeten, Graphic Artist; **Brenna Sink**, Graphics Editor

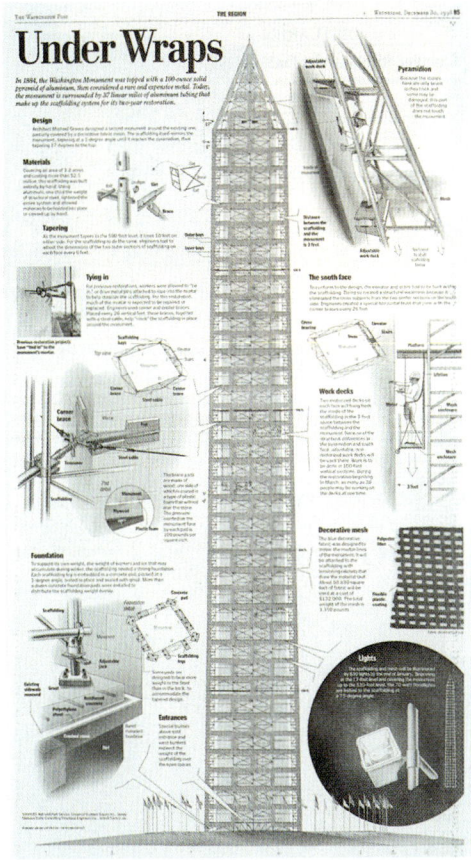

The Philadelphia Inquirer
Philadelphia, PA

Kevin Burkett, Graphic Artist; **David Milne**, A.M.E. Design

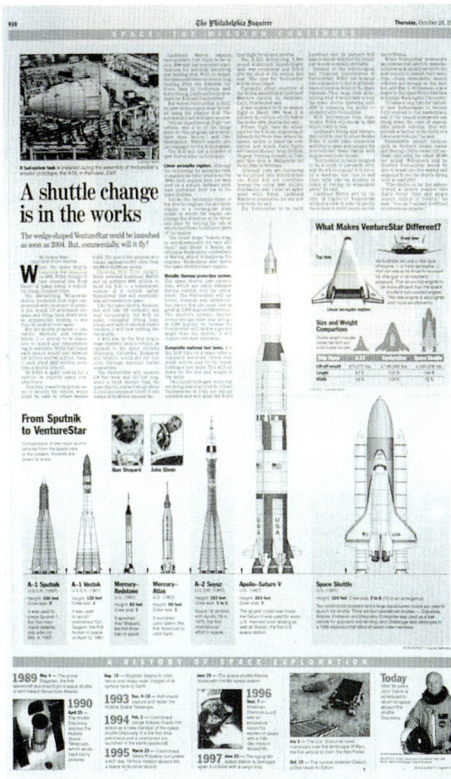

The New York Times
New York, NY

Mika Grondhl, Illustrator

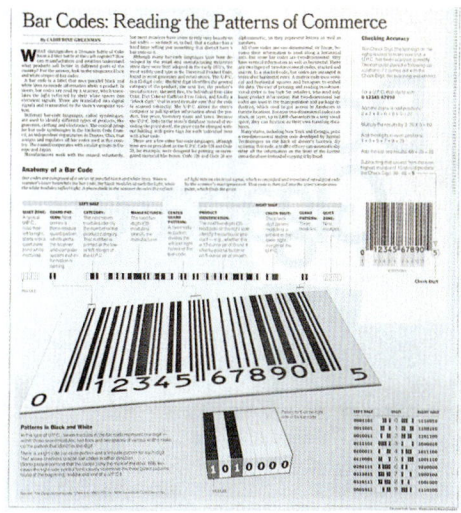

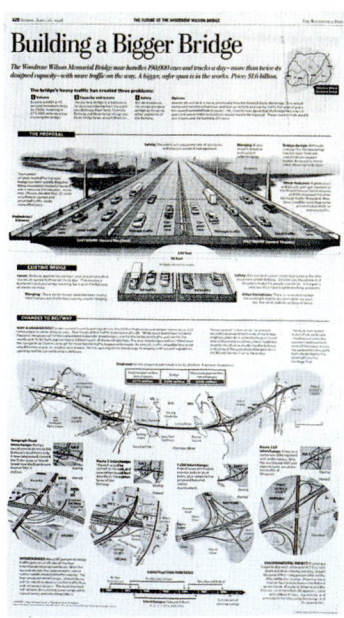

The Washington Post
Washington, DC

Lon Tweeten, Graphic Artist; **Brenna Sink**, Metro Graphics Editor

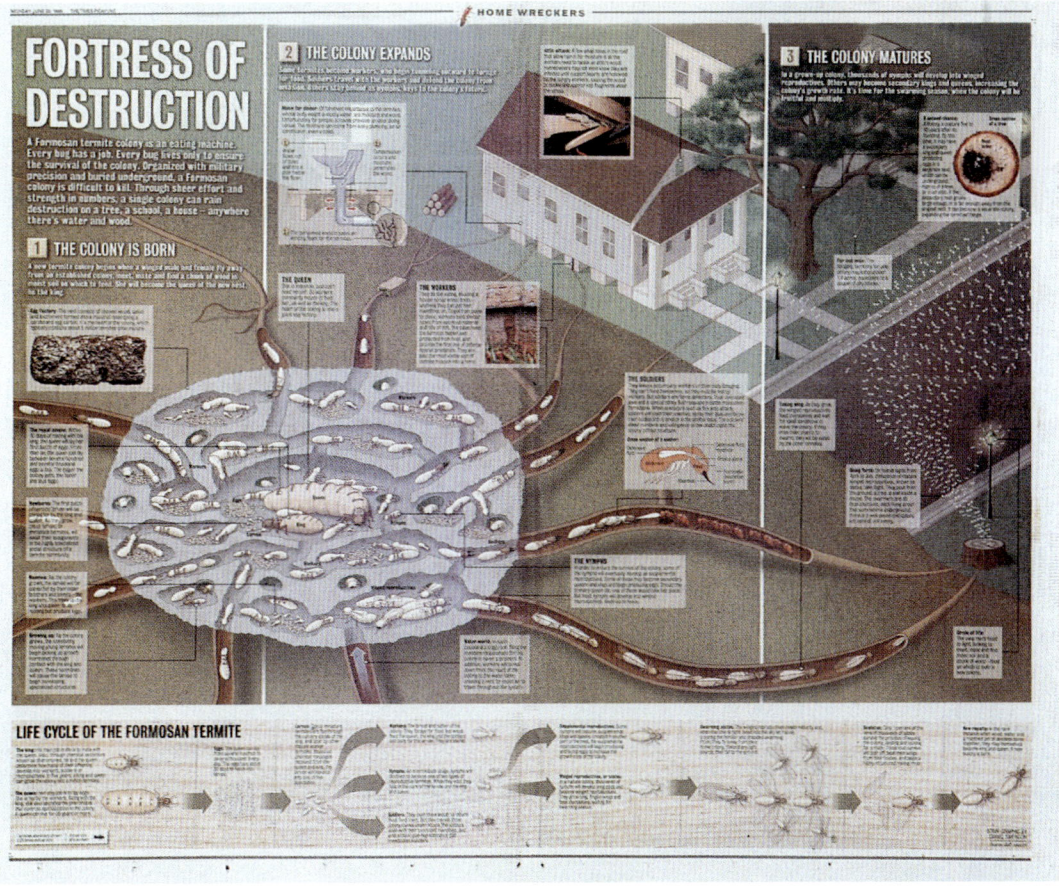

Silver
The Times-Picayune
New Orleans, LA

Daniel Swenson, Graphic Artist; **Angela Hill**, Graphics Editor; **James O'Byrne**, Sunday Editor; **George Berke**, Design Director

TWENTIETH EDITION ■ 247

INFOGRAPHICS ■ Three or More Colors

Gold
Clarín
Buenos Aires, Argentina
Iñaki Palacios, Art Director; **Jaime Serra**, Graphic Director;
Lucas Varela, Artist; **Stella Bin**, Researcher

This entry exceeded the qualifications for a Gold because it dealt with a subject that was vital, yet stayed within the parameters of good taste. It combined great technique and content while conveying emotion. There was a clarity in organization and execution.

Este concursante sobrepasó los requisitos de la medalla de oro, porque trató un tema que era vital y, sin embargo, no se salió de los parámetros del buen gusto. Combinó una técnica y un contenido excelentes, y a la vez trasmitió la emoción. Tuvo claridad en la organización y en la ejecución.

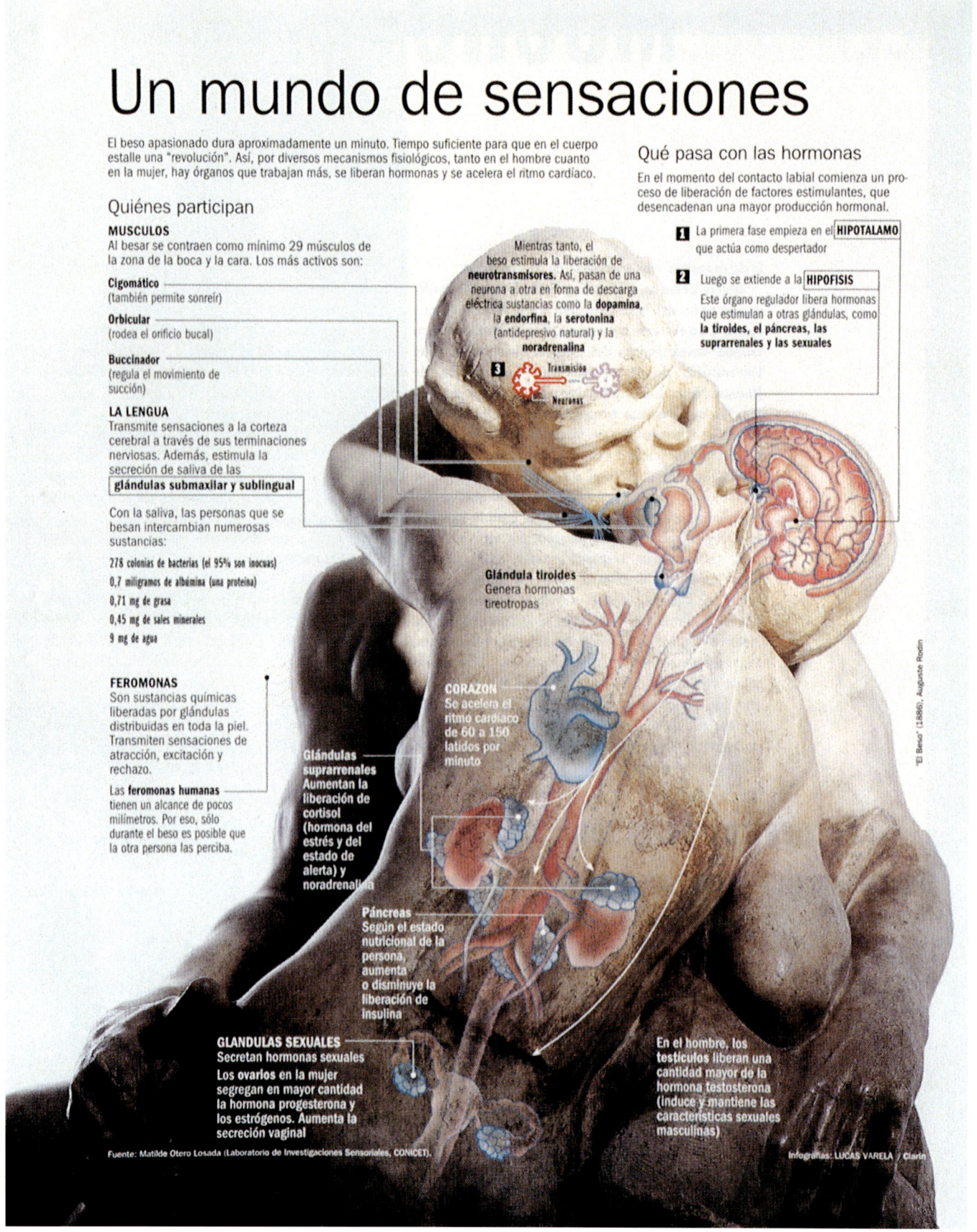

Three or More Colors ■ INFOGRAPHICS

The Charlotte Observer
Charlotte, NC
William Pitzer, News Graphics Editor; **Joanne Miller,** Art Director; **Danielle Parks,** Designer

The Charlotte Observer
Charlotte, NC
William Pitzer, News Graphic Editor; **Joanne Miller,** Art Director; **Brenda Pinnell,** Designer; **David Perlmutt,** Staff Writer; **Jean Marie Brown,** Metro Editor; **Tom Tozer,** Project Editor

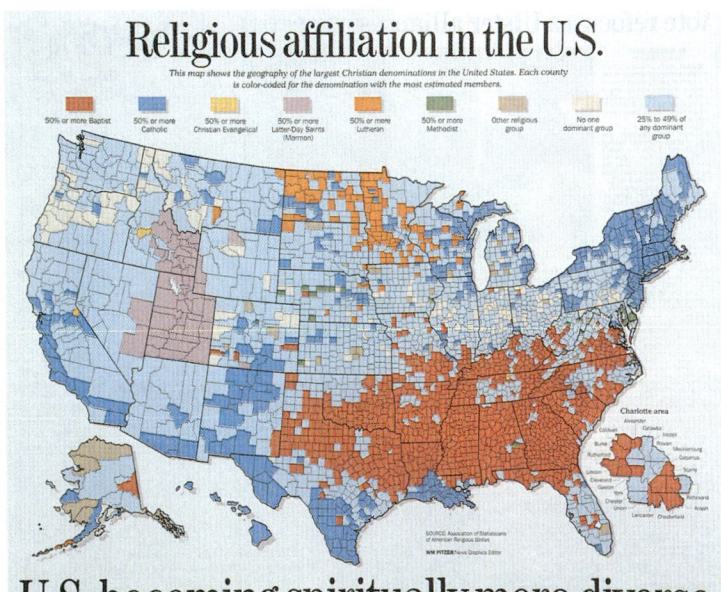

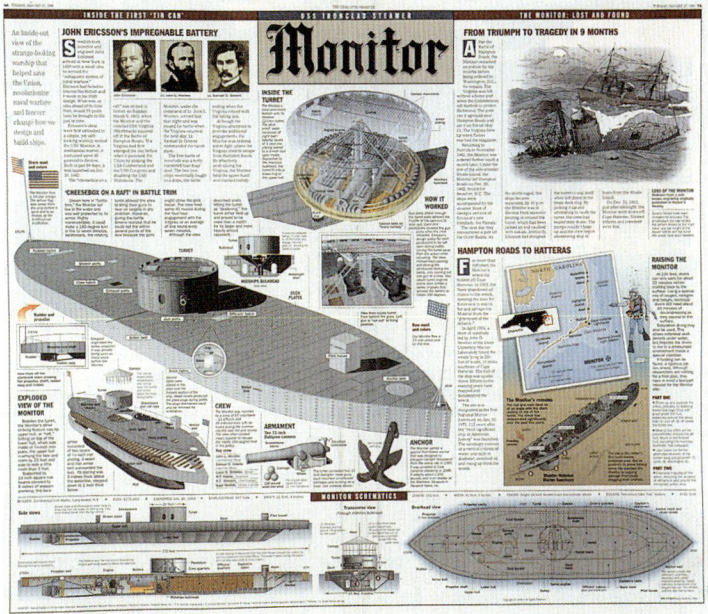

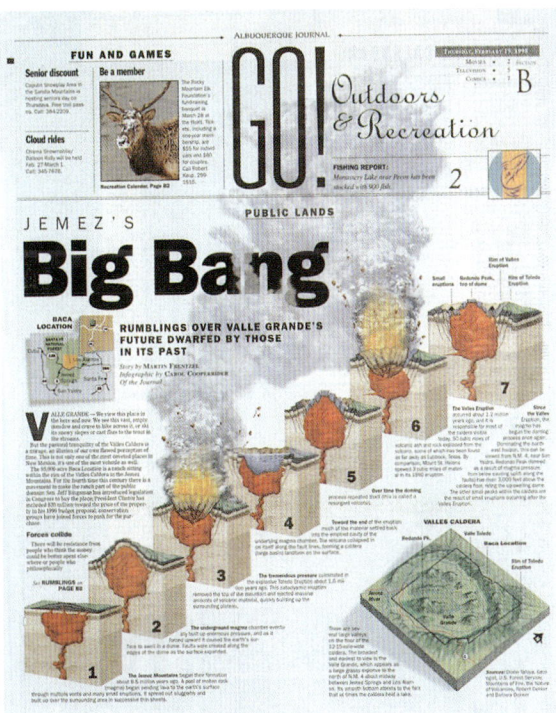

Clarín
Buenos Aires, Argentina
Iñaki Palacios, Art Director; **Jaime Serra,** Graphic Director; **Pablo Loscri,** Artist; **Alejandro Tumas,** Artist; **Stella Bin,** Researcher

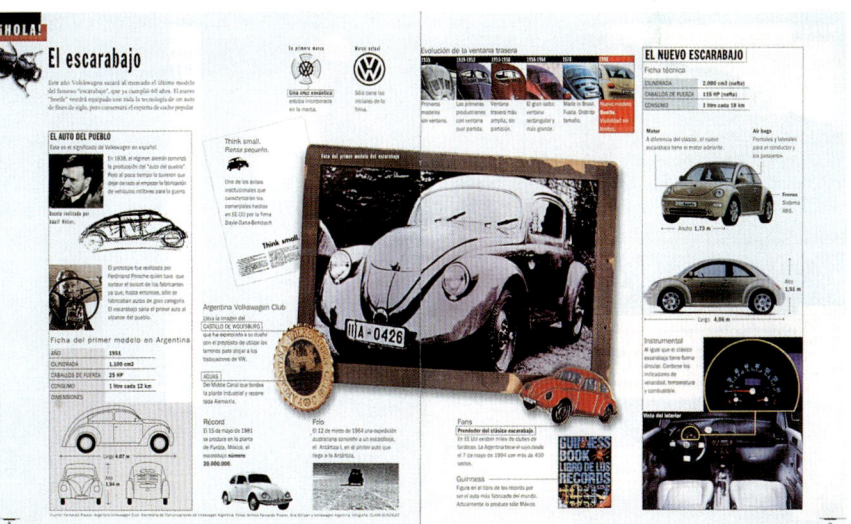

Clarín
Buenos Aires, Argentina
Iñaki Palacios, Art Director; **Jaime Serra,** Graphic Director; **Clara González,** Artist/Researcher; **Alejandro Tumas,** Artist

Albuquerque Journal
Albuquerque, NM
Carol Cooperrider, Artist; **Carolyn Flynn,** A.M.E. Photo/Design; **Joe Kirby,** Design Director; **George Gibson,** Graphics Artist; **Catherine Whipple,** Designer; **Wendy Cromwell,** Assistant Design Director

INFOGRAPHICS ■ Three or More Colors

The Cleveland Plain Dealer
Cleveland, OH
William Neff, Graphic Artist

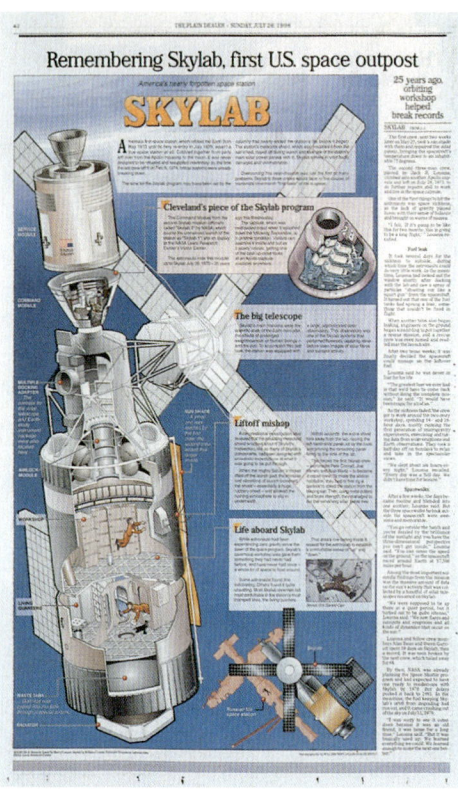

The Honolulu Star-Bulletin
Honolulu, HI
David Swann, Graphic Artist; **Dan Woods**, Graphics Editor

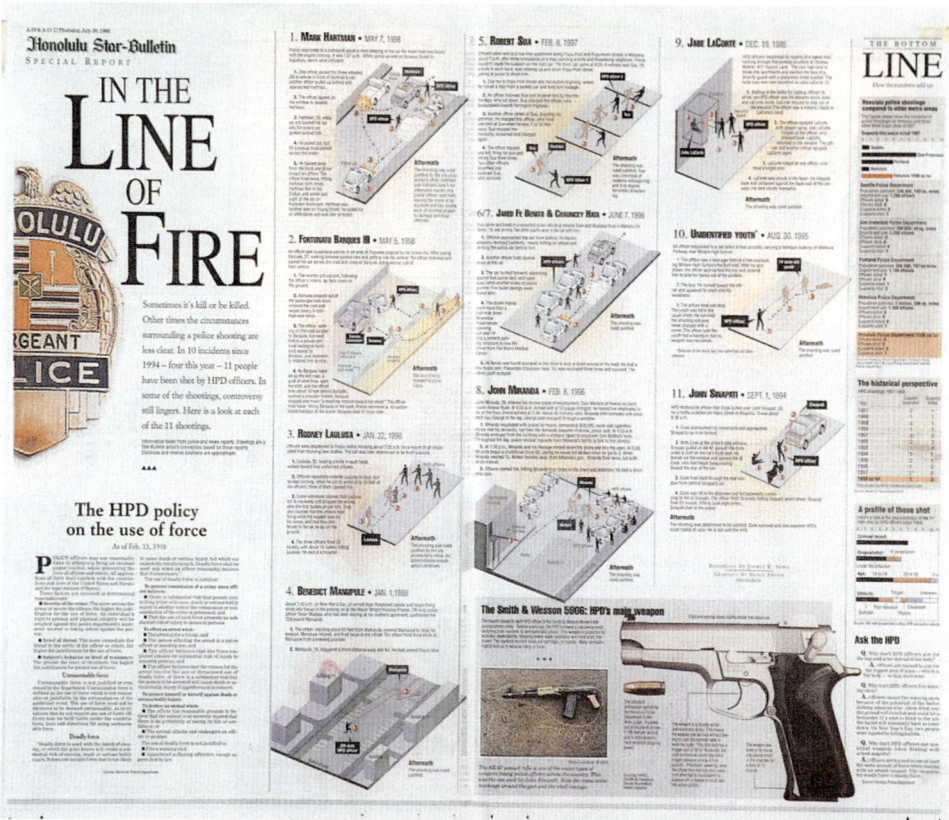

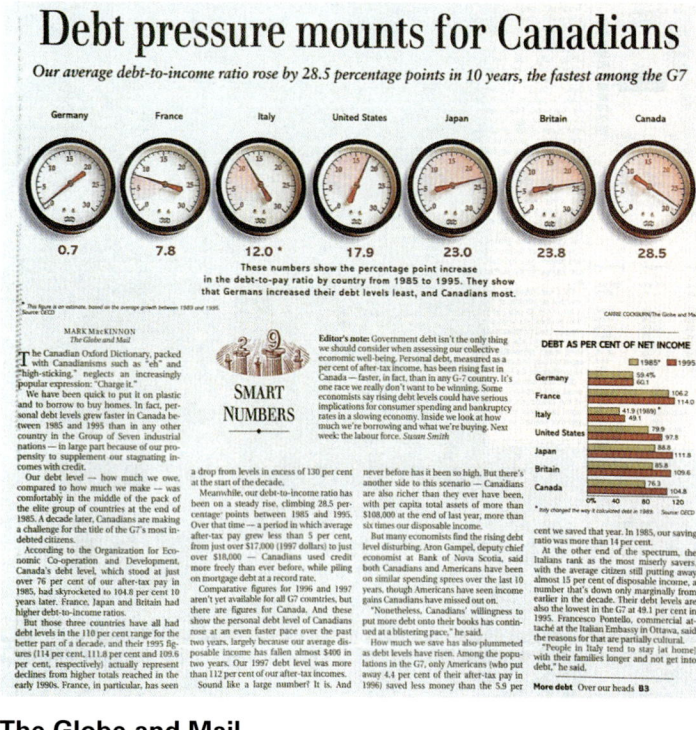

The Globe and Mail
Toronto, Canada
Carrie Cockburn, Graphic Artist; **David Pratt**, Designer

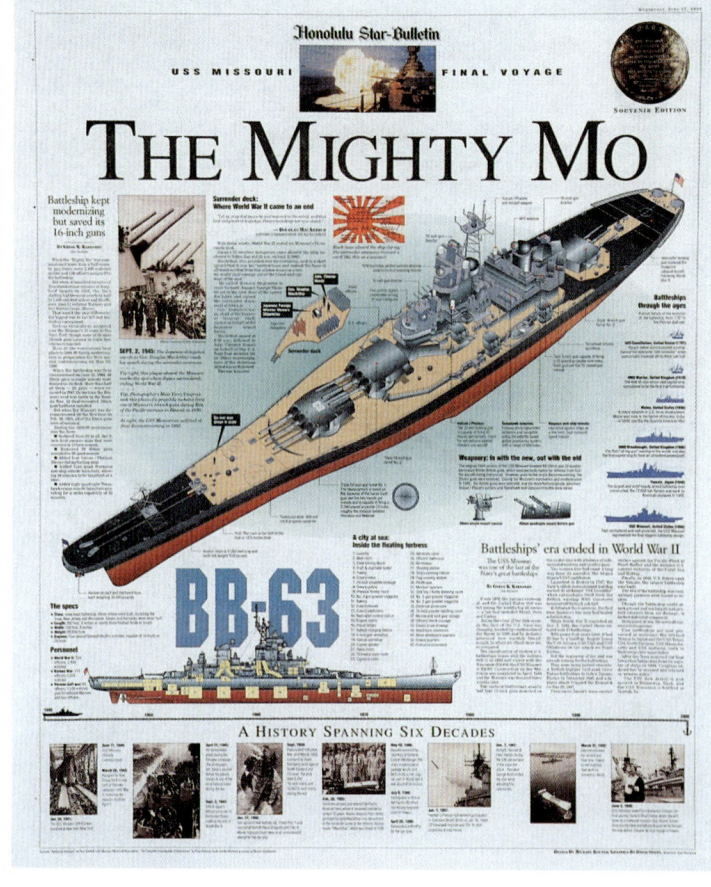

The Honolulu Star-Bulletin
Honolulu, HI
David Swann, Graphic Artist; **Michael Rovner**, A.M.E.
• also for Infographics Portfolio One Artist

250 ■ THE BEST OF NEWSPAPER DESIGN

Three or More Colors — INFOGRAPHICS

The Los Angeles Times
Los Angeles, CA
Paul Carbo, Artist; **Tom Reinken**, Graphics Editor; **Tia Lai**, Art Director

The Philadelphia Inquirer
Philadelphia, PA
Kevin Burkett, Graphic Artist; **David Milne**, A.M.E. Design

The New York Times
New York, NY
John Grimwade, Graphics Editor

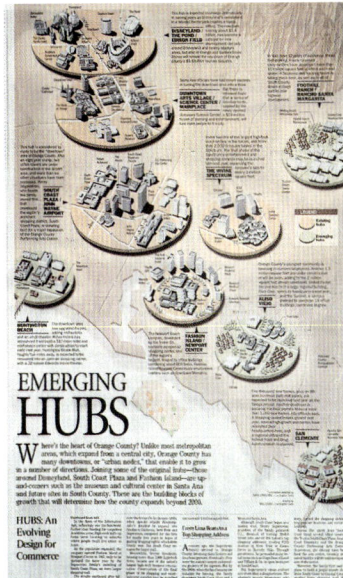
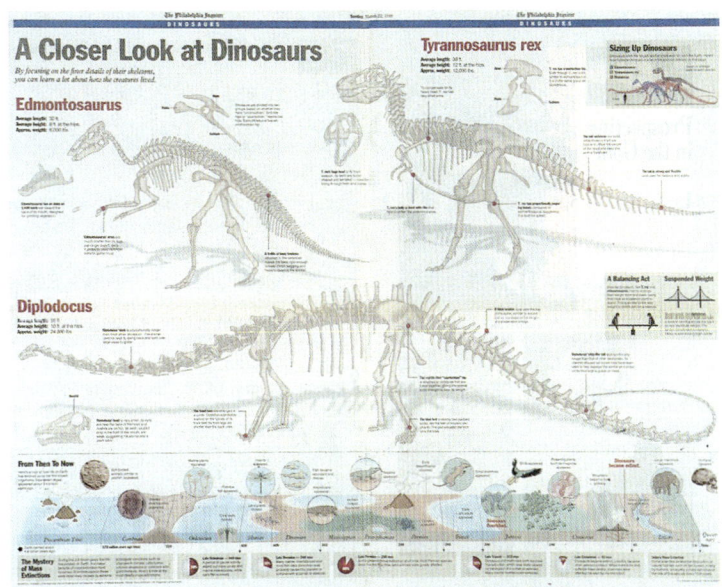
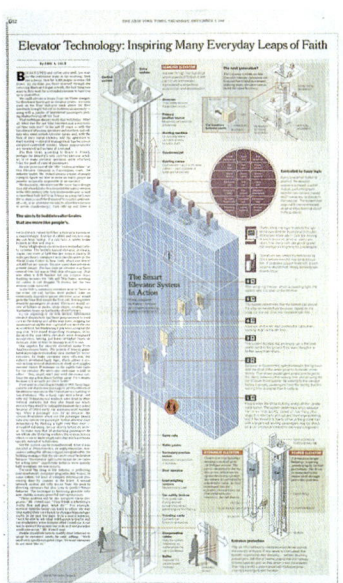

El Mundo Del Siglo XXI
Madrid, Spain
Carmelo Caderot, Art Director; **Gorka Sampedro**, Graphics Editor; **Staff**

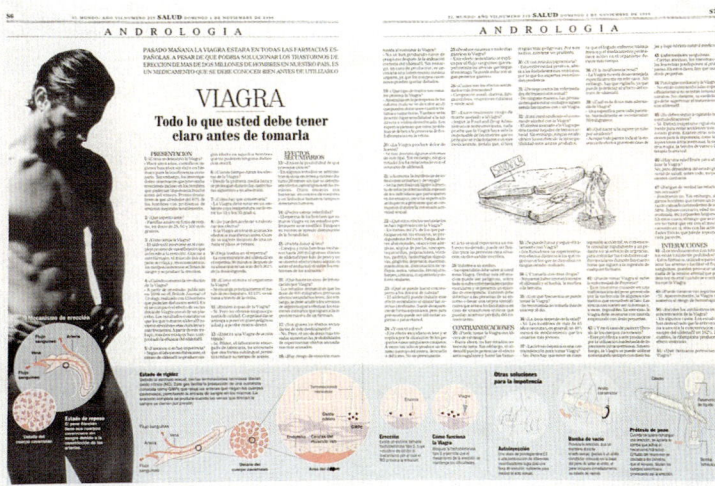

The Oregonian
Portland, OR
Steve Cowden, Graphic Artist; **Katy Muldoon**, Writer; **Steve McKinstry**, Art Director

NRC Handelsblad
Rotterdam, The Netherlands
Fokke Gerritsma, Graphic Artist

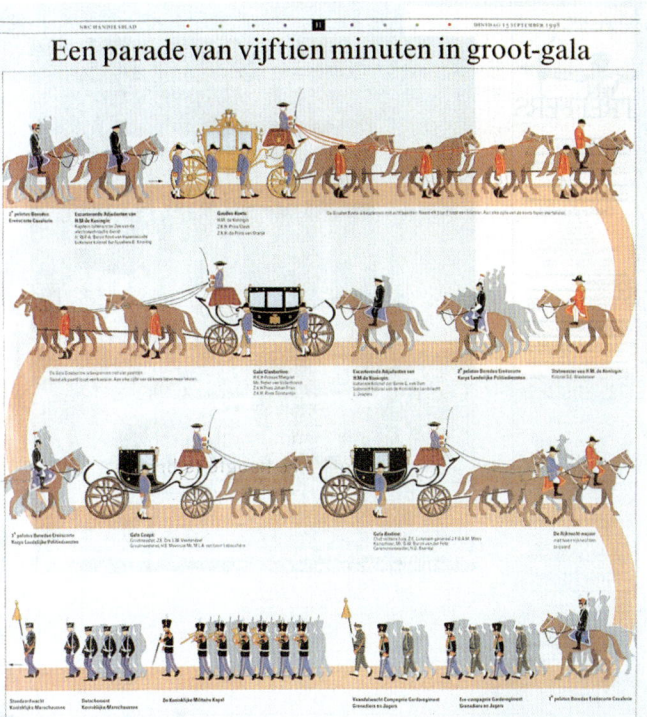
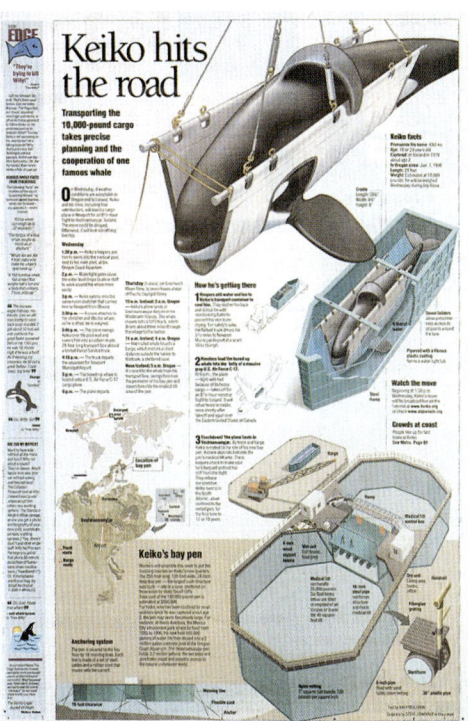

TWENTIETH EDITION ■ 251

INFOGRAPHICS ■ Three or More Colors

The Sacramento Bee
Sacramento, CA
Sean McDade, Artist; **Nam Nguyen**, Assistant Art Director; **Howard Shintaku**, Art Director; **Mort Saltzman**, A.M.E. Graphics; **William Enfield**, Project Editor; **William Endicott**, M.E.; **Rick Rodriguez**, Executive Editor

The San Bernardino County Sun
San Bernardino, CA
Raoul Rañoa, Graphic Artist; **Lynn Anderson**, Reporter; **Betts Griffone**, Graphics Editor

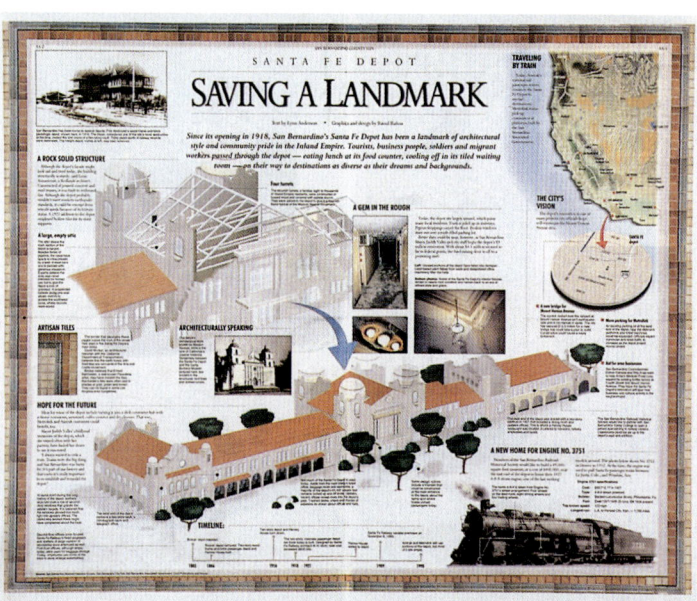

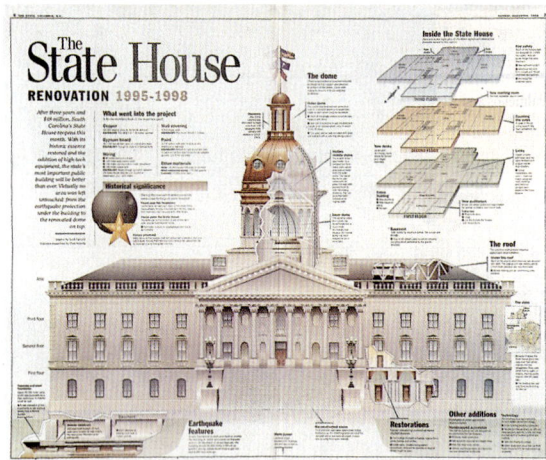

The State
Columbia, SC
Scott Farrand, Graphics Editor; **Steve Long**, Graphic Artist

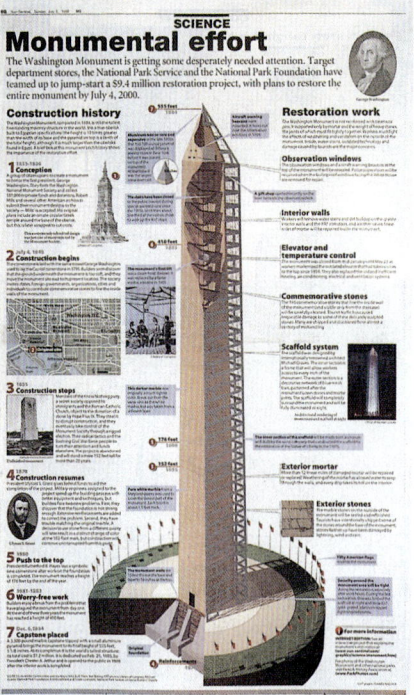

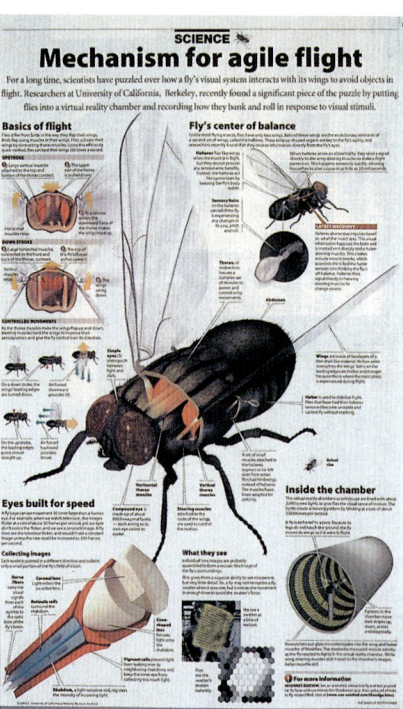

Sun-Sentinel
Ft. Lauderdale, FL
Daniel Niblock, Graphic Journalist; **Don Wittekind**, Graphics Director

Sun-Sentinel
Ft. Lauderdale, FL
R. Scott Horner, Assistant Graphics Director; **Don Wittekind**, Graphics Director

252 ■ THE BEST OF NEWSPAPER DESIGN

Three or More Colors, Portfolio One Artist ■ INFOGRAPHICS

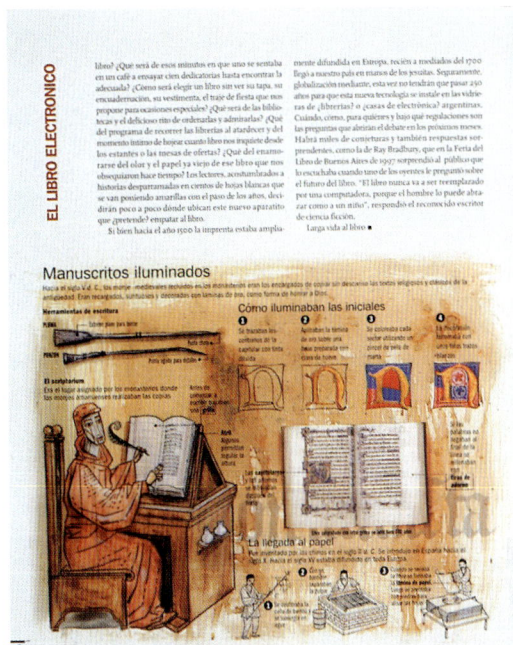
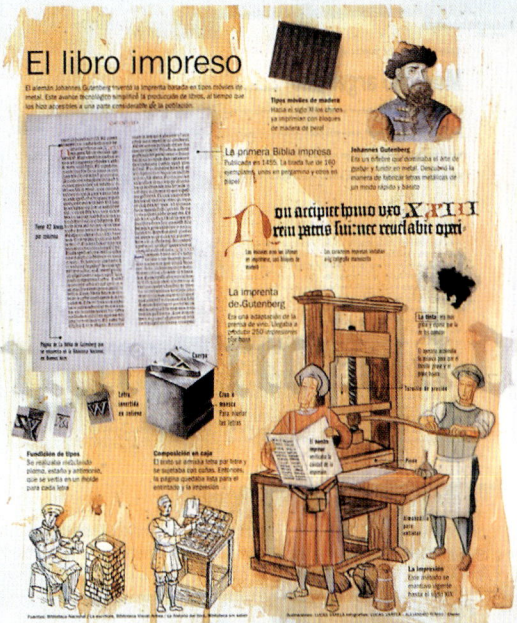

Silver
Clarín
Buenos Aires, Argentina
Iñaki Palacios, Art Director; **Jaime Serra**, Graphic Director; **Lucas Varela**, Artist/Researcher; **Alejandro Tumas**, Artist; **Stella Bin**, Researcher
• for Portfolio and Infographics, Three or More Colors

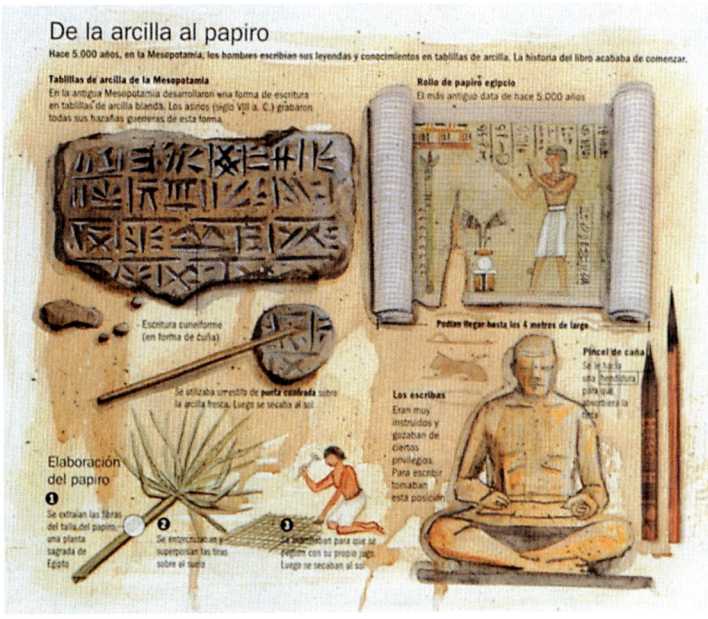
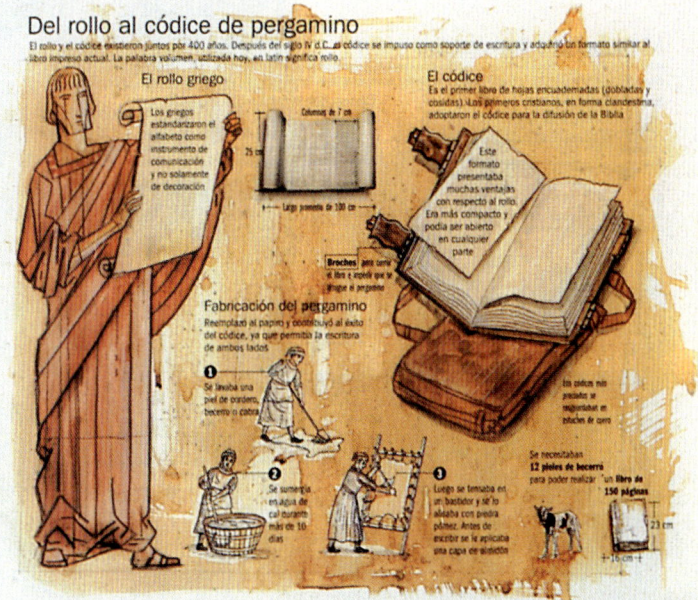

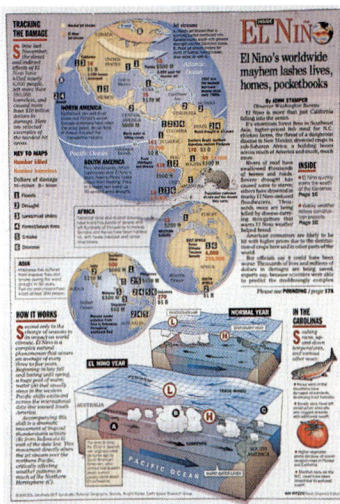

The Charlotte Observer
Charlotte, NC
William Pitzer, News Graphics Editor

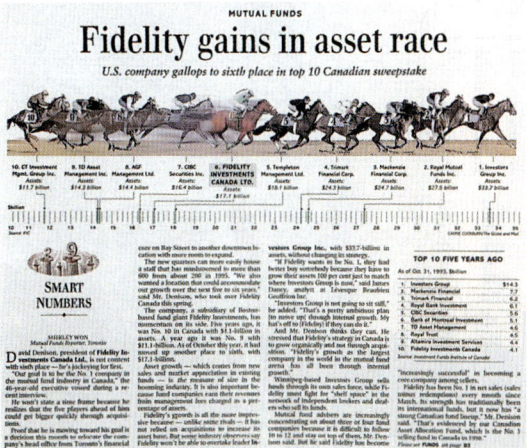

The Globe and Mail
Toronto, Canada
Carrie Cockburn, Graphic Artist

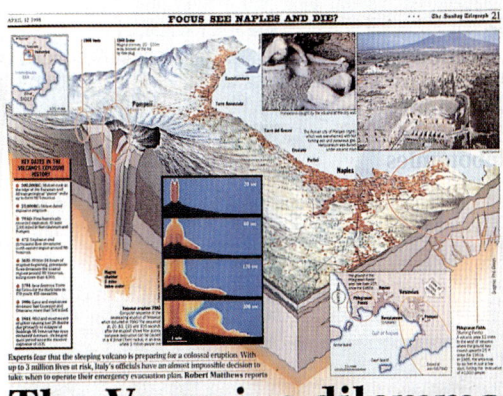

The Sunday Telegraph
London, England
Phillip J. Green, Graphics Editor

INFOGRAPHICS ■ Portfolio One Artist, More than One Artist

The New York Times
New York, NY
Juan Velasco, Graphics Editor

El Mundo Del Siglo XXI
Madrid, Spain
Rafael Ferrer, Graphic Journalist

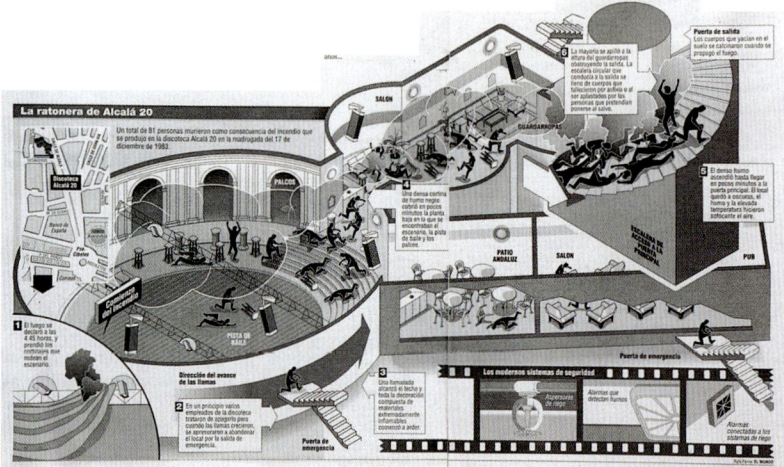

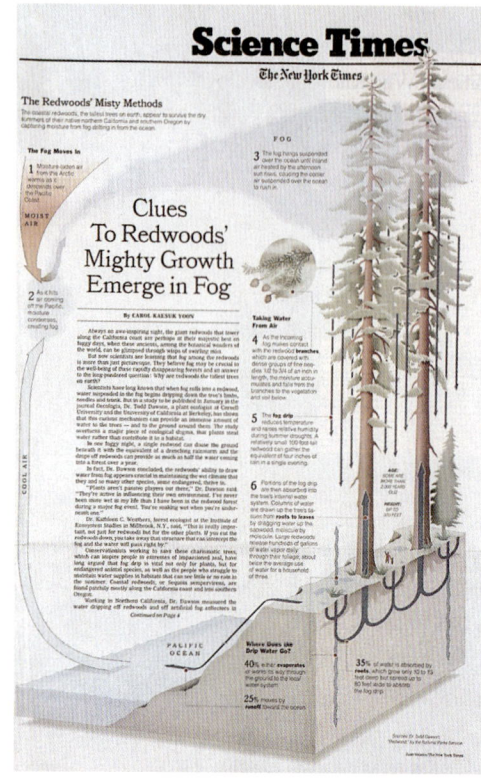

Clarín
Buenos Aires, Argentina
Iñaki Palacios, Art Director;
Jaime Serra, Graphic Director;
Staff

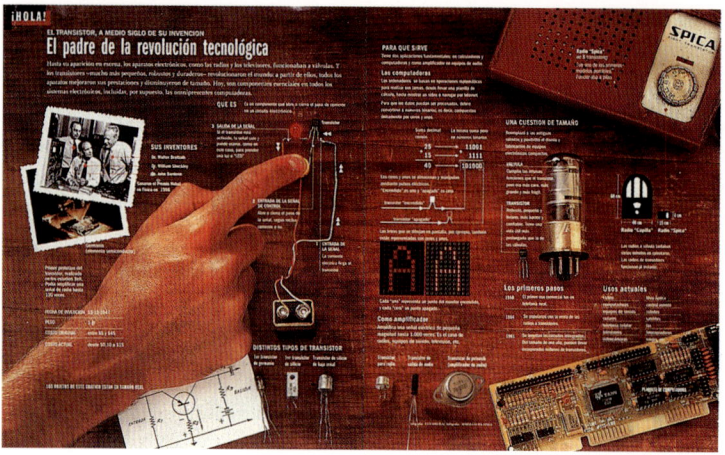

Clarín
Buenos Aires, Argentina
Iñaki Palacios, Art Director;
Jaime Serra, Graphic Director;
Staff

El Periódico de Catalunya
Barcelona, Spain
Francina Cortés, Designer

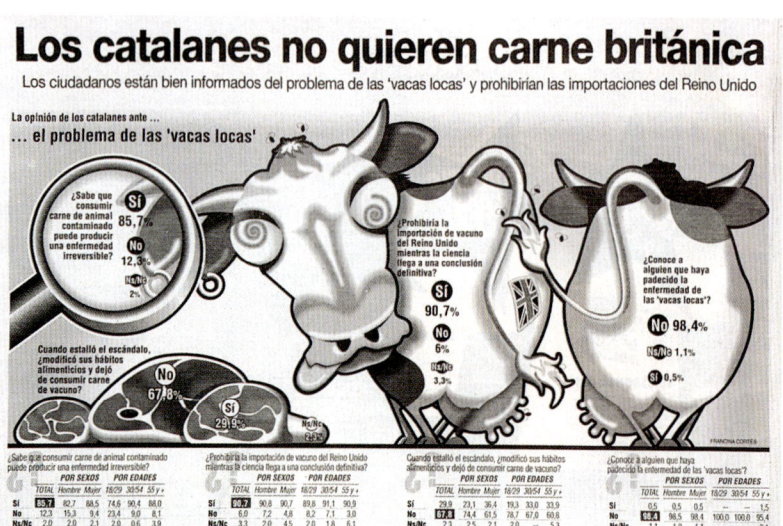

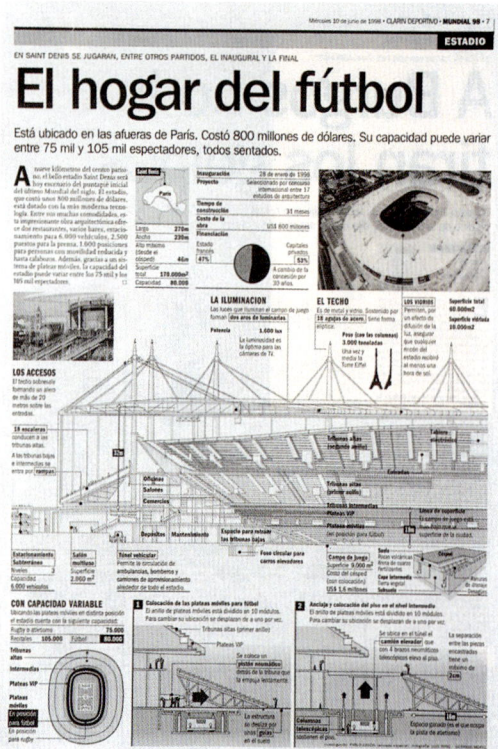

Portfolio More than One Artist ■ INFOGRAPHICS

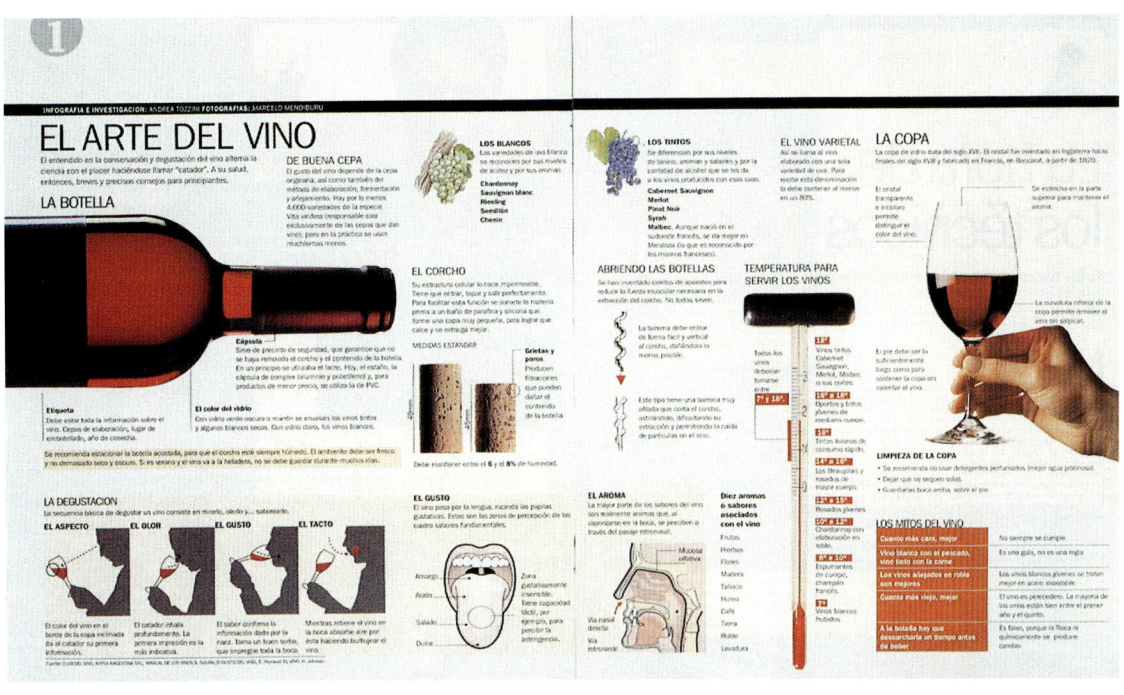

**Gold
Clarín**
Buenos Aires, Argentina
Iñaki Palacios, Art Director; **Jaime Serra,** Graphic Director; **Staff**

The staff captured the tone and the feel for each of the stories. Graphics were not type-heavy and had good balance. The staff showed a commitment to high quality visual reporting. By being involved early in the process, the staff understood the content so well the presentation became second nature.

El plantel del diario captó el tono y el estilo de cada una de las historias. Los gráficos no incluían muchos tipos y tenían un equilibrio adecuado. El plantel demostró su dedicación al reportaje visual de alta calidad. Mediante su participación en las etapas iniciales del proceso, el equipo comprendió el contenido tan bien que la presentación pasó a ocupar un segundo plano.

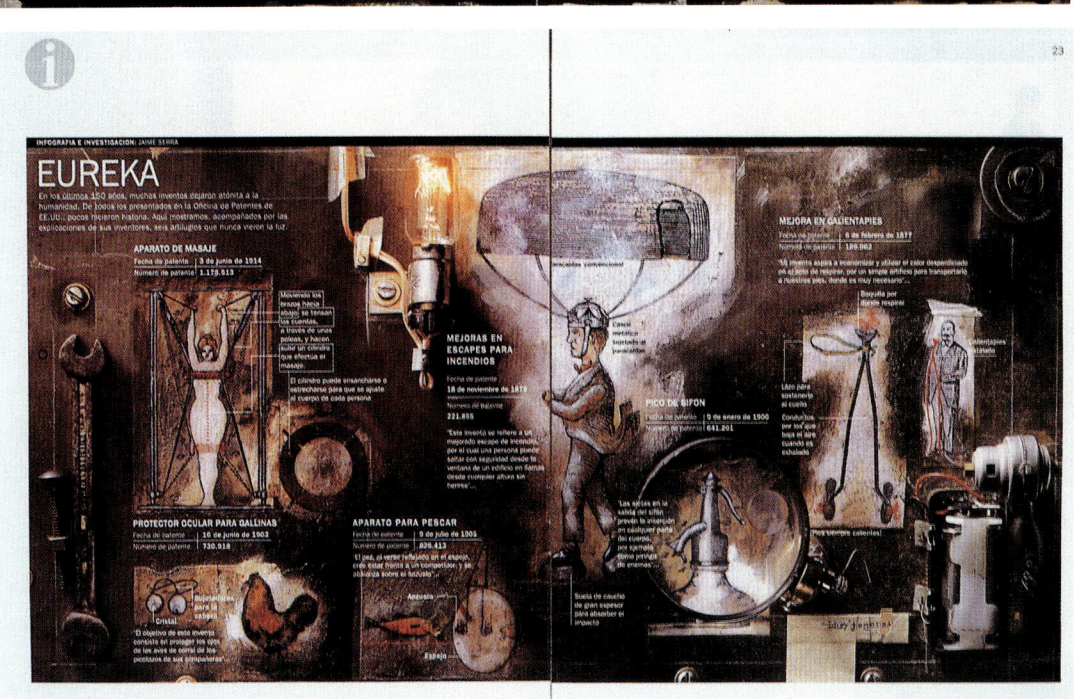

INFOGRAPHICS ■ Portfolio More than One Artist

The Times-Picayune
New Orleans, LA

Daniel Swenson, Graphic Artist; **Angela Hill**, Graphics Editor; **Emmet Mayer, III**, Graphic Artist

The Washington Post
Washington, DC

John Anderson, Graphic Journalist; **Robert Dorrell**, Graphic Journalist; **Seth Hamblin**, Graphics Coordinator

El Correo
Bilbao, Spain

Fernando G. Baptista, Infographic Artist; **Javier Zarracina**, Infographic Editor

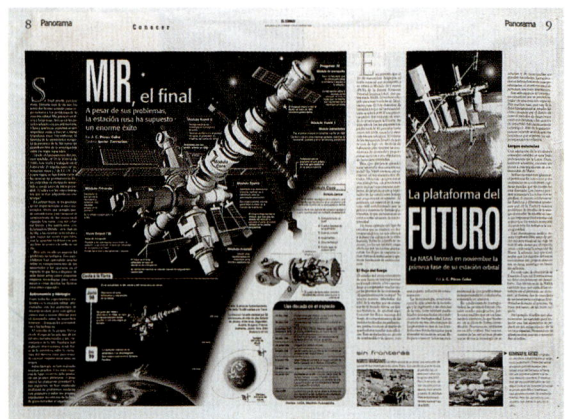

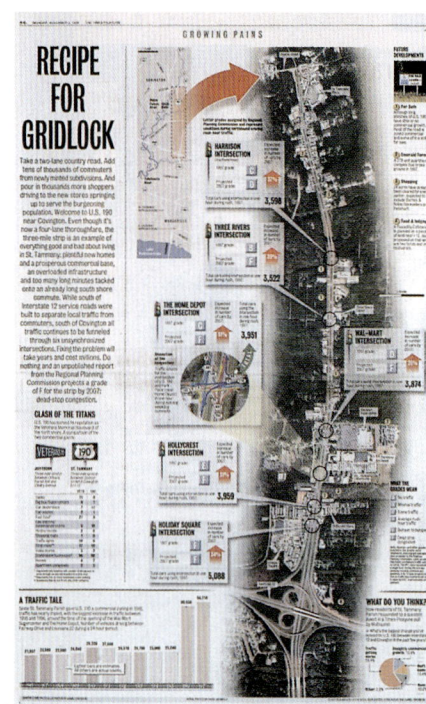

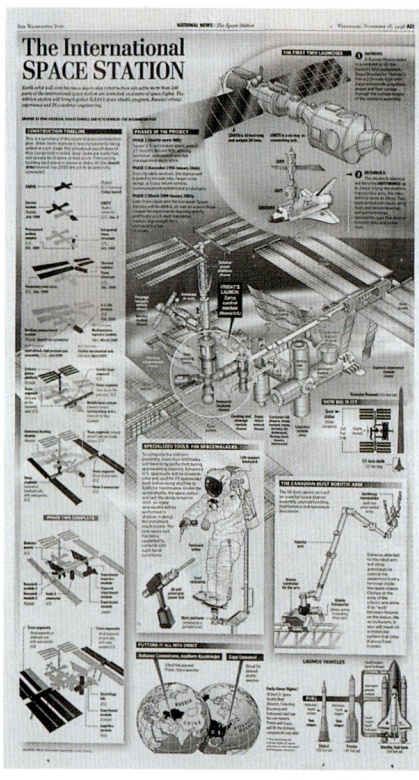

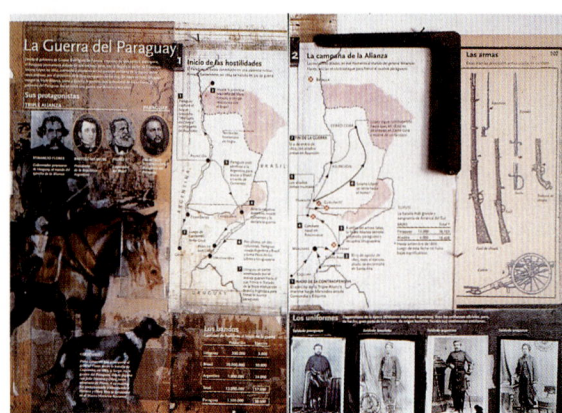

El Observador
Montevideo, Uruguay

Jaime Serra, Graphics Editor Artist; **Pablo Loscri**, Artist Researcher

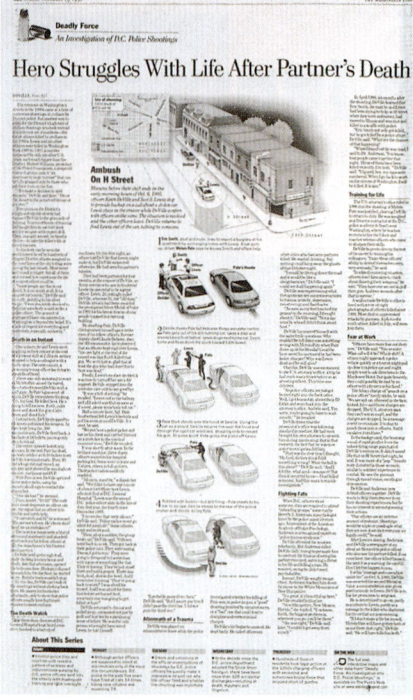

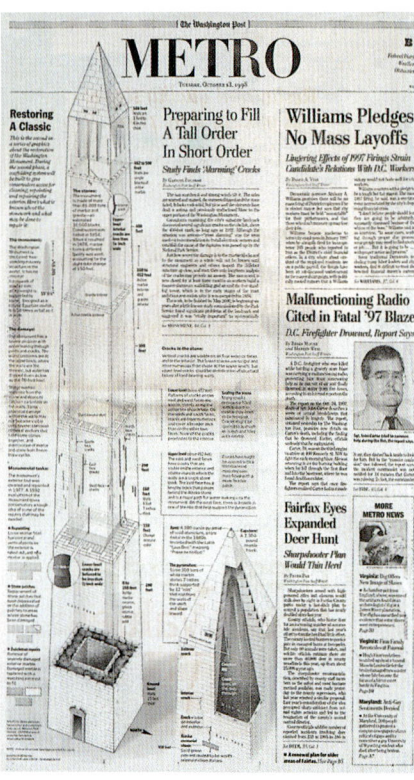

The Washington Post
Washington, DC

Laura Stanton, Graphic Artist; **Lon Tweeten**, Graphic Artist; **Jackson Dykman**, Art Director & Designer

The Washington Post
Washington, DC

Robert Dorrell, Graphic Journalist; **Brenna Sink**, Metro Graphics Editor; **Laura Stanton**, Graphic Artist; **Lon Tweeton**, Graphic Artist
• also for Infographics Black or Black and One Color

MISCELLANEOUS

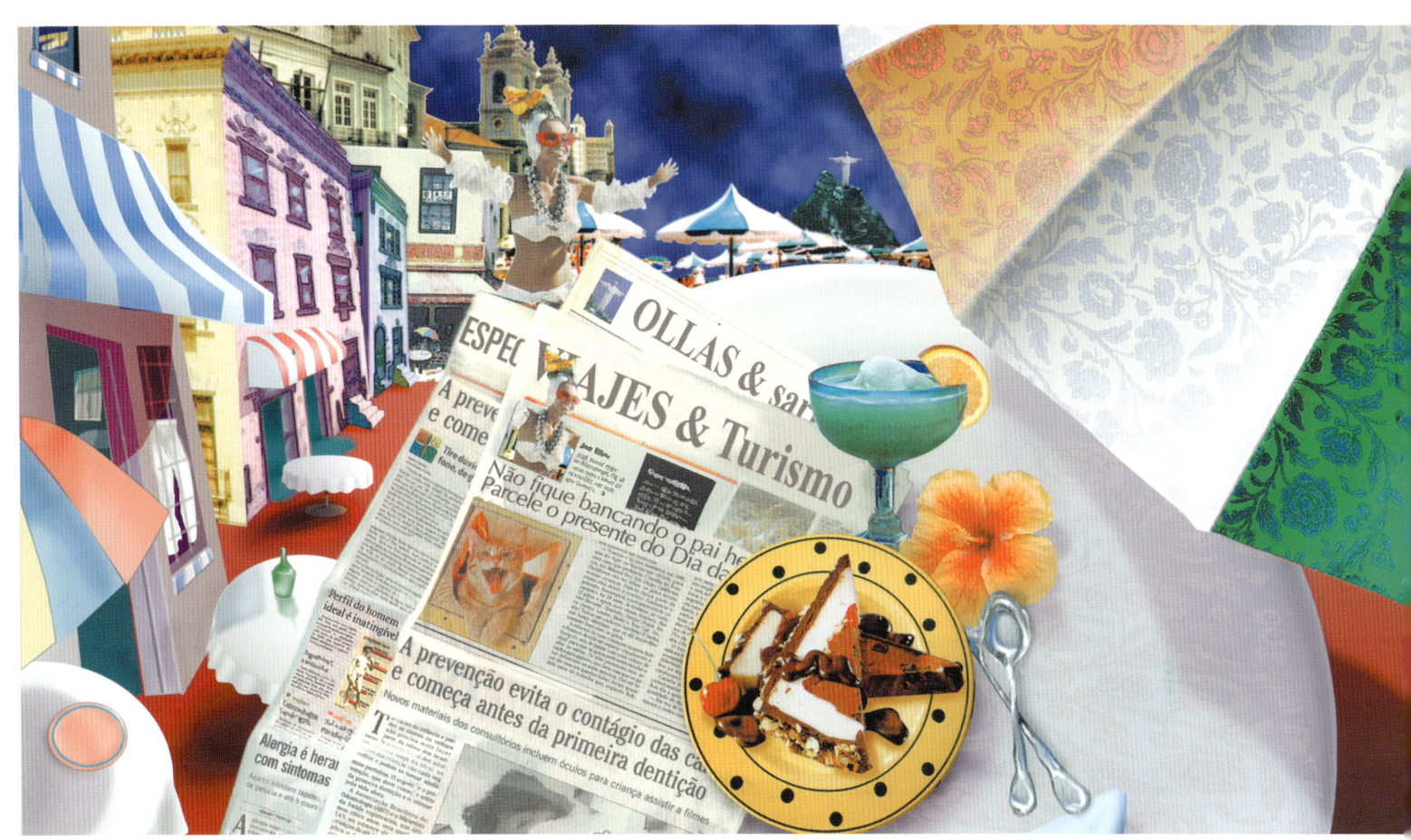

CHAPTER TEN

REDESIGN

REPRINTS

JUDGES

INDEX

MISCELLANEOUS ■ Overall Redesign

Gold
The National Post
Don Mills, Canada

Kenneth Whyte, Editor-in-Chief; **Martin Newland**, Deputy Editor; **Kirk Lapointe**, Executive Editor; **Lucie Lacava**, Design Consultant; **Gayle Grin**, Design Editor; **Roland-Yves Carignan**, Design Editor

The design of this publication is crisp, elegant, wonderful, dynamic, open, clean and fresh. This paper has a look most designers would've loved to be a part of creating. Its presentation is a tonic for the overdose of loud, bold and busy publications. The readers win.

El diseño de esta publicación es nítido, elegante, maravilloso, dinámico, abierto, limpio y refrescante. Este diario tiene un aspecto en cuya creación a la mayoría de los diseñadores les encantaría participar. Su presentación es un bálsamo contra el exceso de publicaciones chillonas, atrevidas y recargadas. Los lectores ganan.

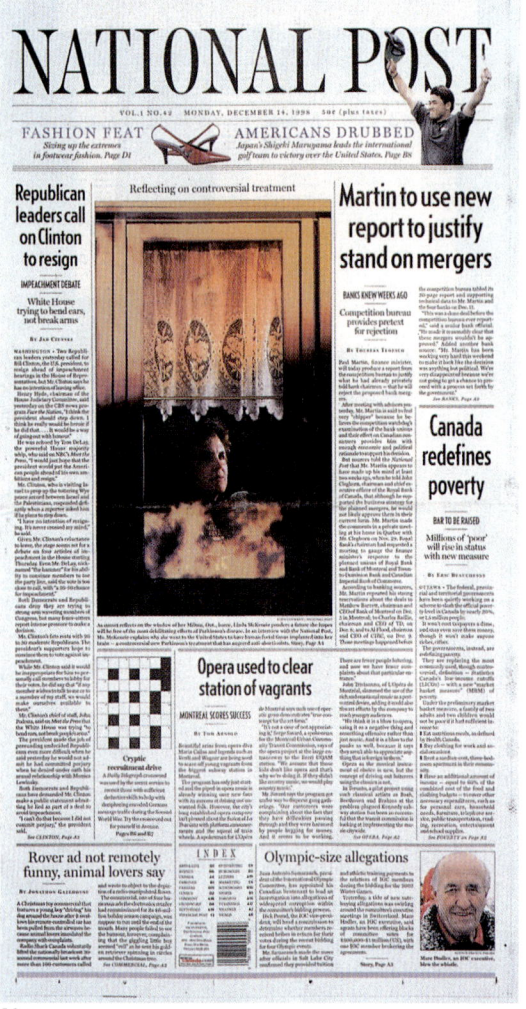

After

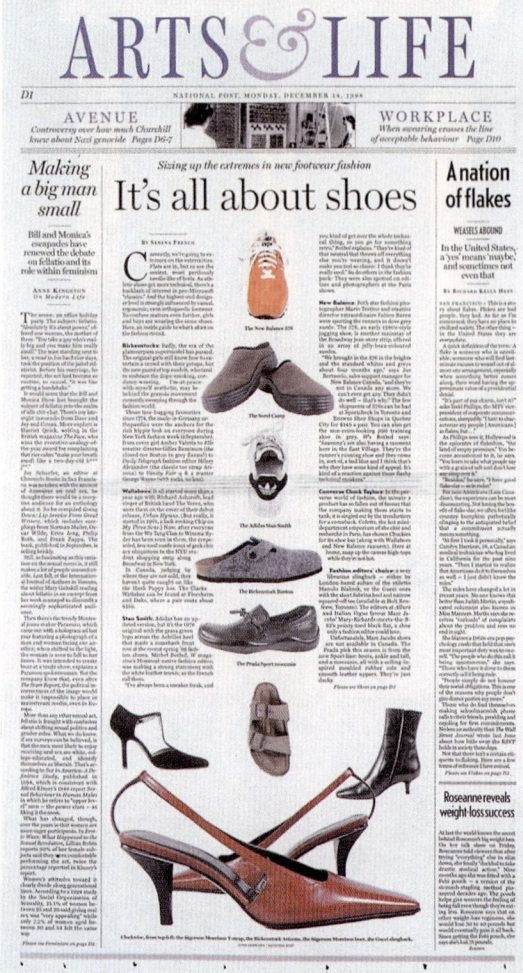

After

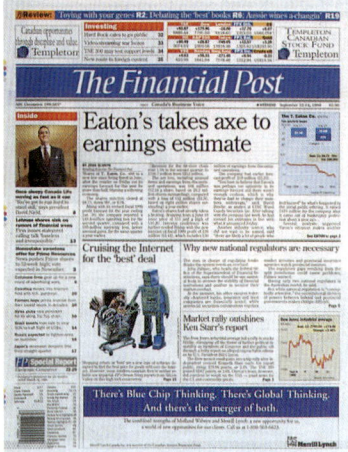

Before

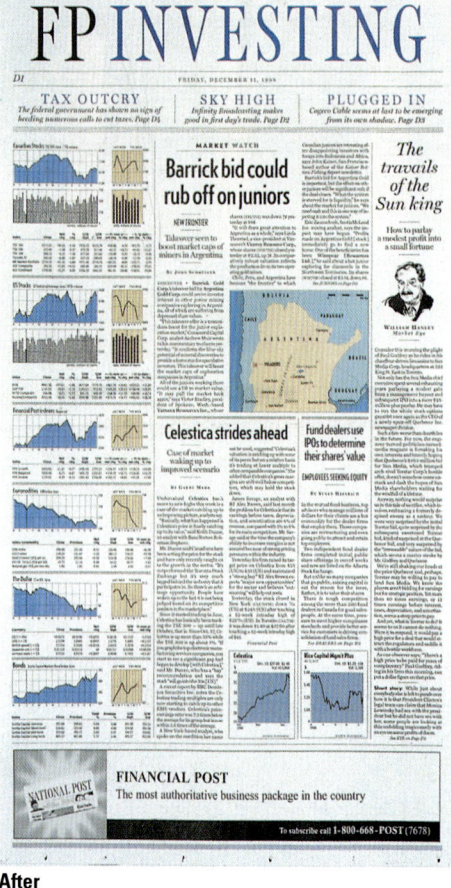

After

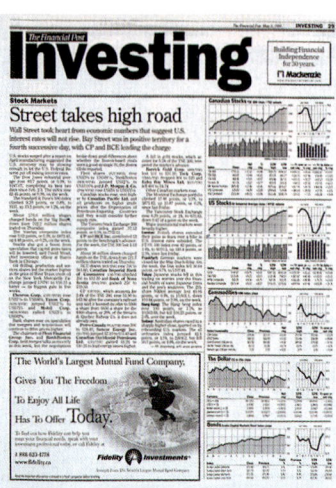

Before

258 ■ THE BEST OF NEWSPAPER DESIGN

Overall Redesign ■ MISCELLANEOUS

Silver
The Globe and Mail
Toronto, Canada
Staff

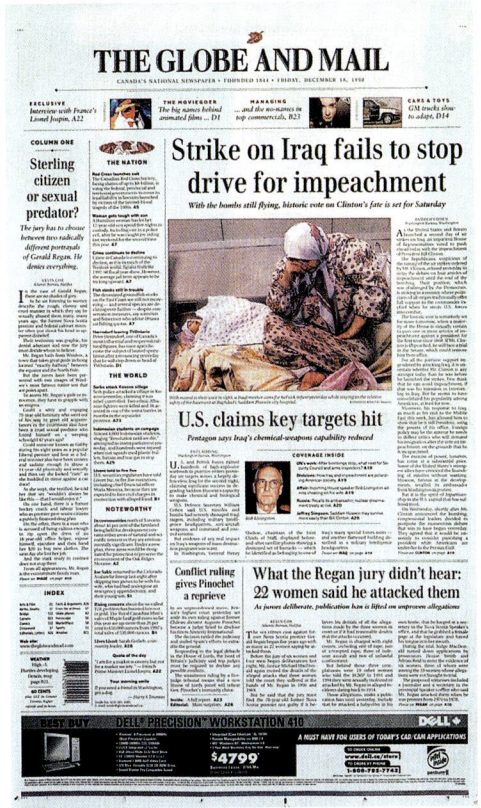
After

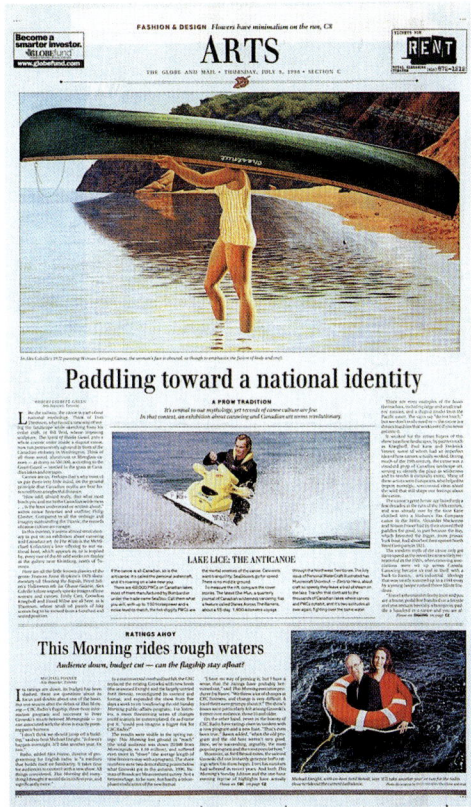
After

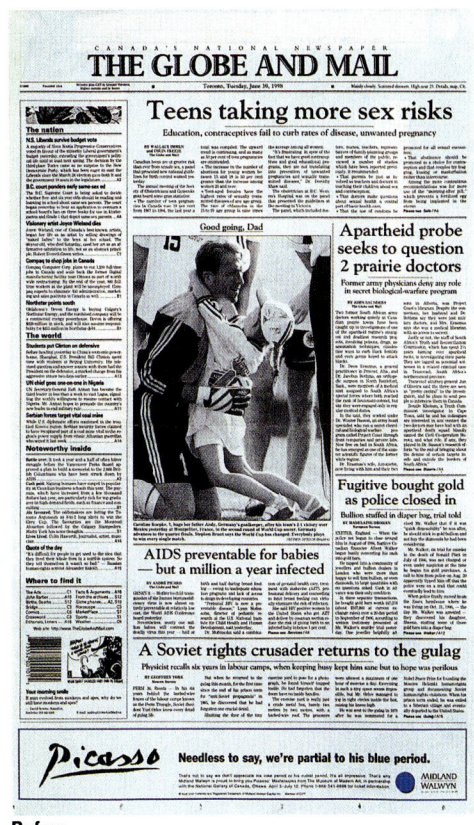
Before

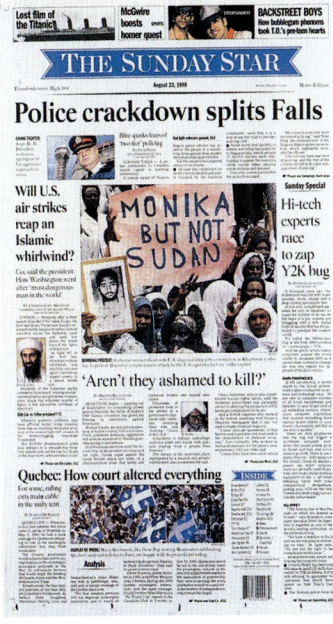
Before

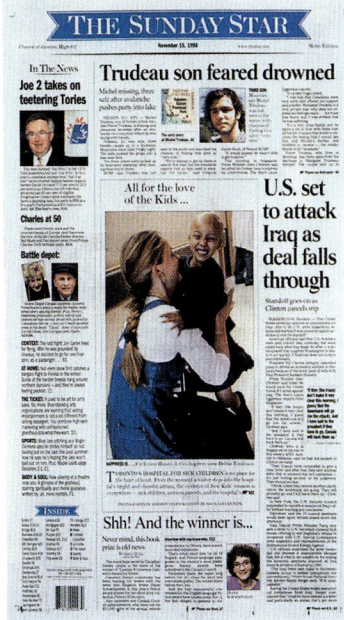
After

The Toronto Star
Toronto, Canada
Staff

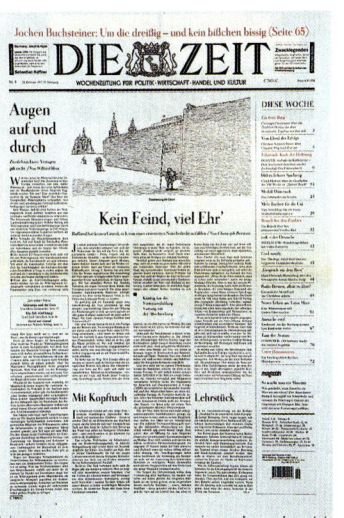
Before

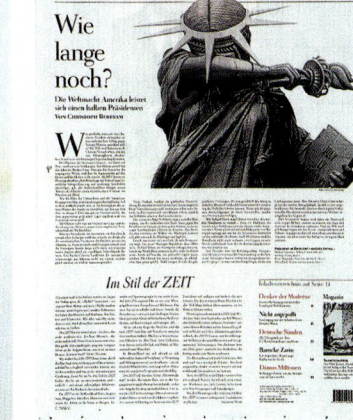
After

Die Zeit
Hamburg, Germany
Arwed Voss, Art Director; **Thomas Brackvogel**, Project Leader; **Mario García**, Design Consultant

TWENTIETH EDITION ■ 259

MISCELLANEOUS ▪ Section Redesign

Silver
El Mundo
Madrid, Spain
Carmelo Caderot, Art Director & Designer; **Manuel de Miguel,** Assistant Art Director & Designer

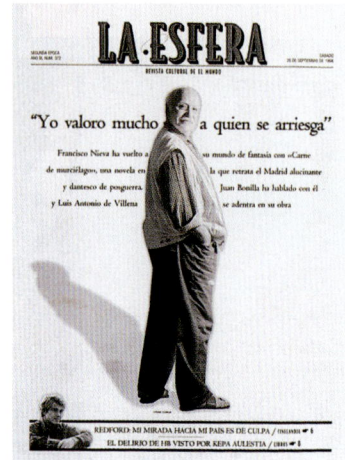
Before

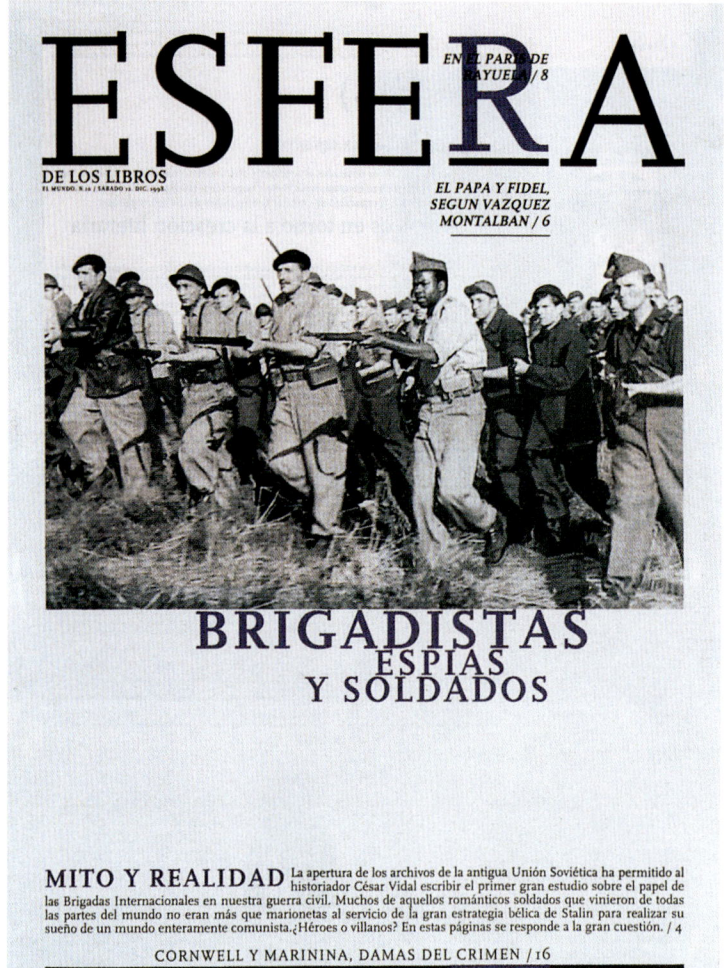
After

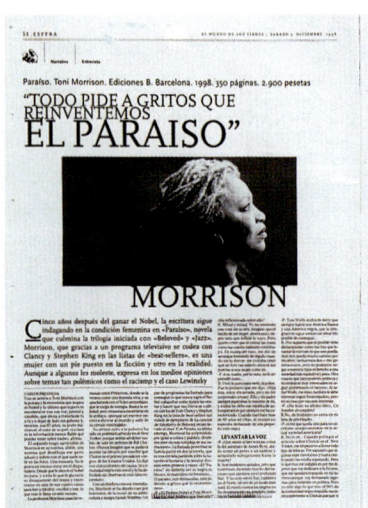 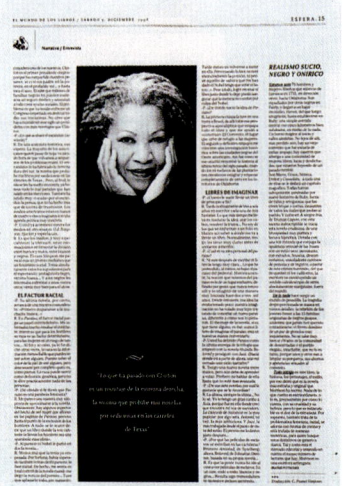
After

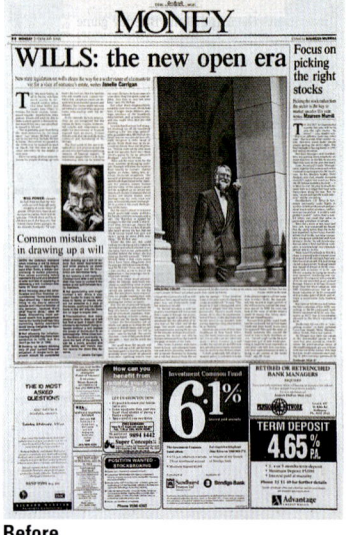
Before

After

The Age
Melbourne, Australia
Ray Gill, Editor; Janelle Carrigan, Deputy Editor; Andrew Wolf, Designer

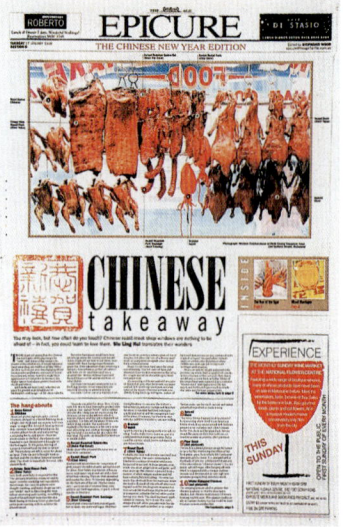
Before

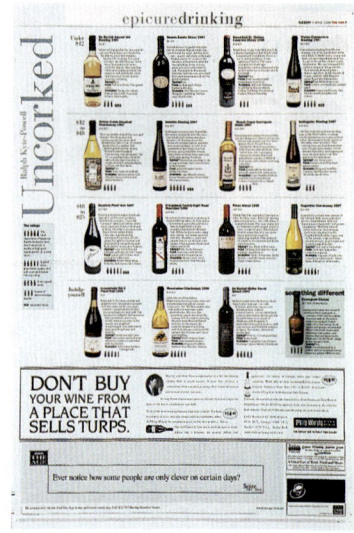
After

The Age
Melbourne, Australia
Judy Green, Designer; Stephanie Wood, Editor/Epicure

Section Redesign ■ MISCELLANEOUS

Berlingske Tidende
Copenhagen, Denmark
Gregers Jensen, Designer Editor; **Bettina Kofmann**, Page Designer; **Mikael Hjorth**, Sub-Editor; **Søren Østergaard Sørensen**, Editor; **Carsten Gregersen**, Design Editor

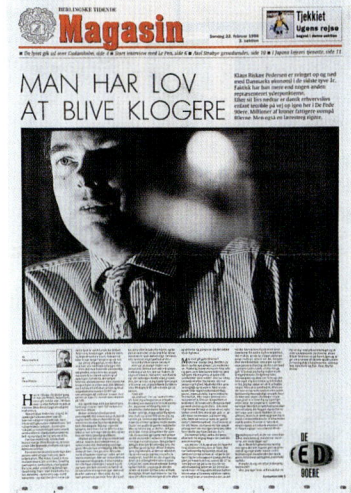

Before

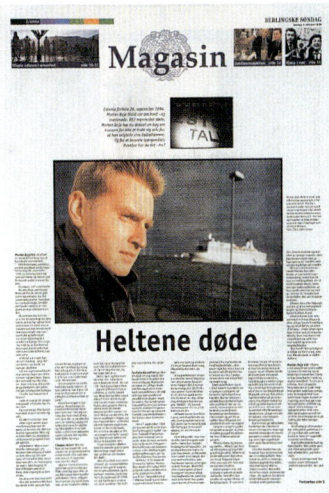

After

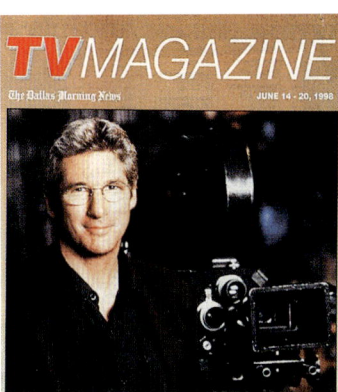

Before

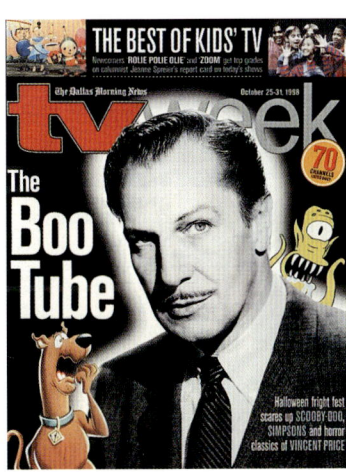

After

The Dallas Morning News
Dallas, TX
G. Noel Gross, Designer; **Norma Cavazos**, Staff; **Susan Verhault**, Staff

Expansión
Madrid, Spain
José Juan Gámez, Art Director & Designer; **Pablo Mª Ramírez**, Designer; **Antonio Martin**, Designer; **Cesar Galera**, Designer

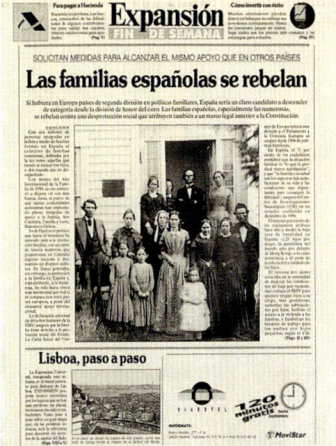

Before

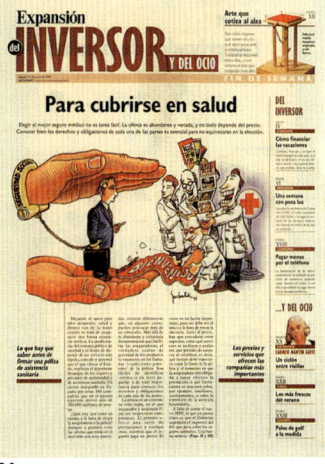

After

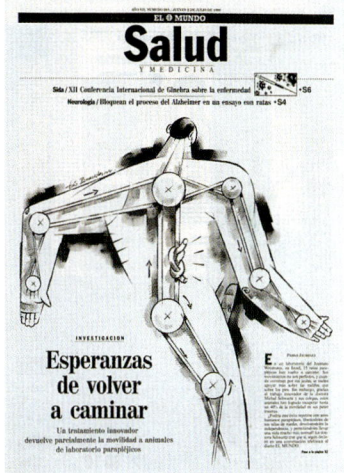

Before

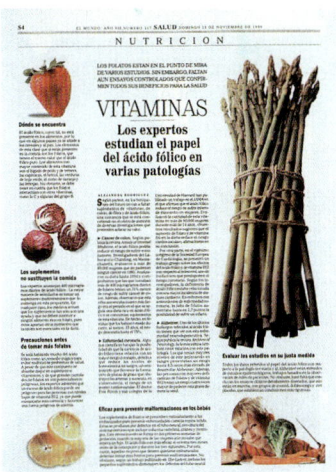

After

El Mundo
Madrid, Spain
Carmelo Caderot, Art Director & Designer; **Manuel de Miguel**, Assistant Art Director & Designer

MISCELLANEOUS ■ Section Redesign, Page Redesign

Clarín
Buenos Aires, Argentina

Iñaki Palacios, Art Director; **Juan Elissetche,** Design Editor; **Vicente Dagnino,** Design Editor; **Federico Sosa,** Design Editor; **Carlos Vazquez,** Graphic Designer; **Maureen Holboll,** Graphic Designer; **Osvaldo Estevao,** Graphic Designer; **Victoria Quintiero,** Graphic Designer

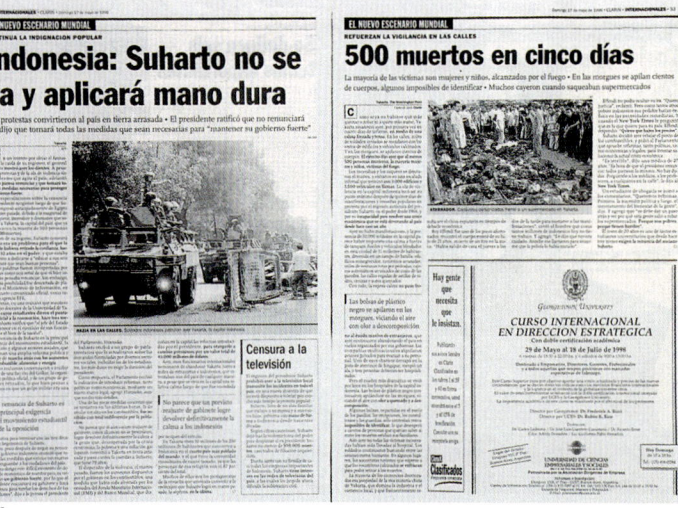

Before

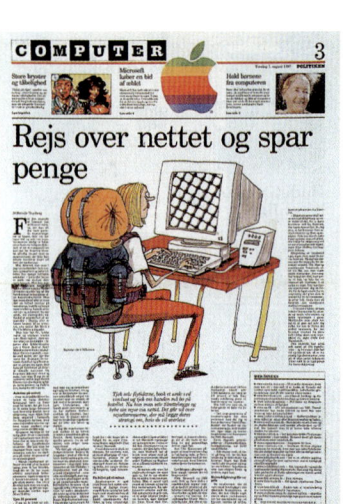

Before

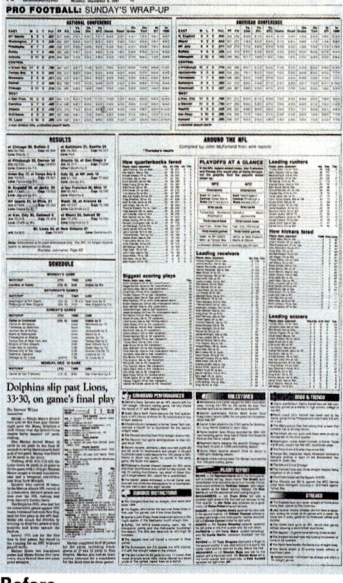

Before

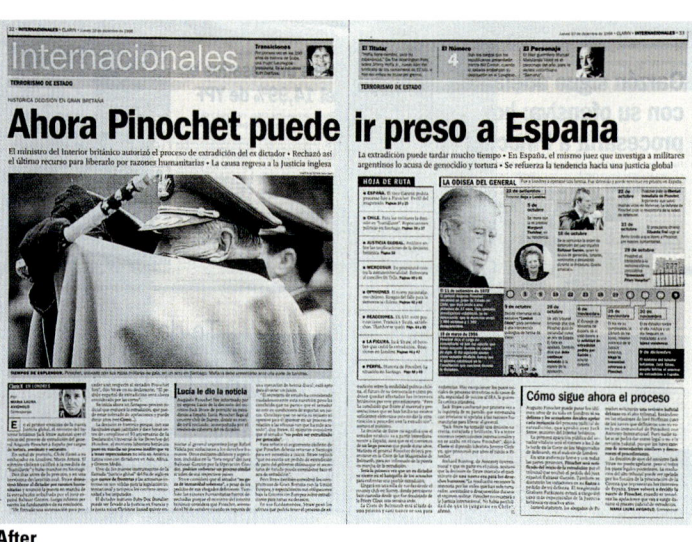

After

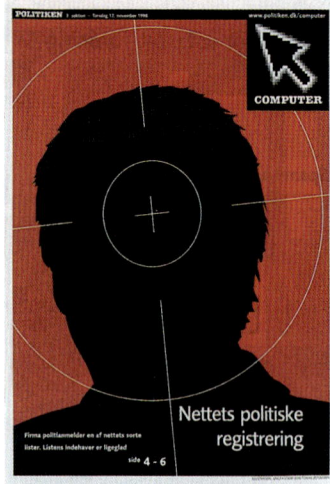

After

Politiken
Copenhagen, Denmark

Søren Nyeland, Design Editor; **Tomas Østergren,** Designer; **Mikkel Henssel,** Designer; **Leif Jonasson,** Editor; **Peter Lembo,** Copy Edito

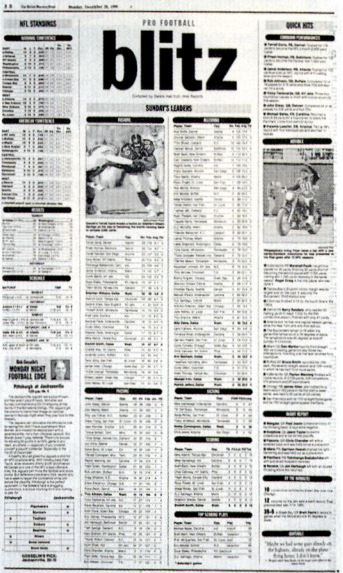

After

The Dallas Morning News
Dallas, TX

Dave Wilson, Designer; **John Banks,** Assistant Sports Editor

262 ■ THE BEST OF NEWSPAPER DESIGN

Page Redesign, Reprints ■ MISCELLANEOUS

The Atlanta Journal & Constitution
Atlanta, GA

Gary Pomerantz, Writer; **Jim Walls,** Project Editor; **Thomas Oliver,** A.M.E. Special Projects; **Ellen Voss,** News Design Desk Manager; **Sheri Taylor,** Art Director; **Tony De Feria,** A.M.E. Graphics/Photography; **Micheal Dabrowa,** Graphics Editor/Artist; **Sarah Hicks,** Designer; **Rich Adicks,** Photographer

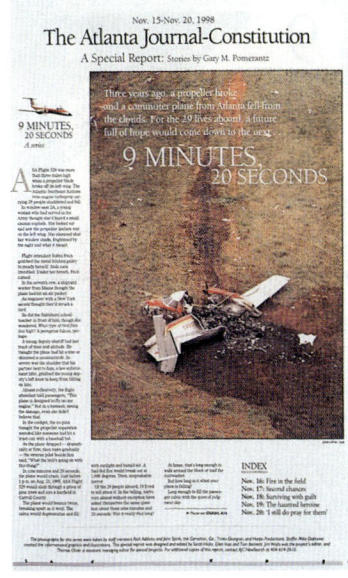

The Philadelphia Inquirer
Philadelphia, PA

Lisa A. Zollinger, Page Designer; **David Milne,** A.M.E. Design; **Bill Marsh,** Art Director; **Alen Mallot,** Photo Editor; **Don Sapatkin,** Weekend Editor

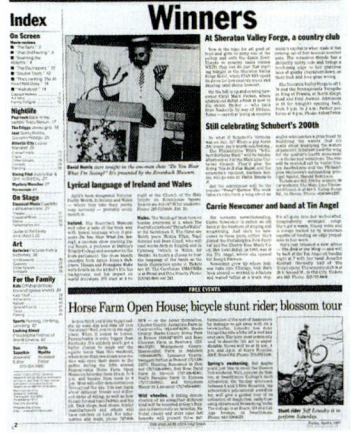

Before

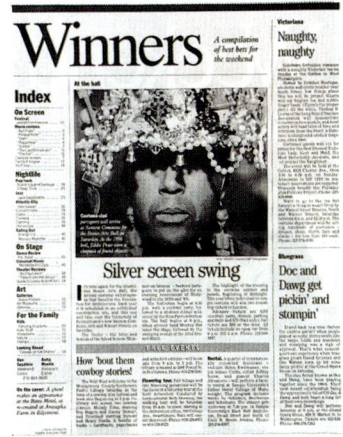

After

The Sun
Baltimore, MD

Jay Judge, News Page Designer; **Joseph Hutchinson,** A.M.E. Graphics/Design; **Andre F. Chung,** Photographer; **Jim Preston,** A.M.E./Photography; **Amy Deputy,** Picture Editor

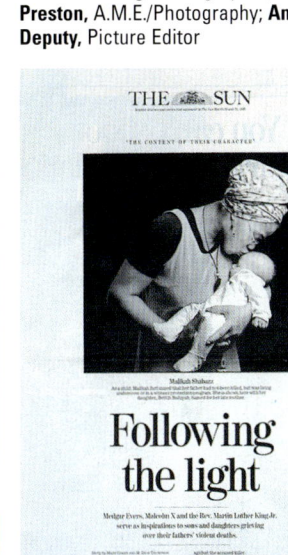

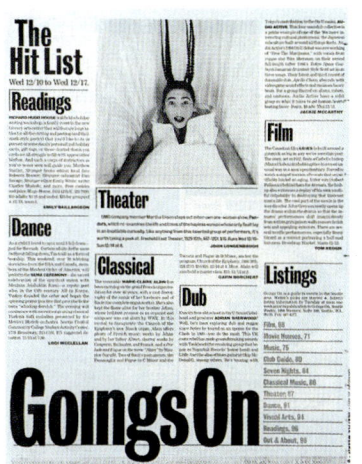

Before

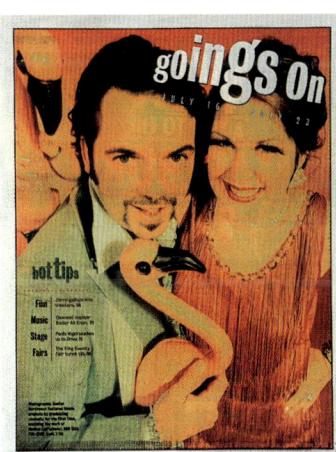

After

Seattle Weekly
Seattle, WA

Barbara Dow, Art Director & Designer

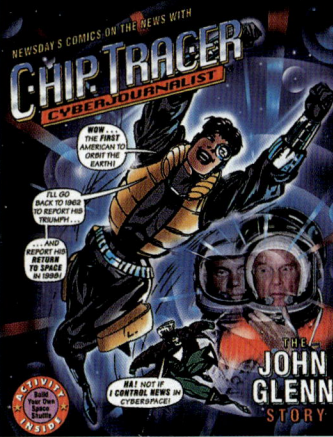

Newsday
Melville, NY

Ned Levine, Art Director & Designer; **Bill Zimmerman,** Editor; **Peggy Brown,** Writer; **Jonalyn Schuon,** Copy Editor; **Steve Geiger,** Artist; **Anthony Castrillo,** Artist; **Rod Eyer,** Diagram Artist

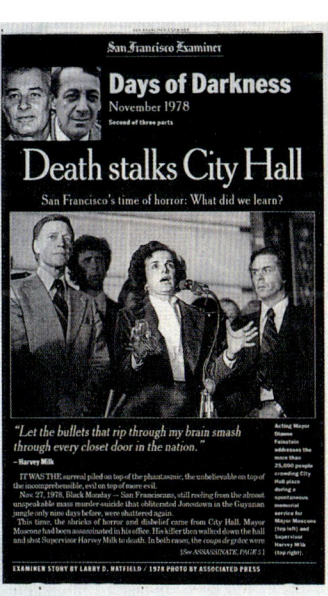

San Francisco Examiner
San Francisco, CA

Kelly Frankeny, A.M.E. Design; **Liz Mangelsdorf,** Photo Editor; **Greg Robinson,** Photographer; **Richard Paoli,** Director/Photography

TWENTIETH EDITION ■ 263

MISCELLANEOUS ■ Other

Clarín
Buenos Aires, Argentina
Iñaki Palacios, Art Director; **Sebastian Garcia,** Graphic Project; **Pablo Ruiz,** Graphic Project; **Alejandra Bliffeld,** Designer; **Alejandro Sokolowski,** Designer; **Victoria Ximenes,** Designer

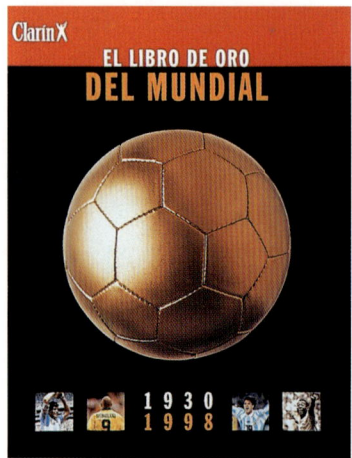

Expansión
Madrid, Spain
Pablo Mª Ramirez, Designer; **Antonio Martín Hervás,** Designer; **Jose Juan Gámez,** Art Director; **Esteban Iglesias,** Designer

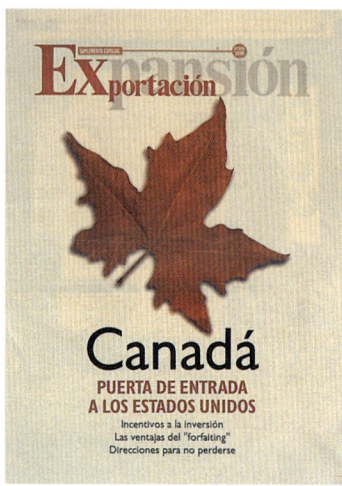

The Sacramento Bee
Sacramento, CA
Sean McDade, Artist; **Nam Nguyen,** Assistant Art Director; **Howard Shintaku,** Art Director; **Mort Saltzman,** A.M.E. Graphics; **William Enfield,** Project Editor; **William Endicott,** M.E.; **Rick Rodriguez,** Executive Editor

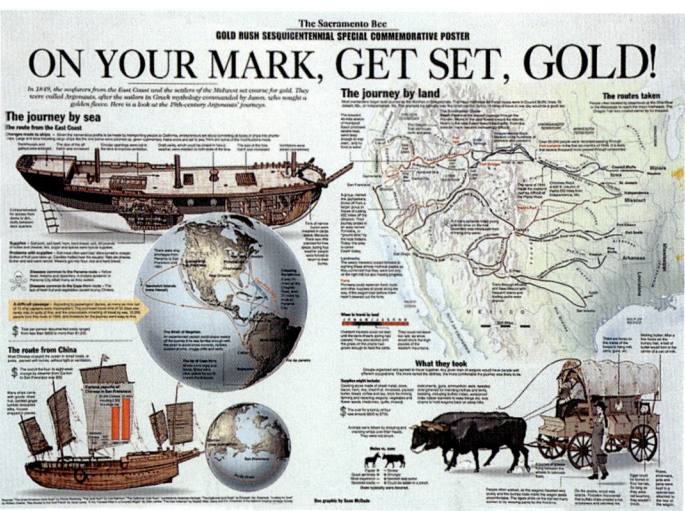

The Times-Picayune
New Orleans, LA
George Berke, Design Director; **Scott Threlkeld,** Photographer

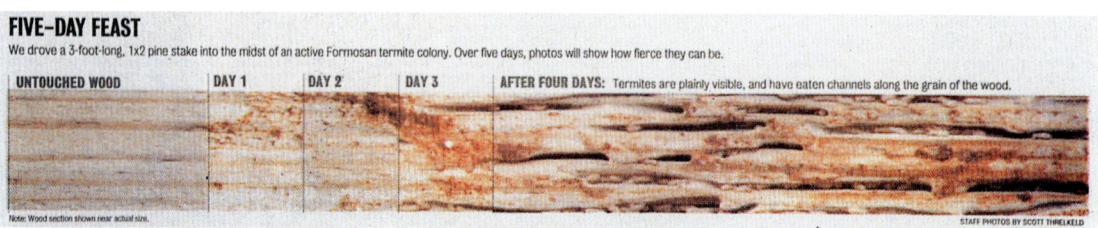

Marca
Madrid, Spain
José Juan Gámez, Graphics Editor & Designer; **Staff**

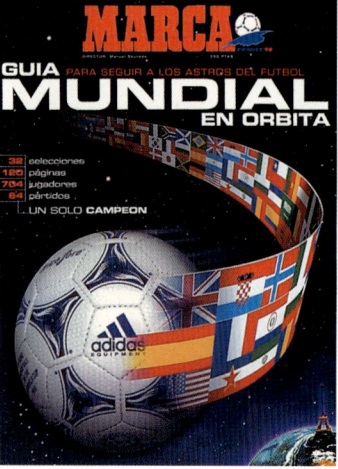

El Observador
Montevideo, Uruguay
Liz Brande, Designer

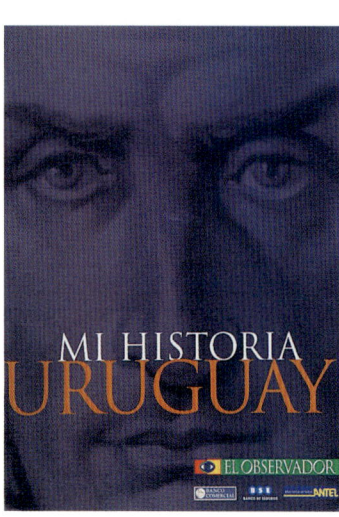

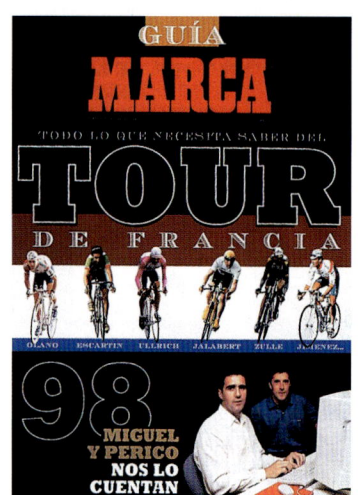

Expansión
Madrid, Spain
Ignacio de Haro, Graphic Artist; **Antonio Martín Hervás,** Designer; **Jose Juan Gámez,** Art Director

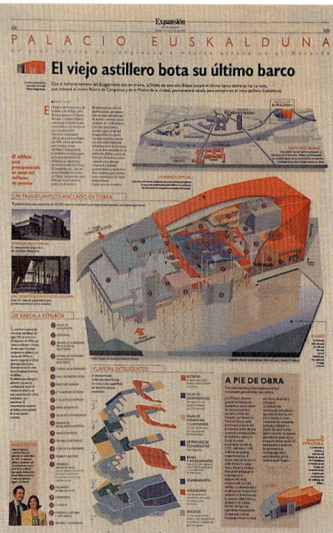

Marca
Madrid, Spain
José Juan Gámez, Graphics Editor & Designer; **Staff**

The Charlotte Observer
Charlotte, NC
William Pitzer, News Graphic Director; **Joanne Miller,** Art Director; **Foon Rhee,** Staff Writer; **Jean Marie Brown,** Metro Editor

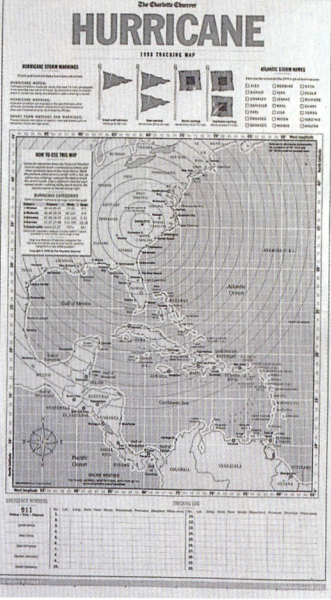

JUDGES

JUDGES' BIOGRAPIES

Two groups of judges decide on the winning entries.

The first group of five judges (this page) looked only at the competition's overall design category (category 1), studying the entries as a whole. They determined the World's Best-Designed Newspapers for information and design presentation for all three circulation sizes.

A second group of 16 judges (next pages) for the general competition was organized into three teams of five judges each, with a "floater judge" to resolve conflicts of interest and act as a backup judge to the three groups. They judged the remaining 20 categories of the overall competition in categories 2 through 21.

BIOGRAFIA DE LOS MEIMBROS DEL JURADO

Dos jurados decidirán quiénes son los ganadores del concurso.

El primer jurado, de cinco miembros, (en esta página) se encargó únicamente de la categoría de diseño general (categoría 1) y estudiaron las obras de los concursantes en su conjunto. Este jurado determinó cuáles fueron los Diarios de Mejor Diseño del Mundo en cuanto a presentación de la información y del diseño según los tres tamaños de tirada.

El segundo jurado, de 16 miembros, a cargo del concurso general, se dividió en tres equipos de cinco miembros cada uno, con un juez "sustituto" que resolviese los conflictos de interés y actuara para apoyar a los tres grupos. Ellos evaluaron las 20 categorías restantes de la competencia general, designadas con los números del 2 al 21.

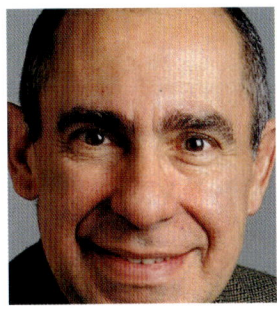 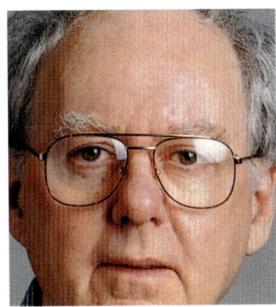 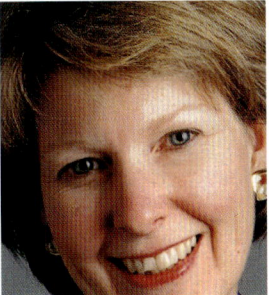 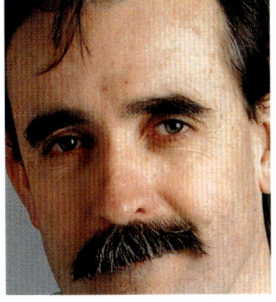 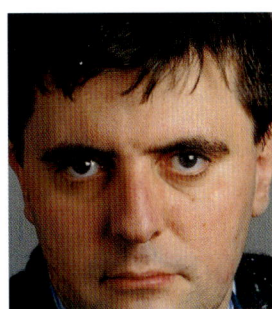

Mario García, Sr., faculty affiliate at the Poynter Institute for Media Studies, was founder and director of the Institute's graphics and design programs from 1982 to 1990. As president and senior designer of Mario Garcia New Media Design International, with offices in Tampa, Fla., Hamburg, Germany and Buenos Aires, Argentina, he spends much of his time traveling as a newspaper and on-line design consultant. He has worked with nearly 400 news organizations worldwide. He is author of several design books.

■ ■ ■

Mario García, Sr., asociado del plantel docente del Poynter Institute for Media Studies, fue fundador y director de los programas de diseño y gráficos del instituto desde 1982 hasta 1990. En calidad de presidente y diseñador jefe de Mario García New Media Design International, con sede en Tampa, Fla.; Hamburgo, Alemania; y Buenos Aires, Argentina, dedica gran parte de su tiempo viajando como consultor de periódicos y diseño en línea. Ha colaborado con casi 400 medios noticiosos de todo el mundo y es autor de varios libros sobre diseño.

Robert Lockwood is president of Robert Lockwood Inc. and has designed more than 70 newspapers worldwide. He continues to work with several long-time clients including The Associated Press. He is a cofounder and first president of the SND and speaks at many international design workshops. In addition, he serves on the advisory board of the Virginia Commonwealth University School of Mass Communications. He is the author of "News by Design: A Survival Guide for Newspapers."

■ ■ ■

Robert Lockwood es presidente de Robert Lockwood, Inc., y ha diseñado más de 70 periódicos de todo el mundo. Continúa trabajando con varios viejos clientes como The Associated Press. Es cofundador y primer presidente de la Society for News Design (SND) y es orador en muchos talleres internacionales de diseño. Además, es miembro del consejo asesor de Virginia Commonwealth University School of Mass Communications. Es autor de "News by Design: A Survival Guide for Newspapers."

Pam Luecke is the editor and vice president of the Lexington Herald-Leader. She also has worked at the Hartford Courant, the Louisville Courier-Journal and Times. During her positions at both the Courier-Journal and the Hartford Courant, she was the supervising editor for work that received a Pulitzer Prize.

■ ■ ■

Pam Luecke es editora y vicepresidente de The Lexington Herald-Leader. También ha trabajado en el Hartford Courant y The Louisville Courier-Journal and Times. Tanto en el Hartford Courant como en el Courier-Journal fue redactora supervisora del trabajo que fue galardonado con el Premio Pulitzer.

Chris Peck is editor of The Spokesman-Review, Spokane, Wash., where he started in 1979 as a columnist. He supervises overall news and editorial operations for the newspaper. In 1982 he was named managing editor. Prior to coming to Spokane he was managing editor of The Times-News in Twin Falls, Idaho, and editor of the Wood River Journal in Hailey, Idaho.

■ ■ ■

Chris Peck es editor de The Spokesman-Review, Spokane, estado de Washington, donde comenzó su labor en 1979 como columnista. Supervisa operaciones editoriales y de noticias en general para este diario. En 1982 fue nombrado redactor gerente. Antes de llegar a Spokane, fue editor ejecutivo de The Times-News en Twin Falls y editor de The Wood River Journal en Hailey, ambos en el estado de Idaho.

Mario Tascón is infographics and internet director of El Mundo, Madrid, Spain. He teaches at the School of Communications at the University of Navarra and is chair of the international infographics seminar "Show, Don't Tell." He is a consultant for the Corriere della Sera (Italy), La Nacion (Argentina), El Mercurio (Chile), O Día (Brasil), Grupo Abril (Brasil), Revista Semana (Colombia), El País (Uruguay) and El Universal (Venezuela). He has won several SND awards for his work.

■ ■ ■

Mario Tascón es director de infografía e Internet de El Mundo, Madrid, España. Enseña en la Facultad de Comunicaciones de la Universidad de Navarra y es presidente del seminario internacional de infografía "Show, Don't Tell." Es consultor de Corriere della Sera (Italia), La Nación (Argentina), El Mercurio (Chile), O Dia (Brasil), Grupo Abril (Brasil), Revista Semana (Colombia), El País (Uruguay) y El Universal (Venezuela). Ha sido galardonado con varios premios de la SND por su labor

JUDGES

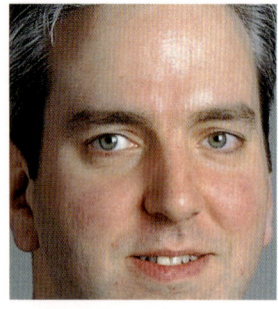 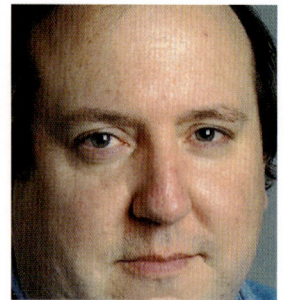 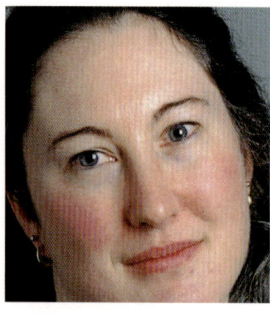 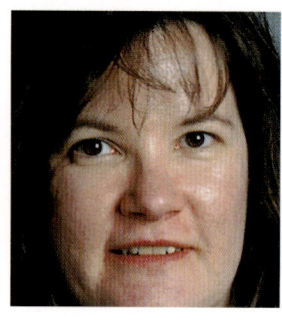 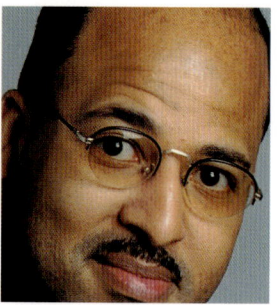

Roland-Yves Carignan, senior design editor, was part of the team that launched Canada's new coast-to-coast daily, the National Post. He was previously art director of Le Devoir, which has been named one of SND's "World's Best-Designed Newspaper" four times.

■ ■ ■

Roland-Yves Carignan, editor jefe de diseño, integró el equipo que lanzó el nuevo diario nacional de Canadá, The National Post. Con anterioridad fue director de arte de Le Devoir, que ha sido nombrado uno de los "Periódicos con Mejor Diseño del Mundo" por la SND en cuatro ocasiones.

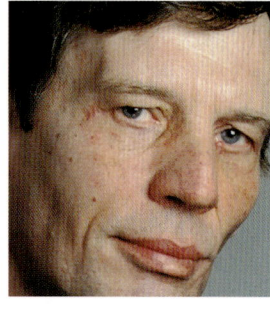

Gregers Jensen is sub-editor/graphic designer at the Berlingske Tidende newspaper in Copenhagen, Denmark. For more than 10 years he has worked with the front page of the newspaper's feature/culture section and has received several SND awards.

■ ■ ■

Gregers Jensen es subdirector y diseñador gráfico del diario Berlingske Tidente de Copenhagen, Dinamarca. Durante más de 10 años ha trabajado en la primera plana de la sección de cultura y artículos del periódico, y ha sido galardonado con varios premios de la SND.

Carl Davaz is The Register-Guard's assistant managing editor for graphics and technology. He is responsible for his newspaper's visual presentation and coordinated his newsroom's transition to pagination. As a photojournalist he has photographed and designed three books. Davaz worked at newspapers in Kansas and Montana before going to Eugene, Ore. in 1986.

■ ■ ■

Carl Davaz es redactor gerente auxiliar de The Register-Guard a cargo del diseño gráfico y tecnología. Es responsable de la presentación visual de dicho diario y coordinó la transición de la sala de redacción a la paginación. Como periodista gráfico, ha fotografiado y diseñado tres libros. Davaz trabajó en diarios de Kansas y Montana antes de partir para Eugene, estado de Oregón, en 1986.

■ ■ ■

Kyle Keener ha sido fotógrafo de artículos de Detroit Free Press durante cuatro años y ha sido nombrado "Fotógrafo Regional del Año" por la National Press Photographer's Association en cinco ocasiones. Comenzó su profesión en el plantel del Kansas City Times en 1984 y posteriormente trabajó en el diario Philadelphia Enquirer durante nueve años. Ha cubierto la problemática del SIDA en Uganda, la liberación de Nelson Mandela en Sudáfrica y el período que siguió al genocidio ocurrido en Ruanda.

Pamela Dunlap-Shohl has worked at the Anchorage Daily News as a graphic artist and designer since 1984. She has won many SND awards. Her work also has been represented in "SPD 32 Publication Design Annual," Print's "1996 Regional Design Annual" and "Best Typography 2" and the 1992 "Best of the West Competition."

■ ■ ■

Pamela Dunlap-Shohl ha trabajado en el Anchorage Daily News como artista gráfica y diseñadora desde 1984, y ha sido galardonada con varios premios de la SND. Su obra también ha sido representada en "SPD 32 Publication Design Annual," "1996 Regional Design Annual" de Print y "Best Typography 2" y en el concurso "Best of the West Competition" de 1992.

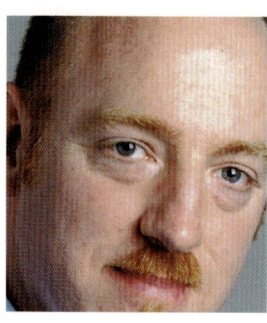

Kyle Keener has been a Detroit Free Press features photographer for four years. He has been named the National Press Photographer's Association Regional Photographer of the Year five times. He started his career on the staff of the Kansas City Times in 1984 before going to the Philadelphia Inquirer for nine years. He has covered AIDS in Uganda, Nelson Mandela's release in South Africa and the aftermath of the Rwandan genocide.

Lara Edge is the assistant managing editor of graphics at The Knoxville News-Sentinel. She has served as news editor, reporter and designer at various newspapers in the U.S. In addition, she has worked as the on-line graphics director for the E.W. Scripps Co. Her work has been recognized with several SND awards.

■ ■ ■

Lara Edge es la redactora ejecutiva auxiliar a cargo de gráficos de The Knoxville News-Sentinel. Ha laborado como editora de noticias, reportera y diseñadora en varios diarios estadounidenses. Además, ha trabajado como directora de gráficos en línea de E.W. Scripps Co. Su labor ha sido galardonada con varios premios de la SND.

■ ■ ■

Ed Kohorst, SND's president, is design editor of the Dallas Morning News. Kohorst, who was named on the News' 1994 Pulitzer Prize for international reporting and also shared in its 1989 Pulitzer for explanatory journalism, served as news art director of the News during 1986-1993. Prior to that, he had worked as staff artist and later assistant graphics editor at the St. Louis (Mo.) Post-Dispatch and as the one-person news art department of The Everett (Wash.) Herald.

■ ■ ■

Ed Kohorst, presidente de la SND, es editor de diseño de The Dallas Morning News. Kohorst fue mencionado en el Premio Pulitzer de 1994 que recibió este diario por la labor de reportaje internacional así como también el

Kenneth Irby is an associate in visual journalism at the Poynter Institute for Media Studies where he teaches photojournalism, leadership, ethics and managing diversity. He conducts research and workshops for news organizations. Irby has been deputy director of photography at Newsday, Inc., and assistant photo editor at The Oakland Press.

■ ■ ■

Kenneth Irby es asociado en periodismo visual del Poynter Institute for Media Studies, donde enseña cursos de periodismo gráfico, liderazgo, ética y aprovechamiento de la diversidad. Irby ha sido director adjunto de fotografía de Newsday, Inc., editor auxiliar de fotografía de The Oakland Press.

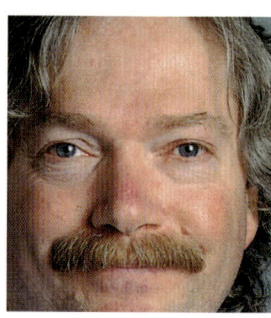

Premio Pulitzer de 1989 en la categoría de periodismo de análisis. Trabajó como director artístico de noticias de The Dallas Morning News durante el período de 1986-1993. Con anterioridad, había sido artista interno y después editor auxiliar de gráficos en el St. Louis Post-Dispatch, estado de Missouri. Por sí solo, estuvo a cargo del departamento artístico de noticias del The Everett Herald, estado de Washington.

JUDGES

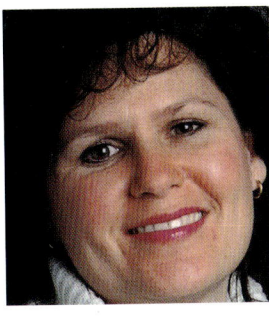 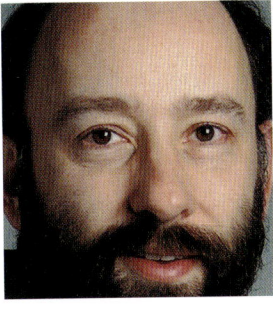 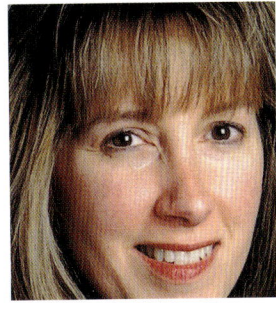 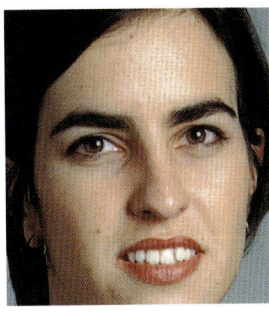 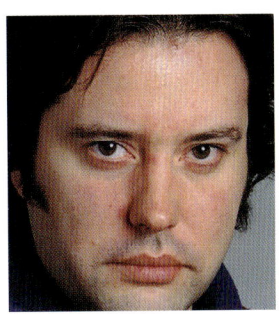

Suzette Moyer is a features page designer at The Hartford Courant. She previously worked at The Sun in Bremerton, Wash. as a designer and presentation editor. During this time, SND recognized the paper twice as one of the "World's Best-Designed Newspapers." She has also worked for several newspapers in Florida.

■ ■ ■

Suzette Moyer es diseñadora de página de artículos de The Hartford Courant. Con anterioridad trabajó para The Sun en Bremerton, estado de Washington, como diseñadora y editora de presentación. Durante este período, SND reconoció a este diario como uno de los "Periódicos con Mejor Diseño del Mundo." También ha trabajado para varios periódicos de la Florida.

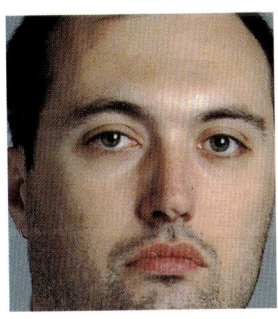

Jaime Serra Palou is graphics director at Clarín newspaper in Buenos Aires. The newspaper won more than 20 awards during the last SND judging. Before joining Clarín, he worked at El Periódico de Cataluña, Spain, from 1990-1994. He is a consultant to newspapers throughout Latin America and is a member of the organizing committee for SND's annual Fall Workshop and Exhibition in Buenos Aires in 2002.

Bill Ostendorf is managing editor/visuals at The Providence Journal. He is also managing editor of NEWS, a regional wire service, and has worked as a reporter, news editor and graphics director at several newspapers. Ostendorf has led hundreds of seminars and has worked as a consultant to many media companies in 18 countries. He created SND's Quick Course and Management Camp workshops and served SND as a regional director.

■ ■ ■

Bill Ostendorf es editor ejecutivo a cargo de materiales visuales de The Providence Journal. También es editor ejecutivo de NEWS, un servicio cablegráfico regional, y ha trabajado de reportero, editor de noticias y director gráfico en varios periódicos. Ha dirigido cientos de seminarios y ha sido consultor de muchas empresas de medios de difusión de 18 países. Fue el artífice de los talleres Quick Course y Management Camp, y ha ocupado el cargo de director regional de SND.

■ ■ ■

Jaime Serra Palou es director gráfico del diario Clarín de Buenos Aires. Este diario obtuvo más de 20 premios en el último concurso de la SND. Antes de trabajar para El Clarín, desempeñó diversas tareas en Periódico de Cataluña, España, de 1990 a 1994. Es consultor de varios periódicos latinoamericanos y es miembro del comité organizador del Taller y Exposición de Otoño anual de la SND que tendrá lugar en Buenos Aires en el año 2002.

Rhonda Prast is a features and news designer at the Minneapolis Star Tribune. She previously worked as art director of Pacific Northwest, the Seattle Times' Sunday magazine, and ran the design desk at the Miami Herald, where she was responsible for 13 sections. She's worked as a section editor, a picture editor and has designed several books. Her work has been recognized by SND, POY and the Sunday Magazine Editors Association.

■ ■ ■

Rhonda Prast es diseñadora de noticias y artículos del Minneapolis Star Tribune. Con anterioridad trabajó como directora artística de Pacific Northwest, la revista dominical de The Seattle Times, y dirigió el departamento de diseño de The Miami Herald, donde tenía a su cargo 13 secciones. Ha desempeñado los cargos de editora de secciones, editora de fotografía y ha diseñado varios libros. Su labor ha sido reconocida por la SND, POY y la Sunday Magazine Editors Association.

■ ■ ■

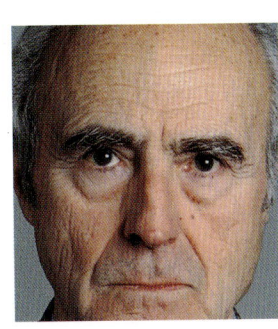

Miguel Urabayen, a Ph.D. in law and journalism, has been a professor of journalism at the University of Navarra (Spain) since 1970. He is a visiting professor at the Poynter Institute for Media Studies. In 1990 he initiated the course "Visual Culture for Journalists"

Maria Rodríguez Alcobendas is design editor for special projects for El Territorio, in Posadas, Argentina. Previously she worked at La Ley, a law publishing group, where she was responsible for the redesign of its publications. She has been features designer at La Nación newspaper in Buenos Aires.

■ ■ ■

María Rodríguez Alcobendas es editora de diseño de proyectos especiales de El Territorio, en Posadas, Argentina. Previamente trabajó en La Ley, una editora de temas legales, donde se responsabilizó del rediseño de sus publicaciones. Ha sido diseñadora de artículos del diario La Nación de Buenos Aires.

■ ■ ■

at the University of Navarra. He has been a judge at the Malofiej Infographic Awards.

■ ■ ■

Miguel Urabayen, con doctorados en Derecho y Periodismo, ha sido profesor de periodismo de la Universidad de Navarra (España) desde 1970. También es profesor visitante del Poynter Institute for Media Studies. En 1990, inició el curso "Cultura visual para periodistas" en la Universidad de Navarra. Ha sido miembro del jurado de los Premios de Infografía Malofiej.

■ ■ ■

Ellen Voss is the design desk manager for The Atlanta Journal-Constitution. She has won a number of SND awards and served as a presenter at many workshops. During the 1996 Olympic Games she was a news editor and manager of the design desk for a special team

Rodrigo Sánchez is the art director of El Mundo in Madrid, Spain. During his seven years there he has designed Sunday supplements including Magazine, La Revista, the weekly Metropoli and the new supplement of La Luna. Before joining El Mundo, he worked with ABC and El Sol newspapers and the magazine Cambio 16.

■ ■ ■

Rodrigo Sánchez es director artístico de El Mundo, diario de Madrid, España. Durante sus siete años de trabajo en dicho diario, ha diseñado suplementos dominicales como Magazine, La Revista, el semanario Metrópoli y el nuevo suplemento de La Luna. Antes de trabajar para El Mundo, trabajó con los diarios ABC y El Sol, y con la revista Cambio 16.

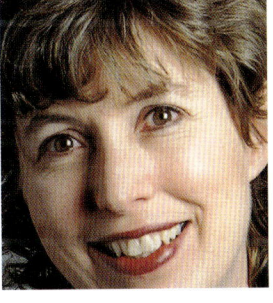

that covered the games.

■ ■ ■

Ellen Voss es gerente del departamento de diseño de The Atlanta Journal-Constitution. Ha sido galardonada con numerosos premios de la SND. Durante los Juegos Olímpicos de 1996, desempeñó los cargos de editora de noticias y gerente de la sección de diseño de un equipo especial conformado por personal de The Atlanta Journal-Constitution, quienes tuvieron a cargo la cobertura de los Juegos.

INDEX

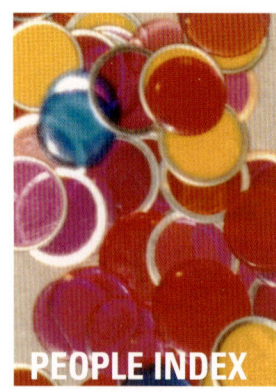

PEOPLE INDEX

A
Aagaard, Lars Henrik, 55
Abrams, Kerri, 140
Abundis, James, 62, 74
Adams Smith, Jeanie, 88
Adams, Steve, 142, 211
Adelino, João Bosco, 74
Adicks, Rich, 263
Adolfo, Luiz, 81, 213
Agins, Michele V., 233
Aicher, Julie, 65
Alberg, Kari, 222
Albert, Scott, 75
Alberti, Tea, 70, 72, 90
Alberto Garza, Ramón, 62, 72, 80, 127, 133, 136, 138, 157, 206
Aldrich, Catherine, 157, 163, 232
Alenäs, Peter, 90, 127
Alimbau, Tori, 146
Alonso, Antonio, 245
Alós, Ernest, 240
Alost, Stan, 61
Alvarado, Martin, 206
Álvarez, Patricia, 149, 167
Alvarez, Patty, 130
Alvarez, Verónica, 206
Alvarus, Fernando Alvim, 238
Álverez Ramallo, Emilio, 147
Amade, Emilio, 245
Amaral, Francisco, 58, 74, 79
Andén, Nina, 99
Anderian, Raffi, 213
Anderson Sokolow, Rena, 92, 111, 115, 176
Anderson, Betty, 92
Anderson, Christopher, 85, 225
Anderson, Dan, 174, 231
Anderson, Dennis, 199
Anderson, Jenny, 98, 102
Anderson, John, 256
Anderson, Lynn, 252
Anderson, Mark, 48
Anderson, Steve, 56
Andersson, Lars, 85-88
Andersson, Thomas, 100, 226
Anding, Bettye, 103
Andreotti, Claudio, 93
Andrews, Joanne, 76
Añeli, Pablo, 207
Angles, Daphne, 88
Anthony Robertson, Blair, 84
Antonuccio, Mark, 131
Antunes, António, 209
Apple, Charles, 170
Arambillet, Diego, 70
Arambula, Anita L., 126
Araujo, Juan F., 157
Arce, Carlos, 62, 72
Arias, Raul, 117, 151, 207, 219
Arisman, Marshall, 222
Armstrong, Cathy, 174
Arnett, Alison, 125
Arteaga, Victor Hugo, 227

Askergren, Jonas, 244
Assur, Jens, 100
Asta, Eudardo, 88
Atchison, Mark, 176
Auch, Herm, 175
Augusto Gonçalves, Marcos, 74, 80-81
Ayart, Jesús, 61
Azevedo e Silva, Francisco, 175

B
Bach, John, 92
Bachtell, Tom, 48
Baird, Jim, 88
Baker, Greg, 142
Bambach, Mike, 88
Banks, John, 79, 262
Bannon, Tim, 115, 209
Banuet, Alejandro, 157
Baptista, Fernando G., 61, 245, 256
Barber, Chris, 66
Barkat, Jonathan, 118
Barret, Deborah, 208
Bartholomay, Lucy, 246
Baseman, Gary, 228
Becker, Lesley, 172
Beckett, Joelle, 75
Beedell, Mike, 138
Bega Communicación, 93
Beguán, Oscar, 107, 109-110, 139
Bejarano, Oscar, 70, 72, 90
Belman, Gustavo, 73
Belmonte, José, 207
Benavides, Toño, 145, 212, 220
Benioff, Carol, 222
Benítez, Carlos, 157
Bennett, Jamie, 100
Benson, Heidi, 109
Berg, Christer, 172
Bergen, Michael, 68
Berger, Eric, 130
Bergin, Erik, 79
Bergsbo, Per, 90, 105
Berke, George, 61, 76, 170, 174, 247, 264
Bernasconi, Francisco, 79
Berry, Pam, 170
Berthet, Jacqueline, 125, 135
Bertram, Charles, 75
Bertran, Albert, 150
Bertrand, Frederique, 222
Best, Patricia, 211
Betts Ford, Laura, 127
Beyrau, Caroline, 99
Biagioni, Marcello, 211
Bianchi, Diego, 65-66
Bigelow, Richard, 135
Bin, Stella, 238, 242, 245, 248, 249, 253
Birch, Christine A., 65
Bissinger, Manfred, 93, 110
Bjørn, Else, 90, 124
Black, Geoff, 76
Blechman, Nicholas, 205
Blechman, R.O., 140-141
Bleck, Cathie, 211
Bliffeld, Alejandra, 264
Blow, Charles M., 243
Bodkin, Tom, 88, 243
Bodo, Sandor, 142
Boerner, Steve, 175
Bogert, Bob, 129
Boites, Jaime, 73
Boom, Wilfred, 142
Borchers, Karen T., 236
Borchuck, James, 173
Bordsen, John, 130
Borgman, Tom, 85-86
Bosler, Clif, 131

Boster, Mark, 224
Boswell, Mark, 243
Bower, Tim, 222
Boyd, G. Andrew, 170, 174, 236
Boyd, Kevin, 205
Boyd, Terri, 79
Boyd, Thomas, 59, 124
Boyles, Dee, 101, 118, 131
Braccio, Silvia, 213
Brackvogel, Thomas, 259
Brande, Liz, 264
Brandenburg, Claudia, 208, 228, 233
Brandt, Harry, 79
Branson, Greg, 57, 75, 243
Brasileiro, Joana, 88
Braulio Martínez, Raúl, 62, 72, 80, 127, 133, 136, 138, 206
Breisacher, George, 81
Brelis, Matthew, 92
Breme, Kurt, 93, 110
Brewer, Linda, 88
Brown, Jean Marie, 249, 264
Brown, Mark, 125
Brown, Peggy, 263
Bruno, Torry, 75
Bruzelius, Nils, 132
Bryant, Michael, 167
Buchmann, Anna, 76
Buck Spears, Audra, 171
Buck, Fielding, 62
Bukh, Katinka, 90-91, 97, 104, 124
Bullard, Mark, 73
Burell, Håkan, 99, 100
Burke, Philip, 208
Burke, Phillip, 119
Burkett, Kevin, 177, 247, 251
Burnside, Scott, 64
Buzek, Mark, 101
Bzdak, Zbigniew, 234

C
Cabiedes, Victor, 72
Cabrera, Gustavo, 68, 73
Caceres, Francisco, 122
Caceres, Rancisco, 115
Caderot, Carmelo, 42-44, 113, 114, 116-117, 140, 142, 145, 150-153, 155-158, 161-162, 165-166, 168, 173, 175-176, 183, 186-188, 193, 196-197, 251, 260-261
Cagayat, Gerard, 174
Cairney, Joan, 48
Cajas, Pancho, 73
Callage, Isabel, 213
Calleja, Raul F. Loredanto, 221
Calzada, Marta, 71
Camacho, Olga, 171
Cameron, Al, 210
Campanario, Gabriel, 63, 67
Campo, Iban, 93
Candellero, Javier, 107, 109-10, 139
Caparrós, Mònica, 147
Carbo, Paul, 246, 251
Cardon, Michele, 85, 231
Carignan, Roland-Yves, 52, 55, 180, 193, 258, 266
Carlson, Chris, 231
Carmody, Elizabeth, 244
Carnevali, Rogério, 61, 90, 92
Carpentier, Janice, 175, 178
Carrasco, Modesto J., 245
Carrigan, Janelle, 260
Carrillo, David, 60, 79, 200
Carrillo, Ernesto, 68, 73
Carrillo, Ismael, 222
Carrillo, Maria, 71
Carter, Paul, 59

Carvalho, Renato, 238
Casey, Nancy, 118, 131
Castañeda, Roberto, 73
Castresana, Valeria, 70, 72, 90
Castrillo, Anthony, 263
Castro, Humberto, 62
Castronuovo, William, 180
Català, Jordi, 240
Catalan, Nacho, 240, 245
Catalão, T. T., 79
Cavalcante, 210
Cavanah, Scott, 128
Cavazos, Norma, 261
Cavendish, Steve, 57, 74, 76
Ceballos, Hector, 245
Cerda, Martin Pérez, 62, 72, 80
Cesarino Costa, Paula, 88
Chambers, Bruce, 231
Champagne, Tony O., 118
Chan, Ron, 212
Chandler, David, 132
Chapman, Terry, 68
Charlon, Aldona, 181
Charlson, Fredson, 74
Chávez, José Antonio, 62
Chávez, Miguel Angel, 127
Chimirri, Héctor, 150
Chin, Barry, 88
Ching Wei, Pai, 175
Chinlund, Chris, 92
Christiansen, Per M. E., 92
Chung, Andre, 86, 231, 263
Chung, Andre F., 86, 263
Chung, Julien, 142
Cieslewicz, Bill, 232
Cinco, Zaida, 140
Cirenza, Fernanda, 74, 80-81
Clark, Patterson, 205
Clarke, Greg, 211
Clinch, Danny, 117
Cobb, Nathan, 170
Cobos, Julián, 93
Cockburn, Carrie, 250, 253
Coelho, Alexandre, 90, 92, 220
Cofan, Marcelo, 93
Coimbra, David, 81
Colbert, Marcel, 55
Collins, Chris, 57
Collins, Jim, 57, 79
Collins, Kit, 91, 137-138
Colon, Pablo, 135
Concannon, Jim, 92
Conner, K.C., 98, 101
Cook, Gary, 244
Cooper, Charles, 57
Cooperrider, Carol, 249
Corbitt, John, 68
Cornatzer, Mary, 68
Cornick, Matthew, 240
Corral, Guillermo, 73
Cortés, Francina, 254
Côté, Geneviève, 111
Couig, Caroline E., 75
Council, Jerold, 238
Cousins, Patricia, 140, 210
Cowan, Lisa, 57, 76
Cowart, Leita, 63
Cowden, Steve, 239, 251
Cowles, David, 48
Cragin, Brian, 63, 67, 74
Crevler, Glen, 80
Cromwell, Wendy, 65, 249
Cronin, Brian, 213
Cross, Robert, 91, 137
Cruz, 123, 125, 129, 133, 239, 245
Cruz, Juancho, 239, 245
Cudmore, Doug, 119
Culebro, Ulises, 142, 161, 176, 203, 205, 220-221, 239, 245

Cunningham, Bill, 75
Curwen, Randy, 131
Cuyler, Joele, 159, 162, 227

D
Da Costa, Beatriz, 165
Dabrowa, Micheal, 263
Dagnino, Vicente, 76, 78-79, 262
Dahl, Ann, 244
Dahl, Arm, 244
Dahm, Bob, 199
Dahrén, Barbro, 132
Dahrling, Deb, 82, 92
Dalton, Julie, 92, 209
Damon, Mark, 57, 74
Daniels, Cindy, 132, 184
Danilo, Eduardo, 62, 68, 73, 138-139, 204, 212, 227-228
Darmon, Reed, 118
Davaz, Carl, 59, 66, 266
Davidson, Gina, 88
Davidson, Larry, 88
Davidson, Matthew, 213
Davies, Brian, 172
Davies, Chuck, 55
Davies, Tom, 76
Davis, Jim, 63, 88
Davis, Patrick, 84
Davison, Pat, 229
Davy, Howard, 175
Dawson, Bill, 88
Dawson, Sue, 67, 111
de Coss, Isaac, 206
de Dios Ferreira, Juan, 243
de Fenoyl, Diane, 96, 100, 188, 227
De Feria, Tony, 263
de Haro, Ignacio, 69, 264
de Jesús Arce, José, 204
de la Rosa, Lourdes, 127
de la Torre, Iosu, 240
de las Alas, Luis, 117, 187
de León Reyes, Luzma Diaz, 138
de León, Beatriz, 138-139
de León, Sandra, 80
De Lorenzi, Miguel, 107, 109, 110, 139
de Luis, Silvia, 127
de Menezes, Thales, 74, 80-81
de Miguel, Manuel, 145, 166, 173, 188, 260-261
de Oliveira, Jair, 74, 80-81, 88
De Repentigny, Yves, 118
de Villegas, Jr., Jose L. Diaz, 224-225
DeGarmo, Kelly, 127
Deheza, Emilio, 62, 68, 73, 138-139, 204, 212, 227-228
Del Castillo, Ricardo, 62, 204, 212, 227
del Castillo, Ricardo, 62, 204, 212, 227
Del Poio, David, 62
del Río, Chano, 42, 113-114, 116-117, 175, 183, 187
Delagrave, Marie, 125
Delessert, Etienne, 222
Delgado, Réne, 204, 212
Dempsey, Crystal, 224
Denk, James, 55, 60, 66-68, 111
Denney, Dave, 57, 174, 177
Deputy, Amy, 86, 263
DeVito, Nicole, 59
Dias, Luís Silva, 51, 144, 148, 157, 161, 163-164, 166, 230
Díaz de León Reyes, Luzma, 139
Diez, Cherie, 171
DiMarzo, Dean, 243

268 ■ THE BEST OF NEWSPAPER DESIGN

INDEX

Dine, Scott, 85
DiNuzzo, Nuccio, 75
Dionisi, Sandra, 209
Dishal, Peter, 129-130
Doctorian, Sonya, 171
Dodds, Jo-Ann, 119
Doe, Kelly, 163, 165, 168, 198, 222
Dohm, Anne Marie, 175
Domingo, Maripaz, 149, 167
Doneiger, Jorge, 65-66
Dorado, Francisco, 42, 113, 114, 116-117, 175, 183, 187
Dorrell, Robert, 256
Dorsey, Steve, 75, 228
Dos Remedios, Anne Marie, 175
Doussard, Robin, 174
Dow, Barbara, 59, 192, 263
Downes, Stephen, 68
Doyle, Hélio, 74, 79
Doyles, Dee, 101
Driggs, Helen, 135
Drummond, Leonardo, 100, 132
Drury, Christian P., 61, 74, 81, 100, 116, 125, 132-133
Dryer, Kim, 224
Duarte, Álvaro, 61, 90, 92
Duarte, Claudio, 112, 116
Duarte, Pedro Rolo, 51, 144, 148, 157, 161, 163-164, 166, 230
Dubson, Geof, 85
Dufalla, Anita, 212
Duffy, Bob, 85
Duffy, Bryce, 168
Dufour, Liz, 232
Dunlap-Shohl, Pamela, 126, 157, 266
Dunleavy, Christine, 167, 197, 211, 222
Dunn, Bill, 57, 75, 80, 243
Duplain, Marc, 200
Duplantier, Alain, 44
Dybdahl, Carmen, 76
Dyer, Leigh, 99
Dykman, Jackson, 256
Dyre, Stig, 90, 124
Dzielak, Kathy, 137

E
Earle, John, 79
Eastburn, Wayne, 59
Eckler, Rebecca, 100
Edelson, Mark, 235
Elazegui, Kate, 131
Elissetche, Juan, 76, 78-79, 262
Ellison, Jake, 60
Elman, Julie, 78, 180
Emmert, Mark, 75
Endicott, William, 252, 264
Enfield, William, 252, 264
Enriquez, Nariano, 146
Epkes, Greg, 119, 122
Epstein, Susan, 125
Erbetta, Dante, 126
Ericson, Matthew, 81
Escalona, Alejandro, 122
Escobedo, Carmen, 127
Esperanza, Cristina, 114
Esqueda, Daniel, 62
Estevao, Osvaldo, 76, 78-79, 262
Estrada, Rafael, 245
Estrin, James, 243
Everly, Katherine, 132
Eyer, Rod, 263

F
Fabela, Alberto, 62
Fader, Carole, 84
Falck, Jørgen, 55
Farr, Bill, 172
Farrand, Scott, 252
Fecht, Steve, 170, 173
Fella, Andrea, 160, 227
Felsing, Alix, 99
Ferguson, John, 111, 115
Fernandes, Rodolfo, 56
Fernandez, Jose Ismael, 224, 225
Fernández, Rubelio, 62
Fernandez, Sergio, 68, 93, 106, 108, 120-123, 126, 135-137, 191
Ferrer, Pablo, 123
Ferrer, Rafael, 244-245, 254
Ferri, John, 119
Ferronato, Oscar, 121, 123, 126
Ferroni, Antonio, 108
Fessier, Bruce, 74
Fila, Bob, 128
Filho, Melchiades, 74, 80-81
Fillion, Kate, 146, 208, 210-211
Finch, Rob, 66
Finch-Kellar, Toni, 61
Fincke, Carl, 68
Fine, Pam, 57, 75
Finley, Denis, 57, 76, 79
Fischer Krentz, Jeri, 84
Fischhoff, Marty, 170, 173
Fisher, Greg, 75
Fitzsimons, Matt, 63
Fladung, Thom, 56
Fleming, Bob, 71, 103
Flinn, John, 131, 191, 212
Floss, Dennis R., 76, 175
Flowers, Shanna, 170
Flynn, Carolyn, 65, 249
Foglia, Efraín, 138, 228
Fontanarrosa, Daniel, 68, 108, 121, 126, 135
Franco, Ramón, 63
Frank, Rickard, 88, 244
Frankeny, Kelly, 109, 129, 131, 191-192, 212, 263
Franklin, Michael, 88
Fraser, Jean, 131
Fratus, Ken, 63, 88
Frazier, David, 98, 102, 129
Frederick, George, 57
Freitas, Conceição, 74
French, Thomas, 171
Friede, Eva, 173
Frisella, Chris, 59
Froelich, Janet, 147, 154, 159, 160, 162, 164, 166-167, 208, 227-228, 230, 233-234
Fuchs, Thomas, 222
Fuda, Silvina, 70, 72, 90
Fuentes, Manuel M., 71

G
Gabrenya, Mark, 62
Galán, Luis, 70-71, 221
Galera, Cesar, 261
Gallegos, Eric, 62
Gallo, Héctor Reinoso, 108, 135
Gallop, Roy, 76
Gallopo, Roy, 241
Gámez, Jose Juan, 69-70, 264
García Quintero, Delgar Antonio, 94
García, David, 146, 149, 167
García, Marcela, 136, 138
García, Mario, 68, 93, 106-110, 120-123, 126, 135-137, 139, 191, 213, 259, 265
Garcia, Sebastian, 264
Garda, Cynthia, 79
Garrison, Ron, 228
Garza, Ramón Alberto, 62, 72, 80, 127, 136, 138, 157, 206
Gaspard, Bill, 88
Gastaldo, John, 88
Gauss, Fredericke, 146, 208, 210-211
Gee, Martin, 101, 118
Gefter, Philip, 88
Geib, Phil, 170
Geiger, Steve, 263
Gelgud, Elizabeth, 67
Gentieu, Penny, 59
Germosek, Kim, 68, 77
Gerritsma, Fokke, 251
Giacobetti, Francis, 149
Gibson, George, 249
Gilbert, Susan, 83-84, 88, 99, 228, 232
Gill, Ray, 260
Gilliland, Alan, 242
Gilmore-Barnes, Catherine, 167, 234
Godfrey, Michael, 174
Goertzen, Jeff, 172
Goldman, Scott, 88
Gomes, Lea Cristina, 129
González, Clara, 249
González, Eugenio, 149, 167
Gonzalez, Gonzalo, 157
González, Isabel, 245
González, Juan Carlos, 107, 109-110
Gonzalez, Julian H., 75
González, Marcela Rivas, 38-139
González, Maria, 194
González, María, 43-44, 145, 150-153, 155-158, 161-162, 165, 168, 196-197
Good, Epha, 54, 59, 76
Goodfellow, Kris, 243
Gordon, Mike, 81
Gorrie, Peter, 213
Goulding, Mike, 231
Gràcia, Ricard, 240
Graham, Jack, 209
Grahn, Geoff, 222
Grajeda, José, 80
Graustark, Barbara, 90
Greco, Joe, 56
Green, Judy, 260
Green, Neville, 171
Green, Phillip J., 240, 253
Green, Tracey, 74
Green, Tracy, 63
Greenfield-Sanders, Timothy, 162
Gregersen, Carsten, 54-55, 261
Griffin, Anna, 84, 96
Griffin, Brian A., 118
Griffin, Jean, 175
Griffone, Betts, 173, 252
Grimwade, John, 251
Grin, Gayle, 52, 54-55, 57, 64, 96, 100, 140, 186, 188, 199, 227, 258
Grippi, Vince, 46, 174
Griswold, Doug, 205
Gritchen, Jeff, 231
Grondhl, Mika, 247
Grosch, Connie, 59
Gross, G. Noel, 261
Grumney, Ray, 57, 75, 243
Guillermo Abad, José, 146
Gunn, Steve, 84
Gurzinski, John, 226
Gustafsson, Marco, 170
Gutiérrez, Fernando, 146
Guzmán, José Luis, 62

H
Haddi, Michel, 168
Haffey, Sean M., 88
Haglund, Birgitta, 244
Haines, Steve, 56
Hajek, Olaf, 222
Hajratwala, Minal, 205
Haley, Peter, 76
Hall, Rebecca, 102, 200
Hamann, Amanda, 140
Hamblin, Seth, 256
Hand, Kevin, 170
Hansen, Søren-Mikael, 58
Hansen, Steen, 56
Hansson, Dan, 87
Hansson, Lena, 79
Hansson, Riber, 206
Hara, Helio, 125
Harker, Laurie, 126, 132-133
Harris, Nancy, 162, 233
Harrison, James, 213
Harrison, Kenneth, 103
Harrison, Mark, 82, 171
Hartford, Rick, 116
Hartig, Dennis, 78
Harvey, Lamont W., 238
Hedengren, Pompe, 90, 127
Heisler, Stephanie, 74
Helguera, Florencia, 91, 137
Heller, Steven, 208, 211, 222
Hellyer, Kevin, 79
Henke, Karolina, 127
Hennessy, Kathleen, 234
Henningsen, Kim, 71
Hensel, Mikkel, 128
Henssel, Mikkel, 90, 262
Heredia, Ricardo, 126
Hergott, Daniel, 146
Hermoso, Gustavo, 240, 245
Hernández, Gustavo Adolfo, 62
Herppich, Steven M., 232
Hervás, Antonio Martín, 63, 64, 69, 264
Hicks, Sarah, 263
Hill, Angela, 170, 174, 244, 247, 256
Hill, Veronica, 124
Hinojosa, Mark, 88
Hippertt, André, 60
Hjerrild, Niels, 54
Hjorth, Mikael, 261
Hoffmann, Duane, 103
Holboll, Maureen, 76, 78-79, 262
Holland, Brad, 222
Holmes, Emily, 238
Holmgren, Mia, 56
Holt, Dean, 75
Hong, Min Jae, 188
Hopkins, M.B., 129
Hopley, Claire, 125
Horn, Dave, 84
Horner, R. Scott, 74, 252
Houston, Luci S., 57
Houston, Susan, 126
Howard, Henry, 76
Howell, Len, 74
Huff, Ron, 198
Huldt, Maria, 99
Hundley, Sam, 71, 103, 140
Hunt, Brian, 140-141
Hurst, Ann, 57
Hutchinson, Joseph, 86, 111, 129-130, 231, 238, 263

I
Iglesias Brickles, Eduardo, 93
Iglesias, Esteban, 264
Ilic, Mirko, 205
Innerst, Stacy, 213, 221-222
Intrator, Howard, 55

Irish, Len, 190
Isip, Jordin, 176-177

J
Jackson, April, 85
Jackson, Lance, 212
Jackson, Ted, 61, 76
Jacobs, Deb, 170
Jakobson, Nina, 90
James, Brian, 63, 242
Jankowsky, Dorothy, 192
Jarnestad, Johan, 79, 242
Jauch, Jill, 109
Jayne, Laura, 76
Jenkins, Tony, 206
Jensen, Gregers, 55, 77, 108, 261, 266
Jerichow, Rie, 77
Jerome-Cohen, Deborah, 129
Jesús Cortes, Juan, 62
Jiménez, Arturo, 122
Joerges, Hans-Ulrich, 93, 110
Johansson, Sören, 56
Johnson, John, 76
Johnson, Richard, 96
Johnson, Scott, 67, 80, 100, 132-133
Johnston, Andrew, 99
Johnston, Robin, 126, 192
Johnston, Steve, 81
Jonasson, Leif, 262
Jones, Charles, 238
Jones, Katherine, 84
Jones, Latané, 103
Jones, Sam, 122
Jonsson, Bengt, 244
Jordan, Jeanne, 74
Jorge, Carlos, 175
Jornet, Carlos, 107, 109-110, 139
Joyce, Dennis, 84
Juan, Ana, 209, 212, 217, 219
Juárez, Moramay, 138
Juby, Jordan, 91
Judge, Jay, 86, 263
Juhl, Morten, 77
Júnior, Amaro, 74
Juul Steen, Annette, 175

K
Kafentzis, John, 59
Kamidoi, Wayne, 80, 180
Kanno, Mario, 74, 80-81
Kapustin, Doug, 231
Karaian, Jim, 80, 88
Karnopp, Kris, 173
Katzenelson, Bob, 97
Keebler, Paul, 229
Keenan, Rakefet, 48
Keener, J. Kyle, 235, 266
Kellams, Michael, 65, 171
Kellams, Mike, 82
Kelley, Gary, 213
Kelso, Karen, 75, 174
Kenner, Herschel, 76
Kennicott, Philip, 85
Kent, Nancy, 90
Kent, Vivian, 242
Kerchelich, Karen, 82
Kerr, Kelly, 125
King, Jeff, 82
King, Nick, 170
King, Nick, 170
Kirby, Joe, 65, 249
Kirby, Joe, 65, 249
Kirkman, Chris, 74, 180
Kirschenbaum, Matías, 65-66
Kitada, Michael, 231
Kitagaki, Jr., Paul, 225
Kitchens, Marilyn S., 228
Kjærhus, Ole, 58
Kjellstrand, Torsten, 83
Klingsick, Norma, 213

INDEX

Klinkenberg, Karen, 82
Knapp, Susan, 228
Knittle, Charles, 81
Knowles, Joe, 79
Koch, Finn, 100, 175
Koci Hernandez, Richard, 118, 236
Koenig, Susan, 170, 174, 236
Kofmann, Bettina, 103, 190, 261
Kofoed, Karina, 90
Kolar, Barry, 67
Kolarik, Kim, 72, 84
Komives, Stephen D., 59, 109
Kopans, Daniel B., 92
Kordalski, David, 56, 170
Kover, Becky, 176
Krabbe, Lars, 56
Kraus, Orlie, 176, 188, 213
Kremer, Lisa, 241
Kress, Alice, 129
Kriegsman, Teresa, 55
Kroencke, Anja, 222
Krogh, Bodil, 95, 97
Kroninger, Stephen, 48
Krueger, Gail, 109
Krumhardt, Pete, 128
Kryger, Matt, 75
Kucer, Marilyn, 54, 76
Kuehn, Karen, 159
Kumata, Michelle, 82
Ku-Ying, Tung, 135, 200
Kuykendall, Jim, 198

L
LaBrosse, Celeste, 65
Lacava, Lucie, 52, 54-55, 57, 64, 96, 140-141, 227, 258
Lai, Tia, 246, 251
Laird, Diedra, 224
Lancaster, Craig, 65
Lapointe, Kirk, 52, 55, 57, 258
Larios, Guilermo, 204, 212
Larrañaga, Germán, 93
Larsen, Hans, 79
Larson, Fredic, 234
Larsson Ask, Bjorn, 244
Latova, Jose, 153
Lauer, Ralph, 127
Lauridsen, Mads Holm, 91
Lauritzen, Kirsten, 55
Lautens, Richard, 227
Layton, Steve, 79, 170
Lee, Dan, 76
Leeds, Greg, 176-178, 188, 213
Leeth, Dan, 130
Lehmann, John, 227
Leida, Edward, 175, 178
Leigh, Anne, 88, 210
Leite, Adi, 88
Lekander, Lance, 119, 190
Lembo, Peter, 262
Leonard, Mary, 92
Leoni, Ricardo, 56
LePage, Jocelyne, 142
Leung, Lewis, 101
Levin, Susan, 209
Levine, Ned, 263
Libreros, Adriana, 137, 188
Lillash, Richard, 176
Lim, Stephanie Grace, 56, 228
Lin, Yvonne, 76, 175
Lindgren, Lennart, 242
Lindquist, David, 76
Linke, Dirk, 93, 110
Liu, John, 243
Loek, Dick, 227
Logan, Cathy, 125
Logsdon, Tracey, 61
Long, Steve, 252
López, Luis Enrique, 138
Lopez, Raphael, 131

Lorenzen, Søren, 100
Loscri, Pablo, 242, 245, 249, 256
Louie, Eugene, 102
Løve Østerbye, Kristoffer, 58, 90
Lovett, Greg, 235
Lovett, O. Rufus, 234
Lucena, Toni, 79
Lucio, Sergio, 94
Luis, Fiona, 125
Lula, 207
Lund, Rick, 82
Lundborg, Beatrice, 99
Lussier, Marc-André, 142
Luxor, Scott, 94
Ly, Tan, 74

M
Ma Ramírez, Pablo, 63, 69-70, 181, 261
MacDonald, Brady, 246
Macdonald, Sally, 171
Macías, Eddie, 62
Mackenzie, Hillary, 137
MacQueen, Brian, 60
Macri, Domenic, 168
Macri, Dominic, 211
Madrid, Jennifer, 211
Majeri, Anthony, 122
Majors, Dan, 77
Makaoui, Sean, 150
Makemson, Harlen, 75
Mallot, Alen, 263
Malok, Andre, 135
Manchess, Gregory, 222
Mancuso, Jo, 129, 192
Maneschy, Renata, 115
Mangelsdorf, Liz, 109, 192, 263
Manning, Jack, 243
Mansfield, Matt, 54, 59, 76
Mantilla, Jorge, 73
Mar, Rod, 82
Maraggi, Sergio, 65-66
Marcelo, Carlos, 74
Marcos, Diana, 127
Marotta, Martín, 65-66
Márquez, Agustín, 62
Marquez, Augustin, 227
Marsh, Bill, 81, 263
Marshall, Ken, 170
Marshall, Richard, 226
Marsula, Daniel, 206, 212
Martel, Claude, 162, 164, 166
Martín Cucurulo, Juan, 66
Martin Grier, Jo-Anne, 211
Martín Hervás, Antonio, 63 64, 69, 264
Martin, Antonio, 261
Martin, Dan, 213
Martin, Ian, 73
Martin, Jane, 92, 170
Martin, Tim, 77
Martines, Jesus, 70, 221
Martinez, Jesus, 71
Martinez, José Luis, 138
Martinez, Ricardo, 42, 45, 202 205, 214
Martins, Marilia, 100, 132
Martinsen, André, 116
Mascotti, Corina, 70
Matchan, Linda, 170
Mather, Mike, 73
Matiá, Chema, 245
Matos, Albano, 175
Matsushita, Elaine, 128-129
Mattsson, Jonny, 226
Max, Andrea, 93
Mayer, III, Emmet, 256
McAllister, Molly, 77

McAuley, Lynn, 91, 137-138
McBride, Robbie, 59
McCartney, Don, 109, 129, 131, 191-192, 212
McClure, Liz, 171
McCollester, Darren, 62
McCormick, Patrick, 115
McCusker, John, 61
McDade, Sean, 252, 264
Mcdonald, Bill, 74
McFarlane, James, 65, 82
McFarlin, Ken, 176, 211
McGuire, Thom, 236
McIntosh, Catherine, 234
McIntosh, Jean, 103, 118
McKinstry, Steve, 101, 239, 251
McLaughlin, Joan, 67
McLelland, Patrick, 101
McMillan, Bill, 56
Meade, Annette, 76
Medel, Ariel, 140, 204
Medrano, Alexandro, 62, 72, 80, 136, 138, 206
Meehan, Mary Beth, 59
Mehegan, David, 209
Meighan, Chris, 66
Meilvang, Nils, 224
Mellon, Steve, 225
Melton, Brian, 56
Mendoza, Carlos, 94
Mendoza, José Manuel, 138, 228
Mertins, Lisa, 101
Meshew, Joanne, 84
Meurice, Stephen, 57
Meuse, Stephen, 125
Michalowski, Jim, 174
Michaud, Janet, 63, 80, 88, 176, 180, 246
Migielicz, Geri, 236
Milette, Paul J., 235
Millener, George, 59
Miller, David, 65, 82, 92, 103, 115, 118, 171
Miller, Joanne, 81, 84, 88, 130, 181, 249, 264
Miller, Ken, 84
Miller, Rich, 75
Miller, Steve, 94
Mills, Russell, 91, 137
Milne, David, 81, 247, 251, 263
Mina, Frank, 234
Miner, Mike, 94, 139-140
Minister, Scott, 176
Miquel, Núria, 150
Mirko, Mark, 235
Mitchell, Lin, 126
Mitchell, Pat, 74
Mizraji, Paula, 70
Mode, Michael, 239
Møldrup, Torben, 56
Molén, Thomas, 79
Molina, Walter, 93
Mollering, David, 132
Monroe, Bryan, 57, 74, 76, 175
Monteith, Kenny, 59
Montes de oca, Ernesto, 228
Montesino, David F., 68
Montgomery, Robb, 60
Monti, Guillermo, 122-123
Moore, Angela, 222
Moore, Buddy, 76, 78
Moore, Chris, 132-133, 171
Moores, Ian, 240
Moose, Debbie, 126
Morales, Irineo, 72
Morales, Luis Miguel, 138
Moré, José, 88
Moreira, Julio, 61

Morel, Gerardo, 238, 241-242, 245
Moreno, Ponto, 73
Morla, Jennifer, 154
Morris, Don, 61, 171
Morris, Tim, 170, 174
Morrow, Sue, 98, 102, 118
Moses, Karen, 65
Moses, Monica, 56, 67, 81, 83 84, 88, 96, 99, 115, 181, 224, 232
Motta, Cesar, 61
Moyer, Bruce, 61, 80
Mueller, Ingrid, 81
Mueller, Laura, 96
Muiña, Nuria, 146
Muldoon, Katy, 251
Mullaney, Paul, 54
Muller, Ingrid, 74, 81, 180
Mulvany, Colin, 46, 174
Mundet Poch, Rosa, 147
Murphey, Lance, 88
Murphy, Courtney, 57, 73, 76
Murphy, Richard, 65
Murray, Clem, 81
Murray, Dave, 61
Murray, Tom, 56
Myers, Gene, 63
Myers, Reggie, 210, 241

N
Naddermier, Kia, 127
Naddermier, Magnus, 90, 99, 127
Naftolin, Lisa, 162
Nagy, Melissa, 170
Naja, Angel, 245
Nakagaw, Carol, 171
Nanetti, Ygnacio, 85
Nania, Gina, 96, 130
Nash, Adelaide, 68
Naughton, Vera, 177-178
Navega, Telio, 112
Nead, Julia, 103, 118
Nease, Rick, 56, 242
Neff, William, 250
Nelson, Hulda, 212
Nelson, John, 46, 109, 174
Nelson, Paul, 57, 79
Neumann, Jeff, 115, 118, 171, 188
Newland, Martin, 52, 55, 57, 258
Newman, Craig, 54, 59, 200
Newsom, Shirley, 135
Nguyen, Nam, 252, 264
Nguyen, Peter, 118
Niblock, Daniel, 252
Nichols, Greg, 75
Nickle, John, 178, 211
Niedziela, Ken, 75
Nielsen, Jane, 79
Niemann, Christoph, 160, 216
Ning, Amy, 131, 211, 221
Noblat, Ricardo, 58, 74, 79
Nordlund, Anders, 79
Nordström, Jockum, 220
Noronha, Luiz, 134
Nowlin, Mark, 133
Nuñez, Mariano, 65-66
Nyeland, Søren, 58, 90-92, 97, 104-105, 124, 128, 262

O
O'Byrne, James, 76, 170, 174, 247
O'Donall, James, 208
O'Neill, Michael, 167, 227
Obregón, Jorge, 72
Ocañas, Pedro, 72
Ochoa, Rui, 233
Odéen, Mars, 79
Oelerich, Ken, 65

Ogris, Armin, 93, 110
Olesen, Stig, 95
Oliveira, Eduardo, 213
Olivella, Omar, 70, 72, 90
Oliver, Thomas, 263
Oliveros, Maltilde, 70
Oliveros, Matilde, 70, 72, 90
Olmeda, Perla, 136, 138
Olsen, Dana E., 228
Olsen, Jeanne, 90-92
Olsen, Kent, 79
Olsen, Michael, 224
Oriol Roca, Ma José, 147
Oropeza, Margarita, 140
Ortega, Arturo, 80
Ortiz, Gabriel, 68
Osgood, Charles, 128
Ostendorf, Bill, 77, 267
Østergaard Sørensen, Søren, 61
Østergren, Tomas, 262
Oswaldo, Angelo, 90, 92
Otamendi, Alberto, 93
Øvad, Winnie, 79
Overgaard, Lotte, 79, 175
Owen, Gerald, 55
Oxford, Troy, 133

P
Pablos, Pedro, 69
Pabst, Marcel, 128
Paddock, Craig, 56
Pãez, Alejandro, 68, 73
Page-Trim, Debra, 142
Palacios, Iñaki, 70, 72, 76, 78 79, 90, 238-239, 241-242, 245 246, 248-249, 253-255, 262, 264
Pang, Deborah, 206
Panichkul, Victor, 111, 129 130, 231
Paoli, Richard, 109, 192, 263
Paquin, Denis, 52, 227
Parker, Bill, 75, 88
Parker, Doug, 61, 76, 170, 174, 236
Parker, Robert Andrew, 222
Parker, Steve, 86
Parks, Danielle, 81, 84, 249
Parley, Graham, 54, 64
Partridge, Thea, 146
Paslay, Jeff, 65
Payne, C.F., 211
Peake, Nicole, 62-63, 74
Pearce, Sara, 232
Peattie, Peggy, 88
Pedersen, Jes Stein, 91
Pedroso, Miguel, 51, 144, 148, 157, 161, 163-164, 166, 230
Péna, Ricardo, 68, 73
Peña, Rodrigo, 62
Penix, Tom, 59, 66, 124
Pereira Gontijo, Adailton, 74, 80-81
Pérez Cerda, Martín, 62, 72, 80, 157
Pérez de Rozas, Carlos, 147
Perez Diaz, Carlos, 90, 92
Pérez Martínez, Martin, 136, 206
Pérez, Antonio, 122
Perez, Gregory, 103
Perlmutt, David, 249
Pernau, Jordi, 240
Perry, Helayne, 85, 131
Perry, Jim, 88
Persall, Steve, 103
Pérsico, Gastón, 65-66
Pestana, Paulo, 74
Peters, Sherry, 116, 132-133
Peterson, D.A., 163
Pett-Ridge, Christopher, 77

INDEX

Pham, The', 96, 99, 224, 228
Phillips, Andrew, 57
Photonica, Neo Vision, 130
Piaggio, Carmen, 173
Pierce, Gene, 162
Pietsch, Chris, 59
Pilgrim, Mike, 174, 231
Pilgrim-Waters, Suzy, 125
Pilon, Alain, 210
Piñeyro, Jorge, 163
Pinilla, Beiman, 65
Pinnell, Brenda, 81, 181, 249
Pires, Toni, 74, 80-81
Pisani, Fernanda, 211
Pitts, Patty, 75, 101
Pitts, Ted, 129
Pitzer, William, 81, 130, 249, 253, 264
Plonka, Brian, 111
Poali, Richard, 109
Poehl, Florian, 93, 110
Poisson, Cloe, 73, 171
Pollak, David, 175
Pomerantz, Gary, 263
Poortinga, Kevin, 54, 76, 181
Portaz, Jorge, 242, 245
Porter, Tracy, 82, 103
Porter, Vikki, 62, 67, 74
Potosky, Gary, 65
Potter, Mitch, 115
Potts, Leanne, 60
Powell, Cory, 81
Powell, Kristen, 115, 181
Powers, Scott, 111, 115
Prados, Alfredo, 64
Prast, Rhonda, 234, 267
Pratt, David, 250
Preece, Jenny, 240
Prendiamano, Andrew, 137
Prendimano, Andrew, 65
Prestamo, Cecilia, 59, 73, 75, 171, 200
Preston, Jim, 86, 263
Pricer, Jamie Lee, 62
Priego, Harold, 93
Pritchard, Jennifer, 128
Prochnow, Bill, 109
Prouse, Marcia, 75, 231
Prouse, Marcia Joy, 231
Prudente, Claudio, 56
Pryds, Lars, 97, 100
Pullen, Crary, 163, 168

Q
Quenzer, Derrik, 241
Quinn, James, 128-129
Quinn, Sara, 139
Quintiero, Victoria, 76, 78-79, 262
Quist Møller, Michael, 91

R
Racovali, John, 52
Ràfols, Maria, 150
Ramberg, Anders, 57, 75, 80, 199, 243
Ramírez, Granada, 157
Ramirez, José, 62
Ramírez, Pablo Ma, 63, 69-70, 181, 261, 264
Ramos, Alejandro, 62
Rangel, Arturo, 136, 206
Rañoa, Raoul, 252
Rauscher, Alexander, 242
Ravenscraft, Stephen, 115, 209
Ravn, Dorthe, 55
Ray, Dan, 68
Raycraft, Patrick, 61
Reagan, Denise M., 103, 174, 177
Rech, Marcelo, 81
Reck, Tim, 66-67

Record, Christopher A., 83
Redondo, Amparo, 44, 145, 150, 165, 168, 196, 198
Reed, Rita, 174, 177
Reese, Tom, 171
Reeves, Janet, 229
Reid, Paulina, 76
Reinken, Tom, 251
Reinoso Gallo, Héctor, 108, 135
Renato Malvar, André, 60
Resendes, Mário B., 51, 144, 148, 157, 161, 163-164, 166, 175, 230
Reynolds, Neil, 91, 137-138
Reynoso, Alejandro, 241
Rhee, Foon, 264
Ribeirinho, José Maria, 51, 144, 148, 157, 161, 163-164, 166, 175, 230
Ricardo, Feriche, 222
Rice, Steve, 75
Riera, Alejandro, 122
Rife, Susan, 139
Ringman, Steve, 82, 171, 235
Ritts, Herb, 183
Ritzau, Helle-Lise, 78
Rivas González, Marcela, 138-139
Rivest, André, 118
Rizzo, Jesica, 146
Robbins, Richard, 88
Roberts, Bill, 73
Roberts, David, 61
Roberts, Randall K., 229
Roberts, Rob, 57
Robinson, Gaile, 127
Robinson, Greg, 263
Robinson, Jamila, 99
Robinson, Katy, 84
Robinson-Chavez, Michael, 232
Robiou, Claudia, 224-225
Rodgers, Dinah, 76
Rodríguez Peña, Rosalinda, 157
Rodríguez Ramos, Ramón, 221
Rodriguez, Gustavo, 106, 108, 122-123
Rodriguez, Ignacio, 162
Rodríguez, Lucía, 94
Rodríguez, Miguel, 157
Rodriguez, Norma, 62
Rodriguez, Paul E., 231
Rodriguez, Rick, 252, 264
Rodriques, André, 74
Roe, Dale, 111
Roennebaek, Lise, 209, 218
Rogers, Kurt, 109
Rognsvoog, Lynn, 77
Roig, Alex M., 149, 167
Rolston, Matthew, 119
Román, Marco Antonio, 138
Romanelli, Jack, 173
Romanowich-Smith, Judy, 57, 75
Rombach, Robin, 227
Romero, Manuel, 63-64
Romero, María Jesús, 140
Romig, Rob, 59
Ros, Alejandro, 91, 137-138
Rose, Devin, 48
Rosenbaum, Daniel, 128
Rosenbloom, Steve, 170
Rossato, Juliana, 93
Rosso, Sebastián, 93, 106, 108, 120-123, 126, 136-137, 189, 210
Rostrum, Tim, 96, 100, 188, 227
Rovner, Michael, 250

Ruben, Falci, 108, 122-123, 135, 191
Rudolph, Jane, 225
Ruis, Thomas, 81
Ruiz, Pablo, 70, 72, 90, 264
Russell, Jack, 130
Russell, Karl, 243
Russo, Lisa, 101
Rutz, Dean, 82, 171
Ryan, Kathy, 147, 159, 162, 164, 166-167, 227-228, 230, 233-234
Ryg Olsen, Lone, 175

S
Saari, Laura, 174
Sætternissen, Peter, 97
Saidon, Ana, 65-66
Sale, John, 46, 174
Salomonson, Bengt, 244
Saltzman, Mort, 252, 264
Sampedro, Gorka, 251
Sánchez, Dina, 245
Sánchez, Gustavo, 149, 167
Sanchez, Richard, 63, 88, 246
Sánchez, Rodrigo, 42-44, 113, 114, 116-117, 145, 150-153, 155-158, 161-162, 165, 168, 175, 182-183, 185, 187, 193, 195-196, 198, 267
Sánchez, Victor, 122
Santacruz, Beatriz, 70
Santiago Méndez, Oscar, 62
Santiago, Enrique, 68, 73
Sapatkin, Don, 263
Sargent, Chris, 244
Sauer, Terry, 57, 75
Sawicki, Bridget, 109
Sayles, John, 131
Scales, Jeffrey, 90
Scarpellini, Vincenzo, 74, 80, 81, 88
Schaben, Al, 224
Schafer, Kevin, 130
Scheef, Justin, 55
Schelin, Maria, 127
Schierlitz, Tom, 162
Schimitschek, Martina, 102
Schlegel, Erich, 172
Schmid, Paul, 92
Schneider, Patrick, 84, 232
Scholl, Tami, 133
Schomberg, Andreas, 93, 110
Schreiber, Lisa, 165, 168
Schulz-Schaeffer, Reinhard, 93, 110
Schuon, Jonalyn, 263
Schutz, David, 80, 246
Schwab Studio, Michael, 210
Schwab, Gary, 88
Schwarz, Glenn, 212
Schweitzer, Alison, 125
Scopin, Joseph W., 128
Scott, John, 61, 75, 111
Scowen, Peter, 96, 100, 188
Secco, Adilson, 74, 80-81
Sedlar, Pat, 109, 129
Sednaoui, Stephane, 164
Seidman, Eric, 57, 78-79
Seifert, Channon, 75
Seixas, Wagner, 61
Sejer Pedersen, Charlotte, 124
Sejer, Charlotte, 90, 124
Seliger, Mark, 42
Semrau, Stefan, 93, 110
Sendra, Ferran, 150
Senechal, Jessaca, 55
Serra, Jaime, 238-239, 241, 242, 245-246, 248-249, 253, 256, 267
Serrano, Sergio, 140, 204

Shafer, Norm, 78
Shaffer, Melanie, 100, 116, 125, 185
Shankweiler, Linda, 239
Shanley, Bob, 235
Shapiro, Marilyn, 88
Shapton, Leanne, 140-141
Shaunessy, Janet, 76
Shechter, Therese, 79, 88
Shellito, Brian, 170
Sherlock, John, 171
Shintaku, Howard, 252, 264
Shirley, Julie, 172
Shomer, Gayle, 99
Shoun, Brenda, 174
Siegel, Harris G., 65, 137
Sikes, Bill, 81
Silva, Rodrigo, 245
Simmons, Derek, 80, 139
Simpson, Karen, 146, 208, 210-211
Sink, Brenna, 247, 256
Sjöberg, Mats, 79
Skoett, Helle, 72
Skwar, Don, 88
Skwish, Andrew, 48, 109, 131, 191-192, 212
Slota, Gerald, 162, 228
Smith, Bill, 222
Smith, James, 111
Smith, John, 240, 244
Snibbe, Kurt, 239
Snyder, Jon, 171
Sokolow, Rena, 80, 92, 111, 115, 176
Sokolowski, Alejandro, 264
Solarz, A. Hugo, 122
Solbrekke, Torfinn, 116
Soloman, Melissa, 62
Soltes, Harley, 235
Somerville, Ian, 115, 119, 213
Soprych, Chris, 170
Sosa, Federico, 76, 78-79, 262
Soto, Antonio, 147
Souza, Heliane, 90, 92
Souza, Pete, 129
St. Angelo, William, 81
St. John, Rob, 75
Stanczak, Ray, 173
Stanford, Chris, 60
Stanton, Laura, 256
Staublin, Grant, 244
Steade, Susan, 74
Steen, Anneli, 170
Stein, Ruthie, 119
Steininger, Otto, 176
Stephenson, David, 228
Stermer, Dugald, 222
Stevenson, Mark, 55
Stockwell, Martin, 67
Stoddard, Scott, 83, 85
Stoles, Harley, 234
Stone, Tony, 59
Storey, John, 192
Stoynoff, Evelyn, 115
Strawser, Kris, 75
Stromberg, Henrik, 232
Stubbe, Glen B., 57
Sullivan, Bartholomew, 88
Sullivan, Cleo, 233
Sumlin, Todd, 181
Summers, Tim, 170
Sutter, Mike, 181
Svegfors, Mats, 244
Sveningson, Ulf, 220
Swann, David, 250
Sweat, Stacy, 75, 88
Swenson, Daniel, 170, 174, 244, 247, 256
Swisher, Molly, 239
Sylvia, George, 75

Syomin, Vladimir, 167, 234
Syrek, David, 125
Syrnick, Susan, 167, 211, 222
Szalkowicz, Cecilia, 65-66

T
Taborda, Felipe, 135
Talbutt, Brad, 84
Talton, Jon, 67
Tanaka, Karen, 165
Tapounet, Rafael, 222
Taylor, Sheri, 263
Taylor-Gist, Karen, 118
Tehan, Patrick, 236
Terstroet, Marc, 142
Testino, Mario, 116
Thanner, Lisa, 232
Thiery, Martha, 242
Thomas, Eddie, 92
Threlkeld, Scott, 61, 170, 174, 236, 264
Tiffet, Christian, 111, 125, 140
Tigano, Catherine, 77
Tines, Charles V., 56
Tlumacki, John, 88
Tornvig, Bo, 57
Torregros, Alberto, 61
Torres, Hugo, 65
Tovar, Rodrigo, 212
Tozer, Tom, 81, 249
Treio, Carmen, 240, 245
Treviño, Diego, 73
Treviño, Martha, 127, 136, 138
Trigo, Guillermo, 146
Tuma, Rick, 170
Tumas, Alejandro, 242, 245, 246, 249, 253
Turner, Lane, 163, 232
Turney, George, 238
Türpe, Federico, 93, 123
Tusa, Susan, 99
Tustin, Steve, 176
Tweed, Dean, 173
Tweeten, Lon, 247, 256

U
Udesen, Betty, 171, 233, 235
Uncles, Alison, 52

V
Valdilena, Ángela, 74, 79
Vale Frogner, Eirik, 135
Valverdi, Raul, 123, 136, 191
Valverdi, Raúl, 108
Van Dyke, Tom, 235
Vanden Broeck, Fabricio, 204
Varela, Lucas, 238, 241, 246, 248, 253
Vargas, Ricardo, 62
Vargas, Yesid, 65
Vaughn, John, 56
Vazquez, Annette J., 57
Vazquez, Carlos, 76, 78-79, 262
Vázquez, Luis, 157
Vega, Herman, 128-129
Velasco, Juan, 239, 254
Veliz, Maria Ester, 108
Verhault, Susan, 261
Versiani, Cláudio, 58, 74, 82
Vest, David, 99
Vestergaard, Anette, 91
Vien, Christian, 192
Viesselman Onuigbo, Kris, 85, 101, 118, 131, 211, 238-239
Vincent, Louise, 173
Vinterberg, Søren, 91, 97
Vitt, Shawn, 118
Voros, Bob, 78
Voss, Arwed, 259
Voss, Ellen, 263, 267

W
Wadden, Ron, 54, 64

INDEX

Wahl, Cynthia, 127
Waigand, Lee, 76
Wainsztok, Carolina, 70, 72, 90
Walker, John, 224
Walls, Jim, 263
Wang, Chin, 67
Ward, Joe, 64, 80
Washington, Ruby, 243
Waters, Lannis, 235
Watson, Chris, 55
Webb, Keith A., 94, 130, 184
Weber, Lara, 170
Weiderer, Ed, 88
Weinstein, Mike, 96
Weissman, Beth, 101
Wernhamn, Gunilla, 128, 181
Wheatley, Tim, 80
Whipple, Catherine, 249
Whitacre, Dianne, 81
White, Brad, 100
White, James, 113
Whitley, Michael, 55, 57, 66 67
Whitley, Michael W., 55
Whyte, Kenneth, 52, 54-55, 57, 64, 96, 100, 140-141, 188, 227, 258
Widebrant, Mats, 142
Wiederer, Ed, 80, 246
Wigstrand, Kerstin, 242
Wikström, Linda, 56
Williams, Greg, 74
Williamson, Michael, 168
Wilson, Dave, 79, 262
Wilson, George, 74
Wilson, Mark, 232
Wilson, Wade, 86
Winge, Todd, 56
Winter, Jessica, 93, 110
Wirsén, Stina, 99, 215, 218, 220
Wischnowski, Stan, 76
Witmer, Jim, 129
Wittekind, Don, 252
Wojcik, James, 162
Wolden, Karen, 60
Wolf, Andrew, 260
Wolleman, Mark, 80
Wood, Stephanie, 260
Woods, Dan, 250
Wright, Randy, 73, 84

X
Ximenes, Victoria, 264
Xin, Liu, 235

Y
Yablonski, Patricia, 175
Yáñez, Oscar, 62, 227
Yarnold, David, 76
Yarosh, Lee, 80
Yee, Ted, 96, 99
Yofre, Alejandro, 150
Yong, Luis, 242, 245
York, Robert, 88, 222
Yuill, Peter, 111

Z
Zagor, Karen, 140
Zamarrón, Héctor, 62, 227
Zambrano, Beatriz, 73
Zamie, Rene, 96
Zarracina, Javier, 61, 245, 256
Zedek, Dan, 80
Zerrizuela, Rubén, 138
Zicarelli, Carlos, 93
Zimmerman, Bill, 263
Zisk, Molly, 85
Zivitz, Marvin, 52, 57
Zollinger, Lisa A., 81, 263

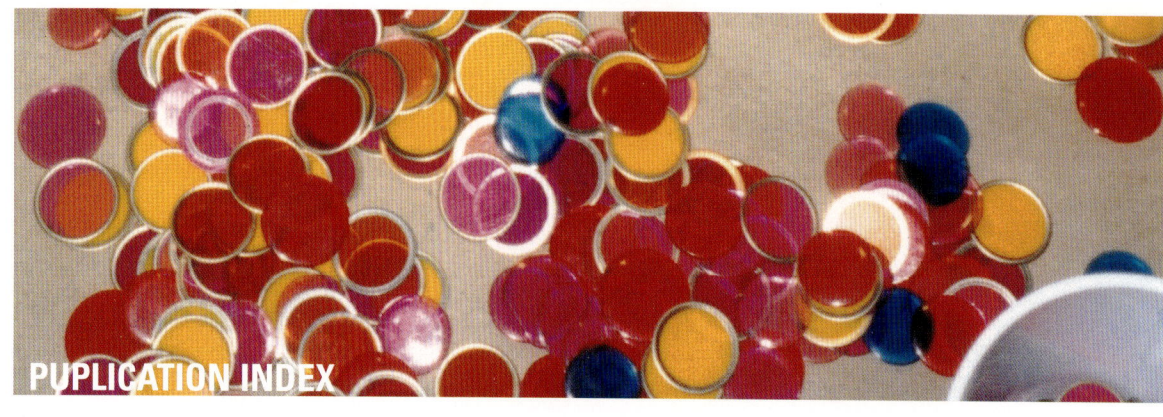

PUBLICATION INDEX

A
Age, 48, 172, 260
Albuquerque Journal, 65, 249
Albuquerque Tribune, 60, 79, 200
Allston/Brighton Tab, 62
a.m. De León, 8, 73, 80, 138-139
Anchorage Daily News, 200, 119, 122, 126, 157, 190
Appeal-Democrat, 172
Arkansas Democrat-Gazette, 210
Asbury Park Press, 65, 137, 188
Atlanta Journal & Constitution, 263
Austin American-Statesman, 181

B
B. T., 71-72, 78, 224
Ball State Daily News, 66
Beacon-News, 55, 60, 66-68, 111
Berlingske Tidende, 54-55, 57, 77, 103, 108, 190, 209, 218, 261
Boston Globe, 63, 67, 80, 88, 92, 94, 111, 115, 125, 130, 132, 135, 157, 163, 170, 176, 180-181, 184, 209, 232, 246
Boulder Daily Camera, 60, 94

C
Cape Cod Times, 140, 210
Centre Daily Times, 10
Charlotte Observer, 56, 67, 81, 83-84, 88, 96, 99, 115, 130, 181, 224, 228, 232, 249, 253, 264
Chicago Tribune, 48-49, 75, 79, 88, 115, 125, 128-129, 131, 170, 209
Cincinnati Enquirer, 198, 232
Citizen, 174
Clarín, 70, 72, 76, 78-79, 90, 238-239, 241 242, 245-246, 248-249, 253-255, 262, 264
Cleveland Plain Dealer, 250
Columbus Dispatch, 176
Comercio, 73
Commercial Appeal, 88
Correio Braziliense, 14, 58, 74, 79
Correo, 16, 61, 245
Correspondenten, 172
Courier-Journal, 72, 84

D
Dagbladet, 116, 135
Dagens Nyheter, 56, 79, 90, 99-100, 127, 170, 215, 218, 220, 242
Daily Telegraph, 242
Dallas Morning News, 79, 127, 172, 261 262, 266
Dayton Daily News, 129
Democra and Chronicle, 76, 175
Denver Rocky Mountain News, 229
Desert Sun, 62-63, 67, 74
Detroit Free Press, 56, 63, 75, 99, 235, 242
Detroit News, 56, 63, 170, 173, 235, 242, 250
Devoir, 111, 125, 140, 192-193
Dia, 60, 115
Diario de Noticias, 12, 127, 175
Diario de Noticias / DNA, 51, 144, 148, 157, 161, 163-164, 166, 230

E
Estado de Minas, 61, 90, 92, 220
Exito, 122
Expansión, 69-70, 181, 261, 264
Expresso, 209, 233

F
Florida Times-Union, 84, 133
Folha de São Paulo, 74, 80-81, 88
Fort Worth Star-Telegram, 127, 131
Fox Valley Villages, 140
Fresno Bee, 224

G
Gaceta, 68, 93, 106, 108, 120-123, 126, 135-137, 189, 191, 210
Gainesville Sun, 18
Globe and Mail, 34, 54, 56, 206, 211, 250, 253, 263
Globo, 56, 100, 112, 116, 125, 129, 132-135, 207, 210, 238
Göteborgs-Posten, 50, 100, 128, 132, 142, 181, 220, 226, 232

H
Hartford Courant, 61, 67, 73-74, 80-81, 84, 100, 116, 125, 132-133, 171, 180, 185, 198, 236
Honolulu Advertiser, 68
Honolulu Star-Bulletin, 250
Houston Chronicle Magazine, 234

I
Idaho Statesman, 73, 84
Imparcial, 140, 204
Indianapolis Star, 75
Irish News, 188, 85

J
Jackson Hole News, 192
Jacksonville Journal-Courier, 94, 139-140

L
L. A. Weekly, 222
Las Vegas Review-Journal, 131, 226
Lexington Herald-Leader, 20, 75, 228, 265
Liberty Times, 200
Listin Diario, 93, 123
Los Angeles Times, 222, 224, 251
Luna, 42, 113-114, 116-117, 175, 182-183, 185, 187, 267

M
Marca, 63-64, 243, 264
Miami Herald, 75
Missoulian, 60
Montreal Gazette, 173
Morgenavisen Jyllands-Posten, 56, 79, 95, 97, 100, 175
Mundo, 42-46, 140, 142, 145, 149-153, 155-158, 161-162, 165-166, 173, 176, 186 188, 193-197, 202-205, 207, 209, 214, 217, 219-221, 239, 244-245, 251, 254, 260-261
Mundo Del Siglo XXI, 45, 166, 202-205, 207, 214, 219-221, 239, 244-245, 251, 254
Mundo Magazines, 145, 161
Mundo Metropoli, 42-43, 151-153, 155 158, 161-162, 193, 195-196, 207
Mundo Siete Leguas, 145, 197
Mundo SU Dinero, 221

N
Nacion, 146, 173, 265
Naperville Sun, 60
National Post, 36, 52, 54-55, 57, 64, 96, 100, 140-141, 146, 180, 186, 188, 199, 208, 210-211, 227, 259
New York Daily News, 81
New York Times, 38, 52, 64, 80, 88, 90, 176, 180, 205, 208, 210-211, 216, 228, 239, 243, 247, 251, 254
New York Times Magazine, 147, 154, 159 160, 162, 164, 166-167, 208, 222, 227, 230, 233-234
News & Observer, 22, 55, 68, 126, 192
News Tribune, 57, 60, 74-76, 79-80, 88, 170, 200, 210, 241, 267
Newsday, 263, 266
Norte, 62, 72, 80, 127, 136, 138, 157, 206
NRC Handelsblad, 142, 251

O
Observador, 256, 264
Olé, 65-66
Orange County Register, 114, 124, 101, 118, 131, 174, 211, 221, 231, 238-239, 246
Oregonian, 101, 118, 131, 225, 228, 236, 239, 251
Ottawa Citizen, 91, 137-138

P
País, 70-71, 146, 149, 167, 221, 240, 245
País Semanal, 149, 167
Palabra, 94
Palm Beach Post, 236, 235
Página/12, 91, 93, 95, 104-105, 112-113, 120, 134, 137-138, 141, 189, 194
Periódico de Catalunya, 222, 240, 254
Periódico de Catalunya/El Dominical, 150
Philadelphia Daily News, 171
Philadelphia Inquirer, 81, 247, 251, 263
Philadelphia Inquirer Magazine, 167, 197, 211, 222
Pittsburgh Post-Gazette, 68, 77, 98, 101, 206, 212, 225, 227
Politiken, 54, 58, 90-92, 97, 104-105, 124, 128, 262
Poughkeepsie Journal, 243
Press-Enterprise, 124
Presse, 118, 142
Providence Journal, 59, 75, 77, 142, 200

R
Reforma, 62, 68, 73, 138-139, 204, 212, 227-228
Register-Guard, 59, 66, 124
Report on Business Magazine, 168, 211
Revista, 163
Revista de El Mundo, 44, 145, 150, 165, 168, 194, 196-198, 209, 212, 217, 219

S
Sacramento Bee, 252, 264
San Bernardino County Sun, 173, 252
San Diego Union-Tribune, 57, 88, 102, 126, 131-133
San Francisco Chronicle, 212, 234
San Francisco Examiner, 109, 129, 131, 191-192, 212, 263
San Jose Mercury News, 57, 74, 76, 98, 102, 118, 129, 175, 200, 205, 235-236
Savannah Morning News, 59, 109
Scotsman, 47
Seattle Post-Intelligencer, 103, 213, 221
Seattle Times, 59, 65, 82, 92, 103, 115, 118, 171, 188, 233-235
Seattle Weekly, 59, 192, 263
Soleil, 24, 55, 125, 200
Spokesman-Review, 26, 46, 59, 83, 85, 109, 174, 225
St. Louis Post-Dispatch, 85-86, 213, 225
St. Paul Pioneer Press, 226
St. Petersburg Times, 61, 103, 171
Star Tribune, 57, 75, 80, 92, 103, 174, 177, 199, 243
Star-Ledger, 57, 129, 135
Sun, 32, 86, 111, 129-130, 231, 238, 263
Sun-Sentinel, 74, 85, 180, 252
Sunday Magazine, 213
Sunday Telegraph, 240, 253
Sunday Times, 261, 264
Svenska Dagbladet, 85-88, 206, 244

T
Tampa Tribune, 74
Tiempo, 65, 141
Times, 54, 59, 76, 80, 85, 181, 200
Times-Picayune, 61, 76, 86, 103, 118, 170, 174, 236, 244, 247, 256, 264
Tomskaya Nedelya, 28
Toronto Star, 54, 115, 119, 176, 213, 227, 259
Tulsa World, 125

V
Vanguardia, 57, 147
Vanguardia Magazine, 147
Virginian-Pilot, 57, 68, 71, 73, 76, 78-79, 103, 180
Voz del Interior, 107, 109-110, 139

W
Wall Street Journal Reports, 176-178, 188, 213
Washington Post, 129, 205, 247, 256
Washington Post Magazine, 163, 165, 168, 198, 222
Washington Times, 128, 205, 222, 247
Women's Wear Daily, 175, 178
Wichita Eagle, 139
Woche, 30, 93, 110

Z
Zeit, 40, 259
Zero Hora, 81, 213